LYNNE GAETZ
Lionel Groulx College

SUNEET
St. Jerome College

RHONDA SANDBERG
George Brown College

The Canadian Writer's World

Paragraphs and Essays

SECOND CANADIAN EDITION

PEARSON

Toronto

Acquisitions Editor: David S. Le Gallais
Marketing Manager: Loula March
Senior Developmental Editor: Paul Donnelly
Program Manager: Joel Gladstone
Project Manager: Marissa Lok
Production Services: Heidi Allgair, Cenveo® Publisher Services
Media Editor: Marisa D'Andrea
Media Producer: Simon Bailey
Permissions Project Manager: Sue Petrykewycz
Photo Permissions Research: Carly Bergy, PreMedia Global
Text Permissions Research: Haydee Hidalgo, Electronic Publishing Services Inc.
Cover and Interior Designer: Anthony Leung
Cover Image: Fotolia

Credits and acknowledgments for material borrowed from other sources and reproduced, with permission, in this textbook appear on the appropriate page within text, or on page 606.

10 9 8 7 6 5 4 3 2 1 [CKV]

Library and Archives Canada Cataloguing in Publication

Gaetz, Lynne, 1960-, author
The Canadian writer's world : paragraphs and essays
/ Lynn Gaetz, Suneeti Phadke, Rhonda Sandberg.—Second edition.

Includes bibliographical references and index.
ISBN 978-0-205-90934-6 (pbk.)

1. English language—Paragraphs—Textbooks. 2. English language—Rhetoric—Textbooks. 3. English language—Grammar—Textbooks. 4. Report writing—Textbooks. I. Phadke, Suneeti, 1961—, author II. Sandberg, Rhonda, 1962-, author III. Title.

PE1439.G33 2014   808'.042   C2014-900079-0

PEARSON

ISBN 978-0-205-90934-6

Brief Table of Contents

Contents

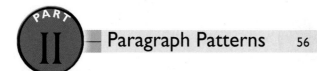

Chapter 5 Narration 69

Chapter 6 Description 83

Chapter 7 Process 95

Chapter 8 Definition 109

Chapter 9 Classification 123

Chapter 10 Comparison and Contrast 137

Chapter 11 Cause and Effect 152

Chapter 12 Argument 164

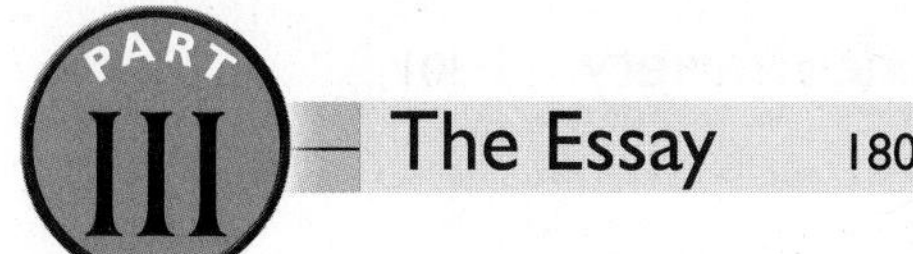

PART III The Essay 180

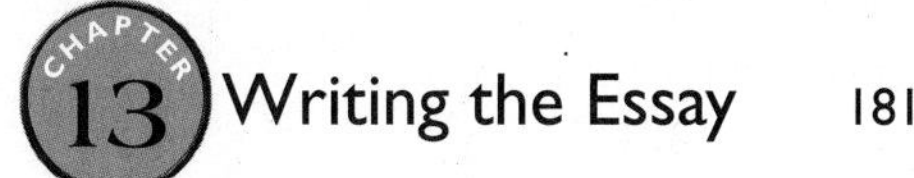

CHAPTER 13 Writing the Essay 181

CHAPTER 14 Essay Patterns 205

CHAPTER 15 Enhancing Your Writing with Research 243

PART IV The Editing Handbook 264

SECTION 1 Effective Sentences ▪ *Theme:* CULTURE

CHAPTER 16 Simple Sentences 266

CHAPTER 17 Compound Sentences 278

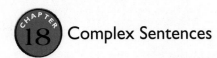

SECTION 8 **Punctuation and Mechanics** ▪ *Theme:* **THE WORKPLACE**

Readings Listed by Rhetorical Mode

Welcome to the Second Canadian Edition of *The Canadian Writer's World: Paragraphs and Essays*

Thank you for making the first Canadian edition of *The Canadian Writer's World* a resounding success. We are delighted that the book has been able to help so many students across the country. The second edition, too, can help your students produce writing that is technically correct and richly detailed whether they have varying skill levels, are native or nonnative speakers of English, or learn better through the use of visuals. When we started the first Canadian edition, we set out to develop practical and pedagogically sound approaches to these challenges, and we are pleased to hear that the book is helping students succeed in their writing courses.

For those new to the book, here is some background information to give a more complete picture.

A Research-Based Approach

We began with the idea that this project should be a collaboration with other developmental writing teachers. So we met with more than forty-five instructors from around North America, asking for their opinions and insights regarding (1) the challenges posed by the course, (2) the needs of today's ever-changing student population, and (3) the ideas and features we were proposing in order to provide them and you with a more effective teaching and learning tool. Pearson Education also commissioned detailed manuscript reviews from instructors, asking them to analyze and evaluate each draft of the manuscript. These reviewers identified numerous ways in which we could refine and enhance our key features. Their invaluable feedback was incorporated throughout *The Canadian Writer's World.* The text you are seeing is truly the product of a successful partnership involving the authors, the publisher, and well over a hundred developmental writing instructors.

How We Organized ***The Canadian Writer's World***

The Canadian Writer's World is separated into five parts for ease of use and convenience.

Part I: The Writing Process teaches students (1) how to formulate ideas (Exploring); (2) how to expand, organize, and present those ideas in a piece of writing (Developing); and (3) how to polish writing so that it conveys their message as clearly as possible (Revising and Editing). The result is that writing a paragraph or an essay becomes far less daunting because students have specific steps to follow.

Part II: Paragraph Patterns gives students a solid overview of the patterns of development. Using an easy-to-understand process (Exploring, Developing, and Revising and Editing), each chapter in this part explains how to convey ideas using one or more writing patterns. As they work through the practices and write their own paragraphs, students begin to see how using a writing pattern can help them achieve their purpose for writing.

Part III: The Essay covers the parts of the essay and explains how students can apply the nine patterns of development to essay writing. This part also discusses the role research plays in writing and explains some ways that students can incorporate research into their essays.

Part IV: The Editing Handbook is a thematic grammar handbook. In each chapter, the examples correspond to a theme, such as popular culture, college life, or the workplace. As students work through the chapters, they hone their grammar and editing skills, while gaining knowledge about a variety of topics. In addition to helping build interest in the grammar practices, the thematic material provides a spark that ignites new ideas that students can apply to their writing.

Part V: Reading Strategies and Selections offers tips, readings, and follow-up questions. Students learn how to write by observing and dissecting what they read. The readings relate to the themes found in Part IV: The Editing Handbook, thereby providing more fodder for generating writing ideas.

How *The Canadian Writer's World* Meets Students' Diverse Needs

We created this textbook to meet your students' diverse needs. To accomplish this, we asked both the instructors in our focus groups and the reviewers at every stage not only to critique our ideas but also to offer their suggestions and recommendations for features that would enhance the learning process of their students. The result has been the integration of many elements that are not found in other textbooks, including our **visual program, coverage of nonnative speaker material,** and **strategies for addressing the varying skill levels students bring to the course.**

The Visual Program

A stimulating, full-colour book with more than seventy photos, *The Canadian Writer's World* recognizes that today's world is a visual one, and it encourages students to become better communicators by responding to images. Chapter-opening visuals in Parts I, II, and III help students think about the chapter's key concept in a new way. For example, in the Chapter 9 opener, a photograph of a candy store sets the stage for classification. Chocolates are grouped by type, which helps students understand the premise of classification. In Part IV, chapter-opening photos help illustrate the theme of the examples and exercises. These visual aids can also serve as sources for writing prompts.

Each of the At Work boxes in Part II features an image from the workplace, along with content on how that particular pattern of development is utilized on the job.

Throughout *The Canadian Writer's World*, words and images work together to encourage students to explore, develop, and revise their writing.

Seamless Coverage for Nonnative Speakers

Instructors in our focus groups noted the growing number of nonnative/English as a Second Language (ESL) speakers enrolling in developmental writing courses. Although some of these students have special needs relating to the writing process, many of you still have a large portion of native speakers in your courses whose more traditional needs must also be satisfied. In order to meet the challenge of this rapidly changing dynamic, we have carefully implemented and integrated content throughout to assist these students. This textbook does not have separate ESL boxes, ESL chapters, or tacked-on ESL appendices. Instead, information that traditionally poses a challenge to nonnative speakers is woven seamlessly throughout the book. In our extensive experience teaching writing to both native and nonnative speakers of English, we have learned that both groups learn best when they are not distracted by ESL labels. With the seamless approach, nonnative speakers do not feel self-conscious and segregated, and native speakers do not tune out detailed explanations that may also benefit them. Many of these traditional problem areas receive more coverage than you would find in other textbooks, arming the instructor with the material to effectively meet the needs of nonnative speakers.

Issue-Focused Thematic Grammar

In surveys, many of you indicated that one of the primary challenges in teaching your course is finding materials that are engaging to students in a contemporary context. This is especially true in grammar instruction. **Students come to the course with varying skill levels,** and many students are simply not interested in grammar. To address this challenge, we have introduced **issue-focused thematic grammar** into *The Canadian Writer's World.*

Each chapter centres on a theme that is carried out in examples and activities. These themes include topics related to popular culture and college life, psychology and health care, great discoveries and the workplace, and political intrigue and the legal world. The thematic approach enables students to broaden their awareness of subjects important to Canadian life, such as understanding advertising and consumerism and thinking about health-care issues and alternative medicine. The thematic approach makes reading about grammar more engaging. And the more engaging grammar is, the more likely students are to retain key concepts—raising their skill level in these important building blocks of writing.

We also think that it is important to teach grammar in the context of the writing process. Students should not think that grammar is an isolated exercise. Therefore, **each grammar chapter includes**

a warm-up writing activity. Students write and edit their paragraphs, paying particular attention to the grammar point covered in the chapter. The end of each grammar section also contains paragraph and essay writing topics that are related to the theme of the section and that follow different writing patterns. Suggestions are given in these chapters for readings in Part V that relate to the grammar themes.

What Tools Can Help Students Get the Most from *The Canadian Writer's World?*

Overwhelmingly, focus group participants and reviewers asked that both a larger number and a greater diversity of exercises and activities be incorporated into *The Canadian Writer's World.* In response, we have developed and tested the following learning aids in *The Canadian Writer's World.* We are confident they will help your students become better writers.

Hints In each chapter, **Hint** boxes highlight important writing and grammar points. Hints are useful for all students, but many will be particularly helpful for nonnative speakers. For example, in Chapter 12, one Hint encourages students to state an argument directly, and another points out the need to avoid circular reasoning. In Chapter 21, a Hint discusses checking for consistent voice in compound sentences. Hints include brief discussions and examples so that students will see both concept and application.

> **Hint** **Be Direct**
>
> You may feel reluctant to state your point of view directly. You may feel that it is impolite to do so. However, in academic writing, it is perfectly acceptable, and even desirable, to state an argument in a direct manner.
>
> In argument writing, you can make your topic debatable by using *should, must,* or *ought to* in the topic sentence or thesis statement.
>
> Although daily prayer is important for many people in Canada, it **should** not take place in the classroom.

Vocabulary Boost Throughout Part II of *The Canadian Writer's World,* Vocabulary Boost boxes give students tips to improve their use of language and to revise and edit their word choices. For example, the Vocabulary Boost in Chapter 4 asks students to replace repeated words with synonyms, and the one in Chapter 5 gives specific instructions for how to vary sentence openings. These lessons give students concrete strategies and specific advice for improving their diction.

> **vo•cab•u•lar•y BOOST**
>
> **Using Varied Language**
>
> 1. Underline the opening word of every sentence in your first draft. Check to see if some are repeated.
> 2. Replace repeated opening words with an adverb, such as *Usually, Generally,* or *Fortunately,* or a prepositional phrase, such as *On the other hand* or *Under the circumstances.* You can also begin sentences with a modifier, such as *Leaving the door open.* In other words, avoid beginning too many sentences with a noun or transitional expression.
>
> **Repeated First Words**
>
> We opened the door of the abandoned house. We looked nervously at the rotting floorboards. We thought the floor might collapse. We decided to enter. We walked carefully across the kitchen floor to the bedroom, one by one.
>
> **Variety**
>
> My cousins and I opened the door of the abandoned house. Nervously, we looked at the rotting floorboards. Leaving the door open, we decided to enter. One by one, we walked across the kitchen floor to the bedroom.

The Writer's Desk Parts I, II, and III include **The Writer's Desk** exercises that help students get used to practising all stages and steps of the writing process. As the chapter progresses, students warm up with a prewriting activity and then use specific methods for developing, organizing (using paragraph and essay plans), drafting, and, finally, revising and editing to create a final draft.

> *The Writer's Desk* **Warm Up**
>
> Think about the following questions and write the first ideas that come to your mind. Try to think of two or three ideas for each topic.
>
> **EXAMPLE:**
>
> What are some effective ways to market a product?
>
> *use colourful packaging*
>
> *create a funny advertisement*
>
> *give free samples*
>
> 1. What are some really silly fads or fashions?
>
> 2. What are some traits of an effective leader?
>
> 3. What are some qualities that you look for in a mate?

Paragraph Patterns at Work To help students appreciate the relevance of their writing tasks, Chapters 4–12 highlight authentic writing samples from work contexts. Titled **Illustration at Work, Narration at Work,** and so on, this feature offers a glimpse of how people use writing patterns in different workplace settings.

Illustration at Work

Patti Guzman is a registered nurse at a large hospital. She was invited to speak to nursing students in a local university. In the following excerpt from her speech, she gives examples to explain why a nurse must be in good physical health.

Physically, the job of a nurse is demanding. On a daily basis, we must lift patients and move them. When patients are bedridden for prolonged periods, we must change their positions on their beds. When new patients arrive, we transfer them from stretchers to beds or from beds to wheelchairs. If patients fall, we must be able to help them stand up. If patients have difficulty walking, we must assist them. Patients who have suffered paralysis or stroke need to be lifted and supported when they are bathed and dressed. Keep in mind that some patients may be quite heavy, so the job requires a good level of physical strength.

The topic sentence expresses the main idea.

Supporting sentences provide details and examples.

The concluding sentence brings the paragraph to a satisfying close.

Robert Kneschke/Shutterstock

Reflect on It Each **Reflect on It** is a chapter review exercise. Questions prompt students to recall and review what they have learned in the chapter.

REFLECT ON IT

Think about what you have learned in this chapter. If you do not know an answer, review that topic.

1. In an illustration paragraph, you ____________________
2. There are two ways to write illustration paragraphs. Explain each of them.
   a. Using a series of examples: ____________________
   b. Using an extended example: ____________________
3. List three transitional expressions that indicate an additional idea.
   ____

The Writer's Room **The Writer's Room** contains writing activities that correspond to general, college, and workplace topics. Some prompts are brief to allow students to freely form ideas, while others are expanded to give students more direction.

There is something for every student writer in this end-of-chapter feature. Students who respond well to visual cues will appreciate the photo writing exercises in **The Writer's Room** in Part II: Paragraph Patterns. Students who learn best by hearing through collaboration will appreciate the discussion and group-work prompts in **The Writers' Circle** section of selected **The Writer's Rooms**. In Part III: The Essay, students can respond to thought-provoking quotations. To help students see how grammar is not isolated from the writing process, there are also **The Writer's Room** activities at the end of Sections 1 to 8 in Part IV: The Editing Handbook.

The Writer's Room

Choose one of the following topics, and write a paragraph or an essay. Remember to follow the writing process.

1. Have you ever been to an acupuncturist, a massage therapist, a naturopath, a homeopath, or any other alternative healing practitioner? Describe the treatment that you received.
2. Do you have a scar, or have you ever had an accident? Explain what happened.
3. Right now, millions of Americans are uninsured for medical care. Should the government of the United States provide health care for all citizens, just as Canada and many European nations do? Why or why not?
4. Should terminally ill patients have the right to die? What are the possible problems if euthanasia is legalized? Write about euthanasia.

Work with a group of students on the following activity.

STEP 1 Write down adjectives, adverbs, and phrases that describe the following people.

EXAMPLE: A good boss: *honest, listens well, supportive*

a. A good doctor: ____________________

b. A bad doctor: ____________________

STEP 2 Rank the qualities from most important to least important.

STEP 3 As a team, write a paragraph about doctors. Compare the good with the bad.

STEP 4 When you finish writing, edit your paragraph and ensure that you have written all the adjectives and adverbs correctly.

***The Canadian Writer's World* eText** Accessed through MyWritingLab (www.MyWritingLab.com), students now have the eText for *The Canadian Writer's World* at their fingertips while completing the various exercises and activities with MyWritingLab. Students can highlight important material and add notes to any section for further reflection and/or study throughout the semester.

New to the Second Canadian Edition

Visualizing the Mode

Chapters 4–12 cover nine paragraph patterns. To help students visualize how to use each pattern, they complete a Visualizing activity. For example, in Chapter 4, Visualizing Illustration includes the topic sentence "Some workers risk their lives daily . . . ." Photos of workers, including a high-rise window cleaner, an electrician, a fisherman, and police officers, are shown. Chapter 8 includes the topic statement "Timeless fashions remain popular and will not go out of style." Students see images of a bobbed haircut, a little black dress, and a classic black suit. These visual examples help students get an overview of the paragraph mode.

Annotations for At Work Paragraphs

In Chapters 4–12, each paragraph pattern includes a real-world example. Each of the At Work paragraphs now contains callouts pointing out the paragraph's key features: the topic sentence, the supporting ideas, and the concluding sentence.

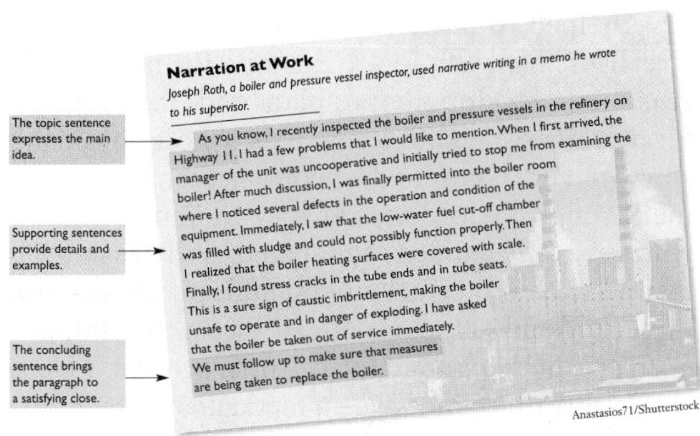

Narration at Work

Joseph Roth, a boiler and pressure vessel inspector, used narrative writing in a memo he wrote to his supervisor.

As you know, I recently inspected the boiler and pressure vessels in the refinery on Highway 11. I had a few problems that I would like to mention. When I first arrived, the manager of the unit was uncooperative and initially tried to stop me from examining the boiler! After much discussion, I was finally permitted into the boiler room where I noticed several defects in the operation and condition of the equipment. Immediately, I saw that the low-water fuel cut-off chamber was filled with sludge and could not possibly function properly. Then I realized that the boiler heating surfaces were covered with scale. Finally, I found stress cracks in the tube ends and in tube seats. This is a sure sign of caustic imbrittlement, making the boiler unsafe to operate and in danger of exploding. I have asked that the boiler be taken out of service immediately. We must follow up to make sure that measures are being taken to replace the boiler.

The topic sentence expresses the main idea.
Supporting sentences provide details and examples.
The concluding sentence brings the paragraph to a satisfying close.

Anastasios71/Shutterstock

New Photos

Several new opening photos and photo writing prompts appear throughout the book. Each grammar chapter has an opening photo that helps to show the thematic content.

Media Writing

Every paragraph pattern chapter now ends with a media writing activity. Students are invited to view a television program, film, or online video and to use the content as a writing prompt.

Updated High-Interest Paragraph Models and Practices

Throughout the book, you will notice new examples, sample paragraphs, writing practices, The Writer's Desk topics, and grammar practices. In fact, to make the content more topical and appealing, roughly 30 percent of the book's content has been updated.

The Writers' Exchange

The Writers' Exchange opens each Part II chapter to give students an activity they can work on together that will help them understand a writing pattern. These collaborative activities also help students build confidence about their knowledge before having to apply it in writing. The Writers' Exchanges are particularly helpful for students who like to listen to acquire knowledge.

Expanded Research Coverage

Chapter 15, "Enhancing Your Writing with Research," has coverage on gathering information using library and Internet sources, as well as expanded coverage of evaluating sources. The discussions of paraphrasing and summarizing have been expanded, and the Works Cited information has been revised. A new sample student paper on e-sports is annotated with comments about MLA style and formatting.

Thematic Organization in Part Five

The thematic organization in Part V groups readings into four broad categories: Popular Culture and College Life, Psychology and Health Care, Great Discoveries and the Workplace, and Political Intrigue and the Legal World. Eleven new readings update the selections with multicultural perspectives and high-interest topics.

Readings Listed by Rhetorical Mode

The Part V readings are grouped in the table of contents by theme and on the Part V opener by theme and dominant writing pattern. A new table of contents has been added directly after the regular table of contents so that you can see which readings are organized in whole or in part by the various rhetorical modes.

Supplements

Annotated Instructor's Edition

The Annotated Instructor's Edition is a collection of teaching tips available to instructors electronically in the eText within MyWritingLab. By clicking on the "i" icons in the eText, instructors can access hundreds of tips to help them teach using The Canadian Writer's World. (Students who view the eText will not see the instructor icons and content; this content is available only within instructor accounts.) The Annotated Instructor's Edition also includes over 75 ESL teaching tips. Many of these were derived from the author's firsthand experience teaching nonnative speakers in the classroom, while others have been suggested by users of The Canadian Writer's World and 16 experts in the field of English language training.

MyWritingLab

MyWritingLab is a state-of-the-art interactive and instructive solution designed to help students meet the challenges of their writing courses and to assist them in all their future writing. MyWritingLab provides access to a wealth of resources, all geared to meet students' learning needs.

MyWritingLab will give users access to the **Pearson eText**. The eText gives students access to the text whenever and wherever they have access to the Internet. eText pages look exactly like the printed text, offering powerful new functionality for students and instructors. Users can create notes, highlight text in different colours, create bookmarks, zoom, click hyperlinked words and phrases to view definitions, and see the text in single-page and two-page views.

Learning Solutions Managers

Pearson's Learning Solutions Managers work with faculty and campus course designers to ensure that Pearson technology products, assessment tools, and online course materials are tailored to meet your specific needs. This highly qualified team is dedicated to helping schools take full advantage of a wide range of educational resources by assisting in the integration of a variety of instructional materials and media formats. Your local Pearson Education sales representative can provide you with more details on this service program.

CourseSmart

CourseSmart is a new way for instructors and students to access textbooks online anytime, from anywhere. With thousands of titles across hundreds of courses, CourseSmart helps instructors choose the best textbook for their class and give their students a new option for buying the assigned textbook as a lower cost eTextbook. For more information, visit www.coursesmart.com.

Acknowledgments

The authors and the publisher would like to thank the following reviewers for their input during the development of the second Canadian edition:

Rose Caruso, Seneca College
Chandra Hodgson, Humber College
Ingrid Hutchison, Fanshawe College
Val Innes, Kwantlen Polytechnic University
Jennifer Mei, Centennial College

Several individuals have helped me in producing the second Canadian edition of *The Canadian Writer's World: Paragraphs and Essays.* I would like to express my great appreciation to Lynne Gaetz and Suneeti Phadke for their pedagogically sound text on which to build Canadian content. I am indebted to the team of dedicated professionals at Pearson Canada, who have helped to make the second Canadian edition a reality. Thanks to Joel Gladstone for his carefully reasoned developmental plan and inspirational ideas and to David S. Le Gallais, whose invaluable support and continued encouragement propelled me through the project. Thanks to Paul Donnelly, who not only guided, supported, and trusted my instincts but also contributed significant vision to the project. Thanks to Heidi Allgair for her patient, wise oversight of the production editorial process. Thanks to Marissa Lok, whose keen, meticulous suggestions during the production process helped greatly, and to Sue Petrykewycz for her superb management of permissions. Thanks to Carly Bergy (PreMedia Global) for her tremendous help with photo permissions research. Thanks as well to Anthony Leung for his cover and interior design and to Marisa D'Andrea and Simon Bailey for their splendid work on media. Special thanks to Joanne Di Ciaula for her promotion of both the first and second Canadian editions (and of the GBC custom text) and to Jordan MacDonald for his technical expertise.

I would like to express my deep appreciation to my exceptional George Brown College academic and administrative colleagues and friends, who contributed their insights, support, and encouragement throughout my writing process. Special thanks to Corinne Abba, Richard Almonte, Stella Bastone, William Basztyk, Md., Jalal Bhuiyan, Sandi Blackburn, Adrian Bond, Pat Bowness, Derek Brown, Julie Bulmash, Peter Burgess, Jon Callegher, Jan Carter, Avanti Chakraverti, Jean Choi, Jacqui Cook, Michael Cooke, Kathy Dumanski, Jill Edmondson, Paul Finlayson, Bernie Gaidosch, Angie Gorassi, John Gudmundson, Karen Hamilton, Anne Hardacre, Avrille Headley, Susan Heximer, Rona Kaushansky, Joyce Kraay, Sam Lampropoulos, Shirley Lesch, Peter Lovrick, Maureen Loweth, Alexandra MacLennan, Heather McAfee, M. J. Perry, Olga Ponichtera, Georgia Quartaro, Jitendra Shalin,

Elizabeth Speers, Frances Steciuk, Don St. Jean, John Swiderski, Barbara Thistle, Lauralynn Tomassi, Helene Vukovich, and Adrienne Weiss.

I would like to express my gratitude for my past and current students for their constant inspiration and honest feedback. Their words and ideas are included in the second Canadian edition of *The Canadian Writer's World: Paragraphs and Essays.*

I would also like to extend my sincere appreciation to my wonderful colleagues and friends at other academic institutions and businesses. Special thanks to Janna Ramsay Best, Kim DiSalle, Kimberly Fahner, Susan Fowler, Rachael Frankford, Robin Frattini, Jack Heffron, Shannon Hengen, Carlos Lopes, Ron Menard, Peter Miller, Kathryn T. Molohon, John Riddell, Melanie Rubens, Susan Serran, Anita Shack, Mira Staples, and Kevin Taylor.

Finally, I would like to dedicate the second Canadian edition of *The Canadian Writer's World: Paragraphs and Essays* to my children, Skyelar and Dylan, who are my light and my love.

Rhonda Sandberg

A Note to Students

Your knowledge, ideas, and opinions are important. The ability to clearly communicate those ideas is invaluable in your personal, academic, and professional life. When your writing is error-free, readers will focus on your message, and you will be able to persuade, inform, entertain, or inspire them. *The Canadian Writer's World* includes strategies that will help you improve your written communication. Quite simply, when you become a better writer, you become a better communicator. It is our greatest wish for this book to make you excited about writing, communicating, and learning.

Enjoy!

Call for Student Writing!

Do you want to be published in *The Canadian Writer's World*? Send your paragraphs and essays to us along with your complete contact information. If your work is selected to appear in the next edition of *The Canadian Writer's World*, you will receive an honorarium, credit for your work, and a copy of the book!

Lynne Gaetz
Suneeti Phadke
Rhonda Sandberg

The Writing Process

An Overview

The writing process is a series of steps that most writers follow to get from thinking about a topic to preparing the final draft. Generally, you should follow the process step by step; however, sometimes you may find that your steps overlap. For example, you might do some editing before you revise, or you might think about your main idea while you are prewriting. The important thing is to make sure that you have done all of the steps before preparing your final draft.

Before you begin the chapters that follow, review the steps in the writing process.

Exploring

Step 1: Think about your topic.

Step 2: Think about your audience.

Step 3: Think about your purpose.

Step 4: Try exploring strategies.

Developing

Step 1: Narrow your topic.

Step 2: Express your main idea.

Step 3: Develop your supporting ideas.

Step 4: Make a plan or an outline.

Step 5: Write your first draft.

Revising and Editing

Step 1: Revise for unity.

Step 2: Revise for adequate support.

Step 3: Revise for coherence.

Step 4: Revise for style.

Step 5: Edit for technical errors.

Exploring

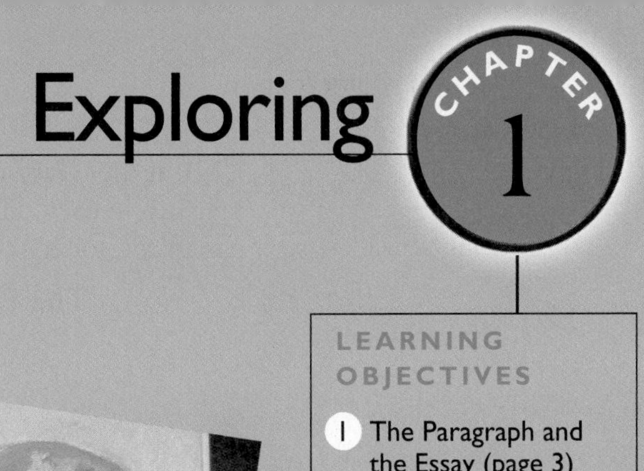

LEARNING OBJECTIVES

Lynne Gaetz

Before creating a final image, a pastel artist takes the time to consider what to create. Similarly, before developing a draft, a writer needs to explore the topic.

The Paragraph and the Essay

Most of the writing that we do—email messages, work reports, school papers—is made up of paragraphs and essays. A **paragraph** is a series of sentences that are about one central idea. Paragraphs can stand alone, or they can be part of a longer work such as an essay, a letter, or a report. An **essay** is a series of paragraphs that are about one central idea. Both the paragraph and the essay are divided into three parts.

Characteristics of a Paragraph	Characteristics of an Essay
▪ The **topic sentence** introduces the subject of the paragraph and shows the writer's attitude toward the subject.	▪ The **introduction** engages the reader's interest and contains the **thesis statement.**
▪ The **body** of the paragraph contains details that support the topic sentence.	▪ The **body** paragraphs each support the main idea of the essay.
▪ The paragraph ends with a **concluding sentence.**	▪ The **conclusion** reemphasizes the thesis and restates the main points of the essay. It brings the essay to a satisfactory close.

Look at the relationship between paragraphs and essays. Both examples are about real-life heroes. However, in the essay, each supporting idea is expanded into paragraph form.

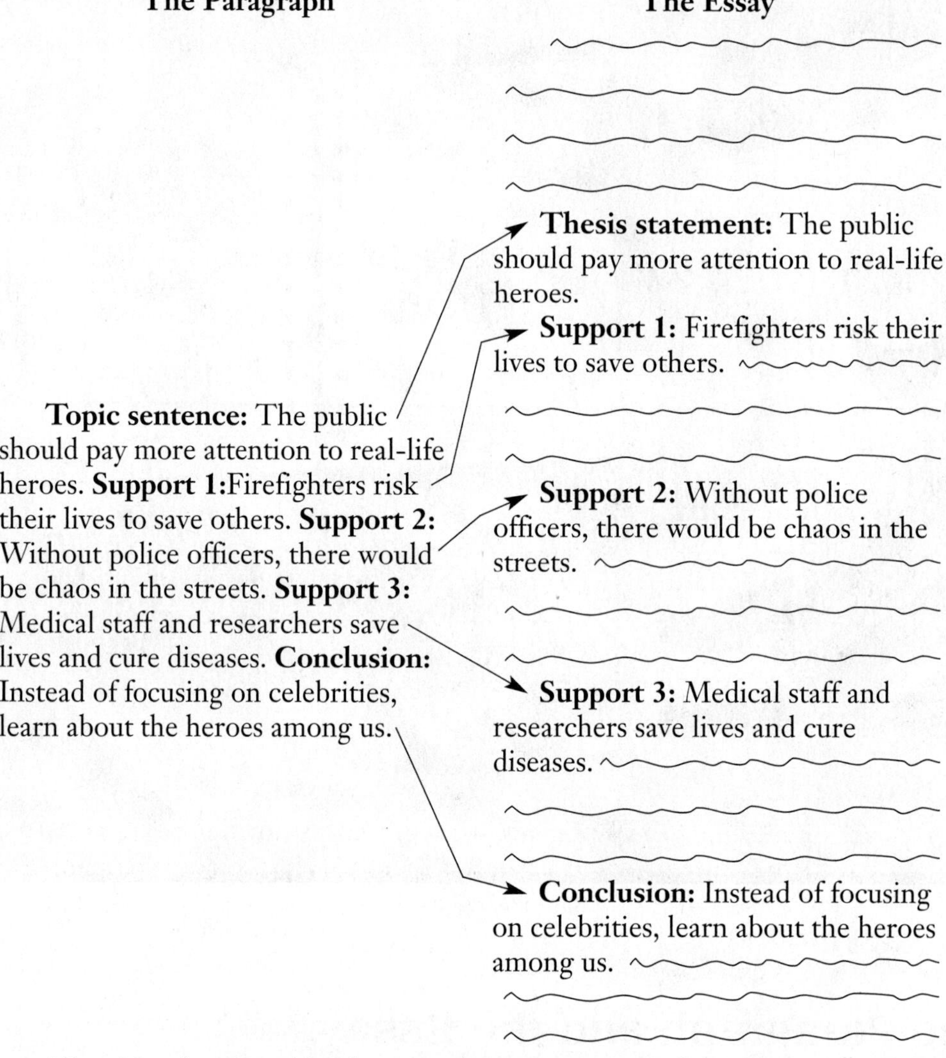

The Paragraph
The Essay
Topic sentence: The public should pay more attention to real-life heroes. Support 1: Firefighters risk their lives to save others. Support 2: Without police officers, there would be chaos in the streets. Support 3: Medical staff and researchers save lives and cure diseases. Conclusion: Instead of focusing on celebrities, learn about the heroes among us.
Thesis statement: The public should pay more attention to real-life heroes.
Support 1: Firefighters risk their lives to save others.
Support 2: Without police officers, there would be chaos in the streets.
Support 3: Medical staff and researchers save lives and cure diseases.
Conclusion: Instead of focusing on celebrities, learn about the heroes among us.

All writing begins with ideas. In the next section of this chapter, you will practise ways to explore ideas.

Visualizing the Writing Process

Wade Vong, a college student, was asked to write a paragraph about cities. Follow the writing process that Wade used to write his paragraph.

Exploring

Wade's topic was "cities." First, Wade narrowed the topic by listing ideas related to cities. Then he chose the narrowed topic "Montreal, my hometown." His audience was his college instructor, and his purpose for writing was to entertain. In the exploring stage, there are several prewriting techniques that can help a writer develop a topic. Wade used a prewriting technique called brainstorming. He listed some ideas and did not worry about his grammar, spelling, or punctuation.

- lots of tourists
- beautiful parks including Mount Royal Park

- Montreal Jazz Fest
- variety of great entertainment, dining, and shopping on rue Ste. Catherine
- close to Quebec City
- Musée des Beaux Arts (oldest museum in Canada)
- sea of neon lights

Developing

In the developing stage, Wade wrote a sentence that expressed the idea that he would develop in his paragraph. Then he created a plan and organized his ideas logically. Below is the first complete draft of his paragraph.

You may notice that Wade's paragraph has errors. He will correct these when he gets to the revising and editing stage of the process.

> Montreal is a vibrant city of extremes. Peaceful suburbs integrate the city landscape. There are beautifull parks. Mount Royal Park is one. Other parts of the city are extremely fast-paced and glitzy. On the busiest streets of Montreal, neon lights illuminates the night sky. Crowds of tourists gaze at paintings, exhibits, and art collections at the Musee Des Beaux Arts. The city, which is close to Quebec City, is also vibrant because of the great entertainment available, including the annual Montreal International Jazz Festival. The city reflects cultural diversity and joie de vivre (joy of life). Dining and Shopping on Rue Ste. Catherine. If you would like to visit a truly unique city, go to Montreal.

Revising and Editing

In the revising stage, Wade removed some sentences that did not relate to his topic, and he added other sentences to make his paragraph more complete. He also added words to help link his ideas. Look at his revisions for unity, support, coherence, and style.

First, peaceful
Montreal is a vibrant city of extremes. ~~P~~eaceful suburbs integrate

the city landscape. There are beautifull parks, including Mount Royal

In contrast, other
Park which is an oasis above the city. ~~O~~ther parts of the city are

extremely fast-paced and glitzy. On the busiest streets of Montreal,

for instance, *jostling*
neon lights illuminates the night sky. Crowds of tourists gaze at

paintings, exhibits, and art collections at the Musee Des Beaux Arts.

The city, which is close to Quebec City, is also vibrant because of the

great entertainment available, including the annual Montreal

International Jazz Festival. The city reflects cultural diversity and

, as you can see in the variety of
joie de vivre (joy of life)~~. There is~~ Dining and Shopping on rue Ste.

Catherine. If you would like to visit a truly unique city, go to Montreal.

In the editing stage, Wade corrected errors in grammar, spelling, punctuation, capitalization, and mechanics.

Montreal is a vibrant city of extremes. First, peaceful suburbs integrate the stunning city landscape. There are *beautiful* beautiful~~l~~ parks, including Mount Royal Park which is an oasis above the city. In contrast, other parts of the city are extremely fast-paced and glitzy. On the busiest streets of Montreal, for instance, neon lights *illuminate* illuminate~~s~~ the night sky. Crowds of jostling tourists gaze at paintings, exhibits, and art collections at the *é* Muse~~e~~ des Beaux Arts. The city, which is close to Quebec City, is also vibrant because of the great entertainment available, including the annual Montreal International Jazz Festival. The city reflects cultural diversity and joie de vivre (joy of life), as you can see in the variety of *dining* ~~D~~ining and *shopping* ~~S~~hopping on rue Ste. Catherine. If you would like to visit a truly unique city, go to Montreal.

When he finished editing, Wade typed a final draft of his paragraph.

Montreal is a vibrant city of extremes. First, peaceful suburbs integrate the stunning city landscape. There are beautiful parks, including Mount Royal Park, which is an oasis above the city. In contrast, other parts of the city are extremely fast-paced and glitzy. On the busiest street of Montreal, for instance, neon lights illuminate the night sky. Crowds of jostling tourists gaze at paintings, exhibits, and art collections at the Musée Des Beaux Arts. The city, which is close to Quebec City, is also vibrant because of the great entertainment available, including the annual Montreal International Jazz Festival. The city reflects cultural diversity and joie de vivre (joy of life). Visitors can enjoy exceptional dining and shopping on rue Ste. Catherine. If you would like to visit a truly unique city, go to Montreal.

Before handing in his assignment, Wade read it through one last time to check for typos.

What Is Exploring?

Have you ever been given a writing subject and then stared at the blank page, thinking, "I don't know what to write?" Well, it is not necessary to write a good paragraph or essay immediately. There are certain things that you can do to help you focus on your topic.

Understand Your Assignment

As soon as you are given an assignment, make sure that you understand what your task is. Answer the following questions about the assignment.

- How many words or pages should I write?
- What is the due date for the assignment?
- Are there any special qualities my writing should include?

After you have considered your assignment, follow the four steps in the exploring stage of the writing process.

ESSAY LINK

When you plan an essay, you should follow the four exploring steps.

EXPLORING

STEP 1 ► **Think about your topic.** Determine what you will write about.

STEP 2 ► **Think about your audience.** Consider your intended readers and what interests them.

STEP 3 ► **Think about your purpose.** Ask yourself why you want to write.

STEP 4 ► **Try exploring strategies.** Experiment with different ways to generate ideas.

Topic

Your **topic** is what you are writing about. When an instructor gives you a topic for your writing, you can give it a personal focus. For example, if the instructor asks you to write about "travel," you can take many approaches to the topic. You might write about the dangers of travel, describe a trip that you have taken, or explain the lessons that travel has taught you. When you are given a topic, find an angle that interests you and make it your own.

When you think about the topic, ask yourself the following questions.

- What about the topic interests me?
- Do I have special knowledge about the topic?
- Does anything about the topic arouse my emotions?

Audience

Your **audience** is your intended reader. In your personal, academic, and professional life, you will often write for a specific audience; therefore, you can keep your readers interested by adapting your tone and vocabulary to suit them. **Tone** is your general attitude or feeling toward a topic. You might write in a tone that is humorous, sarcastic, serious, friendly, or casual. For example, in an email to your friend, you might use a very casual tone, with abbreviations such as *ttyl*, which means *talk to you later*. In an email to your employer, you would use a more formal, businesslike tone.

When you consider your audience, ask yourself the following questions.

- Who will read my assignment—an instructor, other students, or people outside the college?
- Do my readers have a lot of knowledge about my topic?
- Will my readers expect me to write in proper, grammatically correct English?

In academic writing, your audience is generally your instructor or other students, unless your instructor specifically asks you to write for another audience such as the general public, your employer, or a family member.

Instructor as the Audience

When you write for your instructor, use standard English. In other words, try to use correct grammar, sentence structure, and vocabulary. Also, do not leave out information because you assume that your instructor is an expert in the field. Generally, when your instructor reads your work, he or she will expect you to reveal what you have learned or what you have understood about the topic.

PRACTICE 1

Email messages A and B are about career goals. As you read the messages, consider the differences in both the tone and the vocabulary the writer uses. Then answer the questions that follow. Circle the letter of the correct answer.

1. Who is the audience for Email A?

   a. A friend　　b. A family member
   c. A potential employer　　d. An instructor

2. Who is the audience for Email B?

   a. A friend　　b. A family member
   c. A potential employer　　d. An instructor

3. In a word or two, describe the tone in each email.

   Email A: ____________　　Email B: ____________

4. **Language clues** are words or phrases that help you determine the audience. What language clues helped you determine the audience of Emails A and B? The first clue in each email message has been identified for you.

Email A:	Email B:
hey macro, sup?	*Dear Mr. Elliot:*

Email A

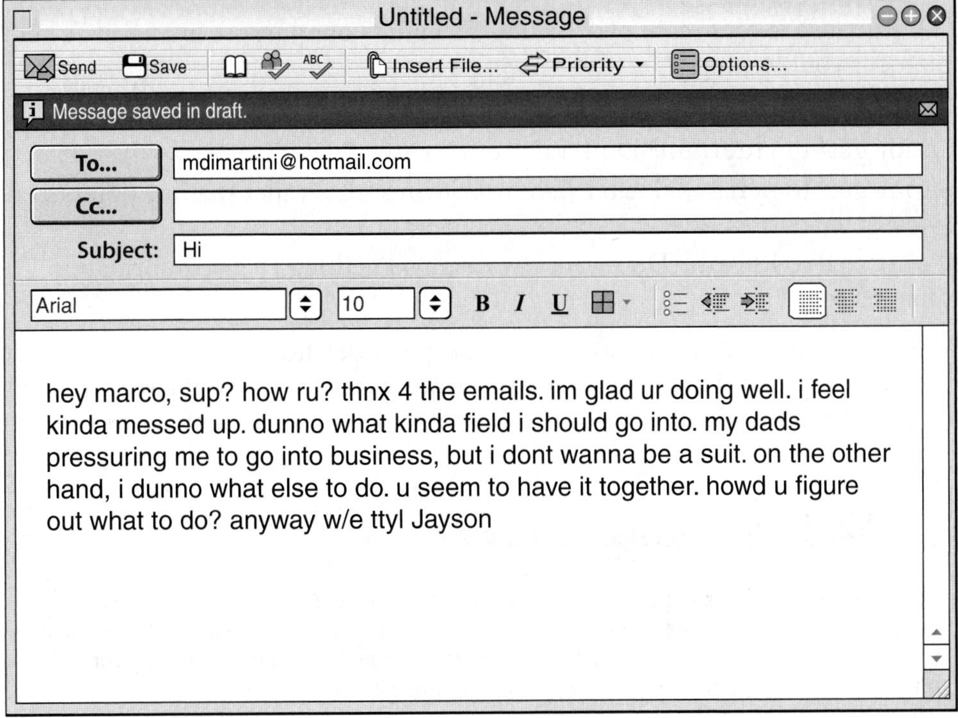

Untitled - Message
Send
Save
Insert File...
Priority
Options...
Message saved in draft.
To...
mdimartini@hotmail.com
Cc...
Subject:
Hi
Arial
10
B
I
U
hey marco, sup? how ru? thnx 4 the emails. im glad ur doing well. i feel kinda messed up. dunno what kinda field i should go into. my dads pressuring me to go into business, but i dont wanna be a suit. on the other hand, i dunno what else to do. u seem to have it together. howd u figure out what to do? anyway w/e ttyl Jayson

Email B

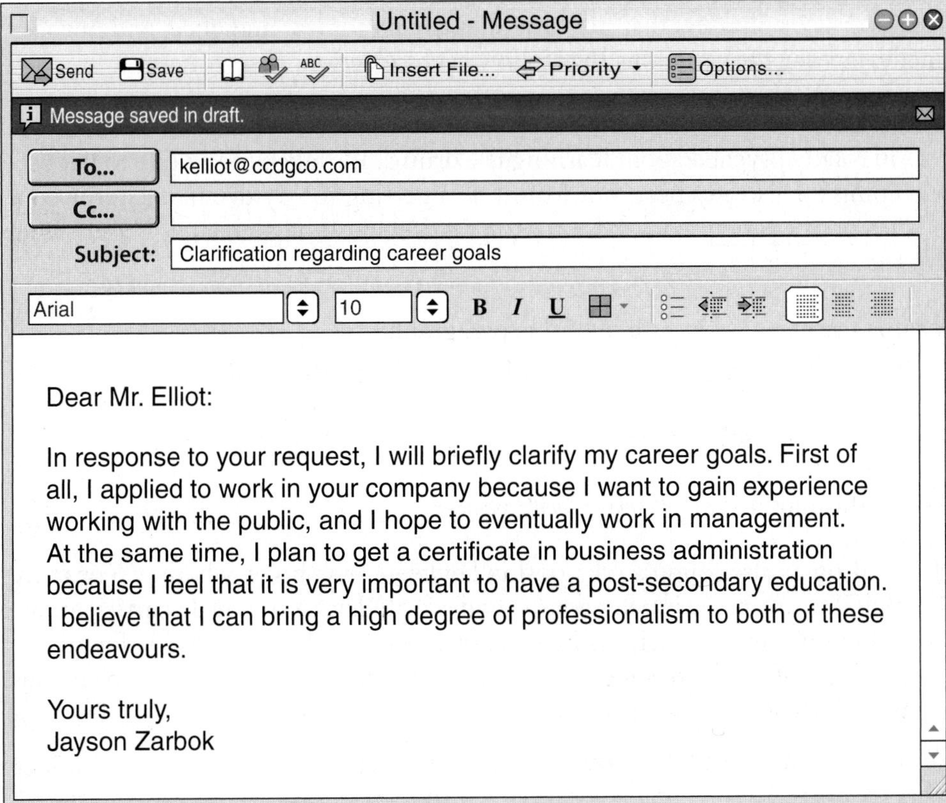

Untitled - Message
Send
Save
Insert File...
Priority
Options...
Message saved in draft.
To...
kelliot@ccdgco.com
Cc...
Subject:
Clarification regarding career goals
Arial
10
B
I
U
Dear Mr. Elliot:
In response to your request, I will briefly clarify my career goals. First of all, I applied to work in your company because I want to gain experience working with the public, and I hope to eventually work in management. At the same time, I plan to get a certificate in business administration because I feel that it is very important to have a post-secondary education. I believe that I can bring a high degree of professionalism to both of these endeavours.
Yours truly,
Jayson Zarbok

Purpose

Your **purpose** is your reason for writing. Keeping your purpose in mind will help you focus your writing.

When you consider your purpose, ask yourself the following questions.

- Is my goal to **entertain?** Do I want to tell a story?
- Is my goal to **persuade?** Do I want to convince the reader that my point of view is the correct one?
- Is my goal to **inform?** Do I want to explain something or give information about a topic?

Sometimes you may have more than one purpose. For example, a narrative paragraph or essay about a personal experience can also inform the reader about something interesting. It is possible to write for a combination of reasons.

General and Specific Purposes

Your **general purpose** is to entertain, to inform, or to persuade. Your **specific purpose** is your more precise reason for writing. For example, imagine that you have to write a piece about music. Your general purpose may be to inform, while your specific purpose may be to explain how to become a better musician.

PRACTICE 2

Selections 1 to 3 are about music; however, each has a different purpose, has been written for a different audience, and has been taken from a different source. To complete this practice, read each selection carefully. Then underline any language clues (words or phrases) that help you identify its source, audience, and purpose. Finally, answer the questions that follow each selection.

EXAMPLE:

Slang ➢ I'm totally psyched about learning the drums. It's taken me awhile to get used to keeping up a steady beat, but I think I'm getting it. My drum teacher is cool, Slang, informal tone ➢ and he's pretty patient with me. I try to practise, but it bugs the neighbours when I hit the cymbals.

What is the most likely source of this paragraph?

a. Website article b. Textbook (c.) Personal letter

What is its purpose? *To inform*

Who is the audience? *Friend or family member*

1. Lomax also found a relationship between polyphony, where two or more melodies are sung simultaneously, and a high degree of female participation in food-getting. In societies in which women's work is responsible for at least half of the food, songs are likely to contain more than one simultaneous melody, with the higher tunes usually sung by women.

   What is the most likely source of this paragraph?

   a. Novel b. Textbook c. Personal letter

What is its purpose? ____

Who is the audience? ____

____

2. When dealing with club managers, it is *imperative* that you act professionally. Get all the details of a gig in advance. Doing so will eliminate any confusion or miscommunication that could result in a botched deal. It will also instantly set you apart from the legions of flaky musicians that managers must endure on a daily basis. That's a good thing.

What is the most likely source of this paragraph?

a. Website article b. Novel c. Personal letter

What is its purpose? ____

Who is the audience? ____

____

3. But there was no reason why everyone should not dance. Madame Ratignolle could not, so it was she who gaily consented to play for the others. She played very well, keeping excellent waltz time and infusing an expression into the strains which was indeed inspiring. She was keeping up her music on account of the children, she said, because she and her husband both considered it a means of brightening the home and making it attractive.

What is the most likely source of this paragraph?

a. Novel b. Textbook c. Personal letter

What is its purpose? ____

Who is the audience? ____

____

PRACTICE 3

View the following cartoon. What is the topic? Who is the audience? What is the purpose? Does the cartoon achieve its purpose?

"Oh no, not homework again."

Arnie Levin/The New Yorker Collection/The Cartoon Bank

Exploring Strategies

After you determine your topic, audience, and purpose, try some **exploring strategies**—also known as **prewriting strategies**—to help get your ideas flowing. The four most common strategies are freewriting, brainstorming, questioning, and clustering. It is not necessary to do all of the strategies explained in this chapter. Find the strategy that works best for you.

You can do both general and focused prewriting. If you have writer's block and do not know what to write, use **general prewriting** to come up with possible topics. Then, after you have chosen a topic, use **focused prewriting** to find an angle of the topic that is interesting and that could be developed in your paragraph.

When to Use Exploring Strategies

You can use exploring strategies at any stage of the writing process.

- To find a topic
- To narrow a broad topic
- To generate ideas about your topic
- To generate supporting details

Watch the **Video** Prewriting: Freewriting **MyWritingLab**

Freewriting

Freewriting is writing for a limited period of time without stopping. The point is to record the first thoughts that come to mind. If you have no ideas, you can indicate that fact in a sentence such as "I don't know what to write." As you write, do not be concerned with your grammar or spelling. If you use a computer, let your ideas flow and do not worry about typing mistakes.

TECHNOLOGY LINK

On a computer, try typing without looking at the screen or with the screen turned off. Don't worry about mistakes.

SANDRA'S FREEWRITING

College student Sandra Ahumada did general freewriting about work. During her freewriting, she wrote everything that came to mind.

> Work. I've only worked in a restaurant. A lotta reasons to work in a restaurant. Schedules are good for college students. Can work nights or weekends. Serving people so different from studying. You can relax your brain, go on automatic pilot. But you have to remember people's orders so it can be hard. And some customer are rude, rude, RUDE. What else . . . It is hard to juggle a job and college work. But it forces me to organize my time. What types of jobs pay a good salary? Day-care work? In some jobs, you get tips in addition to the salary. Should people always tip servers? Don't know. The tips can be very good. Like for hairdressers. Taxi drivers.

SANDRA'S FOCUSED FREEWRITING

After Sandra did her general freewriting, she underlined the ideas that she thought could be expanded into a complete paragraph. Then she looked at her underlined ideas to decide which one to write about. Her purpose was to persuade, so she chose a topic that she could defend. She did focused freewriting about tipping.

> I think people should always tip in restaurants. Why. Well, the waitresses need the cash. I dont earn a lot, so the tips are really important. I gotta lot a bills, and can't pay everything with minimum wage. What else? Diners should just consider the tip as a part of the cost of eating out. If they don't wanna tip, they should cook at home.

Also, lots of other service people get tips and nobody cares. And bad service. It could be the cook's fault. Some customers blame me when the restaurant is really crowded and I'm run off my feet. They should be more understanding. We need those tips. Sure do.

The Writer's Desk Freewriting

Choose one of the following topics, and do some freewriting. Remember to write without stopping.

The family Travel Sports

Brainstorming

Watch the Video
Prewriting: Brainstorming
MyWritingLab

Brainstorming is like freewriting except that you create a list of ideas and you can take the time to stop and think when you create your list. As you think about the topic, write down words or phrases that come to mind. Do not be concerned about grammar or spelling; the point is to generate ideas.

Chul's Brainstorming

College student Chul Yee brainstormed about cities. He made a list of general ideas.

- living in a city vs. living in a town
- my favourite cities
- the bad side of city life
- reasons people move to large cities
- Toronto full of pollution
- reasons to get out of cities

Chul's Focused Brainstorming

After he had brainstormed some general ideas, Chul chose one idea and did some focused brainstorming about the reasons people move out of cities.

- cities are too crowded and impersonal
- smaller towns everybody knows each other
- cities are too dangerous (car jacking last week in this neighbourhood)
- cost of living in the city is higher, rents are higher
- want to know neighbours and feel like a part of a community
- desire the slower pace of life in the country

The Writer's Desk Brainstorming

Choose one of the following topics, and brainstorm. Write down a list of ideas.

Ceremonies Gossip Good or bad manners

Watch the **Video**
Prewriting: Questioning
MyWritingLab

Questioning

Another way to generate ideas about a topic is to ask yourself a series of questions and write responses to them. The questions can help you define and narrow your topic. One common way to do this is to ask yourself *who, what, when, where, why,* and *how* questions. As with other exploring strategies, questioning can be general or focused.

CLAYTON'S QUESTIONING

College student Clayton Rukavina used a question-and-answer format to generate ideas about binge drinking.

What is binge drinking?	having too much alcohol in a short time
Who binge-drinks?	students who are away from home for the first time, or insecure students
Why do students drink too much?	peer pressure, want to be more relaxed, don't think about consequences
When do students drink too much?	spring break, weekends, to celebrate legal age
How dangerous is binge drinking?	may get alcohol poisoning, may choke, and may drink and drive
Where does it happen?	dorm rooms, house parties, fraternities
Why is it an important topic?	can die from binge drinking or drunk driver can kill somebody else

The Writer's Desk Questioning

Choose one of the following topics, and write questions and answers. Try to ask *who, what, when, where, why,* and *how* questions.

Beliefs Patriotism Health

Clustering

Clustering is like drawing a word map; ideas are arranged in a visual image. To begin, write your topic in the middle of the page, and draw a box or a circle around it. That idea will lead to another, so write the second idea and draw a line connecting it to your topic. Keep writing, circling, and connecting ideas until you have groups or "clusters" of them on your page. You can cluster to get ideas about a general or a specific topic.

MAHAN'S CLUSTERING

College student Mahan Zahir used clustering to explore ideas about crime. He identified some main topics.

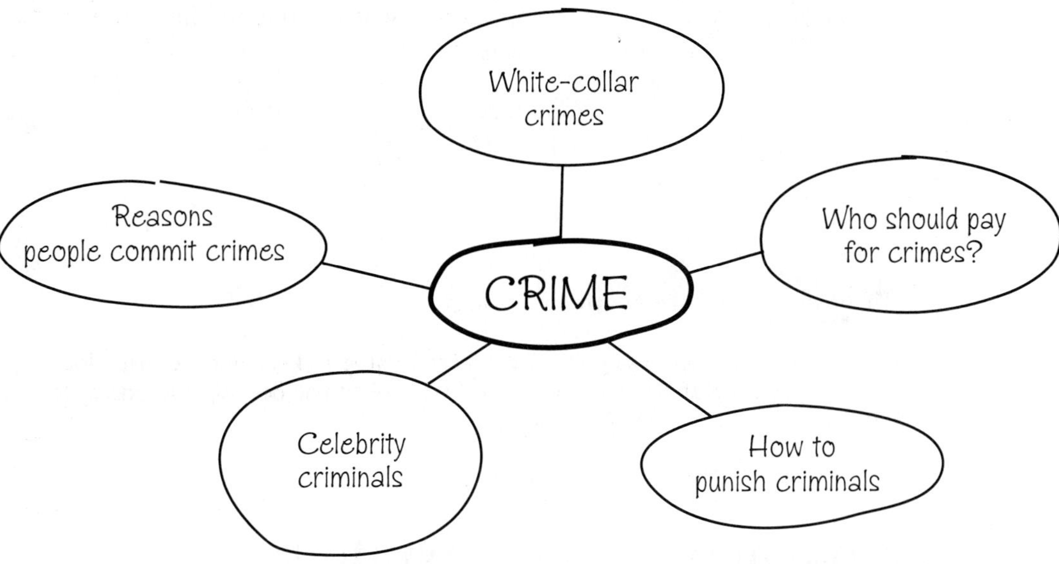

MAHAN'S FOCUSED CLUSTERING

Mahan decided to write about the reasons that people commit crimes. He added clusters to that topic.

The Writer's Desk Clustering

Choose one of the following topics, and make a cluster on a separate sheet of paper. Begin by writing the key word in the middle of the space. Then connect related ideas.

Jobs College Relationships

Hint **More about Exploring**

When you explore a topic using any of the listed strategies, keep in mind that a lot of the ideas you generate may not be useful. Later, when you develop your ideas, be prepared to cut irrelevant information.

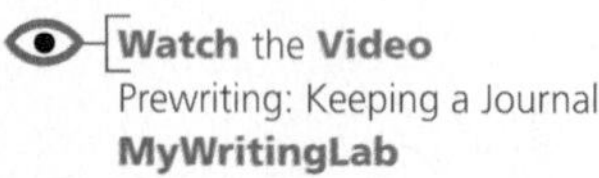

Watch the **Video**
Prewriting: Keeping a Journal
MyWritingLab

Journal and Portfolio Writing

Keeping a Journal

You may write for work or school, but you can also practise writing for pleasure. One way to practise your writing is to keep a journal. A **journal** is a book, a computer file, or a blog (web log) where you record your thoughts, opinions, ideas, and impressions. Journal writing gives you a chance to practise your writing without worrying about your readers and what they might think about it. It also gives you a source of material when you want to write about a topic of your choice. According to the author Anaïs Nin, "Keeping a diary is a way of making everyday life seem as exciting as fiction."

In your journal, you can write about any topic that appeals to you. Here are some topics for journal writing.

- Anything related to your personal life, such as your feelings about your career goals, personal problems and solutions, opinions about your university courses, reflections about past and future decisions, or feelings about your job
- Your reactions to controversies in the world, in your country, in your province, in your city, or in your university
- Facts that interest you
- Your reflections on the opinions and philosophies of others, including your friends or people that you read about in your courses

Keeping a Portfolio

A **writing portfolio** is a binder or an electronic file folder where you keep samples of all of your writing. The purpose of keeping a portfolio is to have a record of your writing progress. In your portfolio, keep all drafts of your writing assignments. When you work on new assignments, review your previous work in your portfolio. Identify your main problems, and try not to repeat the same errors.

REFLECT ON IT

Think about what you learned in this chapter. If you do not know an answer, review that topic.

1. Before you write, you should think about your topic, audience, and purpose. Explain what each one is.
   a. Topic: ______________________________
   b. Audience: ______________________________
   c. Purpose: ______________________________
2. Briefly define each of the following exploring strategies.
   a. Freewriting: ______________________________
   b. Brainstorming: ______________________________
   c. Questioning: ______________________________
   d. Clustering: ______________________________

Writing Activity 1: Topics

Choose one of the following topics, or choose your own. Then generate ideas about the topic. You may want to try the suggested exploring strategy.

General Topics

1. Try freewriting about a strong childhood memory.
2. Try brainstorming and list any thoughts that come to mind about anger.
3. Try clustering. First, write "Rules" in the middle of the page. Then write clusters of ideas that connect to the general topic.
4. Ask and answer some questions about cosmetic surgery.

College- and Work-Related Topics

5. Try freewriting about a comfortable place. Include any emotions or other details that come to mind.
6. Try brainstorming about study habits. List any ideas that come to mind.
7. To get ideas, ask and answer questions about recent celebrity scandals.
8. Try clustering. First, write "cellphones" in the middle of the page. Then write clusters of ideas that relate to the general topic.

Writing Activity 2

Look carefully at the poster. First, determine the topic, audience, and purpose. Whom is the poster trying to convince? What is the purpose? Is the purpose fulfilled? Then try exploring the topic. Use questioning as your exploring strategy. Ask and answer *who, what, when, where, why,* and *how* questions.

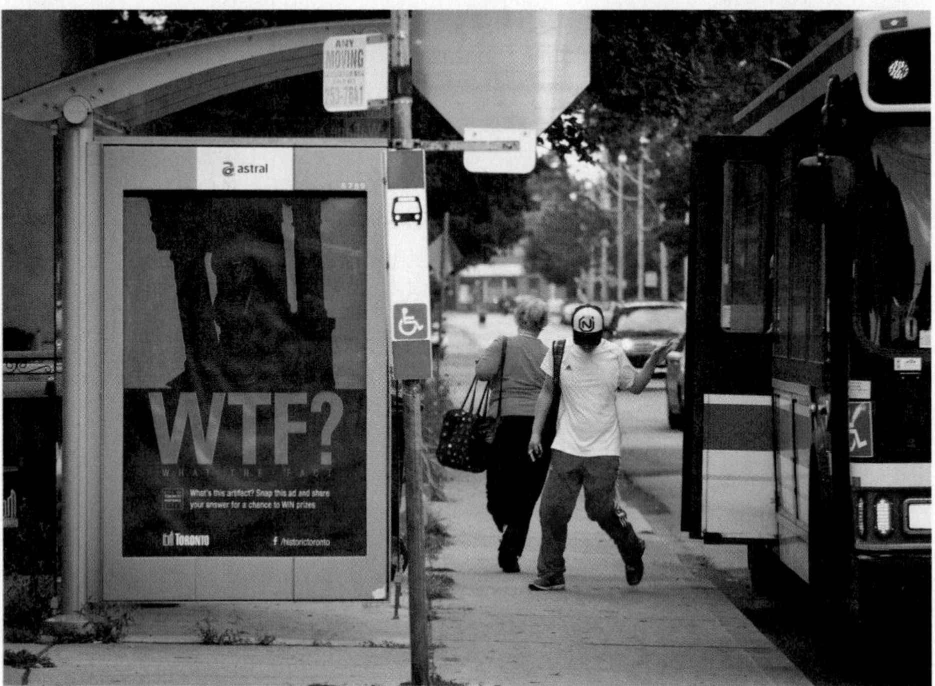

Lucas Oleniuk/Toronto Star via Getty Images

EXPLORING CHECKLIST

As you explore your topics, ask yourself the following questions.

- ☐ What is my topic? (Consider what you will write about.)
- ☐ Who is my audience? (Think about your intended reader.)
- ☐ What is my purpose? (Determine your reason for writing.)
- ☐ How can I explore? (You might try freewriting, brainstorming, questioning, or clustering.)

How Do I Get a Better Grade?

Visit MyWritingLab for audiovisual lectures and additional practice sets about prewriting strategies.

Developing

Lynne Gaetz

After finding an idea, an artist begins to define shapes and layer on colours. Like an artist, a writer shapes ideas to create a solid paragraph or essay.

LEARNING OBJECTIVES

What Is Developing?

In Chapter 1, you learned how to use exploring strategies to formulate ideas. In this chapter, you will focus on the second stage of the writing process: **developing**. There are five key steps in the developing stage.

DEVELOPING

STEP 1 ➤ **Narrow your topic.** Focus on some aspect of the topic that interests you.

STEP 2 ➤ **Express your main idea.** Write a topic sentence (for a paragraph) or a thesis statement (for an essay) that expresses the main idea of the piece of writing.

STEP 3 ➤ **Develop your supporting ideas.** Find facts, examples, or anecdotes that best support your main idea.

STEP 4 ➤ **Make a plan or an outline.** Organize your main and supporting ideas, and place your ideas in a plan or an outline.

STEP 5 ➤ **Write your first draft.** Communicate your ideas in a single written piece.

Watch the **Video**
Paragraphs: Recognizing a Paragraph
MyWritingLab

ESSAY LINK

When you develop an essay, you follow similar steps. For details about essay writing, see Chapter 13.

Watch the **Video**
Essays: Essay Writing
MyWritingLab

Watch the Video
Revising the Paragraph: A Checklist
MyWritingLab

Reviewing Paragraph Structure

Before you practise developing your paragraphs, review the paragraph structure. A **paragraph** is a series of related sentences that develop one central idea. Because a paragraph can stand alone or be part of a longer piece of writing, it is the essential writing model. You can apply your paragraph writing skills to longer essays, letters, and reports.

A stand-alone paragraph generally has the following characteristics.

- A **topic sentence** states the topic and introduces the idea the writer will develop.
- **Body sentences** support the topic sentence.
- A **concluding sentence** ends the paragraph.

Catherine's Paragraph

University student Catherine Niatum wrote the following paragraph. Read her paragraph and notice how it is structured.

The topic sentence expresses the idea that Catherine develops in the paragraph. ➢

Catherine supports the paragraph with examples. ➢

The concluding sentence brings the paragraph to a satisfying close. ➢

The commercialization of traditional holidays helps our economy. First, toy stores and other gift shops benefit when people buy presents for loved ones. Toys "R" Us, for instance, posted record profits during December's gift-giving season. Second, it helps the clothing industry because people spend money on new outfits. Marie Senko, a fashion store owner, says, "During the winter holiday season, we do almost the entire year's business." Moreover, specialty stores see their sales increase when customers buy lights, candles, and other decorations for their homes. Grocery stores and restaurants also profit because people prepare feasts, and companies have staff parties in restaurants and hotels. A Vancouver accounting firm, for example, celebrates every New Year's Eve in a local restaurant. Finally, the travel industry has a financial windfall during celebrations because people cross the nation to visit their loved ones. According to Air Canada employee Annie Sung, seat sales increase by 70 percent during Thanksgiving. The next time someone complains about the commercialization of holidays, remind the person that holiday spending is very beneficial for our economy.

Hint **Paragraph Form**

When you write a paragraph, make sure that it has the following form.

- Always indent the first word of a paragraph. Move it about one inch, or five spaces, from the left-hand margin.
- Try to leave a margin of an inch to an inch and a half on each side of your paragraph.

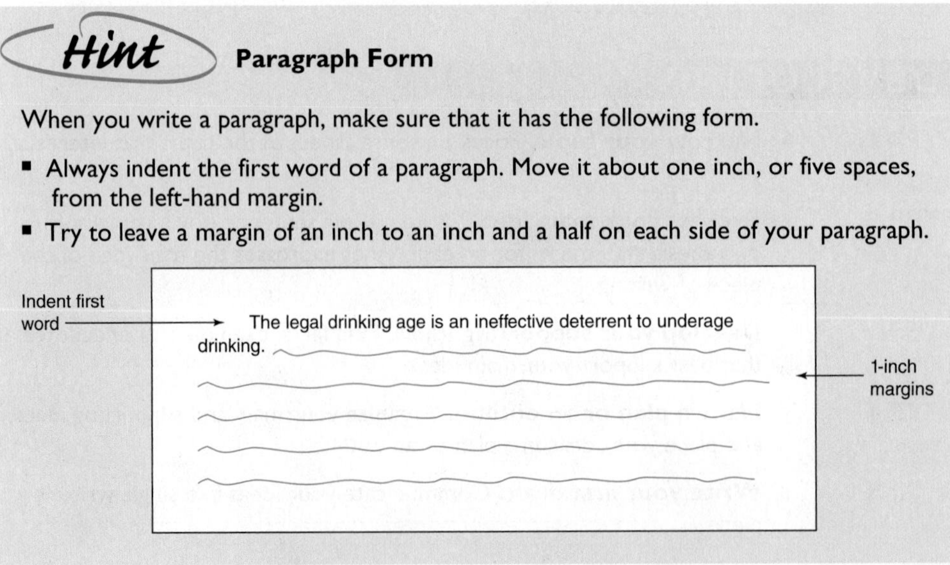

Narrow the Topic

A paragraph has one main idea. If your topic is too broad, you might find it difficult to write only one paragraph about it. When you **narrow** your topic, you make it more specific.

To narrow your topic, you can use exploring strategies such as freewriting, brainstorming, and questioning. These strategies are explained in more detail in Chapter 1, "Exploring."

Review the following examples of general and narrowed topics.

General Topic	Narrowed Topic
The job interview	How to dress for a job interview
College	My misconceptions about college life
Rituals	The high school prom

ESSAY LINK

An essay contains several paragraphs and can have a broader topic than a paragraph.

Narrowing the Topic

One way to narrow your topic is to break it down into smaller categories.

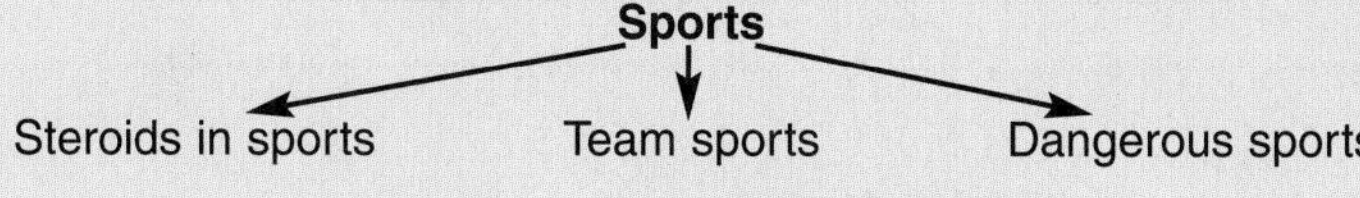

Sandra's Example of Narrowing a Topic

College student Sandra Ahumada practised narrowing a topic by thinking of ideas about work.

- types of work: paid work, housework, homework
- jobs I have done in the service industry: server, cashier
- reasons to work in a restaurant
- how to find a job
- bad jobs that I have had
- finding the right career
- dangerous jobs such as firefighter, police officer
- are online job sites useful?

The Writer's Desk Narrow the Topic

Topics 1 to 5 are very broad. Practise narrowing topics by writing three ideas for each one.

EXAMPLE:

Crime: *white-collar crime*
why people steal
types of punishment

1. The family: ______
______
______

2. Gossip: ______________________

3. Travel: ______________________

4. Sports: ______________________

5. Jobs: ______________________

Watch the Video
Paragraphs: The Topic Sentence
MyWritingLab

The Topic Sentence

After you have narrowed the topic of your paragraph, your next step will be to write a topic sentence. The **topic sentence** has specific characteristics.

- It introduces the topic of the paragraph.
- It states the paragraph's controlling idea.
- It is the most general sentence in the paragraph.
- It is followed by other sentences that provide supporting facts and examples.

ESSAY LINK

Just as a topic sentence expresses the main point of a paragraph, the thesis statement expresses the main point of an essay. Both have a controlling idea.

Watch the Video
Writing a Thesis Statement
MyWritingLab

The **controlling idea** makes a point about the topic and expresses the writer's opinion, attitude, or feeling. You can express different controlling ideas about the same topic. For example, the following topic sentences are about youth offenders, but each sentence makes a different point about the topic.

narrowed topic — controlling idea

Youth offenders should not receive special treatment from the correctional system.

controlling idea

Rehabilitation and education are the best ways for the province to handle **youth offenders.** narrowed topic

PRACTICE 1

Read each topic sentence. Underline the topic once and the controlling idea twice.

EXAMPLE:

Learning to play the guitar requires practice, patience, and perseverance.

1. Music education is essential in public schools.
2. My furnished room has everything a student could need.
3. You can learn to make decisions and think critically with a liberal arts education.

4. Several interesting events happened during the Stanford Prison Experiment.
5. The new youth centre has a very impressive design.
6. There should not be a lower legal drinking age in our province.
7. We encountered many problems on our journey to Prince Edward Island.
8. Rory was known for his rumpled, unfashionable clothing.
9. IQ tests are not always accurate and valid.
10. The Tragically Hip went through many musical phases.

Identifying the Topic Sentence

Before you write topic sentences, practise finding them in paragraphs by other writers. To find the topic sentence of a paragraph, follow these steps.

- Read the paragraph carefully.
- Look for a sentence that sums up the paragraph's subject. Professional writers may place the topic sentence anywhere in the paragraph.
- After you have chosen a sentence, see if the other sentences in the paragraph provide evidence that supports that sentence.

If you find one sentence that sums up what the paragraph is about and is supported by the other sentences in the paragraph, then you have identified the topic sentence.

PRACTICE 2

Underline or highlight the topic sentences in paragraphs A and B. Remember that the topic sentence is not always the first sentence in the paragraph.

EXAMPLE:

Taking a proactive approach is especially important when you consider who the victims of workplace bullying typically are and the effects bullying can have on them. Employees suffering at the hands of bullies are typically those in the organization that are well-liked, dedicated and those who have years of experience and success under their belt. In other words, your stars may very well be the ones targeted and bullying can have devastating effects on their personal and professional lives.

—Naomi Brown, "Filling in the Gaps: How Emotional Intelligence Training Can Combat Workplace Bullying," *HR Professional*

A. Runners are a different breed. With much of our modern athletic world catering to convenience—fitness clubs, treadmills, protection from the elements—it can be hard to understand why someone would pull on a pair of sneakers, open the front door and start running. It's not weather-permitting but weather-*embracing*. Never is this more true than in winter. One person's insanity is another's inspiration, and perhaps it takes a little bit of both to wake up in that morning darkness to face the snow, ice and sub-zero temperatures with nothing but two feet and that voice in your head that whispers, "Go."

—Jeff Beer and Jordan Timm, "Dashing through the Snow," *Canadian Business*

B. Cosmetic surgery is not like fooling around with a bottle of hair dye or getting a set of fake fingernails. The procedures are invasive, the recovery sometimes painful, and mistakes, while not common, can be difficult or impossible to correct. Breast implants may rupture, noses sink inward, and smiles turn unnaturally tight. People who merely wanted fat vacuumed from their thighs have died, while balding men have found themselves sporting new hair in symmetrical rows like tree farms. Stephen Katz, a sociologist at Trent University in Ontario, Canada, says, "To have plastic surgery, you have to think of your body as an object. It's a kind of social madness."

—Patricia Chisholm, "The Body Builders," *MacLean's*

C. Imagine a society without laws. People would not know what to expect from one another (an area controlled by the law of contracts), nor would they be able to plan for the future with any degree of certainty (administrative law); they wouldn't feel safe knowing that the more powerful or better armed could take what they wanted from the less powerful (criminal law); and they might not be able to exercise basic rights which would otherwise be available to them as citizens of a free nation (constitutional law).

—Frank Schmalleger, *Criminal Justice Today*

TECHNOLOGY LINK

If you write your paragraph on a computer, make your topic sentence bold (ctrl B). Then you and your instructor can easily identify it.

Writing an Effective Topic Sentence

When you develop your topic sentence, avoid some common errors by asking yourself these three questions.

1. **Is my topic sentence a complete sentence that has a controlling idea?** You might state the topic in one word or phrase, but your topic sentence should always reveal a complete thought and have a controlling idea. It should not announce the topic.

Incomplete: Working in a restaurant.
(This is a topic but *not* a topic sentence. It does not contain both a subject and a verb, and it does not express a complete thought.)

Announcement: I will write about part-time jobs.
(This announces the topic but says nothing relevant about it. Do not use expressions such as *My topic is* … or *I will write about.* …)

Topic sentence: Part-time jobs help post-secondary students build self-esteem.

2. **Does my topic sentence make a valid and supportable point?** Your topic sentence should express a valid point that you can support with your evidence. It should not be a vaguely worded statement, and it should not be a highly questionable generalization.

Vague: Beauty is becoming more important in our culture.
(Beauty is more important than what?)

Invalid point: Beauty is more important than it was in the past.
(Is this really true? Cultures throughout history have been concerned with notions of beauty.)

Topic sentence: Fashion magazines do not provide people with enough varied examples of beauty.

3. **Can I support my topic sentence in a single paragraph?**
Your topic sentence should express an idea that you can support in a paragraph. It should not be too broad or too narrow.

Too broad: Love is important.
(It would be difficult to write a paragraph about this topic. There are too many things to say.)

Too narrow: My girlfriend was born on March 2.
(What more is there to say?)

Topic sentence: During my first relationship, I learned a lot about being honest.

ESSAY LINK

If you find that your topic is too broad for a paragraph, you might want to save it so you can try using it for an essay.

Hint **Write a Clear Topic Sentence**

Your topic sentence should not express an obvious or well-known fact. When you clearly indicate your point of view, your topic sentence will capture your readers' attention and make them want to continue reading.

Obvious: Money is important in our world.
(Everybody knows this.)

Better: There are several effective ways to save money.

PRACTICE 3

Choose the word from the list that best describes the problem with each topic sentence. Correct the problem by revising each sentence.

Announces	Incomplete	Narrow
Broad	Invalid	Vague

EXAMPLE: This paragraph is about television advertisements.

Problem: *Announces*

Revised statement: *Television advertisements should be banned during children's programming.*

1. How to pack a suitcase.
Problem: ______________________
Revised statement: ______________________
2. I will write about negative political campaigns.
Problem: ______________________
Revised statement: ______________________
3. Today's journalists never tell both sides of the story.
Problem: ______________________
Revised statement: ______________________

4. History teaches us lessons.
   Problem: ____________________
   Revised statement: ____________________
5. Deciding to go to college.
   Problem: ____________________
   Revised statement: ____________________
6. The subject of this paragraph is annoying co-workers.
   Problem: ____________________
   Revised statement: ____________________
7. Everybody wants to be famous.
   Problem: ____________________
   Revised statement: ____________________
8. The coffee shop walls are painted green.
   Problem: ____________________
   Revised statement: ____________________

PRACTICE 4

The following paragraphs do not contain topic sentences. Read the paragraphs carefully and write an appropriate topic sentence for each.

1. ____________________

First, computer technology allows people to work from their own homes, curtailing the need to have face-to-face interaction with other people. Business people can do conference calls, receive and send business documents, and access a lot of information without ever having to go to the office. Next, ATMs and online banking make it convenient for people to take out money or pay bills without having to communicate with bank personnel. Before Internet banking, people used to go to the bank regularly to pay bills or take out money. Most bank tellers knew their clients by name and took the time to chat with them. Nowadays, many people simply interact with a machine. Furthermore, consumers can do their shopping online. They never have to go to a store, further reducing their contact with other people. Indeed, modern technology has led to a way of life where people interact with each other less than before.

2. ____________________

Indeed, eye contact is a crucial ingredient to communicate thoughts and feelings. Many people have had their first social interaction with a future partner through eye contact. On the other hand, people discourage social interaction by avoiding eye contact. Next, hand gestures also communicate many messages. Through hand gestures, people greet, insult, or laugh at each other. For example, students show their knowledge by raising a hand to give a response, hitchhikers ask for a lift by using their thumb, and antiwar protesters convey their philosophy of peace with two fingers in the form of a V. Those who are extremely angry gesture with a fist. Most importantly, facial gestures are a fundamental element for nonverbal communication. People reveal their emotions through smiling, frowning, and rolling their eyes. If people really want to know what someone else is thinking or feeling, they should look closely at the person's body language.

The Writer's Desk Write Topic Sentences

Narrow each of the topics in this exercise. Then write a topic sentence that contains a controlling idea. You could look at Writer's Desk: Narrow the Topic on pages 21–22 for ideas.

EXAMPLE: CRIME

Narrowed topic: *Why people steal*

Topic sentence: *People steal for many reasons.*

1. The family

   Narrowed topic: __________

   Topic sentence: __________

2. Gossip

   Narrowed topic: __________

   Topic sentence: __________

3. Travel

   Narrowed topic: __________

   Topic sentence: __________

4. Sports

   Narrowed topic: __________

   Topic sentence: __________

5. Jobs

   Narrowed topic: __________

   Topic sentence: __________

ESSAY LINK

When writing an essay, place the thesis statement in the introduction. Then each supporting idea becomes a distinct paragraph with its own topic sentence.

Watch the **Video**
Developing and Organizing a Paragraph: Developing a Paragraph
MyWritingLab

The Supporting Ideas

Once you have written a clear topic sentence, you can focus on the **supporting details**—the facts and examples that provide the reader with interesting information about the subject matter. There are three steps you can take to determine your paragraph's supporting details.

- Generate supporting ideas.
- Choose the best ideas.
- Organize your ideas.

Generating Supporting Ideas

You can try an exploring strategy such as brainstorming or freewriting to generate ideas.

Mahan's Supporting Ideas

University student Mahan Zahir narrowed his topic and wrote his topic sentence. Then he listed ideas that could support his topic sentence.

People steal for many reasons.

– need money for food
– want luxury items
– for thrills
– addiction
– for drugs
– minimum wage not enough to buy groceries
– alcohol-related crimes
– unemployment
– want to consume
– lack a moral code
– think they deserve something for nothing
– lack of parental attention
– too lazy
– adrenaline rush

The Writer's Desk **List Supporting Ideas**

Choose two of your topic sentences from the previous Writer's Desk. For each topic sentence, develop a list of supporting ideas.

Choosing the Best Ideas

An effective paragraph has **unity** when all of its sentences directly relate to and support the topic sentence. Create a unified paragraph by selecting three or four ideas that are most compelling and that clearly support your topic sentence. You may notice that several items in your list are similar; therefore, you can group them together. If some ideas do not support the topic sentence, remove them.

Watch the Video
Revising the Paragraph: Unity
MyWritingLab

Mahan's Best Supporting Ideas

Mahan grouped together related ideas and crossed out some ideas that did not relate to his topic sentence.

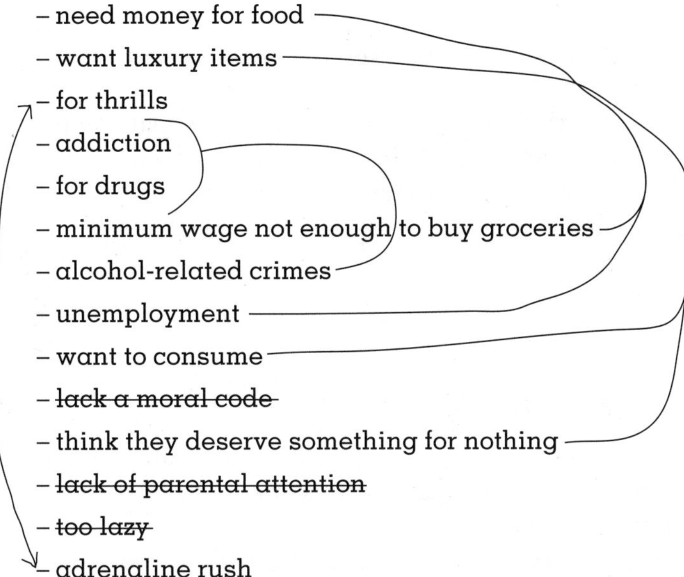

Identifying the Best Ideas

There are many ways that you can highlight your best ideas. You can circle the best supporting points and then use arrows to link them with secondary ideas. You can also use highlighter pens or asterisks (*) to identify the best supporting points.

TECHNOLOGY LINK

On a computer, you can cut (ctrl X) and paste (ctrl V) similar ideas together.

PRACTICE 5

College student Sandra Ahumada brainstormed ideas about tipping. Her purpose was to persuade, so she created a topic sentence that expressed her opinion about the issue.

Underline three ideas from her list that you think are most compelling and that most clearly illustrate the point she is making in her topic sentence. Then group together any related ideas under each of the main subheadings. If any ideas do not relate to her topic sentence, remove them.

Topic Sentence: Customers should always tip restaurant servers.

– part of the cost of going to a restaurant
– shows appreciation for the server's work

- servers need tips to have an adequate standard of living
- their salaries are below the standard minimum wage
- some customers are rude
- servers often don't get benefits such as health care
- you tip hairdressers and taxi drivers
- mistakes aren't always the server's fault
- slow service could be the cook's fault
- sometimes there are not enough servers
- some people in the service industry get good money (cooks, I think)

The Writer's Desk Choose the Best Ideas

Choose *one* of the two lists of supporting ideas that you prepared for the previous Writer's Desk. Identify some compelling ideas that clearly illustrate the point you are trying to make. If any ideas are related, you can group them together. Cross out any ideas that are not useful.

ESSAY LINK

In an essay, you can use time, space, or emphatic order to organize your ideas.

Watch the Video
Developing and Organizing a Paragraph: Organizing a Paragraph
MyWritingLab

Organizing Your Ideas

Organize your ideas in a logical manner so readers can easily follow them. You can use one of three common organizational methods: (1) time order, (2) emphatic order, or (3) space order.

Transitional expressions help guide the reader from one idea to another. A complete list of transitional expressions appears on page 47 in Chapter 3.

TIME ORDER

When you organize a paragraph using **time order (chronological order),** you arrange the details according to the sequence in which they have occurred. When you narrate a story, explain how to do something, or describe a historical event, you generally use time order.

first

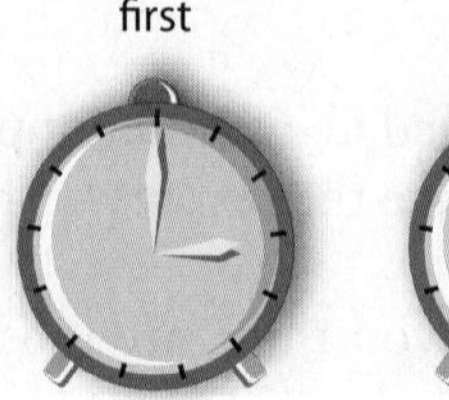

then

after that

Here are some transitional expressions you can use in time-order paragraphs.

after that	first	later	next
eventually	immediately	meanwhile	suddenly
finally	in the beginning	months after	then

The next paragraph is structured using time order.

> One day, some gentlemen called on my mother, and I felt the shutting of the front door and other sounds that indicated their arrival. Immediately, I ran upstairs before anyone could stop me to put on my idea of formal clothing. Standing before the mirror, as I had seen others do, I anointed my head with oil and covered my face thickly with powder. Then I pinned a veil over my head so that it covered my face and fell in folds down to my shoulders. Finally, I tied an enormous bustle round my small waist, so that it dangled behind, almost meeting the hem of my skirt. Thus attired, I went down to help entertain the company.
>
> —Helen Keller, *The Story of My Life*

Emphatic Order

When you organize the supporting details of a paragraph using **emphatic order,** you arrange them in a logical sequence. For example, you can arrange details from least to most important, from least to most appealing, and so on.

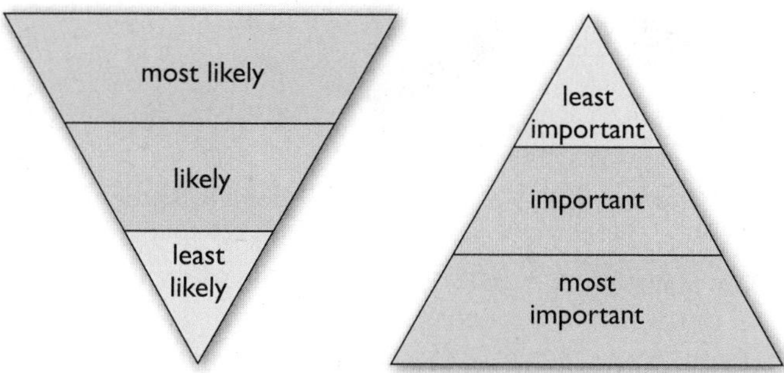

Here are some transitional expressions you can use in emphatic-order paragraphs.

above all	first	moreover	principally
clearly	in particular	most importantly	the least important
especially	last	of course	the most important

The following paragraph uses emphatic order. The writers begin with a somewhat serious condition and end with the most serious one.

> Although our thirst mechanism can trigger us to drink more water, this mechanism alone is not always sufficient: we tend to drink until we are no longer thirsty, but the amount of fluid we consume may not be enough to achieve fluid balance. This is particularly true when we lose body water rapidly, such as during intense exercise in the heat. Because our thirst mechanism has some limitations, it is important that you drink regularly throughout the day and not wait to drink until you become thirsty, especially if you are active. Because our thirst mechanism becomes less sensitive as we age, older people can fail to drink adequate amounts of fluid and thus are at high risk for dehydration. For this reason, older adults should be careful to drink fluids on a regular basis throughout the day. Finally, infants are also at increased risk for dehydration.
>
> —Janice Thompson et al., *Nutrition: A Functional Approach*

Using Emphatic Order

When you organize details using emphatic order, use your own values and opinions to determine what is most or least important, upsetting, remarkable, and so on. Another writer might organize the same ideas in a different way.

Space Order

When you organize ideas using **space order,** you help the reader visualize what you are describing in a specific space. For example, you can describe something or someone from top to bottom or bottom to top, from left to right or right to left, or from far to near or near to far.

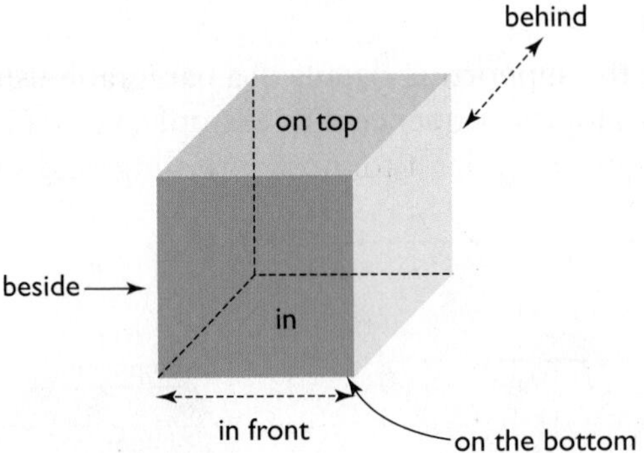

Here are some transitional expressions you can use in space-order paragraphs.

above	beneath	nearby	on top
behind	closer in	on the bottom	toward
below	farther out	on the left	under

In the next paragraph, the writer describes a location beginning at the beach and ending up at the front of the house.

> Their house was even more elaborate than I expected. It was a cheerful red-and-white Georgian Colonial mansion overlooking the bay. The lawn started at the beach and ran toward the front door for a quarter of a mile, jumping over sundials and brick walks and burning gardens—finally, when it reached the house, drifting up the side in bright vines as though from the momentum of its run. The front was broken by a line of French windows.
>
> —F. Scott Fitzgerald, *The Great Gatsby*

PRACTICE 6

Read each paragraph and underline the topic sentence. Then decide what order the writer used: time, space, or emphatic.

A. Five minutes before noon, Dawn left the kitchen full of vinegar clouds and went to stand on the porch beside their brown suitcases. Then she walked to the driveway and looked up and down Sylvan Avenue. Vera said theirs used to be the only house on the street, when the road was a lane and it was all farmland out here. Now it was a subdivision of beige bungalows with sliding glass doors and patios, and theirs was the only house on the street that looked haunted: three storeys of dark brick with cobwebby attachments like trellises and eaves and storm windows. Even the yard looked spooky: gnarled apple trees on one side, tangled forest hiding the creek on the other. In a few minutes, though, Dawn thought happily, she and Jimmy would also live in a home with a patio.

—Jamie Zeppa, *every time we say goodbye*

Order: time

B. Many factors contribute to racist attitudes. First, there are often higher levels of racist incidents in societies that have historically had very little contact with different ethnic groups. According to writer and political analyst Gwynne Dyer, such isolated societies may feel threatened when there is an influx of immigrants. Moreover, racist attitudes become more prevalent when various ethnic communities do not intermingle. If different cultural communities do not work and study together, stereotypes about other groups become entrenched. Most importantly, high levels of poverty contribute to racist reactions; immigrants become easy and available scapegoats when there is competition for limited jobs.

—Eliot Mandel, student

Order: emphatic

C. The tiny interior of the shop was in fact uncomfortably full, but there was almost nothing in it of the slightest value. The floor space was very restricted because all round the walls were stacked innumerable dusty picture-frames. In the window, there were trays of nuts and bolts, worn-out chisels, penknives with broken blades, tarnished watches that did not even pretend to be in going order, and other miscellaneous rubbish. Only on a small table in the corner was there a litter of odds and ends—lacquered snuffboxes, agate brooches, and the like—which looked as though they might include something interesting. As Winston wandered towards the table, his eye was caught by a round, smooth thing that gleamed softly in the lamplight, and he picked it up.

—George Orwell, *1984*

Order: space

PRACTICE 7

Read the following topic sentences. Decide what type of order you can use to develop the paragraph details. Choose space, time, or emphatic order. (There may be more than one correct organizational method.)

EXAMPLE:

Learning to play the guitar requires practice, patience, and perseverance. *Emphatic*

1. Music education is essential in public schools. ______
2. My furnished room has everything a student could need. ______
3. You can learn to make decisions and think critically with a liberal arts education. ______

4. Several interesting events happened during the Stanford Prison Experiment. ____________
5. The new youth centre has a very impressive design. ____________
6. There should not be a lower legal drinking age in our province. ____________
7. We encountered many problems on our journey to Prince Edward Island. ____________
8. Rory was known for his rumpled, unfashionable clothing. ____________
9. IQ tests are not always accurate and valid. ____________
10. The Tragically Hip went through many musical phases. ____________

Watch the Video
Paragraphs: Drafting a Paragraphs
MyWritingLab

The Paragraph Plan

A **plan**, or **outline**, of a paragraph is a map showing the paragraph's main and supporting ideas. To make a plan, write your topic sentence, and then list supporting points and details. Remember to use emphatic, time, or space order to organize the supporting points. In a more formal outline, you can use letters and numbers to indicate primary and secondary ideas.

Mahan's Paragraph Plan

Mahan completed his paragraph plan. He narrowed his topic, wrote a topic sentence, and thought of several supporting details. Here is his paragraph plan.

ESSAY LINK

Make a plan when you write an essay. In essay plans, each supporting idea becomes a separate paragraph.

Watch the Video
Paragraph: How to Write a Successful Paragraph
MyWritingLab

Topic Sentence: People steal for many reasons.
Support 1: Poverty is a primary motivation for people to steal.
Details: —some people are unemployed
—others working at low-paying jobs
—need money for food, rent, clothing
Support 2: Some criminals are greedy.
Details: —want to live a life of luxury
—crave to conspicuously consume
—wish for a larger yacht or faster jet
Support 3: Some people steal due to drug or alcohol addictions.
Details: —addicts steal to buy drugs
—alcohol ruins good judgment
Support 4: Some people steal for the kicks.
Details: —experience the thrill
—receive an adrenaline rush when stealing

Hint Adding Specific Details

When you prepare your paragraph plan, ask yourself if the details clearly support your topic sentence. If not, then you could add details to make your points stronger. For example, when Mahan first brainstormed a list of supporting details (page 28), he did not think of specific details to support his point about greed. In his paragraph plan, however, he added a couple of details (larger yacht, faster jet) to make that point stronger and more complete.

The Writer's Desk Write a Paragraph Plan

Look at the topic sentence and the organized list of supporting ideas that you created for the Writer's Desk exercises on page 27. Now, in the space provided, make a paragraph plan. Remember to include details for each supporting idea.

Topic sentence: ______________________________

____

Support 1: ______________________________

Details: ______________________________

____

Support 2: ______________________________

Details: ______________________________

____

Support 3: ______________________________

Details: ______________________________

____

Writing the Concluding Sentence

A stand-alone paragraph may have a **concluding sentence** that brings it to a satisfactory close. There are several ways to write a concluding sentence.

- Restate the topic sentence in a new, refreshing way.
- Make an interesting final observation.
- End with a prediction, suggestion, or quotation.

ESSAY LINK

Essays end with a concluding paragraph. For more information, see pages 196–197.

Watch the Video Essay Introductions, Conclusions and Titles: Conclusions **MyWritingLab**

Hint Problems with Concluding Sentences

When you write your concluding sentence, do not introduce a contradictory idea or change the focus of the paragraph. For example, in Mahan's paragraph about crime, he should not end with a statement that questions or contradicts his main point.

Weak: But nobody really understands why people break the law. (This concluding sentence undermines the main point, which is that people steal for many reasons.)

Better: Knowing why people steal may help social services and lawmakers deal with criminals more effectively. (This prediction brings the paragraph to a satisfactory close.)

PRACTICE 8

The topic sentences in paragraphs A and B are underlined. For each paragraph, circle the letter of the most effective concluding sentence, and then explain why the other choice is not as effective.

EXAMPLE:

Picasso painted many different types of people that he saw in the Paris neighbourhood of Montmartre. He painted musicians, prostitutes, street vendors, circus performers, and fellow artists, as well as his many lovers. During his blue period, he was drawn to emaciated figures; impoverished mothers and hungry children populated his art.

a. Picasso painted many different types of people.

(b.) The human body was ultimately the most important and repeated image in his paintings and sculptures.

Why is the other choice not as effective?

Sentence "a" just repeats the topic sentence.

A. Our province should insist that daycare centres provide more flexible hours for families. Today, in many families, both parents work outside the home. These parents do not necessarily work from nine to five. For example, nurses and factory employees work in shifts. For such parents, flexible daycare is very important. Also, many parents who are in the service and retail industry work on weekends. For these parents, it is important to have adequate child-care facilities during their work hours.

a. The current opening hours of most daycare centres do not meet the needs of a great number of families.

b. However, maybe daycare owners do not want to open on nights and weekends.

Why is the other choice not as effective?

____

B. College students should find part-time jobs that require them to exercise different muscles. If a business student spends hours sitting in front of a computer screen, then he should try to find a job that requires physical activity. If an engineering student has to do advanced calculus, then maybe her part-time job should allow her to rest her brain. Students who do a lot of solitary study could try to find jobs that allow them to interact socially.

a. Some college students should not take part-time jobs because they need to concentrate on their studies.

b. Humans need to do a variety of activities to be mentally and physically strong, so college students should keep that in mind when they look for work.

Why is the other choice not as effective?

____

PRACTICE 9

Read the next paragraph. Then answer the questions that follow.

Leonardo Da Vinci exemplified the characteristics of the Renaissance archetype. Da Vinci is most famous for being a master painter. His paintings *The Mona Lisa* and *The Last Supper* are two of the most admired in the world. Da Vinci was also an inventor, having been credited for an early model of a helicopter. He also made designs for a tank, a calculator, the double hull for ships, and a hang glider. Furthermore, Leonardo Da Vinci was a scientist. He studied anatomy by dissecting corpses, which helped him to draw human figures more precisely. He was also interested in animal and plant studies. His scientific writings are found in four journals kept in famous museums such as the Louvre and the British Museum.

1. What is the topic of this paragraph?

   ____

2. Underline the topic sentence.
3. List the supporting details.

   ____

   ____

   ____

4. Write two possible concluding sentences for this paragraph.

   a. ____

   ____

   b. ____

   ____

The First Draft

Watch the Video Developing and Organizing a Paragraph: Drafting a Paragraph **MyWritingLab**

After making a paragraph plan, you are ready to write your first draft, which is a very important step in the writing process. Your first draft includes your topic sentence, some supporting details, and a concluding sentence.

As you write your first draft, you might find it difficult sometimes to say what you mean. If you are having trouble, underline that section or put a check mark beside it so that you can come back to revise it later. If possible, put your first draft aside for a few hours before rereading it. Then, when you revise your paragraph, you will read it with a fresh perspective. The next chapter contains information about revising a paragraph.

MAHAN'S FIRST DRAFT

Here is Mahan Zahir's first draft. You may notice that his paragraph has errors. He will correct these when he gets to the revising and editing stage of the process.

People steal for many reasons. Poverty is a primary motivation for people to steal. Because some people are unemployed and others may be underemployed. They may not have enough money for food, clothing rent. Stealing money or food may be very tempting. As a means of survival. Some criminals do fraud because they are greedy. In fact, some extremly wealthy people steal simply because they want to acquire a larger yacht or a faster jet. Another important reason that people engage in stealing is due to addiction to drugs or alcohol. Addicts steal to buy drugs and overuse of alcohol may lead to poor judgement. Finally, people also steal for kicks. Criminals get an adrenaline rush when they outwit the cops.

The Writer's Desk Write Your First Draft

In the previous Writer's Desk, you made a paragraph plan. Now use the plan's information to type or write the first draft of your paragraph.

REFLECT ON IT

Think about what you have learned in this chapter. If you do not know an answer, review that topic.

1. What is a topic sentence? ______________________________

____

2. What is time order? ______________________________

____

3. What is emphatic order? ______________________________

____

4. What is space order? ______________________________

____

Are the following sentences true or false? Circle the better answer.

5. A paragraph has more than one main idea. True False
6. A paragraph's details support its topic sentence. True False

The Writer's Room

Writing Activity 1: Topics

In the Writer's Room in Chapter 1, "Exploring," you used various strategies to find ideas about the following topics. Select one of the topics, and write a paragraph. Remember to follow the writing process.

General Topics

1. A childhood memory
2. Anger
3. Rules
4. Cosmetic surgery

College- and Work-Related Topics

5. A comfortable place
6. Study or work habits
7. College life
8. Cellphones

Writing Activity 2

Choose a topic that you feel passionate about, and write a paragraph. Your topic could be an activity (painting, basketball) or an interest (music, politics). Your topic sentence should make a point about the topic.

Blend Images/Shutterstock

Watch the **Video**
Paragraphs: Revising the Paragraph—A Checklist
MyWritingLab

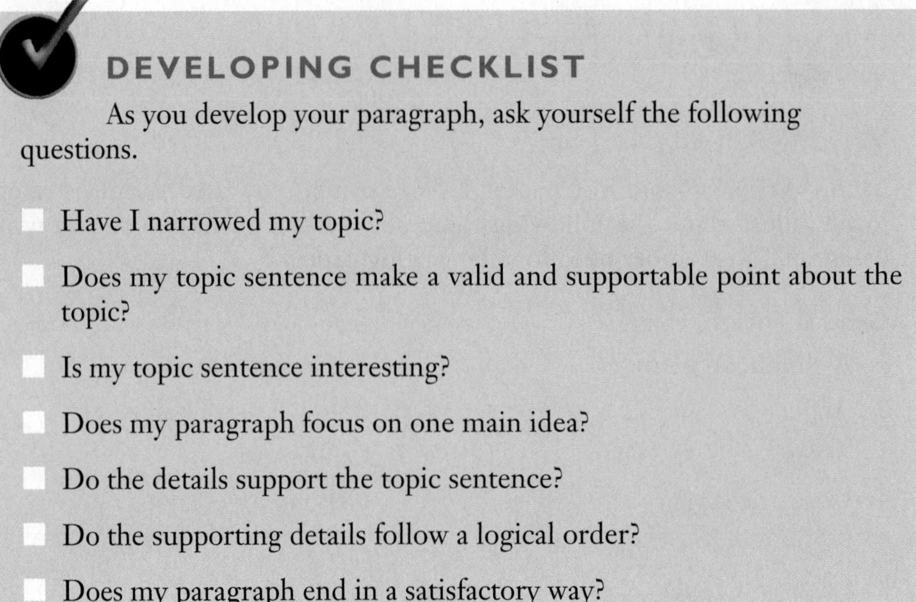

DEVELOPING CHECKLIST

As you develop your paragraph, ask yourself the following questions.

- ☐ Have I narrowed my topic?
- ☐ Does my topic sentence make a valid and supportable point about the topic?
- ☐ Is my topic sentence interesting?
- ☐ Does my paragraph focus on one main idea?
- ☐ Do the details support the topic sentence?
- ☐ Do the supporting details follow a logical order?
- ☐ Does my paragraph end in a satisfactory way?

How Do I Get a Better Grade?

Visit MyWritingLab for audiovisual lectures and additional practice sets about developing paragraphs.

Revising and Editing

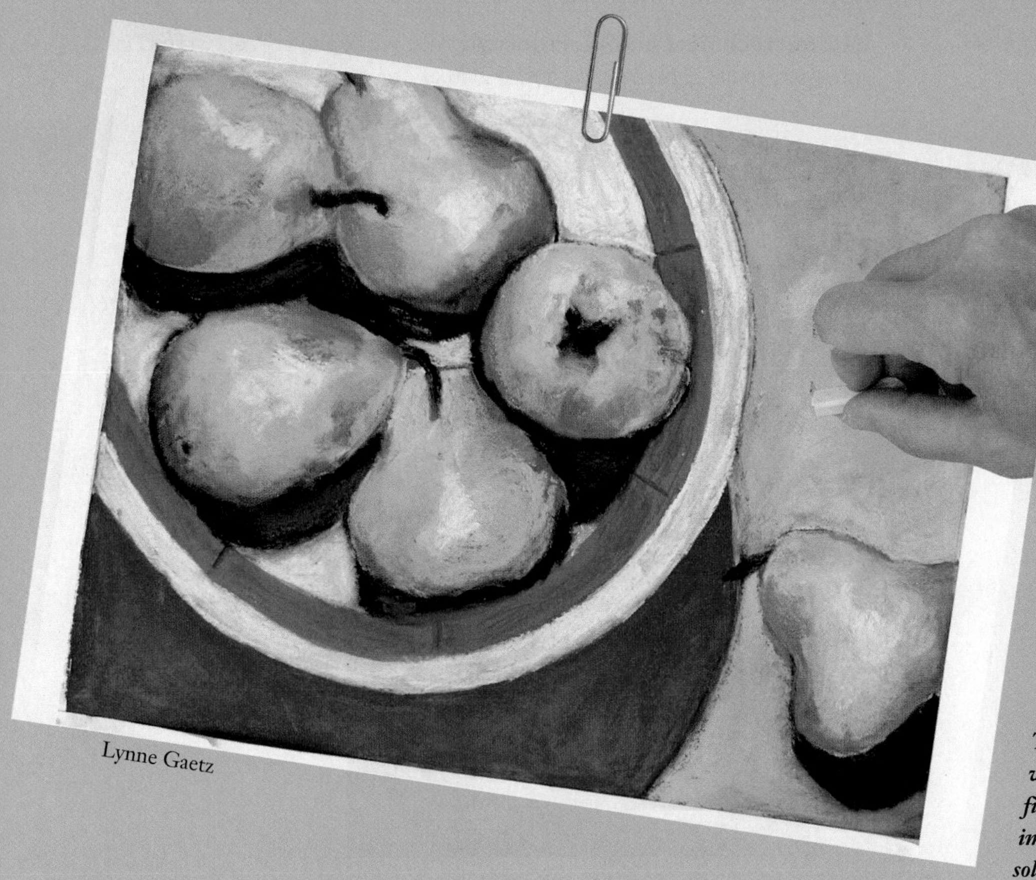
Lynne Gaetz

LEARNING OBJECTIVES

The revising and editing stage of the writing process is similar to adding the finishing touches to an artwork. Small improvements can make the work more solid and complete.

What Is Revising and Editing?

After you have written the first draft of your paragraph, the next step in the writing process is to revise and edit your work. When you **revise**, you modify your writing to make it stronger and more convincing. You do this by reading your first draft critically, looking for faulty logic, poor organization, or poor sentence style. Then you reorganize and rewrite it, making any necessary changes. When you **edit**, you proofread your final draft for errors in grammar, spelling, punctuation, and mechanics.

There are five key steps to follow during the revising and editing stage.

Listen to the **Audio**
Lesson: Writing, Revising, and Editing
MyWritingLab

Watch the **Video**
Revising and Editing Your Own Paragraphs
MyWritingLab

Watch the **Video**
Editing: Writing Paragraphs
MyWritingLab

REVISING AND EDITING

STEP 1 ➤ **Revise for unity.** Ensure that all parts of your work relate to the main idea.

STEP 2 ➤ **Revise for adequate support.** Determine that your details effectively support the main idea.

STEP 3 ►	**Revise for coherence.** Verify that your ideas flow smoothly and logically.
STEP 4 ►	**Revise for style.** Ensure that your sentences are varied and interesting.
STEP 5 ►	**Edit for technical errors.** Proofread your work and correct errors in grammar, spelling, mechanics, and punctuation.

ESSAY LINK

When revising and editing your essay, check that the body paragraphs support the thesis statement. Also, ensure that each body paragraph has unity.

Watch the **Video**
Revising the Paragraph: Unity
MyWritingLab

Revise for Unity

Art Photography by Prindiville/Fotolia

Every idea in a paragraph should move in the same direction just as this bridge goes straight ahead. There should be no forks in the road.

Unity means that all of the sentences in a paragraph support the topic sentence. If a paragraph lacks unity, then some sentences drift from the main idea that a writer has expressed in the topic sentence. To check for unity, ensure that every sentence in the body of the paragraph relates to one main idea.

PARAGRAPH WITHOUT UNITY

In the next paragraph, the writer drifted away from his main idea. One sentence does not relate to the topic sentence. If the highlighted sentence is removed, then the paragraph has unity.*

> The discovery of insulin was certainly the most important event in the life of Charles Herbert Best. One can talk of fate or chance, or of being in the right place at the right time, but the fact is that he accepted an opportunity to work on fundamental research of a very important medical problem, with a young doctor of apparently limited potential who had a burning desire to succeed where many others had failed. On 15 December, a group of physicians at the Toronto General Hospital (TGH), including Drs. Walter Campbell, Duncan Graham, and Almon Fletcher, took part in a discussion with the researchers. The result could well have been just

J.D.S/Shutterstock

The writer took a detour here. ➤

*The lack of unity was introduced for illustration purposes and does not occur in the original.

another footnote in the long battle to defeat the scourge of diabetes, perhaps adding a few details to the accumulated knowledge on the subject. Instead, within a matter of a few months in the middle of 1921, Fred Banting and Charles Best discovered the hormone insulin.

—Henry B.M. Best, *Margaret and Charley: The Personal Story of Dr. Charles Best, the Co-discoverer of Insulin*

PRACTICE 1

Paragraphs A and B contain problems with unity. In each paragraph, underline the topic sentence and cross out any sentences that do not support the controlling idea.

A. Car-based cellphones should be banned. One study published by the *New England Journal of Medicine* found that the risk of a collision quadruples if drivers use a cellular phone. The findings indicate that the major problem with cellphones is that they affect the driver's concentration. Jeffrey Blain repairs roads, and he says that sometimes drivers using their phones go through barriers and into road repair sites because they are so distracted. I also hate it when people use their cellphones in movie theatres. At a recent movie, I heard the beeps of various cellphones at least five times during the film. The problem is especially bad in cars, though. Our government should outlaw cellphones in motor vehicles.

B. Orville and Wilbur Wright had an unlikely dream, but they turned it into reality. When the brothers first tried to make a plane fly, they were unsuccessful. In fact, in 1901, a frustrated Wilbur Wright said that humans wouldn't fly for a thousand years. However, just two years later, on December 17, 1903, Wilbur and Orville Wright flew a plane for 105 feet. The brothers were overjoyed; their hard work and planning had finally paid off. Since that time, air travel has changed a lot. Many different types of planes exist today. Jets fly across our skies and can go from London to New York in a few hours. Eventually the Wright brothers produced nineteen types of aircraft. By sticking with an idea and persevering, the Wright brothers made their dream a reality.

Revise for Adequate Support

ESSAY LINK

When revising your essay, ensure that you have adequately supported the thesis statement. Also, ensure that each body paragraph has sufficient supporting details.

Watch the **Video** Revising the Paragraph: Development **MyWritingLab**

maxdigi/Fotolia

A bridge is built using several well-placed support columns. Like a bridge, a paragraph requires adequate support to help it stand on its own.

A paragraph has **adequate support** when there are enough details and examples to make it strong, convincing, and interesting. The following paragraph attempts to persuade, but it does not have any specific details that make a strong point.

PARAGRAPH WITHOUT ADEQUATE SUPPORT

In European films, the star can be wrinkled or overweight. **Unfortunately, Canadian filmmakers have not figured out that people like to see reflections of themselves on screen.** To get a job, Canadian movie actors must be in perfect shape and have perfect bodies. It is often hard to believe that the beautiful actor is really the waiter or car mechanic that is pictured on screen. The problem is especially acute when the star is older. You can be sure that he or she has had a lot of surgery to look as young as possible. Ordinary audience members have trouble identifying with surgically enhanced actors. Perhaps one day Canadian producers will use regular-looking people in their films.

PRACTICE 2

When the preceding paragraph about film stars is expanded with specific details and examples, the paragraph becomes more convincing. Try adding details on the lines provided. You can do this alone or with a partner.

In European films, the star can be wrinkled or overweight. Unfortunately, Canadian filmmakers have not figured out that people like to see reflections of themselves on screen. To get a job, Canadian movie actors must be in perfect shape and have perfect bodies. For example, ______________________ and ______________________ are incredibly good-looking. It is often hard to believe that the beautiful actor is really the waiter or car mechanic that is pictured on screen. In the movie titled ______________________, the actor ______________________ looks too perfect to be a ______________________. The problem is especially acute when the star is older. You can be sure that he or she has had a lot of surgery to look as young as possible. For instance, ______________________ looks much younger than his or her real age. Ordinary audience members have trouble identifying with surgically enhanced actors. Perhaps one day Canadian producers will use regular-looking people in their films.

Avoiding Circular Reasoning

Circular reasoning means that a paragraph restates its main point in various ways but does not provide supporting details. The main idea goes in circles and never progresses. Avoid using circular reasoning by providing a clear, concise topic sentence and by supporting the topic sentence with facts, examples, statistics, or anecdotes.

Circular reasoning in a paragraph is like a Ferris wheel. The main idea of the paragraph does not seem to progress.

CELIA'S PARAGRAPH

Celia Raines, a student, wrote the following paragraph about a popular proverb. In the paragraph, she repeats her main point over and over and does not provide any evidence to support her topic sentence.

Circular

Those who make the most noise usually get what they want. People sometimes shout and make a fuss and then others listen to them. Those who are quiet get ignored and their opinions do not get heard. It is important for people to speak up and express their needs. This attitude is expressed in the proverb, "The squeaky wheel gets the grease."

In the second version of this paragraph, Celia added a specific example (an anecdote) that helped illustrate her main point.

Revised Paragraph

Those who make the most noise usually get what they want. Those who are quiet get ignored, and their opinions do not get heard. For example, two years ago, the local government started a passenger train service that helped local commuters get into the city. Many citizens loved commuting by train, but those who live near the train tracks complained about the noise. They made petitions, wrote to newspapers, and lobbied the local government to cancel the train service. Those people were so loud and persistent that they got their wish, and the train service was cancelled. The silent majority disagreed with that lobby group, but as the proverb says, "The squeaky wheel gets the grease."

PRACTICE 3

Paragraphs A and B use circular reasoning. There is no specific evidence to support the topic sentence. List supporting examples for each paragraph. With numbers, indicate where you would place the supporting examples.

EXAMPLE:

Canadian teenagers go through several rites of passage. These rites of passage help the teenager navigate the transition from childhood to adulthood. *(1)* Some rites of passage are shared with the community. *(2)* These rites are an important part of every youth's life.

Examples: *(1) The first date and the first kiss are important.*

The first job is also a special step.

(2) During the high school prom, the community members gather together.

A. Police officers have an important function in our society. They provide many useful and necessary services in the community. If there were no police officers, there would be anarchy in the streets. Law-enforcement officers deserve our respect and appreciation.

Examples: ______________________________

____

____

____

____

____

B. When you move out of your family home and live on your own, you should plan your budget carefully. There are many things that you will have to pay for, and a lot of items will be expensive. You will need to pay for services. Even small household items add up. It is expensive to live on your own.

Examples: ______________________________

____

____

____

____

____

ESSAY LINK

To create coherence in an essay, you can place transitional expressions at the beginning of each body paragraph.

Revise for Coherence

When you drive along a highway and you suddenly hit a pothole, it is an uncomfortable experience. Readers experience similar discomfort if they encounter potholes in a piece of writing. Make your writing as smooth as possible by ensuring that it has **coherence:** the sentences should flow smoothly and logically.

Rhonda Sandberg

Just as bolts link pieces of a bridge, transitional expressions can link ideas in a paragraph.

Transitional Expressions

Transitional expressions are linking words or phrases, and they ensure that ideas are connected smoothly. Here are some common transitional expressions.

Watch the **Video**
Revising the Paragraph: Coherence
MyWritingLab

Function	Transitional Expression	
Addition	again also besides finally first (second, third) for one thing furthermore	in addition in fact last moreover next then
Comparison and contrast	as well equally even so however in contrast instead	likewise nevertheless on the contrary on the other hand similarly
Concession of a point	certainly even so indeed	no doubt of course to be sure
Effect or result	accordingly as a result consequently hence	otherwise then therefore thus
Example	for example for instance in other words in particular	namely specifically to illustrate
Emphasis	above all clearly especially first in fact in particular indeed	least of all most important most of all of course particularly principally
Reason or purpose	for this purpose for this reason	the most important reason
Space	above behind below beneath beside beyond closer in farther out inside	near nearby on one side/on the other side on the bottom on the left/right on top outside to the north/east/south/west under
Summary or conclusion	generally in conclusion in other words in short on the whole	therefore thus to conclude to summarize ultimately
Time	after that at that time at the moment currently earlier eventually first (second, etc.) gradually immediately in the beginning in the future in the past	later meanwhile months after now one day presently so far subsequently suddenly then these days

GRAMMAR LINK

For more practice using transitions in sentences, see Chapter 17, "Compound Sentences," and Chapter 18, "Complex Sentences."

Use Transitional Expressions with Complete Sentences

When you add a transitional expression to a sentence, ensure that your sentence is complete. Your sentence must have a subject and a verb, and it must express a complete thought.

Incomplete: For example, the rules posted on the wall.

Complete: For example, the rules were posted on the wall.

PRACTICE 4

The next paragraph contains eight transitional expressions that appear at the beginning of sentences. Underline each expression, and then, in the chart, indicate its purpose. The first one has been done for you.

For those who love eating out, a new type of dining experience is rearing its ugly head. Indeed, service with a sneer is popping up in Canada and the United States. For instance, in the New York City teahouse Tea and Sympathy, customers must follow a rigid list of rules. Those who plan to wait for friends are sharply told to leave. Moreover, patrons who manage to get a table are kicked out as soon as they finish their tea. Similarly, in Vancouver, the Elbow Room Café posts rules on the wall, including one that asks customers to get their own coffee and water. Also, the owner and staff members ridicule customers who order decaf tea or butter-free toast. Even so, clients keep coming back, comparing the experience to going to a show. The bad service trend has always been there. However, people in previous decades would have left such eateries without leaving a tip. These days, customers line up to be abused.

Transitional Expression	Function
1. *Indeed*	*Emphasis*
2.	
3.	
4.	
5.	
6.	
7.	
8.	

PRACTICE 5

Add appropriate transitional expressions to the following paragraph. Choose from the following list, and use each transitional word once. There may be more than one correct answer for each blank.

consequently	first	on the other hand
for example	furthermore	therefore

Workplace gossip has both positive and negative effects. ____________________, when two colleagues share secrets about others, it helps build trust and creates intimacy. ____________________, in large organizations, gossip helps form small social groups that provide workplace support systems. ____________________, overly negative gossip can undermine employee morale. An employee who hears malicious gossip may suspect that he or she is also the subject of office chatter. ____________________, Latisha Bishop, an employee at CR Industries, says that she felt devastated when she realized that her co-workers were spreading information about her private life. ____________________, she seriously considered leaving her job. ____________________, when office workers gossip, they should try to do so without malice.

Revise for Style

When you revise for sentence **style**, you ensure that your paragraph has concise and appropriate language and sentence variety. You can ask yourself the following questions.

- Have I used a **variety of sentence patterns?** (To practise using sentence variety, see Chapter 19.)
- Have I used **exact language?** (To learn about slang, wordiness, and overused expressions, see Chapter 31.)
- Are my sentences **parallel in structure?** (To practise revising for parallel structure, see Chapter 21.)

ESSAY LINK

You should revise your essays for style, ensuring that sentences are varied and parallel. Also, ensure that your language is exact.

Watch the Video Varying Sentence Structure **MyWritingLab**

Watch the Video Using Exact Language **MyWritingLab**

Watch the Video Parallelism **MyWritingLab**

Mahan's Revision

On pages 37–38 in Chapter 2, you read the first draft of student Mahan Zahir's paragraph about crime. Look at his revisions for unity, support, coherence, and style.

> People steal for many reasons. *First, poverty* ~~Poverty~~ is a primary motivation for people to steal. Because some people are unemployed and others may be underemployed. They may not have enough money for food, clothing, rent. Stealing money or food may be very tempting. As a means of survival. *Next, some* ~~Some~~ criminals *perpetrate* ~~do~~ fraud because they are greedy. In fact, some extremely wealthy people steal simply because they want to acquire a larger yacht or a faster jet. *For example, the directors of Enron and WorldCom were found guilty of stealing from shareholders, none of these directors*

< Transition

< Transition

Better word

< Add specific examples

Add indirect quotation ➢ *lacked personal wealth. According to Lisa Bloom, a reporter for court tv, the rich steal for the same reason as the poor: they love getting something for nothing.* Another important reason that people engage in stealing is due to addiction to drugs or alcohol. Addicts steal to buy drugs and overuse of alcohol

Add statistic ➢ may lead to poor judgment. *According to Canadian prison warden Ron Wiebe, "We know that 80 per cent of our offenders either abuse substances or are in prison because of substance-abuse-related crime."* In addition, people steal for kicks. *Martin Jeffs, a twenty three year old mugger who spoke to BBC News, say that*

Add quotation ➢ *excitement is a major motivation for many street criminals: "It gives a lot of people a buzz to know that they have got the power to overpower someone and take his possessions."* Criminals get an adrenaline rush when they outwit the

Better word ➢ ~~cops~~ *police*. *Knowing the different reasons that people steal may help social workers and*

Add concluding sentence ➢ *lawmakers deal with criminals more effectively.*

Adding Strong Support

When you revise, look at the strength of your supporting details. Ask yourself the following questions.

- Are my supporting details interesting, and do they grab the reader's attention? Should I use more vivid words?
- Is my concluding sentence appealing? Could I end the paragraph in a more interesting way?

PRACTICE 6

In Chapters 1 and 2, you saw examples of Sandra Ahumada's prewriting and planning. Now look at the first draft of Sandra's paragraph, and revise it for unity, support, and coherence. Also, ask yourself what you could do to enhance her writing style.

Customers should always tip restaurant servers. Servers need tips to live. Their salary is very low. They depend on tips to pay for food, housing, and other necessities. They do not get benefits such as paid sick days. If you do not like the service, remember that mistakes are not always the server's fault. Poor service could be the cook's fault. Sometimes there are not enough servers. I work as a server in a restaurant, I know how hard it is when customers leave bad tips. Always tip your restaurant server.

Edit for Errors

When you **edit,** you reread your writing and make sure that it is free of errors. You focus on the language, and you look for mistakes in grammar, punctuation, mechanics, and spelling.

There is an editing guide at the back of this book. It contains some common error codes that your instructor may use. It also provides you with a list of things to check for when you proofread your text.

GRAMMAR LINK

For more editing practice, see Chapter 36.

Editing Tips

The following tips will help you proofread your work more effectively.

- Put your writing aside for a day or two before you do the editing. Sometimes, when you have been working closely with a text, you might not see the errors.
- Begin your proofreading at any stage of the writing process. For example, if you are not sure of the spelling of a word while writing the first draft, you could either highlight the word for later verification or immediately look up the word in the dictionary.
- Keep a list of your common errors in a separate grammar log. When you finish a writing assignment, consult your error list and make sure that you have not repeated any of those errors. After each assignment has been corrected, you can add new errors to your list. For more information about grammar and spelling logs, see Appendix 7.

TECHNOLOGY LINK

Word processors have spelling and grammar checkers. Do not always choose the first suggestion for a correction. Make sure that suggestions are valid before you accept them.

Mahan's Edited Paragraph

Mahan Zahir edited his paragraph about crime. He corrected errors in spelling, capitalization, punctuation, and grammar.

People steal for many reasons. First, poverty is a primary motivation
for people to steal. Because some people are unemployed and others
, they
may be underemployed~~. T~~hey may not have enough money for food,
, and *as*
clothing ^ rent. Stealing money or food may be very tempting~~. As~~ a
means of survival. Next, some criminals perpetrate fraud because
extremely
they are greedy. In fact, some ~~extremly~~ wealthy people steal simply
because they want to acquire a larger yacht or a faster jet. For example, the directors of Enron and WorldCom were found guilty of stealing
. N
from shareholders~~, n~~one of these directors lacked personal wealth.
Court TV
According to Lisa Bloom, a reporter for ~~court tv~~, the rich steal for the

same reason as the poor: they love getting something for nothing. Another important reason that people engage in stealing is due to addiction to drugs or alcohol. Addicts steal to buy drugs and over-use of alcohol may lead to poor judgment. According to the Bureau of Justice Statistics in the United States, 68 per cent of jailed inmates reported that their substance abuse problems contributed to ~~there~~ *their* decisions to commit crimes. In addition, people steal for kicks. Martin Jeffs, a ~~twenty three year~~ *twenty-three-year-* old mugger who spoke to *BBC News*, ~~say~~ *says* that excitement is a major motivation for many street criminals: "It gives a lot of people a buzz to know that they have got the power to overpower someone and take his possessions." Criminals get an adrenaline rush when they outwit the police. Knowing the different reasons that people steal may help social workers and lawmakers deal with criminals more effectively.

The Writer's Desk **Revise and Edit**

Choose a paragraph that you wrote for Chapter 2 or for another assignment. Carefully revise and edit the paragraph. You can refer to the Revising and Editing Checklist at the end of this chapter.

Watch the **Video**
Paragraphs: Peer Revising and Editing Workshops
MyWritingLab

Peer Feedback

After you write a paragraph or essay, it is useful to get peer feedback. Ask another person such as a friend, family member, or fellow student to read your work and give you comments and suggestions on its strengths and weaknesses.

Offer Constructive Criticism

When you peer-edit someone else's writing, try to make your comments useful. Phrase your comments in a positive way. Look at these examples.

Instead of saying . . .	**You could say . . .**
Your sentences are boring.	Maybe you could combine some sentences.
Your supporting ideas are weak.	You could add more details here.

You can use the following peer feedback form to evaluate written work.

Peer Feedback Form

Written by: ____________________ Feedback by: ____________________

Date: ____________________

1. What is the main point of the written work?

____

2. What details effectively support the topic sentence?

____

____

3. What, if anything, is unclear or unnecessary?

____

____

4. Give some suggestions about how the work could be improved.

____

____

5. What is an interesting or unique feature of this written work?

____

____

Write the Final Draft

When you have finished making revisions on the first draft of your paragraph, write the final draft. Include all of the changes that you have made during the revision and editing phases. Before you hand in your final draft, proofread it one last time to ensure that you have caught any errors.

The Writer's Desk **Write Your Final Draft**

You have developed, revised, and edited your paragraph. Now write the final draft. Before you offer it to readers, proofread it one last time to ensure that you have found all of your errors.

Spelling, Grammar, and Vocabulary Logs

- **Keep a spelling and grammar log.** You probably repeat, over and over, the same types of grammar and spelling errors. You will find it very useful to record your repeated grammar mistakes in a spelling and grammar log. You can refer to your list of spelling and grammar mistakes when you revise and edit your writing.
- **Keep a vocabulary log.** Expanding your vocabulary will be of enormous benefit to you as a writer. In a vocabulary log, you can make a list of unfamiliar words and their definitions.

See Appendix 7 for more information about spelling, grammar, and vocabulary logs.

REFLECT ON IT

Think about what you have learned in this chapter. If you do not know an answer, review that topic.

1. What are four things that you should look for when revising?

   ______________________ ______________________

   ______________________ ______________________

2. Circle the best answer(s). A paragraph is unified if
   a. There are no irrelevant supporting details.
   b. There are many facts and statistics.
   c. All details support the topic sentence.
3. Circle the best answer: Transitional words are _____ that help ideas flow in a logical manner.
   a. Links b. Sentences c. Verbs
4. The Editing Handbook in Part IV includes information about grammar, spelling, and punctuation errors. In what chapter would you find information about the following topics? Look in the table of contents to find the chapter number.
   a. Capitalization ____________
   b. Subject–verb agreement ____________
   c. Faulty parallel structure ____________
   d. Commas ____________
   e. Commonly confused words ____________

Writing Activity 1: Topics

Choose a paragraph that you have written for your job or for another course. Revise and edit that paragraph, and then write a final draft.

Writing Activity 2

Choose any of the following topics, or choose your own topic. Then write a paragraph. Remember to follow the writing process.

General Topics

1. Interesting things about yourself
2. How to write a paragraph
3. Heroes in the media
4. Recruitment
5. Bad service

College- and Work-Related Topics

6. Something you learned in a college course or on campus
7. An unusual work experience
8. Reasons to turn down a job
9. Telemarketing
10. An interesting job

REVISING AND EDITING CHECKLIST

When you revise and edit, ask yourself the following questions. (For a more detailed editing checklist, refer to the inside back cover of this book.)

Unity

- ☐ Is my paragraph unified under a single topic?
- ☐ Does each sentence relate to the topic sentence?

Support

- ☐ Does my paragraph have an adequate number of supporting details?

Coherence

- ☐ Is my paragraph logically organized?
- ☐ Do I use transitional expressions to help the paragraph flow smoothly?

Style

- ☐ Do I use a variety of sentence styles?
- ☐ Is my vocabulary concise?
- ☐ Are my sentences parallel in structure?

Editing

- ☐ Do my sentences contain correct grammar, spelling, punctuation, and mechanics?

How Do I Get a Better Grade?

Visit MyWritingLab for audiovisual lectures and additional practice sets about revising and editing skills.

Paragraph Patterns

What Is a Paragraph Pattern?

A *pattern or mode* is a method used to express one of the three purposes for writing: to inform, to persuade, or to entertain. Once you know your purpose, you will be able to choose which writing pattern or patterns can help you express it.

Patterns can overlap, and it is possible to use more than one pattern in a single piece of writing. For example, imagine you are writing a paragraph about bullying and your purpose is to inform the reader. You might use *definition* as your predominant pattern, but in the supporting details, you might use *comparison and contrast* to compare a bully and a victim. You might also use *narration* to highlight an incident in which a bully harassed a victim.

Before you work through the next chapters, review the paragraph patterns.

Illustration
To illustrate or prove a point using specific examples

Narration
To narrate or tell a story about a sequence of events that happened

Process
To inform the reader about how to do something, how something works, or how something happened

Description
To describe using vivid details and images that appeal to the reader's senses

Definition
To define or explain what a term or concept means by providing relevant examples

Classification
To classify or sort a topic to help readers understand different qualities about that topic

Comparison and contrast
To present information about similarities (compare) or differences (contrast)

Cause and effect
To explain why an event happened (the cause) or what the consequences of the event were (the effects)

Argument*
To argue or to take a position on an issue and offer reasons for your position

*Argument is included as one of the nine patterns, but it is also a purpose in writing.

Illustration

LEARNING OBJECTIVES

Tupungato/Fotolia

Vendors offer many examples of a product to interest consumers and to make a sale. In illustration writing, you give examples to support your point.

Writers' Exchange

Work with a team of two or three other students. You have three minutes to list as many words as you can that are examples of the following parts of speech.

Noun	Verb	Adjective	Pronoun

EXPLORING

Watch the Video
Paragraph Development: Illustrating
MyWritingLab

What Is Illustration?

When you write using **illustration**, you include specific examples to clarify your main point. You illustrate or give examples any time you want to explain, analyze, narrate, or give an opinion about something. As a writer, you can use many different types of examples to help your reader acquire a deeper and clearer understanding of your subject. You can include personal experience or factual information, such as a statistic.

You give examples every day. When telling a friend why you had a good day or a bad day, you might use examples to make your story more interesting. At school, you might give an oral presentation using examples that will help your audience better understand your point. At work, you might give examples to show clients where or how they might market their products.

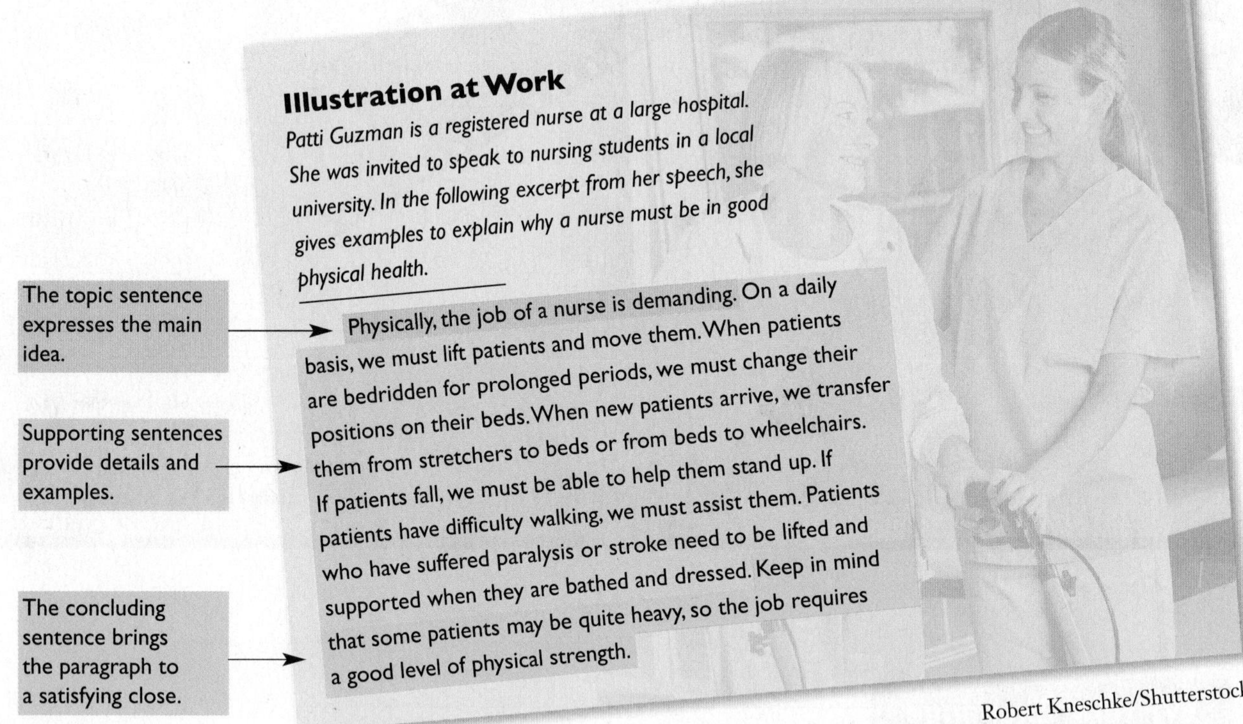

Illustration at Work
Patti Guzman is a registered nurse at a large hospital. She was invited to speak to nursing students in a local university. In the following excerpt from her speech, she gives examples to explain why a nurse must be in good physical health.
The topic sentence expresses the main idea.
Supporting sentences provide details and examples.
The concluding sentence brings the paragraph to a satisfying close.
Physically, the job of a nurse is demanding. On a daily basis, we must lift patients and move them. When patients are bedridden for prolonged periods, we must change their positions on their beds. When new patients arrive, we transfer them from stretchers to beds or from beds to wheelchairs. If patients fall, we must be able to help them stand up. If patients have difficulty walking, we must assist them. Patients who have suffered paralysis or stroke need to be lifted and supported when they are bathed and dressed. Keep in mind that some patients may be quite heavy, so the job requires a good level of physical strength.

Robert Kneschke/Shutterstock

ESSAY LINK

You can develop illustration essays with a series of examples or extended examples.

The Illustration Paragraph

There are two ways to write an illustration paragraph.

- **Use a series of examples** to illustrate your main point. For example, if you are writing a paragraph about an innovative teacher that you had, you might list things that the teacher did, such as wear a costume, let students teach parts of the course, and use music to make a point.
- **Use an extended example** to illustrate your main point. The example can be an anecdote or a description of an event. For example, if you are writing about a stressful vacation, you might describe what happened when you lost your wallet.

PRACTICE 1

Read the next paragraph and answer the questions.

Having integrity puts your **ethics** into day-to-day action. When you act with **integrity**, you earn trust and respect from others. If people can trust you to be honest, to be sincere in what you say and do, and to consider the needs of others, they will be more likely to encourage you, to support your goals, and reward your work. Living with integrity helps you believe in yourself and in your ability to make good choices. A person of integrity isn't a perfect person, but is one who makes the effort to live according to values and principles, continually striving to learn from mistakes and to improve. Take responsibility for making the right moves, and you will follow your mission with strength and conviction. Aim for your personal best in everything you do. As a lifelong learner, you will always have a new direction in which to grow and a new challenge to face. Seek constant improvement in your personal, educational, and professional life. Dream big, knowing that incredible things are possible for you if you think positively and act with successful intelligence. Enjoy the richness of life by living each day to the fullest, developing your talents and potential into the achievement of your most valued goals.

—Carol Carter et al., *Keys to Success*

ethics:
a set of moral guidelines

integrity:
honesty

1. Underline the topic sentence of this paragraph. (The topic sentence expresses the main idea of the paragraph.)
2. What type of illustration paragraph is this? Circle the best answer.
   a. A series of examples b. An extended example
3. What example(s) do the writers give to illustrate their point?

____

____

____

____

PRACTICE 2

Read the next paragraph and answer the questions.

Self-reliance is a trait that students require to be successful in post-secondary education. For example, as students select their choice of program, it is **imperative** that they feel passionate about what they want to study. Usually in a core program of study, such as Human Resources, students will need to demonstrate proficiency in other subject areas as well. If students can try their best to attend classes regularly, study textbooks and lecture notes, and connect with their professors around material that needs clarification, they will demonstrate self-reliance and willingness to learn.

imperative:
vital or important

1. Underline the topic sentence.
2. What does the writer use to present his supporting details? Circle the best answer.

   a. A series of examples   b. An extended example

3. What example(s) does the writer give to illustrate his point?

   ____

   ____

   ____

   ____

4. What are the main events in the narrative? List them.

   ____

   ____

   ____

   ____

   ____

   ____

Watch the Video
Pre-writing: Brainstorming
MyWritingLab

Explore Topics

In the Warm Up, you will try an exploring strategy to generate ideas about different topics.

The Writer's Desk Warm Up

Think about the following questions and write the first ideas that come to your mind. Try to think of two or three ideas for each topic.

EXAMPLE:

What are some effective ways to market a product?

use colourful packaging

create a funny advertisement

give free samples

1. What are some really silly fads or fashions?

   ____

   ____

   ____

2. What are some traits of an effective leader?

   ____

   ____

   ____

3. What are some qualities that you look for in a mate?

   ____

   ____

   ____

DEVELOPING

The Topic Sentence

The topic sentence of the illustration paragraph is a general statement that expresses both your topic and your controlling idea. To determine your controlling idea, think about what point you want to make.

> **ESSAY LINK**
>
> In an illustration essay, the thesis statement expresses the controlling idea.

topic — controlling idea

Part-time jobs teach students valuable skills.

controlling idea — topic

Our father became anxious **when my sister started dating.**

Watch the Video
Paragraphs: The Topic Sentence
MyWritingLab

The Writer's Desk Write Topic Sentences

Write a topic sentence for each of the following topics. You can look for ideas in the previous Writer's Desk. Remember to narrow your topic. Each topic sentence should contain a general statement that expresses both your topic and your controlling idea.

EXAMPLE:

Topic: Effective marketing strategies

Topic sentence: *Advertisers have many clever ways to interest consumers.*

1. Topic: Silly fads or fashions

   Topic sentence: ______________________________

2. Topic: Traits of an effective leader

   Topic sentence: ______________________________

3. Topic: Qualities you look for in a mate

   Topic sentence: ______________________________

The Supporting Ideas

After you have developed an effective topic sentence, generate supporting ideas. In an illustration paragraph, you can give a series of examples or an extended example.

Watch the Video
Developing and Organizing a Paragraph: Developing a Paragraph
MyWritingLab

When you use a series of examples, you can arrange your examples in emphatic order. Emphatic order means that you can place your examples from the most to the least important or from the least to the most important. If you use an extended example, you can arrange your ideas using time order.

Visualizing Illustration

PRACTICE 3

Brainstorm supporting ideas for the following topic sentence. Give examples of how people risk their lives.

Topic sentence: Some workers risk their lives daily.

Scott Speakes/Spirit/Corbis

window washer

Karin Lau/Alamy

electrician

Andreas G. Karelias/Shutterstock

fisher

Stockbyte/Getty Images

police officer

The Writer's Desk Generate Supporting Ideas

Generate some supporting examples under each topic. Make sure your examples support the topic sentences that you wrote for the previous Writer's Desk.

EXAMPLE:
Effective marketing strategies

—use a catchy, memorable jingle

—offer free samples

—have a contest or sweepstakes

—do product placement in television shows

1. Silly fads or fashions

____

____

____

____

2. Traits of an effective leader

____

____

____

____

3. Qualities you look for in a mate

____

____

____

____

The Paragraph Plan

A paragraph plan helps you organize your topic sentence and supporting details before writing a first draft. When you write a paragraph plan, ensure that your examples are valid and relate to the topic sentence. Also include details that will help clarify your supporting examples. Organize your ideas in a logical order.

TOPIC SENTENCE: Advertisers have many clever ways to interest consumers.

Support 1: Relate the product to an interesting character.

Details: —The Pillsbury Doughboy is cute.

—Ronald McDonald appeals to children.

Support 2: Give free samples to consumers.

Details: —Shampoo samples and granola bars come with junk mail.

—Perfume samples are passed out on street corners.

Support 3: Put the product in popular movies or television programs.

Details: —*So You Think You Can Dance Canada* judges drink particular brands.

—Car companies have their products in reality shows.

ESSAY LINK

In an illustration essay, place the thesis statement in the introduction. Then structure the essay so that each supporting idea becomes a distinct paragraph with its own topic sentence.

The Writer's Desk Write a Paragraph Plan

Choose one of the topic sentences that you wrote for the Writer's Desk on page 61. Write a paragraph plan using some of the supporting ideas that you generated in the previous Writer's Desk. Include details for each supporting idea.

Topic sentence: ______________________________

____

Support 1: ______________________________

Details: ______________________________

____

Support 2: ______________________________

Details: ______________________________

____

Support 3: ______________________________

Details: ______________________________

____

Watch the **Video**
Paragraphs: Drafting a Paragraph
MyWritingLab

The First Draft

After you outline your ideas in a plan, you are ready to write the first draft. Remember to write complete sentences. You might include transitional expressions to help your ideas flow smoothly.

Watch the **Video**
Revising the Paragraph: Coherence
MyWritingLab

Transitional Expressions

Transitional expressions can help you introduce an example or show an additional example. The following transitional expressions are useful in illustration paragraphs.

To Introduce an Example		To Show an Additional Example	
for example	namely	also	in addition
for instance	specifically	first (second, etc.)	in another case
in other words	to illustrate	furthermore	moreover

The Writer's Desk Write the First Draft

In the previous Writer's Desk, you developed a paragraph plan. Now write the first draft of your illustration paragraph. Before you write, carefully review your paragraph plan, and make any necessary changes.

Watch the Video
Editing: Writing Paragraphs
MyWritingLab

REVISING AND EDITING

Revise and Edit an Illustration Paragraph

When you finish writing an illustration paragraph, review your work and revise it to make the example(s) as clear as possible to your readers. Check to make sure that the order of ideas is logical, and remove any irrelevant details. Before you work on your own paragraph, practise revising and editing a student paragraph.

PRACTICE 4

Read the next student paragraph, and answer the questions.

Advertisers have many clever ways to get the consumer's attention. First, to make the product memorable, they can link it with an interesting character. When people see the character, they instantly remember the product. For example, any child will recognize Ronald McDonald, the Energizer Bunny, or the Green Giant. Also, the Pillsbury Doughboy. Furthermore, free samples help consumers become familiar with the item. Sometimes, when people are walking downtown, somebody gives you a snack or a perfume sample. Who can resist getting something for nothing? Another smart advertising method is to place products in popular television shows and movies. On *So You Think You Can Dance Canada*, for instance, the judges promote certain soft drinks. In reality shows such as *Survivor*, the contestants win particular car models, and millions of people hear about the car's features. The best marketing strategy is somewhat devious, though. Many companies, especially in the high-tech field, offer mail-in rebates. Consumers are lured by the possibility of a large discount. For instance, I bought anti-virus software for my computer because there was a $40 rebate, but the method of getting the rebate was time-consuming. I had to photocopy my receipt, fill out a form, and mail it. Apparently, large numbers of consumers simply forget to mail the rebate form in, so they never actually receive the discount. Every year, advertisers come up with better and more innovative marketing ideas.

Revising

1. Underline the topic sentence.
2. List the main supporting points.

____

____

____

____

3. What order does the author use?
   a. Time order
   b. Space order
   c. Emphatic order

GRAMMAR LINK

See the following chapters for more information about these grammar topics:
Pronouns, Chapter 28
Fragments, Chapter 20

Watch the Video
Pronouns
MyWritingLab

Watch the Video
Fragments
MyWritingLab

Editing

4. Underline a pronoun error. Write your correction in the space below.

   Correction: ______________________________

5. This paragraph contains a fragment, which is an incomplete sentence. Underline the fragment. Then correct it in the space below.

   Correction: ______________________________

Writing Complete Sentences

A fragment is an incomplete sentence. When you give an example, ensure that your sentence is complete. Avoid fragment errors.

Fragment: For example, too many parties.

Correction: For example, some students go to too many parties.

Rituals: The high school prom

See Chapter 20 for more information about fragments.

The Writer's Desk Revise and Edit Your Paragraph

Revise and edit the paragraph that you wrote for the previous Writer's Desk. Ensure that your paragraph has unity, adequate support, and coherence. Also, correct any errors in grammar, spelling, punctuation, and mechanics.

vo•cab•u•lar•y BOOST

Avoid Repetition

Read through the first draft of your paragraph and identify some words that you frequently repeat. Replace those words with synonyms.

REFLECT ON IT

Think about what you have learned in this chapter. If you do not know an answer, review that topic.

1. In an illustration paragraph, you ______________________________
2. There are two ways to write illustration paragraphs. Explain each of them.
   a. Using a series of examples: ______________________________
   b. Using an extended example: ______________________________
3. List three transitional expressions that indicate an additional idea.

   ____

The Writer's Room

Writing Activity 1: Topics

Choose any of the following topics, or choose your own topic. Then write an illustration paragraph.

General Topics

1. Activities that relieve stress
2. Great things in life that are free
3. Mistakes parents make
4. Items you have lost
5. Positive personality traits

College- and Work-Related Topics

6. Pressures faced by college students
7. Qualities that help you succeed
8. Claustrophobic work environments
9. Qualities of a good instructor
10. Tools or equipment needed for your job

WRITING LINK

More Illustration Writing Topics

Chapter 21, Writer's Room topic 1 (page 333)

Chapter 24, Writer's Room topic 1 (page 369)

Chapter 28, Writer's Room topic 1 (page 425)

Writing Activity 2: Photo Writing

The image depicts an anxious man who feels like he is walking on a tightrope. What things make you feel worried? Write an illustration paragraph about things that make you feel worried or stressed.

Daniel Matzenbacher/dieKleinert/Alamy

READING LINK

More Illustration Readings

"The Beeps" by Josh Freed (page 570)

Writing Activity 3: Media Writing

Watch a popular television show or movie that deals with students in a high school or college setting. Examples are movies such as *Stories We Tell* and *Take This Waltz* and television programs such as *Saving Hope* and *Being Erica*. You can even go on YouTube, type "self-reflection" into the search bar, and then watch some of the segments. Write a paragraph about the show, movie, or video segment, and explain the ways that characters go through periods of self-reflection. Provide several examples.

Watch the Video
Revising the Paragraph: A Checklist
MyWritingLab

ILLUSTRATION PARAGRAPH CHECKLIST

After you write your illustration paragraph, review the checklist on the inside front cover. Also, ask yourself the following questions.

- Does my topic sentence make a point that can be supported with examples?
- Does my paragraph contain sufficient examples that clearly support the topic sentence?
- Do I use transitions to smoothly connect my examples?
- Have I arranged my examples in a logical order?

How Do I Get a Better Grade?

Visit MyWritingLab for audiovisual lectures and additional practice sets about illustration paragraphs.

Narration

LEARNING OBJECTIVES

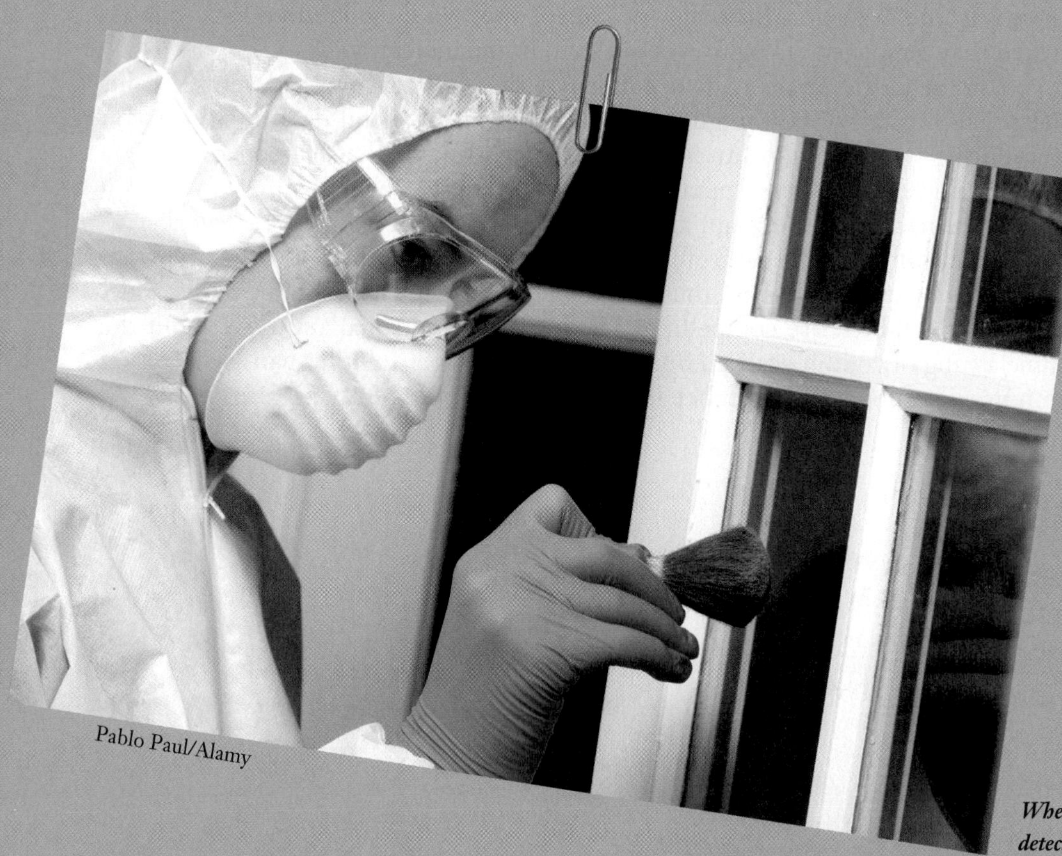

Pablo Paul/Alamy

When investigating a crime scene, a detective must try to find answers to the questions who, what, when, where, why, *and* how. *You answer the same questions when you write a narrative paragraph.*

Writers' Exchange

Work with a team of at least three students, and choose a popular fairy tale. Then you will retell the fairy tale, but you will update it and make it more contemporary. First, one of you begins and says one sentence. Then, switching speakers, each person adds one sentence to the tale.

EXAMPLE: Yesterday, a young woman living in North Bay decided to visit her grandmother.

EXPLORING

Watch the **Video**
Paragraph Development - Narration
MyWritingLab

What Is Narration?

When you **narrate**, you tell a story about what happened. You generally explain events in the order in which they occurred, and you include information about when they happened and who was involved in the incidents.

You use narration every day. You may write about the week's events in your personal journal, or you might send a postcard to a friend detailing what you did during your vacation. At college, you may explain what happened during a historical event or what happened in a novel that you have read. At work, you might use narration to explain an incident involving a customer or co-worker.

Narration not only is useful on its own but also enhances other types of writing. For example, Jason must write an argument essay about youth crime. His essay will be more compelling if he includes a personal anecdote about the time a gang of youths attacked him in a subway station. In other words, narration can provide supporting evidence for other paragraph or essay patterns.

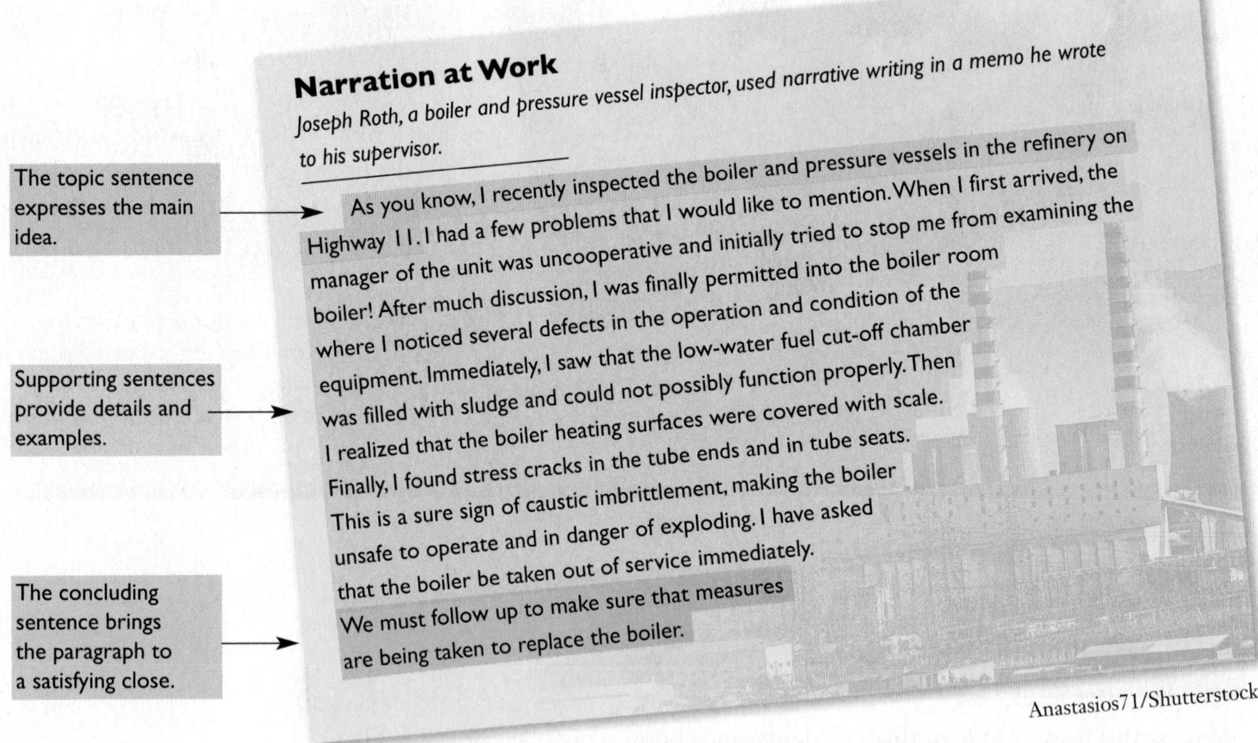

The topic sentence expresses the main idea.
Supporting sentences provide details and examples.
The concluding sentence brings the paragraph to a satisfying close.

Narration at Work

Joseph Roth, a boiler and pressure vessel inspector, used narrative writing in a memo he wrote to his supervisor.

As you know, I recently inspected the boiler and pressure vessels in the refinery on Highway 11. I had a few problems that I would like to mention. When I first arrived, the manager of the unit was uncooperative and initially tried to stop me from examining the boiler! After much discussion, I was finally permitted into the boiler room where I noticed several defects in the operation and condition of the equipment. Immediately, I saw that the low-water fuel cut-off chamber was filled with sludge and could not possibly function properly. Then I realized that the boiler heating surfaces were covered with scale. Finally, I found stress cracks in the tube ends and in tube seats. This is a sure sign of caustic imbrittlement, making the boiler unsafe to operate and in danger of exploding. I have asked that the boiler be taken out of service immediately. We must follow up to make sure that measures are being taken to replace the boiler.

Anastasios71/Shutterstock

The Narrative Paragraph

There are two main types of narrative paragraphs.

ESSAY LINK

In a narrative essay, you can use first- or third-person narration.

1. **Use first-person narration (autobiography).**

   In first-person narration, you describe a personal experience from your point of view. You are directly involved in the story. You use the words *I* (first-person singular) and *we* (first-person plural). For example: "When I was a child, I thought that the world began and ended with me. I didn't know, or care, how other children felt. Thus, when schoolmates ridiculed a shy boy, I gleefully joined in."

2. **Use third-person narration.**

   In third-person narration, you do not refer to your own experiences. Instead, you describe what happened to somebody else. The story is told in the third person using *he*, *she*, *it*, or *they*. You might tell a story about your mother's childhood, or you might explain what happened during the last election. In this type of narration, you are simply an observer or storyteller; you are not a participant in the action. For example: "The students gathered to protest against the war. One student threw a chair through the window of the student centre. Suddenly, people started pushing and shoving."

Choose an Interesting Topic

When you write a narrative paragraph, try to choose a topic that will interest the reader. For example, the reader might not be interested if you write about the act of eating your lunch. However, if you write about a time when your best friend argued with a waiter during a meal, you could create an entertaining narrative paragraph.

Think about a topic that you personally find very interesting, and then share it with your readers. Try to bring your experiences to life so that your readers can share it with you.

Explore Topics

In Writer's Desk: Warm Up, you will try an exploring strategy to generate ideas about different topics.

Watch the **Video**
Prewriting: Questioning
MyWritingLab

The Writer's Desk Warm Up

Think about the following questions, and write down the first ideas that come to your mind. Try to think of two or three ideas for each topic.

EXAMPLE:

What interesting stories have family members told you about their lives?

Life in Frobisher Bay is changing—funny story about meeting new friends from Northern Quebec. People come from all over the world to live in Frobisher. What else? Frobisher is "home" to many people.

1. What are some serious decisions that you have made? Think about decisions related to school, personal relationships, work, and so on.

   ____

   ____

   ____

2. What are some memorable parties or celebrations that you have attended?

____

____

____

3. Think about interesting true events that have happened to family members or friends. Are some stories particularly funny, sad, or inspiring? List some ideas.

____

____

____

PRACTICE 1

The author of the next paragraph was born in 1951 on Baffin Island and went to school in Frobisher Bay, eventually becoming an artist, writer, and photographer. Read the paragraph and answer the questions.

> There are a few memories of my childhood in Frobisher Bay. Life in the Arctic is changing fast and Frobisher has changed along with its people. If Frobisher has a distinct character today, it is that it has become "home" to many Inuit from other communities in the North. On any given day in Frobisher you might meet an Inuk who had come from a town as far away as Port Burwell in the east or from Tuktoyaktuk in the west. There were Inuit from Northern Quebec, from the High Arctic, from the Central Arctic or the Keewatin. Today there is no surprise in meeting an Inuk from Alaska or even from Greenland, on the streets of Frobisher Bay. Who knows, maybe one day we will begin to see whole families coming in from Siberia to live in Frobisher Bay!
>
> —Alootook Ipellie, "Frobisher Bay Childhood"

1. Underline the topic sentence of this paragraph. (Remember, the topic sentence is not always the first sentence.)
2. What type of narration is this? Circle the better answer.

   a. First person b. Third person

3. Who or what is the paragraph about? _______________

   ____

4. In a few words, explain what happened in this paragraph. _______________

   ____

5. When did it happen? _______________
6. Where did it happen? _______________
7. By combining your answers to questions 3 through 6, write a one-sentence summary of the paragraph. Someone who has never read the paragraph

should have a clear idea of the paragraph's content after reading your sentence.

____

____

____

PRACTICE 2

Read the next paragraph and answer the questions.

The economic ups and downs caused by expansion and contraction of the economy constitute the **business cycle.** A typical business cycle runs from three to five years, but could last much longer. Though typically irregular, a cycle can be divided into four general phases: prosperity, recession, depression (which the cycle generally skips), and recovery. During *prosperity*, the economy expands, unemployment is low, incomes rise, and consumers buy more products. Businesses respond by increasing production and offering new and better products. Eventually, however, things slow down, GDP decreases, unemployment goes up, and because people have less money to spend, business revenues decline. This slowdown in economic activity is called a **recession.** Economists often say that we are entering a recession when GDP goes down for two consecutive quarters. Generally, a recession is followed by a *recovery* in which the economy starts growing again. If, however, a recession lasts a long time (perhaps a decade or so), unemployment remains very high, and production is severely curtailed, the economy could sink into a **depression.** Though not impossible, it is unlikely that Canada will experience another severe depression like that of the 1930s.

—Karen Collins and Jackie Shemko, *Exploring Business*

business cycle: recurring periods of increased and decreased economic activity

recession: temporary decline in economic activity

depression: lengthy industrial and financial decline in economic activity

1. Who or what is the paragraph about? ______________________
2. Underline the topic sentence of this paragraph.
3. What point are the authors making about the business cycle?
4. How do the authors support the topic sentence? List the component events that make up this narrative.

____

____

____

____

____

____

____

5. Do the supporting facts provide adequate support for the topic sentence?

____

ESSAY LINK

In a narrative essay, the thesis statement expresses the controlling idea.

Watch the **Video**
Paragraphs: The Topic Sentence
MyWritingLab

DEVELOPING

The Topic Sentence

When you write a narrative paragraph, it is important to express a main point. If you simply describe a list of activities, it is boring for the reader. To make your paragraph interesting, make sure that your topic sentence has a controlling idea.

topic / controlling idea

When somebody broke into my house, I felt totally invaded.

controlling idea / topic

Jay learned to be responsible **during his first job.**

Make a Point

In a narrative paragraph, the topic sentence should make a point. To help you find the controlling idea, you can ask yourself the following questions.

- What did I learn?
- How did I change?
- How did it make me feel?
- What is important about it?

EXAMPLE:

Topic:	Moving out of the family home
Possible controlling idea:	Becoming more independent

topic / controlling idea

When I moved out of the family home, I became more independent.

PRACTICE 3

Practise writing topic sentences. Complete the following sentences by adding a controlling idea.

1. When I moved out of the family home, I felt ____________________

 ____

2. In my first job, I learned ____________________

 ____

3. When I heard the news about ____________________, I realized ________

 ____

The Writer's Desk Write Topic Sentences

Write a topic sentence for each of the following topics. You can look for ideas in Writer's Desk: Warm Up on pages 71–72. Each topic sentence should mention the topic and express a controlling idea.

EXAMPLE:

Topic: A family story

Topic sentence: *When my father found his first job in Canada, there was a humorous misunderstanding.*

1. Topic: A serious decision

   Topic sentence: ______________________________

2. Topic: A celebration or party

   Topic sentence: ______________________________

3. Topic: A story about someone

   Topic sentence: ______________________________

The Supporting Ideas

Watch the **Video**
Revising the Paragraph: Organization
MyWritingLab

A narrative paragraph should contain specific details so that the reader understands what happened. To come up with the details, ask yourself a series of questions. Your paragraph should provide answers to these questions.

- Who is the paragraph about?
- What happened?
- When did it happen?
- Where did it happen?
- Why did it happen?
- How did it happen?

When you recount a story to a friend, you may go back and add details, saying, "I forgot to mention something." When you write a narrative paragraph, however, your sequence of events should be clearly chronological so that your reader can follow your story.

Visualizing Narration

PRACTICE 4

Brainstorm supporting ideas for the following topic sentence. Write some descriptive words and phrases.

Topic sentence: Our camping trip exposed us to new experiences.

Steve Cole/Getty Images

Jeremy Edwards/Getty Images

joste_dj/iStock/Getty Images

______________________ ______________________ ______________________

______________________ ______________________ ______________________

The Writer's Desk Develop Supporting Ideas

Generate supporting ideas for each topic. List what happened.

EXAMPLE:

A family story

dad saw an ad

"busboy" job

bowling alley

dad didn't understand ad

man gave him an apron

1. A serious decision

____

____

____

____

____

2. A celebration or party

____

____

____

____

____

3. A story about someone

____

____

____

____

____

The Paragraph Plan

Before you write a narrative paragraph, it is a good idea to make a paragraph plan. Write down main events in the order in which they occurred. To make your narration more complete, include details about each event.

ESSAY LINK

In a narrative essay, you place the thesis statement in the introduction. Each main event is developed in a supporting paragraph.

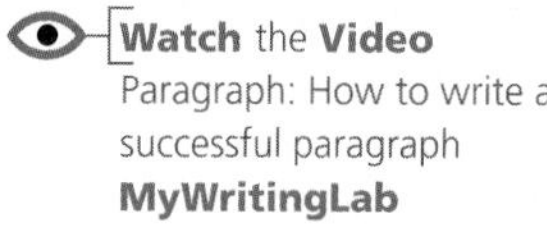

Watch the **Video**
Paragraph: How to write a successful paragraph
MyWritingLab

TOPIC SENTENCE: When my father found his first job in Canada, there was a humorous misunderstanding.

Support 1: In a newspaper, he found an ad for a busboy.

Details: —job was in a bowling alley

—dad didn't speak English very well

Support 2: He went to the bowling alley.

Details: —applied for the job, and got it

—was excited

Support 3: On his first day, his boss asked him to put on an apron and told him to pick up some dishes in the bowling alley's restaurant.

Details: —father was disappointed and asked, "Where's the bus?"

—thought that a "busboy" would work on a bus

The Writer's Desk Write a Paragraph Plan

Choose one of the topic sentences that you wrote for the Writer's Desk on page 75. Write a paragraph plan using some of the supporting ideas that you have generated in the previous Writer's Desk. Include details for each supporting idea.

Topic sentence: ______________________________

____

Support 1: ______________________________

Details: ______________________________

____

____

Support 2: ______________________________

Details: ______________________________

____

____

Support 3: ______________________________

Details: ______________________________

____

____

Watch the Video
Paragraphs: Drafting a Paragraph
MyWritingLab

The First Draft

After you outline your ideas in a plan, you are ready to write the first draft. Remember to write complete sentences. You might include transitional expressions to help your ideas flow smoothly.

Watch the Video
Revising the Paragraph: Development
MyWritingLab

Transitional Expressions

Transitions can help you show a sequence of events. The following transitional words are useful in narrative paragraphs.

To Show a Sequence of Events			
after that	finally	in the end	meanwhile
afterward	first	last	next
eventually	in the beginning	later	then

The Writer's Desk Write the First Draft

In the previous Writer's Desk, you developed a paragraph plan. Now write the first draft of your narrative paragraph. Before you write, carefully review your paragraph plan and make any necessary changes.

REVISING AND EDITING

Watch the Video
Revising and Editing Your Own Paragraphs
MyWritingLab

Revise and Edit a Narrative Paragraph

When you finish writing a narrative paragraph, carefully review your work and revise it to make the events as clear as possible to your readers. Check that you have organized events chronologically, and remove any irrelevant details. Before you revise and edit your own paragraph, practise revising and editing a student paragraph.

PRACTICE 5

Read the next student paragraph, and answer the questions.

When my father found his first job in Canada, there was a humorous misunderstanding. My father, originally from Mexico City, had just moved to Winnipeg, Manitoba and he did not speak English very well. One day, he sees an ad for a busboy job. He wanted the job, so he called the number in the ad. Later that day, he went for an interview in a bowling alley. The restaurant manager spoke with my father and offered him the job. That night, my father went home feeling very excited. The next day, when he arrived for work, the manager gave him an apron and asked him to pick up some dishes in the bowling alley restaurant. My father, feeling confused and dissapointed, asked, "Where is the bus?" He thought that a busboy would work on a bus collecting tickets. The owner laught and explained what a busboy's job is. When my father told the family this story, everybody thought it was funny, but they were also proud of his perseverance because today he has a university degree and a good job.

Revising

1. Write down the two parts of the topic sentence.

   topic + controlling idea

   ____

2. What type of order do the specific details follow? Circle the best answer.

   a. Space b. Time

   c. Emphatic d. No order

3. What are some transitional expressions that the author used?

   ____

4. What type of narration is this?

   a. First person b. Third person

Editing

5. This paragraph contains a tense inconsistency. The tense shifts for no apparent reason. Identify the incorrect sentence. Then write the correct sentence in the space below.

   Correction: ____

   ____

6. This paragraph contains two misspelled words. Identify and correct them.

Misspelled words	Corrections
____________	____________
____________	____________

GRAMMAR LINK

See the following chapters for more information about these grammar topics:
Tense consistency, Chapter 26
Spelling, Chapter 32

Watch the **Video**
Tense
MyWritingLab

Watch the **Video**
Spelling
MyWritingLab

vo•cab•u•lar•y BOOST

Using Varied Language

1. Underline the opening word of every sentence in your first draft. Check to see if some are repeated.
2. Replace repeated opening words with an adverb, such as *Usually, Generally,* or *Fortunately,* or a prepositional phrase, such as *On the other hand* or *Under the circumstances.* You can also begin sentences with a modifier, such as *Leaving the door open.* In other words, avoid beginning too many sentences with a noun or transitional expression.

Repeated First Words

We opened the door of the abandoned house. We looked nervously at the rotting floorboards. We thought the floor might collapse. We decided to enter. We walked carefully across the kitchen floor to the bedroom, one by one.

Variety

My cousins and I opened the door of the abandoned house. Nervously, we looked at the rotting floorboards. Leaving the door open, we decided to enter. One by one, we walked across the kitchen floor to the bedroom.

Using Quotations

When you insert a direct quotation into your writing, capitalize the first word of the quotation, and put the final punctuation inside the closing quotation marks.

- Place a comma after an introductory phrase.
  Vladimir screamed, "The kitchen's on fire."
- Place a colon after an introductory sentence.
  Vladimir watched me coldly: "We have nothing to discuss."

See Chapter 34 for more information about using quotations.

The Writer's Desk Revise and Edit Your Paragraph

Revise and edit the paragraph that you wrote for the previous Writer's Desk. Ensure that your paragraph has unity, adequate support, and coherence. Also, correct any errors in grammar, spelling, punctuation, and mechanics.

REFLECT ON IT

Think about what you have learned in this chapter. If you do not know an answer, review that topic.

1. In narrative writing, you ____________________
2. What are the differences between the two following types of narration?

   First person: ____________________

   ____

   Third person: ____________________

   ____
3. What are some questions that you should you ask yourself when you write a narrative paragraph? ____________________

   ____
4. What organizational method is commonly used in narrative paragraphs? Circle the best answer.

   a. Space order b. Time order c. Emphatic order

The Writer's Room

Writing Activity 1: Topics

Choose any of the following topics, or choose your own topic. Then write a narrative paragraph.

General Topics

1. An interesting decade
2. A risky adventure
3. A move to a new place
4. An unforgettable holiday
5. A disturbing news event
6. An unexpected gift

College- and Work-Related Topics

7. An embarrassing incident at college or work
8. An inspiring teacher or instructor
9. A positive or negative job interview
10. A difficult co-worker
11. Your best experience at work
12. A proud moment at work or college

WRITING LINK

More Narrative Writing Topics

Chapter 28, Writer's Room topic 2 (page 425)
Chapter 30, Writer's Room topics 1 and 2 (page 450)

READING LINK

More Narrative Readings

"The Sanctuary of School" by Lynda Barry (page 563)

Writing Activity 2: Photo Writing

Have you ever lived through an earthquake, a tornado, a flood, a large storm, an extended power outage, or any other event caused by nature? What happened? What did you do? Write a narrative paragraph about a big storm or a natural event that you have lived through.

Minerva Studio/Shutterstock

Writing Activity 3: Media Writing

Watch a popular television show or movie in which a character overcomes a challenge. Examples are the movie *Picture Day* and television programs such as *Dragon's Den*, *7th Heaven*, and *The Hour*. You can even go on YouTube and watch some videos about people who have overcome challenges to meet their personal goals.

Watch the **Video**
Paragraphs: Revising the Paragraph—A Checklist
MyWritingLab

NARRATIVE PARAGRAPH CHECKLIST

As you write your narrative paragraph, review the checklist on the inside front cover. Also, ask yourself the following questions.

- ☐ Does my topic sentence clearly express the topic of the narration?
- ☐ Does my topic sentence contain a controlling idea that is meaningful and interesting?
- ☐ Does my paragraph answer most of the following questions: *who*, *what*, *when*, *where*, *why*, *how*?
- ☐ Do I use transitional expressions that help clarify the order of events?
- ☐ Do I include details to make my narration more interesting?

How Do I Get a Better Grade?

Visit MyWritingLab for audiovisual lectures and additional practice sets about narration paragraphs.

Description

LEARNING OBJECTIVES

Glen Stubbe/MCT/Landov

When professional photographers prepare for a session, they adjust the lighting, the model, and the camera angle to make a visual impression. In descriptive writing, you use words to create a distinct image.

Writers' Exchange

Work with two or three students. First, think about a famous person. Then describe that person, but do not name him or her. Speak nonstop about that person for about twenty seconds. Your teammates must guess the person that you are describing. Then switch speakers.

EXPLORING

Watch the Video
Paragraph Development—Describing
MyWritingLab

What Is Description?

Description creates vivid images in the reader's mind by portraying people, places, or moments in detail.

You use description every day. At home, you might describe a new friend to your family, or you might describe an object that you bought. At school, you might describe the structure of a cell or the results of a lab experiment. At work, you may describe a new product to a client, or you could describe the qualities of potential clients to your boss.

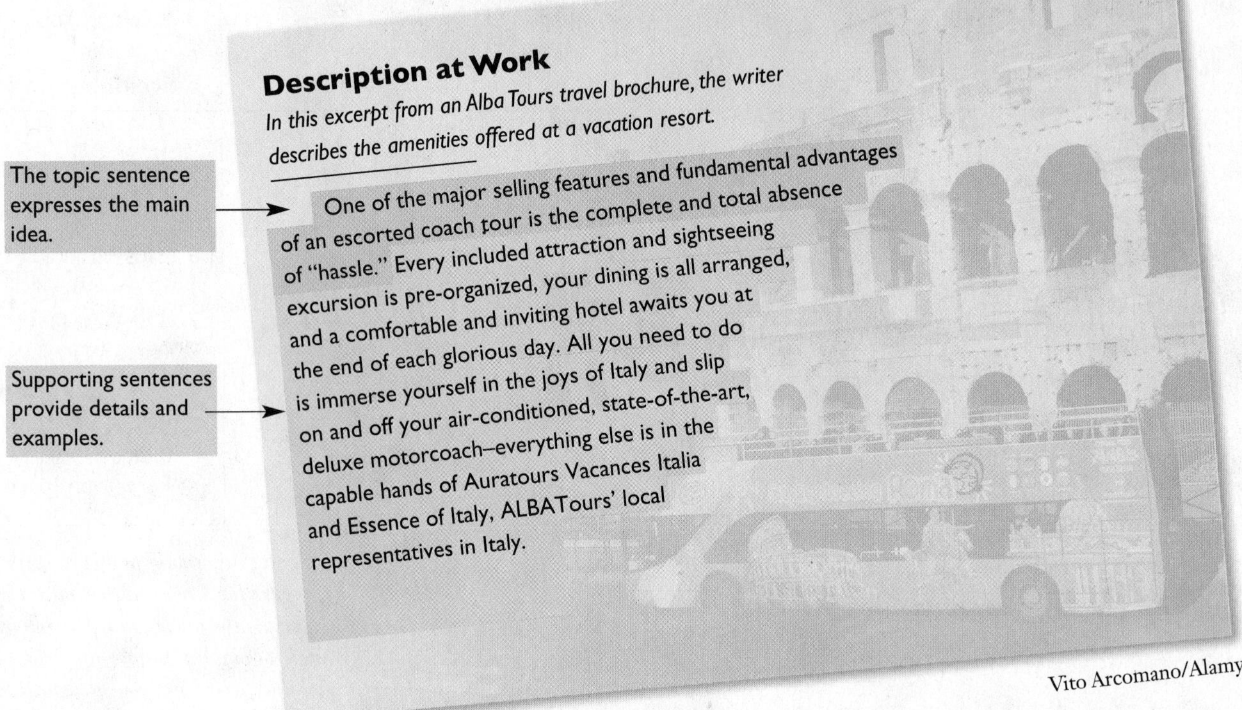

The topic sentence expresses the main idea.
Supporting sentences provide details and examples.
Description at Work
In this excerpt from an Alba Tours travel brochure, the writer describes the amenities offered at a vacation resort.
One of the major selling features and fundamental advantages of an escorted coach tour is the complete and total absence of "hassle." Every included attraction and sightseeing excursion is pre-organized, your dining is all arranged, and a comfortable and inviting hotel awaits you at the end of each glorious day. All you need to do is immerse yourself in the joys of Italy and slip on and off your air-conditioned, state-of-the-art, deluxe motorcoach–everything else is in the capable hands of Auratours Vacances Italia and Essence of Italy, ALBATours' local representatives in Italy.

Vito Arcomano/Alamy

The Descriptive Paragraph

When you write a descriptive paragraph, focus on three main points.

ESSAY LINK

In descriptive essays, you should also create a dominant impression, express your attitude toward the subject, and include concrete details.

1. **Create a dominant impression.**

   The dominant impression is the overall atmosphere that you wish to convey. It can be a strong feeling, mood, or image. For example, if you are describing a business meeting, you can emphasize the tension in the room.

2. **Express your attitude toward the subject.**

   Do you feel positive, negative, or neutral toward the subject? For example, if you feel positive about your best friend, then the details of your paragraph should convey the good feelings you have toward him or her. If you describe a place that you do not like, then your details should express how uncomfortable that place makes you feel. You might write a neutral description of a science lab experiment.

3. **Include concrete details.**

   Details will enable a reader to visualize the person, place, or situation that is being described. You can use active verbs and adjectives so that the reader imagines the scene more clearly. You can also use **imagery,** which is description using the five senses. Review the following examples of imagery.

Sight We had crossed featureless purple deserts and shrieked recklessly down mile after scrubby mile of dusk-bordered nothingness scattered with lonely oil rigs, telephone poles with their sagging wires loping along beside us, silhouettes leaning irregularly into the flat sky.

—Nick Massey-Garrison, "We Turned Some Sharp Corners: A Marriage Proposal in Durango"

Sound They hooked wrist-thick hanks of laghmien noodles and shoveled them into their mouths, slurping, sucking, inhaling, and chomping off portions....

—Jeffrey Tayler, "A Cacophony of Noodles"

Smell For several days the wind blew, full of dust scents and the dryness of sagebrush, carrying eastward our own autumn smell of falling maple leaves, green walnuts, and the warm lemon odor of quince and yellow apples.

—Josephine Johnson, "September Harvest"

Touch She felt a cool breeze on her back and sat upright and turned around.

—Maya Angelou, "Aunt Tee"

Taste I baked a delicious strawberry-rhubarb pie and could taste the sweet strawberries contrasted with the tart rhubarb in one bite.

PRACTICE 1

Read the next paragraph and answer the questions.

As the weeks passed, Lily struggled to stay still and contained in the farmhouse. She worked on her book about the Boston sisters, one of whom was now discovering Manitoulin sixty summers earlier. This had not been part of Lily's plan, but she was delighted by the way the character of Amanda, the society wife and art patron, seemed to have a mind of her own. In defense, Lily haunted the library in Gore Bay and studied the accounts of early Manitoulin settlers, delighting in their epic tales of adaptation. The quest was, she thought, to appreciate the journey and move slowly. Lily did her exercises and stretches every morning and walked two miles daily to the post office, the air smelling green and wet as March became April. She and Will were both seeking something, she felt, but the process was not one of reaching mutual conclusions, but in being together for the journey. Her hands weren't empty. She filled them, writing about a woman of her great-aunt's generation in Manitoulin, cooking, getting out when she could to have lunch with her friends. She loved hearing stories about how people came to Manitoulin, and stayed. She wondered at the way that Will seemed to own serenity and loneliness at the same time.

—Bonnie Kogos, *Manhattan Manitoulin*

1. What is the attitude of the writer toward the subject of the paragraph? Circle the best answer.

   a. Positive b. Negative c. Neutral

2. Write at least two examples to support your answer to question 1.

3. What is the dominant impression the author creates about her experience on the ocean?

   a. Boredom b. Fear c. Wonder d. Surprise e. Sorrow

4. Write at least two examples from the text that show the dominant impression.

Watch the Video
Prewriting: Questioning
MyWritingLab

Explore Topics

In Writer's Desk: Warm Up, you will try an exploring strategy to generate ideas about different topics.

The Writer's Desk Warm Up

Think about the following questions, and write down the first ideas that come to your mind. Try to think of two or three ideas for each topic.

EXAMPLE:

What are some activities that you would like to try?

Arc welding fascinates me. Although it seemed intimidating at first, with the sparks and heat, I would attempt it again in a flash.

1. What were some very emotional moments in your life? (Think about two or three moments when you felt extreme joy, sadness, excitement, anxiety, or other strong emotions.)

2. Describe your food quirks. What are your unusual tastes or eating habits? Which foods do you really love or hate?

3. What are some very busy places?

DEVELOPING

When you write a descriptive paragraph, choose a subject that lends itself to description. In other words, find a subject to describe that appeals to the senses. For example, you can describe the sounds, sights, and smells in a bakery.

ESSAY LINK

In a descriptive essay, the thesis statement expresses the controlling idea.

The Topic Sentence

In the topic sentence of a descriptive paragraph, you should convey a dominant impression about the subject in the controlling idea. The dominant impression is the overall impression or feeling that the topic inspires.

Watch the Video Paragraphs: The Topic Sentence **MyWritingLab**

topic / controlling idea

The abandoned buildings in our neighbourhood are an eyesore.

topic / controlling idea

Lady Patricia was a perfect example of beauty that is but skin deep.

—Nancy Mitford, *Love in a Cold Climate*

How to Create a Dominant Impression

To create a dominant impression, ask yourself how or why the topic is important.

Poor: The parade was noisy.

(Why should readers care about this statement?)

topic / controlling idea

Better: **The parade participants** loudly celebrated the arrival of the New Year.

The Writer's Desk Write Topic Sentences

Write a topic sentence for each of the following topics. You can look for ideas in the previous Writer's Desk. Remember to narrow each topic. Each topic sentence should state what you are describing and contain a controlling idea.

EXAMPLE:

Topic: Arc welding

Topic sentence: *My first attempt at arc welding filled me with awe.*

1. Topic: An emotional moment

   Topic sentence: ______________________

2. Topic: Food quirks

   Topic sentence: ______________________________

   ____

3. Topic: A busy place

   Topic sentence: ______________________________

   ____

Watch the Video
Revising the Paragraph: Organization
MyWritingLab

The Supporting Ideas

After you have developed an effective topic sentence, generate supporting details. The details can be placed in space, time, or emphatic order.

Visualizing Description

PRACTICE 2

Brainstorm supporting ideas for the following topic sentence. Write some descriptive words or phrases.

Topic Sentence: During my canoe trip, the scenery fascinated me.

Polka Dot/Thinkstock

Steve Allen/Stockbyte/Getty Images

Jeremy Woodhouse/Photodisc/Getty Images

______________ ______________ ______________

______________ ______________ ______________

Show, Don't Tell

Your audience will find it more interesting to read your written work if you *show* a quality of a place or an action of a person rather than just stating it.

Example of Telling: I remember my fifth-grade teacher fondly because she was very nice.

Example of Showing: My fifth grade teacher, at the time she taught me, was already beloved of two generations. What I chiefly remember is how she brought her own life's interests into our classroom. Back in the days when "opening exercises" included five or ten minutes of hymn singing, this teacher—a barbershop singer—graced those minutes by teaching us the hymns in four-part harmony. She had founded her own chapter of barbershoppers, quitting her original group in protest when it barred a black singer from joining. This story, too, she shared with us.

—Robyn Sarah, "Notes that Resonate a Lifetime"

PRACTICE 3

Choose one of the following sentences, and write a short description that shows—not tells—the quality of the person, place, thing, or event.

1. The food smelled delicious.
2. It was a hot day.
3. The child's room was messy.

List Sensory Details

To create a dominant impression, think about your topic, and make a list of your feelings and impressions. These details can include imagery (images that appeal to sight, sound, hearing, taste, and smell).

ESSAY LINK

When you plan a descriptive essay, it is useful to list sensory details.

TOPIC: An abandoned building

Details:
—damp floors
—boarded-up windows
—broken glass
—graffiti on the walls
—musty odour
—grey bricks
—chipping paint

vo•cab•u•lar•y BOOST

Using Vivid Language

When you write a descriptive paragraph, try to use **vivid language**. Use specific action verbs and adjectives to create a clear picture of what you are describing.

The lawyer was ~~not nice~~ *vulgar*.
(Use a more vivid, specific adjective.)

The boss ~~shouted~~ *barked* at the employee.
(Use a more vivid, specific verb or image.)

Think about more effective words or expressions for the following:

Hungry: ____________________

Not friendly: ____________________

Cry: ____________________

Speak: ____________________

The Writer's Desk List Sensory Details

Think about images, impressions, and feelings that the following topics inspire in you. Refer to your topic sentences from the previous Writer's Desk, and make a list under each topic.

EXAMPLE:
Arc welding:

flashing light
burning smell
bright sparks
smell of rust
bending wire
popping sound

1. An emotional moment: ______

2. Food quirks: ______

3. A busy place: ______

Watch the **Video**
Paragraph: How to Write a Successful Paragraph
MyWritingLab

ESSAY LINK

In a descriptive essay, place the thesis statement in the introduction. Then develop each supporting idea in a body paragraph.

The Paragraph Plan

A descriptive paragraph should contain specific details so that the reader can clearly imagine what is being described. When you make a paragraph plan, remember to include concrete details. Also, think about the organizational method that you will use.

Topic Sentence: My first attempt at arc welding filled me with awe.

Support 1: At first, the flashing lights frightened me.
Details: —popping and cracking sound
—like a roaring brush fire
—bright sparks

Support 2: The smell of burning newspaper filled the air.
Details: —oxidized metal
—odour of a rusty boat hull

Support 3: I was able to shape the raw metal.
Details: —red-hot wire
—bent like licorice

The Writer's Desk Write a Paragraph Plan

Choose one of the topic sentences that you wrote for the Writer's Desk on page 87, and write a detailed paragraph plan. You can include some of the sensory details that you have generated in the previous Writer's Desk.

Topic sentence: ______________________________

____

Support 1: ______________________________

____

Details: ______________________________

____

____

Support 2: ______________________________

Details: ______________________________

____

____

Support 3: ______________________________

Details: ______________________________

____

____

The First Draft

After you outline your ideas in a plan, you are ready to write the first draft. Remember to write complete sentences. You might include transitional expressions to help your ideas flow smoothly.

Watch the Video Paragraphs: Drafting a Paragraph **MyWritingLab**

Transitional Expressions

You can use space order to describe a person, place, or thing. The following transitions are useful in descriptive paragraphs.

Watch the Video Revising the Paragraph: Development **MyWritingLab**

To Show Place or Position			
above	beyond	in the distance	outside
behind	closer in	nearby	over there
below	farther out	on the left/right	under
beside	in front	on top	underneath

The Writer's Desk Write the First Draft

In the previous Writer's Desk, you developed a paragraph plan. Now write the first draft of your descriptive paragraph. Before you write, carefully review your paragraph plan, and make any necessary changes.

REVISING AND EDITING

Watch the **Video**
Revising and Editing Your Own Paragraphs
MyWritingLab

Revise and Edit a Descriptive Paragraph

When you finish writing a descriptive paragraph, carefully review your work and revise it to make the description as clear as possible to your readers. Check that you have organized your steps logically, and remove any irrelevant details.

PRACTICE 4

Read the following student paragraph, and answer the questions.

> Eight years ago, my first attempt at arc welding filled me with awe. I was fearful, yet I felt as if I had uncover a great secret. At first, the flashing lights frightened me. They made a popping and crackling noise that sounded like a roaring brush fire. Imagine charging a car battery and accidentally knocking the clamps. Sparks flew, yet I could control and maintain the sparking. An odour like that of burning newspaper filled the air. Also, the oxidized metal. It smelled like a rusty boat hull after a rainfall. I felt so powerful because I could make raw metal take shape. Using a vise, the red-hot steel bent as easily as a piece of licorice.
>
> —Kelly Bruce

Revising

1. Underline the topic sentence.
2. Highlight three vivid images in the paragraph.
3. The paragraph ends abruptly. Add a concluding sentence.

____

____

GRAMMAR LINK

See the following chapters for more information about these topics:
Past Participles, Chapter 23
Fragments, Chapter 20
Modifiers, Chapter 30

Editing

4. Identify and correct one past participle error.
   Error: ________________ Correction: ________________
5. A fragment lacks a subject or verb and is an incomplete sentence. Identify and correct one fragment. Write the correction on the line.

   ____
6. The paragraph contains a dangling modifier. Write the correction on the line. (See the Grammar Hint below for more information about modifier errors.)

   ____

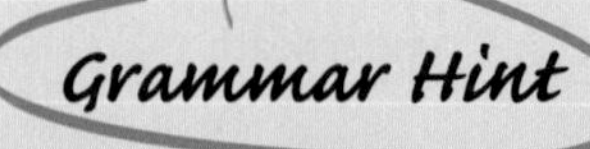

Using Modifiers

When you revise your descriptive essay, check that your modifiers are placed near the items that they are modifying.

Incorrect: The young man drank the coffee slowly wearing a blue suit.

Correct: The young man wearing a blue suit drank the coffee slowly.

See Chapter 30 for more information about misplaced modifiers.

The Writer's Desk Revise and Edit Your Paragraph

Revise and edit the paragraph that you wrote for the previous Writer's Desk. Ensure that your paragraph has unity, adequate support, and coherence. Also, correct any errors in grammar, spelling, punctuation, and mechanics.

REFLECT ON IT

Think about what you have learned in this chapter. If you do not know an answer, review that topic.

1. What are the main features of a descriptive paragraph? ______________________

____

____

2. Define imagery. ______________________________________

3. Look at the familiar words below. Write down at least two more descriptive ways to say each word. Try to find words that are more specific.

a. Cute ____________________ b. Angry ____________________
c. Sad ____________________ d. Mean ____________________

Watch the **Video**
Paragraphs: Revising the Paragraph—A Checklist
MyWritingLab

The Writer's Room

Writing Activity 1: Topics

Choose any of the following topics, or choose your own topic. Then write a descriptive paragraph.

General Topics

1. A coffee shop
2. An interesting house or building
3. A useless product or item
4. An evening out
5. A scene from nature
6. A silly fashion trend

College- and Work-Related Topics

7. A quiet area on campus
8. An unusual student or co-worker
9. A loud place
10. An uncomfortable uniform
11. A place with a good or bad odour
12. An embarrassing moment at work

WRITING LINK

More Descriptive Writing Topics

Chapter 26, Writer's Room topic 1 (page 389)
Chapter 30, Writer's Room topic 2 (page 450)

Writing Activity 2: Photo Writing

Visit a public place and take notes about the sights, sounds, and smells. Then write a paragraph describing that place. Include vivid details.

CREATISTA/Shutterstock

Writing Activity 3: Media Writing

Watch a popular television show or movie that depicts the future or that depicts mysterious places. For example, you can choose the movie *Mystery, Alaska* or a television show such as *Murdoch Mysteries* or *Da Vinci's Inquest*. In a paragraph, describe the setting or main characters. Use imagery that appeals to the senses.

DESCRIPTIVE PARAGRAPH CHECKLIST

As you write your descriptive paragraph, review the checklist on the inside front cover. Also, ask yourself the following questions.

- ☐ Does my topic sentence clearly show what I will describe?
- ☐ Does my topic sentence have a controlling idea that makes a point about the topic?
- ☐ Does my paragraph make a dominant impression?
- ☐ Does my paragraph contain supporting details that appeal to the reader's senses?
- ☐ Do I use vivid language?

READING LINK

More Descriptive Readings

"The Great Offside" by James Mirtle (page 538)
"The Catcher of Ghosts" by Amy Tan (page 548)

How Do I Get a Better Grade?

Visit MyWritingLab for audiovisual lectures and additional practice sets about description paragraphs.

Process

LEARNING OBJECTIVES

A sushi chef follows a process to create a tasty meal. In process writing, you describe how to do something.

Writers' Exchange

Choose one of the following topics, and have a group or class discussion. Describe the steps you would take to complete that process.

1. How to go grocery shopping
2. How to be a bad date
3. How to bathe your dog or cat
4. How to annoy your parents or children

EXPLORING

Watch the Video Paragraph Development—Process **MyWritingLab**

What Is a Process?

A **process** is a series of steps done in chronological order. In process writing, you explain how to do something, how an incident took place, or how something works.

You explain processes every day. At home, you may explain to a family member how to use an electronic appliance. You may need to give written instructions to a babysitter or caregiver. At college, you may explain how to perform a scientific experiment or how a new product was invented. At work, you may explain how to operate a machine or how to do a particular job.

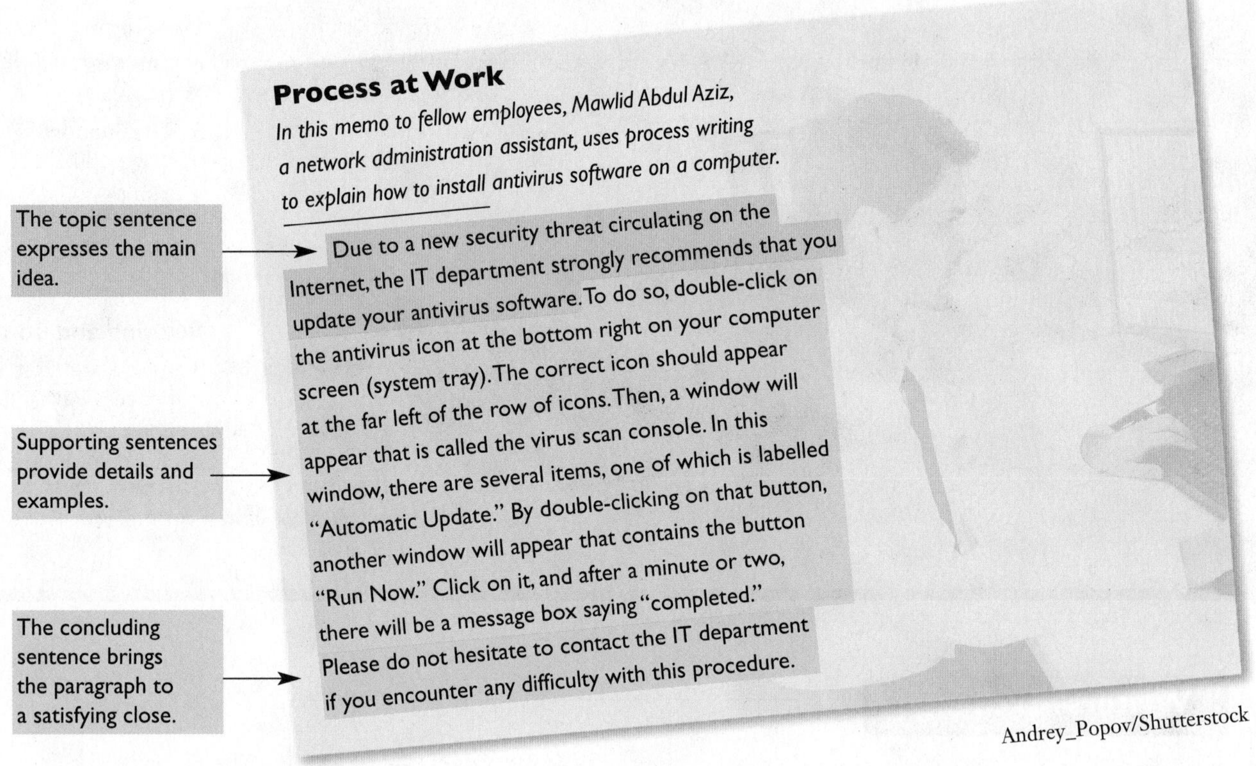

The topic sentence expresses the main idea.
Supporting sentences provide details and examples.
The concluding sentence brings the paragraph to a satisfying close.
Process at Work
In this memo to fellow employees, Mawlid Abdul Aziz, a network administration assistant, uses process writing to explain how to install antivirus software on a computer.
Due to a new security threat circulating on the Internet, the IT department strongly recommends that you update your antivirus software. To do so, double-click on the antivirus icon at the bottom right on your computer screen (system tray). The correct icon should appear at the far left of the row of icons. Then, a window will appear that is called the virus scan console. In this window, there are several items, one of which is labelled "Automatic Update." By double-clicking on that button, another window will appear that contains the button "Run Now." Click on it, and after a minute or two, there will be a message box saying "completed." Please do not hesitate to contact the IT department if you encounter any difficulty with this procedure.

Andrey_Popov/Shutterstock

ESSAY LINK

Process essays also focus on completing or understanding a process.

The Process Paragraph

There are two main types of process paragraphs.

- **Complete a process.** This type of paragraph contains directions on how to complete a particular task. For example, a writer might explain how to paint a picture, how to repair a leaky faucet, or how to get a job. The reader should be able to follow the directions and complete the task.
- **Understand a process.** This type of paragraph explains how something works or how something happens. In other words, the goal is to help the reader understand a process rather than completing a process. For example, a writer might explain how the heart pumps blood to other organs in the body or how a country elects its political leaders.

PRACTICE 1

A framed painting hanging on a wall creates its own imaginary world. Understanding and responding to a painting does not have to be difficult. First, get up close. When you approach a picture, step into its universe. Put your nose up close and observe the picture as a physical object. Drink in its visual and physical properties. Next, take a step back and look at the picture as a whole. Look at the arrangement or composition of the picture's elements: background or foreground, implied movement, and dramatic action. Is there a story? Who are the human figures? Are there symbols? What feelings or ideas does it stimulate in you? Then, think and apply what you know. Study the picture in historical context. This knowledge can help identify the style or movement to which a picture belongs. It can tell you the work's patron or something significant about the artist's life and how this work fits into that story. Finally, respond with your own thoughts and feelings. Look at what it shows you and listen to what it says and record that experience for yourself in a journal or notebook. This personal reflection fixes the impression and helps you recall this picture as something you've become acquainted with.

—Philip E. Bishop, *A Beginner's Guide to the Humanities*

1. a. What is the topic of this paragraph? ______________________________

____

   b. What is the controlling idea in the topic sentence? ________________

____

2. List the main steps the author suggests to understand a painting.

____

____

____

____

PRACTICE 2

Read the next paragraph and answer the questions.

> Tsunamis, like the one that occurred in Indonesia in 2004, are caused by shifting layers in the Earth's crust. The plates of hard rock, which fit together like a puzzle, overlap and move slowly over time. As the plates push against each other, pressure builds up. When the plates finally buckle, or if one plate pushes under another, built-up energy is released. When this happens underwater, seawater gets pushed up to the surface. Waves then spread in different directions. The waves can move at over 200 miles per hour in the deep ocean. As they near the shore and get squeezed in inlets, the waves increase in size and can attain 90 feet in height. At the same time, they slow down but can still move at 50 miles per hour, which is faster than a person can run. When the tsunami hits the shore, it strips the sand off beaches, rips away trees and bushes, and pounds buildings.
>
> —Natalia MacDonald, student

1. Underline the topic sentence.
2. What type of process paragraph is this? Circle the better answer.
   a. Complete a process b. Understand a process
3. List the steps or stages in the process. The first one has been done for you.

   plates push against each other

   ____

   ____

   ____

PRACTICE 3

For each of the following topics, write *C* if it explains how to complete a process, or write *U* if it explains how to understand a process (how something works or how something happens).

1. How to train a pet dog _____
2. The stages in a child's development _____
3. How a child learns to read _____
4. How to avoid being mugged _____
5. Five steps to keep your motorcycle in top condition _____

Watch the Video
Prewriting: Questioning
MyWritingLab

Explore Topics

In Writer's Desk: Warm Up, you will try an exploring strategy to generate ideas about different topics.

The Writer's Desk Warm Up

Think about the following questions, and write down the first ideas that come to your mind. Try to think of two or three ideas for each topic.

EXAMPLE:

Imagine that you have a new opportunity and want to leave your current job. What are some things that you should do before you quit your job?

—give supervisor a lot of notice (needs time to hire someone else)

—ask for a reference letter (I might need it later)

—have a going-away party, and thank co-workers and supervisor

1. How do you do a particular activity at your workplace?

____

____

____

2. What are some things you should do to succeed in college?

____

____

____

3. Think about a particular holiday or celebration that you enjoy. What are some things you do to prepare for that holiday?

____

____

____

DEVELOPING

When you write a process paragraph, choose a process that you can easily cover in a single paragraph. For example, you might be able to explain how to send an email message in a single paragraph; however, you would need much more than a paragraph to explain how to use a particular computer software program.

ESSAY LINK

In a process essay, the thesis statement expresses the controlling idea.

The Topic Sentence

In a process paragraph, the topic sentence states what process you will be explaining and what readers will be able to do or understand after they have read the paragraph.

Watch the Video Paragraphs: The Topic Sentence **MyWritingLab**

topic / controlling idea

To calm your child during a tantrum, follow the next steps.

controlling idea / topic

With inexpensive materials, **you can redecorate a room in your house.**

Make a Point

Your topic sentence should not simply announce the topic. It should make a point about the topic.

Announces: This is how you do speed dating.

controlling idea / topic

Correct: It is surprisingly easy and efficient **to meet someone using speed dating.**

The Writer's Desk Write Topic Sentences

Write a topic sentence for each of the following topics. You can look for ideas in the previous Writer's Desk. Remember to narrow each topic. Each topic sentence should state the process and should contain a controlling idea.

EXAMPLE:

Topic: How to leave a job:

Topic sentence: *If you want to leave your job on a positive note, there are a few things that you should consider.*

1. Topic: How to do an activity at work

   Topic sentence: ______________________________

2. Topic: How to succeed in college

   Topic sentence: ______________________________

3. Topic: How to prepare for a holiday or celebration

   Topic sentence: ______________________________

Watch the Video Revising the Paragraph: Organization **MyWritingLab**

ESSAY LINK

In an essay, each body paragraph could describe a process. For example, in an essay about how to get rich, one body paragraph could be about buying lottery tickets, and another could be about inventing a product.

The Supporting Ideas

A process paragraph contains a series of steps. When you develop supporting ideas for a process paragraph, think about the main steps that are necessary to complete the process. Most process paragraphs use time order.

Give Steps, Not Examples

When you explain how to complete a process, describe each step. Do not simply list examples of the process.

Topic: How to Get Rich

List of Examples	Steps in the Process
Write a best seller	Do market research
Win the lottery	Find a specific need
Invent a product	Invent a product to fulfill that need
Inherit money	Heavily promote the product

Visualizing Process

PRACTICE 4

Brainstorm supporting ideas for the following topic sentence. List some steps that you should take.

Topic sentence: Putting in contact lenses is not a difficult procedure.

verdateo/Fotolia

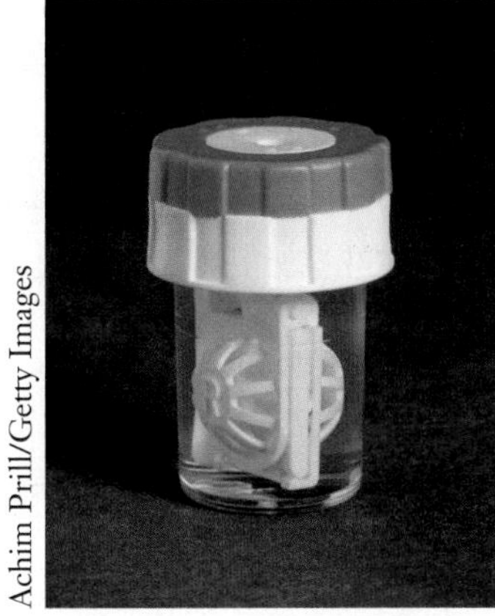

Achim Prill/Getty Images

jocic/Shutterstock

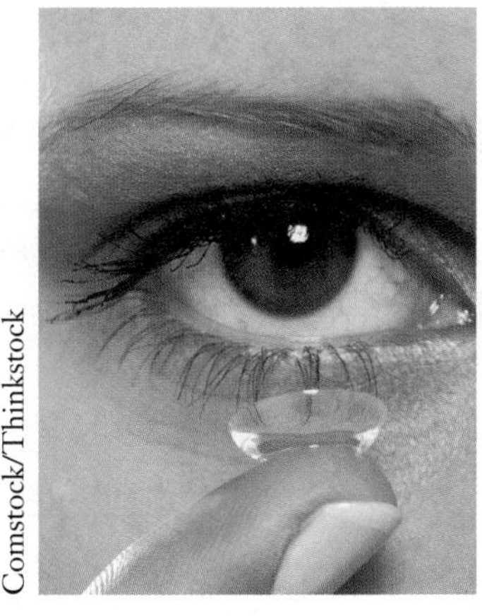

Comstock/Thinkstock

The Writer's Desk List the Main Steps

Think about three or four essential steps in each process. Make a list under each topic.

EXAMPLE:
How to leave a job

explain your reason for going
give enough notice
ask for a reference letter
find out about benefits

1. How to do an activity at work

____
____
____
____

2. How to succeed in college

____
____
____
____

3. How to prepare for a holiday or a celebration

____
____
____
____

Watch the **Video**
Paragraph: How to Write a Successful Paragraph
MyWritingLab

ESSAY LINK

In a process essay, place the thesis statement in the introduction. Then use each body paragraph to explain a step in the process.

The Paragraph Plan

A paragraph plan helps you organize your topic sentence and supporting details before writing a first draft. Decide which steps and which details your reader will really need to complete the process or understand it. Write down the steps in chronological order.

Topic Sentence: If you want to leave your job on a positive note, there are a few things that you should consider.

Step 1: Give positive reasons for leaving.
Details: —do not complain about the company
—say you need a new challenge
Step 2: Give your employer enough notice.
Details: —the company might need time to hire a replacement
Step 3: Ask for a reference letter.
Details: —may need it in the future
Step 4: Find out about employee benefits.
Details: —might get unused vacation pay

Include Necessary Tools or Supplies

When you are writing a plan for a process paragraph, remember to include any special tools or supplies a reader will need to complete the process. For example, if you want to explain how to pack for a move, you should mention that you need boxes, felt-tip markers, newsprint, twine, scissors, and tape.

The Writer's Desk Write a Paragraph Plan

Choose one of the topic sentences that you wrote for the Writer's Desk on page 100, and then list the main steps to complete the process. Also, add details and examples that will help explain each step.

Topic sentence: ______________________________

____

Supporting points:

Step 1: ______________________________

Details: ______________________________

____

Step 2: ______________________________

Details: ______________________________

____

Step 3: ______________________________

Details: ______________________________

____

Step 4: ______________________________

Details: ______________________________

____

Step 5: ______________________________

Details: ______________________________

____

The First Draft

After you outline your ideas in a plan, you are ready to write the first draft. Remember to write complete sentences. You might include transitional expressions to help your ideas flow smoothly.

Watch the **Video**
Revising the Paragraph: Development
MyWritingLab

Transitional Expressions

Most process paragraphs explain a process using time (or chronological) order. The following transitions are useful in process paragraphs.

To Begin a Process	To Continue a Process		To End a Process
(at) first	after that	later	eventually
initially	afterward	meanwhile	finally
the first step	also	second	in the end
	furthermore	then	ultimately
	in addition	third	

The Writer's Desk Write the First Draft

In the previous Writer's Desk, you developed a paragraph plan. Now write the first draft of your process paragraph. Before you write, carefully review your paragraph plan, and make any necessary changes.

REVISING AND EDITING

Watch the **Video**
Revising and Editing Your Own Paragraphs
MyWritingLab

Revise and Edit a Process Paragraph

When you finish writing a process paragraph, carefully review your work and revise it to make the process as clear as possible to your readers. Check to make sure that you have organized your steps chronologically, and remove any irrelevant details.

PRACTICE 5

Read the following student paragraph, and answer the questions.

> If you want to leave your job on a positive note, there are a few things that you should consider. First, give a positive reason for leaving. Instead of complaining about something in the company, you could say that you need a change and want a different challenge. Give as much notice as possible, this will leave a favourable impression. It will also give your boss time to find a replacement. If you think you deserve it, ask for a reference letter. Even if you already have a new job, the reference letter could be useful at a future date. Find out if you are entitled to benefits. You may be eligible for back pay or vacation pay. Business consultant Cho Matsu says "The impression you make when you leave a job could have an impact on your future career."

Revising

1. Underline the topic sentence.
2. The author uses *first* to introduce the first step. Subsequent steps would be more clearly recognizable if the writer had used more transitions. Indicate, with a number, where more transitional expressions could be added, and write possible examples on the lines provided.

   ____

   ____

   ____

3. How does the writer conclude the paragraph?

   a. With a prediction   b. With a suggestion   c. With a quotation

Editing

4. This paragraph contains a type of run-on sentence called a comma splice. Two complete sentences are incorrectly connected with a comma. Identify and correct the comma splice.
5. Identify and correct a pronoun shift.
6. This paragraph contains two punctuation errors in the direct quotation. Correct the mistakes directly on the paragraph.

GRAMMAR LINK

See the following chapters for more information about these grammar topics:
Run-Ons, Chapter 20
Quotations, Chapter 34

Pronoun Shifts

Keep your pronouns consistent. For example, if your process paragraph is addressed to *you*, then do not shift unnecessarily to *we* or *they*.

When you use natural cleaning products, ~~we~~ you help the environment.

vo•cab•u•lar•y BOOST

Look at the first draft of your process essay. Underline the verb that you use in each step of the process. Then, when possible, come up with a more evocative or interesting verb. Use your thesaurus for this activity.

The Writer's Desk **Revise and Edit Your Paragraph**

Revise and edit the paragraph that you wrote for the previous Writer's Desk. Ensure that your paragraph has unity, adequate support, and coherence. Also, correct any errors in grammar, spelling, punctuation, and mechanics.

Watch the **Video**
Paragraphs: Revising the Paragraph—A Checklist
MyWritingLab

REFLECT ON IT

Think about what you have learned in this unit. If you do not know an answer, review that topic.

1. What are the two types of process paragraphs? Briefly explain each type.

   a. ____

   b. ____

2. What organizational method is generally used in process writing? Circle the best answer.

   a. Space order   b. Time order   c. Emphatic order

3. Why are transitional expressions important in process writing?

   ____

The Writer's Room

WRITING LINK

More Process Writing Topics

Chapter 19, Writer's Room topic 3 (page 312)

Chapter 26, Writer's Room topic 2 (page 389)

Chapter 32, Writer's Room topic 4 (page 477)

Writing Activity 1: Topics

Choose any of the following topics, or choose your own topic. Then write a process paragraph.

General Topics

1. How to make your home safe
2. How to decorate a room with very little money
3. How to find a good roommate
4. How to break up with a mate
5. How to train a pet
6. How to build or fix something

College- and Work-Related Topics

7. How to choose a college
8. How to stay motivated at college
9. How to prepare for a job interview
10. How to get along with your co-workers
11. How to organize your desk or tools
12. How something was discovered

Writing Activity 2: Photo Writing

Pop artist Andy Warhol once said that everyone would be famous for fifteen minutes. Think of some processes related to fame. Some ideas might be how to become famous, how to stay famous, how to lose fame, how to survive fame, and how to meet a celebrity. Then write a process paragraph.

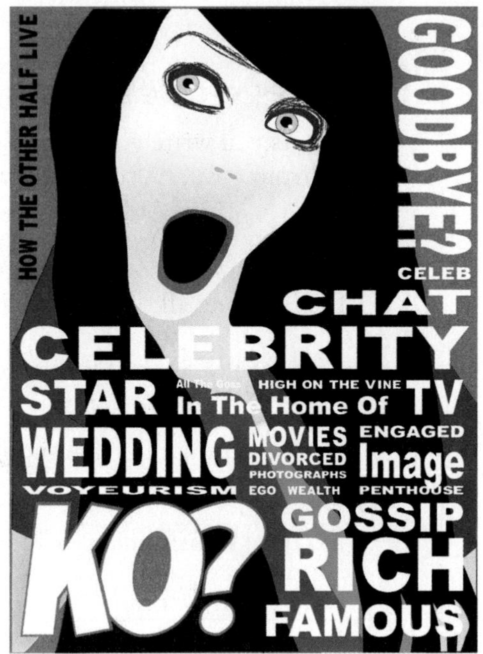

Al/Fotolia

READING LINK

More Process Reading

"Like It or Not, Yoga Is Here to Stay" by Aparita Bhandari (page 566)

Writing Activity 3: Media Writing

Watch a reality television show such as *Project Runway Canada*, *Top Chef Canada*, *Canada's Next Top Model*, or *The Amazing Race Canada*. Describe the process the contestants go through to win the prize.

Hand-out/CTV/Newscom

PROCESS PARAGRAPH CHECKLIST

As you write your process paragraph, review the checklist on the inside front cover. Also, ask yourself the following questions.

- ☐ Does my topic sentence make a point about the process?
- ☐ Do I include all of the steps in the process?
- ☐ Do I clearly explain each step so my reader can complete the process or understand it?
- ☐ Do I mention all of the supplies that my reader needs to complete the process?
- ☐ Do I use transitions to connect all of the steps in the process?

How Do I Get a Better Grade?

Visit MyWritingLab for audiovisual lectures and additional practice sets about process writing.

Definition

Peter Weber/Shutterstock.com

LEARNING OBJECTIVES

Exploring

Developing

Revising and Editing

For many people, the definition of happiness is listening to great music. In definition writing, you define what a term means.

Writers' Exchange

Work with a partner or a team of students. Try to define the following terms. Think of some examples that can help define each term.

netiquette chick flick carnivore texting

EXPLORING

What Is Definition?

When you **define**, you explain the meaning of a word. Some terms have concrete meanings, and you can define them in a few words. For example, a pebble is "a small stone." Other words, such as *culture*, *happiness*, and *evil*, are more abstract and require longer definitions. In fact, it is possible to write a paragraph, an essay, or even an entire book on such concepts.

The simplest way to define a term is to look it up in a dictionary. However, many words have nuances that are not necessarily discussed in dictionaries. For example, suppose that your boss calls your work "unsatisfactory." You might need clarification of that term. Do you have poor work habits? Do you miss deadlines? Is your attitude problematic? What does your boss mean by "unsatisfactory"?

The ability to define difficult concepts is always useful. At home, a friend or loved one may ask you to define *commitment*. If you mention that a movie was *great*, you may need to clarify what you mean by that word. In a political science class, you might define *socialism*, *capitalism*, or *communism*. At work, you might define your company's *winning strategy*.

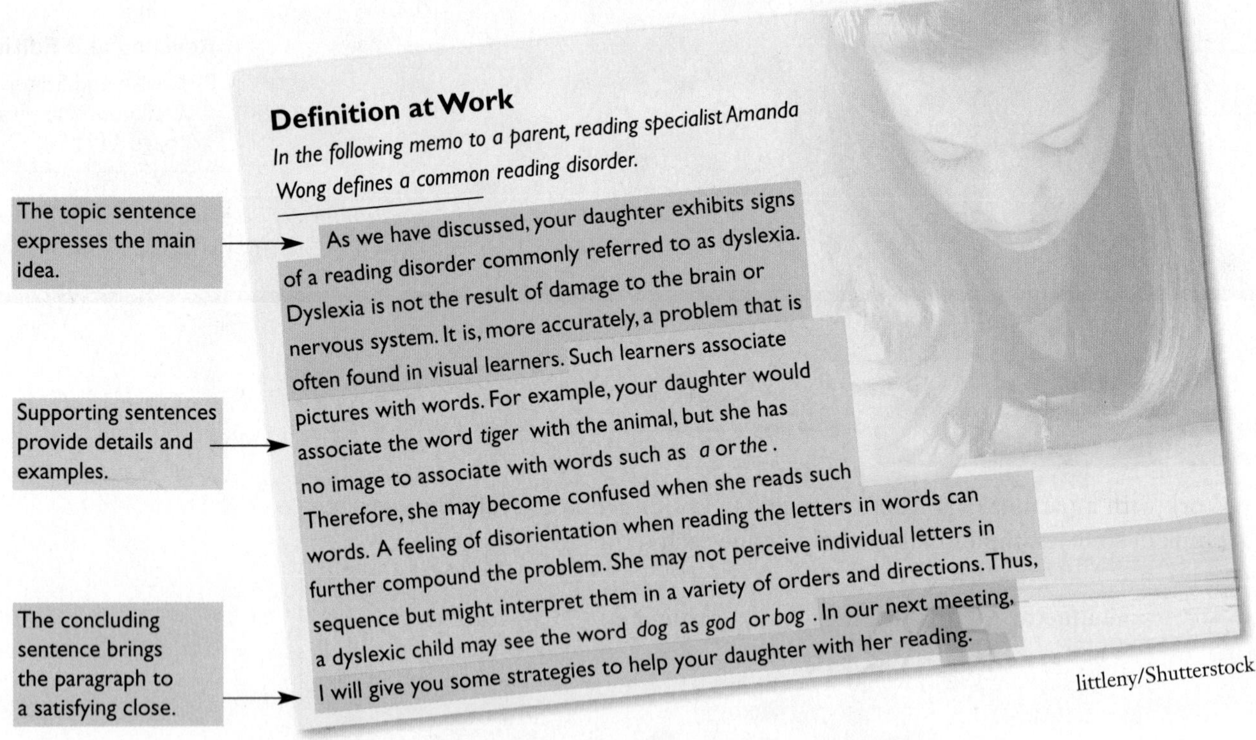
The topic sentence expresses the main idea.
Supporting sentences provide details and examples.
The concluding sentence brings the paragraph to a satisfying close.

Definition at Work

In the following memo to a parent, reading specialist Amanda Wong defines a common reading disorder.

As we have discussed, your daughter exhibits signs of a reading disorder commonly referred to as dyslexia. Dyslexia is not the result of damage to the brain or nervous system. It is, more accurately, a problem that is often found in visual learners. Such learners associate pictures with words. For example, your daughter would associate the word *tiger* with the animal, but she has no image to associate with words such as *a* or *the*. Therefore, she may become confused when she reads such words. A feeling of disorientation when reading the letters in words can further compound the problem. She may not perceive individual letters in sequence but might interpret them in a variety of orders and directions. Thus, a dyslexic child may see the word *dog* as *god* or *bog*. In our next meeting, I will give you some strategies to help your daughter with her reading.

littleny/Shutterstock

The Definition Paragraph

When you write a definition paragraph, try to explain what a term means to you. For example, if someone asks you to define *bravery*, you might tell stories to illustrate the meaning of the word. You may also give examples of acts of bravery. You might even explain what bravery is not.

When you write a definition paragraph, remember the following two points.

- **Choose a term that you know something about.** You need to understand a term in order to say something relevant and interesting about it.
- **Give a clear definition.** In your first sentence, write a definition that is understandable to your reader, and support your definition with examples. Do not simply give a dictionary definition, because your readers are capable of looking up the word themselves. Instead, describe what the word means to you.

Consider Your Audience

When you write a definition paragraph, consider your audience. You may have to adjust your tone and vocabulary, depending on who reads the paragraph. For example, if you write a definition paragraph about computer viruses for your English class, you will have to use easily understandable terms. If you write the same paragraph for your computer class, you can use more technical terms.

PRACTICE 1

Read the paragraph and then answer the questions.

> A standard baseball pitch—slider, curveball, fastball—seems to slavishly follow the laws of physics, making it possible to predict where a ball will go and how it will get there. The knuckleball is different. It appears to dip suddenly, dart to one side or the other, or—when you least expect it—to float in straight over the plate. Hitters are left flailing desperately at it. . . . As the pitch rotates extremely slowly, the orientation of the seams is actually visible to the batter, instead of being the usual blur. It may be that the seams' movement is confused with that of the ball. "Knuckleballs," he [Physicist Alan Nathan] ventures, "are more like bullets than butterflies." Only further experiments will tell us for sure. In the meantime, we can be certain of one thing: that the knuckler is the most beautifully bizarre phenomenon in all of baseball.
>
> —Jay Ingram, "Pitch Perfect," *The Walrus*

1. Underline the topic sentence.
2. What is the writer defining? ____________________
3. Who is the likely audience for this paragraph? ____________________
4. What two examples does the author give to develop the definition?

   ____

   ____
5. Think of another example to add to this paragraph.

   ____

   ____

Watch the Video
Prewriting: Questioning
MyWritingLab

Explore Topics

In Writer's Desk: Warm Up, you will try an exploring strategy to generate ideas about different topics.

The Writer's Desk Warm Up

Think about the following questions, and write down the first ideas that come to your mind. Try to think of two or three ideas for each topic.

EXAMPLE:

What is slang? Think of some examples of slang.

—words people use for effect

—cool, dude, bro

—different cultural groups have their own slang terms

1. What is a white lie? Give some examples of white lies.

2. What is social networking? Give some examples of social networking.

3. What are some characteristics of a workaholic?

Watch the Video
Paragraphs: The Topic Sentence
MyWritingLab

DEVELOPING

ESSAY LINK

In a definition essay, the thesis statement expresses the controlling idea. In the thesis, you can define the term by synonym, category, or negation.

The Topic Sentence

A clear topic sentence for a definition paragraph introduces the term and provides a definition. There are three basic ways to define a term.

- By synonym
- By category
- By negation

Definition by Synonym

The easiest way to define a term is to supply a synonym (a word that has a similar meaning). This type of definition is useful if the original term is difficult to understand and the synonym is a more familiar word.

term +	synonym
A pseudonym	is a false name.
I am a procrastinator,	which means I tend to put things off.

Definition by Category

A more effective way to define a term is to give a definition by category (or class). When you define by category, you determine the larger group to which the term belongs. Then you determine what unique characteristics set the term apart from others in that category.

term +	category +	detail
Netiquette is	proper behaviour	regarding communication on the Internet.
Luddites are	people	who are skeptical about new technology.

Definition by Negation

When you define by negation, you explain what a term *does not* mean. You can then include a sentence explaining what it does mean. Definition by negation is especially useful when your readers have preconceived ideas about something. Your definition explains that it is not what readers thought.

term +	what it is not +	what it is
Alcoholism	is not an invented disease;	it is a serious physical dependency.
Hackers	are not playful computer geeks;	they are criminals.

PRACTICE 2

A. Write a one-sentence definition by synonym for each of the following terms. Your definition should include the term and a synonym. If necessary, you can look up the terms in the dictionary; however, define each one using your own words.

EXAMPLE:

To capitulate *means to give up or surrender.*

1. To procrastinate ______________________________
2. A celebrity ______________________________

B. Write a one-sentence definition by category for the following terms. Make sure that your definition includes the term, a category, and details.

EXAMPLE:

A cockroach *is an insect that lives in the cracks and crevices of buildings.*

3. A knockoff ______________________________

____

4. Paparazzi ______________________________

____

C. Write a one-sentence definition by negation for the following terms. Explain what each term is not, followed by what each term is.

EXAMPLE:

A placebo *is not a real drug; it is a sugar pill.*

5. A television addict ______________________________

____

6. A vote ______________________________

____

Watch the **Video**
Using Exact Language
MyWritingLab

Use the Right Word

When you write a definition paragraph, it is important to use the precise words to define the term. Moreover, when you define a term by category, make sure that the category for your term is correct. For example, look at the following imprecise definitions of insomnia.

Insomnia is the inability to sleep well.
(Insomnia is not an ability or an inability.)

Insomnia is when you cannot sleep well.
(*When* refers to a time, but insomnia is not a time.)

Insomnia is the nights when you do not get enough sleep.
(Insomnia is not days or nights.)

Insomnia is where it is hard to fall asleep.
(*Where* refers to a place, but insomnia is not a place.)

Now look at a better definition of insomnia.

category
Insomnia is a **sleeping disorder** characterized by the inability to sleep well.

Make a Point

Definitions of terms by synonym, category, and negation provide the basis for topic sentences of definition paragraphs. Keep in mind that your paragraph will be more interesting if you express an attitude or a point of view in your topic sentence.

No point: Anorexia is an eating disorder.

Point: Anorexia is a tragic eating disorder that is difficult to cure.

PRACTICE 3

Revise each sentence using precise language.

EXAMPLE:

Tuning out is when you ignore something.

Tuning out is the action of ignoring something.

1. Claustrophobia is the inability to be in a small place.

____

____

2. A bully is the abuse of power over others.

____

____

3. Adolescence is where you are between childhood and adulthood.

____

____

4. Ego surfing is when you surf the Internet to find references to yourself.

____

____

The Writer's Desk Write Topic Sentences

Write a topic sentence in which you define each of the following topics. You can look for ideas in the previous Writer's Desk. Remember to use precise language in your definition.

EXAMPLE:

Topic: Slang

Topic sentence: *Slang is informal language that changes rapidly and exists in various forms among different cultural groups.*

1. Topic: A white lie

   Topic sentence: _______________

   ____

2. Topic: Social networking

   Topic sentence: _______________

   ____

3. Topic: A workaholic

   Topic sentence: _______________

   ____

Watch the **Video**
Revising the Paragraph: Organization
MyWritingLab

The Supporting Ideas

After you have developed an effective topic sentence, generate supporting ideas. In a definition paragraph, you can give examples that clarify your definition.

Think about how you will organize your examples. Most definition paragraphs use emphatic order, which means that examples are placed from the most to the least important or from the least to the most important.

Visualizing Definition

PRACTICE 4

Brainstorm supporting ideas for the following topic sentence. Using words or phrases, describe each example of timeless fashion.

Topic sentence: Timeless fashions remain popular and will not go out of style.

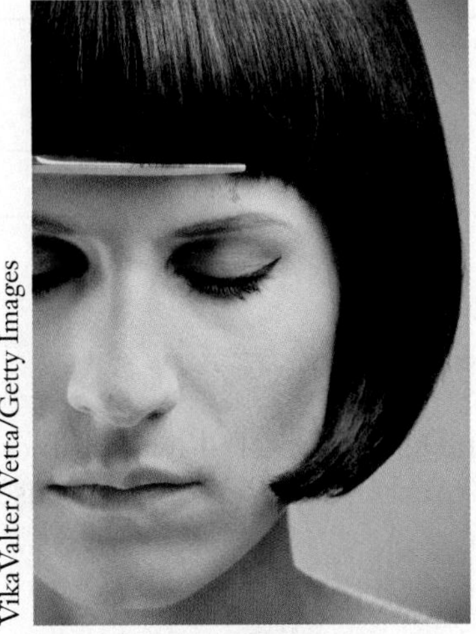

Vika Valter/Vetta/Getty Images

Iveta Angelova/Shutterstock

Szerdahelyi Adam/Fotolia

The Writer's Desk Develop Supporting Ideas

Choose one of your topic sentences from the previous Writer's Desk. List three or four examples that best illustrate the definition.

EXAMPLE:

Slang is informal language that changes rapidly and exists in various forms among different cultural groups.

—words change in different eras

—rappers, punks, goths have own terms

—used like a code between friends

—words show inventive creative thinking

Topic sentence: ______________________________

____

Supports: ______________________________

____

____

____

The Paragraph Plan

A good definition paragraph includes a complete definition of the term and provides adequate examples to support the central definition. When creating a definition paragraph plan, make sure that your examples provide varied evidence and do not just repeat the definition. Also, add details that will help clarify your supporting examples.

ESSAY LINK

In a definition essay, the thesis statement is in the introduction. Each supporting idea is in a distinct body paragraph with its own topic sentence.

TOPIC SENTENCE: Slang is informal language that changes rapidly and exists in various forms among different cultural groups.

Support 1: Slang is a type of code used between friends.

Details: —Punks might call each other emo or poseurs.

—People outside the group might not understand slang.

—Words often help define relationships among group members.

Support 2: Slang words often show very inventive and creative thinking.

Details: —Computer users have come up with a wide variety of net slang terms.

—Some terms are very illustrative and visual.

Support 3: Many slang words come and go quickly.

Details: —In the 1920s, people used words that have gone out of fashion.

—In the 1950s, people used words such as hipster or swell.

—Slang words from the early 2000s, such as homie, are already becoming obsolete.

Watch the Video
Paragraph: How to Write a Successful Paragraph
MyWritingLab

The Writer's Desk Write a Paragraph Plan

Create a detailed paragraph plan using one of the topic sentences that you wrote for the previous Writer's Desk. Arrange the supporting details in a logical order.

Topic sentence: ____________________

____

Support 1: ____________________

Details: ____________________

____

____

Support 2: ____________________

Details: ____________________

____

____

Support 3: ____________________

Details: ____________________

____

____

Watch the Video
Paragraphs: Drafting a Paragraph
MyWritingLab

The First Draft

After you outline your ideas in a plan, you are ready to write the first draft. Remember to write complete sentences. You might include transitional expressions to help your ideas flow smoothly.

Watch the Video
Revising the Paragraph: Development
MyWritingLab

Transitional Expressions

Transitional expressions can show different levels of importance. The following transitions are useful in definition paragraphs.

To Show the Level of Importance	
clearly	next
first	one quality . . . another quality
most important	second
most of all	undoubtedly

The Writer's Desk Write the First Draft

In the previous Writer's Desk, you developed a paragraph plan. Now write the first draft of your definition paragraph. Before you write, carefully review your paragraph plan, and make any necessary changes.

REVISING AND EDITING

Revise and Edit a Definition Paragraph

Watch the **Video** Revising and Editing Your Own Paragraphs **MyWritingLab**

When you finish writing a definition paragraph, carefully review your work and revise it to make the definition as clear as possible to your readers. Check that you have organized your steps logically, and remove any irrelevant details.

PRACTICE 5

Read the following student paragraph, and answer the questions.

Slang is informal language that changes rapidly and exists in various forms among different cultural groups. It is a type of code used between friends. Punks call each other *emo* or *poseurs*. Such words denote a persons status in the group. Often, those outside the group might not understand slang. My grandmother, for example, doesn't know what a homeboy is. Soldiers, athletes, music subcultures, and even wealthy industrialists come up with their own particular jargon. The rich might put down social climbers as *wannabes*. They might call a spouse a *trophy wife* or *husband*. Slang words often show very inventive and creative thinking. Computer users have come up with a wide variety of net slang terms such as *blog*, *flamer*, *troll*, *cyberspook*, or *flamebait*. Some terms are very illustrative. *Jerk* sounds like a fast movement. *Whipped* is similar to the sound a whip makes. Most slang words come and go quick, and they change over time. In the 1920s, men would call a women's legs "gams" and money "clams." In the 1950s, people used words such as *hipster*, *swell*, *hepcat*, or *squaresville*, and those word are outdated. Even slang words from the early 2000s, such as *homie* and *hoser*, are already becoming obsolete.

Revising

1. Underline the topic sentence.
2. What type of definition does the topic sentence contain? Circle the best answer.
   a. Definition by synonym
   b. Definition by category
   c. Definition by negation
3. This paragraph lacks sentence variety. Revise the paragraph to give it more sentence variety by combining sentences or changing the first word of some sentences. (For more information about combining sentences and sentence variety, see Chapters 17–19.)
4. The paragraph lacks transitions to show the order of ideas. Add some transitional expressions.
5. The paragraph needs a concluding sentence. Add a concluding sentence in the lines provided.

____

____

Watch the **Video**
Apostrophes
MyWritingLab

Watch the **Video**
Adjectives
MyWritingLab

GRAMMAR LINK

See the following chapters for more information about these grammar topics:
Apostrophes, Chapter 34
Adjectives and Adverbs, Chapter 29

Editing

6. There is one apostrophe error. Circle and correct the error.
7. There is an error in adverb form. Circle and correct the error.

Watch the **Video**
Adverbs
MyWritingLab

Watch the **Video**
Semicolons, Colons, Dashes and Parentheses
MyWritingLab

Grammar Hint **Using Semicolons**

When you write a definition by negation, you can join the two separate and independent sentences with a semicolon.

Independent clause ; independent clause

Feminists are not man-haters; they are people who want fairness and equality for women.

vo•cab•u•lar•y BOOST

Using Your Thesaurus

Work with a partner and brainstorm synonyms or expressions that can replace each word listed below. If you have trouble coming up with ideas, use your thesaurus.

1. optimist ______________________
2. depressed ______________________
3. lazy ______________________
4. reckless ______________________

When you finish coming up with synonyms, reread your definition paragraph. Circle three words that you have repeated several times. Using your thesaurus, find possible replacements for those words.

The Writer's Desk Revise and Edit Your Paragraph

Revise and edit the paragraph that you wrote for the previous Writer's Desk.

Ensure that your paragraph has unity, adequate support, and coherence. Also, correct any errors in grammar, spelling, punctuation, and mechanics.

Watch the **Video**
Paragraphs: Revising the Paragraph — A Checklist
MyWritingLab

REFLECT ON IT

Think about what you have learned in this chapter. If you do not know an answer, review that topic.

1. In definition writing, what do you do?

   ____

2. Write an example of a definition by synonym.

   ____

3. Write an example of a definition by category.

   ____

4. Write an example of a definition by negation.

   ____

Writing Activity 1: Topics

Choose any of the following topics, or choose your own topic. Then write a definition paragraph.

General Topics

1. A miracle
2. A spoiled child
3. Fashion police
4. Texting addict
5. Mind games

College- and Work-Related Topics

6. Integrity
7. A headhunter
8. An opportunist
9. The glass ceiling

WRITING LINK

More Definition Writing Topics

Chapter 19, Writer's Room topic 1 (page 312)
Chapter 24, Writer's Room topic 4 (page 369)
Chapter 35, Writer's Room topic 1 (page 512)

READING LINK

More Definition Readings

"Ten Beauty Tips You Never Asked For" by Elizabeth Hay (page 541)

Writing Activity 2: Photo Writing

Look at the photo, and think of a term that you can define. Examples are *throwaway society*, *planned obsolescence*, *tech trends*, *digital age*, and *tech trash*.

ifong/Shutterstock

Writing Activity 3: Media Writing

Watch a television show about people who fight to succeed. Examples are *The Office*, *The Apprentice*, *Parks and Recreation*, and *Survivor*. You could watch a documentary such as *The Corporation* or a movie such as *The Godfather*, *There Will Be Blood*, or *Fame*. You can also watch YouTube videos about people who want to become famous. Define the term *blind ambition*, and support your definition with examples or anecdotes from the media.

BLOWN DEADLINE PRODUCTIONS/ HOME BOX OFFICE / Album/Newscom

DEFINITION PARAGRAPH CHECKLIST

As you write your definition paragraph, review the checklist on the inside front cover. Also, ask yourself the following questions.

- ☐ Does my topic sentence contain a definition by synonym, negation, or category?
- ☐ Do all of my supporting sentences relate to the topic sentence?
- ☐ Do I use concise language in my definition?
- ☐ Do I include enough examples to help define the term?

How Do I Get a Better Grade?

Visit MyWritingLab for audiovisual lectures and additional practice sets about definition writing.

Classification

Jiri Hera/Fotolia

LEARNING OBJECTIVES

In a candy store, chocolates are classified according to the amount of cacao in the chocolate and the kind of fillings inside the chocolates. In classification writing, you divide a topic into categories to explain it.

Writers' Exchange

Work with a partner or a group. Divide the following words into three or four different categories. What are the categories? Why did you choose those categories?

mechanic	fertilizer	kitchen
garden	cook	programmer
microwave	landscaper	wrench
office	computer	garage

EXPLORING

Watch the Video
Paragraph Development—Division /Classification
MyWritingLab

What Is Classification?

When you classify, you sort a subject into more understandable categories. Each of the categories must be part of a larger group, yet it must also be distinct. For example, you might write a paragraph about the most common types of pets and sort the subject into cats, dogs, and birds.

Classification occurs in many situations. At home, you could classify the responsibilities of each person in the family, or you could classify your bills. In a biology course, you might write a paper about the different types of cells, or in a commerce course, you may write about the categories in a financial statement. On the job, you might advertise the different types of products or services that your company sells.

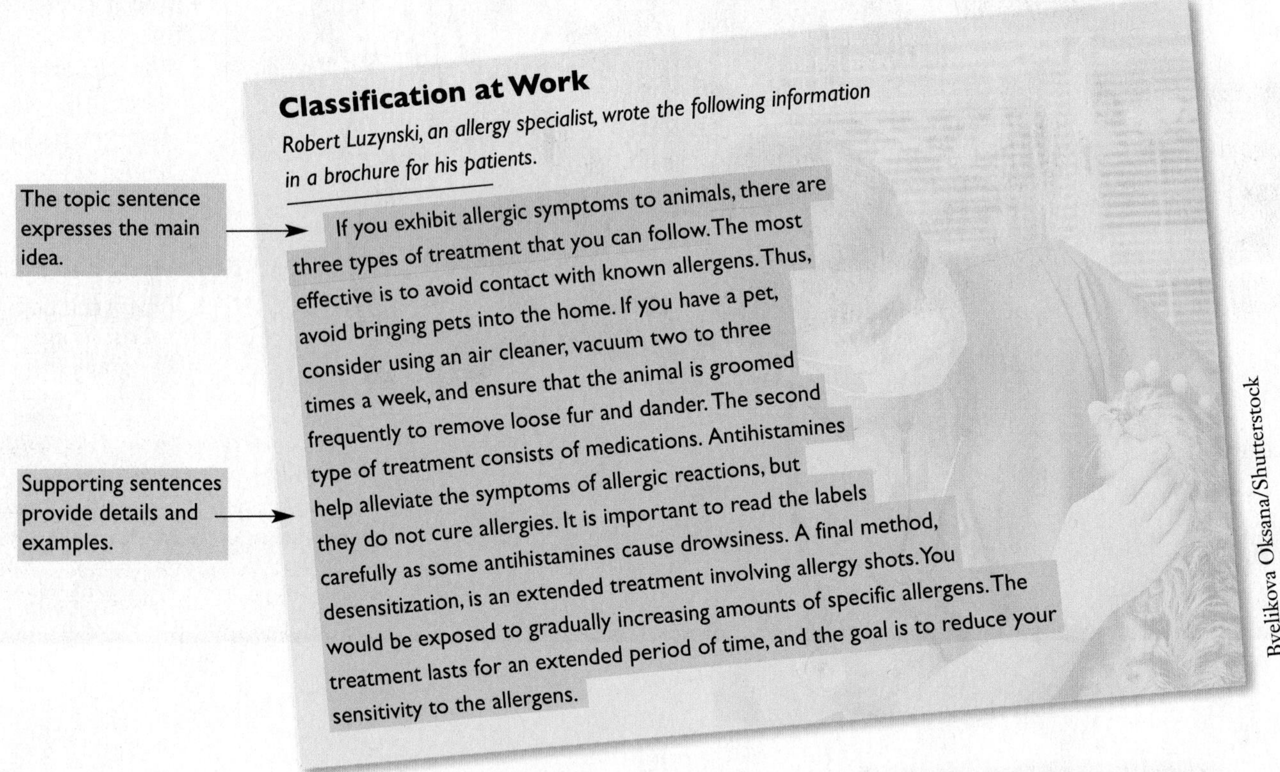

Classification at Work
Robert Luzynski, an allergy specialist, wrote the following information in a brochure for his patients.
The topic sentence expresses the main idea.
Supporting sentences provide details and examples.
If you exhibit allergic symptoms to animals, there are three types of treatment that you can follow. The most effective is to avoid contact with known allergens. Thus, avoid bringing pets into the home. If you have a pet, consider using an air cleaner, vacuum two to three times a week, and ensure that the animal is groomed frequently to remove loose fur and dander. The second type of treatment consists of medications. Antihistamines help alleviate the symptoms of allergic reactions, but they do not cure allergies. It is important to read the labels carefully as some antihistamines cause drowsiness. A final method, desensitization, is an extended treatment involving allergy shots. You would be exposed to gradually increasing amounts of specific allergens. The treatment lasts for an extended period of time, and the goal is to reduce your sensitivity to the allergens.
Byelikova Oksana/Shutterstock

ESSAY LINK

Classification essays also require a classification principle and distinct categories.

The Classification Paragraph

To find a topic for a classification paragraph, think of something that can be sorted into different groups. Also, determine a reason for classifying the items. When you are planning your ideas for a classification paragraph, remember these two points.

1. **Use a common classification principle.** A **classification principle** is the overall method that you use to sort the subject into categories. To find the classification principle, think about one common characteristic that unites the different categories. For example, if your subject is "the telephone," your classification principle might be any of the following:

   – types of annoying telephone calls

   – reasons that people buy cellphones

– types of long-distance services

– types of customer reactions to telephone salespeople

2. **Sort the subject into distinct categories.** A classification paragraph should have two or more categories.

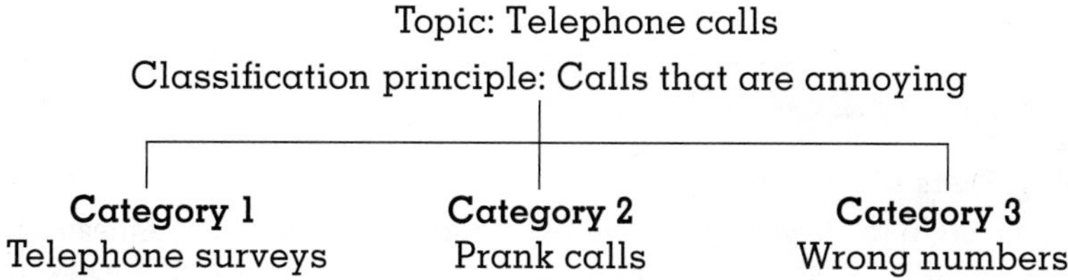

PRACTICE 1

Read the next paragraph and answer the questions.

There may be no way to rid the world of dishonesty, but researchers have learned a great deal about how to tell when someone is lying. Clues to deception are found in four elements of a performance: words, voice, body language, and facial expression. People who are good liars mentally rehearse their lines, but they cannot always avoid inconsistencies that suggest deception. A simple slip of the tongue—something the person did not mean to say in quite that way—can occur in even a carefully prepared performance. Secondly, voice is also useful to determine when a person is lying. Tone and patterns of speech contain clues to deception because they are hard to control. Especially when trying to hide a powerful emotion, a person cannot easily prevent the voice from trembling or breaking. Or an individual may speak more quickly, suggesting anger, or slowly, suggesting sadness. A "leak," conveyed through body language, may tip off an observer to deception. Body movements, sudden swallowing, or rapid breathing may show that a person is nervous. Because there are forty-three muscles in the face, facial expressions are even more difficult to control than body language. A real smile is usually accompanied by a relaxed expression and lot of "laugh lines" around the eyes; a phony smile seems forced and unnatural, with fewer wrinkles around the mouth and eyes. We all try to fake emotion, but the more powerful the emotion, the more difficult it is to deceive others.

—John J. Macionis, "Spotting Lies: What Are the Clues," *Sociology*

1. Underline the topic sentence of this paragraph.
2. State the four categories that the author discusses, and list some details about each category.

a. ______________________________

Details: ______________________________

b. ______________________________

Details: ______________________________

c. ______________________________

Details: ______________________________

d. ______________________________

Details: ______________________________

3. Who is the audience for this paragraph?

____

4. What is the purpose of this paragraph? Circle the best answer.

   a. To persuade   b. To inform   c. To entertain

vo•cab•u•lar•y BOOST

Classifying Parts of Words

A prefix is added to the beginning of a word, and it changes the word's meaning. A suffix is added to the end of a word, and it also changes the word's meaning. Review the list of ten common prefixes and suffixes. Then come up with at least two more words using the listed prefix or suffix.

Prefixes	**Example**	
anti = against	antiwar	________
un = not	unable	________
re = again	redo	________
bi = two	bilingual	________
mis = wrong	misspell	________

Suffixes	**Example**	
er = doer	teacher	________
ment = condition	agreement	________
ly = characteristic of	honestly	________
ous = full of	courageous	________
ful = filled with	respectful	________

Explore Topics

In Writer's Desk: Warm Up, you will try an exploring strategy to generate ideas about different topics.

The Writer's Desk Warm Up

Think about the following questions, and write down the first ideas that come to your mind. Try to think of two or three ideas for each topic.

EXAMPLE: What are some challenges college students face?

Organizational challenges—Might become involved in too many activities

____

Emotional challenges—Might become homesick

____

Financial challenges—Might need to work part-time

____

1. List some clothing that you own. You might think about old clothing, comfortable clothing, beautiful clothing, and so on.

____

____

____

2. What are some different types of consumers? To get ideas, you might think about some people you know and the way that they shop.

____

____

____

3. List some skills or abilities people need for different jobs. As you brainstorm ideas, consider manual labour as well as academic office jobs.

____

____

____

Making a Classification Chart

A **classification chart** is a visual representation of the main topic and its categories. Making a classification chart can help you identify the categories more clearly so that you will be able to write more exact topic sentences.

When you classify items, remember to use a single method of classification and a common classification principle to sort the items. For example, if you are classifying movies, you might classify them according to their ratings: General Audience, Parental Guidance, and Restricted. You could also classify movies according to their country of origin: British, Canadian, and French, for example. Remember that one classification principle must unite the group.

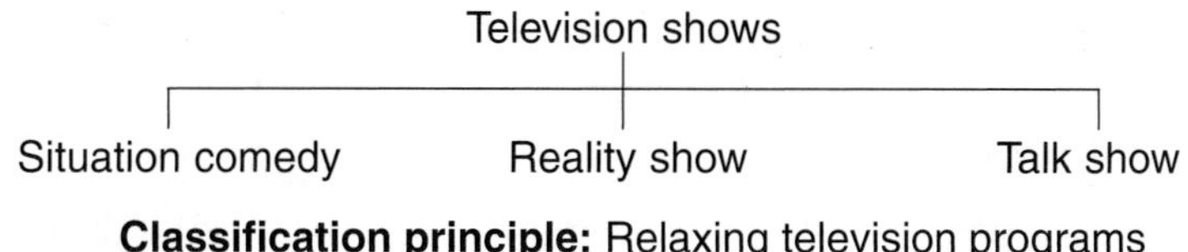

Classification principle: Relaxing television programs

Categories Should Not Overlap

When sorting a topic into categories, make sure that the categories do not overlap. For example, you would not classify drivers as careful drivers, aggressive drivers, or bad drivers because aggressive drivers could also be bad drivers. Each category should be distinct.

PRACTICE 2

In the following classification charts, a subject has been broken down into distinct categories. The items in the group should have the same classification principle. Cross out one item in each group that does not belong. Then write down the classification principle that unites the group.

EXAMPLE:

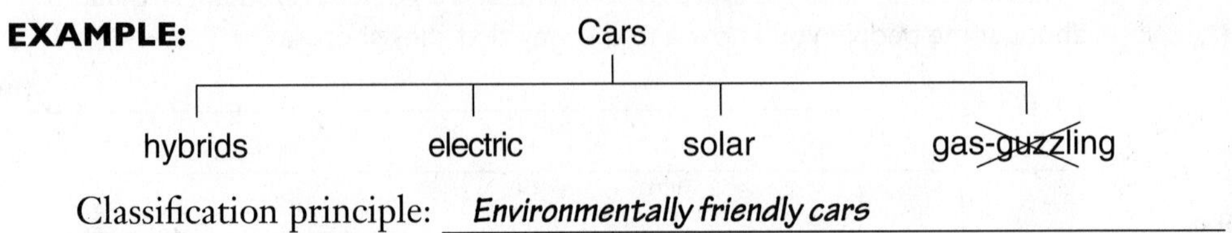

Classification principle: *Environmentally friendly cars*

1.

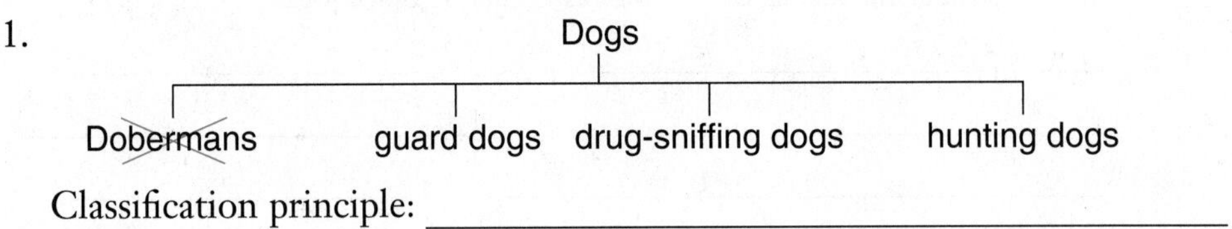

Classification principle: ______________________________

2.

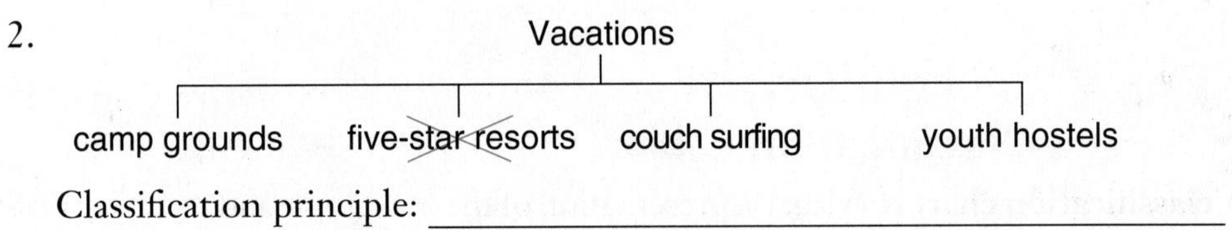

Classification principle: ______________________________

3.

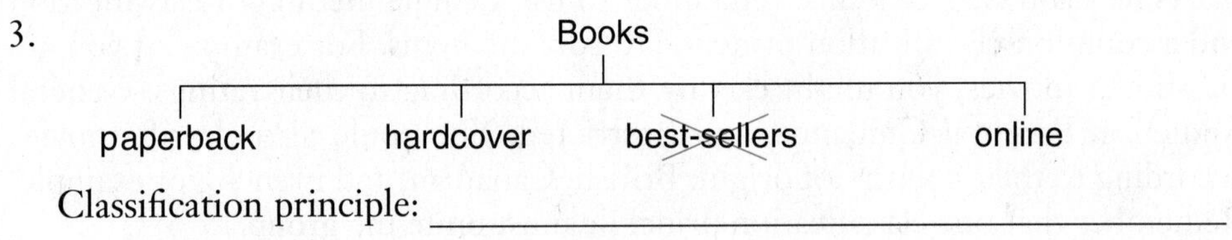

Classification principle: ______________________________

4.

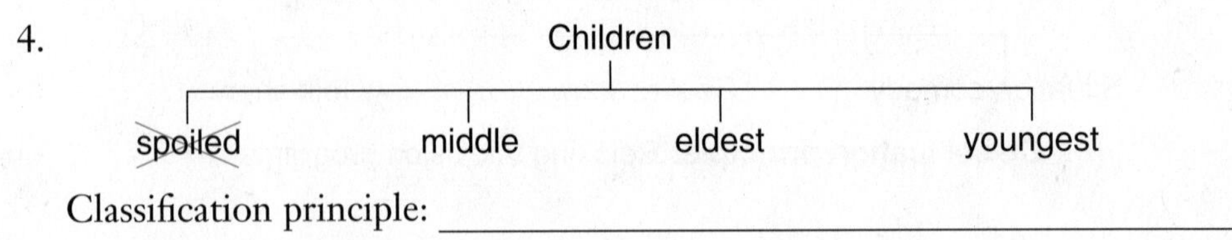

Classification principle: ______________________________

5.

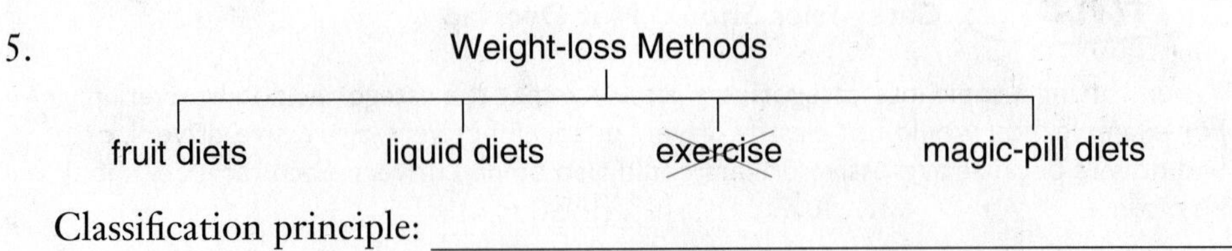

Classification principle: ______________________________

The Writer's Desk Find Distinct Categories

Break down the following topics into three distinct categories. Remember to find categories that do not overlap. You can look for ideas in the previous Writer's Desk.

EXAMPLE:

Challenges for College Students

Organizational Challenges | Emotional Challenges | Financial Challenges

Classification principle: College student challenges

1. Clothing

_______________ _______________ _______________

Classification principle: _______________

2. Consumers

_______________ _______________ _______________

Classification principle: _______________

3. Job skills

_______________ _______________ _______________

Classification principle: _______________

DEVELOPING

The Topic Sentence

The topic sentence in a classification paragraph clearly indicates what you will classify. It also includes the controlling idea, which is the classification principle that you will use.

Several types of students can completely disrupt a classroom.

Topic: Students
Classification principle: Disruptive types

You can also mention the types of categories in your topic sentence.

The most annoying telephone calls are surveys, prank calls, and wrong numbers.

Topic: Telephone calls
Classification principle: Types of annoying calls

ESSAY LINK

In a classification essay, the thesis statement expresses the controlling idea or classification principle.

Watch the **Video**
Paragraphs: The Topic Sentence
MyWritingLab

Make a Point

To make interesting classification paragraphs, try to express an attitude, opinion, or feeling about the topic. For example, you can write a paragraph about types of diets, but it is more interesting if you make a point about the types of diets.

Poor: Types of diets

Better: Types of **dangerous** diets
Types of **effective** diets

Watch the **Video**
Parallelism
MyWritingLab

Use parallel structure when words or phrases are joined in a series.

drug allergies

The three categories of allergies are animal allergies, food allergies, and people who are allergic to medicine.

See Chapter 21 for more information about parallel structure.

The Writer's Desk Write Topic Sentences

Look again at what you wrote in the Writer's Desk on pages 126–127. Also, look at the classification charts that you made for each topic in the previous Writer's Desk. Now write clear topic sentences. Remember that your topic sentence can include the different categories you will be discussing.

EXAMPLE:

Topic: Challenges for college students

Topic sentence: *Some of the most serious problems that college students face are organizational challenges, emotional challenges, and financial challenges.*

1. Topic: Clothing

   Topic sentence: ______________________________

   ____

2. Topic: Consumers

   Topic sentence: ______________________________

   ____

3. Topic: Job skills

   Topic sentence: ______________________________

   ____

The Supporting Ideas

After you have developed an effective topic sentence, generate supporting ideas. In a classification paragraph, you can list details about each of your categories.

Watch the Video
Revising the Paragraph: Organization
MyWritingLab

ESSAY LINK

You can make a detailed classification chart when you develop your classification essay. Each supporting idea would become a distinct paragraph.

Visualizing Classification

PRACTICE 3

Brainstorm supporting ideas for the following topic sentence. List unhealthy ingredients in each type of food.

Topic sentence: Junk food can be classified into three main categories.

ErickN/Shutterstock

Nico Traut/Shutterstock

Barbro Bergfeldt/Shutterstock

Salty ________________ Sweet ________________ Fatty ________________

________________ ________________ ________________

The Paragraph Plan

You can make a standard paragraph plan. You can also create a pie chart to help you visualize the different categories.

Watch the Video
Paragraph: How to Write a Successful Paragraph
MyWritingLab

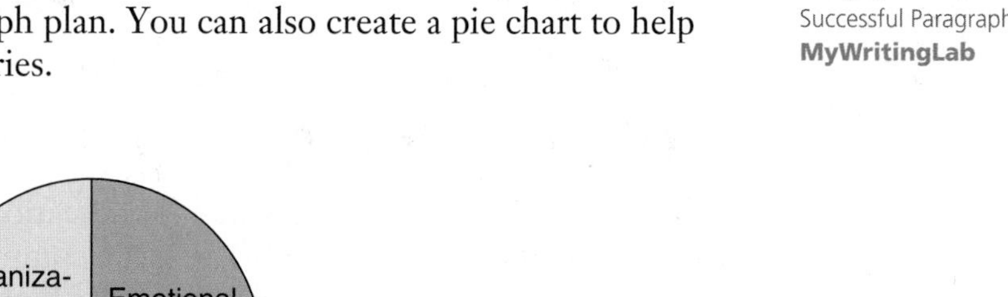

Finally, an effective way to visualize your categories and supporting ideas is to make a detailed classification chart. Break down the main topic into several categories, and then give details about each category.

The Writer's Desk Make a Detailed Classification Chart

Choose one of the topic sentences that you wrote for the previous Writer's Desk, and make a detailed classification chart. Arrange the supporting details in a logical order. You can refer to the information you generated in the Writer's Desk on pages 126–127.

Topic sentence: ____

____

Use the Chart as a Plan

Your classification chart can also serve as your paragraph plan. Like a paragraph plan, your chart contains your topic sentence, your categories, and details about each category.

Watch the **Video**
Paragraphs: Drafting a Paragraph
MyWritingLab

The First Draft

After you outline your ideas in a classification chart or plan, you are ready to write the first draft. Remember to write complete sentences. You might include transitional expressions to help your ideas flow smoothly.

Watch the **Video**
Revising the Paragraph: Development
MyWritingLab

Transitional Expressions

Some classification paragraphs use transitional expressions to show which category is most important and to signal a movement from one category to the next. The following transitions are very useful in classification writing.

To Show Importance	To Show Types of Categories
above all	one kind . . . another kind
clearly	the first/second kind
most of all	the first/second type
particularly	the last category
the most important	

The Writer's Desk Write the First Draft

Write the first draft of your classification paragraph. Before you write, carefully review your detailed classification chart, and make any necessary changes.

REVISING AND EDITING

Revise and Edit a Classification Paragraph

Watch the **Video**
Revising and Editing Your Own Paragraphs
MyWritingLab

When you finish writing a classification paragraph, carefully review your work and revise it to make sure that the categories do not overlap. Check to make sure that you have organized your paragraph logically, and remove any irrelevant details.

PRACTICE 4

Read the following student paragraph, and answer the questions.

> College students often confront many different types of difficulties. But some of the most serious problems that college students face are organizational challenges, emotional challenges, and financial challenges. Many students have difficulty keeping to a strict schedule. Thus, they have difficulty organizing their time. They have to juggle attending classes, working part-time, doing homework, and they socialize. Furthermore, emotional challenges. Some students may feel lonely if they are away from home. They may not like their roommate or their dorm room. Also, students can have financial problems. They may have to work part-time to pay for their education. When students get a scholarship, they may feel extra pressure to keep up their grades.
>
> —Daniel Mirto, college student

Revising

1. What is the classification principle in this paragraph? ______________________

   ____

2. What are the three categories? ______________________________

   ____

3. Add one more supporting example to the following categories:

   Organizational challenges: __________________________

   ____

   Emotional challenges: ______________________________

   ____

   Financial challenges: ______________________________

   ____

GRAMMAR LINK

See the following chapters for more information about these grammar topics:
Fragments, Chapter 20
Pronouns, Chapter 28

Watch the **Video**
Fragments
MyWritingLab

Watch the **Video**
Pronouns
MyWritingLab

Watch the **Video**
Paragraphs: Revising the Paragraph—A Checklist
MyWritingLab

The Writer's Desk Revise and Edit Your Paragraph

Revise and edit the paragraph that you wrote for the previous Writer's Desk. Ensure that your paragraph has unity, adequate support, and coherence. Also, correct any errors in grammar, spelling, punctuation, and mechanics.

REFLECT ON IT

Think about what you have learned in this chapter. If you do not know an answer, review that topic.

1. What is classification? ______________________________

____

2. What is the classification principle? ______________________________

____

3. Give examples of various classification principles that you can use to classify the following items.

EXAMPLE: Cars *Types of owners, degrees of fuel efficiency, price*

a. Animals ______________________________

b. Sports ______________________________

4. Now choose one classification principle for each item in question. Write down three possible categories for that item.

EXAMPLE: Cars

Classification principle: *Types of owners*

Categories: *SUV owners, sports car owners, and tiny eco car owners*

a. Animals

Classification principle: ______________________________

Categories: ______________________________

b. Sports

Classification principle: ______________________________

Categories: ______________________________

5. Why is it useful to make a classification chart? ______________________________

____

The Writer's Room

Writing Activity 1: Topics

Choose any of the following topics, or choose your own topic. Then write a classification paragraph.

General Topics

Types of . . .

1. Problems in a relationship
2. Friends
3. Tech users
4. Games
5. Greetings

College- and Work-Related Topics

Types of . . .

6. Campus fashions
7. Housing
8. Bosses
9. Cheating
10. Co-workers

WRITING LINK

More Classification Writing Topics

Chapter 21, Writer's Room topic 3 (page 333)
Chapter 24, Writer's Room topic 2 (page 369)

Writing Activity 2: Photo Writing

Examine this photo and think about some classification topics. For example, you might discuss types of risky behaviour or dangerous jobs. Then write a classification paragraph based on the photo or your related topic.

READING LINK

Classification Reading

"Advertising Appeals" by Michael R. Solomon (page 578)

Taina Sohlman/Fotolia

Writing Activity 3: Media Writing

Watch a television show or movie about spies. Television shows are *MI5*, *24*, *Chuck*, and *The Unit*, and movies are *Mission Impossible*, *The Good Shepherd*, *Syriana*, and *Duplicity*. You could also watch James Bond or Bourne films. Watch *W-5* for episodes on Canadian spies. Classify spies into types or describe different types of spying, and use examples to support your ideas.

CLASSIFICATION PARAGRAPH CHECKLIST

As you write your classification paragraph, review the checklist on the inside front cover. Also, ask yourself the following questions.

- ☐ Does my topic sentence explain the categories that will be discussed?
- ☐ Do I use a common classification principle to unite the various items?
- ☐ Do I offer sufficient details to explain each category?
- ☐ Do I arrange the categories in a logical manner?
- ☐ Does all of the supporting information relate to the categories that are being discussed?
- ☐ Do I include categories that do not overlap?

How Do I Get a Better Grade?

Visit MyWritingLab for audiovisual lectures and additional practice sets about classification writing.

Comparison and Contrast

Pavel Losevsky/Fotolia

LEARNING OBJECTIVES

In this chapter, you will practise comparing and contrasting.

Writers' Exchange

Work with a partner. Each of you should discuss your food preferences. Then make a short list showing which food preferences you share and which ones you do not share.

Watch the Video
Paragraph Development—Comparing and Contrasting
MyWritingLab

EXPLORING

What Is Comparison and Contrast?

When you want to decide between options, you compare and contrast. You **compare** to find similarities and **contrast** to find differences. The exercise of comparing and contrasting can help you make judgments about things. It can also help you better understand familiar things.

You often compare and contrast. At home, when you watch television, you might compare and contrast different programs. At college, you might compare and contrast different psychological or political theories. On the job, you might need to compare and contrast computer operating systems, shipping services, or sales figures.

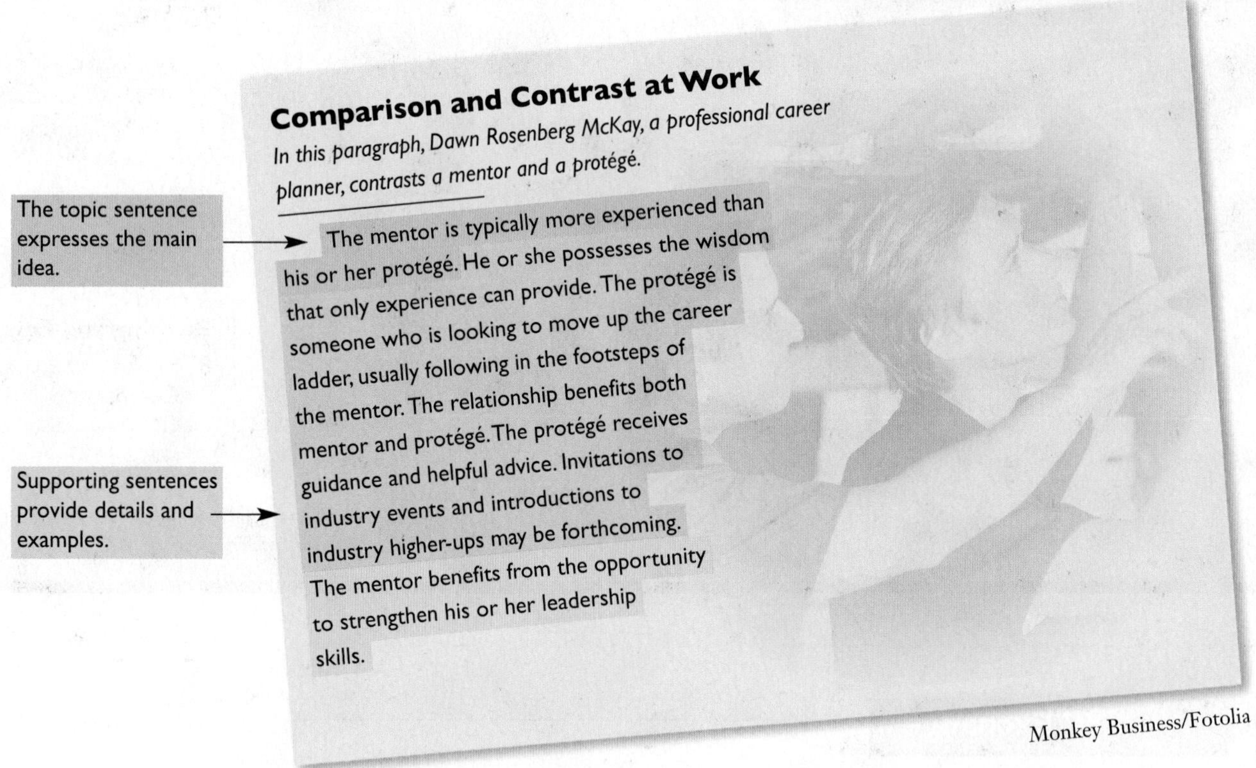

Comparison and Contrast at Work

In this paragraph, Dawn Rosenberg McKay, a professional career planner, contrasts a mentor and a protégé.

The topic sentence expresses the main idea. → The mentor is typically more experienced than his or her protégé. He or she possesses the wisdom that only experience can provide. The protégé is someone who is looking to move up the career ladder, usually following in the footsteps of the mentor. The relationship benefits both mentor and protégé. The protégé receives guidance and helpful advice. Invitations to industry events and introductions to industry higher-ups may be forthcoming. The mentor benefits from the opportunity to strengthen his or her leadership skills.

Supporting sentences provide details and examples. →

Monkey Business/Fotolia

The Comparison and Contrast Paragraph

In a comparison and contrast paragraph, you can compare and contrast two different subjects, or you can compare and contrast different aspects of a single subject. For example, you might contrast married life and single life, or you might write only about marriage but contrast the expectations people have before they get married versus what realistically happens after marriage.

When you write a comparison and contrast paragraph, remember to think about your specific purpose.

- **Your purpose could be to make judgments about two things.** For example, you might compare and contrast two restaurants in order to convince your readers that one is preferable.
- **Your purpose could be to describe or understand two familiar things.** For example, you might compare two stories to help your readers understand their thematic similarities.

Comparison and Contrast Patterns

Comparison and contrast texts follow two common patterns. One pattern is to present the details point by point. Another is to present one topic and then the other topic. When you are thinking about ideas for writing a comparison and contrast paragraph, you can choose one of these two methods to organize your supporting ideas.

Point by Point

Present one point about topic A and then one point about topic B. Keep following this pattern until you have a few points for each topic. You go back and forth from one side to the other like tennis players hitting a ball back and forth across a net.

ESSAY LINK

To write a comparison and contrast essay, organize *each paragraph* in point-by-point or topic-by-topic form.

Topic by Topic

Present all points related to topic A in the first few sentences, and then present all points related to topic B in the last few sentences. You present one side and then the other side, just as lawyers might in the closing arguments of a court case.

Kyle's Example

Kyle is trying to decide whether he should take a job in another city or stay at his current job in his hometown. His goal is to decide whether he should move or stay where he is. Kyle could organize his information using a point-by-point or topic-by-topic method.

Point by Point		Topic by Topic	
Job A	Low salary	Job A	Low salary
Job B	Good salary		Parents nearby
Job A	Parents nearby		Like my colleagues
Job B	Parents far away		
Job A	Like my colleagues	Job B	Good salary
Job B	Don't know colleagues		Parents far away
			Don't know colleagues

PRACTICE 1

Read the next two paragraphs, and answer the questions.

A. As with the work itself, there's always a chasm between my ideal work habits and the reality. Dream: I get up at dawn, write clear and glorious prose undisturbed for five hours and, done by noon, head out for a long walk. Reality: I stumble out of bed around eight, have breakfast, read the paper, read a second paper, make coffee, get to my desk around ten, check e-mail, check more e-mail. I take breaks. I fight with truckers across the street. Stubbornly, I keep working. Days pass. Years pass. Somehow, miraculously, novels get written.

—Catherine Bush, *First Chapter: The Canadian Writers Photography Project* (ed. Don Denton)

1. Underline the topic sentence.
2. What aspects of writing does the author compare? ____________________

____

3. What pattern of comparison does the author follow? Circle the correct answer.

   a. Point by point b. Topic by topic

4. What does this paragraph focus on? Circle the correct answer.

   a. Similarities b. Differences

B. My frontyard in downtown Toronto is covered with dirty white stones. Beneath them lies a layer of black landscaping fabric, and beneath that, soil. So you see, though it is April, nothing will grow here other than the lone maple tree that shoots up from the centre of the yard. Because of the maple, and my swoony melancholy nature, fall is my favourite season. The leaves in their varying shades drop into the yard and cover the dirty white stones, but in spring, every ugly pebble is visible. My frontyard is approximately 10 feet by 15 feet. I have never measured it in the conventional way, but I can imagine two of me lying along the front of the yard and three of me along the side, so I know. A little red fence runs around the edges, perhaps to contain the stones. I don't mind the yard's size, but I do mind its stones, so uniform, so numerous they might be chips of Styrofoam. Which would be better, come to think of it, because wind alone could erase them, at least from my yard. If this were my home, not a rented one, the stones would be the first to go. The smothering black fabric would be lifted, and the soil would be tilled. Ferns would unfurl in the shade, and every possible herb would stretch out to the sun. A tiny postage stamp of green. Such a garden would have made my Opa smile.

—Kristen den Hartog, "Sugar Beets & Roses," *Notes from Home: 20 Canadian Writers Share Their Thoughts of Home*

5. Underline the topic sentence.
6. What does this paragraph compare? ____________________________

____

7. What pattern of comparison does the author follow? Circle the correct answer.

   a. Point by point b. Topic by topic

8. What does the author focus on? Circle the correct answer.

   a. Similarities b. Differences

vo•cab•u•lar•y BOOST

Brainstorming Opposites

Work with a partner and brainstorm words that have the opposite meaning to the words listed below. Try to come up with as many antonyms (words that have the opposite meaning) as possible.

Example: tiny *huge, immense, gigantic*

shy __________

ugly __________

happy __________

run __________

spicy __________

Explore Topics

In Writer's Desk: Warm Up, you will try an exploring strategy to generate ideas about different topics.

Watch the **Video**
Prewriting: Questioning
MyWritingLab

The Writer's Desk Warm up

Think about the following questions, and write down the first ideas that come to your mind. Try to think of two or three ideas for each topic. Then decide if a good paragraph would be about similarities or differences.

EXAMPLE:

What are some key features of two cultural traditions?

My mother's tradition: Diwali	My father's tradition: Hanukkah
festival of lights	*festival of lights*
share gifts with siblings	*light the Menorah*
great desserts	*gold-wrapped chocolates*

My paragraph will focus on __*X*__ similarities ______ differences.

1. What are some stereotypes about your nationality? What is the reality about your nationality?

Stereotypes	Reality
__________	__________
__________	__________
__________	__________

This paragraph will focus on ______ similarities ______ differences.

2. What were your goals when you were a child? What are your goals today?

Goals in childhood	**Goals today**
____________________	____________________
____________________	____________________
____________________	____________________

This paragraph will focus on ______ similarities ______ differences.

3. Write down the names of two famous or prominent actors, politicians, or music stars. Choose one who is accomplished and respected, and choose another who is less respected. List some interesting characteristics of each person.

Person 1: ____________________	**Person 2:** ____________________
____________________	____________________
____________________	____________________
____________________	____________________

This paragraph will focus on ______ similarities ______ differences.

When you plan your comparison and contrast paragraph, decide whether you want to focus on comparing (looking at similarities), contrasting (looking at differences), or both. In a paragraph, it is usually best to focus on either comparing or contrasting. In a larger essay, you could more easily do both.

ESSAY LINK

In a comparison and contrast essay, the thesis statement expresses the main point of the essay.

Watch the **Video**
Paragraphs: The Topic Sentence
MyWritingLab

DEVELOPING

The Topic Sentence

In a comparison and contrast paragraph, the topic sentence indicates what is being compared and contrasted and expresses a controlling idea.

Although all dogs make good house pets, large dogs are much more useful than small dogs.

Topic: Large dogs versus small dogs

Controlling idea: One is more useful than the other.

PRACTICE 2

Read each topic sentence and then answer the questions that follow. State whether the paragraph would focus on similarities or differences.

EXAMPLE:

Before the baby comes people expect a beautiful world of soft coos and sweet smells, but the reality is quite different.

a. What is being compared? *Expectation versus reality of life with a baby*

b. What is the controlling idea? *Reality not as pleasant as expectation*

c. What will the paragraph focus on? Circle the correct answer.

Similarities Differences

1. Many media pundits complain about reality television; however, reality shows are just as good as regular scripted shows.
   a. What is being compared? ______________________________
   b. What is the controlling idea? ______________________________
   ____
   c. What will the paragraph focus on? Circle the correct answer.

   Similarities Differences

2. Women's sports lag behind men's in media attention, prize money, and salaries.
   a. What is being compared? ______________________________
   b. What is the controlling idea? ______________________________
   ____
   c. What does the paragraph focus on? Circle the correct answer.

   Similarities Differences

3. Teenagers are as difficult to raise as toddlers.
   a. What is being compared? ______________________________
   b. What is the controlling idea? ______________________________
   ____
   c. What will the paragraph focus on? Circle the correct answer.

   Similarities Differences

Comparing with Adjectives and Adverbs

When comparing or contrasting two items, ensure that you have correctly written the comparative forms of adjectives and adverbs. For instance, never put *more* with an adjective ending in *-er*.

Living alone is ~~more~~ quieter than living with a roommate.

If you are comparing two actions, remember to use an adverb instead of an adjective.

My roommate cleans ~~quicker~~ *more quickly* than I do.

See Chapter 29 for more information about making comparisons with adjectives and adverbs.

Watch the **Video**
Adjectives
MyWritingLab

Watch the **Video**
Adverbs
MyWritingLab

The Writer's Desk Write Topic Sentences

For each topic, write whether you will focus on similarities or differences. Then write a topic sentence for each one. You can look for ideas in the previous Writer's Desk. Your topic sentence should include what you are comparing and contrasting as well as a controlling idea.

EXAMPLE:

Topic: Two cultural traditions

Focus: *Similarities*

Topic sentence: *Diwali and Hanukkah have some surprising similarities.*

1. Topic: Stereotypes and reality about my nationality

   Focus: ______________________________

   Topic sentence: ______________________________

   ____

2. Topic: Goals in childhood and goals in adulthood

   Focus: ______________________________

   Topic sentence: ______________________________

   ____

3. Topic: Two famous people

   Focus: ______________________________

   Topic sentence: ______________________________

   ____

Watch the **Video**
Revising the Paragraph: Organization
MyWritingLab

ESSAY LINK

In a comparison and contrast essay, place the thesis statement in the introduction. Each supporting idea becomes a distinct paragraph with its own topic sentence.

The Supporting Ideas

After you have developed an effective topic sentence, generate supporting ideas. In a comparison and contrast paragraph, think of examples that help clarify the similarities or differences. To generate supporting ideas, you might try using a Venn diagram. In this example, you can see how the writer draws two circles to contrast Diwali and Hanukkah. Where the circles overlap, the writer includes similarities. If you are focusing only on similarities or differences, then you can make two separate circles.

Visualizing Comparison and Contrast

PRACTICE 3

Brainstorm supporting ideas for the following topic sentence. Compare and contrast the types of heroes.

Topic sentence: My childhood heroes were very different from my current heroes.

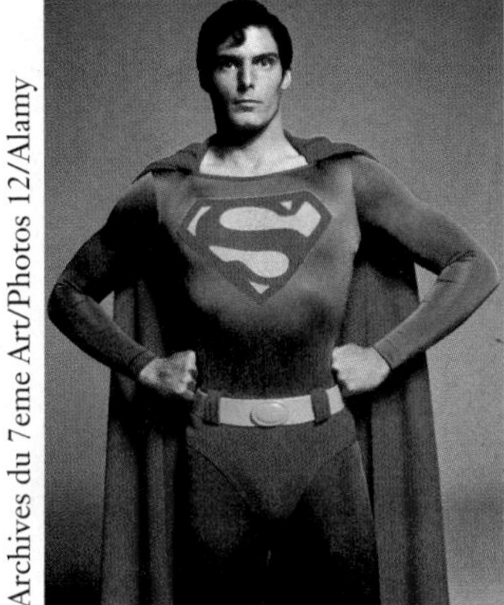

Archives du 7eme Art/Photos 12/Alamy

alens/Shutterstock

Childhood heroes

Rob/Fotolia

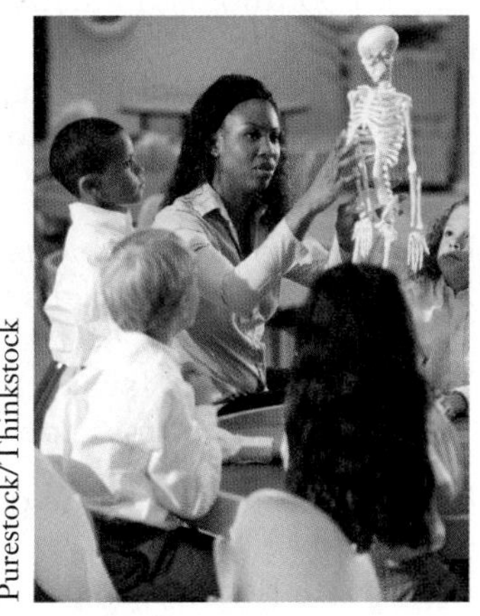

Purestock/Thinkstock

Current heroes

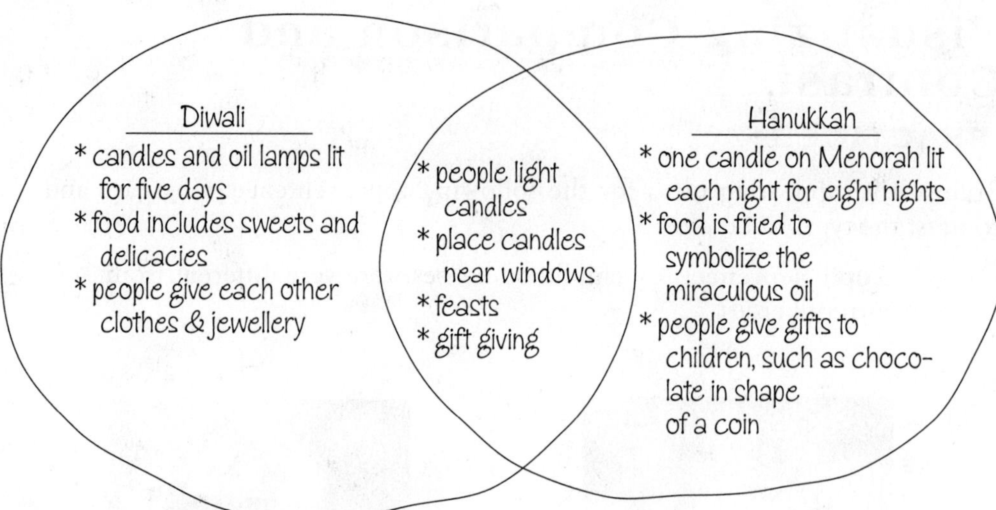

Diwali
* candles and oil lamps lit for five days
* food includes sweets and delicacies
* people give each other clothes & jewellery
* people light candles
* place candles near windows
* feasts
* gift giving
Hanukkah
* one candle on Menorah lit each night for eight nights
* food is fried to symbolize the miraculous oil
* people give gifts to children, such as chocolate in shape of a coin

Watch the **Video**
Paragraph: How to Write a Successful Paragraph
MyWritingLab

The Paragraph Plan

Before you write a comparison and contrast paragraph, it is a good idea to make a paragraph plan. Decide which pattern you will follow: point by point or topic by topic. You can write "**A**" and "**B**" alongside your topics to indicate which side they support. Then add supporting details. Make sure that each detail supports the topic sentence.

TOPIC SENTENCE: Diwali and Hanukkah have some surprising similarities.

POINT BY POINT

A/B Both celebrations are festivals of light.
Details: -People light candles.
-They place candles near windows.

A/B Both have traditions of feasts.
Details: -People eat fried sweets for Diwali.
-Everyone loves fried food for Hanukkah.

A/B Both celebrations include gift giving.
Details: -In Hanukkah, people give gifts of money to children.
-In Diwali, people give clothing and jewellery to each other.

TOPIC BY TOPIC

A Diwali is a festival of light.
Details: -Candles and oil lamps are lit for five days.

A Diwali includes feasts.
Details: -Food includes sweets and delicacies.

A During one day of the Diwali festival, people give gifts to each other.
Details: -Clothes and jewellery are given.
-Children get the most gifts.

B Hanukkah is a festival of light.
Details: -Menorah has eight candles.
-People light one candle each night.

B People have feasts during Hanukkah.
Details: -Food is fried to symbolize the miraculous oil.

B People give gifts to children during Hanukkah.
Details: -Gifts usually resemble money such as chocolate in the shape of a coin.

The Writer's Desk Write a Paragraph Plan

Write a detailed paragraph plan in a point-by-point or side-by-side pattern. You can refer to the information you generated in previous Writer's Desk exercises. You can use the letters **A** and **B** to indicate which side you are discussing in your plan. Include details about each supporting idea.

Topic sentence: ______________________________

____

Support 1: ______________________________

Details: ______________________________

____

Support 2: ______________________________

Details: ______________________________

____

Support 3: ______________________________

Details: ______________________________

____

Support 4: ______________________________

Details: ______________________________

____

Support 5: ______________________________

Details: ______________________________

____

Support 6: ______________________________

Details: ______________________________

____

The First Draft

After you outline your ideas in a plan, you are ready to write the first draft. Remember to write complete sentences. You might include transitional expressions to help your ideas flow smoothly.

Watch the **Video**
Paragraphs: Drafting a Paragraph
MyWritingLab

Transitional Expressions

In comparison and contrast paragraphs, there are some transitional expressions that you might use to explain either similarities or differences.

Watch the **Video**
Revising the Paragraph: Development
MyWritingLab

To Show Similarities		To Show Differences	
additionally	in addition	conversely	nevertheless
at the same time	in the same way	however	on the contrary
equally	similarly	in contrast	then again

The Writer's Desk Write the First Draft

Write the first draft of your comparison and contrast paragraph. Before you write, carefully review your paragraph plan to see if you have enough support for your points and topics.

REVISING AND EDITING

Watch the **Video**
Revising and Editing Your Own Paragraph
MyWritingLab

Revise and Edit a Comparison and Contrast Paragraph

When you finish writing a comparison and contrast paragraph, carefully review your work and revise it to make the comparison or contrast as clear as possible to your readers. Check that you have organized your paragraph logically, and remove any irrelevant details.

PRACTICE 4

Read the following student paragraph, and answer the questions.

The Hindu and Jewish faiths have distinct religious celebrations. However, Diwali and Hanukkah have surprising similarities. For Hindus, Diwali is known as the festival of light, and it symbolizes the victory of good over evil. For five nights, celebrators are lighting as many small oil lamps as possible to symbolize hope and the victory of good over evil. Similarly, Hanukkah is a festival of lights, and people light a Menorah containing eight candles or oil lamps, one per night for eight nights. In Hanukkah, the candles celebrate the miracle of an oil lamp found in the Temple, which burned for eight days and nights even though it only had a day's worth of oil in it. Furthermore, both Hindu and Jewish faithful place the lights near windows so that people passing by can see them. Another similarity: feasts. People celebrating Diwali and Hanukkah have special meals. The Diwali feast includes fried sweets and other desserts. In the same way, during Hanukkah, people eat food fried in oil, such as potato pancakes and donuts. Finally, both Hanukkah and Diwali involve gift giving, with children as the major beneficiaries of the largesse. Hanukkah celebrants give gifts of money or coin-shaped chocolate. During Diwali, children receive gifts of clothing or jewellery, and siblings give gifts to each other. Thus, people of the Jewish and Hindu faiths celebrate some festivals in a similar way.

Revising

1. What is the writer comparing? ______________________________
2. What does the writer focus on?
   a. Similarities b. Differences
3. Number the three main points.
4. Underline six transitional words or expressions that appear at the beginnings of sentences.

Editing

5. This paragraph contains one fragment, or incomplete sentence. Identify and correct the fragment.
6. Identify and correct one verb-tense error.
7. Find and correct one error with an adjective or adverb.

GRAMMAR LINK

See the following chapters for more information about these grammer topics:
Fragments, Chapter 20
Verb Tenses, Chapter 22

Watch the **Video**
Fragments
MyWritingLab

Watch the **Video**
Verb Tenses
MyWritingLab

Watch the **Video**
Paragraphs: Revising the Paragraph—A Checklist
MyWritingLab

The Writer's Desk Revise and Edit Your Paragraph

Revise and edit the paragraph that you wrote for the previous Writer's Desk. Ensure that your paragraph has unity, adequate support, and coherence. Also, correct any errors in grammar, spelling, punctuation, and mechanics.

REFLECT ON IT

Think about what you have learned in this chapter. If you do not know an answer, review that topic.

1. Define the words *comparing* and *contrasting.*
   a. Comparing: ______________________________
   b. Contrasting: ______________________________
2. Explain the following comparison and contrast patterns.
   a. Point by point: ______________________________
   ____
   b. Topic by topic: ______________________________
   ____

The Writer's Room

WRITING LINK

More Comparison and Contrast Writing Topics

Chapter 21, Writer's Room topic 2 (page 333)
Chapter 28, Writer's Room topic 3 (page 425)
Chapter 32, Writer's Room topic 1 (page 477)

READING LINK

More Comparison and Contrast Readings

"The Market and The Mall" by Stephen Henighan (page 528)
"This Boat Is My Boat" by Drew Hayden Taylor (page 573)
"Gone with the Windows" by Dorothy Nixon (page 576)

Writing Activity 1: Topics

Choose any of the following topics, or choose your own topic. Then write a comparison and contrast paragraph.

General Topics

Compare or contrast . . .

1. Two types of music
2. People from two different regions
3. Your current home and a home that you lived in before
4. Expectations about marriage and the reality of marriage
5. Two websites

College- and Work-Related Topics

Compare or contrast . . .

6. High school and college
7. Two career options
8. Working indoors and working outdoors
9. Leaving a child in daycare and leaving a child with a family member
10. Working mainly with your hands and working mainly with your head

Writing Activity 2: Photo Writing

Examine the following photos and brainstorm ideas about the similarities or differences between two places that you go to in order to relax. For example, you can compare a park with your bedroom, a campus coffee shop with a bookstore, or two public parks. After developing your ideas, write a comparison and contrast paragraph.

Sklep Spozywczy/Shutterstock.com

tioloco/ E+/Getty Images

Writing Activity 3: Media Writing

Compare another country to Canada. Watch a foreign film such as *Paradise Now* (Palestine), *Close to Home* (Israel), *Volver* (Spain), *The Queen* (Great Britain), *The Kite Runner* (Afghanistan), or *Slumdog Millionaire* (India). You can also watch YouTube videos about foreign places. You can compare the clothing, music, attitudes, and landscapes of the two places.

COMPARISON AND CONTRAST PARAGRAPH CHECKLIST

As you write your comparison and contrast paragraph, review the checklist on the inside front cover. Also, ask yourself the following questions.

- ☐ Does my topic sentence explain what I am comparing and/or contrasting?
- ☐ Does my topic sentence make a point about the comparison?
- ☐ Does my paragraph have a point-by-point or topic-by-topic pattern?
- ☐ Does my paragraph focus on either similarities or differences?
- ☐ Do all of my supporting examples clearly relate to the topics that I am comparing or contrasting?

How Do I Get a Better Grade?

Visit MyWritingLab for audiovisual lectures and additional practice sets about comparison and contrast writing.

Cause and Effect

LEARNING OBJECTIVES

Library of Congress Prints and Photographs Division [LC-DIG-highsm-13019]

Pollution is a major problem in our world. What causes dirty air, water, and soil? What are the results of a contaminated environment? Cause and effect writing helps to explain the answers to these types of questions.

Writers' Exchange

Your instructor will divide the class into two groups. You should work with a partner or a team of students. Your group will discuss one of the following topics.

What are some reasons that students go to college?

What effects does a college education have on a person's life?

EXPLORING

What Is Cause and Effect?

Watch the Video
Paragraph Development—Cause and Effect
MyWritingLab

Cause and effect writing explains why an event happened or what the consequences of such an event were. A cause and effect paragraph can focus on causes, effects, or both.

You often analyze the causes or effects of something. At home, you may worry about what causes your siblings or your own children to behave in a certain manner, or you may wonder about the effects of certain foods on your health. In a Canadian history course, you might analyze the causes of the Great Depression, or you might write about the effects of industrialization on Canadian society. At work, you may wonder about the causes or effects of a promotion or a pay cut.

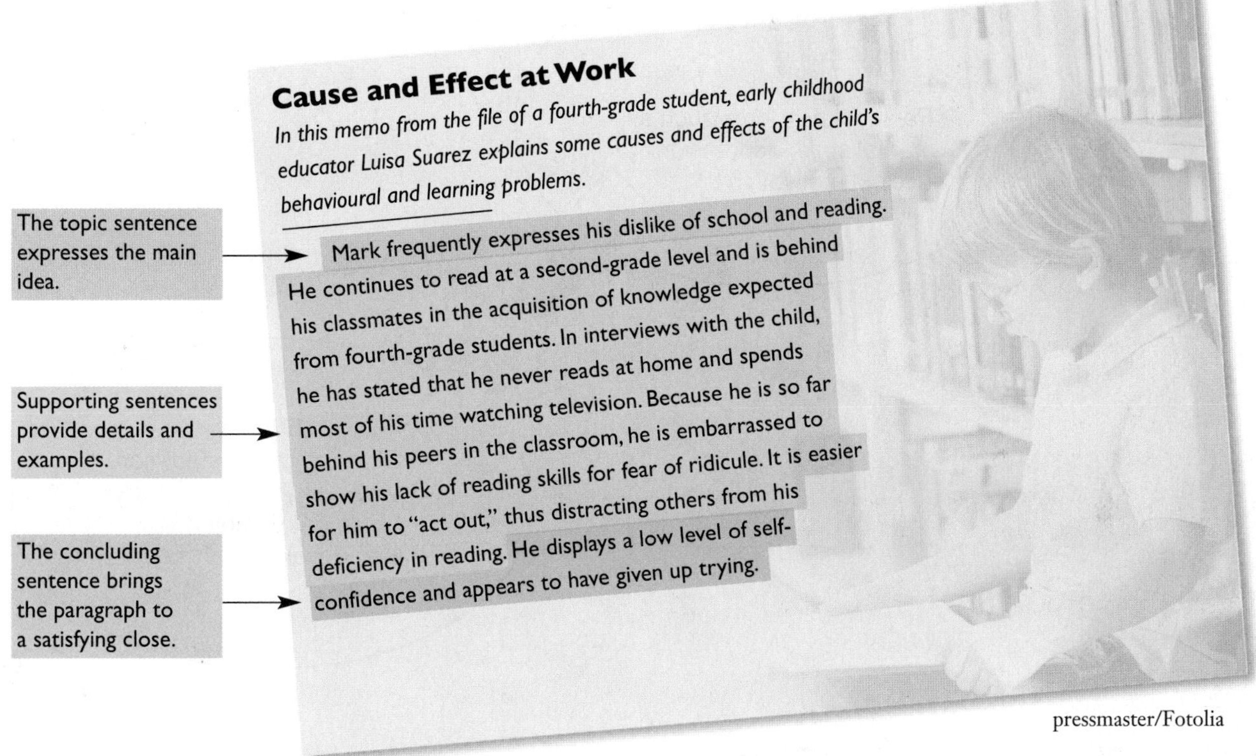
Cause and Effect at Work
In this memo from the file of a fourth-grade student, early childhood educator Luisa Suarez explains some causes and effects of the child's behavioural and learning problems.
The topic sentence expresses the main idea.
Mark frequently expresses his dislike of school and reading. He continues to read at a second-grade level and is behind his classmates in the acquisition of knowledge expected from fourth-grade students. In interviews with the child, he has stated that he never reads at home and spends most of his time watching television. Because he is so far behind his peers in the classroom, he is embarrassed to show his lack of reading skills for fear of ridicule. It is easier for him to "act out," thus distracting others from his deficiency in reading. He displays a low level of self-confidence and appears to have given up trying.
Supporting sentences provide details and examples.
The concluding sentence brings the paragraph to a satisfying close.

pressmaster/Fotolia

The Cause and Effect Paragraph

When you write a cause and effect paragraph, focus on two main points.

1. **Indicate whether you are focusing on causes, effects, or both.** Because a paragraph is not very long, it is often easier to focus on either causes or effects. If you do decide to focus on both causes and effects, make sure that your topic sentence announces your purpose to the reader.
2. **Ensure that your causes and effects are valid.** Determine real causes and effects, and do not simply list things that happened before or after the event. Also, verify that your assumptions are logical.

Illogical: The product does not work because it is inexpensive.
(This statement is illogical; quality is not always dictated by price.)

Better: The product does not work because it is constructed with poor-quality materials.

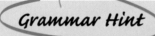

Watch the **Video**
Prewriting: Questioning
MyWritingLab

Explore Topics

In Writer's Desk: Warm Up, you will try an exploring strategy to generate ideas about different topics.

Imagine that you had to write a cause and effect paragraph about employee absenteeism. You might brainstorm and think of as many causes and effects as possible.

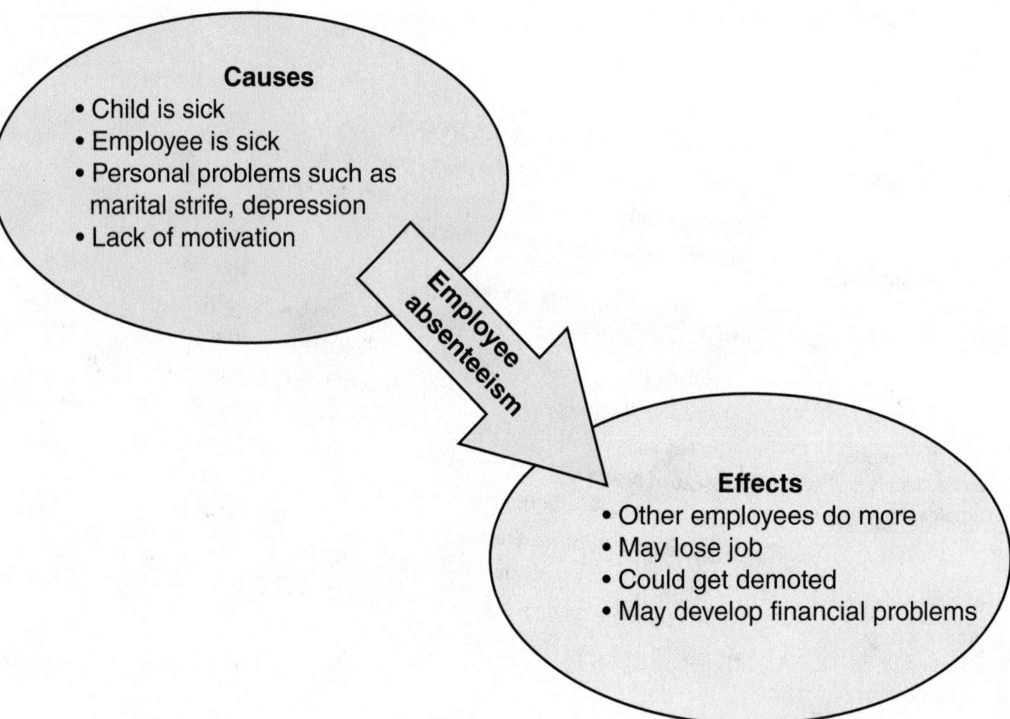

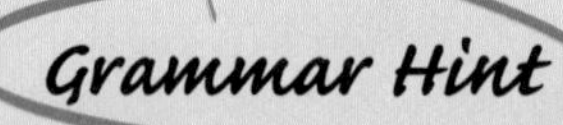

Do Not Confuse *Effect* and *Affect*

Generally, *affect* is used as a verb, and *effect* is used as a noun. *Affect* (verb) means "to influence or change," and *effect* (noun) means "the result."

verb
How will your new job affect your family?

noun
What effect will moving to a new city have on your spouse's career?

Effect can also be used as a verb that means "to cause or to bring about." It is generally used in the following phrases: "to effect a change" and "to effect a plan."

The union members demonstrated to effect changes in their working conditions.

The Writer's Desk Warm Up

Write some possible causes and effects for the following topics. Then decide if your paragraph will focus on causes or effects.

EXAMPLE:

Smoke-free work zones

Causes	Effects
workers complain about smoke	*employees smoke in entrances*
new legislation	*cigarette litter outside building*
lobby groups asking for smoke-free zones	*smokers influence nonsmokers*
lack of ventilation in offices	*smokers take long breaks*

Focus on: *Effects*

1. Cheating

Causes	Effects

Focus on: ____________________

2. Popularity of fast food

Causes	Effects

Focus on: ____________________

3. Teenage rebellion

Causes	Effects

Focus on: ____________________

ESSAY LINK

In a cause and effect essay, the thesis statement expresses whether the essay will focus on causes, effects, or both.

Watch the **Video**
Paragraphs: The Topic Sentence
MyWritingLab

DEVELOPING

The Topic Sentence

The topic sentence in a cause and effect paragraph must clearly state whether the focus is on causes, effects, or both. Also, make sure that you have clearly indicated your controlling idea. Read the following examples of topic sentences. Notice that the controlling ideas are underlined.

topic — controlling idea (causes)

The Great Depression <u>was caused by many factors.</u>

topic — controlling idea (effects)

The Great Depression <u>changed the values of Canadian society in a profound way.</u>

topic — controlling idea (causes and effects)

The Great Depression, <u>which was caused by many factors, changed the values of Canadian society in a profound way.</u>

PRACTICE 1

Carefully read the following topic sentences. Decide whether each sentence focuses on causes, effects, or both. Look for key words that give you clues. Circle the best answer.

1. People become homeless due to difficult life circumstances.
   a. Causes b. Effects c. Both
2. Homeless people must deal with difficult situations in their day-to-day lives.
   a. Causes b. Effects c. Both
3. Because of many problems at the Chernobyl nuclear site, the environment in Ukraine has changed forever.
   a. Causes b. Effects c. Both
4. Scientists have proposed many theories that explain the disappearance of the dinosaurs.
   a. Causes b. Effects c. Both

vo•cab•u•lar•y BOOST

Using your thesaurus, come up with three synonyms for *cause* and three synonyms for *effect*.

The Writer's Desk Write Topic Sentences

Write a topic sentence for each of the following topics. You can look for ideas in the previous Writer's Desk. Determine whether you will focus on causes, effects, or both in your paragraph.

EXAMPLE:

Topic: Smoke-free work zones

Topic sentence: *Smoke-free work zones, implemented for obvious reasons, have had surprising consequences for employees.*

1. Topic: Cheating

 Topic sentence: ______________________________

 ____

2. Topic: Popularity of fast food

 Topic sentence: ______________________________

 ____

3. Topic: Teenage rebellion

 Topic sentence: ______________________________

 ____

The Supporting Ideas

Watch the **Video**
Revising the Paragraph: Organization
MyWritingLab

After you have developed an effective topic sentence, generate supporting ideas. When planning a cause and effect paragraph, think of examples that clearly show the causes or effects. Then arrange your examples in emphatic order. **Emphatic order** means that you can place your examples from the most to the least important or from the least to the most important.

Do Not Oversimplify

Avoid attributing a simple or general cause to a complex issue. When you use expressions such as *it appears that* or *a possible cause is,* you show that you are aware of the complex factors involved in the situation.

Oversimplification:	The high murder rate in cities is caused by easily obtained firearms.
	(This is an oversimplification of a complicated problem.)
Better:	A possible cause of the high murder rate in cities is the abundance of easily obtained firearms.

Visualizing Cause and Effect

PRACTICE 2

Brainstorm supporting ideas for the following topic sentence. Explain how a dam might affect the environment.

Topic sentence: A dam has profound effects on the environment.

Jupiterimages/Photos.com/Getty Images/ Thinkstock

Stephen Finn/Shutterstock

David Woods/Shutterstock

The Writer's Desk Generate Supporting Ideas

Choose one of the topic sentences from the previous Writer's Desk. Then list either causes or effects.

EXAMPLE:

Topic sentence: *Smoke-free work zones, implemented for obvious reasons, have had surprising consequences for employees.*

Supports: *polluted entrances of buildings*

smokers need long breaks

smokers influence nonsmokers

Topic sentence: ______________________________

____

Supports: ______________________________

____

____

____

The Paragraph Plan

In many courses, instructors ask students to write about the causes or effects of a particular subject. Plan your paragraph before you write your final version. Also, think about the order of ideas. Arrange the supporting details in a logical order. As you make your plan, ensure that you focus on causes, effects, or both.

ESSAY LINK

In a cause and effect essay, place the thesis statement in the introduction. Then use body paragraphs, each with its own topic sentence, to support the thesis statement.

Watch the **Video**
Paragraph: How to write a successful paragraph
MyWritingLab

TOPIC SENTENCE: Smoke-free work zones, implemented for obvious reasons, have had surprising consequences for employees.

Support 1: Smokers stand at entrances to have their cigarettes.

Details: —drop their cigarette butts on the ground

—heavy smoke at the entrances

Support 2: Smokers take more breaks.

Details: —need frequent cigarette breaks

—not fair to others who must do extra work

Support 3: Smoking culture influences nonsmokers.

Details: —nonsmokers take breaks with their smoking friends

—some nonsmokers become smokers

The Writer's Desk Write a Paragraph Plan

Refer to the information you generated in previous Writer's Desk exercises, and create a paragraph plan. If you think of new details that will explain your point more effectively, include them here.

Topic sentence: ______________________________

____

Support 1: ______________________________

Details: ______________________________

____

____

Support 2: ______________________________

Details: ______________________________

____

____

Support 3: ______________________________

Details: ______________________________

____

____

Watch the Video
Paragraphs: Drafting a Paragraph
MyWritingLab

Watch the Video
Revising the Paragraph: Development
MyWritingLab

The First Draft

After you outline your ideas in a plan, you are ready to write the first draft. Remember to write complete sentences. You might include transitional expressions to help your ideas flow smoothly.

Transitional Expressions

The following transitional expressions are useful for showing causes and effects.

To Show Causes	To Show Effects
for this reason	accordingly
the first cause	as a result
the most important cause	consequently

The Writer's Desk Write the First Draft

Write the first draft of your cause and effect paragraph. Before you write, carefully review your paragraph plan, and make any necessary changes.

REVISING AND EDITING

Watch the Video
Revising and Editing Your Own Paragraphs
MyWritingLab

Revise and Edit a Cause and Effect Paragraph

When you finish writing a cause and effect paragraph, review your work and revise it to make the examples as clear as possible to your readers. Make sure that your sentences relate to the topic sentence and flow together smoothly.

PRACTICE 3

Read the next student paragraph, and answer the questions.

Smoke-free work zones, implemented for obvious reasons, have had surprising consequences for employees. First, smokers light up outside the main entrances of buildings, and nonsmokers must pass through a cloud of heavy smoke to get inside. Additionaly, the ground outside entrances is littered with cigarette butts, which smokers do not consider as pollution. Moreover, smokers get more breaks because they frequently leave their workstations to have cigarettes. Some people smoke cigars, and others smoke pipes. The nonsmokers must work more harder to cover for their smoking colleagues, and this makes the nonsmokers resentful. An other surprising consequence is that the smoking culture influences nonsmokers. Former smokers, or those who have never smoked, sometimes get into the habit of smoking in order to socialize with their colleagues during the many breaks. Although nosmoking rules are in the public interest, the consequences of such rules should be examined more thoroughly.

Revising

1. Does the paragraph focus on causes, effects, or both? ________________
2. List the causes or effects given. ________________________________

____

____

____

3. There is one sentence in the paragraph that does not relate to the topic sentence. Cross out that sentence.

Editing

4. There is one error with the comparative form. An adverb is incorrectly formed. Correct the error directly on the text.
5. This paragraph contains three misspelled words. Identify and correct them.

GRAMMAR LINK

See the following chapters for more information about these grammar topics:
Adjectives and Adverbs, Chapter 29
Spelling, Chapter 32

Watch the **Video**
Adjectives
MyWritingLab

Watch the **Video**
Adverbs
MyWritingLab

Watch the **Video**
Spelling
MyWritingLab

Watch the **Video**
Paragraphs: Revising the Paragraph—A Checklist
MyWritingLab

The Writer's Desk Revise and Edit Your Paragraph

Revise and edit the paragraph that you wrote for the previous Writer's Desk. Ensure that your paragraph has unity, adequate support, and coherence. Also, correct any errors in grammar, spelling, punctuation, and mechanics.

REFLECT ON IT

Think about what you have learned in this chapter. If you do not know an answer, review that topic.

1. What is the difference between the words *affect* and *effect?*

   Affect: ________________________________

   Effect: ________________________________

2. Brainstorm three possible causes for each option.

   a. Starting to smoke ________________________________

   ____

   b. A car crash ________________________________

   ____

3. Brainstorm three possible effects for each option.

   a. Pollution: ________________________________

   ____

   b. War: ________________________________

   ____

The Writer's Room

Writing Activity 1: Topic

Choose any of the following topics, or choose your own topic. Then write a cause and effect paragraph.

General Topics

Causes and/or effects of …

1. Having a close friendship
2. Having a caffeine addiction
3. Getting a higher education
4. Having a poor body image
5. Spoiling a child
6. Displaying voter apathy

College- and Work-Related Topics

Causes and/or effects of …

7. Having low (or high) marks in college
8. Not keeping up with college workload
9. Skipping classes
10. Working with a family member
11. Working at home
12. Getting a promotion

WRITING LINK

More Cause and Effect Writing Topics

Chapter 19, Writer's Room topic 2 (page 312)
Chapter 26, Writer's Room topic 3 (page 389)
Chapter 35, Writer's Room topic 2 (page 512)

READING LINK

More Cause and Effect Readings

"We Turned Some Sharp Corners: A Marriage Proposal in Durango" by Nick Massey-Garrison (page 530)
"A Shift in Perception" by Cynthia Macdonald (page 551)
"What Adolescents Miss When We Let Them Grow Up in Cyberspace" by Brent Staples (page 581)
"Is Anything Private Anymore?" by Sean Flynn (page 584)

Writing Activity 2: Photo Writing

How has the technological world helped or hindered personal relationships?

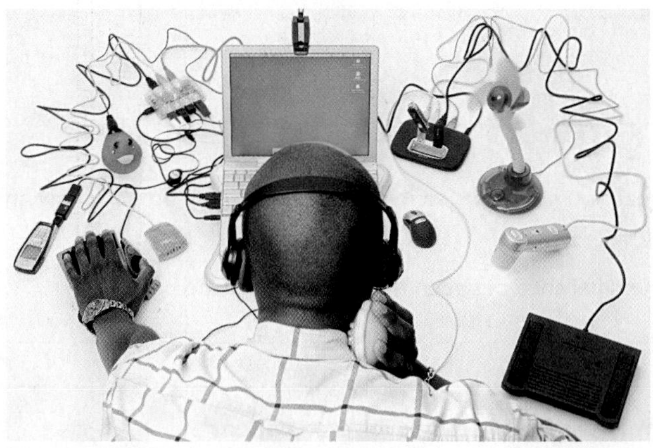

Tony Cenicola/The New York Times/rEDUX

Writing Activity 3: Media Writing

Watch a television show or movie that deals with falling in love or breaking up. You could watch any television soap opera or a romance movie such as *Passchendaele*, *The Proposal*, *Love Happens*, *Take This Waltz*, or *17 Again*. You could also listen to love songs. Describe the causes or effects of falling in love or breaking up, and use examples to support your point.

SANDRA BULLOCK RYAN REYNOLDS
THE PROPOSAL
HERE COMES THE BRIBE...

Photos 12 / Alamy

CAUSE AND EFFECT PARAGRAPH CHECKLIST

As you write your cause and effect paragraph, review the checklist on the inside front cover. Also, ask yourself the following questions.

- ☐ Does my topic sentence indicate clearly that my paragraph focuses on causes, effects, or both?
- ☐ Do I have adequate supporting examples of causes and/or effects?
- ☐ Do I make logical and valid points?
- ☐ Do I use the terms *effect* and/or *affect* correctly?

How Do I Get a Better Grade?

Visit MyWritingLab for audiovisual lectures and additional practice sets about cause and effect writing.

Chapter 12 Argument

LEARNING OBJECTIVES

Allen Furmanski/Shutterstock

Teenagers often argue with their parents. In argument writing, you try to convince readers to agree with your point of view.

Writers' Exchange

For this activity, you and a partner will take turns debating an issue. To start, choose which one of you will begin speaking. The first speaker chooses one side of any issue listed below and then argues about that issue, without stopping, for a set amount of time. Your instructor will signal when to switch sides. After the signal, the second speaker talks nonstop about the other side of the debate. If you run out of ideas, you can switch topics when it is your turn to speak.

Possible topics:

Dogs are better than cats.	Cats are better than dogs.
It's better to be married.	It's better to be single.
Life is easier for men.	Life is easier for women.

EXPLORING

What Is Argument?

Watch the Video
Paragraph Development—Argument
MyWritingLab

When you use **argument**, you take a position on an issue and try to defend your position. You try to convince somebody that your point of view is the best one.

Argument is both a writing pattern and a purpose for writing. In fact, it is one of the most common aims or purposes in most post-secondary and work-related writing. For example, in Chapter 10, there is a paragraph about the writing life, and the author uses comparison and contrast as the predominant pattern. At the same time, the author uses argument to convince the reader that writing can depict intent versus reality. In most of your college- and work-related writing, your purpose will be to persuade the reader that your ideas are compelling and valid.

You use argument every day. You might write a persuasive letter to a newspaper to express your views about public policy. At college, in a sociology class, you might take a position on capital punishment or on gun control. At work, you might have to convince your manager to give you a raise.

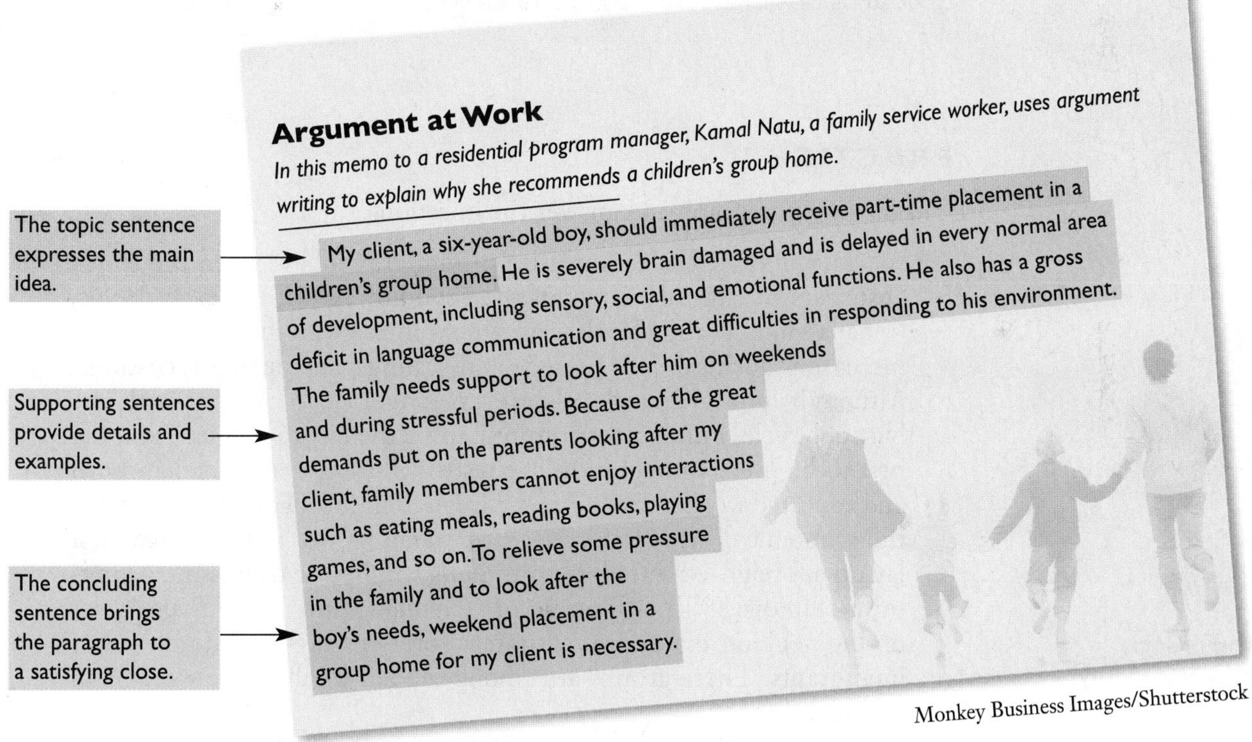

Argument at Work

In this memo to a residential program manager, Kamal Natu, a family service worker, uses argument writing to explain why she recommends a children's group home.

The topic sentence expresses the main idea. → My client, a six-year-old boy, should immediately receive part-time placement in a children's group home. He is severely brain damaged and is delayed in every normal area of development, including sensory, social, and emotional functions. He also has a gross deficit in language communication and great difficulties in responding to his environment. Supporting sentences provide details and examples. → The family needs support to look after him on weekends and during stressful periods. Because of the great demands put on the parents looking after my client, family members cannot enjoy interactions such as eating meals, reading books, playing games, and so on. The concluding sentence brings the paragraph to a satisfying close. → To relieve some pressure in the family and to look after the boy's needs, weekend placement in a group home for my client is necessary.

Monkey Business Images/Shutterstock

The Argument Paragraph

When you write an argument paragraph, remember the following four points.

ESSAY LINK
When you write argument essays, also keep these four points in mind.

- **Choose a subject that you know something about.** It would be very difficult to write a good text about space research funds, capital punishment, or conditions in federal prisons, for example, if you have never had experience with, or read about, these issues. On the other hand, if you, or someone close to you, cannot find good daycare, then you could likely write a very effective paragraph about the necessity of having better daycare services.

- **Consider your readers.** What do your readers already know about the topic? Will they likely agree or disagree with you? Do they have specific concerns? Consider what kind of evidence would be most effective with your audience.
- **Know your purpose.** In argument writing, your main purpose is to persuade readers to agree with you. Your specific purpose is more focused. You may want readers to take action, you may want to support a viewpoint, you may want to counter somebody else's argument, or you may want to offer a solution to a problem. Ask yourself what your specific purpose is.
- **Take a strong position and provide supporting evidence.** The first thing to do in the body of your paragraph is to prove that there is, indeed, a problem. Then back up your point of view with a combination of facts, statistics, examples, and informed opinions.

Be Passionate!

When you are planning your argument paragraph, try to find a topic that you feel passionate about. If you care about your topic, and if you express your enthusiasm, your audience will be more likely to care about it, too.

PRACTICE 1

Read the next paragraph and answer the questions.

Throughout Canadian history, immigrants have been the shock absorbers of clinical swings of the economy. Until the early 1990s, Canada's immigration levels were synchronized with the business cycle, increasing during boom periods and scaling back during recessions. Although immigration levels are no longer co-ordinated with the business cycle, immigrants continue to be the last to be hired and the first to be fired. Immigration creates the illusion that Canadian-born and educated workers are more secure in their jobs. For example, when the economic downturn forces a firm to cut its workforce, it may first lay off a foreign-educated, recent immigrant before dismissing a long-term employee with a lifetime of Canadian experience. Even lower on the **pecking order** are temporary foreign workers and non-status immigrants. These groups are among the most vulnerable workers in Canada.

pecking order: hierarchy of authority

—Harald Bauder, "Economic Crisis Bears Down on Vulnerable Immigrants"

1. Underline the topic sentence.
2. Who is the author's audience? ______________________________
3. What is the author's specific purpose? ______________________________

____

____

4. What economic issues might concern the audience?

5. Underline some examples that the author gives to show that there is a problem.
6. Look at the author's supporting evidence, and circle a statistic.

Explore Topics

In Writer's Desk: Warm Up, you will try an exploring strategy to generate ideas about different topics.

Watch the **Video**
Prewriting: Questioning
MyWritingLab

The Writer's Desk Warm Up

Think about the following questions, and write down the first ideas that come to mind. Try to think of two or three ideas for each topic.

EXAMPLE:

Should officials place more speed bumps on city streets?

Yes, I think so. Then speeding cars would have to slow down. Kids often play on the streets. Speeding cars are dangerous for kids who often play on the streets. Of course, speed bumps may create traffic jams. But in the long term, I think speed bumps are necessary.

1. Sometimes minors steal, vandalize, go joyriding, and do other illegal acts. Should parents be required to pay for damages when their children break the law?

2. In some countries, all youths must do two years of military service. What do you think about compulsory military service?

3. What are some of the major controversial issues in your neighbourhood, at your workplace, at your college, or in the news these days?

DEVELOPING

Watch the Video
Paragraphs: The Topic Sentence
MyWritingLab

The Topic Sentence

In the topic sentence of an argument paragraph, state your position on the issue. In the following topic sentence, notice that the controlling idea has been underlined.

controlling idea — topic

<u>Our government should severely punish</u> **corporate executives who commit fraud.**

Your topic sentence should be a debatable statement. It should not be a fact or a statement of opinion.

Fact: In some public schools, students wear uniforms.
(This is a fact. It cannot be debated.)

Opinion: I think that it is a good idea for public school students to wear uniforms.
(This is a statement of opinion. Nobody can deny that you like school uniforms. Therefore, do not use a phrase such as *In my opinion, I think*, or *I believe* in your topic sentence.)

Argument: Public school students should wear uniforms.
(This is a debatable statement.)

PRACTICE 2

Evaluate the following statements. Write *F* for a fact, *O* for an opinion, or *A* for a debatable argument.

1. I think that competitive sports are unhealthy. _____
2. The legal driving age is too low in Alberta. _____
3. Greedy athletes have hurt professional sports. _____
4. In most provinces, the legal drinking age is nineteen. _____
5. In my opinion, some college students drink too much. _____
6. Some students engage in binge drinking on our university campus. _____
7. The proposed "No Binge Drinking" campaign should be scrapped because underage drinking is not a serious problem in our college. _____
8. I believe that most students are responsible and do not abuse alcohol. _____

Be Direct

You may feel reluctant to state your point of view directly. You may feel that it is impolite to do so. However, in academic writing, it is perfectly acceptable, and even desirable, to state an argument in a direct manner.

In argument writing, you can make your topic debatable by using *should, must*, or *ought to* in the topic sentence or thesis statement.

> Although daily prayer is important for many people in Canada, it **should** not take place in the classroom.

The Writer's Desk Write Topic Sentences

Write a topic sentence for each of the following topics. You can look for ideas in the previous Writer's Desk. Make sure that each topic sentence clearly expresses your position on the issue.

EXAMPLE:

Topic: More speed bumps on city streets

Topic sentence: *With the increased traffic flow in Ottawa, speed bumps should be put in place to decrease the number of speeders and to increase public safety.*

1. Topic: Parents paying for children's crime sprees

   Topic sentence: ______________________________

   ____

2. Topic: Compulsory military service

   Topic sentence: ______________________________

   ____

3. Topic: A controversial issue in your neighbourhood, at work, at college, or in the news

   Topic sentence: ______________________________

   ____

The Supporting Ideas

When you write an argument paragraph, it is important to support your point of view with examples, facts, statistics, and informed opinions. It is also effective to think about some answers you can give to counter the opposition's point of view, and you can consider the long-term consequences if something does not occur. Therefore, try to use several types of supporting evidence.

- **Examples** are pieces of information that illustrate your main argument. For instance, if you want to argue that there are not enough daycare centres in your area, you can explain that one centre has over one hundred children on its waiting list.

  Another type of example is the **anecdote.** To support your main point, you can write about a true event or tell a personal story. For example, if you think that rebellious teenagers hurt their families, you might tell a personal story about your brother's involvement with a gang.

- **Facts** are statements that can be verified in some way. For example, the following statement is a fact: "According to the World Health Organization, secondhand smoke can cause cancer in nonsmokers." **Statistics** are another type of fact. When you use statistics, ensure that the source is reliable, and remember to mention the source. For example, if you want to argue that underage drinking is a problem, you could mention the following statistic

Watch the **Video**
Revising the Paragraph: Organization
MyWritingLab

ESSAY LINK

In an argument essay, body paragraphs should contain supporting details such as examples, facts, informed opinions, logical consequences, or answers to the opposition.

from Statistics Canada's *The Daily*: "Young people were most at risk of dependence. While 9% of 20- to 24-year-olds were dependent on alcohol, the figure at age 55 or older was less than 1%."

- Sometimes experts in a field express an **informed opinion** about an issue. An expert's opinion can give added weight to your argument. For example, if you want to argue that the courts treat youths who commit crimes too harshly or leniently, then you might quote a judge who deals with juvenile criminals. If you want to argue that secondhand smoke is dangerous, then you might quote a lung specialist or a health organization.
- Solutions to problems can carry **logical consequences.** When you plan an argument, think about long-term consequences if something does or does not happen. For example, in response to the terrorist attacks of September 11, 2001, many governments enacted antiterrorism legislation. However, in some cases, the new laws could be used to suppress legitimate dissent or free speech. Also, those new laws could be misused or misinterpreted by future governments.
- In argument writing, try to **answer the opposition.** For example, if you want to argue that drinking laws are ineffective, you might think about the arguments that your opposition might make. Then you might write, "Drinking age laws do a fine job of keeping young people out of clubs and bars; however, these laws do nothing to keep young people from getting access to alcohol from other places." Try to refute some of the strongest arguments of the opposition.

Visualizing Argument

PRACTICE 3

Brainstorm supporting ideas for the following topic sentence. Write a sentence explaining why each activity is dangerous.

Topic sentence: There are several activities you should never do when driving.

bart78/Shutterstock

Putting on makeup

____

____

StockLite/Shutterstock

Texting

____

____

Jupiterimages/Getty Images

Eating

____

____

Avoid Circular Reasoning

When you write an argument paragraph, ensure that your main point is supported with facts, examples, informed opinions, and so on. Do not use circular reasoning. Circular reasoning means that you restate your main point in various ways.

Circular The abundance of spam is not harmless; in fact, a lot of junk email is offensive. People receive many copies of junk mail, and the content offends them. Most people complain when they receive too much junk email, and they feel especially unhappy when the junk email has offensive images.

Not Circular The abundance of spam is not harmless; in fact, a lot of junk email is offensive. According to Odin Wortman of Internet Working Solutions, about 30 percent of unwanted email is pornographic. Children and older people open such mail hoping for a message from a friend, only to see an offensive picture. Another 30 percent of junk mail advertises fraudulent schemes to get rich quickly and hawks products of questionable value or safety.

PRACTICE 4

You have learned about different methods to support a topic. Read each of the following topic sentences, and think of a supporting reason for each item. Use the type of support suggested in parentheses.

1. Boys should be encouraged to express their emotions.

   (Logical Consequence) ______________________________________

   ____

   ____

2. Unleashed dogs should not be allowed on public streets.

   (Example) ____

   ____

   ____

3. The attendance policy at this college is (or is not) effective.

   (Fact) ____

   ____

   ____

4. Teen magazines should not show ads with extremely thin models.

   (Logical Consequence) ______________________________________

   ____

   ____

5. When a couple goes on a date, the person who earns the most money should always pay the bill.

   (Answer the Opposition) _____________________________________

   ____

   ____

READING LINK

For more information about avoiding plagiarism and evaluating and documenting sources, refer to Chapter 15, "Enhancing Your Writing with Research."

Watch the **Video**
Research: Avoiding Plagiarism
MyWritingLab

Listen to the **Audio**
Lesson: Working With Sources and Avoiding Plagiarism
MyWritingLab

Using Research

Watch the **Video**
Research: Finding Sources
MyWritingLab

You can enhance your argument essay with **research** by including information from an informed source. You can look for information in textbooks, newspapers, and magazines and on the Internet.

When you use the Internet for research, make sure that your sources are from the websites of legitimate organizations, reputable magazines or newspapers, or government agencies. For example, for information about the spread of AIDS, you might find statistics on the World Health Organization's website. You would not go to someone's personal rant or conspiracy theory site.

Consider Both Sides of the Issue

Once you have decided what to write about, try to think about both sides of the issue. Then you can predict arguments that your opponents might make, and you can plan your answer to the opposition.

EXAMPLE: Speed bumps

For	**Against**
—slow down speeders	—slow down emergency vehicles
—increase safety in residential neighbourhoods	—increase noise from braking cars
—allow children to play freely without being hit by a speeding car	—increase wear and tear on cars
—may reduce traffic accidents	—may increase traffic jams
—may discourage heavy traffic in residential neighbourhoods	—may cause some drivers back pain

The Writer's Desk Consider Both Sides of the Issue

Write arguments for and against each of the following topics.

1. Parents paying for children's crimes

For	**Against**
______________________	______________________
______________________	______________________
______________________	______________________
______________________	______________________

2. Compulsory military service

For	**Against**
______________________	______________________
______________________	______________________
______________________	______________________
______________________	______________________

3. A controversial issue: ___________________________

For	Against
____________	____________
____________	____________
____________	____________
____________	____________

Avoid Common Errors

When you write an argument paragraph or essay, avoid the following pitfalls.

Do not make generalizations. If you begin a statement with *Everyone knows* or *It is common knowledge*, then readers may mistrust what you say. You cannot possibly know what everyone else knows. It is better to refer to specific sources.

Generalization: Everyone knows that sending Canadian troops to Afghanistan was necessary.

Better: Prominent politicians, such as John Manley, stated that sending Canadian troops to Afghanistan was necessary.

Use emotional arguments sparingly. Certainly, the strongest arguments can be emotional ones. Sometimes the most effective way to influence others is to appeal to their sense of justice, humanity, pride, or guilt. However, do not rely on emotional arguments. If you use emotionally charged words (for example, if you call someone *ignorant*) or if you try to appeal to base instincts (for example, if you appeal to people's fear of other ethnic groups), then you will seriously undermine your argument.

Emotional: Bleeding-heart liberals did not want Canada to send troops to Afghanistan.

Better: Many sectors of society, including student activists, actors, educators, and business groups, did not want Canada to send troops to Afghanistan.

Do not make exaggerated claims. Make sure that your arguments are plausible.

Exaggerated: If Canadian military forces had not participated in training Afghan troops in Kandahar, eventually Afghanistan would have been destroyed.

Better: If Canadian military forces had not participated in training Afghan troops in Kandahar, the Taliban would have continued to terrorize the people.

vo•cab•u•lar•y BOOST

Looking at Associated Meanings

Some words have neutral, positive, or negative associations. With a partner, try to find the most neutral word in each list. Categorize the other words as positive or negative.

1. macho, jerk, hunk, lout, hottie, man, stud, sweetheart, bully
2. large boned, shapely, plump, fat, big, monstrous, heavy, muscular, curvy
3. nation, homeland, refuge, kingdom, fatherland, country, motherland, axis of evil
4. childish, young, immature, innocent, naïve, gullible, inexperienced, youthful, pure
5. freedom fighter, terrorist, anarchist, believer, radical, fanatic, revolutionary, rebel, soldier, activist

Watch the **Video**
Paragraph: How to Write a Successful Paragraph
MyWritingLab

The Paragraph Plan

Before you write your argument paragraph, make a plan. Think of some supporting arguments, and think about details that can help illustrate each argument. Ensure that every example is valid and that it relates to the topic sentence. Also, arrange your ideas in a logical order.

TOPIC SENTENCE: With the increased traffic flow in Ottawa, speed bumps should be put in place to decrease the number of speeders and to increase public safety.

Support 1: By constructing speed bumps, pedestrians will not have to worry about being hit by speeding cars.

Details: —Often children play sports on streets.

—Sometimes people cross the street without looking both ways.

Support 2: Speed bumps can help unify a community.

Details: —A community can petition the city to put speed bumps on certain streets.

—Neighbours form friendships based on a common cause.

Support 3: Speed bumps may reduce traffic accidents.

Details: —Traffic accidents are often caused by excess speed.

—Some drivers have no regard for the speed limits.

The Writer's Desk Write a Paragraph Plan

Choose one of the topic sentences that you wrote for the Writer's Desk on page 169, and write a detailed paragraph plan. You can refer to the information you generated in previous Writer's Desk exercises, and if you think of examples that will explain your point more effectively, include them here.

Subject: ____________________

Topic sentence: ____________________

____

Support 1: ____________________

Details: ____________________

____

____

Support 2: ____________________

Details: ____________________

____

____

Support 3: ______________________

Details: ______________________

____

____

The First Draft

After you outline your ideas in a plan, you are ready to write the first draft. Remember to write complete sentences. You might include transitional expressions to help your ideas flow smoothly.

Watch the Video Paragraphs: Drafting a Paragraph **MyWritingLab**

Transitional Expressions

The following transitional expressions can introduce an answer to the opposition or a statement supporting your argument.

Watch the Video Revising the Paragraph: Development **MyWritingLab**

To Answer the Opposition	To Support Your Argument
admittedly	certainly
however	consequently
nevertheless	furthermore
of course	in fact
on one hand/on the other hand	obviously
undoubtedly	of course

The Writer's Desk **Write the First Draft**

Write the first draft of your argument paragraph. Before you write, carefully review your paragraph plan, and make any necessary changes.

REVISING AND EDITING

Revise and Edit an Argument Paragraph

When you finish writing an argument paragraph, carefully review your work and revise it to make the supporting examples as clear as possible to your readers. Check that the order of ideas is logical, and remove any irrelevant details.

Watch the Video Revising and Editing Your Own Paragraphs **MyWritingLab**

PRACTICE 5

College student Craig Susanowitz wrote the following paragraph. Read the paragraph and answer the questions.

With the increased traffic flow in Ottawa, speed bumps should be put in place to decrease the number of speeders and to increase public safety. Of course, some people argue that speed bumps increase the wear and tear on a car, cause drivers back pain, and increase traffic jams. But such arguments are idiotic when it comes to public safety. By constructing speed bumps in residential neighbourhoods, pedestrians will not have to worry about being hit by speeding cars. Often, in such residential areas, children play sports on the street. As children, my friends and I often played street hockey on roller blades. We wondered why did cars screech to a stop near us. It was a bit scary. In addition, children as well as adults sometimes cross the street without paying attention to the traffic. If a car is going over the speed limit, it may not be able to stop in time if a pedestrian steps into traffic. Next, speed bumps can help unify a community. Neighbours can petition city officials to put speed bumps on certain streets. Being involved in such a worthwhile cause can bring strangers together in a community spirit. Furthermore, speed bumps will prevent car accidents. Traffic accidents are often caused by excess speed because drivers do not have enough time to react to surprises on the road. Many dudes are in a hurry and have no regard for the posted 25 m.p.h. speed limit. So, in closing, speed bumps should be implemented in Ottawa to ensure the safety of our community's residents.

Revising

1. Underline the topic sentence.
2. The writer uses an emotionally charged word. Find and replace the word with a more appropriate word.

   Emotionally charged word: ______________________

   Replacement: ______________________
3. List three arguments that support the topic sentence.

   ____

   ____

   ____
4. The writer also acknowledges the opposition. List the arguments he acknowledges.

   ____

GRAMMAR LINK

See the following chapters for more information about these grammar topics:
Slang versus standard English, Chapter 31
Dangling modifiers, Chapter 30
Embedded questions, Chapter 18

Watch the Video
Standard and Nonstandard English
MyWritingLab

Watch the Video
Dangling Modifiers
MyWritingLab

Editing

5. Find a slang word and replace it with a standard English word.

   Slang: ______________________

   Standard English: ______________________
6. This paragraph contains a dangling modifier. The modifier has no subject. Underline the error and write the correct sentence below.

   ____

   ____
7. This paragraph contains an embedded question error. Underline the error and write the correct phrase below.

   ____

Using Embedded Questions

When you embed a question inside a larger sentence, you do not need to use the question word order. Ensure that your embedded questions are correctly written.

> People wonder why ~~doesn't our country have~~ *our country doesn't have* economic regulations regarding immigrants.

The Writer's Desk **Revise and Edit Your Paragraph**

Revise and edit the paragraph that you wrote for the previous Writer's Desk. Ensure that your paragraph has unity, adequate support, and coherence. Also, correct any errors in grammar, spelling, punctuation, and mechanics.

Watch the **Video**
Paragraphs: Revising the Paragraph—A Checklist
MyWritingLab

REFLECT ON IT

Think about what you have learned in this chapter. If you do not know an answer, review that topic.

1. What is the main purpose of an argument paragraph or essay?

   ____

2. What is the difference between a statement of opinion and a statement of argument?

   ____

   ____

3. What five types of supporting evidence can you use in argument writing?

   ______________ ______________

   ______________ ______________

   ____

4. In argument writing, you should avoid circular reasoning. What is circular reasoning?

   ____

   ____

5. Why is it important to avoid using emotionally charged words?

   ____

   ____

WRITING LINK

More Argument Writing Topics

Chapter 19, Writer's Room topic 4 (page 312)
Chapter 21, Writer's Room topic 3 (page 333)
Chapter 24, Writer's Room topic 3 (page 369)
Chapter 26, Writer's Room topic 4 (page 389)
Chapter 28, Writer's Room topic 4 (page 425)
Chapter 30, Writer's Room topics 3–4 (page 450)
Chapter 32, Writer's Room topics 2–3 (page 477)

READING LINK

More Argument Readings

"Stealing Glances" by Sheila Heti (page 535)
"The Great Offside" by James Mirtle (page 538)
"New Evidence in 'Diefenbaby' Case" by Charlie Gillis (page 546)

The Writer's Room

Writing Activity 1: Topic

Choose any of the following topics, or choose your own topic. Then write an argument paragraph. Remember to narrow your topic and to follow the writing process.

General Topics

1. The voting age
2. Disciplining children
3. Chat room relationships
4. Alternative medical therapies
5. Home schooling

College- and Work-Related Topics

6. Drug testing
7. Value of a post-secondary education
8. Compulsory physical education in college
9. Longer vacations for workers
10. Office relationships

Writing Activity 2: Photo Writing

Examine the photo and think about arguments that you might make about marriage. For example, you might argue about the high cost of weddings, the best type of wedding, why people should or should not marry, or the benefits of premarital counselling. Then write an argument paragraph.

yeo2205/Shutterstock

Writing Activity 3: Media Writing

Watch a television show or movie that deals with health care. You could watch a television show such as *Grey's Anatomy*, *Nurse Jackie*, *Saving Hope*, or *House*. Movies include *My Sister's Keeper* and *Seven Pounds*. Find a controversial issue in the program or movie, and write an argument paragraph. Give examples to support your ideas.

Columbia Pictures/The Everett Collection; Petrol produced by Lost Journey Productions Inc. Created by Ant Horasanli/ Reza Sholeh/Johny Mikhael Directed by Ant Horasanli Written by Ant Horasanli and Reza Sholeh

ARGUMENT PARAGRAPH CHECKLIST

As you write your argument paragraph, review the checklist on the inside front cover. Also, ask yourself the following questions.

- ☐ Does my topic sentence clearly state my position on the issue?
- ☐ Do I make strong supporting arguments?
- ☐ Do I include facts, examples, statistics, logical consequences, or answers to the opposition?
- ☐ Do my supporting arguments provide evidence that directly supports the topic sentence?

How Do I Get a Better Grade?

Visit MyWritingLab for audiovisual lectures and additional practice sets about argument writing.

The Essay

What Is an Essay?

An ***essay*** is a series of paragraphs that support one main or central idea. Essays differ in length, style, and subject, but the structure of an essay generally consists of an ***introductory paragraph***, several ***body paragraphs***, and a ***concluding paragraph.***

Before you begin reading the following chapters, become familiar with the parts of the common five-paragraph essay.

Each body paragraph begins with a topic sentence.

The introductory paragraph introduces the essay's topic and contains its thesis statement.

The title gives a hint about the essay's topic.

The thesis statement contains the essay's topic and its controlling idea.

Alternative Culture

In an era when alternative has become mainstream, what's an angst-ridden teenager to do? Dyeing hair punk colors has become passé. Goths with white face powder, dark lipstick, and lots of eyeliner no longer attract even a second glance. Everyone listens to "alternative" music. It has become increasingly hard for a teenager to rebel against the mainstream.

In other eras, youths had something to rebel about. The 1960s had the hippie era, as young adults rebelled by protesting against injustice, the Vietnam War, and the restrictions of society. LSD, marijuana, and free love reigned. Flash forward to the 1970s, when the punk movement came into existence with bands such as the Sex Pistols, and unemployed youths railed against consumerism. Kurt Cobain in the early 1990s became the rallying cry for a new generation of teenagers disillusioned with the confines of society. But what is happening now? Nobody is in the streets. Nobody is rising up.

Furthermore, bizarre fashion statements have become acceptable. Previously, rebellious teenagers had to resort to shopping in thrift stores or making their own clothes to attain their desired fashion statement. Luckily (or unluckily) for them, society now makes it easy to dress like an individual. Companies make jeans that already have holes in them so they do not have to wait around to have that punk look. If they want to look different, they can try Urban Outfitters, the trendy chain store for people who are fed up with trendy chain stores, where they can look "unique" just like everyone else who shops there.

With this watering down of alternative culture, it has become harder and harder to shock anyone or gain any notorious press. Marilyn Manson, the press's former whipping boy and scapegoat for music as a cause of violence in society (witness the aftermath of the Columbine shootings), has faded from the public's view. Then Eminem became a strange symbol for the increasingly difficult quest to be different from everyone else and to shock society into paying attention. He got some press for his song about killing his wife, but today, nobody is paying attention.

Today's teens, with little to rebel against, find themselves wearing clothing that is mainstream and espousing ideas that shock no one. Perhaps to be truly alternative, adolescents must think for themselves. Authentic is best, no matter what that might be. They can dress as punk or as preppy as they like. They should not let society's version of "alternative" control their actions. The truly cool can think for themselves.

The concluding paragraph brings the essay to a satisfactory close.

Each body paragraph contains details that support the thesis statement.

—*Veena Thomas, student*

Writing the Essay

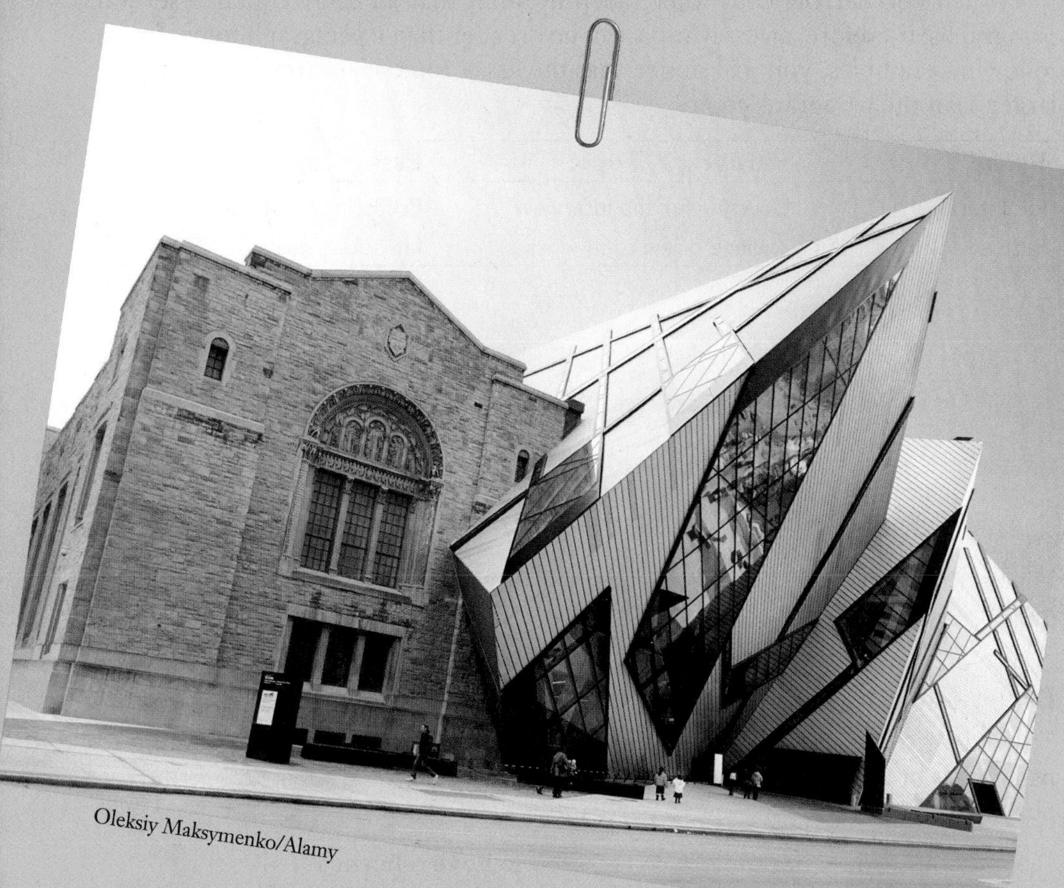

LEARNING OBJECTIVES

Completed in 2007, the Royal Ontario Museum in Toronto has tonnes of concrete, steel, and glass supporting its structure. In the same way, an essay is a sturdy structure that is supported by a strong thesis statement and solid body paragraphs held together by plenty of facts and examples.

EXPLORING

Explore Topics

There are limitless topics for writing essays. Your knowledge and personal experiences will help you find topics and develop ideas when you write your essay.

When you are planning your essay, consider your topic, audience, and purpose. Your **topic** is who or what you are writing about, your **audience** is your intended reader, and your **purpose** is your reason for writing. Do you hope to entertain, inform, or persuade the reader?

WRITING LINK

For more information about exploring strategies, see Chapter 1.

Narrowing the Topic

Your instructor may assign you a topic for your essay, or you may need to think of your own. In either case, you need to narrow your topic (make it more specific) to ensure that it suits your purpose for writing and fits the size of the assignment. To narrow your topic, you can use some exploring methods such as questioning and brainstorming.

When you narrow your topic, keep in mind that an essay contains several paragraphs; therefore, an essay topic can be broader than a paragraph topic. In the following examples, you will notice that the essay topic is narrow but is slightly larger than the paragraph topic.

Broad Topic	Paragraph Topic	Essay Topic
Job interview	Dressing for the interview	Preparing for the interview
Rituals	College orientation week	Initiation rituals

Choosing an Essay Topic

Paragraphs and essays can also be about the same topic. However, an essay has more details and concrete examples to support its thesis.

Do not make the mistake of choosing an essay topic that is too broad. Essays that try to cover a large topic risk being superficial and overly general. Make sure that your topic is specific enough that you can cover it in an essay.

Watch the Video Prewriting: Brainstorming **MyWritingLab**

Watch the Video Prewriting: Questioning **MyWritingLab**

DAVID NARROWS HIS TOPIC

Student writer David Raby-Pepin used both brainstorming and questioning to narrow his broad topic, "music." His audience was his English instructor, and the purpose of his assignment was to persuade.

— Should street performers be required to have a licence?

— downloading music

— difference in earning power between classical and pop musicians

— Why do some rock bands have staying power?

— how to be a successful musician

— What is hip-hop culture?

— the popularity of shows like *So You Think You Can Dance Canada*

— difference between poetry and song lyrics

The Writer's Desk Narrow the Topics

Practise narrowing five broad topics.

EXAMPLE:

Money: *–reasons it doesn't make you happy*

– teach children about value of money

– best ways to be financially successful

1. Crime: ______________________________

____

____

2. Volunteer work: ______________________________

____

____

3. Fashion: ______________________________

____

____

4. Advertising: ______________________________

____

____

5. Education: ______________________________

____

____

DEVELOPING

The Thesis Statement

Once you have narrowed the topic of your essay, develop your thesis statement. The **thesis statement**—like the topic sentence in a paragraph—introduces the topic of the essay and arouses the interest of the reader.

Characteristics of a Good Thesis Statement

A thesis statement has three important characteristics.

- It expresses the main topic of the essay.
- It contains a controlling idea.
- It is a complete sentence that usually appears in the essay's introductory paragraph.

Here is an example of an effective thesis statement.

topic — controlling idea

Marriage has lost its importance for many young people in our society.

Writing an Effective Thesis Statement

Watch the **Video**
Writing a Thesis Statement
MyWritingLab

When you develop your thesis statement, ask yourself the following questions.

1. **Is my thesis statement a complete statement that has a controlling idea?**

   Your thesis statement should always reveal a complete thought and make a point about the topic. It should not announce the topic or express a widely known fact.

Incomplete: Gambling problems.
(This statement is not complete.)

Announcement: I will write about lotteries.
(This statement announces the topic but says nothing relevant about the topic. Do not use an expression such as *I will write about …* or *My topic is …* .)

Thesis statement: A lottery win will not necessarily lead to happiness.

2. **Does my thesis statement make a valid and supportable point?** Your thesis statement should express a valid point that you can support with evidence. It should not be a vaguely worded statement, and it should not be a highly questionable generalization.

Vague: Workplace relationships are harmful.
(For whom are they harmful?)

Invalid point: Women earn less money than men.
(Is this really true for all women in all professions? This generalization might be hard to prove.)

Thesis statement: Before co-workers become romantically involved, they should carefully consider possible problems.

3. **Can I support my thesis statement in an essay?** Your thesis statement should express an idea that you can support in an essay. It should not be too broad or too narrow.

Too broad: There are many museums in the world.
(It would be difficult to write an essay about this topic.)

Too narrow: The Canadian War Museum is in Ottawa.
(What more is there to say?)

Thesis statement: Ottawa's Canadian War Museum contains fascinating artifacts related to the secret world of espionage.

Watch the Video Support for Your Thesis Statement **MyWritingLab**

Give Specific Details

Give enough details to make your thesis statement focused and clear. Your instructor may want you to guide the reader through your main points. To do this, mention both your main point and your supporting points in your thesis statement. In other words, your thesis statement provides a map for the readers to follow.

Weak: My first job taught me many things.

Better: My first job taught me about responsibility, organization, and the importance of teamwork.

Watch the Video Specific Details **MyWritingLab**

PRACTICE 1

Identify the problem in each thesis statement. Then revise each statement to make it more interesting and complete.

Announces	Invalid	Broad
Incomplete	Vague	Narrow

EXAMPLE:

I will write about human misery on television news.

Problem: *Announces*

Revised statement: *Television news programs should not treat personal tragedies as big news.*

1. I think that college friendships are important.

   Problem: ______

   Revised statement: ______

2. Scholarships go to athletes, so academic excellence is not appreciated in colleges.

   Problem: ______

   Revised statement: ______

3. Scientific discoveries have changed the world.

   Problem: ______

   Revised statement: ______

4. The streets are becoming more dangerous.

   Problem: ______

   Revised statement: ______

5. How to use a digital camera.

   Problem: ______

   Revised statement: ______

6. This essay will talk about security and privacy on the Internet.

   Problem: ______

   Revised statement: ______

The Writer's Desk Write Thesis Statements

For each item, choose a narrowed topic from the previous Writer's Desk. Then write an interesting thesis statement. Remember that each thesis statement should contain a controlling idea.

EXAMPLE:

Topic: Money

Narrowed topic: *Winning a lottery*

Thesis statement: *Rather than improving your life, a lottery win can lead to feelings of guilt, paranoia, and boredom.*

1. Topic: Crime

   Narrowed topic: ______________________________

   Thesis statement: ______________________________

   ____

2. Topic: Volunteer work

   Narrowed topic: ______________________________

   Thesis statement: ______________________________

   ____

3. Topic: Fashion

   Narrowed topic: ______________________________

   Thesis statement: ______________________________

   ____

4. Topic: Advertising

   Narrowed topic: ______________________________

   Thesis statement: ______________________________

   ____

5. Topic: Education

   Narrowed topic: ______________________________

   Thesis statement: ______________________________

   ____

The Supporting Ideas

The thesis statement expresses the main idea of the entire essay. In the following illustration, you can see how the ideas flow in an essay. Topic sentences relate to the thesis statement, and details support the topic sentences; therefore, every single idea in the essay is unified and supports the thesis.

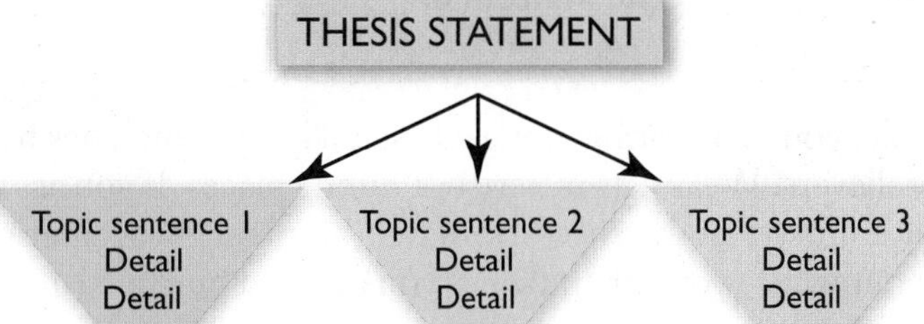

PRACTICE 2

Read the following essay. After you have finished reading, do the following:

1. Create an effective thesis statement. It should sum up the point of the entire essay.
2. Write a topic sentence at the beginning of each body paragraph. The topic sentence should sum up the main point of the paragraph in an interesting way.

Introduction:

Danger has always been synonymous with travel. In past centuries, pirates on the high seas attacked passing ships. Land travellers were not much safer; bandits could attack their covered carriages. Even trains were not safe; in 1904 the outlaw Billy Miner held up a train in Mission Junction and robbed it. Today, with modern communication and with high-speed trains and planes, travel is quick and relatively risk-free. Nonetheless, there are still certain hazards inherent in travelling.

Thesis statement: ______________________________

____

Body paragraph 1 topic sentence: ______________________

____

For example, before you arrive in a new town, find an address and phone number for affordable lodging, and book a room for your first night. If you are a budget traveller, you can always find cheaper accommodations the next day. If you are going to visit a large city, plan to arrive during the daylight hours. It is dangerous to arrive at night and then try to find your way around. Also, make sure that you have a map of your destination. You can download maps on the Internet.

Body paragraph 2 topic sentence: ______________________

____

Do not flash your money in public places. You might wear a money belt under your clothing. One innovative solution is to sew long, extended pockets on the insides of your clothes; you could keep your cheques and passport there. In a small, easily accessible purse or wallet, keep small amounts of local currency for your daily spending.

Body paragraph 3 topic sentence: ______________________________

____

For example, you could bring along a first aid kit that includes bandages and pain relievers. Wear hats in very hot, sunny places. If you are visiting a tropical country, make sure you have the proper vaccinations. Be careful about where you eat and what you eat, and buy bottled drinking water. Your health is important. Obviously, if you get sick, you are not going to enjoy your trip.

Conclusion:

Although robberies can happen, it is unlikely that someone will physically hurt you. If you take risks with your health, if you are careless with your money and passports, or if you underestimate thieves, you may have an unpleasant experience. Of course, if you are careful, you should have a perfectly safe and exciting trip.

Watch the Video Revising the Paragraph: Organization **MyWritingLab**

Generating Supporting Ideas

An effective essay has **unity** when the body paragraphs support the thesis statement. When you develop supporting ideas, make sure that they all focus on the central point that you are making in the thesis statement. To generate ideas for body paragraphs, you could use exploring strategies such as brainstorming, clustering, and freewriting.

Watch the Video Essay Organization: General to Specific Organization **MyWritingLab**

David's Supporting Ideas

David created a list to support his thesis statement. Then he reread his supporting points and removed ideas that he did not want to develop in his essay.

Thesis Statement: Rap and hip-hop artists use their music to share their positive cultural values with others.

— use lyrics to reveal their religious opinions

— Christian lyrics

— ~~hip hop inspired breakdancing~~

— praise Allah

— want to promote peace

— some address issues of violence

— ~~some hip hop artists have been jailed~~

— advise fans about healthy lifestyles

— warn about drugs

— talk about AIDS

The Writer's Desk List Supporting Ideas

Choose two of your thesis statements from the previous Writer's Desk, and create two lists of possible supporting ideas.

Thesis 1: ______________________	Thesis 2: ______________________
______________________	______________________
Support: ______________________	Support: ______________________
______________________	______________________
______________________	______________________
______________________	______________________
______________________	______________________
______________________	______________________
______________________	______________________
______________________	______________________
______________________	______________________
______________________	______________________
______________________	______________________
______________________	______________________

Organizing Your Ideas

An effective essay has organized points that support the thesis statement. After you have brainstormed on your topic, highlight your favourite ideas, and then group together related ideas. Finally, make your essay as clear and coherent as possible by organizing your ideas in a logical manner using time, space, or emphatic order.

WRITING LINK

For more information about time, space, and emphatic order, see Chapter 2, "Developing."

David's Example

David underlined his three best supporting points, and he grouped related ideas using emphatic order.

3
– use lyrics to reveal their religious opinions
– Christian lyrics
~~– hip hop inspired breakdancing~~
– praise Allah
1
– want to promote peace
– some address issues of violence
~~– some hip hop artists have been jailed~~
2
– advise fans about healthy lifestyles
– warn about drugs
– talk about AIDS

Watch the Video Paragraphs: Recognizing a Paragraph **MyWritingLab**

Watch the Video Essay Organization: Specific to General Organization **MyWritingLab**

Watch the Video
Essay Organization: Chronological Organization
MyWritingLab

Watch the Video
Essay Organization: General to Specific Organization
MyWritingLab

Watch the Video
Essay Organization: Importance Order
MyWritingLab

The Writer's Desk Organize Your Ideas

Select one of the lists you produced in the previous Writer's Desk, and then follow these steps.

1. Highlight at least three ideas from your list that are most compelling and that most clearly illustrate the point you are making in your thesis statement.
2. Group together any related ideas with the three supporting ideas.
3. Organize your ideas using time, space, or emphatic order.

Watch the Video
Essays: Recognizing an Essay
MyWritingLab

The Essay Plan

An **essay plan** or an **outline** can help you organize your thesis statement and supporting ideas before writing your first draft. To create an essay plan, follow these steps.

- Look at your list of ideas and identify the best supporting ideas.
- Write topic sentences that express the main supporting ideas.
- Add details under each topic sentence.

In the planning stage, you do not have to develop your introduction and conclusion. It is sufficient to simply write your thesis statement and an idea for your conclusion. Later, when you develop your essay, you can develop the introduction and conclusion.

David's Essay Plan

David wrote topic sentences and supporting examples and organized his ideas into a plan. Notice that he begins with his thesis statement, and he indents his supporting ideas.

Thesis Statement: Rap and hip-hop artists use their music to share their positive cultural values with others.

Body paragraph 1: Many musicians shout out a powerful message of nonviolence.
— They promote peace.
— Some artists address the issue of violence.

Body paragraph 2: Some advise fans about responsible and healthy lifestyles.
— They discuss the importance of good parenting.
— They talk about drug addiction or AIDS.

Body paragraph 3: These urban musicians use their poetry to reveal their religious beliefs.
— Some show their Christian faith through the lyrics.
— Others praise Allah.

Concluding sentence: Ultimately, music is a way for rap musicians to share their personal culture with the world.

Writing a Formal Essay Plan

Watch the Video
Revising the Essay: Development
MyWritingLab

Most of the time, a basic essay plan is sufficient. However, in some of your courses, your instructor may ask you to make a formal plan. A formal plan uses Roman numerals and letters to identify main and supporting ideas.

Thesis statement: ______________________________

I. ______________________________

A. ______________________________

B. ______________________________

II. ______________________________

A. ______________________________

B. ______________________________

III. ______________________________

A. ______________________________

B. ______________________________

Concluding idea: ______________________________

PRACTICE 3

Create an essay plan based on Veena Thomas's essay "Alternative Culture" on page 180.

____
____
____
____
____
____
____
____
____
____
____
____
____

PRACTICE 4

Complete the following essay plan. Add details under each supporting point. Make sure that the details relate to the topic sentence.

Thesis statement: Rather than improving your life, a lottery win can lead to feelings of guilt, paranoia, and boredom.

I. Feelings of guilt are common in newly rich people.

Details: A. ______________________________

____

B. ______________________________

____

C. ______________________________

____

II. Lottery winners often become paranoid.

Details: A. ______________________________

____

B. ______________________________

____

C. ______________________________

____

III. After lottery winners quit their jobs, they commonly complain of boredom and loneliness.

Details: A. ______________________________

____

B. ______________________________

____

C. ______________________________

____

Concluding idea: ______________________________

____

____

Watch the **Video**
Essays: Essay Writing
MyWritingLab

The Writer's Desk Write an Essay Plan

Write an essay plan using the thesis statement and supporting details from the previous Writer's Desk.

Thesis statement: ______________________________

____

I. ______________________________

Details: A. ______________________________

B. ______________________________

C. ______________________________

II. ______________________________

Details: A. ______________________________

B. ______________________________

C. ______________________________

III. ______________________________

Details: A. ______________________________

B. ______________________________

C. ______________________________

Concluding idea: ______________________________

____

The Introduction

After you have made an essay plan, you develop the sections of your essay by creating an effective introduction, linking paragraphs, and writing a conclusion.

The **introductory paragraph** introduces the subject of your essay and contains the thesis statement. A strong introduction will capture your readers' attention and make them want to read on. Introductions may have a lead-in, and they can be developed in several different ways.

The Lead-In

You can begin the introduction with an attention-grabbing opening sentence, or lead-in. There are three common types of lead-ins.

- Quotation
- Surprising or provocative statement
- Question

Introduction Styles

Watch the **Video**
Essay Introductions, Conclusions and Titles: Introductions
MyWritingLab

You can develop the introduction in several different ways. Experiment with any of these introduction styles.

- **Give general or historical background information.** The general or historical information gradually leads to your thesis. For example, in an essay about winning a lottery, you could begin by giving a brief history of lotteries.
- **Tell an interesting anecdote.** Open your essay with a story that leads to your thesis statement. For example, you might begin your lottery essay by telling the story of a real-life lottery winner.
- **Present a vivid description.** Give a detailed description, and then state your thesis. For example, you might describe the moment when a lottery winner realizes that he or she has won.
- **Present an opposing position.** Open your essay with an idea that contradicts a common belief, and build to your thesis. For instance, if most

people want to win the lottery, you could begin your essay by saying that you definitely do not want to be a millionaire.

- **Give a definition.** Define a term and then state your thesis. For example, in an essay about the lottery, you could begin by defining *happiness*.

Watch the Video Revising the Essay: Thesis Statement **MyWritingLab**

Placement of the Thesis Statement

Although a paragraph often begins with a topic sentence, an introduction does not begin with a thesis statement. Rather, most introductory paragraphs are shaped like a funnel. The most general statement introduces the topic. The following sentences become more focused and lead to a clear, specific thesis statement. Therefore, the thesis statement is generally the last sentence in the introduction.

PRACTICE 5

In introductions A through D, the thesis statement is underlined. Read each introduction and then answer the questions that follow. Look at David's example for some guidance.

David's Introduction

Can hip-hop, with its obscene lyrics and violent culture, have any redeeming qualities? Hip-hop and rap music originated from poor, minority-inhabited neighbourhoods located in New York City. Since the residents did not have enough money to buy musical instruments, they began creating beats with their mouths. This raw form of music rapidly became popular within these communities because it gave people a way to express themselves and to develop their creative abilities. <u>Rap and hip-hop artists use their music to share their positive cultural values with others.</u>

1. What type of lead-in does David use? *Question*
2. What introduction style does he use?

   a. Description b. Definition

   (c.) Background information d. Opposing position
3. What is his essay about? *The positive message of hip-hop and rap music*

A. "I never saw the blow to my head come from Huck. Bam! And I was on all fours, struggling for my equilibrium." These are the words of Kody Scott, a former member of a Los Angeles street gang. Kody is describing part of the initiation ritual he endured in order to join a local branch (or "set") of the Crips. First, he stole an automobile to demonstrate his "street smarts" and willingness to break the law. Then he allowed himself to be beaten, showing both that he was tough and that he was ready to do whatever the gang required of him. He completed the process by participating in a "military action"—killing a member of a rival gang. Initiations like this are by no means rare in today's street gangs. Kody, by the way, was just eleven years old.

—Linda L. Lindsey and Stephen Beach, "Joining the Crips," *Essentials of Sociology*

1. What type of lead-in do the authors use? ______________________
2. What introduction style do the authors use?

   a. Anecdote   b. Definition

   c. Background information   d. Opposing position
3. What is this essay about? ______________________________

B. Many practices in conventional medicine are safe and effective. There are, arguably, many that, while effective in the short term, can also have serious adverse consequences. Integrative medicine invites us to look outside our self-imposed box and to begin to understand how there really are no *conventional* and *alternative* distinctions, except in our own minds. Healing is healing. Should not our primary interest be helping our patients to heal safely and effectively? If this is our goal, then we will soon realize that all healing practices, orthodox or alternative, can be complementary if used appropriately and judiciously. This is the goal of integrative medicine. In order to reach this goal, we need to begin a dialogue with other healing practitioners and with our patients, the public, and governments. We need to inform ourselves about other practices and their potential benefits and limitations with an open mind and a healthy scepticism. And we need to encourage appropriate research in these fields in order to evaluate scientifically their potential use in a more holistic model of care.

—Mark Sherman, MD CM, CCFP, "Integrative Medicine: Model for Health Care Reform," *Canadian Family Physician*

4. What type of lead-in does the author use? ______________________
5. What introduction style does the author use?

   a. Anecdote   b. Definition

   c. Description   d. Opposing position
6. What is this essay about? ______________________________

C. High school is a waste of time. In fact, it is a baby-sitting service for teens who are too old to be baby-sat. In England, fifteen-year-olds graduate and can choose technical or university streams of education. They are free to choose what to study, or they can stop schooling and get jobs. In short, they are treated like mature adults. In our country, we prolong the experience of forced schooling much longer than is necessary. We should abolish high schools and introduce a system of technical or pre-university schooling.

—Adelie Zang, student

7. What type of lead-in does the author use? ______________________
8. What introduction style does the author use?

   a. Anecdote   b. Definition

   c. Background information   d. Opposing position
9. What is this essay about? ______________________________

D. The story of how Christianity ultimately conquered the Roman Empire is one of the most remarkable in history. Christianity faced the hostility of the established religious institutions of its native Judea and had to compete not only against the official cults of Rome and the sophisticated philosophies of the educated classes, but also against "mystery" religions like the cults of Mithra, Isis, and Osiris. The Christians also suffered formal persecution, yet Christianity finally became the official religion of the empire.

—Albert M. Craig et al., *The Heritage of World Civilizations*

10. What introduction style do the authors use?

a. Description   b. Definition

c. Historical information   d. Opposing position

11. What is this essay about? formal perscution ______

The Writer's Desk Write Three Introductions

In the previous Writer's Desk, you made an essay plan. Now write three introductions, each in a different style, for your essay. Use the same thesis statement in all three introductions. Later, you can choose the best introduction for your essay.

The Conclusion

A **conclusion** is a final paragraph that rephrases the thesis statement and summarizes the main points in the essay. To make your conclusion more interesting and original, you could close with a prediction, a suggestion, a quotation, or a call to action.

Watch the **Video**
Essay Introductions, Conclusions and Titles: Conclusions
MyWritingLab

David's Conclusion

David concluded his essay by restating his main points.

Ultimately, music is a way for hip-hop and rap musicians to share their personal culture with the world. This cultural facet can be reflected through different values, religious beliefs, and ways of life.

He could then close his essay with one of the following:

Prediction: If you are concerned about hip-hop portraying negative images, don't abandon the music yet. There are many artists who promote and will continue to promote positive values through upbeat lyrics.

Suggestion: Hip-hop fans should encourage musicians to continue to give a positive message through their music.

Call to action: If you are concerned by the negative message of hip-hop music, make your opinions heard by joining the debate on hip-hop blogs and buying CDs from musicians who write only positive lyrics.

Quotation: According to hip-hop artist Doug E. Fresh, "Hip Hop is supposed to uplift and create, to educate people on a larger level, and to make a change."

PRACTICE 6

Read the following conclusion and answer the question.

> As soon as smoking is banned in all public places, we will see the benefits. Our hospitals will treat fewer smoking-related illnesses, and this will save money. Nonsmokers will be saved from noxious fumes, and smokers, who will be forced to smoke outdoors, might feel a greater desire to give up the habit. In the future, we will have a world where a nonsmoker can go through life without having to breathe in someone else's cigarette smoke.
>
> —Jordan Lamott, "Butt Out!"

What method does the author use to end the conclusion?

a. Prediction
b. Suggestion
c. Quotation
d. Call to action

Avoiding Conclusion Problems

In your conclusion, do not contradict your main point, and do not introduce new or irrelevant information. David initially included the next sentences in his conclusion.

> The rap and hip-hop movement is not restrained only to the musical scene. It influences many other facets of art and urban culture as well. It can be found in dance and fashion, for instance. Thus, it is very versatile.

He revised his conclusion when he realized that some of his ideas were new and irrelevant information. His essay does not discuss dance or fashion.

The Writer's Desk Write a Conclusion

In previous Writer's Desks, you wrote an essay plan and an introduction. Now write a conclusion for your essay.

The First Draft

After creating an introduction and a conclusion and after arranging the supporting ideas in a logical order, you are ready to write your first draft. The first draft includes your introduction, several body paragraphs, and your concluding paragraph.

The Writer's Desk Write the First Draft

In previous Writer's Desks, you wrote an essay plan, an introduction, and a conclusion. Now write the first draft of your essay.

REVISING AND EDITING

Revising and Editing the Essay

Revising your essay is an extremely important step in the writing process. When you revise your essay, you modify it to make it stronger and more convincing. You do this by reading the essay critically, looking for faulty logic, poor organization, or poor sentence style. Then you reorganize and rewrite it, making any necessary changes.

Editing is the last stage in writing. When you edit, you proofread your writing and make sure that it is free of errors.

WRITING LINK

To practise revising for unity and support, see Chapter 3, "Revising and Editing."

Watch the **Video**
Revising the Essay: Unity
MyWritingLab

Revising for Unity

To revise for **unity,** verify that all of your body paragraphs support the thesis statement. Also, look carefully at each body paragraph: ensure that the sentences support the topic sentence.

Avoiding Unity Problems

Here are two common errors to check for as you revise your body paragraphs.

- **Rambling paragraphs.** The paragraphs in the essay ramble on. Each paragraph has several topics, and there is no clearly identifiable topic sentence.
- **Artificial breaks.** A long paragraph is split into smaller paragraphs arbitrarily, and each smaller paragraph lacks a central focus.

To correct either of these errors, revise each body paragraph until it has *one* main idea that supports the thesis statement.

Revising for Adequate Support

When you revise for adequate **support,** ensure that there are enough details and examples to make your essay strong and convincing. Include examples, statistics, quotations, or anecdotes.

Watch the **Video**
Revising the Essay: Coherence
MyWritingLab

Revising for Coherence

When you revise for **coherence,** ensure that paragraphs flow smoothly and logically. To guide the reader from one idea to the next or from one paragraph to the next, try using **paragraph links.**

You can develop connections between paragraphs using three methods.

1. **Repeat words or phrases from the thesis statement in each body paragraph.** In the next example, *violent* and *violence* are repeated words.

Thesis statement: Although some will argue that violent movies are simply a reflection of a violent society, these movies actually cause a lot of the violence around us.

Body paragraph 1: Action movie heroes train children to solve problems with violence.

Body paragraph 2: Violent movies are "how to" films for many sick individuals.

2. **Refer to the main idea in the previous paragraph, and link it to your current topic sentence.** In body paragraph 2, the writer reminds the reader of the first point (the newly rich feel useless) and then introduces the next point.

   Thesis statement: A cash windfall may cause more problems than it solves.

   Body paragraph 1: The newly rich often lose their desire to become productive citizens, and they end up feeling useless.

   Body paragraph 2: Apart from feeling useless, many heirs and lottery winners also tend to feel guilty about their wealth.

3. **Use a transitional expression to lead the reader to your next idea.**

   Body paragraph 2: Furthermore, the newly rich often feel guilty about their wealth.

WRITING LINK

Furthermore is a transitional expression. For a list of transitional expressions, see page 47 in Chapter 3.

Revising for Style

Another important step in the revision process is to ensure that you have varied your sentences and that you have used concise wording. When you revise for sentence style, ask yourself the following questions.

- Do I use a variety of sentence patterns? (To practise using sentence variety, see Chapter 19.)
- Do I use exact language? (To learn about slang, wordiness, and overused expressions, see Chapter 31.)
- Are my sentences parallel in structure? (To practise revising for parallel structure, see Chapter 21.)

Editing

When you edit, you proofread your essay and correct any errors in punctuation, spelling, grammar, and mechanics. There is an editing guide on the inside back cover of this book that provides you with a list of things to check for when you proofread your text.

ESSAY LINK

To practise your editing skills, see Chapter 36, "Editing Paragraphs and Essays."

David's Essay

David revised and edited this paragraph from his essay about hip-hop culture.

Watch the Video Essays: How to Edit **MyWritingLab**

~~some~~ *Furthermore, some* rappers advise fans about responsible and healthy lifestyles. Several hip-hop artists divulge the fact that ~~their~~ *they* are parents and discuss the importance of good parenting. Others announce their choice of a monogamous lifestyle~~. They~~ *and* encourage their fans to have respectful relationships. Some rappers mention past drug addictions and advise listeners to ~~be avoiding~~ *avoid* drugs. Others rap about the dangers of sexually transmitted diseases. The rapper Ludacris, for

example,
~~example. He~~ warns his fans about AIDS and HIV and advises them to be careful and to have protected sexual relationships. Such

extremely
messages are ~~extremely~~ important since many young people do not take precautions with their health.

Watch the Video
Essays: Revising and Editing Your Own Essay
MyWritingLab

The Writer's Desk **Revising and Editing Your Essay**

In the previous Writer's Desk, you wrote the first draft of an essay. Now revise and edit your essay. You can refer to the checklist at the end of this chapter.

The Essay Title

ESSAY LINK

For more information about punctuating titles, see pages 499–501 in Chapter 34.

It is a good idea to think of a title after you have completed your essay because then you will have a more complete impression of your essay's main point. The most effective titles are brief, depict the topic and purpose of the essay, and attract the reader's attention.

When you write your title, place it at the top centre of your page. Capitalize the first word of your title, and capitalize the main words except for prepositions (*in*, *at*, *for*, *to*, etc.) and articles (*a*, *an*, *the*). Leave about an inch of space between the title and the introductory paragraph.

Watch the Video
Essay Introductions, Conclusions and Titles: Titles
MyWritingLab

Descriptive Titles

Descriptive titles are the most common titles in academic essays. They depict the topic of the essay clearly and concisely. Sometimes the author takes key words from the thesis statement and uses them in the title. Here are some descriptive titles.

The Importance of Multiculturalism in a Democratic Society
Why Mothers and Fathers Should Take Parenting Seriously

Titles Related to the Writing Pattern

You can also relate your title directly to the writing pattern of your essay. Here are examples of titles for different writing patterns.

Illustration:	The Problems with Elections
Narration:	My Visit to Quebec City
Description:	Graduation Day
Process:	How to Dress for an Interview
Definition:	What It Means to Be Brave
Classification:	Three Types of Hackers
Comparison and contrast:	Fast Food versus Gourmet Food
Cause and effect:	Why People Enter Beauty Pageants
Argument:	Barbie Should Have a New Look

Avoiding Title Pitfalls

When you write your title, watch out for problems.

- Do not view your title as a substitute for a thesis statement.
- Do not put quotation marks around the title of your essay.
- Do not write a really long title because it can be confusing.

PRACTICE 7

1. List some possible titles for the essay about travel in Practice 2 (pages 187–188).

____

____

2. List some alternative titles for David's essay about rap and hip-hop music, which appears below.

____

____

The Final Draft

When you have finished making the revisions on the first draft of your essay, write the final copy. This copy should include all the changes that you have made during the revision phase of your work. You should proofread the final copy of your work to check for grammar, spelling, mechanics, and punctuation errors.

David's Essay

David revised and edited his essay about hip-hop culture. This is his final draft.

Positive Messages in Hip-Hop Music

Can hip-hop, with its obscene lyrics and violent culture, have any redeeming qualities? Hip-hop and rap music mainly originated from poor, minority-inhabited neighbourhoods located in New York City. Since the residents did not have enough money to buy musical instruments, they began creating beats with their mouths. This raw form of music rapidly became popular within these communities because it gave people a way to express themselves and to develop their creative abilities. The rap and hip-hop artists use their music to share their positive cultural values with others.

Many of these musicians shout out a powerful message of non-violence. They promote peace by denouncing the fighting that takes place within their own community. Many leading hip-hop and rap artists are breaking away from the "gangsta rap" lyrics and writing music that shows a productive way to resolve social issues.

Furthermore, some rappers advise fans about responsible and healthy lifestyles. Several hip-hop artists divulge the fact that they are parents and discuss the importance of good parenting. Others announce their choice of a monogamous lifestyle and encourage their fans to have respectful relationships. Some rappers mention past drug addictions and advise listeners to avoid drugs. Others rap about the dangers of sexually transmitted diseases. The rapper Ludacris, for example, warns his fans about AIDS and HIV and advises them to be careful and to have protected sexual relationships. Such messages are extremely important since many young people do not take precautions with their health.

Moreover, these urban musicians also use their lyrics to reveal their religious beliefs. Some show their Christian faith by including God in their texts. "Tommy is on the other side talking with God, understanding why he had it so hard," is from the song "Tommy" by Mathematics. Members of the band Killarmy praise Allah in their lyrics. Hip-hop and rap musicians generally do not criticize other religions through their songs. They only use this form of communication to support their own religious opinions. Hip-hop and rap music can be a way for individuals to show their faith or to pass it on to members of their audience.

Ultimately, music is a way for rap musicians to share their personal culture with the world. This cultural facet can be reflected through different values, religious beliefs, and ways of life. According to hip-hop artist Doug E. Fresh, "Hip Hop is supposed to uplift and create, to educate people on a larger level, and to make a change."

The Writer's Desk Writing Your Final Draft

At this point, you have developed, revised, and edited your essay. Now write the final draft. Before you hand it to your instructor, proofread it one last time to ensure that you have found as many errors as possible.

REFLECT ON IT

Think about what you have learned in this chapter. If you do not know an answer, review that topic.

1. What is a thesis statement? ______________________________

____

2. What are the five different introduction styles?

______________________ ______________________

______________________ ______________________

____

3. What are the four different ways to end a conclusion?

_______________ _______________

_______________ _______________

4. What are the three different ways you can link body paragraphs?

____

____

____

The Writer's Room

Writing Activity 1: Topics

Choose any of the following topics, or choose your own topic. Then write an essay. Remember to follow the writing process.

General Topics

1. Communication
2. An unforgettable experience
3. Differences between generations
4. Advertising
5. Peer pressure

College- and Work-Related Topics

6. Juggling college and family life
7. Having a job and going to college
8. Long-term career goals
9. A current social controversy
10. An important issue in the workplace

Writing Activity 2: Photo Writing

What ideas come to mind when you examine this photo? You may think about celebrities, culture of excess, culture of entitlement, good or bad role models, big business, and so on. Write an essay based on the photo or your related topic.

Helen Filatova/Shutterstock

Watch the Video
Editing: A Checklist
MyWritingLab

REVISING AND EDITING CHECKLIST FOR ESSAYS

Revising

- ☐ Does my essay have a compelling introduction and conclusion?
- ☐ Does my introduction have a clear thesis statement?
- ☐ Does each body paragraph contain a topic sentence?
- ☐ Does each body paragraph's topic sentence relate to the thesis statement?
- ☐ Does each body paragraph contain specific details that support the topic sentence?
- ☐ Do all of the sentences in each body paragraph relate to its topic sentence?
- ☐ Do I use transitions to smoothly and logically connect ideas?
- ☐ Do I use a variety of sentence styles?

Editing

- ☐ Do I have any errors in grammar, spelling, punctuation, and capitalization?

How Do I Get a Better Grade?

Visit MyWritingLab for audiovisual lectures and additional practice sets about writing the essay.

Essay Patterns

LEARNING OBJECTIVES

INSAGO/Shutterstock

Fashion designers choose fabric patterns that are appropriate for the articles of clothing that they wish to make. In the same way, writers choose essay patterns that best suit their purposes for writing.

In Chapters 4 through 12, you read about and practised using nine different paragraph patterns. In this chapter, you will learn how to apply those patterns when writing essays. Before you begin working through this chapter, take a moment to review nine writing patterns.

Pattern	Use
Illustration	To illustrate or prove a point using specific examples
Narration	To narrate or tell a story about a sequence of events that happened
Description	To describe using vivid details and images that appeal to readers' senses
Process	To inform readers about how to do something, how something works, or how something happened
Definition	To define or explain what a term or concept means by providing relevant examples
Classification	To classify or sort a topic to help readers understand different qualities about that topic
Comparison and contrast	To present information about similarities (compare) or differences (contrast)

Cause and effect	To explain why an event happened (the cause) or what the consequences of the event were (the effects)
Argument	To argue or to take a position on an issue and offer reasons for your position

Most college essay assignments have one dominating essay pattern. However, you can use several essay patterns to fulfill your purpose. For example, imagine that you want to write a cause and effect essay about youth crime and that the purpose of the essay is to inform. The supporting paragraphs might include a definition of youth crime and a narrative about an adolescent with a criminal record. You might incorporate different writing patterns, but the dominant pattern would still be cause and effect.

Each time you write an essay, remember to follow the writing process that you learned in Chapter 13, "Writing the Essay."

The Illustration Essay

PARAGRAPH LINK

For more information about developing ideas with examples, refer to Chapter 4, "Illustration."

Watch the Video
Essay Development: Illustrating
MyWritingLab

When writing an illustration essay, you use specific examples to illustrate or clarify your main point. Illustration writing is a pattern that you frequently use in college essays and exams because you must support your main idea with examples.

The Thesis Statement

The thesis statement in an illustration essay controls the direction of the body paragraphs. It includes the topic and a controlling idea about the topic.

topic / controlling idea

A second language provides students with several important advantages.

The Supporting Ideas

In an illustration essay, the body paragraphs contain examples that support the thesis statement. You can develop each body paragraph in two different ways. To give your essay variety, you could use both a series of examples and extended examples.

- **Use a series of examples** that support the paragraph's topic sentence. For example, in an essay about bad driving, one body paragraph could be about drivers who do not pay attention to the road. The paragraph could list the things that those drivers do, such as choosing songs on an iPod, using a cellphone, eating, and putting on makeup.
- **Use an extended example** to support the paragraph's topic sentence. The example could be an anecdote or a description of an event. In an essay about bad driving, for example, one paragraph could contain an anecdote about a driver who always wanted to be faster than other drivers.

An Illustration Essay Plan

Read the next essay plan, and answer the questions.

Introduction
Thesis statement: New technologies have had a profound impact on self-employed workers.

I. Hand-held organizers help such workers maintain a portable office.

A. They store emails, schedules, phone lists, and more.
B. Models are lightweight and fit in a pocket.
C. Messenger services provide means to communicate in real time.

II. Portable computers provide workers with the ability to do complicated things anywhere.
A. They can format and design documents using graphs, tables, and art.
B. They can write, revise, and edit simultaneously.
C. There is no need to carry large paper files; computers can store hundreds of files.
D. The self-employed can access the Internet while travelling.

III. Computer printers have useful features for the self-employed worker.
A. There are integrated scanners and photocopiers.
B. Fax machines allow easy sending and receiving of messages.
C. Laser printers can quickly print out large volumes of documents.

Conclusion: As technologies evolve, more people will be self-employed.

PRACTICE 1

1. Circle the topic and underline the controlling idea in the thesis statement.
2. How does the writer develop each body paragraph? Circle the better answer.
   a. With an extended example b. With a series of examples
3. Write another topic sentence that could support the writer's thesis statement.

____

____

PARAGRAPH LINK

To practise illustration writing, you could develop an essay about one of the topics found in Chapter 4, "Illustration."

Writing Activity 1: Topics

Write an illustration essay about one of the following topics.

General Topics
1. Ridiculous fads or fashions
2. Characteristics of a good friend
3. Stereotypes on television
4. Useless products or inventions
5. Activities that relieve stress

College- and Work-Related Topics
6. Characteristics of a good boss
7. Qualities of an ideal workplace
8. Skills that you need for your job
9. Temptations that college students face
10. Important things to know about doing your job

Writing Activity 2 : Quotations

Read the following quotations. Find one that you agree or disagree with, or find one that inspires you in some way. Then write an illustration essay based on the quotation.

> After climbing a great hill, one only finds that there are many more hills to climb.
>
> —Nelson Mandela, former South African president

> Everything has its beauty, but not everyone sees it.
>
> —Confucius, ancient Chinese philosopher and educator

> We are, for all our diversity, a collective, more than we are individuals.
>
> —Aritha Van Herk, Canadian novelist

ILLUSTRATION ESSAY CHECKLIST

As you write your illustration essay, review the essay checklist on the inside front cover. Also, ask yourself the following questions.

- ☐ Does my thesis statement include a topic that I can support with examples?
- ☐ Does my thesis statement make a point about the topic?
- ☐ Do my body paragraphs contain sufficient examples that clearly support the thesis statement?
- ☐ Do I smoothly and logically connect the examples?

PARAGRAPH LINK

For more information about narrative writing, refer to Chapter 5, "Narration."

Watch the Video
Essay Development: Narrating
MyWritingLab

The Narrative Essay

When you write a narrative essay, you tell a story about what happened, and you generally explain events in the order in which they occurred.

There are two main types of narrative writing. In **first-person narration,** you describe a personal experience using *I* or *we*. In **third-person narration,** you describe what happened to somebody else, and you use *he*, *she*, or *they*.

The Thesis Statement

The thesis statement controls the direction of the body paragraphs. To create a meaningful thesis statement for a narrative essay, you could ask yourself what you learned, how you changed, or how the event is important.

controlling idea — topic

Something wonderful happened (controlling idea) **that summer I turned fifteen.** (topic)

The Supporting Ideas

Here are some tips to remember as you develop a narrative essay.

- Make sure that your essay has a point. Do not simply recount what happened. Try to indicate why the events are important.

- Organize the events in time order (the order in which they occurred). You could also reverse the order of events by beginning your essay with the outcome of the events and then explaining what happened that led to the outcome.
- Make your narrative essay more interesting by using some descriptive language. For example, you could use images that appeal to the senses.

To be as complete as possible, a good narrative essay should provide answers to most of the following questions.

- *Who* is the essay about?
- *What* happened?
- *When* did it happen?
- *Where* did it happen?
- *Why* did it happen?
- *How* did it happen?

Using Quotations

One effective way to enhance your narrative essay is to use dialogue. Include direct and/or indirect quotations.

A **direct quotation** contains the exact words of an author, and the quotation is set off with quotation marks. When you include the exact words of more than one person, you must start a new paragraph each time the speaker changes.

> Sara looked at me sadly: "Why did you betray me?"
>
> "I didn't mean to do it," I answered.
>
> She looked down at her hands and said, "I don't think I can ever forgive you."

An **indirect quotation** keeps the author's meaning but is not set off by quotation marks.

> Sara asked why I had betrayed her.

GRAMMAR LINK

For information about punctuating quotations, see Chapter 34.

Watch the **Video**
Quotation Marks
MyWritingLab

A Narrative Essay Plan

Read the next essay plan, and answer the questions that follow.

Introduction
Thesis statement: Stephen Glass, a promising young writer in Washington, D.C., shocked the world of journalism with his fabricated stories.

I. After his first small falsehood, his lying escalated.
   A. He invented a quotation in 1995.
   B. He invented sources to back up his stories.
   C. He knew about fact checkers, so he created false memos, meeting notes, etc.
   D. Soon entire stories were filled with lies.

II. Glass's career came to a crashing end.
  A. *Forbes* magazine wanted to follow up a Glass story about hackers.
  B. Glass was unable to produce documents about sources.
  C. Glass invented more lies to cover up his initial lies.
  D. Realizing Glass was unethical, the editor of the *New Republic* fired him in 1998.

III. The Glass scandal erupted, shocking publishers and readers.
  A. The story became front-page news.
  B. His editor's competency was questioned.
  C. Fact checkers were exposed as not being thorough enough.
  D. Readers wondered if journalists could be trusted.

Conclusion: The world of journalism is still recovering from the Glass scandal.

PRACTICE 2

1. Who is this essay plan about? ______________________
2. What happened? ______________________
3. When and where did this happen? ______________________
4. What type of narration is this? Circle the better answer.
   a. First person   b. Third person

A Narrative Essay

In the next essay, Jeff Kemp recounts what happened during his early years as a professional football player. Read the essay and answer the questions.

A Lesson in Humility

expediency: convenience; self-interest

1 We live in an age when, too often, rules are scorned, values are turned upside down, principles are replaced by **expediency,** and character is sacrificed for popularity. Individual athletes are sometimes the worst offenders, but not as often as one might think. In fact, sports teach important moral lessons that athletes can apply on and off the playing field.

designated: selected

2 Many people dream of being a professional athlete. For me, the dream seemed to be within reach because my father, Jack Kemp, an outstanding quarterback, played for the American Football League's Buffalo Bills (prior to the AFL's 1970 merger with the National Football League). The trouble was, I was not very good! I was a third-string football player through most of junior high and high school and for two years at Dartmouth College. I was not anyone's idea of a "hot prospect." After graduation, I was passed over by NFL scouts. When I was finally asked to join the Los Angeles Rams in 1981 as a free agent, I was **designated** as fifth-string quarterback.

3 It was a 50-to-1 shot that I would survive training camp. Rookies were the only players required to show up for the first week of camp. There were dozens competing for the few spots open on the team. After two days, a young boy approached me as I was walking off the field. He asked if he could carry my helmet to the locker room. It was a long way, but I said, "Sure, I think you can handle that." The next morning, he showed up before practice and offered

to carry my helmet and shoulder pads, and he was there again after practice offering the same service. So it went for the rest of the week.

4 On the last day, as we were departing the field, my young assistant said, "Jeff, can I ask you a question?" (We were on a first-name basis by then.)

5 I thought, "This is my first fan! He is going to ask me for an autograph."

6 He then inquired, "When do the good football players come to camp?" Right then and there, I learned a lesson in humility from a seven-year-old boy.

7 In my first three NFL seasons, I was forced to learn the same lesson over and over again. During that time, I threw just 31 passes. Nevertheless, by 1984, I had managed to outlast the five NFL quarterbacks who had been ahead of me. With the Rams' record standing at 1–2, I took over for injured quarterback Vince Ferragamo and earned my first start against the Cincinnati Bengals, eventually leading the Rams to nine more victories and a playoff berth.

8 The next season, I returned to the bench as a backup quarterback. Humility, I was compelled to remind myself, was a good thing. It helped me appreciate what I had and avoid dwelling on what I did not have. It prevented complaining, which drains the spirit and unity of any group. It also led me to persevere and be ready whenever opportunity presented itself.

PRACTICE 3

1. What type of narration is this text? Circle the better answer.
   a. First person b. Third person
2. Underline the thesis statement of the essay.
3. What introduction style does Kemp use? Circle the best answer.
   a. Definition b. Anecdote
   c. General information d. Historical information
4. List the main events that Kemp recounts in his essay.

   ____
   ____
   ____
   ____
   ____
   ____
   ____
5. What organizational method does Kemp use? Circle the best answer.
   a. Time order b. Space order c. Emphatic order
6. Write down one example of an indirect quotation from the essay.

   ____
7. Write down one example of a direct quotation from the essay.

   ____

8. Narrative writers do more than simply list a series of events. Kemp explains why the events were meaningful. What did Kemp learn?

____

____

PARAGRAPH LINK

To practise narrative writing, you could develop an essay about one of the topics found in Chapter 5, "Narration."

Watch the **Video**
Paragraph Development: Narration
MyWritingLab

The Writer's Room

Writing Activity 1 : Topics

Write a narrative essay about one of the following topics.

General Topics

1. A family legend
2. An illuminating moment
3. A poor financial decision
4. An important event in the world
5. When you learned to do something new

College- and Work-Related Topics

6. Life lessons that college teaches you
7. What your previous job taught you
8. Your best or worst job
9. Your first job
10. A scandal at work or college

Writing Activity 2 : Quotations

Read the following quotations. Find one that you agree or disagree with, or find one that inspires you in some way. Then write a narrative essay based on the quotation.

> When your mouth stumbles, it's worse than feet.
>
> —Oji proverb

> Those who cannot remember the past are condemned to repeat it.
>
> —George Santayana, Spanish poet and philosopher

> The suburbs are full of heroes.
>
> —Camilla Gibb, Canadian novelist

NARRATIVE ESSAY CHECKLIST

As you write your narrative essay, review the essay checklist on the inside front cover. Also, ask yourself the following questions.

- ☐ Does my thesis statement clearly express the topic of the narration, and does it make a point about that topic?
- ☐ Does my essay answer most of the following questions: *who*, *what*, *when*, *where*, *why*, *how*?
- ☐ Do I use transitional expressions that help clarify the order of events?
- ☐ Do I include details to make my narration more interesting?

The Descriptive Essay

When writing a descriptive essay, use words to create a vivid impression of a subject. Use details that appeal to the five senses: sight, smell, hearing, taste, and touch. You want your readers to be able to imagine all that you are describing.

PARAGRAPH LINK

For more information about descriptive writing, refer to Chapter 6, "Description."

The Thesis Statement

In a descriptive essay, the thesis statement includes what you are describing and makes a point about the topic.

Watch the **Video** Essay Development: Descriptive; Paragraph Development: Describing **MyWritingLab**

topic / controlling idea

Walking down the streets of Vancouver, I was filled with a sense of wonder.

The Supporting Ideas

When you develop your descriptive essay, make sure it gives a **dominant impression.** The dominant impression is the overall feeling that you wish to convey. For example, the essay could convey an impression of tension, joy, nervousness, or anger.

You can place the details of a descriptive essay in space order, time order, or emphatic order. The order that you use depends on the topic of your essay. For example, if you describe a place, you can use space order, and if you describe a difficult moment, you can use time order.

Using Figurative Devices

When writing a descriptive essay, you can use figurative devices such as simile, metaphor, and personification. These devices use comparisons and images to add vivid details to your writing.

- A **simile** is a comparison using *like* or *as*.

  Character, like a photograph, develops in darkness. —Yousuf Karsh

- A **metaphor** is a comparison that does not use *like* or *as*.

  The mind is a battlefield.

- **Personification** is the act of attributing human qualities to an inanimate object or animal.

  The wind kicked the leaves. —Kurt Vonnegut, Jr., "Next Door"

  The sauce hissed on the stove.

PRACTICE 4

Practise using figurative language. Use one of the following to describe each item: simile, metaphor, or personification. If you are comparing two things, try to use an unusual comparison.

EXAMPLE:

Surprising: *Her sudden appearance was as surprising as a 4 a.m. phone call. (simile)*

1. Truck: ____________________
2. Road: ____________________
3. Crowd: ____________________
4. Annoying: ____________________
5. Relaxed: ____________________

A Descriptive Essay Plan

Read the next essay plan, and answer the questions that follow.

Introduction
Thesis statement: Walking down the streets of Vancouver, tourists are filled with a sense of wonder.

I. Granville Street buzzes with bright lights, bustling crowds, and eclectic sounds.
   A. The lights on the billboards glow.
   B. There are bars on every corner.
   C. The streets are filled with the chatter of many different languages.
   D. The smell of hotdogs fills the air.

II. Stanley Park is an oasis on the border of downtown Vancouver.
   A. The skaters and cyclists pass by on the bicycle paths.
   B. The rickshaw drivers wait for passengers.
   C. The air tastes salty near the seawall.
   D. The saxophonist, the mime, and the living statues ply their trades.

III. English Bay, in the west of the city, is impressive.
   A. Visitors hear the roar of the waves crashing.
   B. The chilly wind whips people's faces.
   C. The Rocky Mountains stand tall in the distance.
   D. The shouts of the vendors fill the air.

Conclusion: "There is a legend that when the good people of Toronto die they go to Vancouver. 'Retiring to the west coast,' they call it, to this spawn of mountain and sea, home of the world's heaviest dew—our Vancouver" (Eric Nicol, "First Province on the Left (Vancouver Explained)" by Eric Nicol in *Vancouver: Soul of a City* (edited and with an introduction by Gary Geddes).

PRACTICE 5

1. This essay plan contains imagery that appeals to the senses. Find one example of imagery for each sense.
   a. Sight: ____________________
   b. Sound: ____________________

c. Smell: ______________________________

d. Taste: ______________________________

e. Touch: ______________________________

2. Which type of imagery is most prevalent? ______________________

3. What is the dominant impression of this essay? Circle the best answer.

a. Desire b. Suspicion c. Joy and awe d. Sadness

Writing Activity 1 : Topics

Write a descriptive essay about one of the following topics.

PARAGRAPH LINK

To practise descriptive writing, you could develop an essay about one of the topics in Chapter 6, "Description."

General Topics

1. A celebration
2. A painting or photograph
3. A shopping area
4. A physical and psychological self-portrait
5. A train or bus station or a hospital waiting room

College- and Work-Related Topics

6. Your first impressions of college
7. A gymnasium
8. Your college or workplace cafeteria or food court
9. A memorable person with whom you have worked
10. A pleasant or unpleasant task

Writing Activity 2 : Quotations

Read the following quotations. Find one that you agree or disagree with, or find one that inspires you in some way. Then write a descriptive essay based on the quotation.

> The real voyage of discovery consists not in seeking new landscapes but in having new eyes.
>
> —Marcel Proust, French author

> There is no need to go to India or anywhere else to find peace. You will find that deep place of silence right in your room, your garden, or even your bathtub.
>
> —Elisabeth Kubler-Ross, Swiss author

> Compassion is an act of imagination; a leap of faith into another's closed circle.
>
> —Ann Marie MacDonald, Canadian writer and actor

> Iron rusts from disuse, and stagnant water loses its purity and in cold weather becomes frozen; even so does inaction sap the vigor of the mind.
>
> —Leonardo Da Vinci, Italian artist and inventor

DESCRIPTIVE ESSAY CHECKLIST

As you write your descriptive essay, review the essay checklist on the inside front cover. Also, ask yourself the following questions.

- ☐ Does my thesis statement clearly show what I will describe in the rest of the essay?
- ☐ Does my thesis statement make a point about the topic?
- ☐ Does my essay have a dominant impression?
- ☐ Does each body paragraph contain supporting details that appear to the reader's senses?
- ☐ Do I use figurative language (simile, metaphor, or personification)?

PARAGRAPH LINK

For more information about process writing, refer to Chapter 7, "Process."

Watch the **Video**
Essay Development: Process Analysis; Paragraph Development: Process
MyWritingLab

The Process Essay

A **process** is a series of steps done in chronological order. When you write a process essay, you explain how to do something, how something happens, or how something works. There are two main types of process essays.

1. **Complete a process.** Explain how to complete a particular task. For example, you might explain how to create a sculpture or how to give first aid to a choking victim. Each step you describe helps the reader complete the process.
2. **Understand a process.** Explain how something works or how something happens. In other words, the goal is to help the reader understand a process rather than do a process. For example, you might explain how a law is passed or explain how a previous war began.

The Thesis Statement

The thesis statement in a process essay includes the process you are describing and a controlling idea. In the introduction of a process essay, you should also mention any tools or supplies that the reader would need to complete the process.

topic / controlling idea

Choosing a college requires some careful thinking and planning.

topic / controlling idea

Pregnancy consists of several stages.

List Specific Steps

You can write a thesis statement that contains a map, or guide, to the details that you will present in your essay. To guide your readers, you could mention the main steps in your thesis statement.

topic / controlling idea

It is possible to quit smoking if you focus on your goal, find alternative relaxing activities, and enlist the support of friends and family.

The Supporting Ideas

The body paragraphs in a process essay should explain the steps in the process. Each body paragraph should include details and examples to explain each step.

Using Commands

When writing an essay to help readers complete a process, you can use commands when you explain each step in the process. It is not necessary to write *You should.*

command
First, **introduce** yourself to your roommate.

command
Ask your roommate about his or her pet peeves.

A Process Essay Plan

Read the next essay plan, and answer the questions that follow.

Introduction
Thesis statement: By introducing yourself, joining groups, and organizing events, you will have a better chance of making friends in a new neighbourhood.

I. Introduce yourself to your neighbours.
  A. Find a good moment.
  B. Explain that you are new to the neighbourhood.
  C. Ask a few questions about the area.

II. Have an outdoor party and invite your neighbours.
  A. Find a pretext (holiday, birthday).
  B. Keep the party casual (the point is to have a relaxing time).
  C. Do not worry if some neighbours turn you down.
  D. Aim to find at least one good friend in your area.

III. Get involved in your community.
  A. Volunteer to work at the library.
  B. Become politically active in local elections.

Conclusion: With a bit of effort, you can make friends in any neighbourhood.

PRACTICE 6

1. What kind of process essay is this? Circle the better answer.
   a. Complete a process   b. Understand a process
2. Add another supporting idea to body paragraph 3.

   ____

   ____

3. What organizational method does the writer use? Circle the best answer.

   a. Time   b. Space   c. Emphatic

A Process Essay

In the following essay, Jake Sibley, a musician who maintains an online music site, explains how to become a successful musician. Read the essay and answer the questions.

Steps to Music Success

endeavor: attempt

vital: extremely important

ogling: staring at with desire

1 Before you can achieve anything, you must first imagine it. If you are serious about becoming a successful musician, it will serve you well to look not only at the next step, but also to look down the road to where you ultimately want to be. There is no question that regularly revisiting the fundamentals is critical to success in any long-term **endeavor.** With that in mind, there are some basic things to consider while pursuing your musical dreams.

2 First, setting specific goals and giving them regular attention is **vital** to achieving success at any level in the music business. Goals give direction to your action. Furthermore, achieving goals is a tasty reward that will build your esteem and motivate you to reach even higher. So pick your endpoint, and then write down the steps to get there. If you are just beginning in music, then resolve to take lessons. If you are taking lessons, then resolve to get in a performing band. If you are already performing, then resolve to join a paid project. There is no obstacle that can prevent you from reaching your dream. You just have to plan it and then do it.

3 It is also important to spend time, not money, on your dream. Most likely you have seen rookie musicians with stacks of absurdly expensive gear. Certainly I am guilty of walking into a music store and **ogling** the top-end instruments, convinced that if I could afford that equipment, my sound would improve by leaps and bounds: "If I had that guitar, I would practice *every day.*" If you are not practicing every day already, a new guitar won't change that. The only investment that will improve your success as a musician is *time*—time spent practicing, time spent learning, and time spent pursuing your goals. The lure of expensive gear is a tempting but false road to better musicianship.

4 Furthermore, if you really want to improve, play with others. Music is a form of conversation between human beings. It may well be the oldest language, used for millennia by musically inclined people to jointly convey their own rage, sorrow, hope, and joy to other human beings. Learning music without this community is as futile as learning to play football by yourself. Although hours spent alone with your instrument are certainly necessary for success, engaging in musical conversations and performances is an equally vital element to your progress. A very common weakness among amateur musicians is their inability to make music with other artists—a flaw that can be easily remedied with experience. Even if you are a beginner, get out and play with others and stage a few performances if you can. Without even realizing it, you will begin to assimilate fundamental lessons about listening, interacting, and performing in a live setting that are critical to your future success.

5 Finally, practice, practice, practice! There is simply no other way to ensure your own progress as a musician. Have you been spending hours on the Internet, combing for information on how to market your music, or cheaply record a CD, or win a music competition? That's great, but have you been

spending as least as much time alone with your instrument? If not, you should reconsider your priorities. If you are not practicing several times a week at least, the music you market, or record cheaply, or submit to a competition is not going to get very far. As a musician seeking success at any level, practicing your instrument should be your number-one priority.

6 If you're serious about music, keep focused on your goal. Take the time to learn your craft, and share your gift with others. Do not let anyone else hold you back from what you know you can achieve.

PRACTICE 7

1. Underline the thesis statement of the essay.
2. What type of process essay is this? Circle the better answer.
   a. Complete a process   b. Understand a process
3. In process essays, the support is generally a series of steps. List the steps to music success.

   ____

   ____

   ____

   ____

   ____

4. What organizational method does the author use?
   a. Time order   b. Emphatic order   c. Space order
5. Circle the transitional expressions that Sibley uses to introduce each new paragraph.
6. In which paragraph does Sibley use an anecdote to support his point?

   ____

7. Who is the audience for this essay? ____________________
8. How could this essay have relevance for people who never play music?

   ____

   ____

Writing Activity 1: Topics

Write a process essay about one of the following topics.

PARAGRAPH LINK

To practise process writing, you could develop an essay about one of the topics in Chapter 7, "Process."

Watch the Video
Paragraph Development: Process
MyWritingLab

General Topics

1. How to be a good person
2. How to kick a bad habit
3. How someone became famous
4. How something works
5. How to deal with a problematic teenager

College- and Work-Related Topics

6. How to manage your time
7. How education changed somebody's life
8. How to do your job
9. How to be a better student
10. How to find satisfaction in your work life

Writing Activity 2: Quotations

Read the following quotations. Find one that you agree or disagree with, or find one that inspires you in some way. Then write a process essay based on the quotation.

> Treat the earth well. It was not given to you by your parents; it was loaned to you by your children.
>
> —Native American proverb

> Know how to listen, and you will profit even from those who talk badly.
>
> —Plutarch, ancient Greek philosopher

> Every child is an artist. The problem is how to remain an artist once he [or she] grows up.
>
> —Pablo Picasso, Spanish artist

> If you can spend a perfectly useless afternoon in a perfectly useless manner, you have learned how to live.
>
> —Lin Yutang, Chinese author

PROCESS ESSAY CHECKLIST

As you write your process essay, review the essay checklist on the inside front cover. Also, ask yourself the following questions.

- ☐ Does my thesis statement make a point about the process?
- ☐ Does my essay explain how to do something, how something works, or how something happened?
- ☐ Do I include all of the steps in the process?
- ☐ Do I clearly explain the steps in the process or in the event?
- ☐ Do I mention the tools or equipment that my readers need to complete or understand the process?

The Definition Essay

A definition tells you what something means. When you write a **definition essay,** you give your personal definition of a term or concept. Although you can define most terms in a few sentences, you may need to offer extended definitions for words that are particularly complex. For example, you could write an essay or even an entire book about the term *love.* The way that you interpret love is unique, and you would bring your own opinions, experiences, and impressions to your definition essay.

PARAGRAPH LINK

For more information about definition writing, refer to Chapter 8, "Definition."

Watch the **Video**
Essay Development: Definition; Paragraph Development: Definition
MyWritingLab

The Thesis Statement

In your thesis statement, indicate what you are defining, and include a definition of the term. Look at the three ways you might define a term in your thesis statement.

1. **Definition by synonym.** You could give a synonym for the term.

   term + synonym
   Some consumers insist that Frankenfood, or genetically modified food, be labelled.

2. **Definition by category.** Decide what larger group the term belongs to, and then determine the unique characteristics that set the term apart from others in that category.

   term + category + detail
   A groupie is a fanatical devotee of a musician or band.

3. **Definition by negation.** Explain what the term is not, and then explain what it is.

   term + what it is not + what it is
   Stalkers are not misguided romantics; they are dangerous predators.

The Supporting Ideas

In a definition essay, you can support your main point using a variety of writing patterns. For example, in a definition essay about democracy, one supporting paragraph could give historical background about democracy, another could include a description of a functioning democracy, and a third could compare different styles of democracy. The different writing patterns would all support the overriding pattern, which is definition.

Enhancing a Definition

One way to enhance a definition essay is to begin with a provocative statement about the term. Then, in the body of your essay, develop your definition more thoroughly. This technique arouses the interest of the readers and makes them want to continue reading. For example, the next statement questions a common belief.

According to Dr. W. Roland, attention deficit disorder is an invented disease.

A Definition Essay Plan

Read the next essay plan, and answer the questions that follow.

Introduction
Thesis statement: Depression is not just the blues; it is a serious health problem.

I. A depressed person cannot just "snap out of it."
   A. Depression is not a sign of self-indulgence.
   B. Some people battle the illness for years and need specific treatment.
   C. Offer the example of Katie Rowen, who has been hospitalized several times.
   D. Include quotations from people suffering from depression: William Styron says, "Nightfall seemed more sombre"; Mike Wallace calls it "endless darkness."

II. Symptoms are not always obvious and can be overlooked.
   A. People feel excess fatigue and lack of energy.
   B. They may have unexplained bouts of sadness.
   C. Another symptom is extreme irritability for no obvious reason.
   D. Academic and work performance may suffer.

III. Depression has impacts on a person's physical and emotional life.
   A. A person may neglect nutrition, leading to excess weight gain or weight loss.
   B. He or she may neglect appearance and hygiene.
   C. He or she may alienate family and co-workers.
   D. A depressed person may suffer job loss, leading to financial consequences.

Conclusion: Depression is a serious illness that affects many people in our society.

PRACTICE 8

1. What type of definition does the writer use in the thesis statement? Circle the best answer.
   a. Definition by synonym   b. Definition by category
   c. Definition by negation

2. The writer uses many types of supporting details. Underline a quotation, and circle an anecdote.

3. What organizational strategy does the writer use? Circle the best answer.
   a. Time order   b. Emphatic order   c. Space order

A Definition Essay

In the next essay, student writer Diego Pelaez defines a sports fanatic. Read the essay and answer the questions.

Sports Fanatics

1 The opposing team's greatest player received the ball with time running low. His team down a point, he went to work on his defender. Faking a rush to the basket, he stepped back and rose for the deciding jump shot of the game. He released the ball with a good arc, and sure enough, it found its target, winning the game and the championship. I watched silently and shared the sorrow of my team—the losing team—for I am a sports fanatic. When a beloved team loses, the true sports fanatic feels like he or she has been through a personal tragedy. For sports fanatics, the game is not just a game; it is one of life's most significant events.

2 Sports fanatics never hesitate to show devotion to the team, for devotion is what separates a true sports fanatic from the average, casual sports fan. The casual fan may express **complacency** when the team loses. A sports fanatic feels each defeat with stretches of sorrow and answers each victory with **jubilation.** When my team lost that championship game, I was **despondent** for over a week. I kept going over the game in my head, imagining what might have happened had the game ended a few seconds earlier.

complacency: contentment

jubilation: extreme joy

despondent: miserable

3 Statistics are a vital part to the full understanding of any sport, and sports fanatics know this fact. Fanatics learn everything that they can about the game. They can usually rattle off at least a few statistics that can make regular people question the fanatics' use of their spare time. Yet despite the opinions of others, true sports fans wear their ability to memorize statistics as a badge of honour and as proof of their undying dedication. For example, when I meet a fellow fanatic, I excitedly recite numbers, names, and dates, often competing to show that I have amassed more information about my favourite sport than others.

4 True sports fanatics are not crazy; they simply have an **avid** fantasy life. Millions of kids imitate Wes Cates or Michael Jordan, dreaming of becoming a major leaguer. Even if the sports fanatic is a poor player, he or she has usually played the game in order to fully understand the sport. In essence, the thrill of the sports fanatic is to **live vicariously** through the people talented enough to achieve the fanatic's childhood dreams. I spend many pleasurable moments imagining that I can hear the roar of the crowd when I make that winning jump shot.

avid: full, enthusiastic

live vicariously: to imagine participating in someone else's experience

5 The sports fanatic is a hard creature to understand. Others may wonder why die-hard fans care so much about sports. The point is, fanatics have a purpose in life: they truly care about something, and they express their devotion wholeheartedly. Some of the greatest athletes are sports fanatics too. Growing up, Michael Jordan was passionate about baseball and basketball. Wayne Gretzky spent his childhood absorbing everything that he could about hockey. So instead of regarding sports fanatics as crazy, people should commend them for their commitment and love of the game.

PRACTICE 9

1. Underline the thesis statement of the essay.
2. What introduction style does the writer use? Circle the best answer.
   a. Anecdote   b. Historical information   c. Shocking statement
3. In paragraph 2, the writer compares a fanatic with a casual fan. What is the main difference between the two?

___

___

4. Using your own words, list the main supporting ideas in this essay.
   a. ______________________________
   b. ______________________________
   c. ______________________________
5. Underline an example of definition by negation in the body of the essay.
6. What method does the writer use to end this essay? Circle the best answer.
   a. Quotation   b. Suggestion   c. Prediction

The Writer's Room

PARAGRAPH LINK

To practise definition writing, you could develop an essay about one of the topics found in Chapter 8, "Definition."

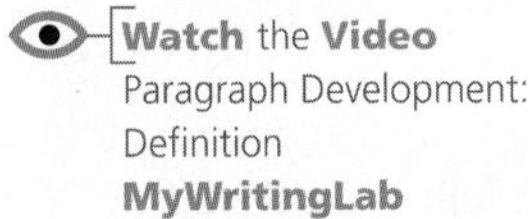

Writing Activity 1: Topics

Write a definition essay about one of the following topics.

General Topics

1. Propaganda
2. A pacifist
3. Street smarts
4. A control freak
5. Our disposable culture

College- and Work-Related Topics

6. A perfectionist
7. A whistle-blower
8. An ineffective boss
9. A conspiracy theory
10. Downsizing

Writing Activity 2: Quotations

Read the following quotations. Find one that you agree or disagree with, or find one that inspires you in some way. Then use it as the basis for a definition essay.

> Rebelling against social control is what youth does.
>
> —Judy Rebick, Canadian journalist and political activist

> Nothing in life makes you feel more in control than having choices.
>
> —Gail Vaz-Oxlade, financial writer

> A leader who does not hesitate before he sends his nation into battle is not fit to be a leader.
>
> —Golda Meir, former Israeli prime minister

> A house is more than the sum of its beams and planks and two-by-fours and wires snaking through the walls.
>
> —Diana Hartog, Canadian poet and novelist

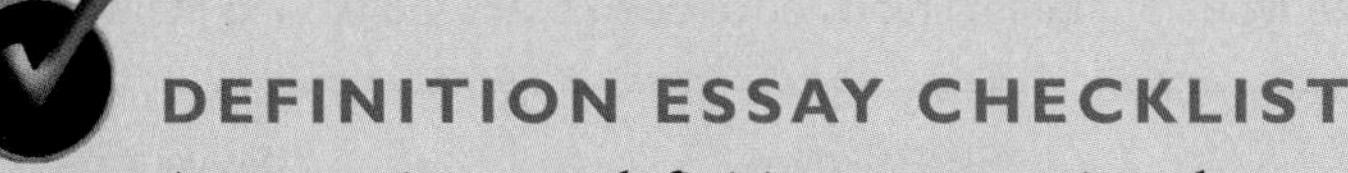

DEFINITION ESSAY CHECKLIST

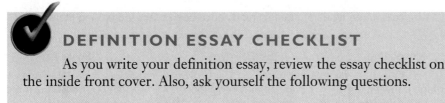

As you write your definition essay, review the essay checklist on the inside front cover. Also, ask yourself the following questions.

- Does my thesis statement explain what term I am defining?
- Does each topic sentence clearly show some aspect of the definition?
- Do my supporting paragraphs include examples that help illustrate the definition?
- Do I use concise language in my definition?

The Classification Essay

Classifying means "to sort a subject into more understandable categories." When you are planning a classification essay, find a topic that you can divide into categories. Each of the categories must be part of a larger group, yet it must also be distinct. For example, if your essay is about types of lawyers, you might sort them into criminal lawyers, divorce lawyers, and corporate lawyers.

PARAGRAPH LINK

For more information about classification writing, refer to Chapter 9, "Classification."

The Thesis Statement

The thesis statement in a classification essay mentions the categories of the subject and contains a controlling idea. In this type of essay, the controlling idea is your classification principle, which is the overall method that you use to sort the items. For example, if your essay topic is "crime," you might sort crime according to types of criminals, categories of violent crimes, or categories of bank-machine crimes.

Watch the Video
Essay Development: Division/Classification; Paragraph Development: Division/Classification
MyWritingLab

controlling idea (classification principle) — topic — categories

There are three very effective types of **bank-machine crimes**: no-tech, low-tech, and high-tech.

List Specific Categories

You can guide your reader by listing the specific categories you will cover in your thesis statement.

topic — controlling idea

Children learn gender roles through the family, the school, and the media.

The Supporting Ideas

In a classification essay, each body paragraph covers one category. To organize your categories and supporting details, you can use a classification chart or a more traditional classification essay plan.

A Classification Chart

A classification chart helps you plan your ideas by providing a visual representation of how you wish to classify a subject. In this sample chart, the thesis statement appears at the top, and all of the categories branch from it.

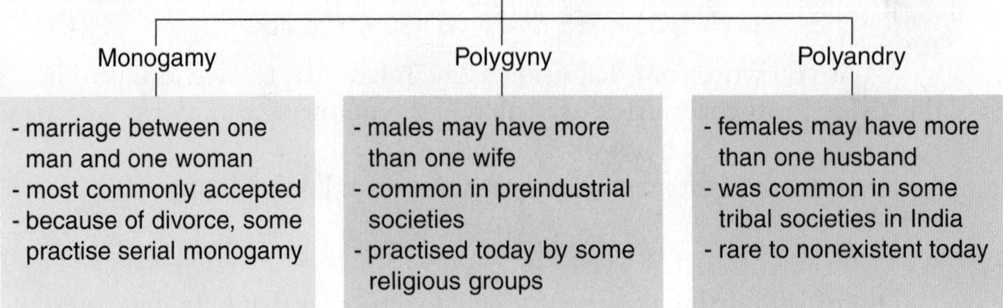

Historically, three types of marital unions have been practised around the world.
Monogamy
Polygyny
Polyandry
- marriage between one man and one woman
- most commonly accepted
- because of divorce, some practise serial monogamy
- males may have more than one wife
- common in preindustrial societies
- practised today by some religious groups
- females may have more than one husband
- was common in some tribal societies in India
- rare to nonexistent today

A Classification Essay Plan

A classification essay plan also helps you organize your essay's categories and details. Read the following essay plan and answer the questions.

Introduction
Thesis statement: There are three main types of bad jokes: overused children's jokes, practical jokes, and insulting jokes.

I. Overused children's jokes bore the listener.
   A. Knock-knock jokes are dull.
   B. The "what is it" jokes are overused.
   C. Nobody likes "Why did the chicken cross the road?" jokes.
   D. Silly riddles are boring.

II. Practical jokes humiliate the victims.
   A. Whoopee cushions can embarrass people.
   B. The plastic wrap on the toilet seat leads to a humiliating mess.
   C. The "paint can over the door" trick can hurt others.
   D. The "kick me" note on a person's back is not funny.

III. Insulting jokes can seriously hurt or offend others.
   A. Jokes about ethnic groups or religious groups can be awful.
   B. Cruel jokes about a person's appearance (big nose jokes, blond jokes) can be hurtful.
   C. Jokes about a profession (lawyer jokes) can insult professionals.

Conclusion: Let's hope that people come up with better jokes.

PRACTICE 10

1. What is the classification principle? That is, what main principle unifies the three categories?

   ____

2. Why is each type of joke considered bad? Underline the reason in each topic sentence.
3. The author organizes the main ideas in emphatic order. How are they arranged? Circle the better answer.

   a. From most to least offensive b. From least to most offensive

4. How does the writer support the main ideas? Circle the best answer.

   a. Examples b. Anecdotes c. Statistics

A Classification Essay

Read the next essay by Saundra Ciccarelli, which is from her textbook *Psychology*.

Phobias

1 Anxiety can take very specific forms. There's a difference between anxiety that is realistic and has a known source and the kind of anxiety found in disorders. If final exams are coming up and a student hasn't studied enough, that student's anxiety is understandable and realistic. But if a student who has studied, has done well on all the exams, and is very prepared still worries excessively, that student is showing an unrealistic amount of anxiety. One of the more specific anxiety disorders is a phobia, an irrational, persistent fear of something. Irrational anxieties, or phobias, come in three categories.

2 Social phobias involve a fear of interacting with others or being in a social situation. People with a social phobia are afraid of being evaluated in some negative way by others, so they tend to avoid situations that could lead to something embarrassing or humiliating. They are very self-conscious as a result. Common types of social phobia are stage fright, fear of public speaking, and fear of urinating in a public restroom. Not surprisingly, people with social phobias often have a history of being shy as children.

3 A specific phobia is an irrational fear of some object or specific situation, such as a fear of darkness or a fear of being enclosed in a small space (claustrophobia). Other specific phobias include a fear of injections, a fear of dental work, a fear of blood, and a fear of heights. Many people experience a fear of specific animals such as a fear of dogs, snakes, or spiders. Mysophobia is a fear of germs, and pyrophobia is a fear of fire.

4 A third type of phobia is agoraphobia, a Greek name that literally means "fear of the marketplace." Although that makes it sound like a social phobia, agoraphobia is a little more complicated. It is actually the fear of being in a place or situation (social or not) from which escape is difficult or impossible if something should go wrong. So agoraphobics are often afraid of not only crowds but also crossing bridges, traveling in a car or plane, eating in restaurants, and sometimes even of leaving the house. To be in any of these situations or to even think about being in such situations can lead to extreme feelings of anxiety and even panic attacks.

5 People with specific phobias can usually avoid the object or situation without too much difficulty, and people with social phobias may simply avoid jobs and situations that involve meeting people face-to-face. But people with agoraphobia cannot avoid their phobia's source because it is simply being outside in the real world. A severe case of agoraphobia can make a person's home a prison, leaving the person trapped inside unable to go to work, shop, or engage in any kind of activity that requires going out of the home.

PRACTICE 11

1. What is the essay's classification principle? ____________________

    ____

2. What are the three main categories? ____________________

    ____

3. Underline the topic sentences in body paragraphs 2, 3, and 4.
4. Do the categories overlap? Explain your answer. ____________________
____
____
5. To better understand how the author organizes this essay, make a classification chart. Write the categories on the lines and examples in the boxes. Use your own words to explain each category.

Types of Phobias

______________ ______________ ______________

6. What is the author's point in the conclusion? ____________________
____
____

The Writer's Room

PARAGRAPH LINK

To practise classification writing, you could develop an essay about one of the topics found in Chapter 9, "Classification."

Watch the **Video**
Paragraph Development: Division/Classification
MyWritingLab

Writing Activity 1: Topics

Write a classification essay about one of the following topics.

General Topics	College- and Work-Related Topics
1. Addictions	7. Annoying customers or clients
2. Marriage ceremonies	8. Competition
3. Extreme sports	9. Success
4. Things that cause allergic reactions	10. Fashions in the workplace
5. Youth subcultures	
6. Punishment	

Writing Activity 2: Quotations

Read the following quotations. Find one that you agree or disagree with, or find one that inspires you in some way. Then write a classification essay based on the quotation.

Work saves us from three great evils: boredom, vice, and need.

—Voltaire, French author and philosopher

There are three kinds of lies: lies, damned lies, and statistics.

—Benjamin Disraeli, British politician

There appears to be three types of politicians: leaders, lobbyists, and professionals.

—R. Ravimohan, Indian journalist

We peer so suspiciously at each other that we cannot see that we Canadians are standing on the mountaintop of human wealth, freedom and privilege.

—Pierre Elliott Trudeau

CLASSIFICATION ESSAY CHECKLIST

As you write your classification essay, review the essay checklist on the inside front cover. Also, ask yourself the following questions.

- ☐ Do I clearly identify which categories I will discuss in my thesis statement?
- ☐ Do I use a common classification principle to unite the various items?
- ☐ Do I include categories that do not overlap?
- ☐ Do I clearly explain one of the categories in each body paragraph?
- ☐ Do I use sufficient details to explain each category?
- ☐ Do I arrange the categories in a logical manner?

The Comparison and Contrast Essay

You **compare** when you want to find similarities and **contrast** when you want to find differences. When writing a comparison and contrast essay, you explain how people, places, things, or ideas are the same or different to prove a specific point.

Before you write, you must make a decision about whether you will focus on similarities, differences, or both. As you explore your topic, make a list of both similarities and differences. Later, you can use some of the ideas in your essay plan.

PARAGRAPH LINK

For more information about this pattern, refer to Chapter 10, "Comparison and Contrast."

Watch the **Video**
Essay Development: Comparing and Contrasting; Paragraph Development: Comparing and Contrasting
MyWritingLab

The Thesis Statement

The thesis statement in a comparison and contrast essay indicates if you are making comparisons, contrasts, or both. When you write a thesis statement, indicate what you are comparing or contrasting and the controlling idea.

Although neat people have a very nice environment, messy people are more relaxed.

Topics being contrasted: Neat people and messy people

Controlling idea: Messy people are more relaxed.

Alice's daughter wants to be her own person, but she is basically very similar to her mother.

Topics being compared: Mother and daughter

Controlling idea: Very similar personalities

The Supporting Ideas

In a comparison and contrast essay, you can develop your body paragraphs in two different ways.

1. In a **point-by-point** development, you present *one* point about topic A and then *one* point about topic B. You keep following this pattern until you have a few points for each topic.

   Paragraph 1: topic A, topic B

   Paragraph 2: topic A, topic B

   Paragraph 3: topic A, topic B

2. In a **topic-by-topic** development, you discuss one topic in detail, and then you discuss the other topic in detail.

   Paragraphs 1 and 2: all of topic A

   Paragraphs 3 and 4: all of topic B

A Comparison and Contrast Essay Plan

Read the next essay plan, and answer the questions that follow.

Introduction

Thesis statement: Soccer is a more exciting, active, and popular sport than baseball.

I. Soccer is fast-paced and thrilling to watch, whereas baseball is boring.
   - A. In soccer, fans watch the ball as it gets kicked constantly around the field.
   - B. In soccer, there are very few quiet moments; the game has constant action.
   - C. In baseball, spectators get bored while watching the pitcher think, consider, and eventually pitch.
   - D. Baseball games have very few seconds of excitement because home runs are so rare.

II. Those who play soccer get more exercise than those who play baseball.
   - A. During soccer games, players constantly run to cover the opposing player.
   - B. After games, soccer players are drenched with sweat.
   - C. Baseball players generally stand on bases or in the outfield simply waiting for action.
   - D. When baseball players are at bat, they spend most of their time waiting for their turn.

III. The World Cup is more popular than the World Series.
   A. Soccer is the number one sport in South America, Africa, Asia, and Europe.
   B. According to Japan's Market Monthly, the number of World Cup viewers is about 40 billion.
   C. Baseball is mainly popular in North America and Japan.
   D. During baseball's 2004 World Series, only 25 million people watched the Boston Red Sox beat the St. Louis Cardinals.

Conclusion: Learn about soccer because it is a fantastic sport.

PRACTICE 12

1. The writer compares and contrasts two things in this essay plan. What are they?

   ____

2. Look at the thesis statement. What is the controlling idea?

   ____

3. What will this essay focus on? Circle the better answer.
   a. Similarities   b. Differences
4. What pattern of comparison does the writer use in this essay? Circle the better answer.
   a. Point by point   b. Topic by topic

A Comparison and Contrast Essay

In this essay, writer Christopher Wolf compares how the process of drying clothes differs from east to west in Canada.

Montrealers, Cherish Your Clotheslines

1 Nobody hangs their laundry out to dry in Calgary. In fact, there are hardly any clotheslines. My grandmother's house had one, but I don't think she ever used it. She, like everyone I knew while growing up there, had a washer and dryer set tucked neatly in a musty corner of her basement, across from a half-century-old furnace.

2 It was an eye-opening experience to travel to Newfoundland as a teenager, where I discovered that St. John's was precisely the opposite of Calgary: everyone had clotheslines. Clothes hung over alleyways and backyards, billowing in the salty Atlantic breeze like flags of chores vanquished. There was something inexplicably romantic, something timeless, about clothes drying on lines, whether in the city or in a stark outport on the Avalon Peninsula.

3 Montreal is similar to St. John's, at least in that regard. Here, the clothesline tradition never really died. Although they're less prevalent today than in the past, you'll still see an abundance of them if you wander down the laneways of just about any neighbourhood. Immigrant neighbourhoods in particular have a ton of clotheslines, probably because they're home to so many people who come from countries where drying your clothes outside is

still the norm. I remember, earlier this fall, driving east through St. Michel on the elevated Metropolitan Expressway, staring at long rows of triplexes tied together by strands of billowing clothes.

4 I wouldn't be surprised if that kind of scene became even more common in the future. That's because clotheslines are no longer just quaint—they're fashionable. The growing marketability of anything "green" has led to a resurgence of interest in drying clothes outside. It's cheaper than clothes dryers, which can consume as much as 900 kilowatt hours of energy per year, and better for your clothes. According to La Presse, which extolled the benefits of clotheslines last summer, the sun eliminates odours and removes stains, and is easier on natural fibres than clothes dryers.

5 But, as much as I like to know that the sun can whiten my whites, it's the clothesline aesthetic that really appeals to me. I'm still charmed by the sight of them, which is good because they're ubiquitous in my back alley from March until November. More than that, though, clotheslines domesticate the street. We've spent so much effort over the past half-century trying to sterilize our cities, to turn them into machines, that we need these kinds of reminders that they are, first and foremost, places where people live, messy as that may be.

6 Still, prejudices linger. Many new subdivisions include provisions in house purchase agreements that ban residents from drying their clothes outside. It's a class thing more than anything else, since clotheslines are still associated by many with poverty. There has been a clear shift in attitude, however. Earlier this month, Ontario's environment minister announced that he wants to override those clothesline bans.

7 I'm not alone in enjoying the look of clotheslines, either. There are plenty of Flickr groups dedicated to clotheslines, including one called "Les cordes à linge de Montréal."

PRACTICE 13

1. Underline the thesis statement of the essay.
2. In the thesis statement, what two things does the writer compare?

   ____

3. What does this essay focus on? Circle the better answer.

   a. Similarities b. Differences

4. What pattern of comparison does the writer follow in paragraph 2? Circle the better answer.

   a. Point by point b. Topic by topic

5. Using your own words, list the writer's main supporting points.

   ____

   ____

   ____

6. In the conclusion, how does the quotation support the writer's main point?

____

____

Writing Activity 1: Topics

Write a comparison and contrast essay about one of the following topics.

General Topics

Compare and/or contrast ...

1. A good host and a bad host
2. Expectations about parenthood versus the reality of parenthood
3. Two different interpretations of an event
4. Living together and getting married

College- and Work-Related Topics

Compare and/or contrast ...

5. Male and female college athletes
6. Working with others and working alone
7. A good manager and a bad manager
8. A stay-at-home parent and an employed parent
9. Student life and professional life
10. Expectations about a job and the reality of that job

PARAGRAPH LINK

To practise comparison and contrast writing, you could develop an essay about one of the topics found in Chapter 10, "Comparison and Contrast."

Watch the **Video**
Paragraph Development: Comparing and Contrasting
MyWritingLab

Writing Activity 2: Quotations

Read the following quotations. Find one that you agree or disagree with, or find one that inspires you in some way. Then write a comparison and contrast essay based on the quotation.

> My grandfather once told me that there are two kinds of people: those who work and those who take the credit. He told me to try to be in the first group; there was less competition there.
>
> —Indira Gandhi, Indian politician

> People are more violently opposed to fur than leather because it is safer to harass rich women than motorcycle gangs.
>
> —Unknown

> Happy families are all alike. Every unhappy family is unhappy in its own way.
>
> —Leo Tolstoy, Russian author

> Soups fall into two camps: quick and simple water, veg, cook and hit the table, or classically made with time and love.
>
> — Trish Magwood, Canadian chef and entrepreneur

COMPARISON AND CONTRAST ESSAY CHECKLIST

As you write your comparison and contrast essay, review the essay checklist on the inside front cover. Also, ask yourself the following questions.

- ☐ Does my thesis statement explain what I am comparing or contrasting?
- ☐ Does my thesis statement make a point about my topic?
- ☐ Does my essay focus on either similarities or differences?
- ☐ Does my essay include point-by-point and/or topic-by-topic patterns?
- ☐ Do all of my supporting examples clearly relate to the topics that are being compared or contrasted?
- ☐ Do I use transitions that will help readers follow my ideas?

PARAGRAPH LINK

For more information about this pattern, refer to Chapter 11, "Cause and Effect."

Watch the **Video**
Paragraph Development: Cause and Effect; Essay Development: Cause and Effect
MyWritingLab

The Cause and Effect Essay

When writing a cause and effect essay, you explain why an event happened or what the consequences of such an event were.

The Thesis Statement

The thesis statement in a cause and effect essay contains the topic and the controlling idea. The controlling idea indicates whether the essay will focus on causes, effects, or both.

topic — controlling idea (causes)
Chronic insomnia is caused by many factors.

topic — controlling idea (effects)
Chronic insomnia can have a serious impact on a person's health.

topic — controlling idea (causes and effects)
Chronic insomnia, which is caused by many factors, can have a serious impact on a person's health.

Thinking about Effects

If you are writing about the effects of something, you might think about both the short-term and the long-term effects. By doing so, you will generate more ideas for the body of your essay. You will also be able to structure your essay more effectively by moving from short-term to long-term effects.

For example, look at the short- and long-term effects of a smoke-free work zone.

Short term: Inside air is cleaner.
The smokers get more coffee breaks.

Long term: Fewer smoke-related illnesses occur in nonsmokers.
Some smokers might quit smoking.

The Supporting Ideas

The body paragraphs in a cause and effect essay focus on causes, effects, or both. Make sure that each body paragraph contains specific examples that clarify the cause and/or effect relationship.

A Cause and Effect Essay Plan

Read the next essay plan, and answer the questions that follow.

Introduction

Thesis statement: People become vegetarians for three important reasons.

I. They cannot justify killing something with a nervous system.
   A. They do not want to hurt living creatures.
   B. Animals with a nervous system suffer horribly when they are killed for food.
   C. Methods used in slaughterhouses are inhumane.

II. A vegetarian diet is healthier than a meat-based diet.
   A. In modern agricultural practices, steroids are given to farm animals.
   B. Meat products have higher cholesterol levels than plant and grain products.
   C. Vegetables and beans ensure an adequate supply of nutrients and proteins.

III. A vegetarian diet is inexpensive.
   A. Vegetables are cheaper than meat.
   B. It is cheaper to produce one pound of vegetables than one pound of beef.
   C. People can grow their own vegetables.

Conclusion: A vegetarian diet is a healthy alternative.

PRACTICE 14

1. In the thesis statement, circle the topic and underline the controlling idea.
2. Does this essay focus on causes or effects? ______________________
3. Who is the audience for this essay? ______________________

A Cause and Effect Essay

Read the next essay by Kevin Bousquet (president of Corpa Group Inc., a private investigation and due diligence firm working for the venture capital industry), and then answer the questions that follow.

Why Canadian Businesses Fail

1 What would happen if you were given a key to a race car for which you had only the manual (a written plan), but you had no previous driving experience?

2 You take your new race car out on to the track and find yourself surrounded by other race car drivers on a fast moving track. You try to follow the manual (your written plan), but you discover it's useless without practical driving experience.

3 Within moments, you crash into a wall and bring down other race car drivers with you. You suffer injuries that affect you and others for a very long time.

4 Banks, lenders, and business development organizations wonder why new start-up businesses in Canada continue to crash into the wall at record rates. Even with the most perfect written business plan, many lenders no longer lend to new start-up businesses simply because the risk for failure is too high.

5 A friend of mine was recently laid off from a job she had for many years. Like most people she went on unemployment benefits while she struggled to look for work. Realising her hope for employment in Canada was bleak she decided to start her own business. She had no previous experience running a business.

6 She discovered a government-sponsored program that would allow her to receive unemployment benefits while starting her own business. The only catch to the deal was she would have to attend and complete the unemployment business training course on how to properly start her own business, or her unemployment benefits would be cut off.

7 While taking the class she came to me almost weekly seeking help with her business plan. I soon realised that her course was very focused on the written business plan, with very little practical training involved.

8 Every business scholar and successful entrepreneur would agree that a written business plan is crucial to the start-up process. Before a building can be built there has to be a solid blueprint. Essentials to a business plan are strategies such as the mission statement, target market, industry analysis, competition, marketing, financial projections and so on.

9 There is, however, a limit to what can be learned in a classroom setting, without hands-on experience or through the examples of successful entrepreneurs.

10 If government lenders, banks and others continue to focus exclusively on well-written business plans, they might as well attach a bankruptcy application form to each loan application.

PRACTICE 15

1. Underline the thesis statement of the essay.
2. Does this essay focus on causes, effects, or both? ____________________
3. Underline a statistic and an anecdote.
4. Using your own words, list the four supporting points.

____

____

____

____

The Writer's Room

Writing Activity 1: Topics

Write a cause and effect essay about one of the following topics.

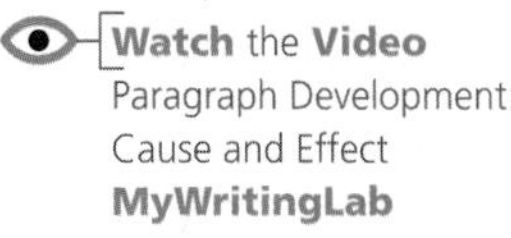

PARAGRAPH LINK

To practise cause and effect writing, you could develop an essay about one of the topics found in Chapter 11, "Cause and Effect."

General Topics

Causes and/or effects of …

1. A new law or policy
2. Rejecting or adopting a religion
3. Patriotism
4. Leaving your home or homeland

College- and Work-Related Topics

Causes and/or effects of …

5. Being a parent and college student
6. Taking time off before college
7. Having an office romance
8. Losing a job
9. Gossiping in the office
10. Changing jobs or career paths

Watch the **Video**
Paragraph Development: Cause and Effect
MyWritingLab

Writing Activity 2: Quotations

Read the following quotations. Find one that you agree or disagree with, or find one that inspires you in some way. Then use it as the basis for a cause and effect essay.

> A word after a word after a word is power.
>
> —Margaret Atwood, Canadian author, poet, critic, essayist

> What I would say to my younger self is this: forget about fear.
>
> —Erica de Vasconcelos, Canadian novelist

> All human actions have one or more of these seven causes: chance, nature, compulsion, habit, reason, passion, and desire.
>
> —Aristotle, ancient Greek philosopher

> One of the symptoms of an approaching nervous breakdown is the belief that one's work is terribly important.
>
> —Bertrand Russell, British author and philosopher

CAUSE AND EFFECT ESSAY CHECKLIST

As you write your cause and effect essay, review the essay checklist on the inside front cover. Also, ask yourself the following questions.

- ☐ Does my essay clearly focus on causes, effects, or both?
- ☐ Do I have adequate supporting examples of causes and/or effects?
- ☐ Do I avoid using faulty logic (a mere assumption that one event causes another or is the result of another)?
- ☐ Do I use the terms *effect* and/or *affect* correctly?

PARAGRAPH LINK

For more information about argument writing, refer to Chapter 12, "Argument."

Watch the Video
Essay Development: Argument; Paragraph Development: Argument
MyWritingLab

The Argument Essay

When you write an **argument essay,** you take a position on an issue, and you try to defend your position. In other words, you try to persuade your readers to accept your point of view.

The Thesis Statement

The thesis statement in an argument essay mentions the subject and a debatable point of view about the subject. Do not include a phrase such as *in my opinion, I think*, or *I am going to talk about* in your thesis statement.

topic / controlling idea

> Building a wall on the Mexican border **is an ineffective way to deal with illegal immigration.**

List Specific Arguments

Your thesis statement can further guide your readers by listing the specific arguments you will make in your essay.

controlling idea / topic / (arguments) 1, 2, 3

> Colleges should implement **work terms** to help students acquire job skills, make professional contacts, and earn money for expenses.

PARAGRAPH LINK

For more detailed information about types of evidence, see pages 169–170 in Chapter 12, "Argument."

The Supporting Ideas

In the body of your essay, give convincing arguments. Try to use several types of supporting evidence.

- **Include anecdotes.** Specific experiences or pieces of information can support your point of view.
- **Add facts.** Facts are statements that can be verified in some way. **Statistics** are a type of fact. When you use a fact, ensure that your source is reliable.
- **Use informed opinions.** Opinions from experts in the field can give weight to your argument.
- **Think about logical consequences.** Consider long-term consequences if something does or does not happen.
- **Answer the opposition.** Think about your opponents' arguments, and provide responses to their arguments.

RESEARCH LINK

For more information about doing research, see Chapter 15, "Enhancing Your Writing with Research."

Watch the Video
Research: Recognizing a Research Paper
MyWritingLab

Quoting a Respected Source

One way to enhance your essay is to include a quotation from a respected source. Find a quotation from somebody in a field that is directly related to your topic. When you include the quotation as supporting evidence, remember to mention the source.

> According to Stats Canada, "Widespread smoking bans in public places appear to have considerably reduced the risk of exposure to second-hand smoke across Canada."

An Argument Essay Plan

Read the next essay plan, and answer the questions that follow.

Introduction

Thesis statement: Canada should institute longer vacation time for employees.

I. Paid vacations in Canada are much shorter than they are in other countries.
   A. My friend Jay complains because he has only one week of paid vacation.
   B. According to Ken Georgetti, president of the Canadian Labour Congress, "[H]ard-working Canadians get a very limited right to paid time off the job relative to workers in similar economies."
   C. Most European countries give employees five weeks of vacation time during their first year of work.
   D. My sister lives in London and gets five weeks off each year.

II. Longer vacations allow employees to have a family life.
   A. Employees with children need time for the children.
   B. With current rules, many children must spend the summer in day camps.
   C. One week is not enough time to have adequate family holidays.

III. Employees with too little time off may burn out.
   A. According to psychologist Brenda Armour, "Employees face stress-related illnesses because they don't get enough time off."
   B. Add anecdote about Ted M., who had a nervous breakdown.
   C. The physical health of employees deteriorates when they lack vacation time.

Conclusion: To improve the health and the morale of employees, the government needs to legislate more vacation time.

PRACTICE 16

1. Circle the topic and underline the controlling idea in the thesis statement.
2. The author uses many types of supporting material. Do the following:
   a. Underline three anecdotes.
   b. Circle two informed opinions.
3. Write a few sentences that could appear in the introduction before the thesis statement. (For ideas about how to write an introduction, look in Chapter 13, "Writing the Essay.")

____

____

____

____

An Argument Essay

The next essay was written by college student Christine Bigras.

The Importance of Music

1 Most parents want their children to receive a well-rounded education. Students study traditional subjects like math, science, English, history, geography, and physical education, but many educators and parents have come to believe that school children should also be taught fine arts subjects. Thus, often school boards offer art, dance, and music, if not as core courses, then at least as extracurricular activities. Although the study and practice of all these arts develop sensitivity and creativity in students, learning music is the most beneficial to all-around student success.

2 First, music makes a child smarter. Everybody has already heard about scientists or doctors who are also musicians. A child who studies music may not become a genius; nevertheless, several research findings have shown that music lessons can enhance IQ and develop intelligence. One of the most recent and conclusive studies, "Music Lessons Enhance IQ," was conducted by E. Glenn Schellenberg from the University of Toronto and was published by *American Psychological Society Magazine* in 2004. This work concluded that there was a link between children who studied music and their academic success because music and schoolwork may develop similar problem-solving skills in children.

3 Furthermore, music education improves a child's physical and psychological health. Playing music is excellent exercise for the heart, especially for those who play a wind instrument. A child will also learn to stand straight and adopt good posture. Playing music also decreases stress and anxiety. Through music, the apprentices will learn concentration and listening skills. Furthermore, high school students who participate in band or orchestra are less interested in the use of all illegal substances (alcohol, tobacco, and drugs) according to the Texas Commission on Drug and Alcohol Abuse Report. The National Data Resource Center states that about 12 percent of students are labelled "disruptive" whereas only 8 percent of students in music programs have that label.

4 Finally, music education helps a child's social development. Playing music may facilitate students to connect to each other better, particularly through participation in orchestra or a choir. No matter if a child is ugly, poor, big, or shy, he or she is as important as any other musician in the group. Music is the great equalizer. Therefore, musicians will learn how to respect each other, how to cooperate, and how to build constructive relationships with others. When Yoko Kiyuka entered my former high school, she was very shy and lonely. The music program changed her life. The connections she made helped her integrate into the school and feel valued. "Music has the power to unite us. It proves that by working together, we can create something truly beautiful," said Pinchas Zukerman, Music Director of the National Arts Centre of Canada. Therefore, music may help a child to become a better citizen, another outstanding reason to encourage children to learn music.

5 Many school boards are removing music education from the curriculum. They argue that music is not a necessary or useful course. However, the benefits conveyed by music education are tremendous. By developing a child's brain, body, and feelings, music gives him or her a better chance to be confident in life. Parents of elementary or secondary school children can play an active role in the success of their children by encouraging them to learn music. Music can make the difference in a child's life.

PRACTICE 17

1. Underline the thesis statement of the essay.
2. What introductory style opens this essay? Circle the better answer.
   a. Definition b. Historical information
   c. General information d. Opposing viewpoint
3. Underline the topic sentence in each body paragraph.
4. In which paragraph does the author address the opposition? ____________
5. Find an example in the essay for each of the following types of evidence.
   a. Statistic: ____
   ____
   b. Anecdote: ____
   ____
   c. Quotation from informed source: __________________________
   ____
6. With what does the writer conclude her essay? Circle the better answer.
   a. Prediction b. Quotation c. Suggestion

Writing Activity 1: Topics

Write an argument essay about one of the following topics. Remember to narrow your topic and follow the writing process.

General Topics

1. Government-sponsored gambling
2. Beauty contests
3. Talk shows
4. Driving laws
5. The health-care system

College- and Work-Related Topics

6. The outsourcing of jobs
7. Great reasons to choose your college
8. The cost of a university education
9. Student activism
10. Dress codes at work

PARAGRAPH LINK

To practise argument writing, you could develop an essay about one of the topics found in Chapter 12, "Argument."

Watch the Video
Paragraph Development: Argument
MyWritingLab

Writing Activity 2: Quotations

Read the following quotations. Find one that you agree or disagree with, or find one that inspires you in some way. Then use it as the basis for an argument essay.

> Advertising is legalized lying.
>
> —H. G. Wells, British author

An eye for an eye leads to a world of the blind.

—Mahatma Gandhi, Indian activist

Our history is partly what makes Canada unique in the world, distinct from other nations with different populations, traditions, political systems, myths and landscapes.

—Charlotte Gray, Canadian professor and writer

ARGUMENT ESSAY CHECKLIST

As you write your argument essay, review the essay checklist on the inside front cover. Also, ask yourself the following questions.

- ☐ Does my thesis statement clearly state my position on the issue?
- ☐ Do I include facts, examples, statistics, logical consequences, or answers to my opponents in my body paragraphs?
- ☐ Do my supporting arguments provide evidence that directly supports each topic sentence?
- ☐ Do I use transitions that will help readers follow my ideas?

How Do I Get a Better Grade?

Visit MyWritingLab for audiovisual lectures and additional practice sets about essay patterns.

Enhancing Your Writing with Research

Goodluz/Shutterstock

LEARNING OBJECTIVES

When you want to seek more information about something, you might talk to other people; look for resources in libraries, bookstores, and museums; make phone calls; search the Internet; and so on. You can use the same tools when looking for details to include in your writing.

What Is Research?

Listen to the **Audio**
Lesson: Researching Your Topic
MyWritingLab

When you **research,** you look for information that will help you better understand a subject. For example, when you plan to see a movie and read movie reviews in the newspaper, you are engaging in research to make an informed decision. At college, you are often asked to quote outside sources in your essays. If you have ever looked for a job, you might have read the newspaper's classified ads, talked to employment counsellors, or spoken to potential employers.

This chapter gives you some strategies for researching information and effectively adding it to your writing.

Research for Academic Writing

Watch the **Video**
Research: Recognizing a Research Paper
MyWritingLab

There is a formal type of writing called the research paper. However, many types of academic essays, especially those with the purpose of persuading, can benefit from research. Additional facts, quotations, and statistics can back up your arguments.

Student writer David Raby-Pepin prepared an argument for an essay about rap music. You may have read his essay in Chapter 13. His purpose was to persuade the reader that rap musicians share positive cultural values. The following paragraph is from his essay.

David's Paragraph without Research

Many of these musicians shout out a powerful message of nonviolence. They promote peace by denouncing the fighting that takes place within their own community. Many leading hip-hop and rap artists are breaking away from the "gangsta rap" lyrics and writing music that shows a productive way to resolve social issues.

David's paragraph, although interesting, is not entirely convincing. He refers to artists who are writing about social issues, but he doesn't mention the names of those artists. David decided to do some research and support his points with specific details. He found many Internet sites about his topic that are run by hip-hop fans, but he worried that his readers might be skeptical if he used those sources. He kept searching and found two quotations from reputable sources.

David's Paragraph with Research

David added two quotations from respected publications. He included the authors' last names in parentheses. Because the publications were on websites, he did not include page numbers in the parentheses.

Many of these musicians shout out a powerful message of nonviolence. They promote peace by denouncing the fighting that takes place within their own community. The hip-hop artists 4Peace write lyrics promoting an end to gun violence; their mission "is to sell peace as aggressively as other rappers peddle sex and violence" (Kahn). To open up the debate on violent behaviour, the National Hip-Hop Summit Youth Council has developed projects to encourage discussion of aggression in the music community. Many leading hip-hop and rap artists support the Council's work and are breaking away from the "gangsta rap" lyrics. They write music that shows a productive way to resolve social issues. Chuck D. of Public Enemy states, "Too often, rap artists focus on the 'gangsta fairy tale' without mentioning the repercussions" (Marks).

Later, at the end of his essay, David also included a Works Cited page with the following information. (You will learn more about the Works Cited page later in this chapter.)

Works Cited

Kahn, Joseph P. "The Message." *Boston Globe*. NY Times Co., 10 Oct. 2006. Web. 23 May 2007.

Marks, Alexandra. "Hip Hop Tries to Break Images of Violence." *Christian Science Monitor*. Christian Science Monitor, 14 Nov. 2002. Web. 23 May 2007.

Avoid Plagiarism!

Plagiarism is the act of using someone else's words or ideas without giving that person credit. Plagiarism is a very serious offence and can result in expulsion from college or termination from work.

The following actions are examples of plagiarism.

"I LOVE YOUR RESUMÉ. IS IT FICTION, NON-FICTION, OR PLAGIARIZED FROM THE INTERNET?"

Schwadron, Harley/CSL, CartoonStock Ltd

- Buying another work and presenting it as your own
- Using another student's work and presenting it as your own
- Failing to use quotation marks or properly set off an author's exact words
- Using ideas from another source without citing that source
- Making slight modifications to an author's sentences but presenting the work as your own

To avoid plagiarism, always cite the source when you borrow words, phrases, or ideas from an author. Include the author's name, the title of the work, and the page number (if it is available).

Listen to the **Audio**
Lesson: Working With Sources and Avoiding Plagiarism
MyWritingLab

Watch the **Video**
Research: Avoiding Plagiarism
MyWritingLab

Gathering Information

To find information that will bolster your essay, consult sources in the library or on the Internet.

Using the Library

When you first enter a library, ask the reference librarian to help you locate information using various research tools, such as online catalogues, CD-ROMs, and microforms.

- **Search the library's online catalogue.** You can search by keyword, author, title, or subject. When you find a listing that interests you, remember to jot down the title, author, and call number. You will need that information when you search the library shelves.
- **Use online periodical services in libraries.** Your library may have access to *EBSCOhost*® or *INFOtrac.* By typing keywords into EBSCOhost®, you can search through national or international newspapers, magazines, and reference books. When you find an article that you need, print it or cut and paste it in a Word file and then email the document to yourself. Remember to print or copy the publication data because you will need that information when you cite your source.

Using the Internet

The Internet is a valuable research tool. You will be able to find information about almost any topic online. Here are some tips to help you with your online research.

- **Use efficient search engines** such as *Google*, *Yahoo!*, and *Ixquick*. Those sites can rapidly retrieve thousands of documents from the Internet. However, most people do not need as many documents as those engines can generate.
- **Choose your keywords with care.** Narrow your search by putting in very specific keywords. For example, to bolster an essay about binge drinking, you might try to find information about deaths due to alcohol poisoning. By placing quotation marks around your keywords, you further limit your search. For example, when you input the words *alcohol poisoning deaths* into Google without quotation marks, you will have over a million hits. When the same words are enclosed with quotation marks, the number of hits is reduced to about five hundred, and the displayed webpages are more relevant.
- **Use bookmarks.** When you find information that might be useful, create a folder where you can store the information so that you can easily find it later. (The bookmark icon appears on the toolbar of your search engine.)
- **Use academic search engines.** Sites such as *Google Scholar* (scholar.google.com) and *Virtual Learning Resources Center* (virtuallrc.com) help you look through academic publications.

Hint **Useful Internet Sites**

The following websites could be useful when you research on the Internet.

Statistics

Statistics from over one hundred United States government agencies	www.fedstats.gov
Statistics Canada	www.statcan.gc.ca
Government of Canada	www.canada.gc.ca

News Organizations

Addresses of hundreds of online magazines	newsdirectory.com
Access to newspapers from all over the world	www.newspapers.com
The Toronto Star site for college students	www.thestar.com/schoolsguide

Other Sites

Job sites	www.monster.ca
	www.jobs.org
Internet Public Library	www.ipl.org
Online encyclopedias	www.encyclopedia.com
	www.britannica.com

Academic Research Sites

Google Scholar	scholar.google.com

Evaluating Sources

Be careful when you use Internet sources. Some sites contain misleading information, and some sites are maintained by people who have very strong and specific biases. Remember that the content of Internet sites is not always verified for accuracy. When you view websites, try to determine who benefits from the publication. What is the site's purpose?

Evaluating a Source

When you find a source, ask yourself the following questions:

- Will the information support the point that I want to make?
- Is the information current? Check the date of publication of the material you are considering.
- Is the source reliable and highly regarded? For instance, is the source from a respected newspaper, journal, or website?
- Is the author an expert on the subject?
- Does the author present a balanced view, or does he or she clearly favour one viewpoint over another? Ask yourself if the author has a financial or personal interest in the issue.
- On various sites, do different authors supply the same information? Information is more likely to be reliable if multiple sources cite the same facts.

PRACTICE 1

Imagine that you are writing an essay about the dangers of online gambling. Your audience is other college students. To enhance your argument, you want to add some facts, statistics, anecdotes, and quotations to your essay. Answer the questions by referring to the list of websites below.

1. Which sites would likely contain useful information? For each site that you choose, explain why it could be useful.

____

____

____

2. Which sites are probably not useful for your essay? For each site you choose, explain why.

____

____

____

____

A. **Gambling Research Addiction Centre to Open at UBC—CBC.ca**
Help for gambling addicts. http://www.cbc.ca/onthecoast/episodes/2013/03/01/gambling-addiction-research-centre-to-open-at-ubc/

B. **ProblemGambling.ca**
Resource for individuals and professionals on gambling.
http://www.problemgambling.ca/EN/Pages/default.aspx

C. **Gender Issues in Gambling**
Studies on gambling across genders.
http://www.nsgamingfoundation.org/pages/Gender-Issues-in-Gambling.aspx

D. **Expansion of Gambling in Canada: Implications for Health and Social Policy—CMAJ.ca**
Public health view on gambling.
http://www.cmaj.ca/cgi/content/full/163/1/61

E. **The Association between Pathological Gambling and Attempted Suicide: Findings from a National Survey in Canada—Canadian Psychiatric Association**
Correlation between problem gambling and suicide.
http://publications.cpa-apc.org/media.php?mid=516

Web Addresses

When you evaluate Internet sites, you can often determine what type of organization runs the website by looking at the last three letters of the Uniform Resource Locator (URL) address.

URL Ending	Meaning	Example
.com	Company	www.canon.com
.edu	Educational institution	canadacollege.edu
.net	Network	www.jobs.net
.org	Organization	www.magazines.org

Keeping Track of Sources

When you find interesting sources, make sure that you record the following information. Later, when you incorporate quotations or paraphrases into your work, you can quickly find the source of the information. (You will learn how to cite sources later in this chapter.)

Book, Magazine, Newspaper	Website
Author's full name	Author's full name
Title of article	Title of article
Title of book, magazine, or newspaper	Title of website
Publishing information (name of publisher, city, and date of publication)	Date of publication or last printing
Pages used	Date you accessed the site
	Complete website address

RESEARCH LINK

To find out more about the MLA and its guidelines, visit the MLA website at www.mla.org.

Finding Complete Source Information

Source information is easy to find in most print publications. It is usually on the second or third page of the book, magazine, or newspaper. On many Internet sites, however, finding the same information can take more investigative work. When you research on the Internet, look for the home page to find the site's title. The Modern Language Association (MLA) recommends that you find and cite as much source information as is available on the website (author's name, title of article, date of publication, etc.).

Add a Paraphrase, Summary, or Quotation

To add research to a piece of writing, you can paraphrase it, summarize it, or quote it.

- When you **paraphrase,** you use your own words to present someone's ideas. A paraphase is about the same length as the original selection.
- When you **summarize,** you briefly state the main ideas of another work. A summary is much shorter than the original selection.
- When you **quote,** you either directly state a person's exact words (with quotation marks) or report them (without quotation marks).

All of these are valid ways to incorporate research in your writing, as long as you give credit to the author or speaker.

Paraphrasing and Summarizing

Both paraphrases and summaries present the ideas that you have found from another source. Before you can restate someone's ideas, you must ensure that you have a very clear understanding of those ideas. Thus, the first thing you must do when you paraphrase or summarize is read the text carefully.

How to Paraphrase

Watch the **Video**
Paraphrasing to Avoid Plagiarism
MyWritingLab

When you paraphrase, you keep the length and order of the original selection, but you restate the ideas using your own words. To paraphrase, follow these steps.

- Read the original text carefully, and underline any key ideas. Ensure that you understand the text.
- Use your own words to restate the key ideas of the original text. To help prevent copying, do not look again at the original source.
- Use approximately the same number of words as the original passage.
- Do not change the meaning of the original text. Do not include your own opinions.
- Document the source. State the author and title of the original text.
- Reread your paraphrase. Verify that you have respected the order and emphasis of the original source.

How to Summarize

A summary is much shorter than a paraphrase, and it presents a global view. To summarize, follow these steps.

- Read the original text carefully. Ensure that you understand the main point.
- Ask yourself *who*, *what*, *when*, *where*, *why*, and *how* questions. These questions will help you to synthesize the ideas of the original text.
- Restate the essential ideas in your own words.
- Maintain the original meaning of the text. Do not include your own opinions.
- Document the source. State the author and title of the original text.
- Reread your summary. Verify that you have explained the central message.

Consider Your Audience

When you decide whether to paraphrase or summarize, think about your audience.

- Paraphrase if your audience needs detailed information about the subject.
- Summarize if your audience needs to know only general information.

PRACTICE 2

Read the following selections and answer the questions. The original selection, written by Jessica Vitullo, appeared in the *National Post* on B2.

Original Selection

Summer barbecues and late-night drinks are a seasonal must for some people, but experts warn they can have a negative impact on the body's internal clock, putting some at risk for weight gain. The body clock, known as the circadian rhythm, controls all of our bodily functions in a 24-hour period, says Andrea D'Ambrosio, a registered dietitian in the GTA. But daily tasks, such as staying up late, eating and drinking at different times in the evening—often a result of summer social outings—throw off this clock. "Any time you're up later and you're out in a social environment, there are opportunities to indulge in things we do as humans," says Nick Bellissimo, an assistant professor of nutrition at Ryerson University. "That's more eating, more drinking, more drinking alcohol."

Paraphrase

Jessica Vitullo, in the *National Post*, reports that in the summer, people tend to upset their natural bodily rhythms by varying their sleep and diet routines. Researchers support this claim by citing individuals' increased social events—often with inconsistent sleep and irregular indulgences as a potential cause (B2).

Summary

Weight gain can occur during the summer months as people's body clocks are impacted by various extracurricular activities, according to Jessica Vitullo in the *National Post* (B2).

1. In the paraphrase and summary, does the writer express an opinion? _____
2. In the paraphrase and summary, the writer gives three pieces of information about the source. What are they?

____

____

____

3. What is the main difference between a paraphrase and a summary?

____

____

Paraphrasing and Summarizing

When you paraphrase or summarize, avoid looking at the original document. After you finish writing, compare your version with the original, and ensure that you have not used too many words from the original document.

PRACTICE 3

Read the following selections and answer the questions. The original selection, written by Martin Seligman, appeared in the *APA Monitor* on page 97.

Original Selection

Unfortunately it turns out that hit men, genocidal maniacs, gang leaders, and violent kids often have high self-esteem, not low self-esteem. A recipe for their violence is a mean streak combined with an unwarranted sense of self-worth. When such a boy comes across a girl or parents or schoolmates who communicate to him that he is not all that worthy, he lashes out.

Summary 1

In the *APA Monitor*, Martin Seligman says that hit men and genocidal maniacs often have high self-esteem. Their mean streak combines with an unwarranted sense of self-worth and creates a recipe for violence (97).

1. How does this summary plagiarize the original piece of writing?

____

____

____

____

Summary 2

Violent youths, like hired assassins and other murderers, often have self-esteem that is too high. Such youths lash out when others question their worthiness.

1. How does this summary plagiarize the original piece of writing?

____

____

____

____

Mention Your Source

When you paraphrase or summarize, remember to mention the name of the author and the title of the publication. If the page number is available, place it in parentheses.

PRACTICE 4

Paraphrase and summarize the original selection. Remember that a paraphrase respects the length and order of the original document, whereas a summary is a very condensed version of the original. This selection, written by Carol R. Ember and Melvin Ember, appeared on page 239 of their book *Cultural Anthropology*.

Original Selection

Religious beliefs and practices are found in all known contemporary societies, and archaeologists think they have found signs of religious belief associated with Homo sapiens who lived at least 60,000 years ago. People then deliberately buried their dead, and many graves contain the remains of food, tools, and other objects that were probably thought to be needed in an afterlife.

Paraphrase: ______________________________

____

____

____

____

____

____

____

Summary: ______________________________

____

____

____

____

Quoting Sources

GRAMMAR LINK

To find out more about using quotations, see Chapter 34.

An effective way to support your arguments is to include quotations. Use quotations to reveal the opinions of an expert or to include ideas that are particularly memorable and important. When quoting sources, remember to limit how many you use in a single paper and to vary your quotations by using both direct and indirect quotations.

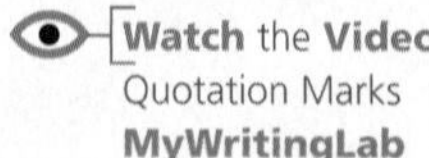

Direct and Indirect Quotations

A **direct quotation** contains the exact words of an author and is set off with quotation marks.

> A CBC news article states, "Some Canadian gun owners are upset their personal information from the national gun registry has been passed by the RCMP to a polling company for a research study."

An **indirect quotation** keeps the author's meaning but is not set off by quotation marks.

> A CBC news article states that some Canadian gun owners are upset with the RCMP about the sharing of their personal gun registry information with a polling company.

How to Introduce or Integrate a Quotation

Quotations should be integrated into sentences. To learn how to introduce or integrate quotations in your writing, read the following original selection, and then view three common methods. The selection, written by John E. Farley, appeared on page 97 of his book *Sociology*.

Original Selection

Human history abounds with legends of lost or deserted children who were raised by wild animals. Legend has it, for example, that Rome was founded by Romulus and Remus, who had been raised in the wild by a wolf.

1. **Phrase introduction**
   You can introduce the quotation with a phrase followed by a comma. Capitalize the first word in the quotation. Place the page number in parentheses.

   In *Sociology*, John E. Farley writes, "Human history abounds with legends of lost or deserted children who were raised by wild animals" (97).

   Alternatively, you can place the phrase after the quotation. End the quotation with a comma instead of a period.

   "Human history abounds with legends of lost or deserted children who were raised by wild animals," writes John E. Farley in *Sociology* (97).

2. **Sentence introduction**
   Introduce the quotation with a sentence followed by a colon. Capitalize the first word in the quotation.

   In his book *Sociology*, John E. Farley suggests that such stories are not new: "Human history abounds with legends of lost or deserted children who were raised by wild animals" (97).

3. **Integrated quotation**
   Integrate the quotation as a part of your sentence. Place quotation marks around the source's exact words. Do not capitalize the first word in the quotation.

   In *Sociology*, John E. Farley mentions a legend about the twin founders of Rome "who had been raised in the wild by a wolf" (97).

Words That Introduce Quotations

One common way to introduce a quotation is to write, "The author says . . . ." However, there are a variety of other verbs that you can use.

admits	concludes	mentions	speculates
claims	explains	observes	suggests
comments	maintains	reports	warns

PRACTICE 5

Practise integrating quotations. Read the following selection and then write direct and indirect quotations. The selection, written by Daniel R. Brower, appeared on page 371 of his book *The World in the Twentieth Century*.

The collapse of German communism began with the regime's desperate decision to grant complete freedom of travel to East Germans.

On the night of November 9, the gates through the Berlin Wall were opened to all. The city became the center of an enormous celebration by East and West Berliners. Some of them climbed the wall itself to celebrate.

1. Write a direct quotation.

____

____

____

____

2. Write an indirect quotation.

____

____

____

____

Cite Sources Using MLA Style

Each time you use another writer's words or ideas, you must **cite the source,** giving complete information about the original document from which you borrowed the material. When quoting, paraphrasing, or summarizing, you can place the source information in parentheses. These **in-text citations**, also known as **parenthetical citations**, allow you to acknowledge where you obtained the information. You must also cite your sources in an alphabetized list at the end of your essay. The Modern Language Association (MLA) refers to the list as Works Cited.

Choose a Documentation Style

The three most common styles for documenting sources are the Modern Language Association (MLA) format, the *Chicago Manual of Style* (CMS) format, and the American Psychological Association (APA) format. Before writing a paper, check with your instructor to see which documentation style you should use and to learn where you can find more information about it.

Citing the Source in the Body of Your Essay

When you introduce a quotation or idea, try to mention the source directly in your paragraph or essay. The next examples show how you can cite some common sources using MLA style.

1. **Mention the author and page number in parentheses.**

   Put the author's last name and the page number in parentheses. Place the final period after the parentheses, not inside the quotation marks.

   > Successful people fight to succeed: "They have determined that nothing will stop them from going forward" (Carson 224).

2. **Mention the page number in parentheses.**

   If you mention the author's name in the introductory phrase, put only the page number in the parentheses. Place the final period after the parentheses.

According to Ben Carson, "Successful people don't have fewer problems" (224).

3. **Mention the author or title of an online source.**

If you are using a web-based source, no page number is necessary. If no author's name is given, put the title of the article in quotation marks. If the title is very long, shorten it beginning with the word you would use to look up the title in the list of works cited.

Furthermore, according to Statistics Canada, university tuition fees have risen over the last year, and on average, undergraduate students paid $5,313 in tuition fees in 2011/2012 compared with $5,581 in 2012/2013 ("Undergraduate Tuition Fees").

Writing Titles for Borrowed Material

Place the title of a short work (article, short story, or individual page on a website) in quotation marks, and italicize the title of a longer work (book, magazine, newspaper, or entire website).

"Addicted to Exercise" appears in *Newsweek*.

GRAMMAR LINK

To find out more about writing titles, see pages 499–501 in Chapter 34.

Preparing a Works Cited Page

Watch the Video Essay Introductions, Conclusions and Titles: Titles **MyWritingLab**

Sometimes called a References list or Bibliography, the Works Cited page gives details about each source you have used and appears at the end of your paper. To prepare a Works Cited page, use this format.

- Write Works Cited at the top of the page, and centre it.
- List each source alphabetically, using the last names of the authors.
- Indent the second line and all subsequent lines of each reference.

Here are some examples of how to cite different types of publications. Notice that the author's name and title are separated by periods, not commas. Also, publishers' names are shortened: for example, Random House is cited as Random.

Book

Last name, First name. *Title of Book*. City of publication: Publisher, Year. Medium.

- **One author**

Moore, Lisa. *Caught*. Toronto: House of Anansi, 2013. Print.

- **Two or more authors**

Ember, Carol R., and Melvin Ember. *Cultural Anthropology*. Upper Saddle River: Prentice, 2002. Print.

- **Essay in an anthology**

Houle, Karen. "Double Arc." *Dropped Threads 2: More of What We Aren't Told*. Ed. Carol Shields and Marjorie Anderson. Toronto: Vintage Canada, 2003. Print.

- **Encyclopedia**

"Fox, (Terry) Terrence Stanley." *The Canadian Encyclopedia*. 2012. Print.

Print

- **Periodical**

> Last name, First name. "Title of Article." *Title of Magazine or Newspaper* Date: pages. Medium.

- **Magazine**

Bickle, Laura. "How to Outsmart Stress." *Chatelaine* May 2013: 139–140. Print.

- **Newspaper**

Hutchinson, Alex. "The Highs and Lows of Altitude Training." *The Globe and Mail* 8 July 2013: L4. Print.

- **Journal**

> Last name, First name. "Title of Article." *Title of Journal* Volume Number.Issue (Year): pages. Medium.

Sorenson, Adam. "Pay for Performance: Rewarding Top Performers through Carve-Outs." *HR Professional* 29.8 (2012): 26–29. Print.

Web

If the information was published on the Internet, include as much of the following information as you can find. Keep in mind that some sites do not contain complete information. Include the URL at the end, surrounded by angle brackets, only if the source would be hard to find without it.

> Author. "Title of Article." *Title of Site or Online Publication*. Name of publisher or sponsor (if not available, put "N.p."), date of publication or most recent update. Medium. Date you accessed the site.

- **Online Periodical**

Slator, Dashka. "It's All Fun and Games." Salon.com. Salon Media Group, 26 Mar. 2013. Web. 15 May 2013.

- **A Document from an Internet Site**

Nankani, Gobind. "Creating Shared Wealth in Africa." *The World Bank*. The World Bank Group, 6 Dec. 2012. Web. 11 June 2013. <http://go.worldbank.org/OR0UE8SGT0>.

Other

- **Personal Interview**

Include the person's name, the words "Personal interview," and the date, as shown below.

Giraldi, Julie. Personal interview. 13 April 2013.

- **Film, Video, or DVD**

Include the name of the film, the director, the studio, the year of release, and the medium.

Mambo Italiano. Dir. Emile Gaudreault. Samuel Goldwyn Company, 2003. Film.

- **Television Program**

Include the segment title, the program name, the network, the broadcast date, and the medium.

"Prescription for Tragedy." *W5*. 13 Oct. 2012. Television.

- **Sound Recording**

  Include the name of the performer or band, the title of the song, the title of the CD-ROM, the name of the recording company, the year of release, and the medium.

  Arcade Fire. "Culture War." *The Suburbs*. Merge, 2010. CD.

Placement and Order of Works Cited

The works cited should be at the end of the research paper. List sources in alphabetical order using the authors' last names. If there is no author, list the title (but ignore *A*, *An*, or *The*, which may appear at the beginning of the title).

Hutchinson, Alex. "The Highs and Lows of Altitude Training." *The Globe and Mail* 8 July 2013: L4. Print.

Slator, Dashka. "It's All Fun and Games." *Salon.com*. Salon Media Group, 26 Mar. 2013. Web. 15 May 2013.

"Test Vote Leaves Immigration Bill in Doubt." *CNN.com*. Cable News Network, 7 June 2013. Web. 7 June 2013.

PRACTICE 6

The four sources below were used in a research paper about humour and creativity. Arrange the sources for a Works Cited list using MLA style.

- Some quotations are from a book called *Creative Intelligence* by Alan J. Rowe. The book was published by Pearson Education in Toronto in 2009.
- A summary is of a newspaper article by Steve Winn called "Offensive Language." It appeared in the April 15, 2013, edition of the *Vancouver Sun* on page A1.
- Some quotations are from a magazine article that Louise Dobson wrote called "What's Your Humour Style?" The article appeared in the August 2013 issue of *Psychology Today* on pages 74 to 77.
- A paraphrase is from an article called "Humour in the Workplace" by Maggie Finefrock. The article was on the website *The Learning Project*, which was last updated on March 9, 2013. The student viewed the article on May 2, 2013.

Works Cited

____

____

____

____

____

____

____

____

____

____

Sample Research Essay Using MLA Style

Read a complete student essay. Notice how the student integrates paraphrases, summaries, and quotations.

Lemieux 1

Double-space your name, instructor's name, course title, and date.

Marie Lemieux
Professor Rhonda Sandberg
COMM 1007
7 December 2012

Title in middle. (Notice that the title is not underlined, boldfaced, or italicized.)

Orcs, Mages, and Zerglings. Oh My!

Double-space the body of the essay.

The crowd is cheering and up on their feet as they look on along with millions of online viewers at an arena packed with fans as the team takes the stage ready to play the game of their life. This could easily be the scene of a basketball or football event, but actually this is a common description of a major E-sports tournament. The most recent was IPL5, a three-day-long tournament held at The Cosmopolitan in Las Vegas, Nevada (*IPL*) which brought in 180k concurrent viewers who watched the grand finals live via video streaming (*Game Streams*). This is the scene of video games being played at a professional level. The industry has grown immensely and rapidly over just the past few years. For many professional players it is no longer just a hobby, but a career. This is possible because of the worldwide spread of acceptance that E-sports are not just games to be played for one's own enjoyment, but a very entertaining medium for spectators to watch. So much so that there is little reason why these games should not be cast on TV and grouped in the same category with other more traditional spectator sports.

Acknowledge sources of borrowed ideas.

The International Olympic Committee (IOC) recognizes some sports that require minimal physical ability, but that involve more mental strength, such as archery and shooting (*Olympic.org*). The ARISF includes Chess and Bridge in their International Sport Federations (*ARISF*). They are all highly competitive and seen by many as viable spectator sports. Some games used heavily in E-sports, such as StarCraft and League of Legends, keep rankings similar to the elo system that is found in Chess. Instead of having categories from Class C up to Grandmaster, they are classified from Bronze up to Diamond. One of the major draws to watching competitive play is to see top Diamond ranked players compete against each other for fortune and glory.

For an internet source, place the title of the article in parenthese.

Another big attraction to E-sports is that anyone can attain that elusive top 10 rank by practicing hard, being disciplined, and having determination just like in any other sport. One of the more appealing attributes to E-sports is that they have very few restrictions on who can participate. The only real equipment needed is a PC or laptop, and according to surveys conducted by Pew Internet & American Ltd., over 50% of American adults own a desktop computer and over 60% own a laptop ("Adult Gadget Ownership"). A restriction for a professional basketball player and other traditional sport players is they can only play effectively for a certain amount of years before their body cannot keep up with the game, but this is not the case in E-sports.

Lemieux 2

A player can be of any age, race, or gender and would be able to compete as long as they possess excellent hand-to-eye coordination abilities. It is also very convenient to start practising. The games are designed for players to easily be matched up with other people to play with and against as opposed to trying to organize twenty-one other people to play a soccer game with. E-sports also offer something unique to the scene in that they give "skilled amateurs a chance to play against professionals, which would be unthinkable in, say, professional football or basketball" ("Gentlemen, Start Your Computers"). This can open up opportunities for amateurs to be noticed by professional teams, possibly get picked up by them, and start their very own professional gamer career which nets the top StarCraft 2 players over $200k USD a year ("Gentlemen, Start Your Computers").

Notice that a paraphrase of someone's idea is acknowledged.

E-sports bend the rules when it comes to paving the way for exciting new spectator sports. Traditional sports have rules that cannot easily be changed which results in a game that is static and always the same. This can lead to predictable outcomes. E-sport games are ever changing by trying to improve and create a challenging, yet fair environment. It also means that no one person can easily master the game and that fans will be able to enjoy the surprises that make each tournament much more interesting to watch. For example, League of Legends has a roster of over a hundred different champions for players to choose from. Every two weeks Riot Games adds another champion to their ranks which causes professional teams to constantly be reworking and coming up with new strategies to win games (*League of Legends*).

There are people that argue that sports are meant to be physical. There are a few reasons behind this. Some say that full body contact sports are more fun to watch because there is the appeal of violence and potential injury, which was why gladiator sports were so popular in Roman times. E-sports only offer this in a virtual sense and without the risk to the players perhaps the thrill is lost on some people. Another reason is that there is a certain amount of amazement that comes with watching people do things that are not easily done, such as a gymnast doing flips on a high beam or a pitcher throwing a ball faster than the average speed limit.

A point that is often debated is that E-sports are not popular enough and that not many people watch the professional scene. This may have been true several years ago as the games that were being used in competitive play were quite dated and not as spectacular looking as current games. There were also problems in trying to transfer a single-player experience to something a viewer could easily watch and enjoy. One of the first E-sports games was CounterStrike, which is a first-person shooter game. The matches were of two teams strategically completing objectives together on a map. The problem was that the viewer could only see through a first-person camera that switched from person to person. This caused some confusion over what exactly was happening as there was no bird's eye view available. It is understandable how some people may have become disinterested with watching professional gaming in the early stages of its development.

While E-sports may not have many physical elements for the viewer, they can still be taxing for the players. Many times during tournaments, in the later ladders, game sets can go for hours with few small breaks in between. It really is a test of endurance both mentally and physically. The physical aspect comes from the pure adrenaline that is experienced from playing with such high stakes and also the finger dexterity needed to win. StarCraft players often boast about the speed at which they can perform tasks in game, which is measured in APM (Actions Per Minute), or the average rate of how quickly their fingers move. Popular StarCraft player Lee "NaDa" Yun Yeoi says, "To win a championship, it should be at least over 200s and in the lower 300s" (CultofRazer). Many techniques have been tried to improve APM, such as using sandbags to weigh down wrists (CultofRazer). Unfortunately, these techniques can be hazardous as there have been cases where players have developed painful carpel tunnel syndrome. The only real way to improve is through "steady and persistent practice" (CultofRazer). This is why Brandon Beck, CEO and co-founder of Riot Games, believes, "There are a lot of skills to master and there's a ton of depth to the experience. It's also fun to watch for the same reason that any traditional sport might be, which is you can be in awe of the super human feats at the highest level of play" (qtd. in Benedetti).

Marie Lemieux—260 (—) ➢

This past year E-sports have grown exponentially in popularity across the world. League of Legends boasts at having 12 million active players daily and as a result is the most played game in the world ("League of Legends' Growth"). A large part of this has to do with the increasing usage of live online streaming. Twitch.tv has led the way for broadcasting E-sports events and supporting its players through their streaming revenue. It allows them to "broadcast their practice sessions online and chat with fans in real time" which appeals to old and new fans ("Gentlemen, Start Your Computers"). Currently the streaming service attracts over 23 million viewers per month and that number is consistently rising as more attention is brought to the scene (*Twitch.tv*). Organizations such as Major League Gaming (MLG) host tournaments year-round that bring together the best players around the world to compete at live events (*Major League Gaming*). Thousands of fans sell out arenas to watch their favourite players battle it out for millions of dollars (Benedetti). In some countries, such as in South Korea, these events

Lemieux 4

are broadcasted live on TV. To them E-sports have achieved the respect they deserve as spectator sports and are celebrated. Local players are treated like celebrities and appear in huge adverts and even have their faces on credit cards. To them it is not an E-sport, but simply a sport (Fitzpatrick and Comiteau). Riot Games hopes to mimic that success in their upcoming 2013 Championship Series. The goal is to provide an experience matched by more traditional spectator sports by creating a regular season comprised of the top 8 teams from around the world to play matches broadcast live every week ("Riot Games Shares"). Stephen "Snoopeh" Ellis of team Counter Logic Gaming EU thinks, "It's really going to take E-Sports to a new level and I hope other companies pick it up… I don't think it's artificially inflating the E-Sports scene, to be honest. They're just doing what developers should do to help grow it" (Thorin).

The potential for E-sports is massive. They have all the key factors needed for successful spectator sports. They are very competitive and require a high skill set to be victorious. They are quickly growing in popularity all over the world and with popularity comes revenue. Right this very moment there are people practicing for a tournament somewhere and no doubt fans viewing a match streamed live online. Big brand names such as Coca-Cola, Red Bull, Samsung and Intel have turned out to sponsor recent events and that awareness is only going to grow ("Gentlemen, Start Your Computers"). There is money to be made in this industry that will help elevate it to the level of other spectator sports. This is the future and the next generation of sports.

Lemieux 5

Centre the title of the Works Cited page. ➢

Double-space sources. ➢

Place sources in alphabetical order. ➢

Indent the second line of each source by .25 cm. ➢

Works Cited

"Adult Gadget Ownership over Time (2006–2012)." *Pew Internet*. Sept. 2012. Web. 2 Dec. 2012.

ARISF. International Olympic Committee, 2009. Web. 2 Dec. 2012.

Benedetti, Winda. "Taipei Assassins Triumph in 'League of Legends' World Finals." *NBCNews.com*. 14 Oct. 2012. Web. 2 Dec. 2012.

CultofRazer. "Razer: The Hax Life." *Vimeo*. Razer, 23 June 2010. Online video. 2 Dec. 2012.

Fitzpatrick, Liam, and Lauren Comiteau. "The Wired Bunch." *Time International (Canada Edition)* 21 July 2008: 68–71. *Canadian Reference Centre*. Web. 2 Dec. 2012.

Game Streams. N.p., 2012. Web. 2 Dec. 2012.

"Gentlemen, Start Your Computers." *Economist* 10 Dec. 2011: 8–9. *Canadian Reference Centre*. Web. 6 Dec. 2012.

IPL: IGN Pro League. IGN Entertainment, Inc., 2012. Web. 6 Dec. 2012.

League of Legends. Riot Games, Inc., 2012. Web. 2 Dec. 2012.

"League of Legends' Growth Spells Bad News for Teemo." *RiotGames.com*. 15 Oct. 2012. Web. 2 Dec. 2012.

Major League Gaming. CBS Interactive Inc., 2012. Web. 2 Dec. 2012.

Olympic.org. International Olympic Committee, 2012. Web. 2 Dec. 2012.

"Riot Games Shares Its Vision for the Future of Esports, Reveals Initial Details of League of Legends Championship Series." *RiotGames.com*. 6 Aug. 2012. Web. 2 Dec. 2012.

Thorin. "'Grilled' Episode 13: Stephen 'Snoopeh' Ellis." *YouTube*. Acer, 25 Nov. 2012. Online video. 2 Dec. 2012.

Twitch.tv. CBS Interactive Inc., 2012. Web. 2 Dec. 2012.

REFLECT ON IT

Think about what you have learned in this chapter. If you do not know an answer, review that topic.

1. What are the differences between a paraphrase and a summary?

Paraphrase	**Summary**
______________________	______________________
______________________	______________________
______________________	______________________
______________________	______________________

2. What are the differences between a direct and an indirect quotation?

Direct	**Indirect**
______________________	______________________
______________________	______________________
______________________	______________________
______________________	______________________

3. What is a Works Cited page?

____

____

____

____

The Writer's Room

Writing Activity 1

Choose a paragraph or an essay that you have written, and research your topic to get more detailed information. Then insert at least one paraphrase, one summary, and one quotation into your work. Remember to acknowledge your sources.

Writing Activity 2

Write an essay about one of the following topics. Your essay should include research (find at least three sources). Include a Works Cited page at the end of your assignment.

1. Write about a contemporary issue that is in the news. In your essay, give your opinion about the issue.
2. Write about your career choice. You could mention job opportunities in your field, and you could include statistical information.
3. Write about the importance of a post-secondary education. Does a post-secondary education help or hurt a person's career prospects? Find some facts, examples, or statistics to support your view.

How Do I Get a Better Grade?

Visit MyWritingLab for audiovisual lectures and additional practice sets about enhancing your writing with research.

The Editing Handbook

Why Is Grammar So Important?

When you speak, you have tools such as tone of voice and body language to help you express your ideas. When you write, however, you have only words and punctuation to get your message across. Naturally, if your writing contains errors in style, grammar, and punctuation, you may distract readers from your message, and they may focus instead on your inability to communicate clearly. You increase your chances of succeeding in your academic and professional life when you write in clear standard English.

The chapters in this Editing Handbook can help you understand important grammar concepts and ensure that your writing is grammatically correct.

Simple Sentences

Section Theme **CULTURE**

LEARNING OBJECTIVES

Skyelar Menard

In this chapter, you will read about topics related to advertising *and* consumerism.

The Writer's Journal

What is your cultural background? How would you identify yourself culturally? Write a paragraph about your cultural identity.

Identify Subjects

A **sentence** contains one or more subjects and verbs, and it expresses a complete thought. Although some sentences can have more than one idea, a **simple sentence** expresses one complete thought. The **subject** tells you who or what the sentence is about. The **verb** expresses an action or state. If a sentence is missing a subject or a verb, it is incomplete.

Singular and Plural Subjects

Subjects may be singular or plural. To determine the subject of a sentence, ask yourself who or what the sentence is about.

A **singular subject** is one person, place, or thing.

Sarah McLachlan is known around the world.

Halifax, Nova Scotia, is her hometown.

A **plural subject** is more than one person, place, or thing.

Contemporary **musicians** try to reach a mass audience.

Many **countries** import Canadian products.

Watch the **Video**
Subjects and Verbs
MyWritingLab

Pronouns

A **subject pronoun** (*he, she, it, you, I, we, they*) can act as the subject of a sentence, and it replaces the noun.

Sandra Oh stars in many films. **She** is known around the world.

Directors make many action films. **They** hope the films will interest young males.

Gerunds (-*ing* words)

Watch the **Video**
Subjects and Verbs
MyWritingLab

Sometimes a gerund (-*ing* form of the verb) is the subject of a sentence.

Relaxing is important.

Business planning is an ongoing process.

Compound Subjects

Many sentences have more than one subject. *Compound* means "multiple." Therefore, a **compound subject** contains two or more subjects.

Men and **women** evaluate products differently.

The **accountants, designers,** and **advertisers** will meet to discuss the product launch.

Recognizing Simple and Complete Subjects

In a sentence, the **simple subject** is the noun or pronoun. The complete name of a person, place, or organization is a simple subject.

he   dancer   Homer Simpson   Sony Music Corporation

The **complete subject** is the noun plus the words that describe the noun. In the next examples, the descriptive words are in italics.

new electric piano   *the old, worn-out* shoes   *Anna's green* convertible

In the following sentence, the simple and complete subjects are identified.

simple subject
The glossy new **magazine** contained interesting articles.
complete subject

PRACTICE 1

Underline the complete subject and circle the simple subject(s).

EXAMPLE:

Academic institutions teach popular culture.

1. Popular music, films, books, and fashions are the sources of our common culture.
2. University professors and administrators did not see the value of popular culture in the past.
3. Classical music, art, and literature were standard subjects.
4. Well-known academics made a distinction between "high" and "low" culture.
5. Opinions changed in the 1980s.
6. Some colleges began offering courses on popular culture.
7. Reality television is considered worthy of study today.
8. An old, highly respected college has a course about television game shows.
9. Alison Anthony and James O'Reilly teach popular culture.
10. They and their students enjoy discussing current trends.

Special Subject Problems

Unstated Subjects (Commands)

In a sentence that expresses a command, the subject is unstated, but it is still understood. The unstated subject is *you*.

Remember to use your coupon.

Pay the cashier.

here/there

Here and *there* are not subjects. In a sentence that begins with *Here* or *There*, the subject follows the verb.

There are five ways to market a product.

(The subject is *ways*.)

Here is an interesting brochure about cosmetics.

(The subject is *brochure*.)

PRACTICE 2

Circle the simple subject(s). If the subject is unstated, then write the subject (*you*) before the verb.

EXAMPLE:

you

To see the announcement, watch carefully.

1. There are many advertisements on the streets of our cities.

2. Look at any bus shelter, billboard, store window, or newspaper.

3. Certainly, some ads appear in surprising places.

4. There are framed announcements on the doors of hotel bathrooms, for example.

5. Furthermore, there are commercials hidden in the middle of the action in movies and television shows.

6. For instance, Telus sponsored the popular reality show *So You Think You Can Dance Canada*.

7. The company provided advertising to run during the show.

8. View advertising with a critical eye.

Identify Prepositional Phrases

Watch the **Video**
Subjects and Verbs
MyWritingLab

A **preposition** is a word that links nouns, pronouns, or phrases to other words in a sentence. It expresses a relationship based on movement or position. Here are some common prepositions.

Common Prepositions

about	before	during	near	through
above	behind	except	of	to
across	below	for	off	toward
after	beside	from	on	under
against	between	in	onto	until
along	beyond	inside	out	up
among	by	into	outside	with
around	despite	like	over	within
at	down			

A **phrase** is a group of words that is missing a subject, a verb, or both and therefore is not a complete sentence. A **prepositional phrase** is made up of a preposition and its object (a noun or a pronoun). In the following phrases, an object follows the preposition.

Preposition	+	Object
in		the morning
among		the shadows
over		the rainbow
with		some friends

Be Careful

Because the object of a preposition is a noun, it may look like a subject. However, the object in a prepositional phrase is *never* the subject of the sentence. For example, in the next sentence, the subject is *child*, not *closet*.

subject
In the closet, the **child** found the hidden gift.

Sometimes a prepositional phrase appears before or after the subject. To help you identify the subject, you can put parentheses around prepositional phrases or mark them in some other way. In each of the following sentences, the subject is in boldface type, and the prepositional phrase is in parentheses.

(In spite of the costs,) **Ruth Handler** took the assignment.

(On a trip to Germany,) **she** saw an interesting product.

Her **company,** (after 1959,) expanded greatly.

Sometimes a sentence can contain more than one prepositional phrase.

prepositional phrase prepositional phrase
(In the late 1950s,) (during a period of prosperity,) a new and original **doll** appeared in North American stores.

According to . . .

When a sentence contains *according to,* the noun that immediately follows the words *according to* is *not* the subject of the sentence. In the following sentence, *Jack Solomon* is not the subject.

subject
(According to Jack Solomon,) **North Americans** are tired of fantasy advertisements.

PRACTICE 3

Place parentheses around the prepositional phrase(s) in each sentence. Then circle the simple subject.

EXAMPLE:

(In 1995,) a successful online company began.

1. In Pierre Omidyar's living room, an idea took shape.
2. With friend and co-founder Jeff Skoll, Omidyar decided to create an online flea market.
3. For several years, the company expanded.
4. Then, in 1998, a Harvard business graduate was asked to join the company.
5. Meg Whitman, with a team of top managers, helped turn eBay into a billion-dollar business.

6. Buyers and sellers, with a click of a mouse, can enter a virtual marketplace.
7. For a small fee, sellers can list items on the site.
8. Buyers, with only a picture and description to evaluate, then bid on the item.
9. At the end of the auction, an eBay employee contacts the buyer and seller.
10. In spite of some initial problems, the online auction has been tremendously successful.

CHAPTER 16

PRACTICE 4

Look at the underlined word in each sentence. If it is the subject, write *C* (for "correct") beside the sentence. If the underlined word is not the subject, then circle the correct subject(s).

EXAMPLES:

In past eras, bustling markets sold consumer goods. ______

Enclosed shopping malls are a fairly recent development. C

1. In West Vancouver, the first indoor mall was built in Canada. ______
2. The world's largest mall has eight hundred stores. ______
3. For some consumers, the local dress shop is a dangerous place. ______
4. On her twenty-second birthday, Amber Wyatt divulged a secret. ______
5. During the previous four years, she had piled up $60 000 in credit card debts. ______
6. She acknowledges, with a shrug, her shopping addiction. ______
7. Today, with a poor credit rating, Amber is unable to get a lease. ______
8. Her brother, boyfriend, and aunt have lent her money. ______
9. Her parents, with some reluctance, allowed their daughter to move back home. ______
10. Many Canadian men and women, according to a recent survey, have a shopping addiction. ______

Identify Verbs

Every sentence must contain a verb. The **verb** either expresses what the subject does or links the subject to other descriptive words.

Listen to the **Audio**
Lesson: Verbs
MyWritingLab

Action Verbs

An **action verb** describes an action that a subject performs.

Watch the **Video**
Tense
MyWritingLab

In 2006, China launched an electric car called the Zap Xebra.

Engineers designed the car's energy-efficient engine.

Linking Verbs

A **linking verb** connects a subject with words that describe it, and it does not show an action. The most common linking verb is *be*.

The marketing campaign is expensive.

Some advertisements are very clever.

Other linking verbs refer to the senses and indicate how something appears, smells, tastes, and so on.

The advertising photo looks grainy.

The glossy paper feels smooth.

Common Linking Verbs

appear	feel	smell
be (am, is, are, was, were, etc.)	look	sound
become	seem	taste

Compound Verbs

When a subject performs more than one action, the verbs are called **compound verbs.**

Good advertising informs, persuades, and convinces consumers.

Members of the public either loved or hated the logo.

Infinitives Are Not the Main Verb

Infinitives are verbs preceded by *to* such as *to fly*, *to speak*, and *to go*. An infinitive is never the main verb in a sentence.

V infinitive V infinitive
Kraft wants **to compete** in Asia. The company hopes **to sell** millions of products.

PRACTICE 5

Underline one or more verbs in these sentences.

EXAMPLE:

Some companies use buzz appeals.

1. Buzz marketers entice consumers to talk about a brand.
2. Some companies hire students to chat about a particular brand of clothing in online forums.
3. To promote *Canada's Next Top Model*, the network gave free makeovers for staff of media agencies and firms.
4. Teenage girls were the target audience for the campaign.

5. The network asked the girls to invite four friends to their homes to watch the series.
6. Occasionally, buzz advertising backfires.
7. A car company placed people in chatrooms to discuss a new SUV model.
8. However, people in the chatroom became angry about the SUVs and criticized them.
9. Guerrilla marketers ambush consumers with promotional content in unexpected places.
10. Smak, representing Koodo Mobile, placed more than one hundred people outfitted in 1980s aerobic attire throughout busy traffic areas in Montreal and Toronto as part of a guerrilla marketing campaign.
11. The campaign *Toronto Sets Bad Drivers Straight* caused a panic.
12. The campaign created havoc but promoted a new cartoon series at the same time.

Identify Helping Verbs

A verb can have several different forms, depending on the tense that is used. **Verb tense** indicates whether the action occurs in the past, present, or future. In some tenses, there is a **main verb** that expresses what the subject does or links the subject to descriptive words, but there is also a helping verb.

The **helping verb** combines with the main verb to indicate tense, negative structure, or question structure. The most common helping verbs are forms of *be*, *have*, and *do*. **Modal auxiliaries** are another type of helping verb; they indicate ability (*can*), obligation (*must*), possibility (*may*, *might*, *could*), advice (*should*), and so on. For example, here are different forms of the verb *open*. The helping verbs are underlined.

<u>is</u> opening	<u>had</u> opened	<u>will</u> open	<u>should have</u> opened
<u>was</u> opened	<u>had been</u> opening	<u>can</u> open	<u>might be</u> open
<u>has been</u> opening	<u>would</u> open	<u>could be</u> opening	<u>could have been</u> opened

The **complete verb** consists of the helping verb and the main verb. In the following examples, the helping verbs are indicated with *HV* and the main verbs with *V*.

HV HV V

Canadian culture <u>has been</u> <u>spreading</u> across the globe for years.

HV HV V

You <u>must have</u> <u>seen</u> the news articles.

In **question forms,** the first helping verb usually appears before the subject.

HV subject HV V

<u>Should</u> the coffee chain <u>have</u> <u>expanded</u> so quickly?

HV subject V

<u>Will</u> the coffee and cakes <u>sell</u> in Moscow?

Interrupting words may appear between verbs, but they are *not* part of the verb. Some interrupting words are *easily*, *actually*, *not*, *always*, *usually*, *sometimes*, *frequently*, *often*, *never*, and *ever*.

HV V
Consumers have often complained about product quality.

HV HV V
The car maker should not have destroyed its electric cars.

GRAMMAR LINK

For information on the position of midsentence adverbs, such as *often*, *sometimes*, and *never*, see page 431 in Chapter 29.

PRACTICE 6

Underline the helping verbs once and the main verbs twice.

EXAMPLE:
The modern consumerism movement has been strong since the 1960s.

1. Marketing and advertising companies need to be aware of the Consumers' Association of Canada.
2. Products should not be dangerous or defective.
3. A single company should never have a monopoly.
4. Businesses must provide consumers with honest information.
5. Some companies have been sued for defective products.
6. Merck, a pharmaceutical company, was forced to remove the drug Vioxx from the market.
7. To protect consumers, the Competition Bureau has implemented rules to prevent misleading advertising.
8. Some companies have been fined for deceptive marketing methods.
9. In a Volvo ad, a monster truck ran over a row of cars and crushed all but the Volvo station wagon.
10. In fact, the Volvo's structure had been reinforced.
11. Volvo was fined $150 000 for deceptive marketing.
12. How should companies respond to consumer complaints?

PRACTICE 7

Circle the simple subjects and underline the complete verbs. Remember to underline all parts of the verb.

EXAMPLE:
Japanese products have captured the imaginations of children around the world.

1. In 1974, a Japanese greeting card company created a white cat with vacant, staring eyes. The cat was given the name "Hello Kitty." Soon, purses, toasters, cameras, and T-shirts had the image of the little animal. For some reason, the strange cat with a bow on one ear and

a missing mouth has become a fashion icon for teenagers worldwide. Thirty years after its debut, Hello Kitty's popularity remains constant.

2. A self-taught illustrator from Japan has created another cute and creepy character. At first glance, you might not notice the details on Mori Chack's bear. The fuzzy pink toy seems to be sweet and cuddly. However, after a closer look, you will see the long, pointed claws and the drop of blood on the bear's mouth. Like Hello Kitty, Gloomy Bear has become trendy. The bear's likeness appears on clothing, key chains, and coffee mugs.

3. Some journalists, including Julia Dault and Kjeld Duits, have written about the trends. They credit Japanese animators with an ability to add a sinister twist to images of saccharine sweetness. Of course, the characters do not simply appeal to children. Gloomy Bear sells briskly to those in their twenties and thirties.

REFLECT ON IT

Think about what you have learned in this chapter. If you do not know an answer, review that topic.

1. What is a sentence? ______________________________

____

2. What does the subject of a sentence do? ______________________________

____

3. Write an example of a simple subject and a complete subject.
   a. Simple: ______________________________
   b. Complete: ______________________________
4. What is a verb? ______________________________

____

5. Write examples of action verbs and linking verbs.
   a. Action: ______________________________
   b. Linking: ______________________________

Circle the better answers.

6.	Can the object of a preposition be the subject of a sentence?	No	Yes
7.	Can a sentence have more than one subject?	No	Yes
8.	Can a sentence have more than one verb?	No	Yes

FINAL REVIEW

Circle the simple subjects and underline the complete verbs. Underline *all* parts of the verb. Remember that infinitives such as *to go* and *to run* are not part of the main verb.

EXAMPLE:

A good name and logo are immensely important.

1. In their book *Marketing: Real People, Real Choices*, Michael R. Solomon, Greg Marshall, and Elnora Stuart discuss brands. 2. With a great deal of care, companies must carefully choose the best name for their products. 3. According to the authors, product names should be memorable. 4. Irish Spring, for instance, is a fresh and descriptive name for soap.

5. Occasionally, mistakes are made. 6. The company Toro called its lightweight snow blower a "snow pup." 7. The product did not sell well. 8. Later, the product was renamed "Snow Master" and then "Snow Commander." 9. The sales have improved tremendously since then.

10. Some brands have become the product name in consumers' minds. 11. Everyone knows popular brands such as Kleenex, Jell-O, Scotch Tape, and Kool-Aid. 12. Without a second thought, many consumers will ask for a Kleenex but not for a tissue with another brand name. 13. Therefore, a great name can be linked to the product indefinitely.

14. According to Solomon, Marshall, and Stuart, there are four important elements in a good brand name. 15. It must be easy to say, easy to spell, easy to read, and easy to remember. 16. Apple, Coke, and Dove are examples of great product names. 17. Good names should also have a positive or functional relationship with the product. 18. Drano is a very functional name. 19. On the other hand, Pampers and Luvs suggest good parenting but have no relation to the function of diapers. 20. Ultimately, large and small businesses put a great deal of care into product branding.

Write about one of the following topics. After you finish writing, identify your subjects and verbs.

1. Describe an effective advertising campaign. List the elements that make the campaign so successful.
2. Compare two online shopping sites. Describe the positive and negative features of each site.

How Do I Get a Better Grade?

Visit MyWritingLab for audiovisual lectures and additional practice sets about simple sentences.

Compound Sentences

Section Theme **CULTURE**

LEARNING OBJECTIVES

Christoph Wilhelm/The Image Bank/Getty Images

In this chapter, you will read about topics related to fads *and* fashions.

The Writer's Journal

Do you have body art such as tattoos and piercings? In a paragraph, explain why you do or do not have body art.

Compare Simple and Compound Sentences

When you use sentences of varying lengths and types, your writing flows more smoothly and appears more interesting. You can vary sentences and create relationships between ideas by combining sentences.

Review the differences between simple and compound sentences.

A **simple sentence** is an independent clause. It expresses one complete idea, and it stands alone. Simple sentences can have more than one subject and more than one verb.

One subject and verb:	Tattooing is not a new fashion.
Two subjects:	Tattooing and body piercing are not new fashions.
Two verbs:	Della McMahon speaks and writes about current trends.

A **compound sentence** contains two or more simple sentences. The two complete ideas can be joined in several ways.

	Trey is a drummer. + He also sings.
Add a coordinator:	Trey is a drummer, **and** he also sings.
Add a semicolon:	Trey is a drummer; he also sings.
Add a semicolon and conjunctive adverb:	Trey is a drummer; **moreover,** he sings.

Combine Sentences Using Coordinating Conjunctions

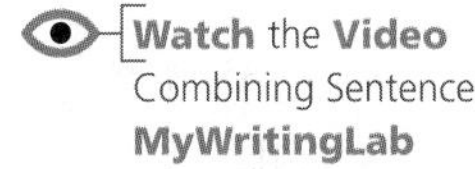

A **coordinating conjunction** joins two complete ideas and indicates the connection between them. The most common coordinating conjunctions are *for*, *and*, *nor*, *but*, *or*, *yet*, and *so*.

Complete idea, **coordinating conjunction** complete idea.

Review the following chart showing coordinating conjunctions and their functions.

Coordinating Conjunction	Function	Example
for	to indicate a reason	Henna tattoos are good options, **for** they are not permanent.
and	to join two ideas	Jay wants a tattoo, **and** he wants to change his hairstyle.
nor	to indicate a negative idea	Cosmetic surgery is not always successful, **nor** is it particularly safe.
but	to contrast two ideas	Tattoos hurt, **but** people get them anyway.
or	to offer an alternative	Jay will dye his hair, **or** he will shave it off.
yet	to introduce a surprising choice	He is good-looking, **yet** he wants to get cosmetic surgery.
so	to indicate a cause and effect relationship	He saved up his money, **so** he will get a large tattoo.

Recognizing Compound Sentences

To be sure that a sentence is compound, place your finger over the coordinating conjunction, and then ask yourself whether the two clauses are complete sentences.

Simple: The fashion model was tall **but** also very thin.

Compound: The fashion model was tall**, but** she was also very thin.

PRACTICE 1

Indicate whether the following sentences are simple (*S*) or compound (*C*). Underline the coordinating conjunction in each compound sentence.

EXAMPLE:

There are many ways to alter your appearance. S

1. Many humans permanently alter their bodies, and they do it for a variety of reasons. _____
2. Body altering is not unique to North America, for people in every culture and in every historical period have found ways to permanently alter their bodies. _____
3. In past centuries, some babies in South America had boards tied to their heads, and their soft skulls developed a long, high shape. _____
4. In Africa, Ubangi women used to extend their lower lips with large, plate-sized pieces of wood. _____
5. In the 1700s, wealthy European men and women ate tiny amounts of arsenic to have very pale complexions. _____
6. Then, in the next century, European and American women wore extremely tight corsets, and they suffered from respiratory and digestive problems. _____
7. Today, some people want to improve their physical appearance, so they sculpt their bodies with cosmetic surgery. _____
8. Others have images tattooed on their skin for decorative, religious, or political reasons. _____
9. Body altering can be painful, but people do it anyway. _____

CHAPTER 17

PRACTICE 2

Read the following passages. Insert an appropriate coordinating conjunction in each blank. Choose from the list below, and try to use a variety of coordinating conjunctions.

for and nor but or yet so

EXAMPLE:

Fashions usually take a while to be accepted, _but_ fads appear and vanish quickly.

1. Have you heard of Harajuku culture? Harajuku is the name of a district in Tokyo, __________ it is also a teen subculture. Every Sunday afternoon, hundreds of Japanese teenagers meet on Jinju Bridge, __________ they engage in "cosplay" (costume play). Some young males dress up, __________ most of the Harajuku kids are female. The girls want to be noticed, __________ they wear homemade frilly dresses and carry parasols. Their costumes require a lot of effort. They might dress up as a cute cartoon character, __________ they can choose to dress in dark gothic costumes.
2. The pop star Gwen Stephani has a perfume brand called "Harajuku," __________ she loves that subculture. Today, the Harajuku district is famous, __________ many visitors go there. Tourists and professional photographers search for the best-dressed youths.
3. Seventeen-year-old Shoshi lives in Tokyo, __________ she visits Jinju Bridge every week. Next Sunday, she might wear a yellow bow in her hair, __________ she may wear a white lace cap. Her costumes are elaborately detailed, __________ she attracts a lot of attention. Tourists stare at her, __________ she is not self-conscious. Shoshi is frequently photographed, __________ she always wears the most eye-catching outfits. She never refuses to pose, __________ do most of her friends.
4. Curiously, participants love to socialize and make friends, __________ they do not use their real names. The teens choose special names, __________ they tell close friends the name. Harajuku culture will probably remain a unique Japanese lifestyle.

jarvis gray/Shutterstock

Stylish and fun

Place a Comma before the Coordinating Conjunction

Add a comma before a coordinating conjunction if you are certain that it joins two complete sentences. If the conjunction joins two nouns, verbs, or adjectives, then you do not need to add a comma before it.

Comma: The word *fashion* refers to all popular styles, **and** it does not refer only to clothing.

No comma: The word *fashion* refers to all popular styles **and** not only to clothing.

PRACTICE 3

Create compound sentences by adding a coordinating conjunction and another complete sentence to each simple sentence. Remember to add a comma before the conjunction.

EXAMPLE:

Many people deny it *, but they worry about their personal style.*

1. My hair is too long ____
2. Today, hairstyles are varied ________________________________
3. Those shoes look uncomfortable _____________________________
4. You may be surprised ______________________________________

Combine Sentences Using Semicolons

Another way to form a compound sentence is to join two complete ideas with a semicolon. The semicolon replaces a coordinating conjunction.

Complete idea	;	complete idea.

Advertisers promote new fashions every year; they effectively manipulate consumers.

PRACTICE 4

Insert the missing semicolon in each sentence.

EXAMPLE:

Tattoos are applied with needles ; ink is inserted under the skin.

1. Primitive tribes used sharp, thin instruments to introduce colour into the skin methods of tattooing have not changed much over the years.
2. In 1990, in the Alps, Austrian hikers found a five-thousand-year-old man they photographed the frozen, tattooed body.
3. The body had long straight lines tattooed on the ankles other lines appeared on the stomach region.
4. An Austrian professor, Konrad Spindler, has a theory about the tattoos he published his ideas in a journal.
5. Perhaps the ancient man received tattoos to cure an illness he may have had intestinal problems.

6. In the past, some tattoos celebrated war victories others honoured religious figures.
7. The warriors of the Marquesas Islands wanted to intimidate their enemies they tattooed a staring eye on the insides of their arms.
8. A tribesman would raise his arm to attack an opponent his enemy would then see the staring eye and feel frightened.
9. In the early twentieth century, in Western cultures, tattoos were often associated with the lower classes sailors, soldiers, and criminals would get tattoos.
10. Tattoos have had a strong resurgence in our culture people from gang members to white-collar professionals have gotten tattoos.

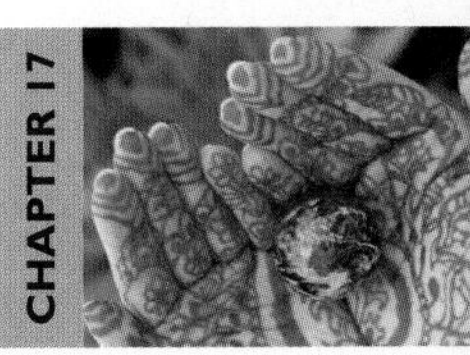

Hint **Use a Semicolon to Join Related Ideas**

Do not use a semicolon to join two unrelated sentences.

Incorrect: Some societies have no distinct word for art; I like to dress in bright colours.
(The second idea has no clear relationship with the first idea.)

Correct: Some societies have no distinct word for art; art is an intrinsic part of their cultural fabric.
(The second idea gives further information about the first idea.)

Watch the **Video**
Semicolons, Colons, Dashes, and Parentheses
MyWritingLab

PRACTICE 5

Write compound sentences by adding a semicolon and another complete sentence to each simple sentence. Remember that the two sentences must have related ideas.

EXAMPLE:

Last year my sister had her tongue pierced; *she regretted her decision.*

1. Youths rebel in many ways ______________________________
____
2. Hair dyes can be toxic ______________________________
____
3. At age thirteen, I dressed like other teens ______________________________
____
4. Running shoes are comfortable ______________________________
____

Watch the Video
Combining Sentences
MyWritingLab

Combine Sentences Using Transitional Expressions

A third way to combine sentences is to join them with a semicolon and a transitional expression. A **transitional expression** can join two complete ideas together and show how they are related. Most transitional expressions are **conjunctive adverbs** such as *however* and *furthermore*.

Transitional Expressions

Addition	Alternative	Contrast	Time	Example or Emphasis	Result or Consequence
additionally	in fact	however	eventually	for example	consequently
also	instead	nevertheless	finally	for instance	hence
besides	on the contrary	nonetheless	later	namely	therefore
furthermore	on the other hand	still	meanwhile	of course	thus
in addition	otherwise		subsequently	undoubtedly	
moreover					

If the second part of a sentence begins with a transitional expression, put a semicolon before it and a comma after it.

Complete idea; **transitional expression,** complete idea.

Miriam is not wealthy**; nevertheless,** she always wears the latest fashions.
; however,
; nonetheless,
; still,

PRACTICE 6

Punctuate the following sentences by adding any necessary semicolons and commas.

EXAMPLE:

A bizarre fashion style can become accepted; however, future generations may find the style ridiculous.

1. Often, a popular personality adopts a fashion later others copy the style.
2. King Louis XIV originally disliked wigs however he started to go prematurely bald and changed his mind about the fashion.
3. The king started to wear high, curly wigs subsequently others copied his style.
4. The heavy, elaborate wigs were expensive hence only middle- and upper-class Europeans wore them.
5. The wigs required constant care in fact they needed to be cleaned, powdered, and curled.

6. Later, the king's mustache started to go grey therefore he shaved it off.
7. Others noticed the king's bare face consequently all the fashionable men removed their mustaches too.
8. Not all new fashions are frivolous in fact some fashions signal a change in a group's status.
9. In the 1920s, women gained the right to vote meanwhile pants became associated with women's new freedom.
10. Other fashions have also made political statements for example in the 1970s, the Afro hairstyle signalled black power.

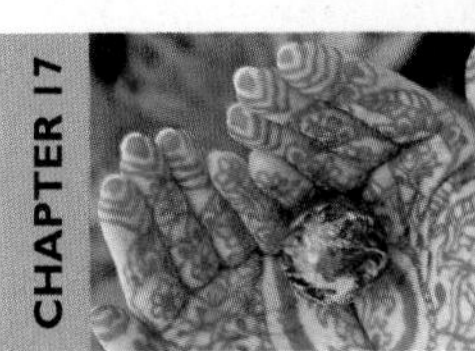

PRACTICE 7

Combine each pair of sentences into one sentence using a transitional expression from the following list. Try to use a different expression in each sentence.

in fact	for example	~~however~~	of course	for instance
therefore	eventually	nevertheless	thus	in contrast

EXAMPLE:

; however, young

Today's parents often complain about their children. ~~Young~~ people are not more violent and rebellious than those of past generations.

1. Youth rebellion is not new. In each era, teenagers have rebelled.
2. Teenagers distinguish themselves in a variety of ways. They listen to new music, create new dance styles, wear odd fashions, and break established social habits.
3. The most visible way to stand out is to wear outrageous fashions. Teenagers try to create original clothing and hairstyles.
4. In the past fifty years, rebellious teens have done almost everything to their hair, including growing it long, buzzing it short, dyeing it, spiking it, shaving it off, and colouring it blue. It is difficult for today's teenagers to create an original hairstyle.
5. Sometimes a certain group popularizes a style. Hip-hop artists wore baggy clothing in the late 1980s.
6. Many parents hated the baggy, oversized pants. Boys wore them.
7. Before the 1990s, most women just pierced their ears. It is now common to see a pierced eyebrow, tongue, or cheek.
8. "Retro" hair and clothing styles will always be popular. People often look to the past for their inspiration.

Subordinators versus Conjunctive Adverbs

A **subordinator** is a term such as *when, because, until,* or *although.* Do not confuse subordinators with conjunctive adverbs. When a subordinator is added to a sentence, the clause becomes incomplete. However, when a conjunctive adverb is added to a sentence, the clause is still complete.

Complete:	She wore fur.
Incomplete (with subordinator):	When she wore fur.
Complete (with conjunctive adverb):	Therefore, she wore fur.

When you combine two ideas using a conjunctive adverb, use a semicolon.

No punctuation:	She was criticized when she wore fur.
Semicolon:	It was very cold; therefore, she wore fur.

PRACTICE 8

Create compound sentences using the following transitional expressions. Try to use a different expression in each sentence.

in fact   however   ~~therefore~~   furthermore   consequently   for example

EXAMPLE:

I have my own style *; therefore, I refuse to spend money following the latest fad.*

1. Many people like to wear fashionable clothing ______________________
____
2. Designer clothing is expensive ______________________
____
3. I cannot sew ______________________
____
4. Some men shave their heads ______________________
____
5. Canadians spend billions of dollars on clothing ______________________
____

REFLECT ON IT

Think about what you have learned in this chapter. If you do not know an answer, review that topic.

1. a. What is a simple sentence? ______________________
____
   b. Write a simple sentence. ______________________

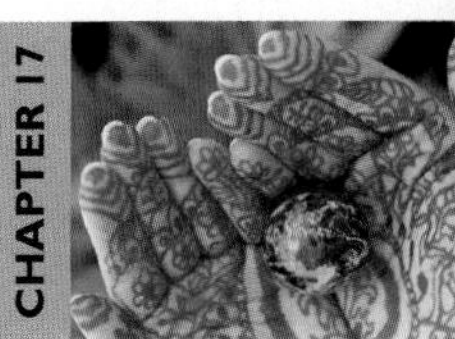

2. a. What is a compound sentence? ______________________

____

b. Write a compound sentence. ______________________

3. What are the seven coordinating conjunctions? ______________________

____

4. Circle the better answer: When two sentences are joined by a coordinating conjunction such as *but*, should you put a comma before the conjunction? Yes No

5. When you join two simple sentences with a transitional expression, how should you punctuate the sentence?

____

____

Final Review

Read the following essay. Create at least ten compound sentences by adding semicolons, transitional expressions (*however*, *therefore*, and so on), or coordinating conjunctions (*for*, *and*, *not*, *but*, *or*, *yet*, and *so*). You may choose to leave some simple sentences.

EXAMPLE:

; for example, top

The fashion industry does not hire average-sized models~~. Top~~ models are very tall and thin.

1. The fashion industry promotes a specific body type. Advertisers also prefer a specific look. They use tall, skinny models to sell fashion. The average person does not have the body dimensions of a top model. This type of appearance is unfeasible for most people. A public backlash has developed against the skinny top model image. People on both sides of the controversy have an opinion. They may love the fashion industry. They may hate it.

2. Critics blame the fashion industry for depicting unrealistic body types. First, top models are far too thin. Their Body Mass Index (BMI) is less than 18.5. A healthy woman should have a BMI between 18.5 and 25. The industry pressures models to remain uncommonly lean. Young girls compare themselves to models. They develop negative body images. Emaciated women are found in fashion magazines, on billboards, and on television. According to psychologists,

such images contribute to eating disorders in adolescents. The images may also lead to yo-yo dieting.

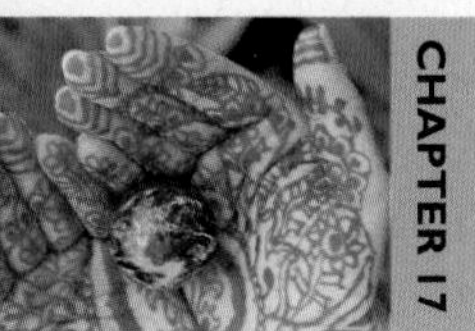

3. Some in the fashion industry have chosen to present more realistic body types. In 2006, one Madrid fashion organizer banned overly skinny models from fashion runways. About 30 percent of the models could not participate in the show. A well-known cosmetics company has launched a regular-women campaign. Dove uses ordinary women to promote a line of body creams. According to a Dove spokesperson, the company wants to encourage debate about body image.

4. However, many in the fashion industry are reacting negatively to the critics' demands. For example, the Dove campaign is hypocritical. Dove sells anti-cellulite creams and anti-aging creams. At the same time, the company tells women to accept their own bodies. Furthermore, according to some critics, clothes look better on thin people. The fashion industry is trying to sell clothes. It must make consumers buy into the fantasy of thin, glamorous models. The models wear beautiful clothes.

5. Clearly, there will be no immediate end to the body image controversy. Such a debate is important. It may never be resolved. Perhaps consumers will influence the direction of the fashion industry in the future.

Write about one of the following topics. Include some compound sentences.

1. Think about some fashions over the last 100 years. Which fashion trends do you love the most? Give examples.
2. List the steps you take when you make a major purchase. For example, what process do you follow when you decide to buy an appliance, car, computer, or house?

How Do I Get a Better Grade?

Visit MyWritingLab for audiovisual lectures and additional practice sets about compound sentences.

Complex Sentences

Section Theme **CULTURE**

LEARNING OBJECTIVES

Germanskydiver/Shutterstock

In this chapter, you will read about topics related to activity fads.

The Writer's Journal

How active are you? Write about some of the physical activities that you do.

What Is a Complex Sentence?

Before you learn about complex sentences, it is important to understand some key terms. A **clause** is a group of words containing a subject and a verb. There are two types of clauses.

An **independent clause** has a subject and a verb and can stand alone because it expresses one complete idea.

Rosie MacLennan won the competition.

A **dependent clause** has a subject and verb, but it cannot stand alone. It "depends" on another clause to be complete.

Although he had injured his heel

A **complex sentence** combines both a dependent and an independent clause.

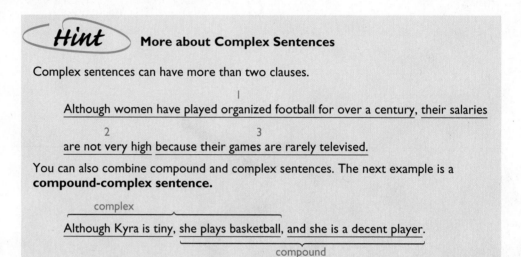

> dependent clause / independent clause
> Although she did not imagine standing on the podium, Rosie MacLennan won the Gold medal in Trampoline at the London 2012 Olympic Games.

Watch the Video
Combining Sentences
MyWritingLab

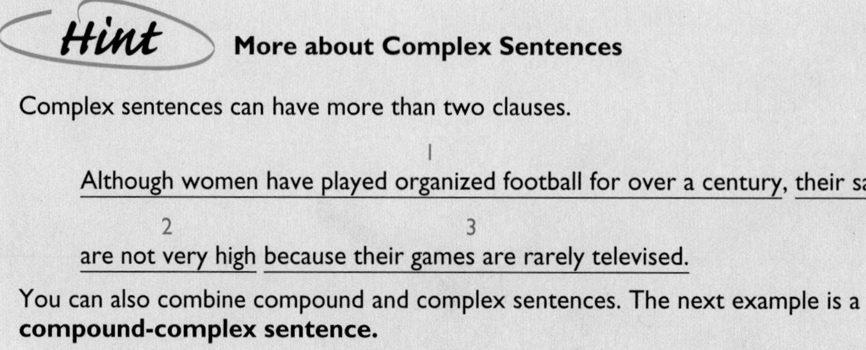

Hint **More about Complex Sentences**

Complex sentences can have more than two clauses.

> 1 / 2 / 3
> Although women have played organized football for over a century, their salaries are not very high because their games are rarely televised.

You can also combine compound and complex sentences. The next example is a **compound-complex sentence.**

> complex
> Although Kyra is tiny, she plays basketball, and she is a decent player.
> compound

Use Subordinating Conjunctions

An effective way to create complex sentences is to join clauses with a subordinating conjunction. When you add a **subordinating conjunction** to a clause, you make the clause dependent. *Subordinate* means "secondary," so subordinating conjunctions are words that introduce secondary ideas. Here are some common subordinating conjunctions followed by examples of how to use these types of conjunctions.

Common Subordinating Conjunctions

after	as though	if	though	where
although	because	provided that	unless	whereas
as	before	since	until	wherever
as if	even if	so that	when	whether
as long as	even though	that	whenever	while

Main idea **subordinating conjunction** secondary idea.

Crowds cheered **whenever** the team won.

Subordinating conjunction secondary idea, main idea.

Whenever the team won, crowds cheered.

PRACTICE 1

The following sentences are complex. In each, circle the subordinating conjunction and then underline the dependent clause.

EXAMPLE:

Even if we cannot know for sure, early humans probably played games and sports.

1. When humans shifted from being food gatherers to hunters, sports probably developed in complexity.
2. It would be important to practise cooperative hunting before humans attacked mammoths or other large creatures.
3. Early humans also practised war games so that they could win battles with other tribes.
4. Spectator sports evolved when societies had more leisure time.
5. In many places, spectators watched while young boys passed through their initiation rituals.
6. Whenever early humans played sports or games, they tested their physical, intellectual, and social skills.

Meanings of Subordinating Conjunctions

Subordinating conjunctions create a relationship between the clauses in a sentence.

	Cause or Reason	Condition or Result	Contrast	Place	Time
Conjunctions	as because since so that	as long as even if if provided that only if so that unless	although even though if though whereas unless	where wherever	after before once since until when whenever while
Example	Eric learned karate **because** he wanted to be physically fit.	He will not fight **unless** he feels threatened.	People learn karate **even though** it is difficult to master.	**Wherever** you travel, you will find karate enthusiasts.	**After** he received his black belt, he became a teacher.

PRACTICE 2

In each of the following sentences, underline the dependent clause. Then indicate the type of relationship between the two parts of the sentence. Choose one of the following relationships.

condition	reason	time
contrast	location	

EXAMPLE:

When Rebeka feels lonely, she goes on her Facebook page. ________

1. After the invention of computers, many new fads emerged. ________
2. Social networking sites are popular because people can stay in touch with their friends. ________
3. A lot of college students use Facebook or Twitter whenever they have spare time. ________
4. Generally students use Facebook whereas professionals use Twitter. ________
5. Wherever Rebeka goes, she can check her Facebook page. ________
6. Rebeka will continue to use Facebook unless a better networking site appears. ________

Punctuating Complex Sentences

If you use a subordinator at the beginning of a sentence, put a comma after the dependent clause. Generally, if you use a subordinator in the middle of the sentence, you do not need to use a comma.

Comma: **Even though** he is afraid of heights, Malcolm tried skydiving.

No comma: Malcolm tried skydiving **even though** he is afraid of heights.

PRACTICE 3

Correct eight errors in the following selection by adding the missing commas. If the sentence has a subordinating conjunction, then underline the conjunction.

EXAMPLE:

Although most sports are quite safe^, some sports are extremely hazardous.

1. Each year, many people are killed or maimed when they practise a sport. Although skydiving and bungee jumping are hazardous extreme sports like base jumping, free diving, and rodeo events are even more dangerous.

2. Even though they may get arrested many people try base jumping. Wherever there are tall structures there may also be base jumpers. The jumpers wear parachutes and dive off buildings and bridges so that they can feel an adrenaline rush. Because the parachute may get tangled on the structure base jumping is an extremely dangerous sport.

3. Another extreme sport is free diving. Free divers hold their breath until they are as deep as possible underwater. So that they can break existing records some free divers have dived almost 120 metres. Sometimes when their brains lack oxygen they have to be resuscitated.

4. Although most rodeo sports can be safe bull riding is dangerous. Many bull riders are injured or even killed because the bull throws them off and tramples them.

5. Surprisingly, most sports-related injuries occur when people participate in an innocent-sounding sport. According to the Canadian Association of Orthopaedic Surgeons, almost half a million people are injured each year when they ride bicycles. So, what is the best policy? When playing a sport take precautions to protect yourself.

PRACTICE 4

Add a missing subordinating conjunction to each sentence. Use each subordinating conjunction once.

although	even though	~~when~~	whereas
because	unless	whenever	

EXAMPLE:

___*When*___ you refer to a "football" in Europe, Africa, or Asia, most people assume you are talking about a round black-and-white ball.

1. British people will assume you are speaking about soccer ____________________ you specifically say "Canadian football."

2. Soccer is the world's most popular sport ____________________ it is inexpensive to play. ____________________ someone decides to join a soccer team, he or she does not require expensive padding or equipment.

3. ____________________ a lot of Canadians love to play soccer, there are not many professional teams in Canada. Sports such as basketball, baseball, and football have professional teams and are shown on network television ____________________ soccer is not widely viewed.

4. ____________________ soccer has yet to become as popular as other sports in Canada, it is this country's fastest-growing sport, according to the Canadian Soccer Association. Perhaps soccer sensation David Beckham will help raise soccer's profile in North America.

Put a Subject after the Subordinator

When you form complex sentences, always remember to put a subject after the subordinator.

Wrestling is like theatre because ^*it* involves choreographed manoeuvres.

Boxers do not know who will win the round when ^*they* enter the ring.

PRACTICE 5

Add four missing subjects to the next paragraph.

EXAMPLE:

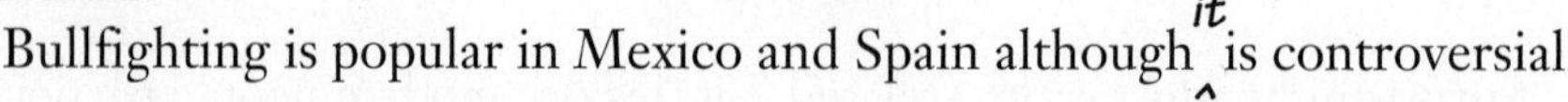

Bullfighting is popular in Mexico and Spain although ^it is controversial.

Each bullfight is an elaborate ceremony with three parts. In the first part, when the matador enters the arena, is dressed in a fine suit embroidered with gold. Holding a red cape, the matador tries to entice the bull. The spectators cheer when see the bull charging at the cape. In the second part, the *banderilleros*, or matador's assistants, push short spears into the bull until is tired and angry. In the third part, the matador enters the ring again holding a smaller cape and a sword. After has performed well, the matador kills the bull.

PRACTICE 6

Combine the following sentence pairs with subordinating conjunctions. Write each sentence twice: once with the dependent clause at the beginning of the sentence, and once with the dependent clause at the end. Properly punctuate the sentences.

Use one of the following conjunctions. Use a different conjunction each time.

~~because~~ while when even though although

EXAMPLE:

I am not athletic. I love football.

Although I am not athletic, I love football.

____

1. Professional football players can achieve fame and fortune. Many students want to play the sport.

____

____

2. Football is a great sport. It has some drawbacks.

____

____

3. Linebackers hit other players. They can develop head injuries.

____

____

4. A player has a concussion. The player should not finish the game.

____

____

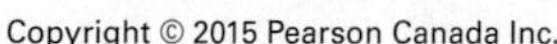

5. Professional football players retire. Some have long-term health problems.

____

____

CHAPTER 18

Use Relative Pronouns

A **relative pronoun** describes a noun or pronoun. You can form complex sentences by using relative pronouns to introduce dependent clauses. Review the most common relative pronouns.

who whom whomever whose which that

Watch the Video Pronoun Case **MyWritingLab**

That

Use ***that*** to add information about a thing. Do not use commas to set off clauses that begin with *that.*

> Randy Carlyle began his hockey career in a town *that is northwest of Sudbury, Ontario.*

Which

Use ***which*** to add nonessential information about a thing. Generally, use commas to set off clauses that begin with *which.*

> Randy Carlyle is the head coach of an NHL hockey team, *which is located in Toronto.*

Who

Use ***who*** (*whom, whomever, whose*) to add information about a person. When a clause begins with *who,* you may or may not need a comma. Put commas around the clause if it adds nonessential information. If the clause is essential to the meaning of the sentence, do not add commas. To decide if a clause is essential or not, ask yourself if the sentence still has clarity without the *who* clause. If it does, the clause is not essential.

> Most women **who** play sports do not earn as much money as their male counterparts.
> (The clause is essential. The sentence would not have clarity without the *who* clause.)
>
> Gold-medal-winning swimmer Michael Phelps, **who** has won many competitions, earns millions of dollars in endorsement deals.
> (The clause is not essential.)

Using *That* or *Which*

Both *which* and *that* refer to things, but *which* refers to nonessential ideas. Also, *which* can imply that you are referring to the complete subject and not just a part of it. Compare the next two sentences.

> Local baseball teams **that** have very little funding can still succeed.
> (This sentence suggests that some teams have good funding but others don't.)
>
> Local baseball teams, **which** have very little funding, can still succeed.
> (This sentence suggests that all of the teams have poor funding.)

GRAMMAR LINK

For more information about punctuating relative clauses, refer to Chapter 33, "Commas."

Watch the Video Commas **MyWritingLab**

PRACTICE 7

Using a relative pronoun, combine each pair of sentences to form a complex sentence.

EXAMPLE:

The Olympic Games celebrate excellence in sports. They occur once every four years.

The Olympic Games, which occur once every four years, celebrate excellence in sports.

1. The Olympic Games are very expensive to produce. They bring benefits to host countries.
2. In 2008, China presented an amazing opening ceremony. The ceremony attracted more than a billion viewers.
3. Michael Phelps is very shy. He won eight gold medals.
4. Some Chinese citizens complained about human rights abuses. They were arrested.
5. Coal-burning plants produce a lot of pollution. They were closed during the games.
6. The 2008 Olympics demonstrated something. China is a modern and vibrant society.

PRACTICE 8

Add a dependent clause to each sentence. Begin each clause with a relative pronoun (*who*, *which*, or *that*). Add any necessary commas.

EXAMPLE:

Teams *that have good leadership* often win tournaments.

1. The player ______________________________ might be hired to promote running shoes.

2. An athlete ______________________________ should be suspended for at least one game.
3. Bungee jumping is an activity ______________________________
4. I would like to try an extreme sport ______________________________
5. Skydiving ______________________________ is a sport I would like to try.
6. Athletes ______________________________ should be warned about the dangers of steroids.

Use Embedded Questions

It is possible to combine a question with a statement or to combine two questions. An **embedded question** is a question that is set within a larger sentence.

Question: How old are the Olympic Games?

Embedded question: The sprinter wonders how old the Olympic Games are.

In questions, there is generally a helping verb before the subject. However, when a question is embedded in a larger sentence, you need to remove the helping verb or place it after the subject. As you read the following examples, pay attention to the word order in the embedded questions.

Combine two questions.

Separate: Do you know the answer? Why **do** they like bullfighting?
(The second question includes the helping verb *do*.)

Combined: Do you know why they like bullfighting?
(The helping verb *do* is removed from the embedded question.)

Combine a question and a statement.

Separate: I wonder about it. When **should** we go to the arena?
(In the question, the helping verb *should* appears before the subject.)

Combined: I wonder when we should go to the arena.
(In the embedded question, *should* is placed after the subject.)

Use the Correct Word Order

When you edit your writing, ensure that you have formed your embedded questions properly. Remove question form structures from the embedded questions.

He wonders why ~~do~~ people like bullfighting. I asked him what ~~did he think~~ *he thought* about the sport.

PRACTICE 9

Correct six embedded question errors.

EXAMPLE:

The writer explains how ~~can people~~ *people can* love dangerous sports.

CHAPTER 18

One activity that generates controversy is bullfighting. Some people wonder why should bulls die for entertainment. They question how can bullfighting be so popular. Many call it a brutal activity because the bull is weakened and then slaughtered. For others, bullfighting is a respected tradition.

Spanish matador Mario Carrión wonders why do some people call bullfighting a sport. In sports, the goal is to win points in a confrontation with an opponent. In Carrión's view, a bullfight is not a sport because a human cannot compete against a thousand-pound beast. He defines bullfighting as "a dramatic dance with death."

Bullfight enthusiasts ask themselves why does bullfighting have a bad reputation. They wonder why is it rejected by so many nations. Do you know what can they do to improve the reputation of bullfighting?

Rick Hyman/ E+/Getty Images

REFLECT ON IT

Think about what you have learned in this chapter. If you do not know an answer, then review that topic.

1. Write six subordinating conjunctions. ______________________________

   ____

2. Write a complex sentence. ______________________________

   ____

3. List six relative pronouns. ______________________________

4. Correct the error in the following sentence.

   Clayton wonders why should he wear a helmet when he goes skateboarding.

Final Review

The following paragraphs contain only simple sentences. To give the paragraphs more variety, form at least ten complex sentences by combining pairs of sentences. You will have to add some words and delete others.

EXAMPLE:

When ~~Some~~ people pierce their tongues *, they* ~~. They~~ risk getting an infection.

1. Many activity fads come and go. Many of these fads are ridiculous. Why do fads become so popular? Nobody knows the answer. There were some unusual fads in the 1950s. College students did phone-booth stuffing. Students entered a phone booth one by one. They tried to stuff as many people as possible into the closed space. Later, hula hoops hit the market. In the 1960s, millions of people bought and used the circular plastic tubes. The hula hoop fad did not last long. It briefly provided people with an innovative way to exercise. People put the hoops around their waists. They would gyrate to keep the hoops spinning.

2. In the spring of 1974, a streaking fad began. It occurred on college campuses in Florida and California. Young people stripped naked. They may have felt embarrassed. They ran through public places such as football stadiums and malls. They wanted to shock people. The actor David Niven was presenting at the 1974 Academy Awards. A nude streaker dashed behind him. The streaker made a peace sign. Millions of viewers were watching the show. They saw the streaker.

3. Flash mobbing, a recent trend, is organized on websites. Flash mobs first appeared in New York City in the summer of 2003. For no obvious reason, a large group of people gathered on a stone wall in Central Park. They chirped like birds. In Berlin, Germany, about forty people shouted "Yes." They were in a subway car. They shouted into their cellphones at exactly the same moment. In Montreal, Canada, a large group of people began quacking. They were throwing rubber ducks into a fountain. Do you know the answer to the following question? Why do certain websites promote flash mobbing? They do it for a simple reason. They hope to add vibrancy to dull modern life.

Write about one of the following topics. Include some complex sentences.

1. Think about a sport that you really enjoy and a sport that you dislike. Compare and contrast the two sports.
2. Why do athletes train for events such as the Olympics? What are some of the effects of being an Olympic athlete? You can write about causes and/or effects.

How Do I Get a Better Grade?

Visit MyWritingLab for audiovisual lectures and additional practice sets about complex sentences.

Sentence Variety

Section Theme **CULTURE**

Skyelar Menard

LEARNING OBJECTIVES

***In this chapter, you will read about topics related to* cultural icons.**

The Writer's Journal

Would you like to be famous? What are some problems that could be associated with fame? Write a paragraph about fame.

What Is Sentence Variety?

In Chapters 17 and 18, you learned how to write different types of sentences. This chapter focuses on sentence variety. **Sentence variety** means that your sentences have assorted patterns and lengths. In this chapter, you will learn to vary your sentences by consciously considering the length of sentences, by altering the opening words, and by joining sentences using different methods.

Combine Sentences

A passage filled with simple, short sentences can sound choppy. When you vary the lengths of your sentences, the same passage becomes easier to read and flows more smoothly. For example, read the following two passages. In the first paragraph, most of the sentences are short, and the style is repetitive and boring. In the second paragraph, there is a mixture of simple, compound, and complex sentences.

GRAMMAR LINK
If you forget what compound and complex sentences are, refer to Chapters 17 and 18.

Watch the **Video**
Combining Sentences
MyWritingLab

Simple Sentences

Canadian corporations are not nearly as advanced as we like to think they are. It comes down to workplace diversity. But that's changing quickly. It is not because executives are particularly broad-minded. They are not sensitive to discrimination. They are finding that the very future of their business now depends on hiring immigrants. Currently, one-fifth of our country's workers are immigrants. By 2011, it's estimated that new Canadians will account for all net labour-force growth. The labour market is particularly tight in Alberta's energy sector. Immigrants account for almost all growth. Prior generations of new Canadians complained of underemployment. The latest wave of highly skilled immigrants has many options. If your firm doesn't welcome their culture or religious beliefs, they'll simply look elsewhere.

Canadian corporations are not nearly as advanced as we like to think they are when it comes to workplace diversity. But that's changing quickly. Not because executives are particularly broad-minded or sensitive to discrimination, but because they're finding that the very future of their business now depends on hiring immigrants. Currently, one-fifth of our country's workers are immigrants, and by 2011, it's estimated that new Canadians will account for all net labour-force growth. In industries where the labour market is particularly tight, such as the Alberta energy sector, immigrants already account for almost all growth. While prior generations of new Canadians complained of underemployment, the latest wave of highly skilled immigrants is finding that in many sectors, they have plenty of options to choose from. In such a market, if they get the impression that your firm doesn't welcome their culture or religious beliefs, they'll simply look elsewhere.

—Rachel Mendelson, "Diversity or Death"

Be Careful with Long Sentences

If a sentence is too long, it may be difficult for the reader to understand. If you have any doubts, break up a longer sentence into shorter ones.

Long and complicated:	Elvis Presley is a cultural icon who achieved the American dream by using his musical skills and his raw sexual energy to transform himself from a truck driver into a rock-and-roll legend, yet he did not handle his fame very well, and by the end of his life, he was unhappy and addicted to painkillers.
Better:	Elvis Presley is a cultural icon who achieved the American dream. Using his musical skills and his raw sexual energy, he transformed himself from a truck driver into a rock-and-roll legend. However, he did not handle his fame very well. By the end of his life, he was unhappy and addicted to painkillers.

PRACTICE 1

Modify the following paragraph so that it has both long and short sentences. Make sure you write some compound and complex sentences.

A cultural icon can be an object, a person, or a place. Cultural icons symbolize a belief or a way of life. Each country has its own icons. They become part of that country's history. For example, the maple leaf is a familiar image. The red leaf on the Canadian flag symbolizes Canadian culture, commerce, and growth. Niagara Falls and the Rocky Mountains are defining places. People can be icons too. In Canada, Pierre Trudeau is a cultural icon. In the United States, Elvis Presley is a cultural icon. These icons reflect a shared cultural experience.

Include a Question, a Quotation, or an Exclamation

The most common type of sentence is a statement. A simple but effective way to achieve sentence variety is to do the following:

- Ask and answer a **question.** You could also insert a **rhetorical question,** which does not require an answer but is used for effect.

  Did Elvis really do anything shocking?

- Include the occasional **exclamation** to express surprise. However, do not overuse exclamations because they make your writing look less academic.

  Elvis's swinging hips were considered obscene!

- Add a **direct quotation,** which includes the exact words that somebody said.

  Elvis said, "I didn't copy my style from anybody."

In the next passage, a question, an exclamation, and a quotation add variety.

Norma Jeane Baker was born to a mentally unstable mother and an absent father. The shy little girl spent her childhood being shuffled between an orphanage and foster parents. From such inauspicious beginnings, a cultural icon was born. Norma, who later changed her name to Marilyn Monroe, bleached her hair, had plastic surgery on her nose, and became one of Hollywood's most recognizable figures. **Why is she remembered?** Perhaps her fame is partly due to her untimely death at the age of thirty-six. She is also remembered for her sensuality and her childlike vulnerability. **Even at the height of fame, she exuded unhappiness and once complained, "Everybody is always tugging at you. They'd like a chunk out of you."** Some argue that she was not talented, and others suggest that people will forget her. **But the truth is, even half a century after her death, her image is one of the most recognized in the United States!**

< Question

< Quotation

< Exclamation

Punctuating Quotations

If you introduce your quotation with a phrase, put a comma after the phrase and before the opening quotation marks. Put the final period inside the closing quotation marks.

Marilyn Monroe once complained, "Everybody is always tugging at you."

If the end of the quotation is not the end of the sentence, place a comma inside the final quotation marks.

"They were terribly strict," she once said.

GRAMMAR LINK

For more information about punctuating quotations, refer to Chapter 34.

Quotation Marks
MyWritingLab

PRACTICE 2

Read the following passage. Change one sentence to a question, one to an exclamation, and one to a quotation.

EXAMPLE:

Why do most ~~Most~~ people want to be famous? ~~.~~

The last one hundred years were a century of celebrities. Many ordinary people achieve almost saintly status. In previous centuries, heroes were those who fought bravely in wars or who rescued others. Today, actors, musicians, politicians, and athletes are routinely deified. Even criminals such as Al Capone and Charles Manson become household names. In the words of Daniel J. Boorstin, celebrity worship and hero worship should not be confused. However, we confuse them every day.

Vary the Opening Words

An effective way to make your sentences more vivid is to vary the opening words. Instead of beginning each sentence with the subject, you could try the following strategies.

Begin with an Adverb

An **adverb** is a word that modifies a verb, and it often (but not always) ends in *-ly*. *Slowly*, *usually*, and *suddenly* are adverbs. Other adverbs include words such as *sometimes*, *never*, *however*, and *often*.

Generally, a cultural icon arouses strong feelings in members of that culture.

Often, an extremely gifted and famous person becomes an icon.

Begin with a Prepositional Phrase

A **prepositional phrase** is a group of words made up of a preposition and its object. *Under the chair*, *in the beginning*, and *after the fall* are prepositional phrases.

> In Stanley Park, Vancouver, the First Nations totem poles welcome visitors.
>
> At dawn, we photographed the totem poles.

Comma Tip

Generally, when a sentence begins with an adverb or a prepositional phrase, place a comma after the opening word or phrase.

> **Cautiously,** the reporter asked the volatile star another question.
>
> **Without any warning,** she stood up and left the room.

PRACTICE 3

Rewrite the following sentences by placing an adverb or a prepositional phrase at the beginning. First, strike out any word or phrase that could be moved. Then, rewrite that word or phrase at the beginning of the sentence. Finally, correctly punctuate your new sentence.

EXAMPLE:

Actually, ______________________ Canada's most recognizable symbol was ~~actually~~ made by the Canadian National Railway.

1. ______________________ The CN Tower in Toronto is the world's second-tallest free-standing structure.
2. ______________________ More than 1500 construction workers actually participated in the building process.
3. ______________________ Construction of the tower began on a sunny day in 1973.
4. ______________________ It finally officially opened in 1976 and attracts millions of visitors annually.
5. ______________________ People can walk onto a 24-square-metre glass floor, which is 342 metres up in the tower.
6. ______________________ They can actually dine in a 360-degree revolving restaurant and enjoy the skyline view.
7. ______________________ Individuals can participate in EdgeWalk, a thrilling hands-free walk around the roof's perimeter.
8. ______________________ The skyscraper is generally the epicentre of Toronto tourism.

PRACTICE 4

Add an opening word or phrase to each sentence. Use the type of opening that is indicated in parentheses. Remember to punctuate the sentence properly.

EXAMPLE:

Adverb
Surprisingly, actors Joshua Jackson and Ellen Page enjoy watching the National Hockey League (NHL) Stanley Cup Playoffs.

1. (Adverb) ______________________________ the Stanley Cup is more than a trophy with engraved names.
2. (Prepositional phrase) ______________________________ the trophy is like a beacon to aspiring amateur and professional hockey players.
3. (Prepositional phrase) ______________________________ thousands of professional athletes have competed with dreams of advancing to the NHL Finals and winning the Stanley Cup.
4. (Adverb) ______________________________ some athletes make it, but many do not.
5. (Adverb) ______________________________ the Stanley Cup is an important symbol in Canada.

Combine Sentences with a Present Participle

You can combine two sentences with a present participle. A **present participle** is a verb that ends in *-ing*, such as *believing*, *having*, and *using*. Combine sentences using an *-ing* modifier only when the two actions happen at the same time.

Separate sentences:	He looked across the harbour. He saw the lighthouse.
Combined sentences:	Looking across the harbour, he saw the lighthouse.

PRACTICE 5

Combine the next sentences by converting one of the verbs into an *-ing* modifier.

EXAMPLE:

George Chuvalo reminisces about his former boxing career and family life. He is armed with advice for youth.

Reminiscing about his former boxing career and family life, George Chuvalo had no idea of how drug-related deaths would haunt him.

Having no idea of how drug-related deaths would haunt him, George Chuvalo reminisces about his former boxing career and family life.

1. George Chuvalo competed for three decades as a famous Canadian heavyweight boxer. He was never knocked out.

____

____

____

2. He used a unique boxing method. Chuvalo won many fights.

3. He was defeated by Muhammad Ali, Joe Frazier, and George Foreman. He fought in 93 professional fights.

4. He was inducted into the Canadian Sports Hall of Fame in 1990. Chuvalo was also inducted into the World Boxing Hall of Fame in 1997.

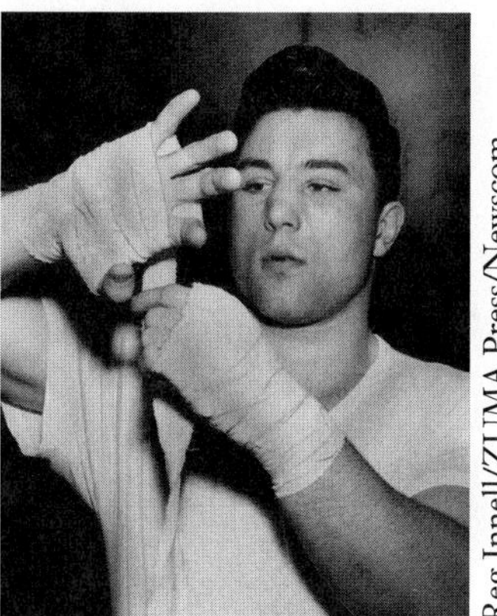

Reg Innell/ZUMA Press/Newscom

George Chuvalo

5. Chuvalo lost three sons and his wife. He suffered when the deaths of those close to him were drug related.

6. He raised another son and daughter. He remarried and is a stepfather to his wife's children.

7. He decided to do public speaking engagements on the danger of drugs. He has toured high schools and young adult centres across Canada promoting a drug-free life.

8. Chuvalo survived devastating personal losses in his life. He regained his balance by sharing his experiences and advice with others.

Combine Sentences with a Past Participle

Another way to combine sentences is to use a past participle. A **past participle** is a verb that has an *-ed* ending (although there are many irregular past participles, such as *gone*, *seen*, *broken*, and *known*).

You can begin a sentence with a past participle. To do this, you must combine two sentences, and one of the sentences must contain a past participle.

Separate sentences: Jesse Owens was raised in Alabama. He became a famous athlete.

Combined sentences: Raised in Alabama, Jesse Owens became a famous athlete.

PRACTICE 6

GRAMMAR LINK

For a complete list of irregular past participles, see Appendix 2.

Combine each pair of sentences into one sentence beginning with a past participle.

EXAMPLE:

Jesse Owens was born in 1913. He was the son of sharecroppers and the grandson of slaves.

Born in 1913, Jesse Owens was the son of sharecroppers and the grandson of slaves.

1. Jesse Owens was excluded from team sports in college. The African-American athlete excelled at individual sports such as track and field.

____

____

____

2. He was invited to the 1936 Olympic Games. He competed in twelve events.

____

____

____

3. The 1936 Olympic Games were held in Berlin. They were a showcase for the Nazi party.

____

____

____

4. Owens went on to win four Gold medals. He was encouraged by his fans.

____

____

____

5. Hitler was surprised at Owens's success. He refused to shake the medal winner's hand.

____

____

____

6. The athlete was treated like a hero upon his return. He basked in glory for a short while.

___

___

___

7. Owens was forbidden to ride in the front of a bus. He expressed sadness about the segregation laws in his state.

___

___

___

8. A Berlin street was renamed Jesse Owens Strasse in 1984. The street leads to the Olympic stadium.

___

___

___

Combine Sentences with an Appositive

An **appositive** is a word or phrase that gives further information about a noun or pronoun. You can combine two sentences by using an appositive. In the example, the italicized phrase could become an appositive because it describes the noun *Bob Marley*.

Two sentences: Bob Marley was *a founding member of The Wailers*. He went on to have a solo career.

You can place the appositive directly before the word that it refers to or directly after that word. Notice that the appositives are set off with commas.

Combined: A founding member of The Wailers (appositive), **Bob Marley** went on to have a successful solo career.

Combined: **Bob Marley,** a founding member of The Wailers (appositive), went on to have a successful solo career.

Finding an Appositive

To find an appositive, look for a word or phrase that describes or renames a noun. The noun could be anywhere in the sentence.

Bob Marley popularized a new fashion trend. He wore dreadlocks.

In the preceding sentences, "dreadlocks" describes the new fashion trend. You could combine the sentences as follows:

Bob Marley popularized **a new fashion trend,** dreadlocks (appositive).

PRACTICE 7

Combine the following pairs of sentences. In each pair, make one of the sentences an appositive. Try to vary the position of the appositive. In some sentences, you could put the appositive at the beginning of the sentence, and in others, you could put the appositive after the word that it describes. The first one has been done for you.

EXAMPLE:

Bob Marley was a Jamaican. He greatly popularized reggae music.

Bob Marley, a Jamaican, greatly popularized reggae music.

1. Bob Marley brought international attention to reggae music. He was a great musician.

2. Marley was biracial. He was born in 1945 in Jamaica.

3. Marley's father was a sailor. His father died when Marley was young.

4. At the age of fourteen, Marley started jam sessions with Joe Higgs. Higgs was a Rastafarian and reggae musician.

5. Jamaicans loved the reggae sound of The Wailers. The group was one of the most famous bands in the country.

6. Bob Marley contributed greatly to twentieth-century music. He is a music icon.

REFLECT ON IT

Think about what you have learned in this chapter. If you do not know an answer, review that topic.

1. Why is sentence variety important?

2. Write a sentence that begins with an adverb.

3. Write a sentence that begins with a present participle. ____________________

____

4. Write a sentence that begins with a past participle. ____________________

____

5. Write a sentence that begins with an appositive. ____________________

____

Final Review

The next essay lacks sentence variety. Use the strategies that you have learned in this chapter to create at least ten varied sentences.

EXAMPLE:

People are obsessed with fame~~. Perhaps they believe~~ *, believing* that fame will make them immortal.

1. Andy Warhol was an artist. He made a fortune with silkscreens of famous icons such as Marilyn Monroe and Mick Jagger. He predicted that everyone would be famous for fifteen minutes. Today, television is filled with ordinary people. They hope to achieve celebrity status. We wonder why this is happening. Our society elevates celebrities above the common human. Certainly, celebrities often have great talent. The talent includes exceptional musical ability, great athletic prowess, or a compelling ability to act. However, many celebrities lack moral character. They are models of bad behaviour. Celebrities often make poor role models.

Alex Timaios USA Photography / Alamy

2. Some celebrities in the twentieth century were emotionally fragile. There are people such as Marilyn Monroe, Jimi Hendrix, and Kurt Cobain. They turned to drugs to cope with their pain. For example, Cobain and Hendrix abused heroin. Monroe abused prescription drugs. Some argue that these celebrities are simply troubled people. They cannot be blamed for their addictions. Others suggest that such celebrities provide children with negative role models. The celebrities make drugs appear glamorous and exciting.

3. Other celebrities have promoted violence. This includes Tupac Shakur and many other rap artists. Shakur certainly had a difficult childhood. He was raised in Baltimore, Maryland. He was accepted to the prestigious Baltimore School for the Arts. He developed his music and writing skills. He also became involved in gangs. He was arrested on several occasions. His rap music often mentioned the thug life. It told stories of gunfights and gang rivalries. He was gunned down during a trip to Las Vegas, Nevada. The rapper died violently.

4. Impressionable youngsters want to emulate their heroes. They do not think about the dangers of drugs or gang life. Some people do not care what celebrities do. Artists are entitled to make mistakes. Others argue that celebrities have a certain responsibility. No matter what your opinion is, people leading public lives will always be under scrutiny.

The Writer's Room

Choose one of the following topics, and write a paragraph or an essay. When you write, remember to follow the writing process.

1. Define *hero*. What makes a person a hero?
2. Why do so many people crave fame? How does celebrity status affect people? Write about the causes or effects of fame.

READING LINK

Culture

"The Market and the Mall" by Stephen Henighan (page 528)
"We Turned Some Sharp Corners: A Marriage Proposal in Durango" by Nick Massey-Garrison (page 530)
"Stealing Glances" by Sheila Heti (page 535)
"The Great Offside" by James Mirtle (page 538)

Collaborative Activity

Work with a team of about three students. Using the six words below, create a paragraph. Include simple, compound, and complex sentences in your paragraph.

hero	disappointment	clothing
talent	leader	icon

When you finish, exchange paragraphs with another team. Verify whether the other team has used a variety of sentences. Then edit the other team's paragraph, looking for any errors in punctuation or sentence form.

How Do I Get a Better Grade?

Visit MyWritingLab for audiovisual lectures and additional practice sets about sentence variety.

Fragments and Run-Ons

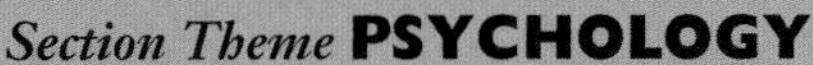

Section Theme **PSYCHOLOGY**

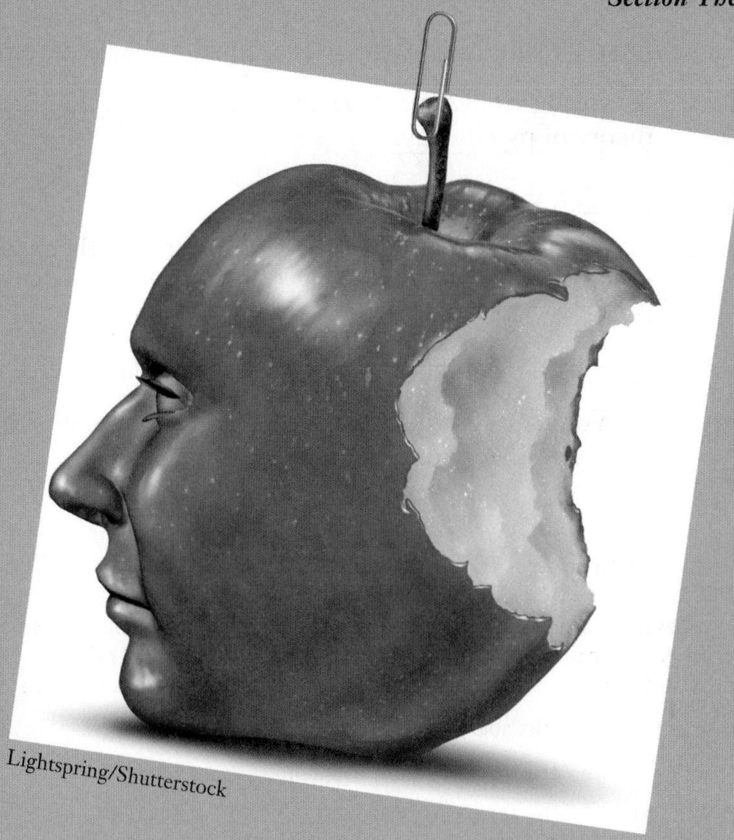

Lightspring/Shutterstock

LEARNING OBJECTIVES

In this chapter, you will read about topics related to **psychological profiles.**

The Writer's Journal

How do men and women deal with personal problems? Do they use different strategies? Write about problem-solving techniques that men and women use.

Fragments

Listen to the **Audio**
Lesson: Correcting Common Errors: Fragments and Run-On Sentences
MyWritingLab

A **sentence** must have a subject and verb, and it must express a complete thought. A **fragment** is an incomplete sentence. Either it lacks a subject or verb, or it fails to express a complete thought. You may see fragments in newspaper headlines and advertisements (*Wrinkle-free skin in one month*). However, in college writing, it is unacceptable to write fragments.

Sentence: Sigmund Freud was a famous psychologist.

Fragment: Considered to be the founder of psychoanalysis.

Phrase Fragments

A phrase fragment is missing a subject or a verb. In the following examples, the fragments are underlined.

No verb: First, Gestalt theory. It focuses on an individual's perceptions.

No subject: Wolfgang Kohler was born in 1887. Founded the Gestalt theory of psychology.

How to Correct Phrase Fragments

To correct a phrase fragment, either add the missing subject or verb, or join the fragment to another sentence. Here are two ways you can correct the phrase fragments in the previous examples.

Join sentences: First, Gestalt theory focuses on an individual's perceptions.

Add word: Wolfgang Kohler was born in 1887. **He** founded the Gestalt theory of psychology.

Watch the **Video**
Fragments
MyWritingLab

Incomplete Verbs

A sentence must have a subject and a complete verb. If a sentence has an incomplete verb, it is a phrase fragment. The following example contains a subject and part of a verb. However, it is missing a helping verb; therefore, the sentence is incomplete.

Fragment: Many books about psychology written by Carl Jung.

To make this sentence complete, you must add the helping verb.

Sentence: Many books about psychology were written by Carl Jung.

PRACTICE 1

Underline and correct six phrase fragments.

EXAMPLE:

A childhood trauma. ~~It~~ can be the source of an irrational fear.

1. First, superstitions. People sometimes have irrational beliefs. Many compulsive gamblers, for example, think that they can control the spin of slot machine reels by carrying good luck charms. Some carry a four-leaf clover. Or a rabbit's foot. The illusion of control.

2. Many athletes have rituals or lucky items of clothing. A lucky number on their jersey. Rams running back Marshall Faulk always wears black to the stadium. Another football player, Chris Hale. He believes that dressing in a particular sequence is lucky. Also, Wayne Gretzky played each game. Without his hockey sticks touching other sticks.

Fragments with *-ing* and *to*

A fragment may begin with a **present participle,** which is the form of the verb that ends in *-ing* (*running*, *talking*). It may also begin with an **infinitive,** which is *to* plus the base form of the verb (*to run*, *to talk*). These fragments generally appear before or after another sentence that contains the subject. In the examples, the fragments are underlined.

-ing fragment: Thinking about positive outcomes. It helps people cope with stress.

***to* fragment:** Michael J. Fox has developed a resilient attitude. To live with Parkinson's disease.

How to Correct *-ing* and *to* Fragments

To correct an *-ing* or *to* fragment, either add the missing words, or join the fragment to another sentence. Here are two ways to correct the previous examples.

Join sentences: Thinking about positive outcomes helps people cope with stress.

Add words: Michael J. Fox has developed a resilient attitude **because he had** to live with Parkinson's disease.

When the *-ing* Word Is the Subject

Sometimes a gerund (*-ing* form of the verb) is the subject of a sentence. In the next example, *advocating* is the subject of the sentence.

Correct: Advocating is an important skill.

A sentence fragment occurs when the *-ing* word is part of an incomplete verb string or when the subject was mentioned in a previous sentence.

Fragment: Michael J. Fox has achieved success. Advocating for a cure for Parkinson's disease.

PRACTICE 2

Underline and correct six *-ing* and *to* fragments.

EXAMPLE:

Living through a childhood trauma. It can be the source of an irrational fear.

Relating characteristics and physical health. Doctors Myer Friedman and Ray Rosenman divided people into personality types. Acting extremely competitive. Type A personalities are workaholics. They feel a strong pressure. To be busy. Type B personalities tend to be easygoing. Feeling relaxed and at peace. They can spend hours lying in the sun. Other researchers identified a Type C personality. Type C people are usually very pleasant but cannot easily express anger. To avoid conflict. They internalize strong emotions. According to Friedman and Rosenman. The personality type at greatest risk of developing heart disease is Type A. However, researchers at Duke University have found that only extremely hostile Type A profiles are at increased risk of coronary disease.

Explanatory Fragments

An **explanatory fragment** provides an explanation about a previous sentence and is missing a subject, a complete verb, or both. Such fragments are sometimes expressed as an afterthought. These types of fragments begin with one of the following words.

also	especially	for example	including	particularly
as well as	except	for instance	like	such as

In each example, the explanatory fragment is underlined.

Fragment: Carl Jung studied with many prominent psychologists. For instance, Sigmund Freud.

Fragment: Psychologists analyze behaviour. Particularly through methods of observation.

How to Correct Explanatory Fragments

To correct explanatory fragments, add the missing words or join the explanation or example to another sentence. Here are two ways to correct the fragments in the previous examples.

Add words: Carl Jung studied with many prominent psychologists. For instance, **he worked with** Sigmund Freud.

Join sentences: Psychologists analyze behaviour, particularly through methods of observation.

PRACTICE 3

Underline and correct six explanatory fragments. You may need to add or remove words.

EXAMPLE:

loyal, especially

Some fans are very ~~loyal. Especially~~ Montreal Canadiens fans.

Stephen Dubner wrote *Confessions of a Hero Worshipper*. He describes the personality of sports fans, and his book has interesting anecdotes. For example, the 1994 World Cup. The saliva in male soccer fans was tested before and after an important match. The chosen fans were from

Brazil. As well as Italy. The testosterone level in the fans of the winning team rose quickly. Particularly during the final minutes of the game. The losing fans' testosterone level decreased. Researcher Paul Bernhardt was surprised. Especially by the percentages. The fans of the winning team, with a 20 percent increase, had the same level of testosterone as the athletes. The findings may explain aggressive episodes. Such as soccer hooliganism. Immediately after a testosterone surge, some males may act more aggressively. Especially when provoked.

Dependent-Clause Fragments

A **dependent clause** has a subject and verb, but it cannot stand alone. It *depends* on another clause to be a complete sentence. Dependent clauses may begin with subordinating conjunctions (subordinators) or relative pronouns. The following are some of the most common words that begin dependent clauses.

Subordinating Conjunctions				Relative Pronouns
after	before	though	whenever	that
although	even though	unless	where	which
as	if	until	whereas	who(m)
because	since	what	whether	whose

The next two examples contain dependent-clause fragments. In each example, the fragment is underlined.

Fragment: Although I cross my fingers for luck. I know that it is a silly superstition.

Fragment: I will not walk under a ladder. That is leaning against a wall.

How to Correct Dependent-Clause Fragments

To correct dependent-clause fragments, either join the fragment to a complete sentence, or add the necessary words to make it a complete idea. You could also delete the subordinating conjunction. Here are two ways to correct the fragments in the previous examples.

Delete the subordinator: I cross my fingers for luck. I know that it is a silly superstition.

Join sentences: Although I cross my fingers for luck, I know that it is a silly superstition.
I will not walk under a ladder that is leaning against a wall.

CHAPTER 20

PRACTICE 4

Underline and correct five dependent-clause fragments.

EXAMPLE:

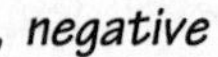

Whenever they blame themselves~~. Negative~~ thinkers make their problems larger.

1. Dr. Michael Ungar is a Dalhousie University researcher. Who directs the International Resilience Research Project. For the project, researchers study how youth can be more resilient in times of adversity. Around the world. Using qualitative and quantitative research, the study focuses on how children cope with difficulties. Such as poverty, drugs, war, and violence.

2. One child in the program who came from a tough inner-city neighbourhood had convinced himself that he would probably end up in a gang. Even though he hated violence. The program taught this boy. That there are other possible outcomes. He learned that he did not have to focus on worst-case scenarios.

PRACTICE 5

The next paragraphs contain phrase, explanatory, *-ing*, *to*, and dependent-clause fragments. Correct fifteen fragment errors.

EXAMPLE:

nightmares when

Many people had ~~nightmares. When~~ they were children.

1. In ancient times. People thought that dreams had heavenly origins. The ancient Egyptians thought that dreams had a prophetic function. The Babylonians and Assyrians also. Some Egyptian pharaohs recorded their strange dreams. For example, Thutmose IV. He dreamed that the Sphinx spoke to him. Using a familiar language. The Sphinx, which was buried in sand, asked Thutmose to remove the sand. If he obeyed. He would then become king. Thutmose cleared the sand off the Sphinx. Soon after, became king.

2. Some psychologists believe that dreams are meaningless. Although others disagree. Dreams have a significant purpose.

andriikoval/Fotolia

According to Sigmund Freud. Freud believed that dreams could lead to understanding the unconscious mind. He proposed that dreams appeared in symbols or in disguised forms. That dreams had hidden meanings. Freud theorized that dream symbols showed the dreamer's desires. Either sexual or aggressive in nature.

3. Two modern theories about dreams. In the first theory, some psychologists propose that dreaming is necessary. Because a dream's purpose is to rid the mind of useless data. We forget our dreams because we no longer need the information in them. The second theory. Dreams have no function at all. Some psychologists believe that the brain is responding to high levels of stimuli. Therefore, people have inexplicable dreams. Such as dreams about someone that they have never met. Certainly, there are many psychological theories. To help explain the meanings of dreams.

Run-Ons

Watch the **Video**
Run-Ons
MyWritingLab

A **run-on sentence** occurs when two or more complete sentences are incorrectly joined. In other words, the sentence runs on without stopping. There are two types of run-on sentences.

- A **fused sentence** has no punctuation to mark the break between ideas.

  Incorrect: Psychologists describe human behaviour they use observational methods.

- A **comma splice** uses a comma incorrectly to connect two complete ideas.

  Incorrect: Wilhelm Wundt was born in 1832, he is often called the founder of modern psychology.

PRACTICE 6

Read the following sentences. Write *C* beside correct sentences and *RO* beside run-ons.

EXAMPLE:

Sigmund Freud and Carl Jung were two famous psychologists they profoundly influenced the field of psychology. *RO*

1. Psychologists study human behaviour, researchers have developed many theories on human nature. ______
2. Instinct theory is one model developed by psychologists it proposes that behaviour is based on biology. ______
3. Learning theory suggests that humans learn through experience. ______
4. Trait theories focus on human characteristics, psychologists describe personality types. ______

5. Freud developed a theory about personality in which he divided the mind into three parts. ______
6. Freud named the parts the *id*, *ego*, and *superego* his theory became enormously influential. ______
7. Psychoanalysis started to lose its popularity by the 1940s, at that time other personality theories were developing. ______
8. One psychologist, William Sheldon, tried to connect personality to body shapes. ______
9. Sheldon's types were mesomorphic or lean, endomorphic or fat, and ectomorphic or tall and thin. ______
10. Human personalities vary greatly it is difficult to categorize them. ______

How to Correct Run-Ons

You can correct run-on sentences in a variety of ways. Read the following run-on sentence, and then review the four ways to correct it.

Run-on: Kerry Jang studies twins he is interested in genetic influences on behaviour.

1. Make two separate sentences by adding end punctuation, such as a period.

   Kerry Jang studies twins. **He** is interested in genetic influences on behaviour.
2. Add a semicolon.

   Kerry Jang studies twins**;** he is interested in genetic influences on behaviour.
3. Add a coordinator (*for*, *and*, *nor*, *but*, *or*, *yet*, *so*).

   Kerry Jang is interested in genetic influences on behaviour**, so** he studies twins.
4. Add a subordinator (*after*, *although*, *as*, *because*, *before*, *since*, *when*, *while*).

   Kerry Jang studies twins **because** he is interested in genetic influences on behaviour.

PRACTICE 7

A. Correct each run-on by making two complete sentences.

EXAMPLE:

. They
The twins are identical~~, they~~ have brown hair and eyes.

1. Until the 1960s, twins put up for adoption were generally separated they were often adopted by two different families.
2. Psychologists are interested in studying twins raised in different families, they want to determine whether genetics or the environment plays a dominant role in behaviour.
3. An amazing case involves Tamara Rabi and Adriana Scott they met each other in 2003.

B. Correct each run-on by joining the two sentences with a semicolon.

EXAMPLE:

The girls are remarkably similar; they both love to dance.

4. Tamara and Adriana were born in Mexico they were separated and raised by different families.
5. The girls were adopted by American families they lived just twenty-five miles apart.
6. Tamara Rabi was raised by a Jewish family in a city Adriana Scott was raised by a Catholic family in a suburb.

C. Correct the next run-ons by joining the two sentences with a coordinator such as *for*, *and*, *nor*, *but*, *or*, *yet*, or *so*.

EXAMPLE:

A boy named Justin dated Adriana, but there was no mutual attraction.

7. Justin still wanted to find a girlfriend, his friend set him up with another girl.
8. Justin met Tamara he was astounded at her similarity to his previous girlfriend, Adriana.
9. Justin convinced the girls to meet each other, they met in a McDonald's parking lot.

D. Correct the next run-ons by joining the two sentences with a subordinator such as *although*, *because*, *where*, or *when*.

EXAMPLE:

The girls were happy to meet because they each wanted a sister.

10. The twins did not go to the same type of school their families were not in the same income bracket.
11. They received different qualities of education, they were both B students.
12. The girls flew to Mexico they met their birth mother.

PRACTICE 8

Write *F* beside fragments, *RO* beside run-on sentences, and *C* beside correct sentences.

EXAMPLE:

The origins of certain fears. ___F___

1. Maggie Juato, a public relations executive, becomes breathless and dizzy whenever she sees one. _____
2. The red nose, the curly green hair, and the large floppy shoes. _____
3. The fear of clowns is known as coulrophobia. _____
4. The clown's painted face is frightening. _____
5. With a large mocking grin painted over the clown's real mouth. _____
6. Professional clowns are aware of the problem they do not approach the fearful. _____
7. Perhaps the phobia is caused by clown horror movies. _____
8. Stephen King's movie *It*, for example. _____
9. In the film, actor Tim Curry plays the evil clown, Pennywise, he smacks his lips every time he is about to murder a child. _____
10. While such movies are terrifying. _____
11. Real clowns are actors and comedians who need the work, they entertain children in hospitals and the elderly in nursing homes. _____
12. Certain psychologists can help patients overcome their clown phobias. _____

PRACTICE 9

Correct the fragment and run-on errors.

EXAMPLE:

About 3 percent of births in Canada are twins ^*, but* the percentage is increasing.

1. For many years, Kerry Jang, director of UBC's Twin Project, has been studying identical and fraternal twins. Who were not necessarily raised apart. He contacted twins or their parents to study their similarities and differences.

2. Studies on twins at UBC's Twin Project include data from more than 1500 sets of twins they reflect differences in attitudes among the individuals. The research on at least 30 subjects suggests attitudes toward issues such as life preservation, equality, and athleticism are not only based on life experience. But also on genetics.

3. Jang's studies however point to attitudes regarding intellectual pursuits (such as reading) as having no genetic influence. The researcher is now able to provide reasoning. For the difficulty in changing a person's behaviour.

4. Another study on twins by Canadian-born Steven Pinker at Harvard University suggests that language development (sometimes slightly delayed with twins) is based more on environmental issues than on genetics. One researcher Jennifer Ganger explains this by linking the interactions the twins have with their caregivers, stating that they are more shared.

5. The twin studies suggest certain possibilities, for example, similar attitudes toward issues may have a genetic component. Twins may also have delayed language development. Possibly related to face-to-face conversation with caregivers. Much more research is needed to know how genes influence behaviour.

REFLECT ON IT

Think about what you have learned in this chapter. If you do not know an answer, review that topic.

1. What is a sentence fragment? ______________________________
2. What are the types of fragments?
   ______________ ______________
   ______________ ______________
3. What is a run-on? ______________________________
4. Define a comma splice. ______________________________
5. Define a fused sentence. ______________________________
6. Explain the four ways to correct a run-on sentence.
   a. ______________________________
   b. ______________________________
   c. ______________________________
   d. ______________________________

FINAL REVIEW

Correct fifteen fragment and run-on errors.

EXAMPLE:

First, dreams express our deepest fears.

~~First, dreams and fears.~~

1. "To sleep, perchance to dream," wrote Shakespeare in his play *Hamlet*. Many great writers have written about dreams. Such as Lewis Carroll. His famous work *Alice in Wonderland* is dreamlike. In the story, Alice has an adventure with a white rabbit. Another bizarre character is the Queen of Hearts. Who wants to cut off Alice's head.

2. Dreams sometimes leave the dreamer feeling uncomfortable. In Franz Kafka's novella *Metamorphosis*, the main character, Gregor Samsa, wakes

up feeling uneasy. Because he has had bad dreams during the night. When he wakes up, Samsa finds himself transformed into a grotesque insect, he realizes that it is not a dream.

CHAPTER 20

3. The meaning of dreams. Sigmund Freud and his student Carl Jung proposed a theory, they wrote that dreams have a specific purpose. Jung believed that dreamers could learn from their dreams. In his book *Memories, Dreams, and Reflections*. Jung wrote that dreams forced him to think about important things. Such as life and death.

4. Dreams have been the source of inspiration to many people. According to the Koran. God revealed many truths to Mohammad through dreams. Mohammad then recorded these revelations. In the Bible. God appeared in dreams to many people. Including Joseph. Others have also drawn inspiration from dreams. For instance, the Japanese filmmaker Akira Kurosawa. He recorded his dreams he stated that man is a genius when he is dreaming.

5. Dreams have inspired artists, writers, and religious figures. If you have recurring dreams, you might write them down, dreams can be the source of fascinating stories.

The Writer's Room

Write about one of the following topics. Check that there are no sentence fragments.

1. Explain why people are superstitious, and give examples to support your point of view.
2. Look again at Practice 2. What personality type are you? Are you Type A, B, or C? Describe your personality.
3. Describe a set of twins. Compare and contrast twins by looking at their similarities and differences. If you don't know any twins, then describe the similarities and differences between siblings (brothers and sisters).

How Do I Get a Better Grade?

Visit MyWritingLab for audiovisual lectures and additional practice sets about fragments and run-ons.

Faulty Parallel Structure

Section Theme **PSYCHOLOGY**

LEARNING OBJECTIVES

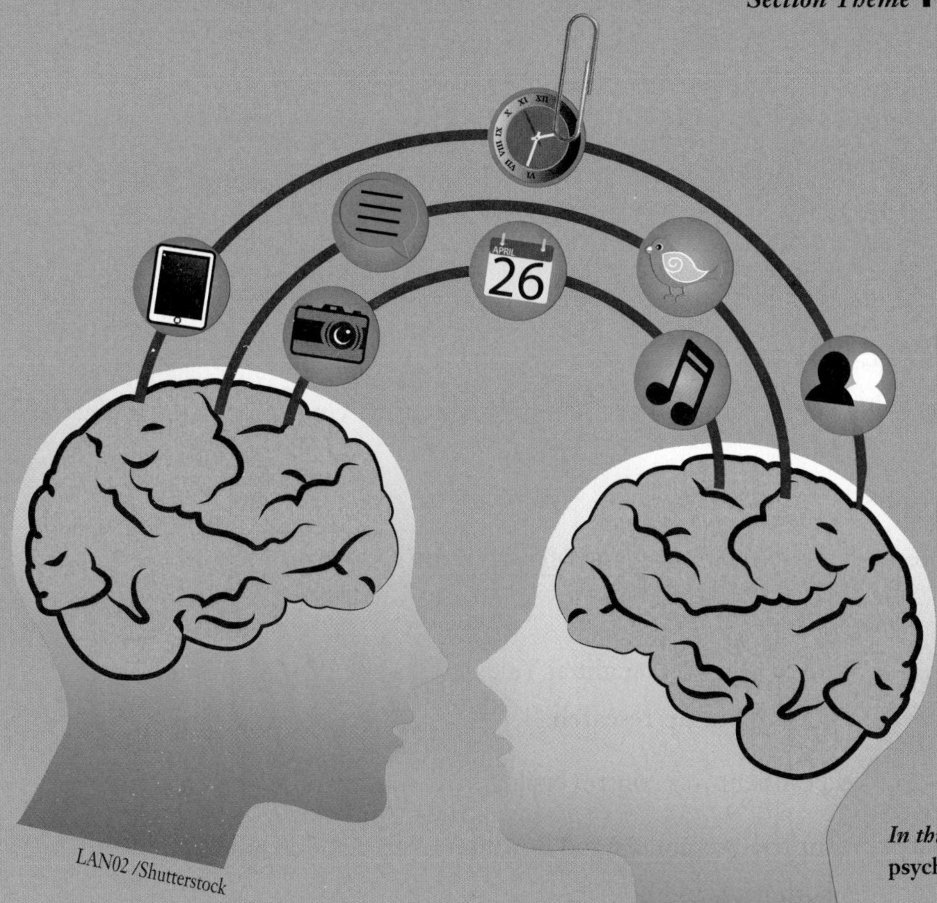

LAN02 /Shutterstock

In this chapter, you will read about topics related to psychological experiments.

The Writer's Journal

Write a short paragraph comparing your personality to that of a family member or friend. Describe how your personalities are similar and different.

What Is Parallel Structure?

Watch the **Video**
Parallelism
MyWritingLab

Parallel structure occurs when pairs or groups of items in a sentence are balanced. In the following sentences, the underlined phrases contain repetitions of grammatical structure but not of ideas. Each sentence has parallel structure.

> Internet sites, magazines, and newspapers published the results of the experiment.
> (The nouns are parallel.)

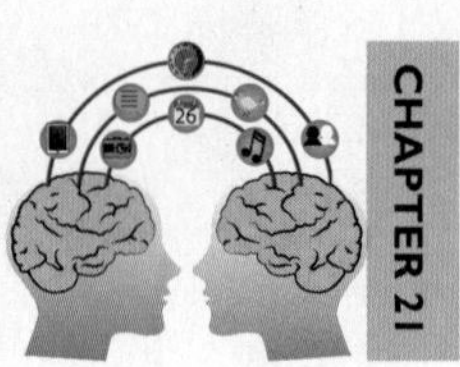

Psychologists observe and predict human behaviour.
(The present tenses are parallel.)

The experiment was fascinating, groundbreaking, and revolutionary.
(The adjectives are parallel.)

To get to the psychology department, go across the street, into the building, and up the stairs.
(The prepositional phrases are parallel.)

There are some test subjects who develop a rash and some who have no reactions.
(The "who" clauses are parallel.)

PRACTICE 1

All of the following sentences have parallel structures. Underline the parallel items.

EXAMPLE:

Students in my psychology class listened to the instructor, took notes, and asked questions.

1. Professor Stanley Milgram taught at Yale, conducted a famous experiment, and wrote a book about his research.
2. Milgram's experiment was controversial, provocative, and surprising.
3. His experiment tried to understand how humans reacted to authority, how they obeyed authority, and how they felt about authority.
4. For his experiment, Milgram used one actor in a lab coat, one actor with glasses, and one unsuspecting subject in street clothes.
5. The psychologist told the subject to sit at the desk, to watch the "patient" behind the glass, and to listen to the experiment "leader."
6. The leader told the subject when to start electric shocks, when to increase the level of shocks, and when to stop the experiment.
7. Milgram's experiment raised important questions, ended in astonishing results, and gave valuable insight into human behaviour.
8. Psychologists continue to perform experiments, give lectures, and debate issues.

Identify Faulty Parallel Structure

It is important to use parallel structure when using a series of words or phrases, paired clauses, comparisons, and two-part constructions.

Series of Words or Phrases

Use parallel structure when words or phrases are joined in a series.

Not parallel: Students, administrators, and people who teach sometimes volunteer for psychology experiments.

Parallel: Students, administrators, and teachers sometimes volunteer for psychology experiments.
(The nouns are parallel.)

Not parallel: I plan to study for tests, to attend all classes, and listening to the instructor.

Parallel: I plan to study for tests, to attend all classes, and to listen to the instructor.
(The verbs are parallel.)

Paired Clauses

Use parallel structure when independent clauses are joined by *and*, *but*, or *or*.

Not parallel: The experimenter placed two probes on her head, and her wrist is where he attached a monitor.

Parallel: The experimenter placed two probes on her head, and he attached a monitor to her wrist.
(The prepositional phrases are parallel.)

Not parallel: She felt dizzy, and she also had a feeling of fear.

Parallel: She felt dizzy, and she also felt afraid.
(The adjectives are parallel.)

Use Consistent Voice

When a sentence has two independent clauses and is joined by a coordinating conjunction, use a consistent voice. In other words, if one part of the sentence is active, the other should also be active.

Not parallel: The researcher conducted the experiment, and then a report was written by him.

Parallel: The researcher conducted the experiment, and then he wrote a report.
(Both parts use the active voice.)

GRAMMAR LINK

To learn more about active and passive voice, see pages 353–355 in Chapter 23.

Watch the **Video**
Active and Passive Voice
MyWritingLab

PRACTICE 2

Correct the faulty parallel structure in each sentence.

EXAMPLE:

Some psychology experiments are bold, pioneering, and ~~show their originality.~~ *original.*

1. Ivan Pavlov was a Russian physiologist, a research scientist, and he won a Nobel prize.

2. Pavlov became interested in dog salivation, and digestion also interested him.
3. To get to his lab, Pavlov walked through the door, up the stairs, and the department is where he entered.

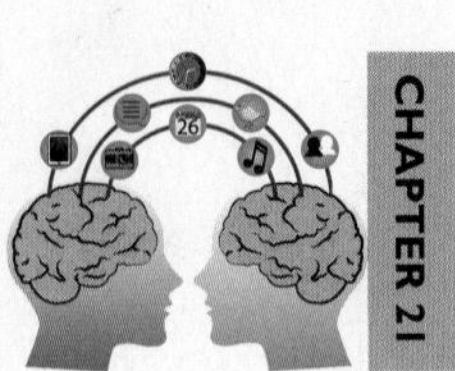

4. Pavlov used many sound-making devices to stimulate his dogs, such as metronomes, whistles, and he also used tuning forks.
5. Pavlov noticed that the dogs heard the noise, saw the food dish, and were salivating.
6. Some of the dogs were excited, nervous, and expressed enthusiasm.
7. Western scientists found Pavlov's experiments to be astounding, innovative, and thought they were important.
8. Ivan Pavlov worked quickly and was very efficient.

Comparisons

Use parallel structure in comparisons containing *than* or *as.*

Not parallel: Creating new experiments is more difficult than to re-create an earlier experiment.

Parallel: Creating a new experiment is more difficult than re-creating an earlier experiment.
(The *-ing* forms are parallel.)

Not parallel: His home was as messy as the way he kept his laboratory.

Parallel: His home was as messy as his laboratory.
(The nouns are parallel.)

Two-Part Constructions

Use parallel structure for the following paired items.

either . . . or	not . . . but	both . . . and
neither . . . nor	not only . . . but also	rather . . . than

Not parallel: My psychology class was both informative and a challenge.

Parallel: My psychology class was both informative and challenging.
(The adjectives are parallel.)

Not parallel: I would rather finish my experiment than leaving early.

Parallel: I would rather finish my experiment than leave early.
(The verbs are parallel.)

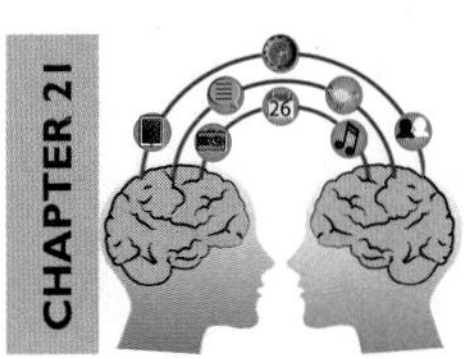

PRACTICE 3

Correct ten errors in parallel construction.

EXAMPLE:

Philip Zimbardo is creative and ~~an interesting person.~~ *interesting.*

1. Philip Zimbardo created an experiment that was both unique and startled others. The Stanford Prison Experiment examined how ordinary people would react when placed in positions of power. He chose twenty-four students who were healthy, stable, and they abided by the law. Each subject would be either a guard or a prisoner for a two-week period.

2. On the first day of the experiment, each guard was told to wear a uniform, carry a baton, and sunglasses were put on. Ordinary people who had committed no crime, who had broken no laws, and been honest were placed in a cold room. The prisoners were not only arrested but the guards also deloused them.

3. Immediately, the experimenters observed shocking behaviour. Some of the guards started to act controlling, sadistic, and they abused the prisoners. On the second day, the prisoners rioted and the guards attacked. Some prisoners decided that they would rather leave than continuing with the experiment.

4. During the next few days, officials, priests, and teachers observed the experiment. Nobody questioned the morality of the proceedings. Then, on the sixth day, another psychologist arrived. She was appalled and she felt horror when she realized what was happening.

5. Zimbardo realized that his student actors were taking the experiment too seriously. Both the prisoners and the people playing the guards had to stop the experiment. Zimbardo worried that the student actors would be seriously hurt, distressed, and suffer from depression.

PRACTICE 4

Correct the errors in parallel construction.

EXAMPLE:

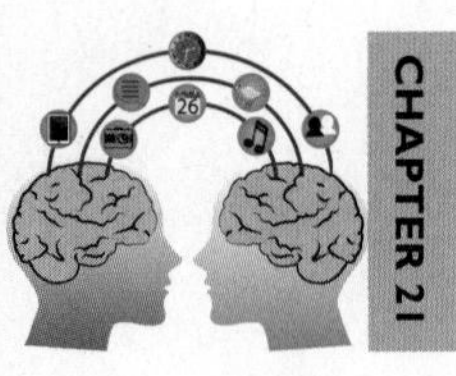

interesting.
Information about bystander apathy is surprising and ~~of interest.~~

1. Bystander apathy is the unwillingness of an individual to help another in an emergency. In the 1960s, psychologists started to collect data, investigate behaviours, and proposing theories about bystander apathy. Many incidents have occurred that appear to demonstrate how people assume it is someone else's responsibility to respond in an emergency.

2. In several large Canadian cities, homelessness is widespread. People on their way to work or when they go to school walk right past individuals sitting or lying down on cold, damp, urban streets. Often people step over huddled, quivering, homeless persons without glancing at their eyes or to see if they are okay. This is an example of bystander apathy.

3. Sadly, people tend to react to out-of-the ordinary events like these by doing what everyone else is doing: not acting. Groups of bystanders often hold back (more so than individuals on their own do) and resist helping others, thinking that someone else will react. This is called "pluralistic ignorance."

4. Many psychologists have studied the phenomenon of bystander apathy, and the results have been published by them. There are many reasons a bystander may not help someone in trouble. Bystanders may not want to risk their own lives, they may not have the skills to help in an emergency, or legal problems could be incurred. In addition, many people do not want to look stupid or be seen as being foolish if there is no real emergency. Psychologists believe that these are only some possible reasons for bystander apathy.

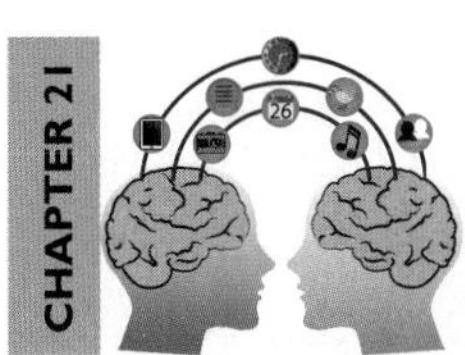

PRACTICE 5

Write sentences using parallel structure with the following grammatical items.

1. Parallel nouns: ______________________________

____

2. Parallel verbs: ______________________________

____

3. Parallel adjectives: ______________________________

____

4. Parallel *who* clauses: ______________________________

____

REFLECT ON IT

Think about what you have learned in this chapter. If you do not know an answer, review that topic.

1. What is parallel structure? ______________________________

____

2. Why is parallel structure important? ______________________________

____

Fill in the blanks of the following sentences. Make sure the grammatical structures are parallel.

3. The college I attend is both ______________________________ and ______________________________.

4. In my spare time, I ______________________, ______________________, and ______________________.

FINAL REVIEW

Correct twelve errors in parallel construction.

EXAMPLE:

counsellors

Psychiatrists, psychologists, and ~~other people who are counsellors~~ help patients deal with their mental health problems.

1. In 1972, psychologist David Rosenhan was young, intelligent, and had enthusiasm. He asked eight of his friends to participate in a psychology experiment. There were some psychologists, a pediatrician, a psychiatrist, a man who was a painter, a homemaker, and a graduate student. Rosenhan told the participants that for five days they had to stop showering, they

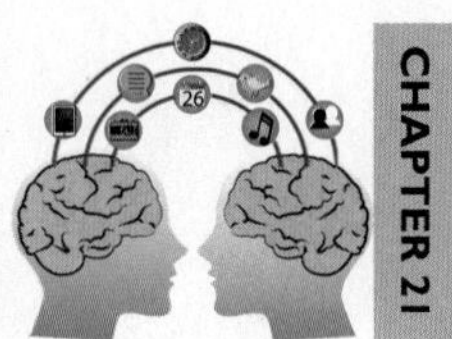

had to look unclean, and to wear old clothes. At the end of the fifth day, the participants travelled to different parts of the country and entered various psychiatric hospital emergency rooms. The psychiatric hospitals were either private and expensive or public and they cost very little. The participants told the admitting psychiatrists that they heard voices. They told the truth about everything else in their lives.

2. Psychiatrists looked for and were finding serious psychological illnesses in the patients. They diagnosed all eight patients with paranoid schizophrenia. The doctors institutionalized the patients from eight to fifty-eight days. Rosenhan's experiment showed that psychiatric evaluation had to be both stringent and have no bias.

3. Lauren Slater is a researcher, psychologist, and she writes. In 2003, she decided to reenact Rosenhan's experiment to see if assessment methods in psychiatry had changed. She became the guinea pig in her own experiment. Like Rosenhan's friends, she looked scruffy, she visited different psychiatric institutions, and told the psychiatrists about voices in her head. Psychiatrists asked her neither about her religious beliefs, nor was she asked anything about her cultural background. The examining psychiatrists asked her some general questions, took her temperature, and she was diagnosed by them with depression.

4. Slater knew she did not really suffer from depression because she had asked her real doctor, her family, and her people who were her friends to assess her mental state. Unlike the psychiatrists in Rosenhan's experiment, Slater's psychiatrists did not admit her to their hospitals, but they all prescribed antipsychotic and antidepressant drugs for her. She wrote about her experiences in her book *Opening Skinner's Box*. Her book is fascinating, illuminating, and it is of interest.

The Writer's Room

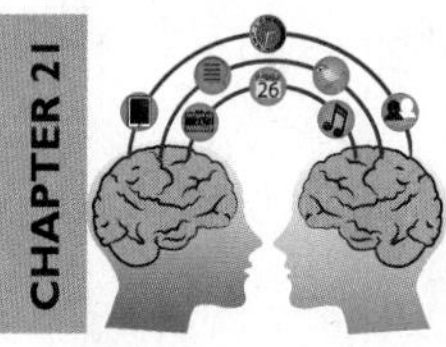

Write about one of the following topics. Make sure that you have not written any run-ons.

1. What makes you happy? Describe some situations or events that make you happy.
2. What are some different ways that people deal with their fears? Classify their responses to fear into three categories.

The Writers' Circle Collaborative Activity

When you apply for a job, the employer often asks you what your strengths and weaknesses are. Work with a team of students to do the following activity.

STEP 1 Think of a successful person. You could choose a person from any of these categories.

A business tycoon	A politician	A movie star
A musician	An athlete	A writer or artist

STEP 2 Brainstorm one list of that person's strengths and another list of that person's weaknesses.

STEP 3 Write a short paragraph about that successful person, discussing the person's strengths and weaknesses.

STEP 4 Exchange paragraphs with another team. Proofread the other team's paragraph, checking especially for fragments, run-ons, and parallel structure.

READING LINK

Psychology

"New Evidence in 'Diefenbaby' Case" by Charlie Gillis (page 546)
"The Catcher of Ghosts" by Amy Tan (page 548)
"A Shift in Perception" by Cynthia Macdonald (page 551)
"The Sage" by Eric Andrew-Gee (page 557)
"The Sanctuary of School" by Lynda Barry (page 563)
"Like It or Not, Yoga Is Here to Stay" by Aparita Bhandari (page 566)

How Do I Get a Better Grade?

Visit MyWritingLab for audiovisual lectures and additional practice sets about faulty parallel structure.

Present and Past Tenses

Section Theme **ESPIONAGE**

LEARNING OBJECTIVES

Dieter Spannknebel/Stockbyte/Getty Images

In this chapter, you will read about topics related to the history of espionage.

The Writer's Journal

Write a short paragraph describing the last spy or suspense movie that you have seen. Describe what happened in the movie.

What Is Verb Tense?

A verb shows an action or a state of being. A **verb tense** indicates when an action occurred. Review the various tenses of the verb *work*.

Present time: She works alone.

Past time: The agent worked in Monaco last summer.

Future: She will work in the Middle East next year.

Use Standard Verb Forms

Nonstandard English is used in everyday conversation, and it may differ according to the region in which you live. **Standard Canadian English** is the common language generally used and expected in schools, businesses, and government institutions in Canada. Most of your instructors will want you to write using Standard Canadian English.

Nonstandard:	He don't have no time.	She be busy.
Standard:	He does not have any time.	She is busy.

The Simple Present Tense

Watch the **Video**
Tense
MyWritingLab

In English, there are two forms of the present tense. The **simple present tense** indicates that an action is a general fact or habitual activity.

Fact: The Spy Museum contains many interesting spy artifacts.

Habitual activity: The undercover agent meets her superiors once a month.

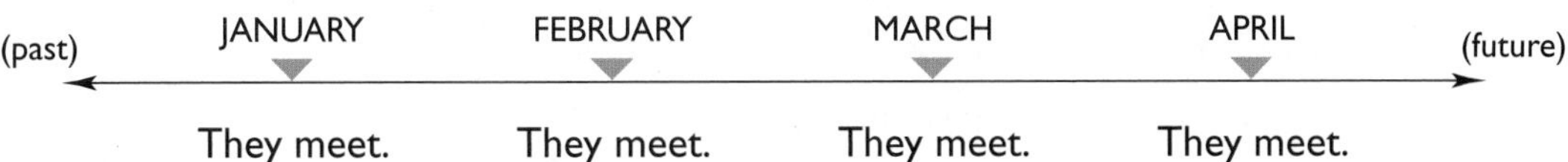

The Present Progressive

The **present progressive tense** indicates that an action is in progress at this moment. In this chapter, you will focus on the simple present and past forms.

present progressive tense
Right now, the agent is taking pictures with her spy camera.

Forms of the Simple Present Tense

GRAMMAR LINK

For more information about progressive forms, see pages 359–361 in Chapter 24.

Simple present tense verbs (except *be*) have two forms.

- **Base form:** When the subject is *I*, *you*, *we*, *they*, or the equivalent (*women*, *the Rocky Mountains*), do not add an ending to the verb.

  Nations rely on spies to gather secret information.

  Many agents speak several languages.

- **Third-person singular form:** When the subject is *he*, *she*, *it*, or the equivalent (*Mark*, *Carol*, *Moncton*), add an *-s* or *-es* ending to the verb.

  That woman works as a spy. She has several code names.

Look at the singular and plural forms of the verb *work*.

Present Tense of *Work*

	Singular	**Plural**
First person:	I work.	We work.
Second person:	You work.	You work.
Third person:	He work**s**.	They work.
	She work**s**.	
	It work**s**.	

Irregular Present Tense Verbs (be and have)

In the present tense, *be* and *have* do not follow the regular pattern for verb endings. Be particularly careful when writing these verbs.

Present Tense of *Be*

I am	He is	You are
	She is	We are
	It is	They are

Present Tense of *Have*

I have	He has	You have
	She has	We have
	It has	They have

GRAMMAR LINK

For more information about subject-verb agreement, see Chapter 25.

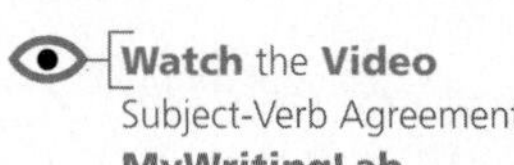

Watch the Video
Subject-Verb Agreement
MyWritingLab

Make Your Subjects and Verbs Agree

In the present tense, the subject and verb must **agree** in number. If the subject is third-person singular (*he*, *she*, *it*), the corresponding verb must have the singular form, too.

Although plural nouns usually end in -*s*, plural verbs do not. Instead, singular verbs have the -*s* or -*es* ending. Notice the errors in subject-verb agreement in the next sentences.

> Edward Rowen ~~work~~ *works* for the Canadian Security Intelligence Service. Why ~~do~~ *does* the service investigate candidates? It ~~do~~ *does* not want to hire people with criminal records.

PRACTICE 1

Circle the correct present tense form of the verbs in parentheses.

EXAMPLE:

Spying (seem, (seems)) like an exciting job.

1. According to Christopher Andrew, co-author of *The Sword and the Shield*, the acronym *mice* (sum, sums) up the reasons why a person may become a traitor.
2. *Mice* (stand, stands) for "money, ideology, compromise, and ego."

3. According to Andrew, the most popular reason (is, are) money.
4. Some agents (receive, receives) millions in cash, jewellery, and so on.
5. Another reason (is, are) ideology.
6. Sometimes people (believe, believes) that another country's way of life is better.
7. Some men and women (become, becomes) spies because they are ashamed of something that they have done.
8. For example, if a government bureaucrat (steal, steals) money and another person (find, finds) out, the bureaucrat can be blackmailed to become a spy.
9. Finally, many people (think, thinks) that spying (is, are) an exciting profession.
10. Andrew (say, says) that "an interesting minority want to be secret celebrities" in their own little world of espionage.

The Simple Past Tense

Watch the Video Tense **MyWritingLab**

The **simple past tense** indicates that an action occurred at a specific past time. In the past tense, there are regular and irregular verbs. **Regular verbs** end in *-d* or *-ed* (*talked*, *ended*, *watched*). **Irregular verbs** do not follow a regular pattern and do not end in any specific letter (*knew*, *saw*, *met*).

Yesterday morning, the spy satellite **passed** over my home.

YESTERDAY MORNING — TODAY

The satellite **passed.**

The Past Progressive

The **past progressive tense** indicates that an action was in progress at a particular past moment. In this chapter, you will focus on the simple past.

While the detectives were watching (past progressive tense) the house, the suspect escaped.

Regular Past Tense Verbs

Regular past tense verbs have a standard *-d* or *-ed* ending. Use the same form for both singular and plural past tense verbs.

Singular subject: One well-known agent **learned** to speak twelve languages.

Plural subject: During World War II, secret agents **used** codes to communicate.

Spell Regular Past Tense Verbs Correctly

Most regular past tense verbs are formed by adding *-ed* to the base form of the verb.

walked questioned

However, there are some exceptions.

- When the regular verb ends in *-e*, just add *-d*.

  realized appreciated

- When the regular verb ends in a consonant + *-y*, change the *y* to *i* and add *-ed*.

  reply, replied try, tried

- When the regular verb ends in a vowel + *-y*, just add *-ed*.

  played employed

- When the regular verb ends in a consonant-vowel-consonant combination, double the last consonant and add *-ed*.

  tap, tapped plan, planned

Do Not Confuse *Past* and *Passed*

Some people confuse *past* and *passed*. *Past* is a noun that means "in a previous time" or "before now."

She has many secrets in her past.

Passed is the past tense of the verb *pass*, which has many meanings.

Many days passed as we waited for her arrival.

(*Passed* means "went by.")

I passed you the butter a moment ago.

(*Passed* means "took something and gave it to someone.")

He passed the entrance test.

(*Passed* means "successfully completed.")

GRAMMAR LINK

See Chapter 32, "Spelling and Commonly Confused Words," for information about the spelling of verbs.

Watch the Video
Easily Confused Words
MyWritingLab

PRACTICE 2

Write the simple past form of each verb in parentheses. Make sure you spell the past tense verb correctly.

EXAMPLE:

The Canadian government (form) ___*formed*___ the Canadian Security Intelligence Service (CSIS) in 1984 to detect enemy spies in the country.

1. In June 2009, CSIS (hire) ______________ Richard B. Fadden to be the director of the organization. Since the start of the Cold War, the RCMP

and then in 1984, CSIS (improve) ____________ training. The agency (plan) ____________ to use modern technological investigative methods.

2. During the Cold War period, the organization (realize) ____________ that Canada was the target of espionage activities. This was a result of a Russian defector who had (work) ____________ at the Soviet Embassy in Ottawa. At that time, the organization (focus) ____________ on using technological gadgets, which were (design) ____________ for espionage activities.

3. Some of the gadgets have been (declassify) ____________ for people to see. Items such as lunch boxes, briefcases, purses, and binoculars were (use) ____________ to conceal tape recorders or cameras. They were (design) ____________ for special agents to engage in activities without being (detect) ____________.

4. These devices reflect the efforts that secret agents went to. They also clearly reveal the danger that Canada (face) ____________ around national security. The artifacts are objects that were (employ) ____________ to prevent foreign countries from discovering Canada's science and military secrets.

5. Currently, CSIS has (expand) ____________ to include other areas of security concern. They are (involve) ____________ in minimizing risks of terrorism, weapons of mass destruction, espionage, transnational criminal activity, information security threats, and security screening.

GRAMMAR LINK

See Appendix 2 for a complete list of irregular verbs.

Irregular Past Tense Verbs

Irregular verbs change internally. Because their spellings change from the present to the past tense, these verbs can be challenging to remember.

Watch the Video
Regular and Irregular Verbs
MyWritingLab

The prisoner wrote with invisible ink. (wrote = past tense of *write*)

The guards sent the letter. (sent = past tense of *send*)

The prisoners began a revolt. (began = past tense of *begin*)

PRACTICE 3

Write the correct past form of each verb in parentheses. Some verbs are regular and some are irregular. If you do not know the past form of an irregular verb, consult Appendix 2.

EXAMPLE:

During the American Revolution, armies (write) *wrote* letters with invisible ink.

1. In 1775, an American soldier named Benjamin Thompson (combine) ____________ ferrous sulphate and water. When mixed together, the substances (turn) ____________ into invisible ink. Later, the reader

of the letter (hold) ____________ it over a candle flame, and the ink (become) ____________ brown. The lines with the invisible ink (appear) ____________ between the lines of the regular letter.

2. More recently, during World War II, a mysterious person (send) ____________ a postcard to Jacob Rosenblum, a resident of Bucharest, Romania. The postcard, dated August 20, 1943, (come) ____________ from a death camp and (have) ____________ one line. In German, the letter (say) ____________, "My darling, I remember you with love" and was signed "Lola." Underneath the black writing, a message (appear) ____________ in invisible ink. In that message, the author (speak) ____________ of "starvation, degradation, killing by gas," and "an agonizing hell." The letter writer also (request) ____________ signal pistols and invisible ink. The letter (end) ____________ with the mysterious words "K is fulfilling his mission. We will do what we have to do."

3. During past wars, people (find) ____________ many ways to make invisible ink, and they (pass) ____________ secret messages to others. For example, soldiers (make) ____________ ink out of acidic liquids such as lemon juice and vinegar. When a soldier (write) ____________ with such substances, the ink would later turn brown when heated. In the past, some prisoners of war even (use) ____________ their own sweat and saliva to make invisible ink.

be (was or were)

Past tense verbs generally have one form that you can use with all subjects. However, the verb *be* has two past forms: *was* and *were*.

Past Tense of Be

	Singular	Plural
First person:	I was	We were
Second person:	You were	You were
Third person:	He was She was It was	They were

PRACTICE 4

Write *was* or *were* in each space provided.

EXAMPLE:

The RCMP and university art students ___*were*___ partners on a project.

1. During 2007, the UCFV Visual Arts students ____________ chosen to work on the RCMP's training site. Chilliwack's Pacific Region Training Centre (PRTC) ____________ the location for the art students to create a huge cityscape mural. The background ____________ designed for police officers to have a lifelike quality to their training since sections ____________ painted to depict similar areas where the officers encounter criminals. Commercial and residential areas and a back alley ____________ replicated on the walls.

2. The RCMP training annex ____________ plain before the art students began their work, and the centre ____________ not able to provide the officers with a real-world setting for their tactical training. The officers ____________ pleased with the results, and the students ____________ contributing not only to an academic art project but to one that had community value as well, as their program mandates.

Problems with be, have, and do

Some writers find it particularly difficult to remember how to use the irregular verbs *be*, *have*, and *do* in the past tense. Here are some helpful guidelines.

Avoiding Common Errors with *be*

- Use *were* in the past tense when the subject is plural. Do not use *was*.

  The officers ~~was~~ *were* encountered by criminals.

- Use the standard form of the verb (*is* or *was*), not *be*.

  The camera ~~be~~ *was* small enough to fit in a pen.

Avoiding Common Errors with *have*

- Use the past form of the verb (*had*), not the present form (*have* or *has*), when speaking about a past event.

  The prisoner ~~has~~ *had* to write messages with invisible ink during the war.

Avoiding Common Errors with *do*

- Use *done* only when it is preceded by a helping verb (*was done*, *is done*, and so on).

  The students ~~done~~ *did* an interview with the press yesterday.

PRACTICE 5

Correct ten verb errors. If the verb is incorrectly formed, or if the verb is in the wrong tense, write the correct form above it.

EXAMPLE:

Some people ~~has~~ *have* very little respect for pigeons.

1. Most city dwellers believes that pigeons are nuisances. For example, at my apartment building, the owner done many things last year to keep

pigeons off the balconies. However, people undervalue pigeons. During past wars, the homing pigeon has an important role in international espionage.

2. During the Napoleonic wars, homing pigeons gived officials a crucial way to communicate. The small birds carried and delivered secret messages because they was able to fly over enemy territories. Those pigeons be able to transmit messages faster than soldiers on horses, and they haved legendary endurance.

3. According to Richard Platt's book *Spy*, Roman emperor Julius Caesar also used birds to send messages. Pigeons be valued for their speed, size, and reliability. Additionally, over half a million pigeons taked messages to soldiers during World War I, and some soldiers actually hided pigeons in their pockets and cared for them on battlefields. We should appreciate pigeons because they played an important role in previous wars.

Negative and Question Forms

In the present and past tenses, you must add a helping verb (*do*, *does*, or *did*) to question and negative forms. In the present tense, use the helping verb *do*, or use *does* when the subject is third-person singular. Use *did* in the past tense.

Questions: **Do** you know about the Canadian War Museum in Ottawa?
Does the museum open on weekends?
Did you visit the war museum last summer?

Negatives: We **do** not live in Ottawa.
The museum **does** not open on holidays.
We **did** not visit the war museum last summer.

When the main verb is *be* (*is*, *am*, *are*), no additional helping verb is necessary.

Questions: **Is** the Camouflage Exhibition boring?
Were copies of war propaganda posters for sale?

Negatives: The Camouflage Exhibition **is not** boring.
Copies of war propaganda posters **were not** for sale.

A Note about Contractions

In informal writing, it is acceptable to contract negative verb forms. However, you should avoid using contractions in your academic writing.

CSIS ~~doesn't~~ *does not* have enough multilingual interpreters.

Use the Correct Question and Negative Forms

In question and negative forms, always use the base form of the main verb, even when the subject is third-person singular.

Why does the Canadian War Museum ~~has~~ *have* so many school visits?

In 1914, Mata Hari did not ~~discussed~~ *discuss* her identity.

PRACTICE 6

Write questions for each answer. Remember to add a helping verb (*do*, *does*, or *did*) when necessary.

EXAMPLES:

Where is the Canadian War Museum?

The Canadian War Museum is in Ottawa.

What does it contain?

It contains thousands of military artifacts.

1. ______________________________

   The Canadian War Museum opened in 2005.

2. ______________________________

   The artifacts document Canada's military history.

3. ______________________________

   No, the museum is not open on Sundays.

4. ______________________________

   Yes, the George Metcalf Archival Collection has original photographs, scrapbooks, and 3-D maps.

5. ______________________________

   Yes, many tourists visit the museum each year.

PRACTICE 7

Combine the words in parentheses to form negatives. Remember to add a helping verb (*do*, *does*, or *did*) when necessary.

EXAMPLE:

Ottawa's Canadian War Museum has thousands of military objects, but it (have, not) *does not have* spy paraphernalia for public viewing.

1. Ottawa's Canadian War Museum contains many interesting artifacts. For example, on display are paintings and sculptures depicting Australia, Britain, and Canada during World War II. These works of art (be, not) ____________ for sale. Rather, the exhibition is an online collection for public viewing. Many of the items on display (be, not) ____________ pleasant to look at because they clearly reflect battle, captivity, and casualties.

2. The museum also displays interesting war propaganda posters online. As well, it offers an interesting permanent exhibition on Canada's peacekeeping and Western defence roles. Visitors (need, not) ____________ to have extensive knowledge of the country's international vision to appreciate this exhibition on the future.

3. Clearly the Canadian War Museum is an extremely interesting place. Tourists (have, not) ______________ to spend the entire day at the museum because it (be, not) ______________ a very large place.

Use the Base Form after To

Remember to use the base form of verbs that follow *to* (infinitive form).

Greenstein wanted to ~~studied~~ *study* the postcard.

PRACTICE 8

The next selection contains verb tense, spelling, and *past* versus *passed* errors. Correct fifteen errors.

EXAMPLE:

Many books ~~describes~~ *describe* the Navajo code talkers of World War II.

1. Navajo be an incredibly complex language with complicated syntax and tonal qualities. It has no alphabet or written forms, and only Native Americans in the Southwest speaks it. During World War II, Navajo natives maked an important contribution to the Allied war effort.

2. During the war, Japanese and German troops tapped Allied communication lines and listen to the messages. Japanese code breakers was particularly capable. They managed to figured every code that the Allies came up with. In 1942, the Marines get hundreds of Navajo volunteers to relayed coded messages about military plans. The Navajos past messages using their language, and they be very efficient code talkers. They call fighter planes "hummingbirds" and submarines "iron fish."

3. The Japanese tought that they could figure out the messages. They work hard, but they did not managed to break the Navajo code. After the war ended, the Navajos did not received recognition for their important work as code talkers until 1969.

Watch the Video
Modifiers
MyWritingLab

Avoid Double Negatives

A double negative occurs when a negative word such as *no*, *nothing*, *nobody*, or *nowhere* is combined with a negative adverb such as *not*, *never*, *rarely*, or *seldom*. The result is a sentence that has a double negative. Such sentences can be confusing because the negative words cancel each other.

The agent does not have no children.
(According to this sentence, the agent has children.)

He didn't know nothing about it.
(According to this sentence, he knows something about it.)

How to Correct Double Negatives

There are several ways to correct double negatives.

- Completely remove one of the negative forms.

accepted no **or** didn't accept
The agent ~~didn't accept no~~ money.

- Change *no* to *any* (*anybody*, *anything*, *anywhere*).

any
The agent didn't accept ~~no~~ money.

PRACTICE 9

Correct the six errors with double negatives. You can correct each error in more than one way.

EXAMPLES:

any
Mata Hari didn't have ~~no~~ close friends.

had
Mata Hari ~~didn't have~~ no close friends.

SZ Photo / Scherl/DIZ Muenchen GmbH, Sueddeutsche Zeitung Photo / Alamy

1. In 1875, Mata Hari's Dutch parents named her Margareta Zelle. At the age of eighteen, she married a much older naval officer. Her husband was an alcoholic, and Zelle didn't see no reason to stay with him. Zelle left, and she didn't take none of her furniture or clothing.

2. Zelle didn't have no marketable skills. She decided to become an exotic dancer. She changed her name to Mata Hari and performed Hindu temple dances. She never said nothing to her parents about her new career choice.

3. Due to her beauty, she attracted many influential men, such as the German crown prince and high-ranking German officers. Their wives didn't say nothing nice about Mata Hari. Her career as a dancer lasted for about ten years.

4. According to her biographer, Erika Ostrovsky, Mata Hari became a spy for the Germans in 1914, and her code name was H 21. One day, French

officials intercepted a German secret service telegram. They identified Mata Hari's code name and accused her of espionage. Mata Hari said that she didn't do nothing wrong. However, the French courts found her guilty of espionage. In 1918, a firing squad executed her.

REFLECT ON IT

Think about what you have learned in this chapter. If you do not know an answer, review that topic.

1. What are the present and past forms of the verb *be*?

	Present	Past
I	______________	______________
he, she, it	______________	______________
you, we, they	______________	______________

2. Write an example of a regular past tense verb. ______________________
3. Write an example of an irregular past tense verb. ______________________
4. What is the simple past form of the following verbs?

   a. think: __________________ b. mention: __________________

   c. have: __________________ d. go: __________________
5. Correct one verb error in each of the following sentences.

   a. In 2012, a Canadian naval officer turned spy was arrest by the RCMP.

   b. Jeffrey Delisle sell secrets to the Russian military intelligence agency.

   c. Delisle attempt to stop selling secrets to the Russian military agency in 2009.

   d. In response, the Russians sent a photo of his daughter walking to school in Halifax.

   e. Delisle has been sentence to 20 years in prison.

FINAL REVIEW

Correct fifteen errors in present and past tense verbs. Also look for and correct a double negative. There are a total of sixteen errors.

EXAMPLE:

When people talk about espionage, they generally ~~thinks~~ *think* about secret agents who work for governments.

1. Industrial espionage occurs when companies spy on each other. It be a major problem. A nation's economic survival depend on its ability to be innovative in the industrial sector. For example, in 1994, a large company develop a new highly efficient engine. It wanted to be the first company to put

that engine on the market. That company had to protected its information so that competitors could not put the product out first.

2. Last year, Max B. worked as a spy, and he easily finded top-secret information. A large corporation hire Max as a temporary worker. He begun his job last August. When he be inside the company, he done an unethical thing. He used his computer to access the company's database. He discover an important new project just by looking at the electronic file folder titled "Priorities." The company directors never knowed what Max was doing. The employers didn't suspect nothing. When Max left the job, he brung home important documents.

3. Governments around the world take industrial espionage seriously. Last year, people in Norway, Israel, and Switzerland was in trouble with the law because they selled company secrets. Today, businesses be more vulnerable than ever.

Write about one of the following topics. Check your verb tenses carefully.

1. Have you ever done volunteer work? Explain what you did.
2. Describe an effective election advertisement.

How Do I Get a Better Grade?

Visit MyWritingLab for audiovisual lectures and additional practice sets about present and past tenses.

Past Participles

Section Theme **ESPIONAGE**

LEARNING OBJECTIVES

Paul Gilligan/Getty Images

In this chapter, you will read about **fictional and real spies.**

The Writer's Journal

Reflect on how children were disciplined in the past and how they are disciplined today. Write a paragraph explaining how the disciplining of children has changed over the years.

GRAMMAR LINK

For a list of irregular past participles, see Appendix 2.

Past Participles

A **past participle** is a verb form, not a verb tense. You cannot use a past participle as the only verb in a sentence; instead, you must use it with a helping verb such as *have*, *has*, *had*, *is*, *was*, or *were*.

	helping verb	past participle
Ian Fleming	was	raised in England.
His novels	have	become very popular.

Regular Verbs

The past tense and the past participle of regular verbs are the same.

Base Form	Past Tense	Past Participle
walk	walked	walked
try	tried	tried
use	used	used

Irregular Verbs

The past tense and the past participle of irregular verbs may be different. For a complete list of irregular past participles, see Appendix 2.

Base Form	Past Tense	Past Participle
begin	began	begun
go	went	gone
speak	spoke	spoken

PRACTICE 1

Each group of verbs contains one error. Underline the error, and write the correct word in the space provided.

EXAMPLE:

	Base Form	Past Tense	Past Participle	
	lose	<u>losed</u>	lost	*lost*
1.	cost	cost	costed	______
2.	come	came	came	______
3.	build	builded	built	______
4.	sink	sank	sank	______
5.	bring	brang	brought	______
6.	write	wrote	wrote	______
7.	choose	choosed	chosen	______
8.	fall	felt	fallen	______
9.	feel	felt	fell	______
10.	blow	blew	blowed	______
11.	tear	tore	tore	______
12.	take	taked	taken	______
13.	bite	bited	bitten	______
14.	sit	sat	sitten	______
15.	grow	grew	growed	______

PRACTICE 2

In the following selection, all irregular past participles are underlined. Correct ten past participle errors.

EXAMPLE:

put
Many parents have ~~putted~~ video cameras in their home.

1. Spying on children is not new; in fact, parents have <u>did</u> it for centuries. Parents have <u>read</u> their children's diaries, and some have <u>gone</u> through

their children's belongings. However, in recent years, the methods used to spy have became more sophisticated.

2. According to John Stossel of ABC News, some parents have bought video cameras and miniature tape recorders to spy on their children. For example, in 2012, the Roy family bought a small video camera. It was hided behind a plant in the living room, and their son, Samuel, was not told that the camera was there. One evening, while his parents were out, Samuel was catched on the video camera smoking and drinking with friends. When the boy was shown the tape, he admitted that he had taked the alcohol. The parents insist that they have teached their child a valuable lesson.

3. Another spy tool can track the speed of a driver. A Regina father, Ed Jarvis, has putted the device in his car so that he can monitor his son's driving. Recently, Ed punished his son, David, when he realized that the boy had broke the law. The device proved that David had drove over the speed limit. David's reaction was harsh: "The only thing my father has done is make me angry. He has no faith in me."

4. The issue about spying on children is controversial. Some people believe that parents should snoop. Parents have the right to know if their teenagers have maked serious mistakes. Others claim that spying can break the bonds of trust between a parent and a child. If you were a parent, would you spy on your children?

The Present Perfect Tense: *have/has* + Past Participle

A past participle combines with *have* or *has* to form the **present perfect tense.** You can use this tense in two different circumstances.

- Use the present perfect to show that an action began in the past and continues to the present time. You will often use *since* and *for* with this tense.

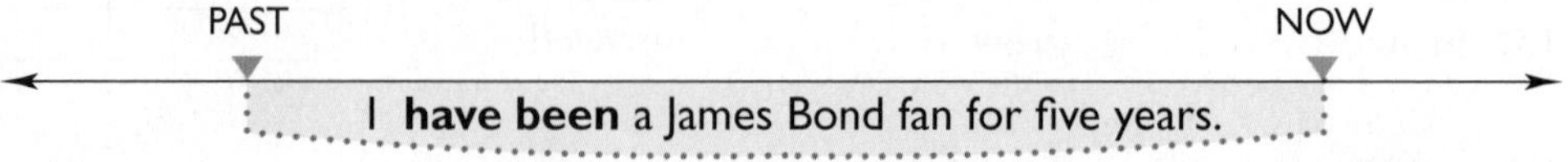

- Use the present perfect to show that one or more completed actions occurred at unspecified past times.

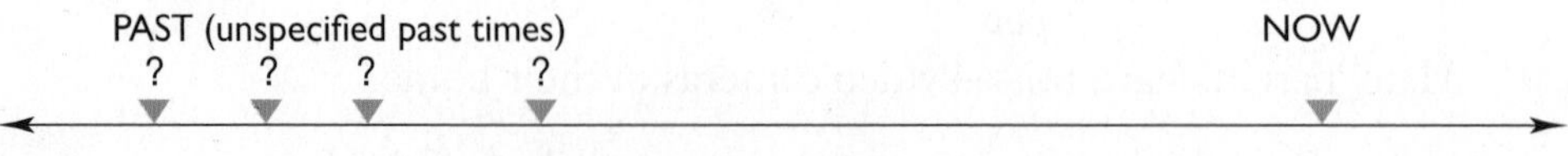

Use Time Markers

Time markers are words that indicate when an action occurred.

Simple Past Tense

- To refer to a completed incident that occurred at a specific past time, use the following time markers.

yesterday	ago	when I was …	last (week, month, year …)
in the past	in 2013	during the 1970s	in the early days of …

Ian Fleming **wrote** his first novel in 1953.

Present Perfect Tense

- To refer to an action that began in the past and is still continuing, use the following time markers.

since	for (a period of time up to now)	ever
up to now	so far	not … yet

Spy films **have been** popular since the 1930s.

- To refer to an action that occurred at unspecified past times, use the following time markers.

once	lately	several times	three times
many	twice	recently	

I have seen *The World Is Not Enough* once and *Skyfall* twice.

CHAPTER 23

Look at the difference between the past and the present perfect tenses.

Simple past: In 1962, Sean Connery appeared in the first James Bond film, *Dr. No.*
(This event occurred at a known past time.)

Present perfect: Many different actors have played James Bond.
(We do not really know when the actors played James Bond.)

James Bond movies have been popular for more than forty years.
(The action began in the past and continues to the present.)

PRACTICE 3

Write the simple past or present perfect form of each verb in parentheses.

EXAMPLE:

For the past six years, my cousin Mike (be) ___*has been*___ a James Bond fanatic.

1. Spy fans around the world (watch) ____________________ James Bond movies since the mid-1960s. Although most people (hear) ____________________ of James Bond, few people know about the man behind the movies.

2. Ian Fleming was born in 1906, and his father (be) ____________________ a successful stockbroker. As a result, Ian (spend) ____________________

Photos 12/Alamy

Daniel Craig, the current James Bond

his youth living a high-class lifestyle. In the 1940s, the British Secret Service (draft) ____________________ Ian Fleming because he could easily mix with upper-class officials.

3. In 1953, Fleming (use) ____________________ his experiences to create his first James Bond book. Since then, James Bond (be) ____________________ extremely popular. Over the last forty years, viewers around the world (see) ____________________ the sophisticated spy in action.

4. Since the first film, the James Bond character (age, never) ____________________. For more than forty years, beautiful women (try) ____________________ to seduce him and villains ____________________ to kill him. Over and over, Bond (escape) ____________________ danger by using his intelligence, his fast cars, and his secret weapons. Since its debut, the James Bond character (capture) ____________________ the audience's imagination.

The Past Perfect Tense: *had* + Past Participle

The **past perfect tense** indicates that one or more past actions happened before another past action. It is formed with *had* and the past participle.

PAST PERFECT — PAST — NOW

The robbers **had left** when the police arrived.

Notice the differences among the simple past, the present perfect, and the past perfect tenses.

Simple past: Last night I watched a documentary on double agents.
(The action occurred at a known past time.)

Present perfect: I have read many articles about spying.
(The actions occurred at unspecified past times.)

Past perfect: The government had suspected the agent for a long time before he was arrested as a spy.
(All of the actions happened in the past, but one action happened before another.)

PRACTICE 4

Underline the correct verb form. You may choose the simple past, the present perfect, or the past perfect tense.

EXAMPLE:

Ben Lee (was / has been) a CSIS agent since 2001.

1. Khaleb and Richard (are / were / have been) friends since they were children. When they (were / had been) eight years old, they (pretended /

have pretended) to work for the CSIS. By the age of ten, they (have made / had made) several paper CSIS badges.

2. By the time Richard turned twenty, he (has been / had been) in trouble with the law several times. For example, in 2006, Richard went out with a friend. Richard did not realize that his friend (brought / had brought) some drugs into the car. The police arrested both men and showed them the drugs. Richard truthfully claimed that he (never saw / had never seen) the drugs. He said that someone else (has put / had put) them in the trunk. However, because Richard was in the car, the officer (charged / had charged) him with possession of narcotics. Now Richard cannot become a CSIS agent because he has a criminal record.

3. Khaleb has good grades in college. He (never failed / has never failed) a course in his entire life. Khaleb is also in good physical condition. During his last medical exam, the doctor said that he (never saw / had never seen) such a healthy young man. Furthermore, Khaleb speaks three languages. By the time he was twelve years old, Khaleb (has already learned / had already learned) to speak Spanish and Arabic. Since the summer, the agency (made / has made) several background checks on Khaleb. Up to now, Khaleb (had passed / has passed) all of the tests. Khaleb has a very good chance of becoming a CSIS agent.

Watch the Video Active and Passive Voice **MyWritingLab**

In sentences with the **passive voice**, the subject receives the action and does not perform the action. Look carefully at the next two sentences.

Active: The diplomat **gave** secret documents to an undercover agent.
(This is active because the subject, *diplomat*, performed the action.)

Passive: Secrets documents **were given** to an undercover agent.
(This is passive because the subject, *documents*, was affected by the action and did not perform the action.)

To form the passive voice, use the appropriate tense of the verb *be* plus the past participle.

Verb Tense	**Active Voice** (The subject performs the action.)	**Passive Voice: *be* + Past Participle** (The subject receives the action.)
Simple present	She writes spy stories.	Spy stories are written (by her).
Present progressive	is writing	are being written
Simple past	wrote	were written
Present perfect	has written	have been written

(Continued)

Verb Tense	Active Voice (The subject performs the action.)	Passive Voice: *be* + Past Participle (The subject receives the action.)
Future	will write	will be written
Modals	can write	can be written
	could write	could be written
	should write	should be written
	would have written	would have been written

PRACTICE 5

Decide whether each underlined verb is active or passive. Write *A* (for "active") or *P* (for "passive") above each verb.

EXAMPLE:

P *A*
Many ordinary citizens have been recruited as spies even though the work is dangerous.

1. During times of war, armies have used both scouts and spies. Army scouts can wear their full uniform. They are sent ahead of advancing forces. Spies, on the other hand, wear disguises and try to blend in with the regular population.
2. Spying is much more dangerous than scouting because captured scouts are treated as prisoners of war. A captured spy, on the other hand, may be executed immediately. In spite of the obvious dangers, many people are attracted to the field of espionage because they love excitement and danger.

The *by* … Phrase

In many passive sentences, it is not necessary to write the *by* … phrase because the noun performing the action is understood.

CSIS agents are selected according to their abilities.
(Adding "by CSIS recruiters" after "selected" is not necessary.)

PRACTICE 6

A. Complete the following sentences by changing each italicized verb to the passive form. Do not alter the verb tense. Note: You do not have to include the *by* … phrase.

EXAMPLE:

The supervisor *spies* on the workers.
The workers *are spied on (by the supervisor).*

1. Sometimes employers *place* spy cameras in their factories.
Sometimes spy cameras ____________________
____

2. Last year, Mr. Roy *installed* three surveillance cameras.
   Last year, three surveillance cameras ______________________________

   ____

3. The video cameras *filmed* some sleeping workers.
   Some sleeping workers ______________________________

   ____

4. As a result, the boss *has fired* three technicians.
   As a result, three technicians ______________________________

   ____

5. The workers will file a complaint.
   A complaint ______________________________

   ____

Hint **Avoid Overusing the Passive Voice**

Generally, use the active voice instead of the passive voice. The active voice is more direct and less wordy than the passive voice. For example, read the next two versions of the same message.

Passive voice: The problem has been rectified by us, and a new order is being prepared for you. You will be contacted by our sales department.

Active voice: We have corrected the problem and are preparing a new order for you. Our sales department will contact you.

In rare cases when you do not know who did the action, the passive voice may be more appropriate.

James Bond's miniature camera was made in Italy.
(You do not know who made the camera.)

PRACTICE 7

Underline examples of the passive voice in the following letter. Then rewrite the letter using the active voice.

Dear Parents,

Security cameras have been installed in our school for several reasons. First, intruders have been seen by students. Also, if fighting is done by students, the scenes will be recorded, and the culprits will be caught. In addition, any vandalism to school property can be viewed by our staff. For further information, we can be contacted at any time during school hours.

Sincerely,
Tony Romano, Principal, Rosedale High School

____

____

____

____

____

____

____

____

The Past Participle as an Adjective

A past participle can function as an adjective when it appears after a linking verb such as *be* or *feel*. In the example, *excited* modifies *agent.*

The young agent was **excited.**

A past participle can also function as an adjective when it describes or modifies the noun that follows it. In the example, *broken* modifies *promises*.

She was angry about the **broken** promises.

Be Careful!

In the passive voice, sometimes the verb *be* is suggested but not written. The following sentence contains the passive voice.

Many Activities [that were] done in the 1920s are still common today.

PRACTICE 8

Underline and correct eight errors in past participles.

EXAMPLE:

Military historians have ~~wrote~~ *written* about Canadian Western defence and peacekeeping.

1. Canada is a strong international peacekeeping force. The country is involve in peacekeeping missions around the world and is prepare to assist countries as mandate by the United Nations.
2. Canada assist countries such as Afghanistan by working with the Afghan authorities to create harmony and security. Canadian troops providing humanitarian aid to those suffering in war-torn areas. They are even equip to help with essential services like water and to establishes security, education, and job opportunities.
3. Overall, Canada assist countries in stabilizing and establishing security when wars occur. In many situations, such as the one in Kandahar, the Canadian government was criticized for not informing the public of the dangers of the mission.

REFLECT ON IT

Think about what you have learned in this chapter. If you do not know an answer, review that topic.

1. Give two circumstances in which you would use the present perfect tense.
____
____
____
____

2. When do you use the past perfect tense? ____________________
____

3. How do you form the passive voice? ____________________
____

4. Identify and correct the errors in the following sentences.
   a. Robert Ludlum's first book was publish in 1971.
   b. By 2000, he had wrote twenty-one spy novels.
   c. Millions of people have buyed his novel *The Bourne Identity*.
   d. Have you ever saw a movie that was based on a book by Ludlum?

FINAL REVIEW

A. Fill in each blank with the appropriate verb tense. The sentence may require active or passive voice.

EXAMPLE:

Cellphone cameras (be) ___*have been*___ on the market since 2003.

1. Since their debut, cellphone cameras (criticize) ____________________ by those who are worried about privacy issues. For example, in 2003, cellphone cameras (ban) ____________________ in many health clubs. In January 2004, in the locker room of a European spa, some women (film) ____________________ by a voyeur. Additionally, since 2003, schoolteachers and others who work with the public (complain) ____________________ to authorities about the possible misuse of cellphone cameras. For instance, in 2006, a teacher's angry outburst (record) ____________________ by a student.

2. On the other hand, since their first appearance, cellphone cameras (help) ____________________ the police. Since 2003, many crimes (solve) ____________________ by members of the public. For example, after a 2007

Montreal hockey riot, most of the vandals (catch) ____________________ because bystanders took cellphone videos. In May 2008, two robbers in Georgia (arrest) ____________________. Police thanked a teenager who (took) ____________________ a picture of the robbers' license plate number.

B. Underline and correct five past participle errors.

EXAMPLE:

The photo was ~~use~~ *used* in court.

3. The cellphone camera has cause a lot of controversy since its appearance. Websites such as Flickr contain images that were took with the tiny cameras. Many cellphones can also take short videos. Films showing people kissing or yawning have been post on YouTube. Last March, a woman's privacy was not respect when someone put a picture of her online. She forced the website to remove the unflattering image. However, cellphone cameras have also help police solve cases. Undoubtedly, the little gadget is both a blessing and a curse.

Write about one of the following topics. Make sure that verb forms are correct.

1. Define an ideal politician. What characteristics should a great politician have?
2. Why do some parents spy on their children? What are the effects of such spying? Write about the causes and effects of spying on children.

How Do I Get a Better Grade?

Visit MyWritingLab for audiovisual lectures and additional practice sets about past participles.

Other Verb Forms

CHAPTER 24

Section Theme **ESPIONAGE**

Monty Rakusen/Cultura /Getty Images

LEARNING OBJECTIVES

In this chapter, you will read about topics related to spy mysteries.

The Writer's Journal

In your opinion, is it ethical to use cameras to spy on nannies, babysitters, or other caregivers? Write a paragraph about the issue.

Problems with Progressive Forms (*-ing* Verbs)

Most verbs have progressive tenses. The **progressive tense** indicates that an action is, was, or will be in progress. For example, the present progressive indicates that an action is happening right now or for a temporary period of time.

Simple present: Detective Jonkala **spies** on cheating spouses every day.

Present progressive: Today, he **is following** Ms. Wang.

Every day, he spies on cheating spouses.

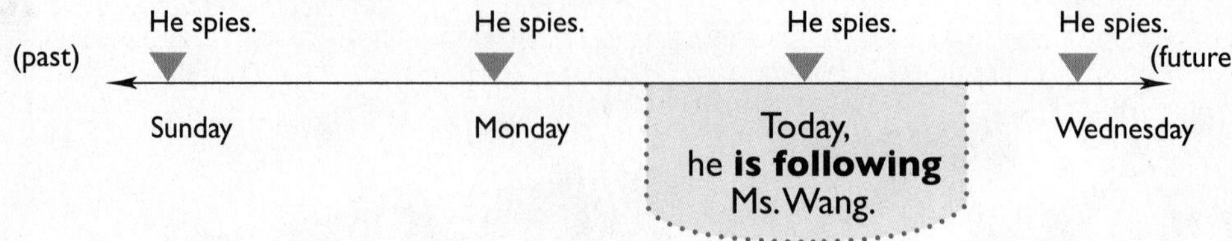

To form the progressive, use the appropriate tense of the verb *be* with the *-ing* verb.

Present progressive:	Right now, Detective Jonkala is watching the suspect.
Past progressive:	He was taking notes when the suspect left the hotel.
Future progressive:	Tomorrow, at 6 a.m., Natasha will be following the suspect.
Present perfect progressive:	Detective Jonkala has been working for the police since 2000.
Past perfect progressive:	Detective Jonkala had been waiting in his car when his partner arrived.

Common Errors with the Progressive Form

- Do not use the progressive form when an action happens regularly.

  Every day he ~~is complaining~~ *complains* about his job.

- In the progressive form, use the correct form of the verb *be*.

  Right now the nanny ~~be~~ *is* playing with the children.

- In the progressive form, always include the complete helping verb.

  Right now, the agents ^*are* examining the photos. They ^*have* been working for hours.

Nonprogressive Verbs

Some verbs do not take the progressive form because they indicate an ongoing state or a perception rather than a temporary action. Here are some examples of nonprogressive verbs.

Perception Verbs	Preference Verbs	State Verbs	Possession
admire	care*	believe	have*
feel*	desire	know	own
hear	doubt	mean	possess
look*	hate	realize	
see	like	recognize	
seem	love	suppose	

smell*	prefer	think*
taste*	want	understand

*The verbs marked with an asterisk have more than one meaning and can also be used in the progressive tense. Compare the next pairs of sentences.

Nonprogressive	**Progressive**
He **has** a video camera. (Expresses ownership)	He **is having** a bad day.
I **think** it is unethical. (Expresses an opinion)	I **am thinking** about you.

PRACTICE 1

Each sentence has errors with progressive forms. Correct each error.

EXAMPLE:

I ~~been~~ *have been* working as a nanny for years.

1. Generally, I am loving my job, but this morning something terrible happened.
2. I was watching TV while the baby be sleeping, and I couldn't believe what was on one of the family's videos.
3. When I pressed the "Play" button, I was shocked because I was recognizing myself on the video.
4. The video had been taken months ago while I be reading to the family's children.
5. There is a hidden video camera in the house, and for months the parents been spying on me.
6. I am a good nanny, and every day I am conducting myself professionally.
7. I do not think that families should spy on nannies unless the children been acting upset or the nanny been displaying strange behaviour.
8. My employer, a local politician, was not wanting a scandal, so he apologized.

Nonstandard Forms: *gonna, gotta, wanna*

Some people commonly say *I'm gonna*, *I gotta*, or *I wanna*. These are nonstandard forms, and you should not use them in written communication.

- Write *going to* instead of *gonna*.

    The nanny is ~~gonna~~ *going to* sue her employer.

- Write *have to* instead of *gotta*.

    The Smiths ~~gotta~~ *have to* go to court to fight the lawsuit.

- Write *want to* instead of *wanna*.

    They ~~wanna~~ *want to* win their case.

PRACTICE 2

Underline and correct eight incorrect verb tenses or nonstandard verbs.

EXAMPLE:

want to
I really ~~wanna~~ solve the mysterious code.

1. Spies have always relied on codes and ciphers to hide and send secret messages. Cryptology refers to systems that use letters of the alphabet to represent other letters. A ciphered message is unintelligible to someone who is not familiar with the code. There are many codes and ciphers that remain unsolved. Code hobbyists are understanding that those who wanna solve codes gotta be very patient and clever.

2. One of the most intriguing examples of work with codes concerns women who worked in radio communications during World War II. These workers were gonna try to break codes they woulda heard over the radio waves. The women worked for The Women's Royal Canadian Naval Service, listening to and transcribing messages. They were gonna decode secret enemy codes as they listened to messages for hours on end.

3. In Oshawa in the 1940s, a spy centre (Camp X) was created. Within the centre was a radio-relay station where female radio operators were gonna attempt to analyze secret messages. Their contribution to the war must be recognized.

Using Gerunds and Infinitives

Sometimes a main verb is followed by another verb. The second verb can be a gerund or an infinitive. A **gerund** is a verb with an *-ing* ending. An **infinitive** consists of *to* and the base form of the verb.

Gerund	Hanssen considered **joining** the FBI. (verb + gerund)
Infinitive	He wanted **to have** a long career. (verb + infinitive)

Do not confuse gerunds with progressive verb forms. Compare the following sentences.

Maria is writing. (The action of writing is in progress right now.)

Some people enjoy **writing**. (Writing is a gerund that follows enjoy.)

Verbs Followed by Gerunds

acknowledge	deny	keep	recall
adore	detest	loathe	recollect
appreciate	discuss	mention	recommend
avoid	dislike	mind	regret
can't help	enjoy	miss	resent
complete	finish	postpone	resist
consider	imagine	practice	risk
delay	involve	quit	tolerate

EXAMPLES:

She would consider **working** for us.

She risks **losing** her job.

Verbs Followed by Infinitives

afford	decide	manage	refuse
agree	demand	mean	seem
appear	deserve	need	swear
arrange	expect	offer	threaten
ask	fail	plan	volunteer
claim	hesitate	prepare	want
compete	hope	pretend	wish
consent	learn	promise	would like

EXAMPLES:

He expected **to keep** his job.

He promised **to be** honest.

Verbs Followed by Gerunds or Infinitives

Some verbs can be followed by either a gerund or an infinitive.

begin continue like love start

Marcus loves **to spy**. Marcus loves **spying**.

Using *Stop*

You can follow *stop* with a gerund or an infinitive, but there is a difference in meaning.

Stop + gerund means "to permanently stop doing something."
Hanssen stopped **selling** information to the Soviets.

Stop + infinitive means "to stop an activity to do something else."
The agent was leaving when he stopped **to talk** to an old friend.

PRACTICE 3

Underline the appropriate verb form. Choose the gerund or the infinitive.

EXAMPLE:

The spy's job involved (passing / to pass) information to the Russians.

1. Robert Hanssen, like many double agents, was a very good liar. Most people can't help (lying / to lie) at one time or another. The psychologist Robert Feldman enjoys (studying / to study) human deception. He says that human beings need (lying / to lie) sometimes. Lying seems (being / to be) a part of human nature.
2. Feldman conducts experiments to learn how people lie. In one test, he places two strangers in a small room. He asks (videotaping / to videotape) the participants. After ten minutes, he stops (taping / to tape), and then he questions the two people. Usually, the subjects deny (to lie / lying). Then, while watching the video, they stop (fooling / to fool) themselves, and they admit that they have made many inaccurate statements. For instance, in one trial, the male participant falsely claimed (being / to be) a musician, and the female pretended (to like / liking) the same music as the male. They justified (being / to be) inaccurate by saying that their lies were not harmful. It appears that humans simply cannot avoid (lying / to lie) sometimes.

Using Conditional Forms

In **conditional sentences,** there is a condition and a result. There are three types of conditional sentences, and each type has two parts, or clauses. The main clause depends on the condition set in the *if* clause.

First Form: Possible Present or Future

The condition is true or very possible.

If + present tense,	... future tense ...
condition (*if* clause)	result

If you **buy** the book, you **will learn** about satellites.

Second Form: Unlikely Present

The condition is not likely and will probably not happen.

If + past tense,	... *would* (expresses a condition) ...
If + past tense,	... *could* (expresses a possibility) ...
condition (*if* clause)	result

If I **saw** a UFO, I **would take** a picture of it.

Note: In formal writing, when the condition contains the verb *be*, always use *were* in the *if* clause.

If Jenna **were** a scientist, she would study UFOs.

Third Form: Impossible Past

The condition cannot happen because the event is over.

If + past perfect tense, ... *would have* (+ past participle) ...

condition (*if* clause) result

If aliens **had visited** the earth in 1947, someone **would have photographed** them.

Be Careful with the Past Conditional

In the third type of conditional sentence, the impossible past, the writer expresses regret about a past event or expresses the wish that a past event had worked out differently. In the *if* part of the sentence, remember to use the past perfect tense.

If + past perfect tense, ... *would have* (past participle) ...

had listened

If CSIS agents ~~would have listened~~ to the tape, they **would have discovered** the agent's identity.

PRACTICE 4

Write the correct conditional form of each verb in parentheses.

EXAMPLE:

If I buy a book about the Cambridge Four, perhaps I (be) _will be_ able to understand why they spied for the Soviets.

1. One of the most interesting spy rings of the twentieth century was known as the Cambridge Four. In the 1930s, if England (be) ____________________ stable economically, perhaps communism (appeal, not) ________________ ________________ to British youth. However, at that time, Russia recruited many young men who were communist sympathizers.

2. The infamous Cambridge Four were recruited as undergraduates from Cambridge University's Trinity College in the 1930s. The Russians wanted recruits who would eventually be in positions of influence. For example, Anthony Blunt came from an upper-class family. If he (come) ______________________ from a working class background, the Russians (recruit, never) _________________________________ him. In college, the four spies behaved normally. If the Cambridge Four (behave)

_______________ erratically, perhaps someone (denounce) _______________ them as spies sooner.

3. During World War II, the four men revealed many American and British secrets to the Russians. By 1951, they fell under suspicion. British code breakers deciphered a message showing that someone had leaked nuclear secrets to the Russians. If this information about the leak (reach, not) _______________ one of the traitors, the British authorities (catch) _______________ the Cambridge Four. Instead, two of the spies successfully fled to Russia, and the other two were never prosecuted.

Nonstandard Forms: *would of, could of, should of*

Some people commonly say *would of, could of,* or *should of.* They may also say *woulda, coulda,* or *shoulda.* These are nonstandard forms, and you should avoid using them in written communication. When you use the past forms of *should, would,* and *could,* always include *have* + the past participle.

If I had been in Ottawa or Montreal during Prime Minister Pierre Elliott Trudeau's political terms, I ~~woulda~~ *would have* tried to meet him.

Unfortunately, he died from cancer in 2000. The prime minister ~~should of~~ *should have* travelled to more colleges and universities in his later years for public speaking engagements.

PRACTICE 5

Correct the eight errors in conditional forms or in the past forms of *could* and *should.*

EXAMPLE:

The assassination should not ~~of~~ *have* happened.

1. One of the biggest political crimes of the twentieth century in Canada was the death of Quebec Minister of Labour and Immigration Pierre Laporte. On October 5, 1970, British Trade Commissioner James Cross was kidnapped in Montreal by the Front de Libération du Québec (FLQ). The violent terrorist

group felt they could of obtained a separate and independent province from the rest of Canada through such criminal actions. What the kidnappers wanted in exchange for Cross was publicly communicated. The FLQ demanded that its detained or convicted members should of been released and given safe transport to Cuba. The kidnappers also thought they should of been able to broadcast their antiauthority manifesto on Radio-Canada.

2. On October 10, the FLQ's requests were granted by the Quebec Minister of Justice, but a dramatic chain of events unfolded. That same day, Quebec Minister of Labour and Immigration Pierre Laporte was kidnapped from the lawn of his home. If Laporte had been out of the country, he possibly could of been protected.

THE CANADIAN PRESS/Montreal Gazette

3. On October 16, after the Quebec government sought the help of the Canadian Armed Forces, the Canadian federal government (under the leadership of Prime Minister Pierre Elliott Trudeau) established a state of "apprehended insurrection" under the War Measures Act, which limited civilian freedom and provided authorities with the power to ban the FLQ in Quebec. In hindsight, perhaps the government could of done something less extreme, since the action was not fully embraced by all Canadians, many of whom thought this kind of action should of only been used in wartime.

4. On October 17, the body of strangled Pierre Laporte was found in a car trunk in St. Hubert, Quebec. In early December, the police located the FLQ members who were holding James Cross. They complied with the kidnappers' requests, but the criminals should of known better. They were arrested four weeks later and tried for kidnapping and murder. This series of events is known as the October Crisis, and although it should of put an end to terrorist activity in Quebec, which some people think it did, a strong separatist movement emerged.

REFLECT ON IT

Think about what you have learned in this chapter. If you do not know an answer, review that topic.

1. When do you use the progressive form of verbs? ______________________

____

2. Write your own examples of the three types of conditional sentences.

   First form: ______________________________________

   ____

   Second form: ____________________________________

   ____

   Third form: ______________________________________

   ____

3. Correct the following sentences by writing the standard form of each nonstandard verb.

   a. If you wanna succeed, you gotta work hard.

   b. Chris Rutkowski, a Canadian astronomer, been studying UFOs since the mid-1970s.

   c. If Pierre Laporte had been out of the country, maybe he woulda lived.

   d. Maybe one day someone is gonna tell the truth about the FLQ's recruitment strategies.

FINAL REVIEW

Underline and correct twenty errors with verbs. Look for nonstandard verbs and errors with conditionals, gerunds, and progressive forms.

EXAMPLE:

have Yes.

Chapman should ~~of~~ changed professions.

1. On a warm June day in 2010, Anna Chapman be sitting in a Manhattan coffee shop. The twenty-eight-year-old woman was gonna meet up with a mysterious stranger. While she waiting, she checked her Facebook account on her iPhone. If you woulda seen her that day, you would of smiled. She coulda passed for the girl next door. But the perky redhead was actually an undercover Russian spy.

2. An FBI agent arrived at the coffee shop and sat at Chapman's table. He be wearing a wire. He pretended being a Russian consulate employee. He asked Chapman to deliver a fake passport to another Russian spy, and she agreed doing it. She shoulda been more careful. Soon after that meeting,

she was arrested along with nine other Russian spies. Of course, they all denied to be part of a spy ring.

3. The Russian spies could of gone to prison. However, the U.S. and Russia didn't wanna hurt their relationship. High-ranking politicians decided that they gotta make a deal. The U.S. returned the ten spies to Russia and were receiving four prisoners in exchange.

4. The deal, which could of appeared to favour the Russians, was actually better for the Americans. The four prisoners had given extremely important information to Western nations. The ten Russians, on the other hand, been producing nothing of value at the time of their arrest. They were called "rank amateurs" by London's *Daily Telegraph* newspaper.

5. If she hadn't been a spy, Chapman could of had a great life in the United States. People who wanna have a peaceful life gotta stay out of trouble.

Write about one of the following topics. Review your verb forms carefully.

1. How would your life have been different if you had lived one hundred years ago? List several ways.
2. Should journalists report on the private lives of politicians? For example, is it important to know if a candidate has committed adultery or has had an addiction to drugs or alcohol? Explain your views.

Work with a group of two or three other students. Choose a scandal that was in the news. It can be a scandal that happened to a celebrity, politician, sports figure, or business person. Discuss what happened. Then, as a team, write a short paragraph about the scandal. Use the past tense.

After writing the paragraph about the scandal, discuss what you would have done if you had been that person. Then, in a second paragraph, write about what you would have done. Explain why, and give some details.

READING LINK

Espionage

"What Adolescents Miss When We Let Them Grow Up in Cyberspace" by Brent Staples (page 581)

"Is Anything Private Anymore?" by Sean Flynn (page 584)

How Do I Get a Better Grade?

Visit MyWritingLab for audiovisual lectures and additional practice sets about other verb forms.

Subject-Verb Agreement

Section Theme **COLLEGE LIFE**

LEARNING OBJECTIVES

wavebreakmedia ltd/Shutterstock

***In this chapter, you will read about topics related to* college issues.**

The Writer's Journal

In a short paragraph, express your opinion about the extracurricular activities on your campus.

Listen to the **Audio** Correcting Common Errors: Subject-Verb Agreement and Parallel Structure **MyWritingLab**

Watch the **Video** Subject-Verb Agreement **MyWritingLab**

Basic Subject-Verb Agreement Rules

Subject-verb agreement simply means that a subject and verb agree in number. A singular subject needs a singular verb, and a plural subject needs a plural verb.

Singular subject: Mr. Connor (S) **teaches** (V) in a community college.

Plural subject: The students (S) **appreciate** (V) his approach.

Simple Present Tense Agreement

Writers use **simple present tense** to indicate that an action is habitual or factual. Review the following rules for simple present tense agreement.

- When the subject is *he*, *she*, *it*, or the equivalent (*Adam*, *Maria*, *New Brunswick*), add an *-s* or *-es* ending to the verb. This is also called the **third-person singular form.**

Singular: Michael **works** in the college bookstore. (one person)

This neighbourhood **needs** a medical clinic. (one place)

The trophy **belongs** to the best athlete in the college. (one thing)

> **GRAMMAR LINK**
> For more information about the present tense, see Chapter 22.

- When the subject is *I*, *you*, *we*, *they*, or the equivalent (*the Zorns*, *the mountains*, *Amber and Tom*), do not add an ending to the verb.

Plural: College students **juggle** many tasks. (more than one person)

Some cities **have** colleges and four-year universities. (more than one place)

The benefits **include** a higher standard of living. (more than one thing)

For example, review the present tense forms of the verb *talk*.

Present Tense of *Talk*

	Singular	Plural
First person:	I talk	We talk
Second person:	You talk	You talk
Third person:	He talks	They talk
	She talks	
	It talks	

PRACTICE 1

Write the correct present tense form of each verb in parentheses.

EXAMPLE:
Mila Zahn's family (live) *lives* near Hamburg, Germany.

1. Mila Zahn is a German exchange student, and she (study) _____________ in a Canadian college.
2. Zahn (see) _____________ many glaring cultural differences between Canadians and Germans.
3. Many Canadian students (juggle) _____________ work and school.
4. For example, Mila's friend Amber (do) _____________ not have much money.
5. Amber (work) _____________ part-time so that she can pay for her studies.

6. However, in Germany, the state (sponsor) ______________ all levels of education, so students (do) ______________ not feel financial pressure.
7. (Do) ______________ the average Canadian student pay too much for higher levels of education?
8. (Do) ______________ you work and go to college?

Troublesome Present Tense Verbs: *be, have, do*

Some present tense verbs are formed in special ways. Review the verbs *be*, *have*, and *do*.

	Be	Have	Do
Singular forms			
First person:	I am	I have	I do
Second person:	You are	You have	You do
Third person:	He is	He has	He does
	She is	She has	She does
	It is	It has	It does
Plural forms			
First person:	We are	We have	We do
Second person:	You are	You have	You do
Third person:	They are	They have	They do

Use Standard Forms of *Be*

Some people use sentences such as *He be ready* or *She ain't happy*. However, those are nonstandard forms and should not be used in written conversation. Review the following corrections.

That man ~~be~~ *is* cool, but he ~~ain't~~ *is not* a good candidate for student council president.

PRACTICE 2

In the next selection, each verb is underlined. Correct twelve errors in subject-verb agreement or the incorrect use of *ain't*.

EXAMPLE:

Many exchange students ~~studies~~ *study* in Canada.

1. Emi Kawamura is a Japanese exchange student. According to Emi, some Canadian students has many misguided ideas about the Japanese. Emi remind people that she do not fit any stereotype. For example, her math skills is poor and she rarely uses computers.

2. The educational system in Japan differ from that in Canada. Japanese students has a longer school year than Canadian students. Japanese college entrance exams is very difficult, and students experience high levels of stress. Emi's brother, Jin, attends a private "cramming" school called a *juku*. He have to study six days a week because he hopes to get into a good university.

3. Because of complaints from parents and students, Japanese officials wants to reform the educational system. One plan is to place less emphasis on entrance exams. The current system ain't healthy for students.

4. Although the average Japanese student have a stressful experience in high school, the situation changes in college. Canadian college courses is more difficult than those in Japan, in Emi's opinion.

Simple Past Tense Agreement

In the past tense, all verbs except *be* have one past form.

Regular:	I worked.	He worked.	You worked.	We worked.	They worked.
Irregular:	I ate.	He ate.	You ate.	We ate.	They ate.

Exception: *Be*

In the past tense, the only verb requiring subject-verb agreement is the verb *be*, which has two past forms: *was* and *were*.

Was	**Were**
I was	We were
He was	You were
She was	They were
It was	

Present Perfect Tense Agreement

When writing in the present perfect tense, which is formed with *have* or *has* and the past participle, use *has* when the subject is third-person singular.

> My college **has** raised tuition fees. Other colleges **have** not raised their fees.

GRAMMAR LINK

For more information about using the present perfect tense, see Chapter 23.

Agreement in Other Tenses

When writing in most other verb tenses and in modal forms (*can*, *could*, *would*, *may*, *might*, and so on), use the same form of the verb with every subject.

Future:	I will **work**; she will **work**; they will **work**; you will **work**; we will **work**.
Past perfect:	I had **met**; she had **met**; they had **met**; you had **met**; we had **met**.
Modals:	I can **talk**; she should **talk**; they could **talk**; you might **talk**; we would **talk**.

PRACTICE 3

Correct twelve subject-verb agreement errors among the underlined verbs, and write *C* above correct verbs.

EXAMPLE:

A problem ~~exist~~ *exists* in many colleges and universities.

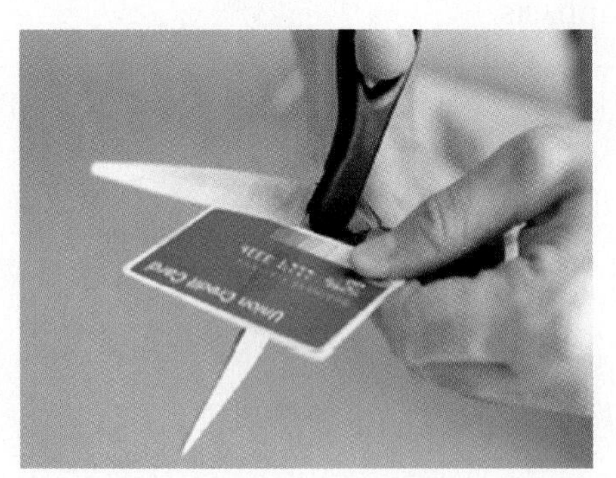
Creatas/Getty Images

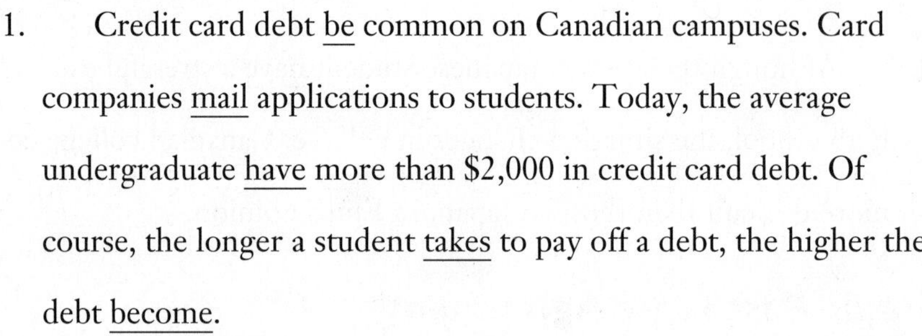
1. Credit card debt be common on Canadian campuses. Card companies mail applications to students. Today, the average undergraduate have more than $2,000 in credit card debt. Of course, the longer a student takes to pay off a debt, the higher the debt become.

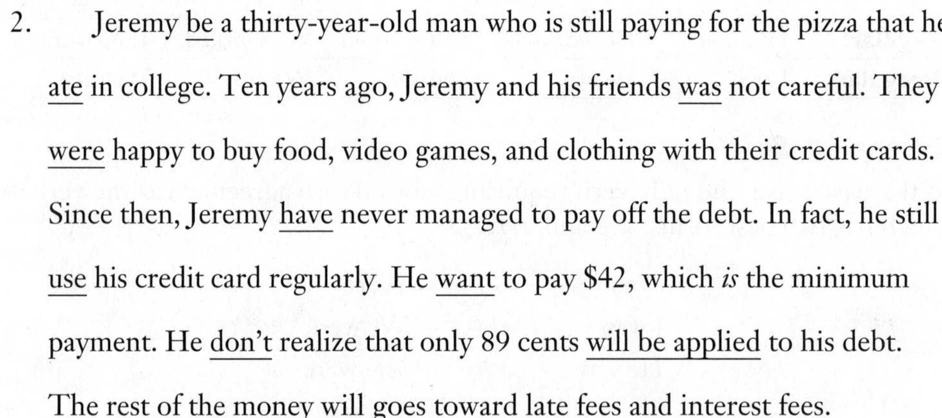
2. Jeremy be a thirty-year-old man who is still paying for the pizza that he ate in college. Ten years ago, Jeremy and his friends was not careful. They were happy to buy food, video games, and clothing with their credit cards. Since then, Jeremy have never managed to pay off the debt. In fact, he still use his credit card regularly. He want to pay $42, which *is* the minimum payment. He don't realize that only 89 cents will be applied to his debt. The rest of the money will goes toward late fees and interest fees.

3. Credit card companies charge extremely high fees. When you receives a credit card, you should pays the balance every month. You can avoid interest rates of about 20 percent.

More Than One Subject

There are special agreement rules when there is more than one subject in a sentence.

and

When subjects are joined by *and*, use the plural form of the verb.

> Colleges, universities, and trade schools **prepare** students for the job market.

or, nor

When two subjects are joined by *or* or *nor*, the verb agrees with the subject that is closer to it.

> Neither Amanda Jackson nor her students (plural) **use** the computer lab.

> Either the students or Amanda (singular) **uses** the department's portable laptop computer.

As Well As and **Along With**

The phrases *as well as* and *along with* are not the same as *and*. They do not form a compound subject. The real subject is before the interrupting expression.

> Joe, Carlos, and Peter **work** in a career college.

> Joe, along with Carlos and Peter, **teaches** business classes.

PRACTICE 4

Circle the correct verb in each sentence. Make sure the verb agrees with the subject.

EXAMPLE:

Colleges and universities (have, has) various interesting programs.

1. Both Theo and Amber (study, studies) nursing.
2. Amber and her mother (live, lives) in Mississauga.
3. Two buses or a train (transport, transports) Amber to her college campus.
4. Theo and his mother (reside, resides) in a small town outside Toronto.
5. Neither of the two local colleges nor the university (offer, offers) nursing programs.
6. Each day, Theo and his girlfriend (travel, travels) to Centennial College in Scarborough.
7. Neither Theo nor his parents (has, have) a lot of money.
8. Each year, either two fast-food restaurants or the local hardware store (sponsor, sponsors) low-income students.
9. Work and careful planning (pay, pays) off for college students.

Special Subject Forms

Some subjects are not easy to identify as singular or plural. Two common types are indefinite pronouns and collective nouns.

Indefinite Pronouns

Indefinite pronouns refer to a general person, place, or thing. Carefully review the following list of indefinite pronouns.

Indefinite Pronouns

Singular	another	each	no one	other
	anybody	everybody	nobody	somebody
	anyone	everyone	nothing	someone
	anything	everything	one	something
Plural	both, few, many, others, several			

Singular Indefinite Pronouns

In the following sentences, the verbs require the third-person singular form because the subjects are singular.

Everyone **knows** that career colleges offer practical, career-oriented courses.

Nothing **stops** people from applying to a career college.

You can put one or more singular nouns (joined by *and*) after *each* and *every*. The verb is still singular.

Each man and woman **knows** the stories about credit card debt.

Plural Indefinite Pronouns

Both, *few*, *many*, *others*, and *several* are all plural subjects. The verb is always plural.

Many **apply** to high-tech programs.

Others **prefer** to study in the field of health care.

PRACTICE 5

Underline the subjects and circle the correct verbs.

EXAMPLE:

Many people (chooses / choose) career colleges to further their studies.

1. Lucas Vigoletti (study / studies) Computer Programming and Analysis at Seneca College. The program (is / are) very demanding, and everyone in his class (work / works) very hard. Everybody (know / knows) that a good grade will help him or her find an interesting career. No one (expect / expects) the program to be easy.

2. Lucas (is / are) married to Virginia, and he (have / has) a part-time job as a telemarketer. Therefore, he (have / has) to schedule his study time well. All courses (require / requires) reading a lot of material, participating in workshops, and engaging in student discussions. Lucas and his classmates (have / has) to learn programming codes, (find / finds) computer viruses, and (review / reviews) notes from the previous day. Many (stay / stays) up past midnight studying.

3. Lucas and his friend Joshua also (practise / practises) interviewing techniques. They (prepare / prepares) lists of questions and (take / takes) turns "interviewing" each other. Some students (do / does) group interviews, while others (observe / observes) taped authentic interviews. Everybody (feel / feels) confident that such preparation will be helpful in a formal interview situation. Nobody (expect / expects) to pass the courses without working hard.

Collective Nouns

Collective nouns refer to a group of people or things. These are common collective nouns.

army	class	crowd	group	population
association	club	family	jury	public
audience	committee	gang	mob	society
band	company	government	organization	team

Generally, each group acts as a unit, so you must use the singular form of the verb.

The jury **is** ready to read the verdict.

If the members of the group act individually, use the plural form of the verb. It is a good idea to use a phrase such as *members of*.

Acceptable: The committee **are** not able to come to an agreement.

Better: The members of the committee **are** not able to come to an agreement.

Police Is Plural

The word *police* is always thought of as a plural noun because the word *officers* is implied but not stated.

The police **have** arrested a suspect.

The police **are** patrolling the neighbourhood.

PRACTICE 6

In each sentence, underline the subject and circle the correct verb.

EXAMPLE:

The government (offer / offers) financial aid for some students.

1. A career college (is / are) a sensible choice for many students wanting practical work skills. Such institutions (offer / offers) a variety of career-related programs. For example, my college (have / has) programs in high-tech, health care, business, and hospitality.
2. My friend Santosh (studies / study) in the hospitality program. Santosh (was / were) a cook in the army, but now he (want / wants) a career in adventure tourism. The army (provide / provides) financial help to Santosh for his studies. In fact, the military (encourage / encourages) its employees to continue education and training. Santosh's family also (give / gives) him encouragement.
3. People (need / needs) social, math, communication, and organizational skills when entering the hospitality business. Everyone (enter / enters) this field knowing that he or she must be able to get along with people during stressful situations. The industry (is / are) growing, but it (is / are) very important to have the right education. Career colleges (give / gives) students an advantage in this highly competitive market.

Verb before the Subject

Usually, the verb comes after the subject, but in some sentences, the verb comes before the subject. In such cases, you must still ensure that the subject and verb agree.

there or here

When a sentence begins with *there* or *here*, the subject always follows the verb. *There* and *here* are not subjects.

V S V S
Here **is** the college course list. There **are** many night courses.

Questions

In questions, word order is usually reversed, and the main or helping verb is placed before the subject. In the following example, the main verb is *be*.

V S V S
Where **is** the cafeteria? **Is** the food good?

However, in questions in which the main verb isn't *be*, the subject usually agrees with the helping verb.

HV S V HV S V
When **does** the library **close**? **Do** students **work** there?

PRACTICE 7

Correct any subject-verb agreement errors. If the sentence is correct, write *C* in the blank.

EXAMPLE:

~~Has~~ you ever won a competition? *Have*

1. There is many athletic scholarships in colleges. ______
2. Has many students benefited from the scholarships? ______
3. Does athletes get preferential treatment? ______
4. Is there a reason to stop giving scholarships to athletes? ______
5. There is many pressures on student athletes. ______
6. Why do Wayne Brydon want to play basketball professionally? ______
7. Do female athletes have the same opportunities? ______
8. According to Selma Rowen, there have not been enough attention given to academically successful students. ______
9. On the other hand, there is many people who support athletes. ______
10. In addition to doing their course work, do college athletes have to train for several hours each day? ______

Interrupting Words and Phrases

Words that come between the subject and the verb may confuse you. In these cases, look for the subject and make sure that the verb agrees with the subject.

S interrupting phrase V
Some rules regarding admission to this college **are** controversial.

S prepositional phrase V
A student in two of my classes **writes** for the college newspaper.

Identify Interrupting Phrases

When you revise your paragraphs, add parentheses around words that separate the subject and the verb. Then you can check to see whether your subjects and verbs agree.

S prepositional phrase V
A student (in two of my classes) **writes** for the college newspaper.

When interrupting phrases contain *of the* or similar words, the subject appears before the phrase.

S prepositional phrase V
One (of my biggest problems) **is** my lack of organization.

PRACTICE 8

Underline the subject in each sentence. Add parentheses around any words that come between each subject and verb. Then circle the correct form of the verb.

EXAMPLE:

One (of the most controversial issues on campus) **is / are** affirmative action.

1. Some colleges in this country **have / has** more relaxed admission standards for students from ethnic minorities. Such colleges, with good reason, **want / wants** to have a vibrant and diverse student population. However, arguing that they have been discriminated against, students from across the nation **have / has** sued their colleges. Judges in courtrooms **have / has** had to consider whether affirmative action is unfair.

2. People in favour of affirmative action (or employment equity, as it is termed in Canada) **have / has** compelling arguments. Historically, some ethnic groups in Canada **has / have** not had access to higher education. Many factors such as poverty **contribute / contributes** to the problem. Literary journalist Wade Rowland, in an article for the *Toronto Star*, **suggest / suggests** that the poor and uneducated suffer in the information world. Additionally, affirmative action **help / helps** create a diverse student body.

3. For some people, regulations to safeguard affirmative action **help / helps** equalize opportunities in our society. For others, such regulations **is / are** unfair to certain groups. What is your opinion?

Interrupting Words: *who, which, that*

If a sentence contains a clause beginning with *who*, *which*, or *that*, then the verb agrees with the subject preceding *who*, *which*, or *that*.

There is a woman in my neighbourhood *who* **counsels** students.

Here are some old newspapers *that* **discuss** steroid abuse.

One article, *which* **contains** stories about hazing, is very interesting.

CHAPTER 25

PRACTICE 9

Underline and correct ten subject-verb agreement errors.

EXAMPLE:

The English department has a help centre that ~~open~~ *opens* weekdays.

1. Students who needs help with their English can go to the help centre. My friend who never speak English at home often goes to the help centre. He does exercises that helps him. He says that the woman who work there is friendly.

2. There is some computers in the help centre. If a student who have an assignment due need to use a computer, one is available. There is also several tutors available who help the students.

3. Sometimes the administrators who control the budget threatens to close the help centre. When that happens, students who uses the centre protest. Then the centre remains open.

REFLECT ON IT

Think about what you have learned in this chapter. If you do not know an answer, review that topic.

1. When should you add *-s* or *-es* to verbs? ______________________________

   ____

2. Look at the following nouns. Circle all the collective nouns.

family	people	army	committee
judge	crowd	brothers	audience

3. When do you use *was* and *were*?

   Use *was* ______________________________

   Use *were* ______________________________

4. Circle and correct any subject-verb agreement errors in the following sentences.
   a. There is many colleges in Ontario.
   b. The University of Toronto apparently have a secret society.
   c. One of our cousins go to University of Toronto.
   d. There is no hazing rituals on our campus.

Final Review

Correct twenty errors in subject-verb agreement.

EXAMPLE:

looks
This college campus ~~look~~ peaceful.

1. Two years ago, Elmira Reed left home for the first time and went to college. Today, Reed, a biology major, has a private dorm room on campus. She admits that she love the feeling of independence. However, last March, Reed's purse and book bag was stolen from her car, and in May, there was robberies in several dorm rooms.

2. College campuses is not always the peaceful and safe places that they appears to be. In fact, according to the Canadian Federation of Students, education and awareness regarding assault and violent crime are essential for students. Even though there is many reported violent crimes per year on college or university campuses, the idea of a police presence in such areas has been rejected. However, if each student take a few simple precautions, he or she can reduce the risk of being a crime victim.

3. First, everyone who live in campus dorms need to act responsibly. Neither Reed nor her roommate take proper precautions. Sometimes, when Reed's roommate go out for the evening, she posts information about her whereabouts on her room door. However, such information provide thieves with an invitation to break in. Students should not leave notes posted on their doors, and they should always lock their room doors even if they plan to be absent for only a short while.

4. Furthermore, students should familiarize themselves with campus security locations. There is usually call boxes in certain buildings, and students should know where to find those emergency phones. Also, if someone want to study in a secluded location at night, he or she should inform campus security. Some campuses has "walk home" services for students who uses the library late at night. New students need to find out what the campus has to offer.

5. Ultimately, anyone who live on campus need to think about security. If nobody take precautions, then more robberies will occur. Remember that colleges are public places, buildings are open late, and there is not always a lot of security guards on campus. Therefore, it is important to be sensible.

The Writer's Room

Write about one of the following topics. Make sure that your subjects and verbs agree.

1. Examine this photo. Define a term that relates to the photo. Some ideas might be *debt*, *interest rates*, *reckless spender*, *cheapskate*, *spendthrift*, and *credit card junkie*.

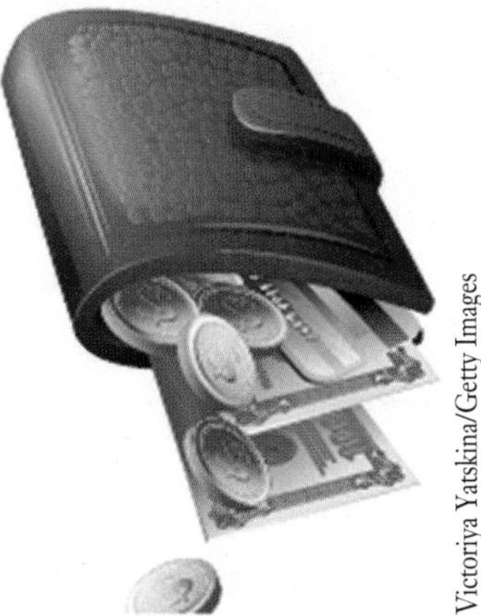

Victoriya Yatskina/Getty Images

2. Should college be free? What could be the advantages or disadvantages of free college?

How Do I Get a Better Grade?

Visit MyWritingLab for audiovisual lectures and additional practice sets about subject-verb agreement.

Tense Consistency

Section Theme **COLLEGE LIFE**

LEARNING OBJECTIVE

1 Consistent Verb Tense (page 384)

In this chapter, you will read about people who have made **difficult choices.**

MARIA TOUTOUDAKI/ E+/Getty Images

The Writer's Journal

How do images in the media influence the way that people judge their own bodies? Write a short paragraph about the media and body image.

Consistent Verb Tense

When you write, the verb tense you use gives the reader an idea about the time when the event occurred. A **tense shift** occurs when you shift from one tense to another for no logical reason.

Tense shift: College reporter Erica Santiago interviewed a protester and asks about his political philosophy.

Correct: College reporter Erica Santiago interviewed a protester and asked about his political philosophy.

Sometimes the time frame in a text really does change. In those circumstances, you would change the verb tense. The following example accurately shows two different time periods. Notice that certain key words (*during my childhood, today*) indicate what tense the writer should use.

> During my childhood, I <u>ate</u> (past) a lot of fast food. Today, I <u>try</u> (present) to eat a healthy diet.

PRACTICE 1

Identify and correct each tense shift. If the sentence is correct, write *C* in the space.

EXAMPLE:

Many adults go back to college and ~~received~~ training in new careers. *receive*

1. Career change is a frightening experience for many people because they lost the security and familiarity of a job and they have to go back to school to become requalified. _______
2. Last year, Lee Kim was at a crossroads in his life because he is about to change careers. _______
3. For the previous ten years, Lee had been working as a computer service technician for a small company, but a year ago, the company downsized, and he lost his job. _______
4. Suddenly, at the age of thirty-five, Lee is faced with having to change careers, and he was scared. _______
5. Lee met with a career counsellor; she advises Lee to check out the different programs in various career colleges. _______
6. Lee researched the courses at different institutions, and he finds that the medical laboratories program was a good option for him. _______
7. Now, Lee is enrolled as a student at Cambrian College, but he admits that going back to college after many years is intimidating. _______
8. Nowadays, Lee had to budget his money and has to relearn how to be a student. _______

Would and Could

When you tell a story about a past event, use *would* instead of *will*, and use *could* instead of *can*.

> In 2013, college wrestler Robert Burzak knew that he ~~can~~ *could* bulk up if he used steriods, but he promised his coach that he ~~will~~ *would* not.

PRACTICE 2

Underline and correct ten tense shifts.

EXAMPLE:

Robert began weight training after he ~~breaks~~ *broke* his leg.

1. In 2011, Robert Burzak joined a health club and tries weightlifting. He knew that he can have a sculpted body if he worked out. After a few months of weight training, he starts to get impatient. He wanted to get larger muscles very quickly, so, after a training partner told him about steroids, he decides to try them.

2. Robert started by taking steroids in pill form. Within weeks he noticed a difference. Soon, he graduated to steroid injections. Others noticed his large muscles, and Robert feels proud of his "six-pack" stomach and his large biceps. He realized that his new look conformed to the images of male beauty seen in the media.

3. Unfortunately, after Robert began to use steroids, side effects kick in. Robert developed acne on his back. Most worrisome, he felt wild mood swings, and he will alternate between violent outbursts and periods of depression. He cannot stop taking the pills because each time he tried to stop, his weight will plummet.

4. Finally, in 2013, Robert gave up steroids. He knew that the risks to his health outweighed the benefits of having a sculpted body. Furthermore, his girlfriend said that she will leave him if he could not stay off the drugs. Today, Robert is drug-free.

REFLECT ON IT

Think about what you have learned in this chapter. If you do not know an answer, review that topic.

1. What is tense inconsistency? ______________________________

____

2. If you are writing a paragraph about a past event, what word should you use instead of these two?

   a. will: ____________________ b. can: ____________________

3. Read the following paragraphs and find five tense inconsistencies. Correct the errors.

   EXAMPLE: Kaitlin diets because she ~~wanted~~ *wants* to look thinner.

   In 2012, college student Amy Heller became severely malnourished. In an attempt to lose weight, Heller ingested diet pills, and she severely restricts her intake of food. When others suggested that she had a problem, Heller will deny it. By July 2014, she weighs only 88 pounds. Heller finally sought treatment, and soon she can eat regular meals.

   In 2013, Wendy Hoyt made a study about body image and college students. She asked more than two hundred students to rate their level of satisfaction with their own bodies. Her results showed that women are more dissatisfied with their weight than men were. She attributed the diverse statistics to the influence of the media.

FINAL REVIEW

Underline and correct the tense shifts in the next student essay.

EXAMPLE:

In the 1970s, many conscientious objectors ~~get~~ *got* involved in politics, and they fled to Canada.

1. In the 1960s and 1970s, many people oppose the Vietnam War and the military draft in the United States. Thousands flee to Canada at that time to avoid being drafted, and they are called “draft dodgers” and “deserters.” In 2002, Eric Longley write an article about draft laws in the

Gale Encyclopedia of Popular Culture. According to Longley, young people of college age south of the border are often forced to participate in wars up until 1973.

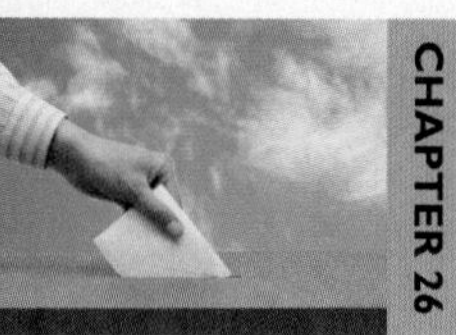

2. Draft dodging is common during the Vietnam War, with 125 000 individuals fleeing to Canada. At that time, many men will register in college to avoid going to war, but when the war escalated, the government introduces a lottery system, and college students can be drafted. In a 2004 interview, V. A. Smith said that he fled to Canada in 1970 when his lottery number is picked because he does not want to fight in Vietnam. Parents of acclaimed author and social activist Naomi Klein come to Canada in 1967 to escape the draft.

3. In 2006, draft dodgers and those who assisted them were honoured at a celebration in Castlegar, British Columbia. Since there is enormous controversy over the bronze "Welcoming Peace" sculpture, it's now housed at a private gallery rather than publicly displayed outside.

4. The Canadian Armed Forces and the U.S. Army National Guard offer excellent educational and career opportunities for their recruits. In 2001, many young men and women enter the National Guard to get a free college education. Then many of them have to fight overseas. For example, Jessica Lynch, a soldier wounded during the Iraq War, said that she just wants to get an education when she enlists.

5. Do the poorest members of society face a larger risk of fighting overseas? Some argue that a military draft penalizes working-class men and women. Others believed that a military draft is the only fair way to ensure that armies have enough soldiers. As long as conflicts between nations exist, the military will need to find recruits.

The Writer's Room

Write about one of the following topics. Ensure that your verb tenses are consistent.

1. Describe your college campus. You might describe an interesting building or area of the campus.
2. What are some things that new students should know about your college? Explain how to survive the first few semesters in college.

READING LINK

College Life
"The Market and the Mall" by Stephen Henighan (page 528)
"We Turned Some Sharp Corners: A Marriage Proposal in Durango" by Nick Massey-Garrison (page 530)
"Stealing Glances" by Sheila Heti (page 535)
"The Great Offside" by James Mirtle (page 538)

The Writers' Circle Collaborative Activity

Work with a team of students, and create a short survey. Formulate at least five interesting questions about college life. For example, you can ask about the food services, the course selection, transportation, student fees, extracurricular activities, fashions, student study habits, or any other topic that you can think of.

For each question that you create, include a list of possible choices. It will be much easier to compile your results if all students choose their responses from the same list. Do not ask open-ended questions. Finally, if a question asks about student knowledge, give an "I don't know" choice. Otherwise, students may simply make a guess, and that would skew your results.

After you have completed your survey questions, then one team member should remain seated, and the other team members should split up and sit with other groups in the class to ask the questions. After each member has gathered information, the original group should get together and write a summary of the results.

How Do I Get a Better Grade?

Visit MyWritingLab for audiovisual lectures and additional practice sets about tense consistency.

Nouns, Determiners, and Prepositions

Section Theme **INVENTIONS AND DISCOVERIES**

LEARNING OBJECTIVES

1 Singular and Plural Nouns (page 390)
2 Count Nouns and Non-count Nouns (page 395)
3 Determiners (page 397)
4 Prepositions (page 400)

Kuzmick/Fotolia

In this chapter, you will read about topics related to **inventions** *and* **discoveries.**

The Writer's Journal

Write a short paragraph describing the most interesting invention from the twentieth century. Explain why the invention is important.

Singular and Plural Nouns

Nouns are words that refer to people, places, or things. Nouns are divided into common nouns and proper nouns.

- **Common nouns** refer to general people, places, or things and begin with a lowercase letter. For example, *books*, *computer*, and *city* are common nouns.
- **Proper nouns** refer to particular people, places, or things and begin with a capital letter. For example, *Alexander Graham Bell*, *Microsoft*, and *Orillia* are proper nouns.

Nouns are either singular or plural. A **singular noun** refers to one of something, while a **plural noun** refers to more than one of something. Regular plural nouns end in *-s* or *-es*.

	Singular	Plural
People:	inventor	inventors
	writer	writers
Places:	town	towns
	village	villages
Things:	computer	computers
	aspirin	aspirins

Adding -*es*

When a noun ends in *s*, *x*, *ch*, *sh*, or *z*, add *-es* to form the plural.

business/business**es** tax/tax**es** church/church**es**

Irregular Plural Nouns

Nouns that do not use *-s* or *-es* in their plural forms are called **irregular nouns.** Here are some common irregular nouns.

Singular	Plural	Singular	Plural
person	people	woman	women
child	children	tooth	teeth
man	men	foot	feet

Some nouns use other rules to form the plural. It is a good idea to memorize both the rules and the exceptions.

- For nouns ending in *f* or *fe*, change the *f* to *v* and add *-es*.

Singular	Plural	Singular	Plural
knife	kni**ves**	thief	thie**ves**
wife	wi**ves**	leaf	lea**ves**

Some exceptions: belief, beliefs; roof, roofs; safe, safes.

- For nouns ending in a consonant + *y*, change the *y* to *i* and add *-es*.

Singular	Plural	Singular	Plural
lady	lad**ies**	baby	bab**ies**
berry	berr**ies**	cherry	cherr**ies**

If a vowel comes before the final *y*, then the word retains the regular plural form.

Singular	Plural	Singular	Plural
day	days	key	keys

- Some nouns remain the same in both singular and plural forms.

Singular	Plural	Singular	Plural
fish	fish	deer	deer
moose	moose	sheep	sheep

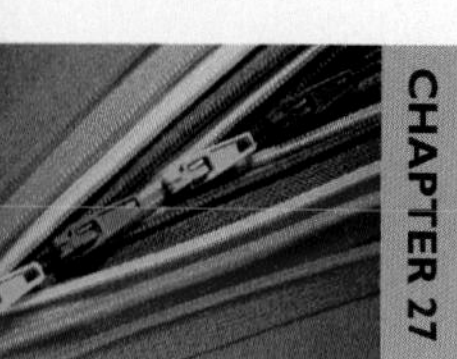

- Some nouns are thought of as being only plural and therefore have no singular form.

Plural Form Only

clothes	goods	proceeds	scissors
eyeglasses	pants	savings	series

- Some nouns are **compound nouns,** which means that they are made up of two or more words. To form the plural of compound nouns, add *-s* or *-es* to the last word of the compound noun.

Singular	Plural	Singular	Plural
bus stop	bus stop**s**	artificial heart	artificial heart**s**
air conditioner	air conditioner**s**	jet airplane	jet airplane**s**

In hyphenated compound nouns, if the first word is a noun, add *-s* to the noun.

Singular	Plural	Singular	Plural
senator-elect	senator**s**-elect	runner-up	runner**s**-up
sister-in-law	sister**s**-in-law	husband-to-be	husband**s**-to-be

- Some nouns that are borrowed from Latin keep the plural form of the original language.

Singular	Plural	Singular	Plural
millennium	millennia	paparazzo	paparazzi
datum	data	phenomenon	phenomena

Persons* versus *People

There are two plural forms of *person*. *People* is the most common plural form.

Some people have great ideas. Many people patent their ideas.

Persons is used in a legal or an official context.

The patent was stolen by persons unknown.

PRACTICE 1

Correct ten errors in plural noun forms.

1. Most inventions are made by ordinary persons who are able to think outside the box. Many inventions are unplanned. Back in 1905, an eleven-year-old boy named Frank Epperson mixed powdered fruit and water with a stick and accidentally left the drink on his back porch. Overnight, the temperature plummeted. In the morning, he pulled his frozen drink out of his glass and showed it to the other childrens at school. When he was

in his twentys, he remembered his invention and patented it. He called his product a "popsicle."

2. In 1869, a wire factory worker named Alan Parkhouse was at a company gathering with several familys. His two sister-in-laws complained about the lack of places to hang their coats. Parkhouse bent a piece of wire into two ovales and created a hook between them, thus inventing the first cloths hanger.
3. In 1853, George Crum, a chef, was cutting potatos when he heard some customers complain about the thickness of his French fries. Then he cut thinner fries, but the two womans still complained. Finally, Crum looked through his selection of knifes and chose the sharpest one. He cut fries that were so thin they could not be eaten with a fork. The potato chip was born!

PRACTICE 2

Fill in the blanks with either the singular or the plural form of the noun. If the noun does not change, put an *X* in the space.

EXAMPLES:

	Singular	**Plural**
	man	*men*
	X	goggles
1.	person	______________
2.	loaf	______________
3.	______________	mice
4.	brother-in-law	______________
5.	lady	______________
6.	______________	pants
7.	______________	jeans
8.	sheep	______________
9.	calf	______________
10.	______________	binoculars
11.	child	______________
12.	______________	shelves
13.	______________	sunglasses
14.	alarm clock	______________
15.	bathing suit	______________

Key Words for Singular and Plural Nouns

Some key words will help you determine whether a noun is singular or plural.

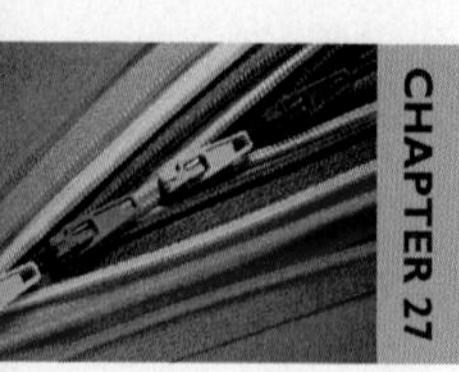

- Use a singular noun after words such as *a*, *an*, *one*, *each*, *every*, and *another*.

  As **a** young mother, Dorothy Gerber prepared homemade baby food for her daughter.

  Gerber tried to sell her product to **every** grocery store in her town.

- Use a plural noun after words such as *two*, *all*, *both*, *many*, *few*, *several*, and *some*.

  Very **few** companies produced food targeted to children.

  Today, **many** babies eat Gerber's baby food.

Using Plural Nouns after *of the*

Use a plural noun after the expressions *one, all, two, each, few, lots, many, most* and *several of the*… .

One of the most useful **items** ever invented is the zipper.

PRACTICE 3

Circle the correct noun in each set of parentheses.

EXAMPLE:

In the future, some of the most useful (invention / inventions) will be in the energy sector.

1. Very few (government / governments) would deny that carbon reduction is important. Every (year / years), engineers try to come up with an automobile (prototype / prototypes) that is fuel efficient and economical. Today, many (person / people) discuss electric cars, but did you know that such automobiles are not a new (invention / inventions)?

2. In 1883, electric (car / cars) roamed Toronto's streets. Lawyer Frederick Bernard Featherstonehaugh (commission / commissioned) the first Canadian electric car to be built. However, during the 1920s, the mass production of combustion (engine / engines) wiped out electric cars for the next forty years.

3. Then, on October 16, 1973, something happened. All of the (member / members) of the Organization of Petroleum Exporting Countries (OPEC) cut production of oil and announced that they would no longer ship oil to Western nations. One of the (result / results) of the crisis was that people discussed electric cars again. Today, engineers in almost every (nation / nations) want to develop an efficient electric (vehicle / vehicles).

Count Nouns and Non-count Nouns

In English, nouns are grouped into two types: count nouns and non-count nouns. **Count nouns** refer to people or things that you can count, such as *engine*, *paper*, or *girl*. Count nouns usually can have both a singular and a plural form.

She read a book about inventions. She read five books about inventions.

Non-count nouns refer to people or things that you cannot count because you cannot divide them, such as *electricity* and *music*. Non-count nouns usually have only the singular form.

The furniture in the inventor's house looked expensive.

Inventors usually have a lot of specialized equipment.

To express a non-count noun as a count noun, refer to it in terms of types, varieties, or amounts.

The patent office has **a variety of** furniture.

My friend works for an entertainment company where he listens to **many styles of** music.

The clerk at the patent office likes to drink coffee with **four cubes of** sugar.

Here are some common non-count nouns.

Common Non-count Nouns

Categories of Objects		Food	Nature	Substances	
clothing	machinery	bread	air	chalk	paint
equipment	mail	fish	earth	charcoal	paper
furniture	money	honey	electricity	coal	
homework	music	meat	energy	fur	
jewellery	postage	milk	radiation	hair	
luggage	software	rice	water	ink	

Abstract Nouns

advice	effort	information	progress
attention	evidence	knowledge	proof
behaviour	health	luck	research
education	help	peace	violence

PRACTICE 4

Change the italicized words to the plural form, if necessary. If you cannot use the plural form, write *X* in the space. If the word ends in *y*, you may have to change the *y* to *i* for the plural form.

EXAMPLE:

In written communication, there have been many useful *discovery* __ies__.

1. Since the beginning of *history* ______, people have used various *method* ______ to compose in written form. Early *human* ______ used *substance* ______ such as *charcoal* ______, *chalk* ______, and *paint* ______ to write on *wall* ______ and *paper* ______. Eventually, a lot of *information* ______ was recorded using ink and a quill.

2. In 1884, Lewis Waterman patented one of the most useful *invention* ______. Although Waterman's fountain *pen* ______ worked reasonably well, they were unreliable, and ink could leak onto *clothing* ______ and *furniture* ______.

3. Since the 1930s, a lot of *progress* ______ has been made in written communication. In 1938, Ladislo Biro was one of the best-known *journalist* ______ in Hungary. He spent a lot of *time* ______ thinking about different *type* ______ of writing *tool* ______. Using quick-drying ink that was common in printing *press* ______, and using a small ball bearing, he created the first ballpoint pen.

4. These days, *company* ______ do a lot of *research* ______ because they want to develop a new, better writing tool. In fact, there are many different *kind* ______ of *pen* ______ on the market.

Determiners

Determiners are words that help to determine or figure out whether a noun is specific or general.

> Arthur Scott used **his** imagination and created **a** new invention, **the** paper towel.

You can use many words from different parts of speech as determiners.

Articles:	a, an, the
Demonstratives:	this, that, these, those, such
Indefinite pronouns:	any, all, both, each, every, either, few, little, many, several
Numbers:	one, two, three
Possessive nouns:	Jack's, the teacher's, a man's
Possessive adjectives:	my, your, his, her, its, our, their, whose

Commonly Confused Determiners

Some determiners can be confusing because you can use them only in specific circumstances. Review this list of some commonly confused determiners.

a, an, the

A and *an* are general determiners, and *the* is a specific determiner.

> I need to find a (general) new car. The (specific) cars in that showroom are expensive.

- Use *a* and *an* before singular count nouns but not before plural or non-count nouns. Use *a* before nouns that begin with a consonant (*a man*), and use *an* before nouns that begin with a vowel (*an invention*).

  > An ordinary woman created a very useful product.

- Use *the* before nouns that refer to a specific person, place, or thing. Do not use *the* before languages (*he studies Greek*), sports (*we played football*), and most city and country names (*Biro was born in Hungary*).

  > In 1885, Karl Benz invented the first automobile while living in the city of Mannheim, Germany.

many, few, much, little

- Use *many* and *few* with count nouns.

  > Many **people** have tried to develop new products, but few **inventions** are really successful.

- Use *much* and *little* with non-count nouns.

  > Manu Joshi spent too much **money** on very little **research.**

this, that, these, those

- Use *this* and *these* to refer to things that are physically close to the speaker or at the present time. Use *this* before singular nouns and *these* before plural nouns.

This **computer** in my purse measures three by five inches. These **days,** computers are very small.

- Use *that* and *those* to refer to things that are physically distant from the speaker or in the past or future. Use *that* before singular nouns and *those* before plural nouns.

In the 1950s, computers were invented. In those **years,** computers were very large. In that **building,** there is a very old computer.

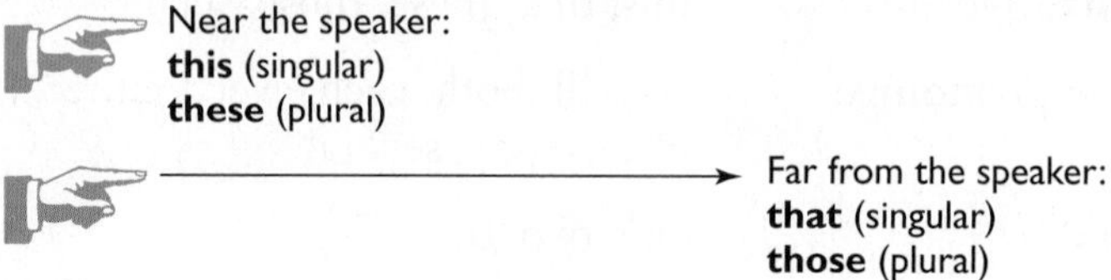

PRACTICE 5

Write *a*, *an*, or *the* in the space before each noun. If no determiner is necessary, write *X* in the space.

EXAMPLE:

A modern convenience like __a__ car can make travelling much easier.

1. Most of us admire ______ beautiful, shiny new automobiles, but we do not give ______ same admiration to ______ windshield wipers. Indeed, we take ______ windshield wiper for granted, yet it is ______ extremely necessary tool when we are driving. In fact, before ______ invention of ______ windshield wiper, drivers had to stop to clean the front window of their vehicles.

2. In 1902, when she was on ______ trip to New York City, Mary Anderson observed that streetcar drivers had to look through open windows when they were driving in bad weather. In 1903, she invented ______ gadget that could clean car windows. Her wipers consisted of rubber blades on ______ outside of the windshield and ______ handle on ______ inside of the car. Drivers could turn ______ wipers by turning the handle.

3. Anderson received ______ patent for her invention, and by 1916, all American-made cars had ______ windshield wipers as ______ regular feature.

PRACTICE 6

Underline the appropriate determiner in parentheses. If the noun does not require a determiner, underline X.

EXAMPLE:

Most inventions begin with (X / a / the) great idea.

1. (This / These) days, (much / many) people want to get rich quickly by developing (a / the / X) great new product. They also hope to make (X / the) life easier for others. (Every / Some / X) inventions are extremely useful, while others are totally absurd.

2. (Few / Little) inventions are as bizarre as (a / X / the) "Twelve Gauge Golf Club." It requires very (few / little) equipment. It contains (the / a) barrel, (the / a) muzzle, and (the / a) trap door to load explosives. (A / The / X) firing pin is in (an / the / X) exact spot where (a / the / X) club is supposed to hit (the / X) ball. (The / An) inventor received (X / a) patent in 1979. There were many odd patents (this / that) year. The device does not cost (much / many) money to produce. However, it has produced very (few / little) interest among consumers.

3. Although (much / many) absurd inventions never earn a penny, a (few / little) of them become successful. In 2005, (a / the) cellphone company in China created a breathalyzer phone. People can program (a / the) phone to block certain numbers such as that of the boss. If the phone user is inebriated, he or she cannot dial (that / those) numbers. Although people in North America do not have (much / many) information about the phone, it is extremely popular in (the / X) Korea. More than 200 000 people bought the phones because they wanted to avoid making (a / the / X) embarrassing phone calls.

4. (This / That) year, thousands of people will patent their ideas. With a (few / little) time and (some / many) research, perhaps you can come up with a great invention.

PRACTICE 7

Correct fifteen errors in singular nouns, plural nouns, and determiners.

EXAMPLE:

ideas
One of the most interesting ~~idea~~ is a self-cleaning house.

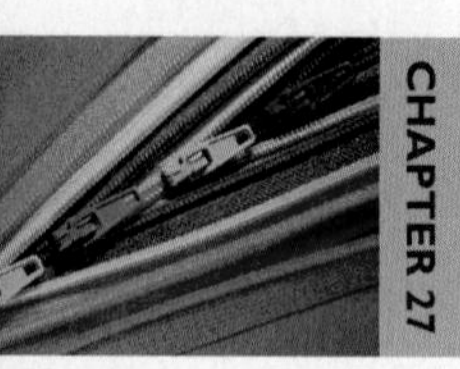

In her autobiography, Agatha Christie wrote that most invention arise from laziness. Peoples invent to save themselves trouble. Christie's comments apply perfectly to Frances Gabe of Newberg, Oregon. Gabe, after a lot of researches, has invented and patented the world's first self-cleaning house. A house will appeal to anyone who hates to clean. On the ceiling of each rooms in Gabe's house, there is a cleaning and drying machines. At the touch of a buttons, each units first sprays soapy water over the room, then rinses and blow-dries the entire area. The rooms' floors are sloped slightly so that excess waters runs to a drain. The furnitures is made of waterproof material, and there are no carpets. There are not much decorations in the house. In the kitchen, all dish are cleaned, dried, and stored inside dishwasher cupboards. Every sink, tub, and toilets is self-cleaning. Gabe created the architectural plans and the designs for the specialized equipments. This days, Gabe actually lives in her patented prototype home.

Watch the Video
Prepositions
MyWritingLab

Prepositions

Prepositions are words that show concepts such as time, place, direction, and manner. They show connections or relationships between ideas.

Scientists made many important discoveries **during** World War II.

Canadian scientists raced **to** build the first atomic bomb.

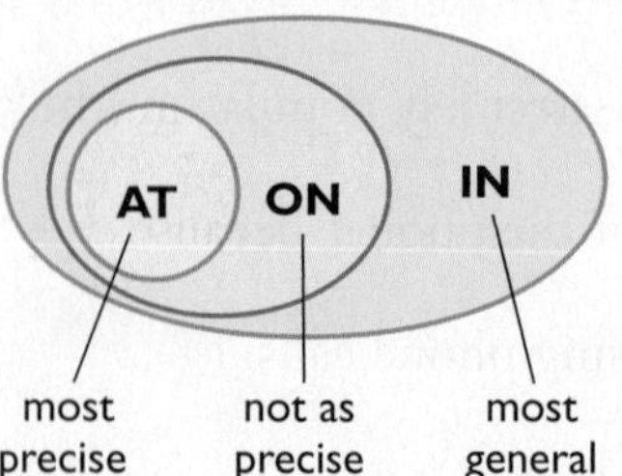

Prepositions	Prepositions of Time	Prepositions of Place
at	at a specific time of day (at 8:30 p.m.) at night at breakfast, lunch, dinner	at an address (at 15 Maple Street) at a specific building (at the hospital)
on	on a day of the week (on Monday) on a specific date (on June 16) on a specific holiday (on Martin Luther King Day) on time (meaning "punctual") on my birthday	on a specific street (on 17th Avenue) on technological devices (on -TV, on the radio, on the phone, on the computer) on a planet (on Earth) on top
in	in a year (in 2005) in a month (in July) in the morning, afternoon, evening in the spring, summer, fall, winter	in a city (in Sault Ste. Marie) in a country (in Spain) in a continent (in Africa)
from … to	from one time to another (from 6 a.m. to 8 p.m.)	from one place to another (from Toronto to Saint John)
for	for a period of time (for six hours)	for a distance (for ten kilometres)

Commonly Confused Prepositions

to versus *at*

Use *to* after verbs that indicate movement from one place to another.

> Each morning, Albert walks **to** the library; he goes **to** the coffee shop; and he returns **to** his office.

Exception: Do not put *to* directly before *home.*

> Albert returned ~~to~~ home after he won his prize. He didn't go to his friend's home.

Use *at* after verbs that indicate being or remaining in one place (and not moving from one place to another).

> In the afternoon, he stays **at** work. He sits **at** his desk and looks **at** his inventions.

for versus *during*

Use *during* to explain when something happens. Use *for* to explain how long it takes to happen.

> **During** the month of August, the patent office closes **for** two weeks.
>
> The inventors of the bomb experimented **for** many years **during** World War II.

PRACTICE 8

Write the correct preposition in each blank. Choose *in*, *on*, *at*, *to*, *for*, *during*, or *from*.

EXAMPLE:

At 5:15 a.m, we heard the news.

1. One of the most influential inventions ______ history was the creation of the atomic bomb.
2. ______ Germany, scientists were trying very hard to develop the atomic bomb ______ the beginning of World War II.
3. Louis Slotin, a young scientist ______ Winnipeg, was invited to participate ______ the Manhattan Project, a plan to create the first atomic bomb ______ the United States.
4. Uranium, a valuable product for creating the bomb, was mined ______ Eldorado Mine ______ Great Bear Lake's shores.
5. The ore was mined and transported ______ river barges ______ the war.
6. Dene miners and their families, who lived and worked ______ the area, were exposed to high levels of radiation ______ and after the war.
7. Not only did Slotin die from the effects of a disastrous mishap ______ a scientific experiment with uranium and plutonium, but the Dene people suffered tremendously as well.
8. Many individuals suffered ______ the effects of uranium poisoning; furthermore, many developed cancer and died.
9. ______ the 1990s the government finally agreed to cleanse the Dene land of radioactive waste.

PRACTICE 9

Correct five errors with prepositions.

EXAMPLE:

for

The zipper has been popular ~~during~~ *for* many years.

Whitcomb Judson patented a new type of fabric fastener on 1893. Several others contributed to the design of the fastener. Today, the zipper is the source of many "fly" jokes. For example, last semester, I went at my science class to make a presentation, and I did not realize that my zipper was down. During twenty minutes, I spoke, and some students giggled. During a month, others teased me. I must have heard "you're flying low" a hundred times. Now, when I go at college, I ensure that my zipper is firmly fastened.

Common Prepositional Expressions

Many common expressions contain prepositions. These types of expressions usually express a particular meaning.

EXAMPLE:

verb preposition

This morning I listened **to** the radio.

Here is a list of common prepositional expressions.

accuse (somebody) of	escape from	prevent (someone) from
acquainted with	excited about	protect (someone) from
add to	familiar with	proud of
afraid of	feel like	provide (someone) with
agree with	fond of	qualify for
angry about	forget about	realistic about
angry with	forgive (someone) for	refer to
apologize for	friendly with	related to
apply for	good for	rely on
approve of	grateful for	rescue from
argue with	happy about	responsible for
ask for	hear about	sad about
associate with	hope for	satisfied with
aware of	hopeful about	scared of
believe in	innocent of	search for
belong to	insist on	similar to
capable of	insulted by	specialize in
care about	interested in	stop (something) from
care for	introduce to	succeed in
commit to	jealous of	take advantage of
comply with	keep from	take care of
concern about	located in	thank (someone) for
confronted with	long for	think about
consist of	look forward to	think of
count on	opposed to	tired of
deal with	participate in	upset about
decide on	patient with	upset with
decide to	pay attention to	willing to

depend on	pay for	wish for
disappointed about	pray for	worry about
disappointed with	prepared for	
dream of	prepared to	

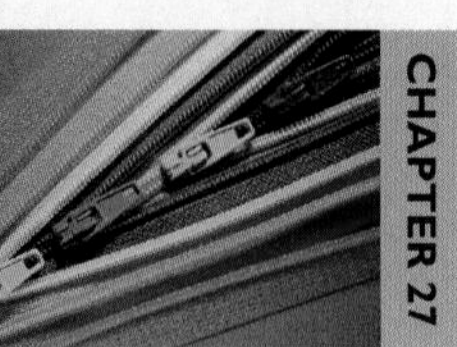

PRACTICE 10

Write the correct preposition in each blank. Use the preceding list of prepositional expressions to help you.

EXAMPLE:

Many U.S. citizens participated ___*in*___ the war effort.

1. During World War II, many people believed ____ science. Canadian Louis Slotin was interested ______ physics. He heard ______ the rise of fascism in Germany. He decided ______ become a scientist with the U.S. government.

2. Slotin was excited ______ working on atomic bombs for the Manhattan Project. Officials searched for a secluded location to develop the bomb and chose a desert area near Los Alamos, New Mexico. Slotin dealt ______ a large team of scientists.

3. With Slotin's experience ______ triggering devices, the young physicist worked ______ plutonium and uranium ______ a dangerous experiment. He attempted ______ bring together hemispheres ______ these chemicals without causing a chain reaction. Observing the "blue glow" of the united chemicals was referred ______ as "tickling the dragon's tail."

4. Unfortunately,______ one day in 1946, the experiment had disastrous effects. Slotin's hand slipped, and the man was exposed ______ a high level of radiation, which took his life nine days later.

5. Because Slotin prevented the others ______ the room from absorbing critical levels of radiation before he had, the man was deemed a hero.

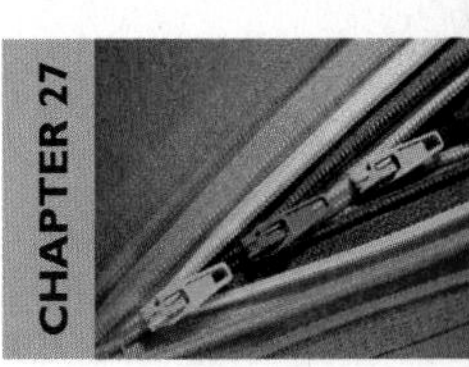

REFLECT ON IT

Think about what you have learned in this chapter. If you do not know an answer, review that topic.

1. What is the definition of a noun? ______________________________

____

2. Give examples of five non-count nouns.

__________ __________ __________ __________ __________

3. Make the following nouns plural.
   a. tooth: ____________________
   b. backseat driver: ____________________
   c. bride-to-be: ____________________
   d. kiss: ____________________
   e. homework: ____________________
   f. loaf: ____________________
4. Correct the errors in the following sentences.

EXAMPLE: Leonardo da Vinci had ~~much~~ *many* ideas.

   a. He invented much things.
   b. He developed a idea for a parachute.
   c. Da Vinci is one of the most famous artist in the world.
   d. Little of his other works are as famous as the *Mona Lisa*.

FINAL REVIEW

Correct fifteen errors in singular nouns, plural nouns, determiners, and prepositions.

EXAMPLE:

George de Mestral had ~~the~~ *a* splendid idea.

One summer day on 1948, George de Mestral decided to go for a hike. As he was walking through some tall weed, burrs stuck to his pants and to his dog's furs. This had happened much times before. However, on that day, de Mestral decided to examine some of the burrs with the microscope, and he discovered some interesting informations. He noticed that each burrs was made up of little hooks that helped it cling to material. He was very interested of this discovery. He thought on a way to use the hook system of the burrs to develop a products

for the home. After much attempts, George patented his invention in 1951 and called it Velcro. This days, Velcro is used on different type of products such as shoes, clothings, and toys. Now, many manufacturers depend of Velcro.

The Writer's Room

Write about one of the following topics. Then review your nouns, determiners, and prepositions.

1. In the past one hundred years, what events have changed the world? List some events.
2. Think about a recent invention. Contrast people's lives before and after that invention.

How Do I Get a Better Grade?

Visit MyWritingLab for audiovisual lectures and additional practice sets about nouns, determiners, and prepositions.

Pronouns

Section Theme **INVENTIONS AND DISCOVERIES**

Steve Allen/Stockbyte/Getty Images

LEARNING OBJECTIVES

***In this chapter, you will read about topics related to* ancient civilizations.**

The Writer's Journal

Write a short paragraph describing a historical figure whom you admire. You could write about a famous politician, actor, writer, artist, scientist, or explorer. Explain what that person did that was admirable.

Pronoun Case

Pronouns are words that replace nouns (people, places, or things), other pronouns, and phrases. Use pronouns to avoid repeating nouns.

> Machu Picchu is an ancient city located high in the Andes. ~~Machu Picchu~~ *It* was discovered in 1911.

Pronouns are formed according to the role they play in a sentence. A pronoun can be the subject or object of the sentence, or it can show possession. The following chart shows the three main pronoun cases: subjective, objective, and possessive.

Pronouns

			Possessives	
Singular	**Subjective**	**Objective**	**Possessive Adjective**	**Possessive Pronoun**
1st person	I	me	my	mine
2nd person	you	you	your	yours
3rd person	he, she, it, who, whoever	him, her, it, whom, whomever	his, her, its, whose	his, hers
Plural				
1st person	we	us	our	ours
2nd person	you	you	your	yours
3rd person	they	them	their	theirs

Subjective Case

A **subject** performs an action in a sentence. When a pronoun is the subject of the sentence, use the subjective form of the pronoun.

> **She** liked to read mystery novels set in ancient times.
>
> **We** watched a horror movie about mummies.

Objective Case

An **object** receives an action in a sentence. When a pronoun is the object in the sentence, use the objective form of the pronoun.

> The audience gave **him** an ovation for the lecture on ancient China.
>
> My sister saw **us** at the lecture.

Possessive Case

A possessive pronoun shows ownership.

- **Possessive adjectives** are always placed before the noun that they modify. In the next sentences, *her* and *their* are possessive adjectives.

> She finished **her** book about the pyramids, but they did not finish **their** books.

- **Possessive pronouns** replace the possessive adjective and noun. In the next sentence, *her* is a possessive adjective, and *theirs* is a possessive pronoun.

> She finished **her** book about the pyramids, but they did not finish **theirs**.

Problems with Possessive Pronouns

When using the possessive pronouns *hers* and *theirs*, be careful that you do not add an apostrophe before the *s*.

> The archaeology book is ~~her's~~ hers. The papyrus map is ~~their's~~ theirs.

Some possessive adjectives sound like certain contractions. When using the possessive adjectives *their*, *your*, and *its*, be careful that you do not confuse them with *they're*, *you're*, and *it's*.

Their is the possessive adjective.	Their flight to Cancun was late.
They're is the contraction of *they are*.	They're not going to be on time for the bus tour.
Your is the possessive adjective.	Your tour guide has a map of the Tulum Mayan ruins.
You're is the contraction of *you are*.	You're going to enjoy visiting this ancient site.
Its is the possessive adjective.	The Temple of the Frescoes has a beautiful mural on its wall.
It's is the contraction of *it is*.	It's an important piece of Mayan history.

GRAMMAR LINK

For more information about apostrophes, see Chapter 34.

Watch the Video
Apostrophes
MyWritingLab

Choosing *His* or *Her*

To choose the correct possessive adjective, think about the possessor (not the object that is possessed).

- If something belongs to a female, use *her* + noun.

  Cecilia packed her luggage.

- If something belongs to a male, use *his* + noun.

  Tony booked his flight.

PRACTICE 1

Underline the correct possessive adjective or possessive pronoun in each set of parentheses.

EXAMPLE:

> Historians often cite Greece and (its / it's) ancient monuments as important to the study of Western civilization.

1. Societies in the ancient world revered (their / there) monuments. The Greeks especially loved (their / theirs). Greek society encouraged (its / it's) philosophers to create lists of wonderful architecture of that time because Greek leaders wanted to encourage (they're / there / their) citizens to be proud of the Greek heritage. Different philosophers put a variety of items on (their / theirs) lists. Unfortunately, many of the lists have not survived up to (our / ours) time.

2. The oldest surviving list of ancient wonders was written by Antipater of Sidon around 140 BCE. Antipater, of course, was a Greek male, and (her / its / his) list mainly consisted of Greek structures. He listed such things as the pyramids at Giza, the Hanging Gardens of Babylon, the statue of Zeus at Olympia, and the Lighthouse of Alexandria, among others. Most of those structures are no longer standing. For example, the Lighthouse was destroyed by an earthquake and (it's / its) aftershocks.

3. My professor, Aspasia Jones, gave a slide show of (her / hers) trip to the pyramids. Many people, of course, have taken photographs of the pyramids, but (her / hers) were particularly interesting. She had permission to go into a chamber closed to the public, and we were able to see (it's / its) contents. Her assistant, Milo, used (his / its) new camera to take the photos.

4. Would you like to go to Aspasia's next slide show? Could we use (your / you're / yours) car? (My / Mine) is getting repaired. Call me on (my / mine) cellphone.

Pronouns in Comparisons with *than* or *as*

Avoid making errors in pronoun case when the pronoun follows *than* or *as*. If the pronoun is a subject, use the subjective case, and if the pronoun is an object, use the objective case.

If you use the incorrect case, your sentence may have a meaning that you do not intend it to have. For example, people often follow *than* or *as* with an objective

pronoun when they mean to follow it with a subjective pronoun. Look at the differences in the meanings of the next sentences.

> objective case
> I like ancient history as much as **him.**
> (I like ancient history as much as I like him.)

> subjective case
> I like ancient history as much as **he.**
> (I like ancient history as much as he likes ancient history.)

Complete the Thought

If you are unsure which pronoun case to use, test by completing the thought. Look at the following examples.

> He likes to visit museums more than **I** (like to visit museums).
>
> He likes to visit museums more than (he likes to visit) **me.**

Pronouns in Prepositional Phrases

In a prepositional phrase, the words that follow the preposition are the objects of the preposition. Therefore, always use the objective case of the pronoun after a preposition.

> To **her,** learning about history is not important.
>
> Between **you** and **me,** our history class is very interesting.

Pronouns with *and* or *or*

Use the correct case when nouns and pronouns are joined by *and* or *or.* If the pronouns are the subject, use the subjective case. If the pronouns are the object, use the objective case.

Subjective: *He and I* ~~Him and me~~ had to do a presentation on the Incas.

Objective: The instructor asked *him and me* ~~he and I~~ to present first.

Finding the Correct Case

An easy way to determine whether your case is correct is to say the sentence with just one pronoun.

> The librarian asked her and (I, me) to speak quietly.
>
> **Choices:** The librarian asked I … *or* The librarian asked me… .
>
> **Correct:** The librarian asked her and me to speak quietly.

CHAPTER 28

PRACTICE 2

Correct any errors with pronoun case. Write *C* in the space if the sentence is correct.

EXAMPLE:

Last summer, my friend and ~~me~~ I visited Mexico.

1. My friend, Maria, is older than me. ______
2. Maria gave me a book on the Maya civilization because she is as interested in the subject as me. ______
3. Maria and me took a bus to Chichén Itzá, an ancient site that was built around the middle of the sixth century. ______
4. At the site, we asked a young man to take a picture of we girls. ______
5. Maria's camera was newer than mine, so we used her's. ______
6. The young man, whose name was Karl, climbed with Maria and me to the top of the pyramid. ______
7. Him and his friend Pedro told us that they were afraid of heights. ______
8. Between you and I, I was also getting a bit dizzy, so we decided to climb down. ______
9. Our tour guide told Pedro and me that the Maya abandoned Chichén Itzá in the tenth century. ______
10. Karl said goodbye to us because him and Pedro had to catch the bus for Belize. ______

KKulikov/Shutterstock

Relative Pronouns (*who, whom, which, that, whose*)

Watch the Video
Nouns
MyWritingLab

Relative pronouns can join two short sentences. Here is a list of relative pronouns.

who	whom	which	that	whose
whoever	whomever			

- *Who* (or *whoever*) and *whom* (or *whomever*) always refer to people. *Who* is the subject of the clause, and *whom* is the object of the clause.

  Subject: The archaeologist **who** specializes in Mayan culture is speaking today.

  Object: The archaeologist **whom** you met is my mother.

GRAMMAR LINK

Clauses with *which* are set off with commas. For more information, see Chapter 33, "Commas."

- *Which* always refers to things.

  The ancient city of Machu Picchu, **which** I have never seen, is located in the Andes.

Watch the Video
Commas
MyWritingLab

Watch the Video
Pronouns
MyWritingLab

- *That* refers to things.

  Hiram Bingham wrote a book **that** is about Machu Picchu.

- *Whose* always shows that something belongs to or is connected with someone or something. It usually replaces possessive pronouns such as *his*, *her*, and *their*. Do not confuse *whose* with *who's*, which means "who is."

  The archaeologist traced the route. His maps were on the table.

  The archaeologist, **whose** maps were on the table, traced the route.

Choosing *Who* or *Whom*

If you are unsure whether to use *who* or *whom*, test yourself in the following way. Replace *who* or *whom* with another pronoun. If the replacement is a subjective pronoun such as *he* or *she*, use *who*. If the replacement is an objective pronoun such as *her* or *him*, use **whom**.

> I know a man **who** works in a museum.
> (He works in a museum.)
>
> The man to **whom** you gave your portfolio is the director of the museum.
> (You gave your portfolio to him.)

PRACTICE 3

Write the correct relative pronoun in each blank.

EXAMPLE:

> The Khmer civilization, ___*which*___ built the temples of Angor, lost its power by the fifteenth century.

1. The Hindu temples of Angkor, ________ are among the most magnificent examples of architecture, were built between the ninth and twelfth centuries. The ancient Khmer kings, ________ kingdom was between present-day Cambodia and the Bay of Bengal, commissioned about a hundred temples at the site. King Suryavaram II, ________ was a devout Hindu, started to build the temples to honour the Hindu god Vishnu. The temple ________ portrays Hindu cosmology is at Angkor Wat.

2. During the powerful reign of the Angkor kings, many people ________ were Vishnu devotees made pilgrimages to the temples. The Angkor kings, to ________ religion was important, preserved these temples for many centuries. The temples were abandoned around 1432 due to political instability.

3. The temples, ________ were very beautiful, were almost forgotten for the next few centuries. Although Buddhist monks for ________ the temples represented an important religious site did visit, it was the French explorer Henri Mouhot ________ popularized the spot for Europeans. Mouhot visited the area ________ the jungle had hidden. On his journey, Mouhot encountered tigers, spiders, and leeches, ________ made his journey difficult.

4. Today, many tourists ________ are interested in ancient monuments visit the site. However, looters, ________ steal priceless objects to sell to collectors and tourists, are destroying the temples, ________ are a world heritage site.

Reflexive Pronouns (*-self/-selves*)

Use **reflexive pronouns** when you want to emphasize that the subject does an action to himself or herself.

I asked **myself** many questions.

History often repeats **itself.**

Do not use reflexive pronouns for activities that people do to themselves, such as washing or shaving. However, you can use reflexive pronouns to draw attention to a surprising or an unusual action.

The little boy fed **himself.**
(The boy probably could not feed himself at a previous time.)

The next chart shows subjective pronouns and the reflexive pronouns that relate to them.

Pronouns That End with *-self* or *-selves*

Singular	Antecedent	Reflexive Pronoun
1st person	I	myself
2nd person	you	yourself
3rd person	he, she, it	himself, herself, itself
Plural		
1st person	we	ourselves
2nd person	you	yourselves
3rd person	they	themselves

Common Errors with Reflexive Pronouns

Hisself and *theirselves* do not exist in English. These are incorrect ways to say *himself* and *themselves.*

> *themselves*
> The tourists went by ~~theirselves~~ to the museum.
>
> *himself.*
> Croesus visited the oracle by ~~hisself.~~

PRACTICE 4

Fill in the blanks with the correct reflexive pronouns.

EXAMPLE:

He wanted to explore the forest by *himself.*

1. Our guide was upset because she had twisted her ankle while walking by ______________ through the jungle. She had forgotten how easily she could hurt ______________ by tripping on a tree root.

2. Our guide looked at us and said, "Go to the temple by ______________. You are all capable of finding it."

3. Because our guide could not go with us, we had to climb the steps of the temple by ______________. One member of the group, Matt, decided we were too slow for him, so he decided to climb up by ______________.

4. I thought to ______________ that he would probably get lost. Sure enough, he did get lost. When we found him, he told us that he had lost his footing and cut ______________ on some of the crumbling pieces of rock. We offered him some first aid supplies so he could patch ______________ up.

5. After we found Matt, we got ______________ back on track. We reached the top of the temple and felt very pleased with ______________.

Watch the Video
Pronoun Reference and Point of View
MyWritingLab

Pronoun-Antecedent Agreement

A pronoun must agree with its **antecedent,** which is the word to which the pronoun refers. Antecedents are nouns, pronouns, and phrases that the pronouns have replaced, and they always come before the pronoun. Pronouns must agree in person and number with their antecedents.

> The archaeologist was frustrated because **she** could not raise enough money for **her** expedition.
>
> *(The archaeologist* is the antecedent of *she* and *her.)*
>
> My instructor went on a vacation to Peru. **He** took **his** family with **him.**
>
> *(My instructor* is the antecedent of *he, his,* and *him.)*
>
> China has many ancient salt mines. **They** date back to the fourth century BCE.
>
> (*Salt mines* is the antecedent of *they.)*

GRAMMAR LINK

For a list of collective nouns, see 377 in Chapter 25.

Using Collective Nouns

Collective nouns refer to a group of people or things. The group acts as a unit; therefore, it is singular.

> The association had **its** meeting on Monday.
>
> The government tried to implement **its** policies.

PRACTICE 5

Fill in the blank spaces with the appropriate pronouns or possessive adjectives.

EXAMPLE:

> Many people are fascinated with the lost city of Troy, and ___*they*___ are curious about the city's history.

1. The archaeologist Heinrich Schliemann believed that finding the lost city of Troy would bring __________ fame and fortune. He was convinced that __________ idea about the location of Troy was correct. Archaeologists at that time thought that the city of Troy was a myth and that they would waste __________ time hunting for __________.

2. Schliemann was a millionaire who spent __________ time and money pursuing __________ archaeological interests. In 1868, Schliemann met Frank Calvert, a businessman who owned land around Hisarlik, Turkey.

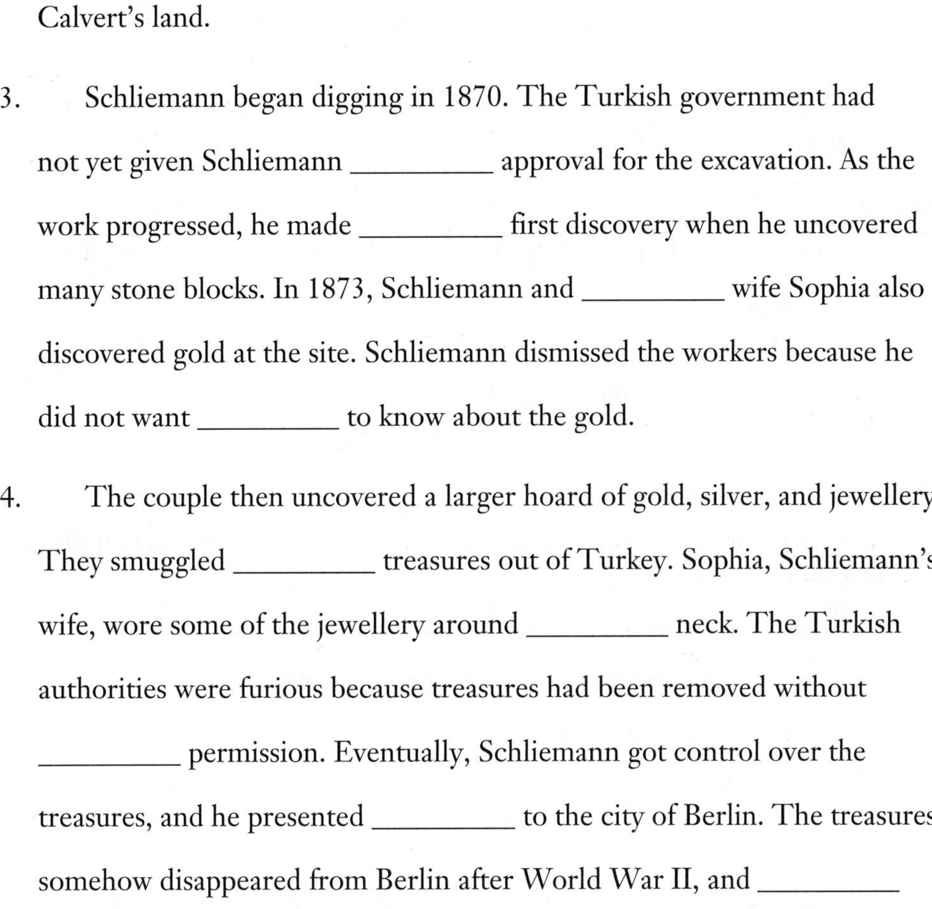

Both men were convinced that __________ could find the lost city of Troy. Calvert provided the funding, and Schliemann began to excavate on Calvert's land.

3. Schliemann began digging in 1870. The Turkish government had not yet given Schliemann __________ approval for the excavation. As the work progressed, he made __________ first discovery when he uncovered many stone blocks. In 1873, Schliemann and __________ wife Sophia also discovered gold at the site. Schliemann dismissed the workers because he did not want __________ to know about the gold.

4. The couple then uncovered a larger hoard of gold, silver, and jewellery. They smuggled __________ treasures out of Turkey. Sophia, Schliemann's wife, wore some of the jewellery around __________ neck. The Turkish authorities were furious because treasures had been removed without __________ permission. Eventually, Schliemann got control over the treasures, and he presented __________ to the city of Berlin. The treasures somehow disappeared from Berlin after World War II, and __________ were recently rediscovered in Moscow.

Indefinite Pronouns

Use **indefinite pronouns** when you refer to people or things whose identity is not known or is unimportant. The following chart shows some common singular and plural indefinite pronouns.

Indefinite Pronouns

Singular	another	each	no one	other
	anybody	everybody	nobody	somebody
	anyone	everyone	nothing	someone
	anything	everything	one	something
Plural	both, few, many, others, several			
Either singular or plural	all, any, half (and other fractions), more, most, none, some			

Singular

When you use a singular indefinite antecedent, also use a singular pronoun to refer to it.

> Everybody feels amazed when **he or she** sees China's terra-cotta army for the first time.
>
> Nobody should forget to visit China's terra-cotta army in **his or her** lifetime.

Plural

When you use a plural indefinite antecedent, also use a plural pronoun to refer to it.

> The two objects are ancient, and both have **their** own intrinsic value.
>
> The world has many illegal excavation sites; there are several operating in China, but **they** cannot be controlled.

Either Singular or Plural

Some indefinite pronouns can be either singular or plural, depending on the noun to which they refer.

> Many archaeologists came to the site. All were experts in **their** field.
>
> (*All* refers to archaeologists; therefore, the pronoun is plural.)
>
> We excavated all of the site and **its** artifacts.
>
> (*All* refers to the site; therefore, the pronoun is singular.)

Using *of the* Expressions

In sentences containing the expression *one of the* … or *each of the* … , the subject is the indefinite pronoun *one* or *each*. Therefore, any pronoun referring to that phrase must be singular.

> One of the statues is missing **its** weapon.
>
> Each of the men has **his** own map.

PRACTICE 6

Identify and correct nine errors in pronoun-antecedent agreement. You may change either the antecedent or the pronoun. If you change any antecedents, make sure that your subjects and verbs agree.

EXAMPLE:

> Some of the soldiers had ~~his~~ *their* own swords.

1. In 1974, in Xi'an, China, some local men were digging a well when they made an astounding discovery. One of the men uncovered a clay

soldier with their bare hands. Then others, using their shovels, discovered more clay soldiers at the site. Someone rode their bicycle to the local communist party headquarters. The worker described what he and the others had found.

2. The local communist party sent some archaeologists to the site. When they arrived, everyone expressed shock at the sight before their eyes. They realized that the find was significant. The central government sent a message to the local peasants. Each had to leave their land and move to another location. Nobody was allowed to remain in their home.

3. Over the next years, specialists excavated the site. They uncovered more than eight thousand terra-cotta soldiers. The soldiers are life-size, and many have his own unique physical features, representing every ethnic group in China. Different male artists sculpted groups of the soldiers. Each engraved their name on the statues.

4. The clay soldiers have been guarding an ancient emperor for more than two thousand years. Everybody in the all-male army, including generals, officers, cavalry, and archers, had their own life-sized weapon. Today, the site is a major tourist attraction in China. Anybody who goes to China on their holiday should try to visit the terra-cotta army.

Avoid Sexist Language

Terms like *anybody*, *somebody*, *nobody*, and *each* are singular antecedents, so the pronouns that follow those words must be singular. At one time, it was acceptable to use *he* as a general term meaning "all people"; however, today it is more acceptable to use *he or she*.

Sexist:	Everyone had to leave his home.
Solution:	Everyone had to leave his or her home.
Better solution:	The citizens had to leave their homes.

Exception: If you know for certain that the subject is male or female, then use only *he* or only *she*.

PRACTICE 7

Circle the correct pronouns in the following paragraphs.

EXAMPLE:

Some people say that history is not important because (its, it's) information is not relevant to people's everyday lives.

1. History courses offer information about the past, but many people wonder whether they should spend (his or her, their) time studying the past. In fact, somebody might feel it is more important to think about (his or her, their) future. In other words, some people may not consider history and (it's, its) lessons to be as important as other subjects that are more practical.

2. In the past, historians and (their, theirs) supporters memorized names and dates. Everybody believed that (his or her, their) knowledge of history indicated a high level of education. Between you and (I, me), I do not think that this reason for studying history is valid. I think that history should be studied for (its, it's) own merits. For example, history tells us about societies and (their, theirs) past behaviours. History also informs us about a critical moment in the past and (its, it's) influence on today's lifestyles. Furthermore, history helps us understand more about (yourselves, ourselves).

3. I like studying history; however, my brother has always liked it far more than (I, me). He became really interested when we were children. (He, Him) and (I, me) used to read stories about World War I. After school, while the other neighbourhood kids were playing outside, my brother preferred to spend hours watching war films (who, that) had great battle scenes.

4. Now my brother is a historian. He is a man (who, whom) believes that everybody should take (his or her, their) history lessons seriously. In fact, my brother met (his, her) future wife in history class. He was sitting by (hisself, himself, herself) when she sat near him. The rest, of course, is history.

Vague Pronouns

Avoid using pronouns that could refer to more than one antecedent.

Vague: Frank asked his friend where his map of ancient Greece was.
(Whose map is it: Frank's or his friend's?)

Clearer: **Frank** wondered where **his** map of ancient Greece was, so he asked his friend about it.

Avoid using confusing pronouns such as *it* and *they* that have no clear antecedent.

Vague: They say that people should get vaccines before travelling to certain countries.
(Who are *they*?)

Clearer: **Health authorities** say that people should get vaccines before travelling to certain countries.

Vague: It stated in the magazine that the tower of Copán in Honduras has more hieroglyphic inscriptions than any other Maya ruin.
(Who or what is *it*?)

Clearer: **The magazine article** stated that the tower of Copán in Honduras has more hieroglyphic inscriptions than any other Maya ruin.

This, *that*, and *which* should refer to a specific antecedent.

Vague: The teacher told us that we should study hard for our history exams because they were going to be difficult. This caused all of us to panic.
(What is *this*?)

Clearer: The teacher told us that we should study hard for our history exams because they were going to be difficult. **This information** caused all of us to panic.

Avoid Repeating the Subject

When you clearly mention a subject, do not repeat the subject in pronoun form.

Egypt's pyramids~~, they~~ are more than four thousand years old.

The book ~~it~~ is really interesting.

PRACTICE 8

Each sentence has either a vague pronoun or a repeated subject. Correct the errors. You may need to rewrite some sentences.

EXAMPLE:

The radio reporter announced
~~They said on the radio~~ that archaeologists have discovered a new burial ground along the Yangzte River.

1. Professor Schmitt told Mark that a book about the Great Wall of China is on his desk.
2. It states that the Great Wall of China is more than two thousand years old.
3. They built the wall to protect the Chinese empire from northern invasions.
4. This also helped unify China.
5. The history book it contains information on the emperor Oin Shi Huang.
6. They say that the emperor ordered construction of the Great Wall.
7. They persecuted anyone who disagreed with the emperor.
8. The book it has many other interesting facts about the Great Wall of China.
9. For example, the wall it is over 2400 kilometres in length.
10. They say the only human-made object that can be seen from space is the Great Wall.

Pronoun Shifts

If your writing contains unnecessary shifts in person or number, you may confuse your readers. Carefully edit your writing to ensure that your pronouns are consistent in number and person.

Making Pronouns Consistent in Number

Pronouns and antecedents must agree in **number**. If the antecedent is singular, then the pronoun must be singular. If the antecedent is plural, then the pronoun must be plural.

> singular — *his or her*
>
> The **director** of the museum encouraged ~~their~~ *his or her* employees to be on time.

> plural — *they*
>
> When **tourists** visit an excavation site, ~~he~~ *they* should be careful not to touch the artifacts.

Making Pronouns Consistent in Person

Person is the writer's perspective. In some writing assignments, you may use first person (*I*, *we*). For other assignments, especially most college and workplace writing, you may use second person (*you*) or third person (*he*, *she*, *it*, *they*).

When you shift your point of view for no reason, your writing may become unclear, and you may confuse your readers. If you begin writing from one point of view, do not shift unnecessarily to another point of view.

> If ~~one~~ *we* considered the expenses involved in visiting another country, **we** would probably never travel.

> **We** visited the pyramids at Teotihuacán, but ~~you~~ *we* could not climb one of them because archaeologists were working on it.

Avoiding Pronoun Shifts in Paragraphs

Sometimes it is easier to use pronouns consistently in individual sentences than it is in larger paragraphs or essays. When you write paragraphs and essays, always check that your pronouns agree with your antecedents in person and in number. In the next example, the pronouns are consistent in the first two sentences; however, they shift in person in the third sentence.

> **We** went to Mexico City last year. **We** travelled around on the subway to visit various archaeological sites. Sometimes the subway was so crowded that ~~you~~ *we* could barely move.

PRACTICE 9

Correct eight pronoun shift errors.

EXAMPLE:

> We visited the pyramids at Giza, Egypt. The lines were so long that ~~you~~ *we* had to wait for hours.

1. An Egyptian pharaoh built the Great Pyramid as a tomb. All the powerful pharaohs believed that material goods must be buried in their tombs to help you on their journey in the afterlife.

2. Napoleon invaded Egypt in 1798. Napoleon and his soldiers were amazed when they saw the pyramids. After the army invaded Egypt, they returned to France with many artifacts. Napoleon thought that you had the right to take anything from a country that you had invaded.

3. One of Napoleon's soldiers discovered the Rosetta Stone but did not realize the importance of their discovery. In 1801, British soldiers invaded

Egypt and found the Rosetta Stone. They took the stone and brought them back to England.

4. When tourists go to the British Museum in London, one may see many antiquities from Egypt. Every year, people go to see the Rosetta Stone because you know it is impressive.

REFLECT ON IT

Think about what you have learned in this chapter. If you do not know an answer, review that topic.

1. What is a pronoun? ______________________________

____
2. Write a sentence that includes an objective pronoun. ______________________________

____
3. When do you use possessive pronouns (*my*, *mine*, *his*, *hers*, etc.)? ______________________________

____
4. Circle the best answer: In a sentence, *whom* replaces
   a. The subject. b. The object
5. What is an antecedent? ______________________________

____
6. Circle the best answer: Pronouns must agree with their antecedents
   a. Only in number. b. Only in person.
   c. Both in number and in person. d. Neither in number nor in person.

FINAL REVIEW

Correct fifteen errors with pronouns in the next paragraphs.

EXAMPLE:

A prominent archaeologist
~~It~~ says that the dispute between many countries is about cultural property rights.

1. People learn important things about history by visiting museums filled with historical artifacts. For example, Britain and France they have obtained antiquities from countries around the world. The British government believes in it's right to keep the treasures who are exhibited

in museums. However, countries such as Greece and Egypt want their treasures back because they view antiquities as a part of its cultural heritage. Returning antiquities to its native countries is a complicated issue.

2. The removal of artifacts such as mummies has created an ethical problem for the Egyptian government and their archaeologists. An interesting science article it says that a lot of information can be acquired from the scientific study of burial sites. Although some people believe it is always unethical to dig up the dead, every archaeologist who studies Egyptian mummies increases their knowledge of ancient Egypt. For example, centuries ago, the pharaohs believed that they could get to heaven faster if you were buried with food and treasures for the voyage. Each pharoah decided for hisself what he would take on his journey to the afterlife. When a pharaoh died, priests mummified the body and buried them in the pyramids. Therefore, archaeologists whom have excavated burial sites not only find mummies but also find valuable artworks and other artifacts.

3. They say that the dispute between countries such as Egypt and Britain will not be resolved. They say that international policy should regulate ownership of national treasures. Everybody has their own opinion about the issue.

Choose one of the following topics, and write a paragraph or an essay. Remember to follow the writing process.

1. In the past one hundred years, what events have changed the world? List some events.
2. Tell a story about an ideal vacation. Where would you go and what would you do? Use descriptive language in your writing.
3. Think about a recent invention. Contrast people's lives before and after that invention.
4. How important is history as a school subject? Should history be a compulsory subject?

Collaborative Activity

Take turns interviewing a partner. Discover at least five interesting things about each other. Then write a paragraph about your partner.

When you have finished, exchange paragraphs with your partner. Proofread your partner's paragraph. Look carefully at nouns, pronouns, and determiners. Discuss any errors that you find.

READING LINK

Great Discoveries

"The Beeps" by Josh Freed (page 570)
"This Boat Is My Boat" by Drew Hayden Taylor (573)
"Gone with the Windows" by Dorothy Nixon (page 576)
"Advertising Appeals" by Michael R. Solomon (page 578)

How Do I Get a Better Grade?

Visit MyWritingLab for audiovisual lectures and additional practice sets about pronouns.

Adjectives and Adverbs

Section Theme **HEALTH CARE**

LEARNING OBJECTIVES

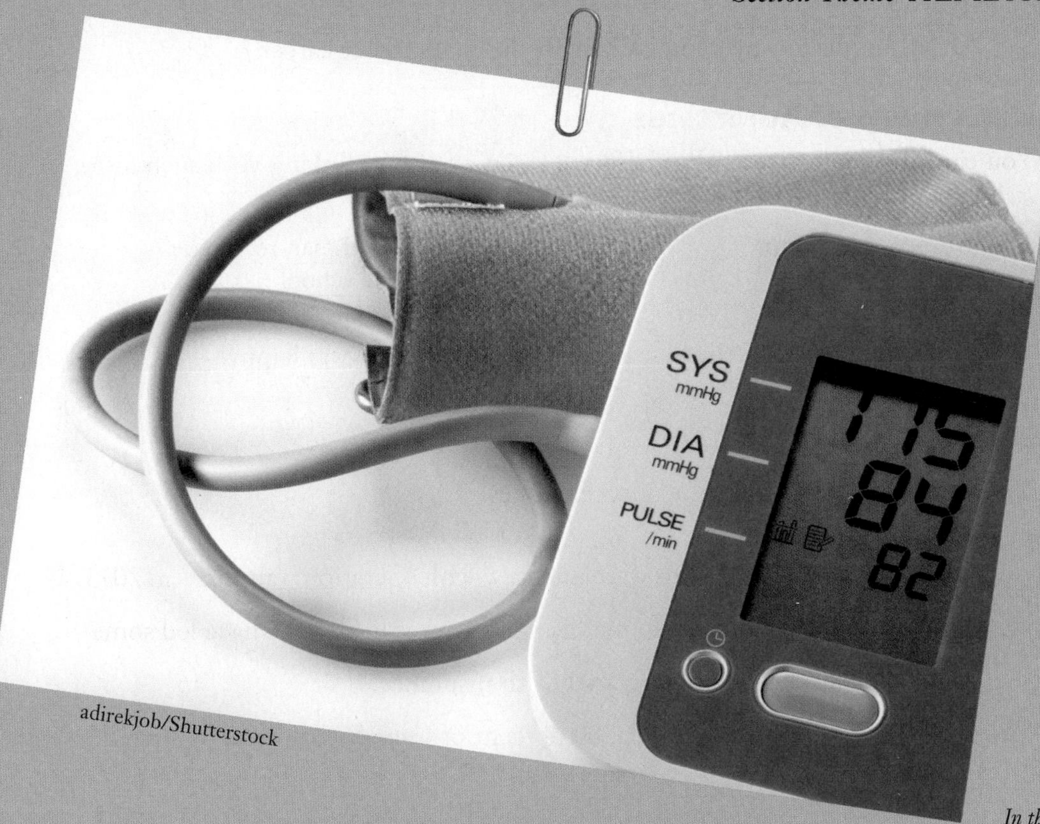

adirekjob/Shutterstock

In this chapter, you will read about topics related to **health care.**

The Writer's Journal

Write a short paragraph describing how people can best protect their health. List several examples in your paragraph.

Adjectives

Adjectives describe nouns (people, places, or things) and pronouns (words that replace nouns). They add information explaining how many, what kind, or which one. They also help you appeal to the senses by describing how things look, smell, feel, taste, and sound.

An **intelligent** woman, Jenny Trout, became the first female in Canada to be a licensed physician.

Jenny Trout established a **reputable medical** college.

Dr. Trout had to overcome **difficult** obstacles in her career.

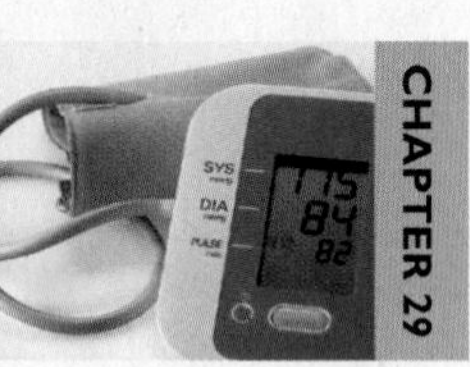

Placement of Adjectives

You can place adjectives either before a noun or after a linking verb such as *be*, *look*, *appear*, *smell*, or *become*.

Watch the Video
Adjectives
MyWritingLab

Before the noun:	The **young unemployed** man received a scholarship for **medical** school.
After the linking verb:	He was (LV) **shocked**, but he was (LV) **happy**.

PRACTICE 1

Underline the adjectives in the next sentences.

EXAMPLE:

About 10 million Canadians were unhappy with operation wait times in 2013.

1. Long waiting lists for certain medical procedures in Canada have led some people to consider buying private health insurance.
2. According to Statistics Canada, 80 percent of Canadians are happy with the public health care system.
3. Government-funded health care has been available in Canada since 1962, but there are still debates over the role of the private sector in the health care industry.
4. Some people find themselves with enormous bills for prescription drugs that they desperately need.
5. Where the average American citizen pays one dollar for a prescription drug, a British citizen pays 64 cents and a Canadian citizen pays only 57 cents.
6. The average annual profit of the top ten drug companies is more than $3 billion.
7. Drug companies argue that they do groundbreaking research on new drugs.
8. Politicians will continue to have many impassioned debates about the future of accessible, fair health care in Canada.

Problems with Adjectives

You can recognize many adjectives by their endings. Be particularly careful when you use the following adjective forms.

Adjectives Ending in *-ful* or *-less*

Some adjectives end in *-ful* or *-less*. Remember that *-ful* ends in one *l* and *-less* ends in double *s*.

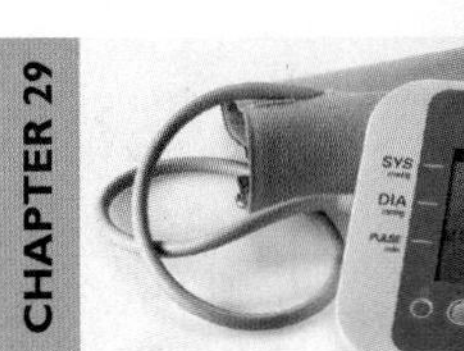

Alexander Fleming, a **skillful** scientist, conducted many **useful** experiments.

His work appeared in **countless** publications.

Adjectives Ending in *-ed* or *-ing*

Some adjectives look like verbs because they end in *-ing* or *-ed*.

- When the adjective ends in *-ed*, it describes the person's or animal's expression or feeling.

  The **overworked** and **tired** scientist presented her findings to the public.

- When the adjective ends in *-ing*, it describes the quality of the person or thing.

  Her **compelling** and **promising** discovery pleased the public.

Keep Adjectives in the Singular Form

Always make an adjective singular, even if the noun following the adjective is plural. In the next example, "year" acts as an adjective.

Paul was a nine-~~years~~ *year*-old boy when he broke his arm while playing with ~~others~~ *other* children.

PRACTICE 2

Correct eight adjective errors. The adjectives may have the wrong form, or they may be misspelled.

EXAMPLE:

Many ~~surprised~~ *surprising* medical findings happen by accident.

1. One of the world's amazed scientifics discoveries happened by pure chance. Born in 1881, Alexander Fleming was a tireles medical doctor. He worked in his small London clinic where he treated famous people for venereal disease. He also conducted many biologicals experiments.

2. One day in 1928, he put some *Staphylococcus* bacteria in a culture dish. Two weeks later, Fleming, who was a carefull researcher, discovered that a clear ring encircled the yellow-green mould on the dish. A mould spore had flown into the dish from a laboratory on the floor below. At that point, Fleming made an insightfull observation. He had an astounded revelation. He realized that the mould somehow stopped the growth of bacteria in the culture dish.

3. Fleming named the new product penicillin. During World War II, the drug saved millions of lives, and it continues to be used today to treat differents infections.

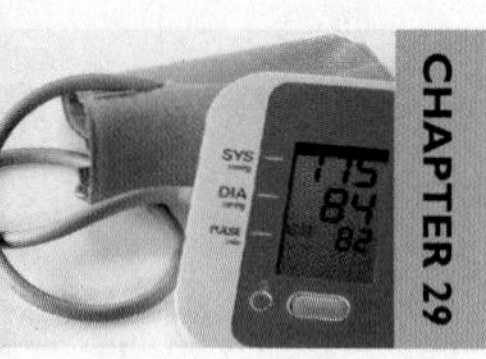

Adverbs

Adverbs add information to adjectives, verbs, or other adverbs. They give more specific information about how, when, where, and to what extent an action or event occurred.

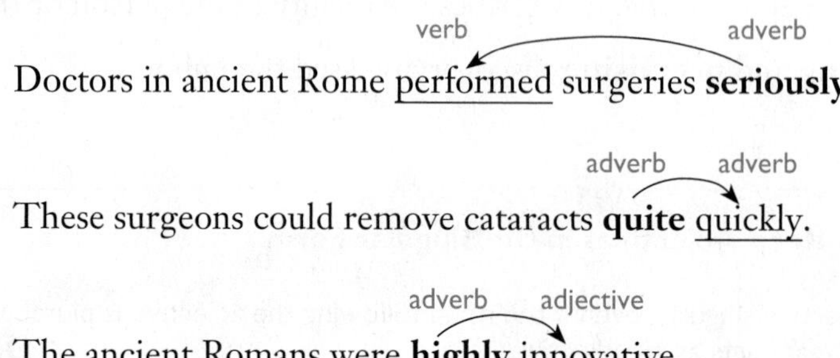

verb → adverb: Doctors in ancient Rome performed surgeries **seriously.**

adverb → adverb: These surgeons could remove cataracts **quite** quickly.

adverb → adjective: The ancient Romans were **highly** innovative.

Forms of Adverbs

Watch the Video
Adverbs
MyWritingLab

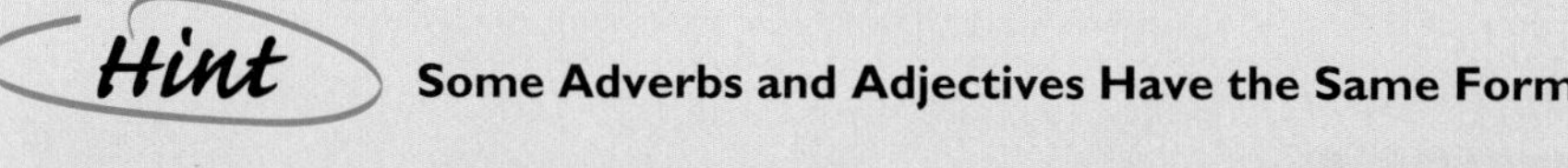

Hint **Some Adverbs and Adjectives Have the Same Form**

Some adverbs look exactly like adjectives. The only way to distinguish them from adjectives is to see what they are modifying or describing. The following words can be either adjectives or adverbs.

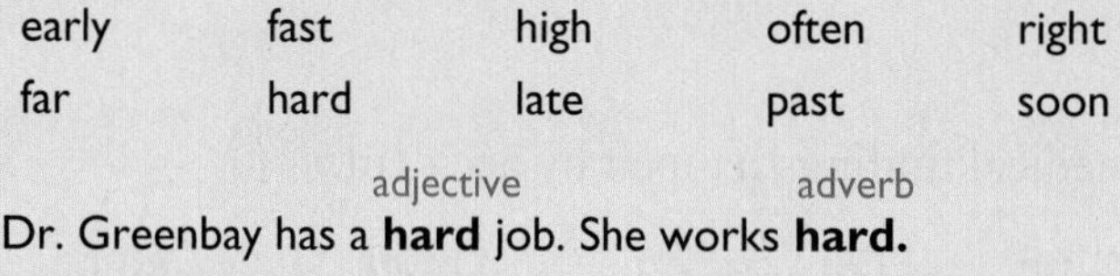

early	fast	high	often	right
far	hard	late	past	soon

Dr. Greenbay has a **hard** job (adjective). She works **hard.** (adverb)

Adverbs often end in *-ly*. In fact, you can change many adjectives into adverbs by adding *-ly* endings.

- If you add *-ly* to a word that ends in *l*, then your new word will have a double *l*.

  Many ancient Romans viewed surgeons **scornfully.** (scornful + ly)

- If you add *-ly* to a word that ends in *e*, keep the *e*. Exceptions to this rule are *truly* and *duly*.

  Doctors were **extremely** (extreme + ly) careful when they operated on patients.

PRACTICE 3

Circle the correct adjectives or adverbs in each sentence.

EXAMPLE:

Many groups (loud, (loudly)) debate the subject of euthanasia.

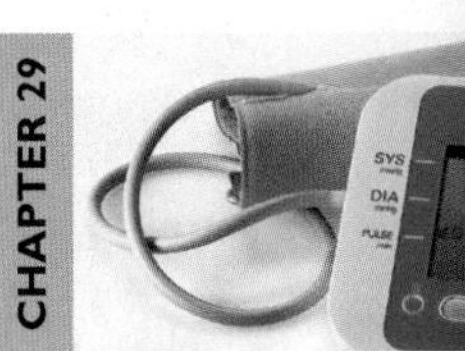

1. The average life span for human beings has increased (great, greatly) due to advances in medical technology. Yet (certain, certainly) debilitating diseases decrease the quality of life. Therefore, society has to deal (frequent, frequently) with the issue of a patient's right to choose to die. A debate has (rapid, rapidly) developed among medical professionals on the ethics of prolonging the life of people with debilitating diseases. Many people have (strong, strongly) opinions on the subject of euthanasia.

2. The term *euthanasia* refers to a third party (intentional, intentionally) causing the death of a patient at the patient's request. For example, a doctor removing a life support machine is committing euthanasia. *Assisted suicide* refers to a third party (clear, clearly) helping a patient commit the act of dying. For example, a family member who (knowing, knowingly) supplies a patient with drugs is assisting suicide if the patient takes the (powerful, powerfully) drugs to die. To date, Canada does not allow people to participate in assisted suicide (legal, legally).

Placement of Frequency Adverbs

Frequency adverbs are words that indicate how often someone performs an action or when an event occurs. Common frequency adverbs are *always*, *ever*, *never*, *often*, *sometimes*, and *usually*. They can appear at the beginning of sentences, or they can appear in the following locations.

- Place frequency adverbs before regular present tense and past tense verbs.

  Medical doctors **always** recite the Hippocratic oath.

- Place frequency adverbs after all forms of the verb *be* (*am*, *is*, *are*, *was*, *were*).

  My patients are **usually** punctual for appointments.

- Place frequency adverbs after helping verbs.

  I have **never** broken any bone in my body.

PRACTICE 4

Correct six errors in the placement of frequency adverbs.

EXAMPLE:

Medical students ~~must take sometimes~~ *must sometimes take* a course on the history of medicine.

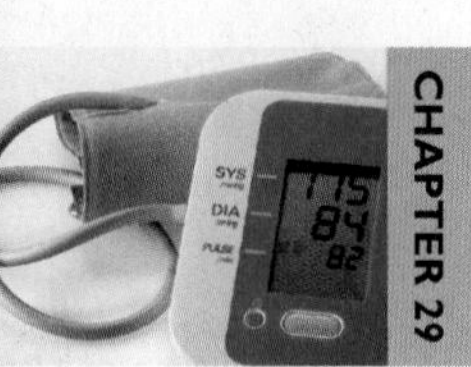

1. Hippocrates was born about 460 BC in Greece. Medical professionals claim generally that Hippocrates is the founder of modern medicine. In ancient Greece, physicians thought that a patient's illness usually was due to evil spirits. Hippocrates rejected often such explanations. He believed that there was a connection between good health and a good diet. He often was criticized for his beliefs.

2. Hippocrates travelled sometimes through Greece teaching medicine. On the island of Cos, Hippocrates founded a school of medicine and also developed his famous oath. To show their respect for Hippocrates, doctors take always the Hippocratic oath before they begin to practise medicine.

Problems with Adverbs

Use the Correct Form

Many times, people use an adjective instead of an adverb after a verb. Ensure that you always modify your verbs using an adverb.

> Ancient Greek medicine advanced ~~real quick~~ *really quickly* after the time of Homer.
>
> However, patients recovered very ~~slow~~ *slowly*.

PRACTICE 5

Correct nine errors in adjective and adverb forms.

EXAMPLE:

> Euthanasia is a ~~realy~~ *really* difficult issue.

1. People who oppose the "right-to-die" movement argue that many patients who wish for euthanasia may be extremelly depressed. Patients may also have incomplete information about other options, such as long-term care and real effective pain control. Opponents of legal euthanasia also suggest that many desperately people could be coerced into committing euthanasia quick.

2. People who want to legalize euthanasia feel profound that the quality of a person's life is the most important consideration in this debate. They say that if a patient has become severe disabled due to illness, his or her quality of life is drastically reduced. They believe that a patient should have the right to

die with dignity if he or she chooses. Proponents of euthanasia have real firm beliefs. They think that laws can prevent abuse or coercion of the patient.

3. Legislators act slow when it comes to making policy decisions about euthanasia. People on both sides of the issue express their opinions forcefuly. There is no consensus.

CHAPTER 29

Using *Good* and *Well*, *Bad* and *Badly*

Watch the Video
Adverbs
MyWritingLab

Good is an adjective, and *well* is an adverb.

Adjective: Louis Pasteur had a **good** reputation.

Adverb: He explained his theories **well.**

Exception: Use *well* to describe a person's health: I do not feel **well.**

Bad is an adjective, and *badly* is an adverb.

Adjective: My father has a **bad** cold.

Adverb: His throat hurts **badly.**

PRACTICE 6

Circle the correct adjectives or adverbs.

EXAMPLE:

Generally, patients who communicate (good, well) with their doctors receive (good, well) advice.

1. Mary Mallon was feeling (good, well) on the day that she was arrested.
2. Her (bad, badly) cooked food made many people ill.
3. The public had some (good, well) luck when authorities found Mary Mallon.
4. Mallon was accused of having (bad, badly) habits in the kitchen and of spreading typhoid fever through food.
5. She reacted (bad, badly) to these accusations.
6. She did not believe that the authorities had (good, well) intentions when they took her to the police station.
7. Although she cooked (good, well), the public health authorities wanted her to stop cooking for others.
8. Mary behaved (bad, badly) and continued to cook for people, so the police forced her to move to an isolated island near the Bronx.
9. She became known as Typhoid Mary and lived in (good, well) conditions in a house on North Brother Island for more than twenty years.

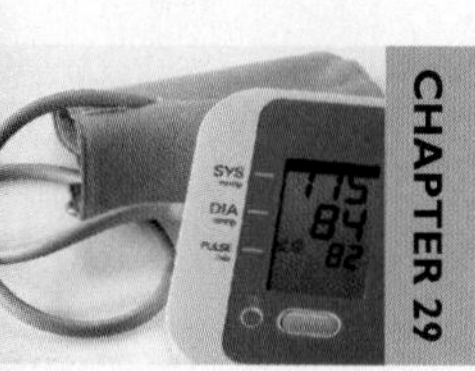

Comparative and Superlative Forms

Use the comparative form to show how two persons, things, or items are different.

Adjectives: Dr. Jonas Salk was a better researcher than his colleague.

Dr. Sabin is more famous for his research on the polio virus than Dr. Enders.

Adverbs: Dr. Salk published his results more quickly than Dr. Drake.

Dr. Salk debated the issue more passionately than his colleague.

Use the **superlative form** to compare three or more items.

Adjectives: Dr. Salk was the youngest scientist to receive funding for polio research at the University of Michigan.

Polio was one of the most destructive diseases of the twentieth century.

Adverbs: Dr. Parekh talked the most rapidly of all the doctors at the conference.

She spoke the most effectively of all of the participants.

How to Write Comparative and Superlative Forms

You can write comparative and superlative forms by remembering a few simple guidelines.

Using *-er* and *-est* endings

Add *-er* and *-est* endings to one-syllable adjectives and adverbs.

Adjective or Adverb	Comparative	Superlative
tall	tall**er** than	the tall**est**
hard	hard**er** than	the hard**est**
fast	fast**er** than	the fast**est**

Double the last letter when the adjective ends in one vowel + one consonant.

hot	ho**tter** than	the ho**ttest**

Using *more* and *the most*

Add *more* and *the most* to adjectives and adverbs of two or more syllables.

Adjective or Adverb	Comparative	Superlative
dangerous	**more** dangerous than	**the most** dangerous
effectively	**more** effectively than	**the most** effectively
nervous	**more** nervous than	**the most** nervous

When a two-syllable adjective ends in *y*, change the *y* to *i* and add *-er* or *-est*.

Adjective	Comparative	Superlative
happy	happ**ier** than	the happ**iest**

Using Irregular Comparative and Superlative Forms

Some adjectives and adverbs have unique comparative and superlative forms. Study this list to remember how to form some of the most common ones.

Adjective or Adverb	Comparative	Superlative
good, well	better than	the best
bad, badly	worse than	the worst
some, much, many	more than	the most
little (a small amount)	less than	the least
far	farther, further	the farthest, the furthest

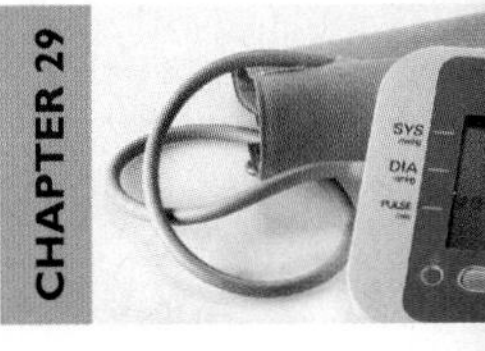

GRAMMAR LINK

Farther indicates a physical distance. *Further* means "additional." For more commonly confused words, see Chapter 32.

PRACTICE 7

Underline the appropriate comparative or superlative form of the words in parentheses.

EXAMPLE:
Some drug ads are (more / most) effective than others.

1. In the past, there was (less, least) drug research than there is today. Anybody could claim to have the (better, best) medicine on the market. For example, in the early twentieth century, one of the (more, most) successful products was Miss Lydia E. Pinkham's Vegetable Compound. The vial, which contained 20 percent alcohol content, promised to cure "female complaints." It had (more, most) alcohol than beer, and it was the (more, most) popular cure of its era.

2. In Canada, the Health Products and Food Branch of Health Canada regulates drug advertising. Companies are not allowed to say that their products are (better, best) than those of their competitors, and they cannot claim to have the (less, least) side effects of all medications.

3. Today drug companies spend billions on advertising. Critics claim that companies spend (more, most) on convincing consumers to buy their products than they do on testing their products. Those who are against drug advertising say that it makes medications (more, most) expensive than they were before. Companies spend billions convincing consumers that their products are the (more, most) effective on the market. Consumers then pressure their doctors to give a certain well-known drug, even if there

are (better, best) alternative products. On the other hand, advertisements must list side effects, so in some respects consumers are (better, best) informed than they were in the past.

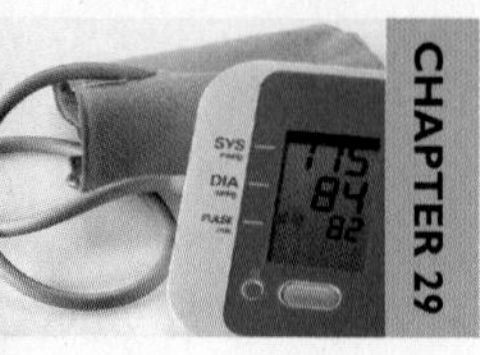

PRACTICE 8

Complete the sentences by writing either the comparative or the superlative form of the word in parentheses.

EXAMPLE:

Some people have (thin) ___thinner___ bones than others.

1. By about age thirty-five, all adults lose some bone mass. Then, as people age, bone deteriorates (rapidly) ____________________ than before. With osteoporosis, bones become (brittle) ____________________ than previously. Some people become (short) ____________________ than they were in their youth because osteoporosis can cause the vertebra in the back to collapse.
2. Osteoporosis is much (common) ____________________ in women than in men because women have (little) ____________________ bone mass than men do. In women, the rate of bone loss is (quick) ____________________ after menopause than it is in premenopausal women.
3. Some in the medical community say that calcium pills are the (effective) ____________________ way to slow the onset of the disease. Yet women from Asian and African nations who consume very little calcium have much (low) ____________________ osteoporosis rates than Canadian women. Osteoporosis is one of the (little) ____________________ understood chronic diseases in the world.

Problems with Comparative and Superlative Forms

Using *more* and *-er*, *most* and *-est*

In the comparative form, never use *more* and *-er* to modify the same word. In the superlative form, never use *most* and *-est* to modify the same word.

Some people thought that Salk's vaccine was ~~more better~~ *better* than Sabin's vaccine. The polio vaccine was one of the ~~most best~~ *best* discoveries of our times.

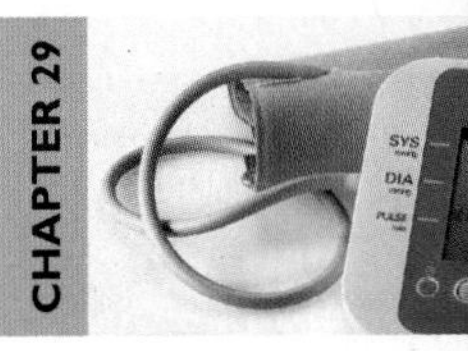

Using *fewer* and *less*

In the comparative form, never use *less* to compare two count nouns. Use *less* to compare two non-count nouns. (Non-count nouns are nouns that cannot be divided, such as *information* and *music*.) Use *fewer* to compare two count nouns.

Today, ~~less~~ *fewer* people get vaccinated than in previous decades because some question the safety of certain vaccinations. ~~Fewer~~ *Less* information about vaccines was available in the 1950s than is available today.

GRAMMAR LINK

For a list of non-count nouns, refer to pages 395–396 in Chapter 27.

Using *the* in the Comparative Form

Although you would usually use *the* in superlative forms, you can use it in some two-part comparatives. In these expressions, the second part is the result of the first part.

The more (action) you exercise, the better (result) your health will be.

PRACTICE 9

Correct fifteen adjective and adverb errors.

EXAMPLE:

Americans ~~continual~~ *continually* debate the ethics of organ transplants.

1. One of the most greatest miracles of modern medicine is organ transplants. Organ transplants save most lives than ever before. With donor organs, many recipients can lead more better lives than previously imagined. However, a public debate about organ transplants is growing rapid.

2. The source of donor organs is a controversial issue. Given the scarcity of organs, some individuals who need transplants quick have obtained organs through unscrupulous methods. For instance, some have bought organs from the most poorest segments of the population in developing

countries. Destitute people sometimes sell their organs to rich buyers because they need money real badly.

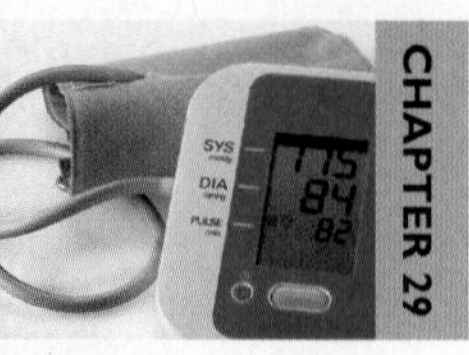

3. Who should receive an organ transplant? Given the scarcity of supply, should a person who smokes heavy or drinks too much receive a lung or liver transplant? Obviously, the more a person smokes, the worst his or her health will be. Should such people be refused access to organ transplants?

4. In addition, money is an issue in this debate. Hospital administrators are concerned about the high cost of transplants. Less people have adequate medical insurance than ever before. Should those with health insurance be treated more better than those without? According to most experts, the richest a patient is, the best his or her chances are to receive a transplant.

5. Waiting for an organ transplant is one of the worse experiences anyone can go through. Hopefully, in future years, the number of people who sign donor cards will be more higher than it is now.

REFLECT ON IT

Think about what you have learned in this chapter. If you do not know an answer, review that topic.

1. What is an adjective? ______________________________

____

2. What is an adverb? ______________________________

____

3. Write the correct adjective or adverb in each blank.
   a. My doctor treats her patients (good, well) ________. She is one of the (better, best) ________ eye surgeons in Berlin.
   b. My brother has (less, fewer) ________ work experience than I do, but he also has (less, fewer) ________ responsibilities.
4. The following sentences contain adjective or adverb errors. Correct each mistake.
   a. We had a real nice time at the medical conference.
   b. Everyone was dressed casual.
   c. My sister changes often her mind about her career.
   d. The advancing medical textbook is my sister's.

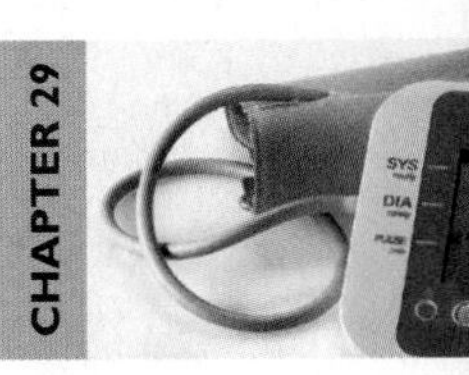

FINAL REVIEW

Underline and correct twenty errors in adjectives and adverbs.

1. Health care is one of the most fastest growing fields in the world. In our nation, the aging population is making the demand for nurses more and more intenser. According to *Canadian Nursing Home Magazine*, an online magazine, there is an acute nursing shortage. Less people enter the nursing profession than in the past. In fact, the number of people in their early twenties entering the nursing profession is at its lower point in forty years. The shortage is worldwide. Canada, England, and many other nations have a more greater shortage than the United States has. As a possible career, more people should consider the nursing profession.

2. First, nurses have a greater responsibility and more diversely role than most people realize. In some jurisdictions, nurses can write prescriptions and nurse midwives can deliver babies. Forensic nurses treat traumatizing victims of violent crime. Furthermore, hospitals are not the only places where nurses can work. Nursing jobs are available in walk-in clinics, schools, vacation resorts, and medical equipment firms. Even film studios hire sometimes on-set nurses.

3. Also, nursing can be an extreme rewarding career. Joan Bowes, a nurse in Prince Edward Island, says that she feels as if she is doing something usefull each day. Occasionally, her actions help to save lives. Last month, a young patient who had been injured really bad was admitted to the hospital where Joan works. A few days later, Joan noticed that the patient was unable to move his head as easy as before. She quick alerted a specialist who then diagnosed a meningitis infection. Joan's observation helped to save the patient's life. Joan's husband, Keith, is a home-care nurse. He is compassionate, and he interacts good with his patients. As one of a growing number of men in the profession, Keith feels that entering nursing was the better decision he has ever made.

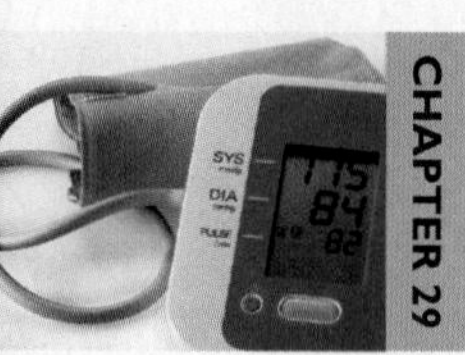

4. Nurses are more better compensated than in the past. In the 1970s, salaries for nurses were much worst than they are today. In fact, nurses were paid the less among health care professionals. Nowadays, because nurses are in such high demand, many hospitals give signing bonuses, decent schedules, and real good salaries.

5. Potential nurses should enjoy helping people. For those who want to have a rewarding career with decent benefits, nursing is an excellent career choice. The more society appreciates nurses, the best health care will be.

The Writer's Room

Write about one of the following topics. Underline adjectives and adverbs.

1. What steps can you take to motivate yourself to exercise regularly?
2. What are some possible problems that may occur if euthanasia is legalized in all provinces?

How Do I Get a Better Grade?

Visit MyWritingLab for audiovisual lectures and additional practice sets about adjectives and adverbs.

Mistakes with Modifiers

Section Theme **HEALTH CARE**

LEARNING OBJECTIVES

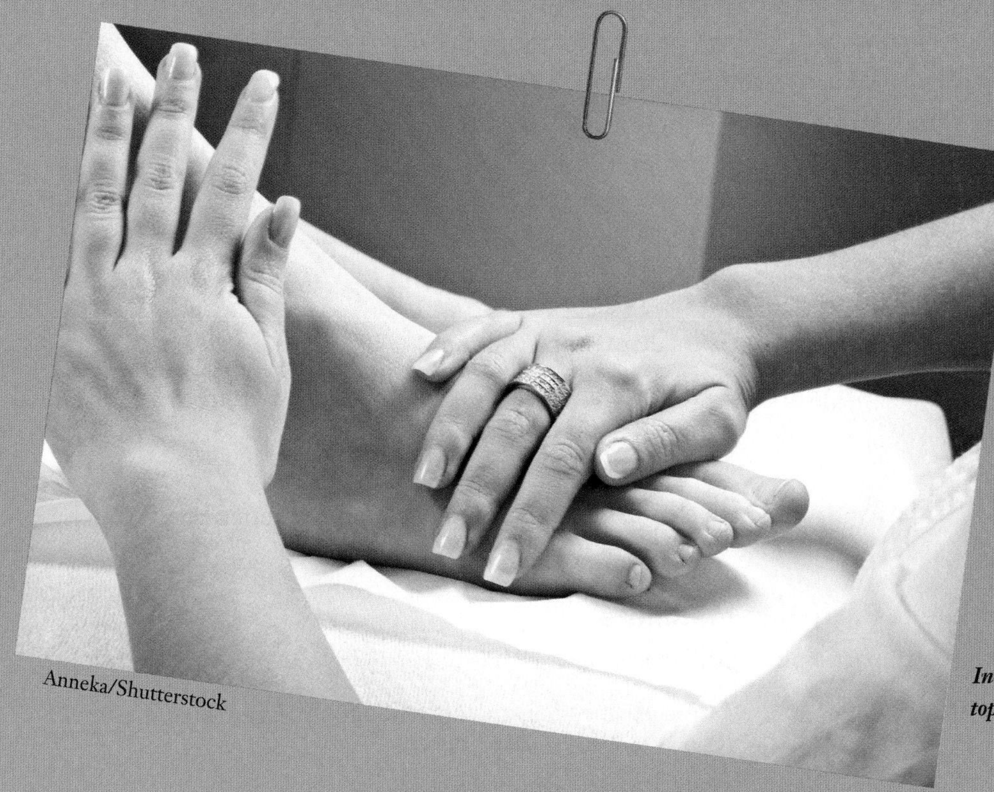

Anneka/Shutterstock

***In this chapter, you will read about topics related to* alternative medicine.**

The Writer's Journal

Would you ever consult an acupuncturist, a homeopath, or any other alternative healing practitioner? Why or why not? Write a paragraph about your attitude toward alternative medicine.

Misplaced Modifiers

Watch the **Video** Misplaced or Dangling Modifiers **MyWritingLab**

A **modifier** is a word, phrase, or clause that describes or modifies nouns or verbs in a sentence. For example, *holding the patient's hand* is a modifier. To use a modifier correctly, place it next to the word(s) that you want to modify.

modifier — words that are modified

Holding the patient's hand, **the doctor** explained the procedure.

A **misplaced modifier** is a word, phrase, or clause that is not placed next to the word it modifies. When a modifier is too far from the word that it is describing, then the meaning of the sentence can become confusing or unintentionally funny.

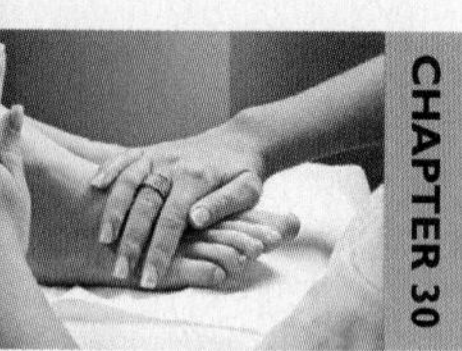

I saw a pamphlet about acupuncture sitting in the doctor's office.
(How could a pamphlet sit in a doctor's office?)

Commonly Misplaced Modifiers

As you read the sample sentences for each type of modifier, notice how the meaning of the sentence changes depending on where the modifier is placed. In the examples, the modifiers are underlined.

Prepositional Phrase Modifiers

A prepositional phrase is made of a preposition and its object.

Confusing: Cora read an article on acupuncture written by reporter James Reston in a café.
(Who was in the café: James or Cora?)

Clear: In a café, Cora read an article on acupuncture written by reporter James Reston.

Present Participle Modifiers

A present participle modifier is a phrase that begins with an *-ing* verb.

Confusing: James Reston learned about acupuncture touring China.
(Can acupuncture tour China?)

Clear: While touring China, James Reston learned about acupuncture.

Past Participle Modifiers

A past participle modifier is a phrase that begins with a past participle (*walked*, *gone*, *known*, and so on).

Confusing: Called meridians, acupuncturists claim there are two thousand pathways on the body.
(What are called meridians: the acupuncturists or the pathways?)

Clear: Acupuncturists claim there are two thousand pathways called meridians on the body.

Limiting Modifiers

Limiting modifiers are words such as *almost*, *nearly*, *only*, *merely*, *just*, and *even*. In the examples, notice how the placement of *almost* changes the meaning.

Almost all of the doctors went to the lecture that disproved acupuncture.
(Some of the doctors did not attend, but most did.)

All of the doctors **almost** went to the lecture that disproved acupuncture.
(The doctors did not go.)

All of the doctors went to the lecture that **almost** disproved acupuncture.
(The lecture did not disprove acupuncture.)

 **Other Types of Modifiers**

There are many other types of modifiers. For example, some modifiers begin with relative clauses, and some are appositives.

Relative Clause

Confusing: The treatments involved acupuncture needles that were expensive.
(What was expensive: the treatment or the needles?)

Clear: The treatments that were expensive involved acupuncture needles.

Appositive

Confusing: A very sick man, Monica helped her uncle find a doctor.
(How could Monica be a very sick man?)

Clear: Monica helped her uncle, a very sick man, find a doctor.

PRACTICE 1

Circle the letter of the correct sentence in each pair. Underline the misplaced modifier in each incorrect sentence.

EXAMPLE:

a. Simon Weiss learned about acupuncture with enthusiasm.
(b) With enthusiasm, Simon Weiss learned about acupuncture.

1. a. Simon read about acupuncture, which is based on an ancient philosophy.
   b. Based on an ancient philosophy, Simon read about acupuncture.
2. a. By licensed practitioners, Canada allows acupuncture to be performed.
   b. Acupuncture can be performed by licensed practitioners in Canada.
3. a. Only Canada allows acupuncturists to practise without medical supervision.
   b. Canada only allows acupuncturists to practise without medical supervision.
4. a. In a hurry, Simon asked for information about acupuncture.
   b. Simon asked for information about acupuncture in a hurry.
5. a. Needing treatment, Mr. Lo examined the patient.
   b. Mr. Lo examined the patient needing treatment.
6. a. Faced with chronic headaches, Mr. Lo was prepared to treat Simon.
   b. Faced with chronic headaches, Simon was prepared to try Mr. Lo's treatment.

7. a. Carefully guiding the needles, Mr. Lo gently pierced Simon's skin.
   b. Carefully guiding the needles, Simon's skin was gently pierced by Mr. Lo.

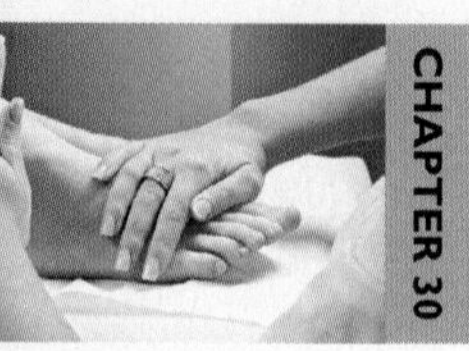

8. a. Mr. Lo treated Simon wearing a mask.
   b. Wearing a mask, Mr. Lo treated Simon.

Correcting Misplaced Modifiers

To correct misplaced modifiers, do the following:

- Identify the modifier.

  Manuel saw the accident walking past the hotel.

- Identify the word or words that are being modified.

  Who walked past the hotel? **Manuel**

- Move the modifier next to the word(s) being modified.

  Walking past the hotel, **Manuel** saw the accident.

PRACTICE 2

Underline the misplaced modifiers in the following sentences. Then rewrite the sentences. You may have to add or remove words to give the sentence a logical meaning.

EXAMPLE:

Acting recklessly, the motorcycle was driven too quickly by the young man.

Acting recklessly, the young man drove the motorcycle too quickly.

1. In a wheelchair, the nurse sat near the patient.

2. The patient took the medication with red hair.

3. Ross was a teenager with a cast on his leg weighing 120 pounds.

4. Dr. Zimboro talked to Ross carrying a medical chart.

5. Not wearing a helmet, the accident could have killed the young man.

6. By all motorcyclists, many medical professionals believe that helmets should be worn.

____

____

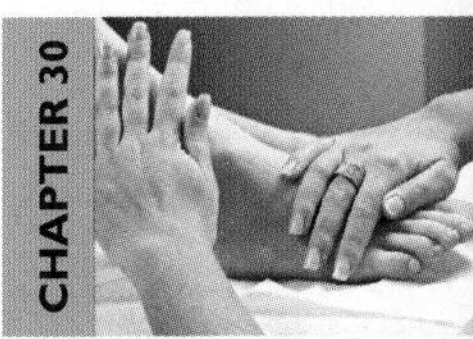

7. Citing freedom of expression, a fight against helmet laws is being proposed by cycling enthusiasts.

____

____

8. Scared of having another accident, the motorcycle will not be driven again by Ross.

____

____

Dangling Modifiers

Watch the **Video** Misplaced or Dangling Modifiers **MyWritingLab**

A **dangling modifier** opens a sentence but does not modify any words in the sentence. It "dangles" or hangs loosely because it is not connected to any other part of the sentence.

To avoid having a dangling modifier, make sure that the modifier and the first noun that follows it have a logical connection.

Confusing: While talking on a cellphone, the ambulance drove off the road.
(Can an ambulance talk on a cellphone?)

Clear: While talking on a cellphone, the ambulance **technician** drove off the road.

Confusing: To get into medical school, high grades are necessary.
(Can high grades get into a school?)

Clear: To get into medical school, **students** need high grades.

PRACTICE 3

Read each pair of sentences. Circle the letter of each correct sentence.

EXAMPLE:

a. Having taken a pill, the results were surprising.
(b.) Having taken a pill, I was surprised by the results.

1. a. With the patient's budget in mind, the least expensive drugs were prescribed.
   b. With the patient's budget in mind, the doctor prescribed the least expensive drugs.
2. a. Believing in their effects, placebos are often given to patients.
   b. Believing in their effects, Doctor Zimboro sometimes gives placebos to patients.
3. a. After taking a sugar pill, patients often feel relieved.
   b. After taking a sugar pill, there is often a feeling of relief.

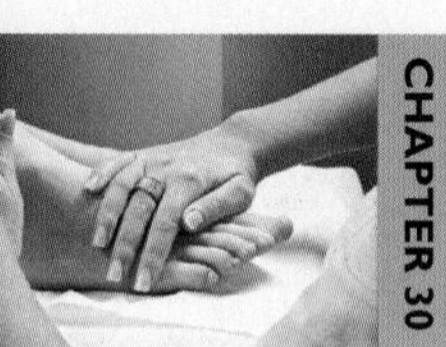

4. a. Surprised, the word *placebo* means "I shall please."
   b. Surprised, I read that the word *placebo* means "I shall please."
5. a. Thinking about the mind-body relationship, scientist Esther Sternberg conducted an experiment.
   b. Thinking about the mind-body relationship, an experiment was conducted.
6. a. Frustrated, Sternberg's temptation was to give up.
   b. Frustrated, Sternberg was tempted to give up.
7. a. Using laboratory rats, Sternberg discovered a link between the mind and body.
   b. Using laboratory rats, a link was discovered between the mind and body.
8. a. Given an antidepressant, the arthritis disappeared.
   b. Given an antidepressant, some rats no longer had arthritis.
9. a. Excited about her discovery, Sternberg wrote an article for a medical journal.
   b. Excited about her discovery, an article was written for a medical journal.

Correcting Dangling Modifiers

To correct dangling modifiers, do the following:

- Identify the modifier.

  While dieting, self-control is necessary.

- Decide who or what the writer aims to modify.

  Whose self-control is necessary? **People's**

- Add the missing subject (and in some cases, also add or remove words) so that the sentence makes sense.

  While dieting, **people** need to have self-control.

PRACTICE 4

In each sentence, underline the dangling modifier. Then rewrite each sentence, adding or removing words to provide a logical meaning.

EXAMPLE:

Worried about their weight, a lot of diet books are bought.

Worried about their weight, Canadians buy a lot of diet books.

1. When dieting, obsessing about food is common.

____

____

2. To buy that diet book, $13.95 is required.

____

____

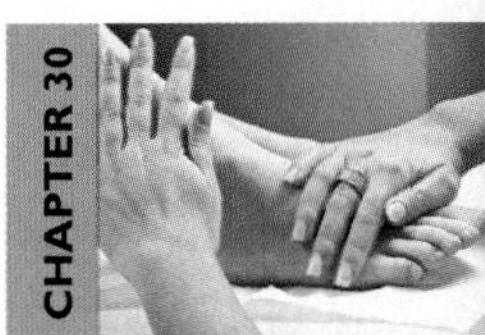

3. The chicken was roasting while reading my diet book.

____

____

4. Not eating any bread, rice, or pasta, weight fell off easily.

____

____

5. Feeling skeptical, the benefits of a meat-based diet are questioned.

____

____

6. Indulging in fatty foods, heart problems can occur.

____

____

7. Working with celebrities, diet books are promoted on television.

____

____

8. When uncertain about which diet to follow, the advice of a nutritionist can be helpful.

____

____

PRACTICE 5

Some sentences in this practice have dangling or misplaced modifiers. Write *M* next to misplaced modifiers, *D* next to dangling modifiers, and *C* next to correct sentences. If the modifier is misplaced, move it. If the modifier is dangling, add words to make the sentence complete.

EXAMPLE:

people try different therapies.
Hoping to live a long life, ~~different therapies are tried.~~ *D*

1. Called Ayurveda therapy, ancient Indians developed a school of medicine. ______

2. Originally written on palm leaves, researchers found 2000-year-old texts. ______

3. Possibly causing diseases, Ayurvedic medicine teaches about an imbalance in mental and physical energies. ______

4. Ayurvedic medicine is widely followed by many people in India. ______

5. Doing meditation and yoga, essential parts of this alternative therapy are learned. ______

6. Dr. Shah spoke about traditional Indian medicine in a state of excitement. ______

7. Called homeopathy, India has produced a therapy that uses plants, animals, and minerals to cure a patient's illness. ______

8. Later, a German doctor organized the rules of homeopathic treatment wearing glasses. ______

9. In the 1800s, homeopathy became popular in Canada. ______

10. Feeling skeptical, the merits of homeopathy are questioned. ______

11. In fact, many conventionally trained doctors do not believe in alternative medical therapies. ______

12. Having tried many different therapies, the effectiveness of the treatments were discussed. ______

REFLECT ON IT

Think about what you have learned in this chapter. If you do not know an answer, review that topic.

1. What is a modifier? ____________________

   ____

2. What is a misplaced modifier? ____________________

   ____

3. What is a dangling modifier? ____________________

   ____

4. What type of modifier error is in each sentence? Write *M* for "misplaced" and *D* for "dangling." Then correct the sentence.

   a. Overeating, a weight problem was developed.

   ____

   b. The doctor examined the X-ray in the lab coat.

   ____

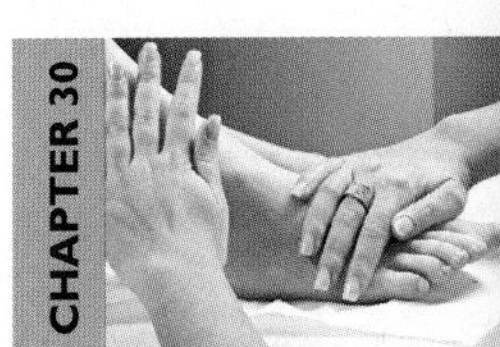

FINAL REVIEW

Underline ten dangling or misplaced modifier errors in the next selection. Then correct each error. You may need to add or remove words to ensure that the sentence makes sense.

EXAMPLE:

young girl got a surprising result.
Working on her school project, a ~~surprising result occurred~~.

1. There are many fraudulent claims in alternative medicine. In fact, feeling desperate, fortunes are spent on suspect therapies. It is difficult for members of the public to determine which therapies are valid and which are pure quackery. At an important medical conference, some doctors discussed healing touch eating lunch together. In recent years, critics have attacked healing touch therapy.

2. Based on several ancient healing practices, Dolores Krieger developed therapeutic touch therapy. According to touch therapists, a skilled practitioner can pass his or her hands over a patient's body and remove obstacles in the energy field. Using the method all over Canada, therapeutic touch is actively promoted.

3. Named Emily Rosa, an experiment at school was conducted by a nine-year-old girl. In 1998, Emily tested twenty-one therapeutic touch practitioners wearing a school uniform. A therapist would place both hands, palms facing up, on the table. A screen prevented the therapist from seeing Emily. Emily then placed her own hand over one of the therapist's hands. Emily asked the therapist which hand was nearest to her own. Unable to see Emily, the guesses were correct only 44 percent of the time.

4. Emily's results were published in a reputable medical journal. Emily's parents proudly read the article drinking coffee. Dr. George D. Lundberg believes that therapeutic touch practitioners should disclose the results of Emily's experiment to patients. However, those in the therapeutic touch community criticize the experiment feeling angry. They believe that Emily

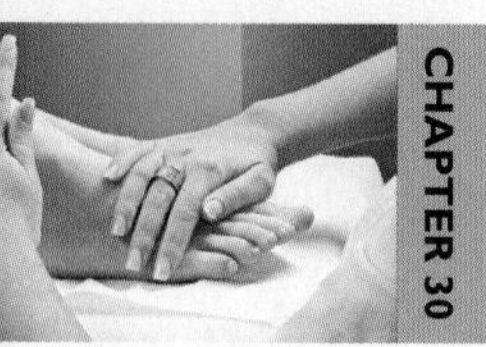

was too healthy for the experiment to work. They also feel that there were too few practitioners in the experiment. Rejecting the results, therapeutic touch continues to be popular.

The Writer's Room

Choose one of the following topics, and write a paragraph or an essay. Remember to follow the writing process.

1. Have you ever been to an acupuncturist, a massage therapist, a naturopath, a homeopath, or any other alternative healing practitioner? Describe the treatment that you received.
2. Do you have a scar, or have you ever had an accident? Explain what happened.
3. Right now, millions of Americans are uninsured for medical care. Should the government of the United States provide health care for all citizens, just as Canada and many European nations do? Why or why not?
4. Should terminally ill patients have the right to die? What are the possible problems if euthanasia is legalized? Write about euthanasia.

The Writers' Circle Collaborative Activity

Work with a group of students on the following activity.

STEP 1 Write down adjectives, adverbs, and phrases that describe the following people.

EXAMPLE: A good boss: *honest, listens well, supportive*

a. A good doctor: ______________________

____

b. A bad doctor: ______________________

____

STEP 2 Rank the qualities from most important to least important.

STEP 3 As a team, write a paragraph about doctors. Compare the good with the bad.

STEP 4 When you finish writing, edit your paragraph and ensure that you have written all the adjectives and adverbs correctly.

READING LINK

Health Care

"New Evidence in 'Diefenbaby' Case" by Charlie Gillis (page 546)
"The Catcher of Ghosts" by Amy Tan (page 548)
"A Shift in Perception" by Cynthia Macdonald (page 551)
"The Sage" by Eric Andrew-Gee (page (page 557)
"The Sanctuary of School" by Lynda Barry (page 563)
"Like It or Not, Yoga Is Here to Stay" by Aparita Bhandari (page 566)

How Do I Get a Better Grade?

Visit MyWritingLab for audiovisual lectures and additional practice sets about mistakes with modifiers.

Exact Language

Section Theme **THE LEGAL WORLD**

Sam Cornwell/Shutterstock

LEARNING OBJECTIVES

In this chapter, you will read about topics related to crimes and criminals.

***The Writer's* Journal**

Write a paragraph that summarizes the events of a well-known crime. Describe what happened.

Use Specific and Detailed Vocabulary

Great writing evokes an emotional response from the reader. Great writers not only use correct grammatical structures but also infuse their writing with precise and vivid details that make their work come alive.

When you proofread your work, revise words that are too vague. **Vague words** lack precision and detail. For example, the words *nice* and *bad* are vague. Readers cannot get a clear picture from them.

Compare the following sets of sentences.

Vague: The movie was bad.

Precise: The crime drama contained violent, gory scenes.

Vague: Our instructor told us about the death of Julius Caesar.

Precise: Our history instructor, Dr. London, recounted how Julius Caesar was murdered in 44 BC.

Creating Vivid Language

When you choose the precise word, you convey your meaning exactly. Moreover, you can make your writing clearer and more impressive by using specific and detailed vocabulary. To create vivid language, try the following strategies.

- **Modify your nouns.** If your noun is vague, make it more specific by adding one or more adjectives. You could also rename the noun with a more specific term.

  Vague: the man

  Vivid: the shopkeeper   the thin, nervous soldier

- **Modify your verbs.** Use more vivid and precise verbs. You could also use adverbs.

  Vague: walk

  Vivid: saunter   stroll   march briskly

- **Include more details.** Add detailed information to make the sentence more complete.

  Vague: Several signs foretold of Caesar's murder.

  Precise: Several ominous signs, such as Caesar's horses getting loose and a soothsayer's warning, foretold of Caesar's impending death.

WRITING LINK

You can find more information about appealing to the five senses in Chapter 6, "Description."

Watch the Video
Paragraph Development—Describing
MyWritingLab

Hint **Use Imagery**

You can make your writing come alive by using **imagery,** which is description using the five senses: sight, sound, smell, touch, and taste. In the example, the underlined words add details to the sentence and contribute to a more exact description.

The one-eyed, scar-faced pirate jabbed his sword at the frightened crew.

PRACTICE 1

Replace the familiar words in parentheses with more vivid words or phrases, and add more specific details. Use your dictionary or thesaurus if you need help.

EXAMPLE:

Graffiti artists (write) *scrawl words and pictures* on walls.

1. Many cities spend a lot of money (cleaning) ____________________________ ____________________________ graffiti.

2. (Youths) ____________________________ spray paint on many (places) ____________________________

3. They worry about getting caught by (someone) ____________________________ ____________________________

4. Some cities permit graffiti artists to paint on (certain locations) ________ ____________________________

5. Sometimes graffiti artists use (bad words) ____________________________ ____________________________

6. Governments could combat the problem (with many solutions) ________ ____________________________

7. Some people think graffiti artists should be (treated harshly) __________ ____________________________

PRACTICE 2

Underline all the words in the paragraph that add vivid details to the description.

EXAMPLE:

The air, <u>cool</u> and <u>fresh</u> and <u>dark</u> after the <u>warm</u>, <u>lighted</u> kitchen, blew upon her face.

You can cycle the entire length of the Beach area in Toronto in a quarter of the time it takes for the 501 Neville Park streetcar to slowly chug its way down Queen Street East. The scenic view along the lakeshore's paved, smooth cycling path is rejuvenating. Lake Ontario glistens on the left while manicured, polished backyard grounds greet you on the right—all the way from the Neville Park loop to the red brick fire station near Woodbine Avenue.

Adding Appositives

An appositive is a word or phrase that gives further information about a noun or pronoun. You can write sentences that are more exact and detailed by adding appositives.

Sherlock Holmes, the famous detective (appositive), was helped by his friend Dr. Watson (appositive).

CHAPTER 31

Watch the Video
Using Exact Language
MyWritingLab

Avoid Wordiness and Redundancy

Sometimes students fill their writing assignments with extra words to meet length requirements. However, good ideas can get easily lost in work that is too wordy. Also, if the explanations are unnecessarily long, then writing becomes boring.

To improve your writing style, use only as many words or phrases as you need to fully explain your ideas.

> The police department was a distance of two blocks from the municipal library. (A block is a measure of a distance, so it is unnecessary to repeat that information.)

Correcting Wordiness

You can cut the number of words needed to express an idea by replacing a wordy phrase with a single word. You can also remove the wordy phrase completely.

> *Because*
> ~~By virtue of the fact that~~ we did a survey, we found that most young college students do not study criminology.

Some Common Wordy Expressions and Substitutions

Wordy	Better	Wordy	Better
at that point in time	then, at that time	gave the appearance of	looked like
big, small in size	big, small	great, few in number	great, few
in close proximity	close *or* in proximity	in order to	to
a difficult dilemma	a dilemma	in spite of the fact	in spite of
due to the fact	because	in the final analysis	finally, lastly
equally as good as	as good as	period of time	period
exactly the same	the same	past history	past *or* history
exceptions to the rule	exceptions	return again	return
final completion	end	still remain	remain
for the purpose of	for	a true fact	a fact

PRACTICE 3

In the next sentences, cross out all unnecessary words or phrases, or modify any repeated words.

EXAMPLE:

> *many*
> In 1995, ~~a great number of~~ people were interested in Paul Bernardo's trial.

1. In 1987, Scarborough citizens were terrified due to the fact that a rapist was in their midst.
2. At that point in time, nobody knew who was ultimately responsible for so many attacks on women.
3. Eventually, the crimes were traced to a couple living in St. Catharines.
4. Although Paul Bernardo and Karla Homolka appeared to be a regular run-of-the-mill couple, they were very dangerous.
5. The pair of killers gave the appearance of being young and carefree.
6. At the final completion of Bernardo's trial, he was sentenced to life in prison for two counts of first-degree murder.
7. Homolka, who testified against her husband, received a twelve-year imprisonment charge for her involvement in the rapes and murders.
8. There were no exceptions to the rule, so Bernardo's appeals for parole have been rejected.
9. In spite of the fact that the couple's crimes were horrific, they have become famous.
10. Bernardo still remains in prison, while Homolka, who pleaded guilty to manslaughter, now lives in the Caribbean.

Avoid Clichés

Clichés are overused expressions. Because they are overused, they lose their power and become boring. You should avoid using clichés in your writing.

She was as busy as a bee.

Local businesses had to cough up money.

Some Common Clichés

a drop in the bucket	easier said than done
as light as a feather	keep your eyes peeled
as luck would have it	last but not least
axe to grind	top dog
between a rock and a hard place	tried and true
break the ice	under the weather
calm, cool, and collected	work like a dog

Correcting Clichés

When you modify a cliché, you can change it into a direct term. You might also try playing with language to come up with a more interesting description.

Cliché:	She was as busy as a bee.
Direct language:	She was extremely busy.
Interesting Description:	She was as busy as an emergency room nurse.

PRACTICE 4

Cross out ten clichéd expressions, and then replace them with fresh or direct language.

EXAMPLE:

Police forces have to ~~bear the burden of~~ *deal with* organized criminal groups.

1. The North American Mafia, also known as the Cosa Nostra, flourished during the years of Prohibition. Criminals hustled and bustled to meet a demand for alcohol and other illegal services, such as prostitution. As Prohibition progressed, Mafia members kept their noses to the grindstone to provide services in cities such as Montreal, Toronto, Hamilton, and Windsor. Law-enforcement agents kept their eyes peeled and tried to stop the Mafia's criminal activities, but that was easier said than done.

2. According to Pierre de Champlain in his book *Mobsters, Gangsters and Men of Honour*, the Cosa Nostra comprises many families, one of which was, until recently, led by Vito Rizzuto in Montreal. In 2004, however, Rizzuto was arrested at his lavish Montreal mansion where he was enjoying the finer things in life. Another Mafia member had become a government informant and implicated Rizzuto in an earlier deadly murder. Each Cosa Nostra family is based on a pyramid-shaped model of authority. The top dog is the Godfather. Under the Godfather, there are lieutenants and, last but not least, soldiers. Soldiers are Mafia members who do the criminal activities.

3. Currently, authorities have arrested many crime bosses, but that is just a drop in the bucket. Other gangs, such as the Russian Mafia, are gaining influence and power in the blink of an eye. The police are now working like dogs to investigate criminal organizations that are made up of many different ethnic groups.

Standard English versus Slang

Watch the Video
Standard and Nonstandard English
MyWritingLab

Most of your instructors will want you to write using **standard English.** The word *standard* does not imply "better." Standard Canadian English is the common language generally used and expected in schools, businesses, and government institutions in Canada.

Slang is nonstandard language. It is used in informal situations to communicate common cultural knowledge. In any academic or professional context, do not use slang.

Slang: My friend and I hang together. Last weekend, we watched a movie that was kinda weird but also pretty sweet. It was called *Eastern Promises,* and it was about the Russian Mafia.

Standard English My friends and I spend a lot of time together. Last weekend, we watched a movie that was unusual but fascinating. It was called *Eastern Promises,* and it was about the Russian Mafia.

Hint **Do Not Use Slang in Academic Writing**

Slang is very informal and should be avoided in academic writing. Keep in mind that slang changes depending on generational, regional, cultural, and historical influences. For example, rather than saying "I have to *leave,*" people in one group might say *scram* or *split,* while those in another group might say *bail* or *bounce.* Avoid using slang expressions in your writing because they can change very quickly—so quickly, in fact, that you might remark that this textbook's examples of slang are "lame."

PRACTICE 5

Replace the underlined slang expressions with the best possible choice in standard Canadian English.

EXAMPLE:

Every day, the cops deal with gangs. ______*police officers*______

1. Gang members can be guys or chicks. ____________
2. Some young people think that gangs are cool. ____________
3. It takes a lot of guts to refuse to join a gang. ____________
4. Someone may join a gang because he or she does not want to look like a wimp. ____________
5. Others join gangs because they want to earn megabucks. ____________
6. Sometimes people hang with gangs because they feel more protected. ____________
7. It is dicey to be in a gang. ____________

8. Police try to keep their cool when they deal with gangs. ____________
9. Gang members are often on the lookout for narcs. ____________
10. Many gang members end up in the joint. ____________

REFLECT ON IT

Think about what you have learned in this chapter. If you do not know an answer, review that topic.

1. What is vivid language? ____________
2. Why should you add details to your writing? ____________
3. Edit the following sentences for wordiness and redundancy. Cross out any unnecessary phrases, or modify them to make them more concise.

   a. The suspect lived in close proximity to the bank that he had robbed.

   b. Hakim wrote the final completion of his paper on *The Great Train Robbery*.
4. Edit the following sentences for clichés and overused expressions. Replace the clichés with your own words.

   a. Peter will be in for a rude awakening if he does not study for his law-enforcement exams.

   b. Peter is feeling under the weather today.
5. Edit the following sentences for slang. Replace the slang words with standard Canadian English.

   a. Replacing the contents of a stolen wallet is such a drag.

   b. I read a cool biography about Al Capone.

FINAL REVIEW

Edit the following paragraphs for slang, clichés, and vague language.

Part A

In the next paragraph, five vague words are underlined. Replace these words with specific details to make the paragraph more interesting. Also correct three wordy expressions.

EXAMPLE:

flamboyant criminal

The ~~man~~ convinced wealthy victims to part with their money.

1. Christopher Rocancourt is a con artist. Small in size, Rocancourt was the son of an alcoholic house painter and a teenage prostitute. He lived in an orphanage, and then he was adopted at age twelve. Perhaps as a result of the fact that he grew up in poverty, Rocancourt decided to reinvent himself. He has pretended to be a venture capitalist, the son of a movie director, and a boxing champion. For more than fifteen years, he has managed to steal money from rich <u>people</u> in Hollywood and elsewhere. He says that he simply wanted to have a <u>better</u> life. Rocancourt claims his life has been <u>interesting</u>. He spent the past few years <u>running</u> from authorities. At this point in time, <u>he</u> is in prison.

Part B
Replace twelve slang or clichéd expressions.

EXAMPLE:

a skilled manipulator
Christopher Rocancourt is <u>a strange dude</u>.

2. While in Hollywood, Rocancourt stayed in the Beverly Wilshire Hotel. He managed to pull the wool over many people's eyes. Some actors knew him as Christopher De Laurentiis, the nephew of filmmaker Dino De Laurentiis. To others, he was Christopher de la Renta, nephew of fashion designer Oscar de la Renta. He claimed to be friends with Robert De Niro, Jean-Claude Van Damme, and the Sultan of Brunei. Posing as an investor, he persuaded his wealthy friends to give him tons of dough. Promising to triple or quadruple their money, he easily messed with people's heads. Rocancourt earned millions with his cons. When his wealthy friends learned the truth about him, they were blown away. Today a lot of his former friends have an axe to grind with Christopher Rocancourt.

3. Nowadays, the con artist is surprisingly unrepentant. While rapping with a journalist from CBS News, Rocancourt said that he is not a thief. He claims that he simply borrows from friends, and then he doesn't repay them. Certainly, he is a slick piece of work who preys on people who are

as dumb as doorknobs. Most of his victims wanted to turn a quick buck, and he was happy to let them believe that they could benefit from his financial expertise. Nowadays, those victims are understandably bummed. It will be a cold day in hell before any of the wealthy friends recoup their money. Rocancourt's sweet gig, which included driving Hummers, dating wealthy women, and befriending millionaires, seems to be over.

The Writer's Room

Write about one of the following topics. Make sure that you use exact and concise language.

1. List some steps that parents can take to prevent their children from joining gangs or breaking laws.
2. What are some different categories of crimes? Classify crimes into three different types.

How Do I Get a Better Grade?

Visit MyWritingLab for audiovisual lectures and additional practice sets about exact language.

Spelling and Commonly Confused Words

Section Theme **THE LEGAL WORLD**

LEARNING OBJECTIVES

nito/Fotolia

In this chapter, you will read about topics related to controversial crimes.

The Writer's Journal

Do you think that celebrities who commit crimes are treated differently than regular people? Write a paragraph expressing your opinion about celebrity criminals.

Spelling Rules

Watch the **Video**
Spelling
MyWritingLab

It is important to spell correctly. Spelling mistakes can detract from good ideas in your work. You can become a better speller if you always proofread your written work and if you check a dictionary for the meaning and spelling of words about which you are unsure. To help you improve your spelling, here are some spelling rules.

Using a Dictionary

If you are unsure about the spelling or meaning of a word, consult a dictionary. Try to use a recent edition. Also, get to know the features of your dictionary.

READING LINK

For more information about using a dictionary, see pages 526–527 in Part V, "Reading Strategies" (Chapter 37).

Writing *ie* or *ei*

Remember the following rule so that you know when to use *ie* or *ei*. Write *i* before *e* except after *c* or when *ei* is pronounced *ay*, as in *neighbour* and *weigh*.

***i* before *e*:**	ach**ie**ve	bel**ie**ve	fr**ie**nd	
***ei* after *c*:**	c**ei**ling	conc**ei**ve	perc**ei**ve	
***ei* pronounced *ay*:**	b**ei**ge	v**ei**n	w**ei**gh	
Exceptions:	effic**ie**nt	**ei**ther	for**ei**gner	h**ei**ght
	l**ei**sure	n**ei**ther	sc**ie**nce	s**ei**ze
	soc**ie**ty	spec**ie**s	th**ei**r	w**ei**rd

PRACTICE 1

Circle the correct spelling of each word.

EXAMPLE:

recieve/receive

1. decieve/deceive
2. foreigner/foriegner
3. grief/greif
4. hieght/height
5. vien/vein
6. science/sceince
7. efficient/efficeint
8. theif/thief
9. deciet/deceit
10. chief/cheif
11. wieght/weight
12. sufficeint/sufficient

Adding Prefixes and Suffixes

A **prefix** is added to the beginning of a word, and it changes the word's meaning. For example, *con-*, *dis-*, *pre-*, *un-*, and *il-* are prefixes. A **suffix** is added to the ending of a word, and it changes the word's tense or meaning. For example, *-ly*, *-ment*, *-ed*, and *-ing* are suffixes.

When you add a prefix to a word, keep the last letter of the prefix and the first letter of the main word.

u**n** + **n**atural = u**nn**atural   di**s** + **s**atisfaction = di**ss**atisfaction

When you add the suffix *-ly* to words that end in *l*, keep the *l* of the root word. The new word will have two *l*'s.

persona**l** + **l**y = persona**ll**y   actua**l** + **l**y = actua**ll**y

Words Ending in *-ful*

Although the word *full* ends in two *l's*, when *-ful* is added to another word as a suffix, it ends in one *l*.

careful successful hopeful

Notice the unusual spelling when *full* and *fill* are combined: fulfill.

PRACTICE 2

Read the following words and decide if they are correctly spelled. If the word is correct, write *C* in the space provided. If the word is incorrect, write the correct word in the space.

EXAMPLES:

factualy *factually* ________ untrue *C* ________

1. naturally	________	7. beautifull	________
2. ilogical	________	8. iresponsible	________
3. continually	________	9. unusual	________
4. imoral	________	10. carefuly	________
5. unecessary	________	11. fataly	________
6. mispell	________	12. fulfilled	________

Adding *-s* or *-es*

Add *-s* to nouns and to present tense verbs that are third-person singular. However, add *-es* to words in the following situations.

- When words end in *s*, *sh*, *ss*, *ch*, or *x*, add *-es*.

  Noun: church–church**es** **Verb:** fix–fix**es**

- When words end with the consonant *y*, change the *y* to *i* and add *-es*.

  Noun: berry–berr**ies** **Verb:** marry–marr**ies**

- When words end in *o*, add *-es* in most cases.

  Noun: hero–hero**es** **Verb:** do–do**es**

  Exceptions: piano–piano**s**; radio–radio**s**; logo–logo**s**; patio–patio**s**.

- When words end in *f* or *fe*, change the *f* to *v* and add *-es*.

  leaf–lea**ves** knife–kni**ves**

  Exceptions: belief–belief**s**; roof–roof**s**.

PRACTICE 3

Add *-s* or *-es* to each word. Write the new word in the space provided.

EXAMPLE:

reach *reaches*

1. hero	______________	7. potato	______________
2. crutch	______________	8. candy	______________
3. fix	______________	9. miss	______________
4. echo	______________	10. fly	______________
5. carry	______________	11. teach	______________
6. dish	______________	12. scarf	______________

Adding Suffixes to Words Ending in -e

When you add a suffix to a word ending in *e*, make sure that you follow the next rules.

- If the suffix begins with a vowel, drop the *e* on the main word. Some common suffixes beginning with vowels are *-ed*, *-er*, *-est*, *-ing*, *-able*, *-ent*, and *-ist*.

  hope–hop**ing** encourage–encourag**ing**

  Exceptions: For some words that end in *ge*, keep the *e* and add the suffix.

  courage–courage**ous** change–change**able**

- If the suffix begins with a consonant, keep the *e*. Some common suffixes beginning with consonants are *-ly*, *-ment*, *-less*, and *-ful*.

  sure–sure**ly** like–like**ness**

  Exceptions: Some words lose their final *e* when a suffix is added.

  argue–argument true–truly

PRACTICE 4

Rewrite each word with the suggested ending.

EXAMPLE:

use + ed *used*

1. achieve + ment	______________	7. large + er	______________
2. strange + est	______________	8. endorse + ment	______________
3. argue + ment	______________	9. argue + ing	______________
4. love + ing	______________	10. nine + ty	______________
5. active + ly	______________	11. write + ing	______________
6. true + ly	______________	12. change + able	______________

Adding Suffixes to Words Ending in -y

When you add a suffix to a word ending in *y*, make sure that you follow the next rules.

- If the word has a consonant before the final *y*, change the *y* to an *i* before adding the suffix.

  beauty–beautiful supply–supplied

- If the word has a vowel before the final *y*, if it is a proper name, or if the suffix is *-ing*, do not change the *y* to an *i*.

  day–days try–trying the Vronsky family–the Vronskys

  Exceptions: Some words do not follow the previous rule.

  day–da**i**ly lay–la**i**d say–sa**i**d pay–pa**i**d

PRACTICE 5

Rewrite each word with the suggested ending.

EXAMPLE:

try + ed *tried* ____________

1. happy + est ____________
2. play + er ____________
3. pretty + er ____________
4. Connolly + s ____________
5. lonely + ness ____________
6. envy + able ____________
7. angry + ly ____________
8. day + ly ____________
9. say + ing ____________
10. dirty + est ____________

Doubling the Final Consonant

Sometimes when you add a suffix to a word, you must double the final consonant. Remember the next tips.

One-Syllable Words

- Double the final consonant of one-syllable words ending in a consonant-vowel-consonant pattern.

  bat–ba**tt**er plan–pla**nn**ed prod–pro**dd**ed

- Do not double the final consonant if the word ends in a vowel and two consonants or if it ends with two vowels and a consonant.

  cool–coolest park–parking clean–cleaner

Words of Two or More Syllables

- Double the final consonant of words ending in a stressed consonant-vowel-consonant pattern.

  pre<u>fer</u>–prefe**rr**ed oc<u>cur</u>–occu**rr**ed

- If the word ends in a syllable that is not stressed, then do not double the last letter of the word.

  <u>hap</u>pen–happened <u>vi</u>sit–visiting

PRACTICE 6

Rewrite each word with the suggested ending.

EXAMPLES:

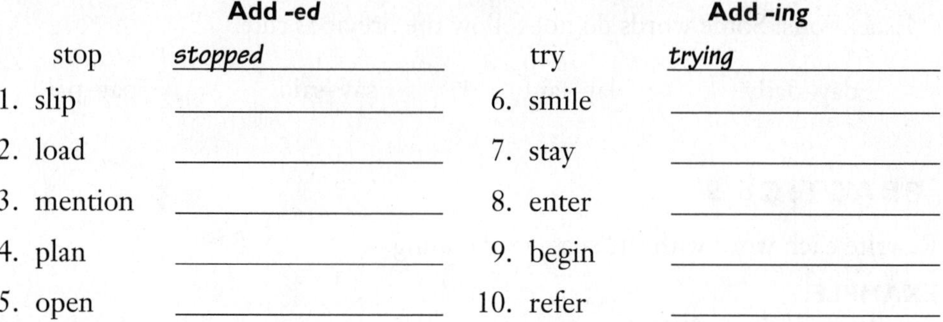

	Add -*ed*		Add -*ing*
stop	*stopped*	try	*trying*
1. slip	__________	6. smile	__________
2. load	__________	7. stay	__________
3. mention	__________	8. enter	__________
4. plan	__________	9. begin	__________
5. open	__________	10. refer	__________

PRACTICE 7

Correct twelve spelling mistakes in the next selection.

EXAMPLE:

The parents reacted ~~angryly~~ *angrily* when they were convicted.

1. In Canada, all provinces have parental responsability statutes. In 2003, the *Youth Criminal Justice Act* replaced the *Young Offenders Act* throughout Canada. Such laws make parents legaly responsible for their children's crimminal acts, which include property damige, loss, or destruction done intentionally.

2. Those who are against such laws argue that holding parents responsible definitly does nothing to stop juvenile delinquints from committing crimes. At a certain age, peer groups become more influential than parents. It is unecessary and unfair to force parents to pay for damages. Such laws are ilogical and simply attempt to fix a problem after the fact, instead of helping the parents deal with the children before any serious crimes occur.

3. Some people, argueing for the laws, say parents must be encouriged to take a more active role in their children's lifes. If parents know that they may be charged for their children's actions, they will likely intervene and try to get their children some help before serious crimes can occurr. Some supporters also argue that taxpayers should not have to pay for vandalism and other damage caused by juveniles.

Spelling Two-Part Words

Some one-word indefinite pronouns sound as if they should be two separate words, but they are not. Here are some examples of one-word indefinite pronouns.

Words with *any*:	anything, anyone, anybody, anywhere
Words with *some*:	something, someone, somebody, somewhere
Words with *every*:	everything, everyone, everybody, everywhere

Spelling *another* and *a lot*

***Another* is always one word:**	Bonnie committed another crime.
***A lot* is always two words:**	She robbed a lot of banks.

PRACTICE 8

Correct ten spelling errors in the next paragraph.

EXAMPLE:

Another
~~An other~~ scandal occurred last year.

Alot of professional athletes have committed criminal acts. Some times the crimes are not serious. For example, in 2005 Derek Dueck, former provincial-level track athlete of Calgary, was fined for smuggling a steroid into Canada. In other instances, such as when Olympic gold-medal swimmer Michael Phelps was charged with driving under the influnce in 2004, the athlete's image can be tarnished. However, some athletes have asaulted, raped, or killed. Ice skater Tonya Harding and her husband hired some body to hit her skatting rival in the knee. Boxer Mike Tyson was accused and eventually convicted of rape, and several professional football payers have been charged with murder. Because television and newspapers present professional athletes as icons, many fans refuse to accept that their heroes have done any thing wrong. Basketball fan Trevor Nixon says, "Any body can make accusations. Unfair attacks on successfull athletes can cause their families much grief." Perhaps the public should accept that athletes are not always heroic.

120 Commonly Misspelled Words

The next list contains some of the most commonly misspelled words in English.

absence
absorption
accommodate
acquaintance
address
aggressive
already
aluminum
analyze
appointment
approximate
argument
athlete
bargain
beginning
behaviour
believable
business
calendar
campaign
careful
ceiling
cemetery
clientele
committee
comparison
competent
conscience
conscientious
convenient
curriculum
definite
definitely
desperate
developed
dilemma
disappoint
embarrass
encouragement
environment
especially
exaggerate
exercise
extraordinarily
familiar
February
finally
foreign
government
grammar
harassment
height
immediately
independent
jewellery
judgment
laboratory
ledge
leisure
license/licence
loneliness
maintenance
mathematics
medicine
millennium
minuscule
mischievous
mortgage
necessary
ninety
noticeable
occasion
occurrence
opposite
outrageous
parallel
performance
perseverance
personality
physically
possess
precious
prejudice
privilege
probably
professor
psychology
questionnaire
receive
recommend
reference
responsible
rhythm
schedule
scientific
separate
sincerely
spaghetti
strength
success
surprise
technique
thorough
tomato
tomatoes
tomorrow
truly
Tuesday
until
usually
vacuum
Wednesday
weird
woman
women
wreckage
writer
writing
written
zealous

Spelling Strategies

Here are some useful strategies to improve your spelling.

- Keep a record of words that you commonly misspell in your spelling log, which could be in a journal or binder. Have a friend read from your list of misspelled words to give you a spelling quiz. See Appendix 7 for more information about spelling logs.
- Use memory cards or flash cards to help you memorize the spelling of difficult words.
- Write down the spelling of difficult words at least ten times to help you remember how to spell them.

PRACTICE 9

Circle the correctly spelled word in each pair.

EXAMPLE:

foreigner/foriegner

1. ceiling/cieling
2. ancient/anceint
3. noticable/noticeable
4. echos/echoes
5. writting/writing
6. accommodate/accomodate
7. definitely/definitly
8. sincerly/sincerely
9. running/runing
10. appealled/appealed
11. comittee/committee
12. embarrassed/embarassed
13. recommend/recommand
14. absence/absense
15. wierd/weird
16. niece/neice
17. personallity/personality
18. exaggerate/exagerate
19. butterflys/butterflies
20. responsible/responsable
21. efficeint/efficient
22. fryed/fried
23. independent/independant
24. appointment/apointment

PRACTICE 10

Correct fifteen spelling mistakes in the next selection.

EXAMPLE:

outrageous
Detectives may never solve some ~~outragous~~ crimes.

1. In 1888, in England, a series of sickening and vicious murders horrifyed London society. A serial killer, known only as Jack the Ripper, attacked women in London's East End with a razor blade. He caught the imagineation of the public.

2. Newspaper articles and editorials on the Ripper's crimes appearred every day, but some of the stories were filled with exagerations. London citizens were extremly afraid of the serial killer, and they wanted to know who was responsable for the crimes. Politicians recommanded that the Ripper be executed for his crimes. As time passed, London police felt embarassed because they could not find the killer.

3. Although there was much speculation at that time, the identity of the Ripper was never discovered. A myth has developped about him, and

today some people are hopefull that the puzzle can be solved. An American crime writer, Patricia Cornwell, has proposed that the well-known British impressionist painter Walter Sickert was the Ripper. In the early 1900s, Sickert made graphic paintings of murdered women, and he had studioes near the crime scenes. In an interview with *ABC News*, Cornwell said, "Some of his paintings, if you juxtapose them with some of the morgue photos, are extraordinarilly chilling." Cornwell has used her own money to verify DNA evidence from a letter supposedly writen by the Ripper. However, her evidence is inconclusive, so the controversy remains.

4. Not everybody beleives Cornwell's theory, and people have offered other explanations about who Jack the Ripper actualy was. Perhaps the case will remain an unsolved mystery.

Using a Spelling Check

The spelling and grammar tool on a computer will highlight most misspelled words and provide suggested corrections. Be aware that a spelling checker's abilities are limited; it cannot verify that you have used commonly confused words accurately. For example, it cannot determine whether you should use *your* or *you're*.

Because a spelling checker is not 100 percent reliable, remember to proofread for spelling errors before you submit your final work.

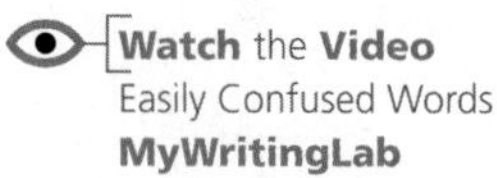

Look-Alike and Sound-Alike Words

Sometimes two English words can sound very much alike but have different spellings and different meanings. For example, two commonly confused words are *defiantly*, which means "to resist or challenge something," and *definitely*, which means "finally" or "decisively." Dictionaries will give you the exact meaning of unfamiliar words. Read the next list to get familiar with many commonly confused words.

Word	Meaning	Example
accept	to receive; to admit	The police sergeant accepted an award for outstanding work.
except	excluding; other than	None of his colleagues, except his wife, knew about the award.
affect	to influence	Writer's block affects a person's ability to write.
effect	the result of something	Writer's block can have bad effects on a person's ability to write.

Word	Meaning	Example
been	past participle of the verb *to be*	Patrick Fitzgerald has been a prosecutor for many years.
being	present progressive form (the *-ing* form) of the verb *to be*	He was being very nice when he signed autographs.
by	preposition meaning *next to*, *on*, or *before*	The defendant sat by her lawyer. By 10 a.m., the jury was getting restless. Everyone hoped the case would be over by the weekend.
buy	to purchase	The lawyer will buy a new car with the client's money.
complement	to add to; to complete	The car will be a nice complement to her other possessions.
compliment	to say something nice about someone	Sudbury's mayor complimented the detectives.
conscience	a personal sense of right or wrong	The robber had no conscience.
conscious	to be aware; to be awake	The robber was conscious of his terrible crime.
disinterested	to be impartial	The trial judge was disinterested, favouring neither side.
uninterested	to lack interest in something	The robber looked uninterested when told of his sentence.
elicit	to get or draw out	The police tried to elicit a confession from the gang member.
illicit	illegal; unlawful	The police found evidence of the gang's illicit activities.
everyday	ordinary; common	Crime is an everyday occurrence.
every day	during a single day; each day	The police watch the gang members every day.
imminent	soon to happen	The police stated that an arrest was imminent.
eminent	distinguished; superior	Patrick Fitzgerald is an eminent prosecutor.
imply	to suggest	The reporter implied that the police need more time to investigate.
infer	to conclude	The police inferred from the clues the gang's whereabouts.
its	possessive case of the pronoun *it*	The judge's desk is large, and its legs are ornate.
it's	contraction for *it is*	It's generally known that he is very good at solving crimes.
knew	past tense of *know*	Fitzgerald knew that the newspaper executive was guilty.
new	recent; unused	He had new evidence to present to the court.
know	to have knowledge of	Many people know about Fitzgerald's work.
no	a negative	The police made no arrests.

(*Continued*)

Word	Meaning	Example
lose	to misplace or forfeit something	The police did not want to lose track of the stolen money.
loose	too big or baggy; not fixed	Detectives sometimes wear loose clothing as part of their disguises.
loss	a decrease in an amount; a serious blow	The company experienced a serious loss when the money was stolen.
peace	calm sensation; a lack of violence	The two rival gangs finally made peace. They felt a sense of peace when hostilities stopped.
piece	a part of something else; one item in a group of items	The thieves ate a piece of cake to celebrate the successful heist.
personal	private	The criminal has a lot of personal problems.
personnel	employees; staff	The police must hire new personnel.
principal	main person; director of a school	The principal detective talked to the principal of our school.
principle	a rule or standard	The police try to follow the principle of law.
quiet	silent	The thieves remained quiet when arrested.
quite	very	The public is becoming quite angry at the increase in crime.
quit	stop	The detective sometimes wants to quit the force.
taught	past tense of *teach*	Drake taught a class on criminology.
thought	past tense of *think*	He thought his students were intelligent.
than	word used in comparisons	Fitzgerald is more determined than other prosecutors.
then	at a particular time; after a specific time	Cornwell investigated the case, and then she wrote about it.
that	word used to introduce a clause	She wrote that Walter Sickert was the Ripper.
their	possessive form of *they*	The police officers went to their favourite restaurant.
there	a place	They went there by police van.
they're	contraction of *they are*	They're both interesting people.
through	in one side and out the other; finished	The police cruiser passed through a tunnel. Then they were through for the day.
threw	past tense of *throw*	Somebody threw a rock at the officer's car.
thorough	complete	They did a thorough investigation of the crime scene.
to	indicates direction or movement; part of an infinitive	I want to go to the film.
too	also; very	The robber was too young to be given a prison sentence. Her friend was, too.
two	the number after one	There were two witnesses to the holdup.

Word	Meaning	Example
where	question word indicating location	The police knew where the diamonds were hidden.
were	past tense of *be*	The diamonds were in a safe place.
we're	contraction of *we are*	We're going to meet the detectives.
write	to draw symbols that represent words	Patricia Cornwell will write about the crime.
right	correct; the opposite of the direction left	The police knew that they had arrested the right criminal. They found the diamonds in her right pocket.
who's	contraction of *who is*	The police sergeant, who's very well known, spoke to reporters.
whose	pronoun showing ownership	Criminals, whose crimes hurt society, must be punished.

PRACTICE 11

Circle the correct word in each sentence.

1. Many people (buy, by) mystery novels.
2. Successful writers of detective fiction receive many (complements, compliments) for their ingenious plots.
3. Edgar Allan Poe and Herman Melville are (excepted, accepted) as being the first American mystery writers.
4. Arthur Conan Doyle and Agatha Christie are two (eminent, imminent) British mystery writers.
5. The (principal, principle) characters in their works are Sherlock Holmes and Hercule Poirot, both of whom are detectives.
6. To solve the mystery, both Holmes and Poirot try to (elicit, illicit) clues by talking to various characters.
7. The public has also (thought, taught) highly of other mystery writers such as Erle Stanley Gardner and Maureen Jennings.
8. Many students were (quite, quiet) when Andrew Pyper started to give his lecture about detective fiction.

PRACTICE 12

Correct twenty-five errors in the following passages. Look for the commonly confused words that are indicated in parentheses.

EXAMPLE:

too
He is ~~to~~ busy these days.

1. (*to, too, two*)

Hollywood has been the centre of many famous crimes. In 1995, the O. J. Simpson criminal trial kept Americans glued too their televisions.

Simpson was accused of killing to people. Nicole Simpson was killed, and her friend Ronald Goldman was killed, to. Some analysts believe that there was to much media coverage during the trial. The police tried to find clues too solve the murder. On October 3, 1995, Simpson was declared not guilty, although he was later convicted in a civil trial.

2. (*then, than, that*)

Another celebrity accused of murder was record producer Phil Spector, a man who produced the Beatles, the Ramones, and others. In recent years, Spector has become more eccentric and reclusive then he was in the past. In 2007, prosecutors stated than Spector murdered a guest in his home. Apparently, Lana Clarkson, a night-club hostess and actress, was visiting Spector on the night of February 3. Spector claimed than she played with his gun, and than she committed suicide. However, immediately after her death, Spector told the police than he had just killed someone. His lawyers stated than his admission of guilt was not valid because Spector had been suffering from prescription drug withdrawal, and the producer was less lucid then he should have been. The case was more highly publicized then most murder cases. On September 26, 2007, the trial ended in a hung jury.

3. (*threw, through, thorough*)

Winona Ryder, another famous Hollywood actor, was accused of shoplifting in 2002. Store detectives claimed that Ryder passed threw the store taking items and then left threw the front doors when she was finished shopping. Store detectives intercepted Ryder as she was leaving and did a through search of her bags. They then charged her with theft of merchandise worth $4800. In court, the judge threw out some evidence, but he accepted testimony from the store detectives. When the trial was threw, the jury found Ryder guilty, but she did not have to spend time in prison.

4. (*it's, its*)

The preceding three celebrities have received a lot of attention from the media and it's readership. Many people think that its wrong for celebrities to profit from crimes they have been accused of doing. Other people think that its fair if celebrities profit in the long term.

5. (*who's, whose*)

People of all ages idolize celebrities who have committed crimes. However, the public should remember that celebrities who commit crimes are criminals. A person whose famous should not behave criminally. Celebrities who's profession puts them in the public spotlight should be aware of the influence they have, especially on young people.

6. (*their, there, they're*)

However, supporters of celebrities who have committed crimes say that although celebrities lead public lives, there human. They should not be punished for the rest of there lives for making a mistake. Their is much debate about this issue.

REFLECT ON IT

Think about what you have learned in this chapter. If you do not know an answer, review that topic.

1. a. In a word containing *ie* or *ei*, when does *i* come before *e*?

   ____

   b. When does e come before *i*?

   ____

2. Circle the correctly spelled words. Correct each misspelled word.

   realy finally unatural illogical plentifull

3. Write down three pairs of words that you commonly confuse.

   ______________ ______________

   ______________ ______________

   ______________ ______________

4. Correct eight mistakes in the next passage.

   Crimes are quiet a common occurrence in my nieghbourhood. The police are planing to increase there surveillance in this area. The public, to, can help. Its important to report any unnusual events. Eventualy, such actions will help lower the crime rate.

FINAL REVIEW

Underline and correct twenty spelling errors and mistakes with commonly confused words in the essay.

EXAMPLE:

applied
Sometimes, laws are unfairly <u>applyed</u>.

1. The Native Women's Association of Canada is concerned about how Aboriginal women are treated in the Canadian judicial system. In a 2007 paper presented at the National Aboriginal Women's Summit in Corner Brook, key problems and reccommendations were proposed.

2. Accordding to the paper, one of the issues facing Aborignal women is with the public preception and treatment of them when they are engaged with all levels of the law, from police and lawyers to the court system. Another problem includes the high incidances of both incarceration and victimization in the courts. There is "an alarmingly high level of Aboriginal women who are missing and/or murdered," the paper states. As well, the percentage of women versus men in Canadian federal prisons is much higher.

3. The authors site reasons for why many Aboriginal women reperesent such a high poportion of those who negativly encounter the legal system. They are often "poor, single parents, first-time offenders, have been victims of prior abuse and experience high rates of mental illness including depression and substance abuse problems." Other causes include "systemic barriers such as lack of knowledge of the system, cultural and language gaps and lack of council representation."

4. Restorative justice or a healing circle for those offencses not as severe as sexual assault or murder would beneffit those involved in criminal activity. Generally, this is a more wholistic approach to crime prevention and rehabilitation since the offenders are provided with the support of elders and the community—and even the victim if he or she agrees to it.

Counselling, community servise, and special healing traditions could assist the offenders as well and would be the bassis of Aboriginal justice.

5. Change in Canada's current juditial system is needed so that Aboriginal women are not percieved in such a neggative manner. The association suggests that if more Aboriginal people were involved in the process, the results would bennefit all.

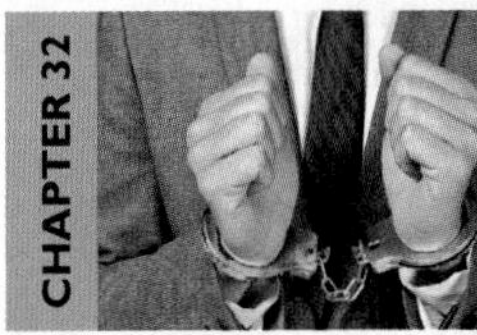

The Writer's Room

Choose one of the following topics, and write a paragraph or an essay. Remember to follow the writing process.

1. Compare and contrast graffiti with another type of art.
2. Do you believe that the holistic justice approach is fair and effective?
3. Should juveniles who commit serious crimes be treated as harshly as adults?
4. What are some steps that parents can take to prevent their children from breaking laws or becoming criminals?

The Writers' Circle Collaborative Activity

Work with a partner or a small group of students, and compose a paragraph about the qualities of a good comic book hero. In your paragraph, tell a story about a heroic action that the superhero does. Use slang words and clichés in your paragraph. Make sure that your paragraph is double-spaced, and make sure that the writing is clear.

When you have finished your paragraph, exchange sheets with another team of students. Edit the other team's paragraph, and imagine that the audience is a college instructor. Change all clichés and slang expressions into standard Canadian English.

READING LINK

The Legal World

"What Adolescents Miss When We Let Them Grown Up in Cybersapce" by Brent Staples (page 581)

"Is Anything Private Anymore?" by Sean Flynn (page 584)

How Do I Get a Better Grade?

Visit MyWritingLab for audiovisual lectures and additional practice sets about spelling and commonly confused words.

Commas

Section Theme **THE WORKPLACE**

LEARNING OBJECTIVES

ZUMA Press, Inc. / Alamy

In this chapter, you will read about **business etiquette and wise business decisions.**

The Writer's Journal

Have you ever thought about having your own business? What type of business would you like to have? Write a paragraph about owning a business.

Watch the **Video**
Commas
MyWritingLab

What Is a Comma?

A **comma** (,) is a punctuation mark that helps keep distinct ideas separate. There are many ways to use a comma. In this chapter, you will learn some helpful rules about comma usage.

Notice how comma placement changes the meaning of the following sentences.

The dog bites, the cat laughs, and then she has a nap.

The dog bites the cat, laughs, and then she has a nap.

Commas in a Series

Use a comma to separate items in a series of three or more items. Remember to put a comma before the final *and* or *or*.

unit 1	,	unit 2	,	and or	unit 3

Toronto, Vancouver, and Edmonton have many employment opportunities.

The job search requires courage, perseverance, and energy.

You can network, contact employers directly, or use a placement service.

Punctuating a Series

In a series of three or more items, do not place a comma after the last item in the series (unless the series is part of an interrupting phrase).

Incorrect: Her poise, simplicity, and kindness, impressed us.

Correct: Her poise, simplicity, and kindness impressed us.

Do not use commas to separate items if each item is joined by *and* or *or.*

It is not possible to study and listen to music and have a conversation at the same time.

PRACTICE 1

Underline series of items in the next selection. Then add eighteen missing commas where necessary.

EXAMPLE:

Some individuals, small-business owners, and home-based workers design and print their own business cards.

1. Many small companies do not have the money to advertise, so their only means of promoting their product is to hand out cards to friends neighbours and strangers who might be interested in the business. The type of card that people carry depends on the type of business that they have. Photographers pastry chefs artists and musicians often have colours and images on their cards. Doctors lawyers and accountants tend to use a simple black-and-white design printed on good-quality paper.

2. Your business card should transmit more than just your name position telephone number and address. According to consultant Frank Yeoman,

people are attracted to cards that have clear simple and direct messages. At the same time, a business card should stand out in some way, so it is a good idea to think about the colour texture and design of the card. The card should be eye-catching.

3. Yeoman says that you should never put your photo on your business cards unless you are a model or an actor. As trends change, you may be embarrassed to have hundreds of business cards depicting you with an unfashionable hairstyle outdated glasses and an unattractive shirt. You get only one chance to make an impression on new customers, so it is important to put some time effort and planning into your business card design.

Commas after Introductory Words and Phrases

Use a comma after an **introductory word.** The introductory word could be an interjection such as *yes*, *no*, or *well*; it could be an adverb such as *usually* or *generally*; or it could be a transitional word such as *however* or *therefore*.

Introductory word(s)	,	sentence.

Yes, I will help you complete the order.

Frankly, you should reconsider your customer service promise.

However, the job includes a lot of overtime.

Use a comma to set off **introductory phrases** of two or more words. The phrase could be a transitional expression such as *of course* or *on the contrary*, or it could be a prepositional phrase such as *on a warm summer evening*. The introductory phrase could also be a modifier such as *running out of fuel* or *born in France*.

On the other hand, his career was not going well.

In the middle of the meeting, I received a phone call.

Speaking to the crowd, the manager explained the stock's performance.

PRACTICE 2

Underline each introductory word or phrase. Then add ten missing commas.

EXAMPLE:

In today's job market, people must remain flexible.

1. For the first time in history workers can expect to outlive the organizations that they work for. For example many high-tech companies came and went during the stock market boom of the late 1990s. Additionally many businesses go bankrupt each year.

2. Furthermore those working in successful companies may see their jobs become obsolete. In fact the majority of the nation's bank tellers were laid off in the 1990s. As a result many people in the banking industry have had to retrain or change jobs.

3. According to Myriam Goldman the average person should plan for three different careers. Of course some people love their jobs and have no desire to look elsewhere. However even those in secure jobs may get bored and long for a career change down the road. Working in a volatile job market workers should remain open and flexible.

Commas around Interrupting Words and Phrases

Interrupting words or phrases appear in the middle of sentences. Such interrupters are often asides that interrupt the sentence's flow but do not affect its overall meaning. Some interrupters are *by the way*, *as a matter of fact*, and *for example*. Prepositional phrases can also interrupt sentences.

My sister, for example, has never invested in stocks.

The market, by the way, has been down recently.

Mrs. Jayson, frankly, never acknowledges her employees.

My manager, in the middle of a busy day, decided to go to a movie!

Using Commas with Appositives

An appositive gives further information about a noun or pronoun. The appositive can appear at the beginning, in the middle, or at the end of the sentence. Set off appositives with commas.

beginning
A large city in Ontario, Toronto has a variety of public learning centres.

middle
Dr. Anex, a senior surgeon, recommends the transplant.

end
The office is next to Graham's, a local eatery.

PRACTICE 3

The next sentences contain introductory words and phrases, interrupters, and series of items. Add the missing commas. If the sentence is correct, write *C* in the space provided.

EXAMPLE:

Email, voice mail, and cellphones are changing the way that people do business. _____

1. Jamaal Khabbaz a marketing manager, complains about high-tech gadgets in the workplace such as pagers, cellphones and personal organizers. _____
2. Many workers in his opinion break rules of basic etiquette. _____
3. He gets annoyed, for example when a lunch meeting is interrupted by a ringing cellphone. _____
4. Unfortunately, many people do not consider it rude to answer a call in the middle of a meal. _____
5. According to Kabbaz the workplace needs new business etiquette rules. _____
6. Electronic mail, a convenient way to send and receive messages is not private. _____
7. Without a doubt, it is offensive to read other people's mail. _____
8. Some people, however have no qualms about standing next to a computer and reading over the shoulder of an email recipient. _____
9. Email junkies, those addicted to electronic messages cause the most problems. _____
10. In the middle of a busy day the email addict sends cartoons, videos and messages to co-workers. _____
11. Most shocking of all, some employees download offensive films and send them to others. _____

12. One company, a producer of electronic surveillance equipment fired six employees for sending pornographic emails to each other. ______

Commas in Compound Sentences

A **compound sentence** contains two or more complete sentences joined by a coordinating conjunction (*for*, *and*, *nor*, *but*, *or*, *yet*, *so*).

Watch the **Video**
Combining Sentences
MyWritingLab

Sentence , and sentence.

I want a job, **so** I will look in the classified ads.

Some interesting companies are nearby, **and** maybe they are hiring.

I will work in an office, **but** I do not want to work from nine to five.

PRACTICE 4

Add six commas that are missing from this letter.

EXAMPLE:

I am punctual, and I am hardworking.

Dear Ms. Graham:

I saw an ad in the *Edmonton Journal* stating that you need a junior accountant. I am interested in the job so I have enclosed a resumé highlighting my skills in this field. I have an aptitude for computers and I am able to solve problems in creative ways.

I have taken several courses in accounting at Grant MacEwan College but I have not completed the program. I am comfortable with spreadsheets and I have worked with income tax preparation programs.

I am available for an interview at any time so please do not hesitate to contact me. Thank you for your consideration and I look forward to hearing from you.

Yours sincerely,

Marcus Fisher

Marcus Fisher

Commas in Complex Sentences

Watch the **Video**
Combining Sentences
MyWritingLab

A **complex sentence** contains one or more dependent clauses (or incomplete ideas). When you add a **subordinating conjunction**—a word such as *because*, *although*, or *unless*—to a clause, you make the clause dependent.

dependent clause — independent clause

When the stock market opened, he sold his shares.

Use a Comma after a Dependent Clause

If a sentence begins with a dependent clause, place a comma after the clause. Remember that a dependent clause has a subject and a verb, but it cannot stand alone. When the subordinating conjunction comes in the middle of the sentence, it is not necessary to use a comma.

	Dependent clause , main clause.
Comma:	After the meeting ends, we will go to lunch.
	Main clause dependent clause.
No comma:	We will go to lunch after the meeting ends.

Use Commas to Set Off Nonrestrictive Clauses

Clauses beginning with *who*, *that*, and *which* can be restrictive or nonrestrictive. A **restrictive clause** contains essential information about the subject. Do not place commas around restrictive clauses.

No commas: The only local company that does computer graphics has no job openings.

(The underlined clause is essential to understand the meaning of the sentence.)

A **nonrestrictive clause** gives nonessential information. In such sentences, the clause gives additional information about the noun but does not restrict or define the noun. Place commas around nonrestrictive clauses.

Commas: Her book, which is in bookstores, is about successful entrepreneurs.

(The underlined clause contains extra information, but if you removed that clause, the sentence would still have a clear meaning.)

Which, That, Who

which

Use commas to set off clauses that begin with *which*.

Groupaction Marketing, **which** was founded in 1982, creates advertising products.

that

Do not use commas to set off clauses beginning with *that*.

The company **that** was at the centre of the federal sponsorship scandal creates advertising products.

who

When a clause begins with *who*, you may or may not need a comma. If the clause contains nonessential information, put commas around it. If the clause is essential to the meaning of the sentence, it does not require commas.

Essential:	People **who** trust their government believe that their best interests are in mind.
Not essential:	Former company head, Jean Brault, **who** was at the centre of the Liberal sponsorship scandal, was sent to prison.

PRACTICE 5

Edit the following practice by adding sixteen missing commas.

EXAMPLE:

Many charitable foundations have donated money, time, and expertise to alleviate inequality.

1. The Stephen Lewis Foundation which began in 2003 is one of Canada's largest charities. Stephen Lewis established the foundation to help reduce the pain and anguish of the catastrophic widespread HIV/AIDS in sub-Saharan Africa. In its first six years the organization raised more than $28 million. Its mandate is to work primarily on several grassroots community projects to assist women with basic needs to supply medicine and to provide counselling care for the sick and dying. The foundation also provides orphans with basic needs schooling and grief counselling. Men women and children are educated on the disease to create awareness, provide treatment and offer prevention strategies associated with HIV/AIDS. The foundation's Grandmothers Campaign offers shelter nutrition financial help and grief support to these main caregivers as they are often in charge of households of ten to fifteen individuals many of whom are sick or dying.

2. A foundation, which is not strictly a business must function like a business to amass enough money to continue its charitable work. Even though a foundation cannot pay its directors it must pay its employees, researchers, and suppliers. Therefore, income that a charitable foundation generates must offset such expenses. Unlike many other charities, the Stephen Lewis Foundation has maintained low (less than 10 percent) operational costs.

Commas in Business Letters

When you write or type a formal letter, ensure that you use commas correctly in the following parts of the letter.

Addresses

In the address at the top of the letter, insert a comma between the following elements.

- The street name and apartment number
- The city and province or country

Do not put a comma before the postal code.

Dr. Brent Patterson

312 Appleby Road, Suite 112

Truro, NS B1A 2Z1

If you include an address inside a complete sentence, use commas to separate the street address from the city and the city from the province or country. If you just write the street address, do not put a comma after it.

Commas: The building at 130 King Street West, Toronto, contains the Stock Exchange.

No comma: The building at 130 King Street West contains the Toronto Stock Exchange.

Dates

In the date at the top of the letter, add a comma between the full date and the year. If you just write the month and the year, then no comma is necessary.

May 21, 2014 January 2014

If you include a date inside a complete sentence, separate the elements of the date with commas.

We visited Halifax on Monday, July 26, 2014.

Writing Numbers

In letters, it is not necessary to write ordinal numbers such as *first* (1st), *second* (2nd), *third* (3rd), or *fourth* (4th). Instead, just write the number: 1, 2, 3, 4, and so on.

February 24, 2015 October 11, 2015

Salutations

Salutations are formal letter greetings. The form "To Whom It May Concern" is no longer used regularly by North American businesses. The best way to address someone is to use his or her name followed by a comma or a colon. The colon is preferred in business letters.

Dear Ms. Lewin: Dear Sir or Madam: Dear Mom,

Complimentary Closings

Place a comma after the complimentary closing. Notice that the first word of the closing is capitalized.

Respectfully,   Yours sincerely,   Many thanks,

Sample Letter of Application

You send a sample letter of application to an employer when you apply for a job. Review the parts of the following letter.

Seamus O'Brien
10 Siksika Boulevard
Edmonton, AB T5A OJ1
(780) 234-5678 ← *Sender's address (name, phone, and possibly an email address)*

September 12, 2014 ← *Date*

Avant Garde Computers
Adelaide and Sinclair Corporation
6116 Greenway Avenue
Edmonton, AB T35 1X3 ← *Recipient's address*

Subject: Position of junior programmer ← *Subject line*

Dear Ms. Roebok: ← *Salutation*

I saw an ad in Saturday's Edmonton Journal stating that you need a junior programmer. I have enclosed a resumé highlighting my skills in this field. I have an aptitude for computers, and, when I was fourteen years old, I created my first game program.

I have just finished a diploma program in computer programming at Grant MacEwan College. I took courses in several computer languages. I have also completed a six-week training program, and I have enclosed a letter of reference from the owner of that company.

If you require further information, please contact me. I am available for an interview at any time and could start work immediately. Thank you for your consideration.

Sincerely, ← *Closing (After the closing, put your handwritten signature followed by your typed name.)*

S. O'Brien

Seamus O'Brien

Enclosures: resumé
letter of reference

CHAPTER 33

PRACTICE 6

The next letter contains ten errors. Add five missing commas and remove five unnecessary commas.

Red River Publications
1440 Cliff Street
Vancouver BC V4A 3W9

April 2 2014

Graham Britt
214 Regents Road,
Victoria, BC, V8N 2S7

Dear Mr. Britt:

On Monday March 12 we received your manuscript. We are pleased to inform you that your article will be published in the May, issue, of *Red River*.

Could you please meet with me at our branch office? I will be at 44 Hillside Road, during the last week of the month. You can stop by the office at any time during that week. We are looking forward to meeting with you.

Yours truly

Lydia Halburton

Lydia Halburton

REFLECT ON IT

Think about what you have learned in this chapter. If you do not know an answer, review that topic.

1. Explain the rules of comma usage in the following situations.

   a. Series of items: ______________________________

   ____

   b. Introductory words or phrases: ______________________________

   ____

   c. Interrupting phrases: ______________________________

   ____

   d. Compound sentences: ______________________________

   ____

2. What is a nonrestrictive clause? ______________________________
____
3. Should you place commas around nonrestrictive clauses? ______ Yes ______ No
4. Write a sentence that contains a nonrestrictive clause.
____
____
5. Write three common closings for a business letter.
____
____

Final Review

Edit the next essay by adding seventeen missing commas and removing three unnecessary commas.

EXAMPLE:

Entertainers, including comedians, actors, and musicians, should consult with a financial advisor.

1. Horace Madison co-founder of Madison Smallwood Financial Group, manages the careers of top urban rappers, hip-hop artists and blues musicians. Madison grew up in Harlem and he had a middle-class childhood. He heard about many high-profile artists and musicians M. C. Hammer, for example, who ended up going broke. When he began to work on Wall Street, he decided to focus on entertainers, who were at risk of mismanaging their funds.

2. Madison handles every aspect of his clients' lives. He helps them pay their bills, collect their revenue and plan their investment portfolios. According to Madison, some of his new artists desperately want to buy expensive jewellery or cars. In many cases they have just signed a million-dollar record deal. The artists, explains Madison do not always realize that they owe the record label for some of the money spent on music videos, marketing and travel. In fact, some artists can sell a million records and still end up owing money to the company. Furthermore new artists face

pressure from family and friends. When their friends see the artist in a music video they call up the artist asking for a handout or a job.

3. Madison helps artists set up a budget and he carefully monitors what his clients spend. If a client wants to waste an outrageous amount on a frivolous luxury item Madison forces the client to sign a "stupid letter." He wants his clients to understand, that they are making a stupid financial move so the letter states that such spending is against the advice of Madison's firm. In an interview with Mitchell Raphael a journalist with the *National Post* newspaper, Madison told an anecdote. He said that a client wanted to rent a Ferrari for $1000 a day. Madison without a pause, asked the client to sign the stupid letter. The client, a rapper rethought his plans and decided to rent a different car for $300 a day.

4. Ultimately, excessive spending is not smart. Hip-hop artists must think about their long-term future, because they have a career span of only three or four years. Madison and Smallwood Financial Group have helped a variety of artists manage the minefield of fame. In fact, Eve, a hip-hop artist has thanked Madison for helping her spend her money wisely.

The Writer's Room

Write about one of the following topics. Verify that your comma usage is correct.

1. Are you a good money manager? Describe how you handle your finances.
2. Categorize spenders into different types. Give examples for each type.

How Do I Get a Better Grade?

Visit MyWritingLab for audiovisual lectures and additional practice sets about commas.

The Apostrophe, Quotation Marks, and Titles

Section Theme **THE WORKPLACE**

LEARNING OBJECTIVES

DenisNata/Fotolia

In this chapter, you will read about topics related to **success stories** *and* **controversies.**

The Writer's Journal

Would you like to own your own business? If so, what type would you like to own? Describe your dream business.

The Apostrophe (')

An **apostrophe** is a punctuation mark showing a contraction or ownership.

ownership / contraction

Daymond **John's** business is very successful, and **it's** still growing.

Using Apostrophes in Contractions

To form a **contraction,** join two words into one and add an apostrophe to replace the omitted letter(s).

Apostrophe replaces *o*	is + not = isn't
Apostrophe replaces *a*	I + am = I'm

Common Contractions

The following are examples of the most common contractions.

- **Join a verb with *not*.** The apostrophe replaces the letter *o* in *not*.

is + not = isn't	has + not = hasn't
are + not = aren't	have + not = haven't
could + not = couldn't	should + not = shouldn't
do + not = don't	would + not = wouldn't
does + not = doesn't	

Exceptions: will + not = won't, can + not = can't

- **Join a subject and a verb.** Sometimes you must remove several letters to form the contraction.

I + will = I'll	she + will = she'll
I + would = I'd	Tina + is = Tina's
he + is = he's	they + are = they're
he + will = he'll	we + will = we'll
Joe + is = Joe's	who + is = who's
she + has = she's	who + would = who'd

Exception: Do not contract a subject with the past tense of *be*. For example, do not contract *he* + *was* or *they* + *were*.

Contractions with Two Meanings

Sometimes one contraction can have two different meanings.

I'd = I had or I would   **he's** = he is or he has

When you read, you should be able to figure out the meaning of the contraction by looking at the words in context.

She's hiring new personnel. (She is)   **She's** seen several interesting candidates. (She has)

PRACTICE 1

Add nine missing apostrophes to the next selection.

EXAMPLE:

Starting a business ~~isnt~~ *isn't* a simple process.

1. Back in 1998, Chip Wilson created his own yoga clothing line after attending a yoga class in Vancouver. When he went to the yoga session,

he noted that the clothing worn for yoga sessions was too bulky and uncomfortable for stretching. Wilson realized that a lighter fabric wouldve suited yoga enthusiasts more, so he began to create and sell fabrics and run a yoga studio, where he sought feedback from his clientele. After the underground clothing business escalated in Kitsilano, a beach area of Vancouver, Wilson created the name Lululemon Athletica, based on a survey. The logo didnt go with the word; rather, its derived from a rejected name for the business: athletically hip.

2. Wilsons business thrived on the promotion of fitness and a healthy lifestyle, but the business owner didnt realize that educating staff and customers would take so much time and energy. Hes constantly aware of whats working and whats not by ensuring that senior managers visit retail stores weekly.

3. Lululemon has expanded now to include spas and wellness centres along with pilates and yoga studios. With the focus on wellness and product improvement, the company continues to thrive—even if the owner isnt worried or focused on the competition.

PRACTICE 2

Look at each underlined contraction, and then write out the complete word.

EXAMPLE:

They weren't ready to start a business. *were not*

1. Carol Simon's very happy with her bridal gown company. ________
2. She's been an entrepreneur for seven years. ________
3. She's an extremely friendly, ambitious woman. ________
4. I wish I'd had the same idea as Carol. ________
5. I'd like to have my own company, too. ________

Using Apostrophes to Show Ownership

You can also use apostrophes to show ownership. Review the next rules.

Possessive Form of Singular Nouns

Add *-'s* to a singular noun to indicate ownership, even if the noun ends in *s*.

Chip's interest in healthy living is the basis of his company.

Somebody's house became a factory.

Dylan's dad has his own business.

Possessive Form of Plural Nouns

When a plural noun ends in *s*, just add an apostrophe to indicate ownership. Add *-'s* to irregular plural nouns.

Many **companies'** websites are down.

The four **friends'** business is very successful.

The **children's** clothing company is expanding.

Possessive Form of Compound Nouns

When two people have joint ownership, add *-'s* to the second name. When two people have separate ownership, add *-'s* to both names.

Joint ownership: Skye and **Jason's** company is successful.

Separate ownership: **Skye's** and **Jason's** offices are in separate buildings.

PRACTICE 3

Write the singular and plural possessive forms.

EXAMPLE:

	Singular Possessive	Plural Possessive
Mr. Cohen	*Mr. Cohen's*	*the Cohens'*
1. client		
2. boss		
3. secretary		
4. Mr. Ness		
5. woman		
6. salesperson		

PRACTICE 4

Write the possessive forms of the following phrases.

EXAMPLE:

the sister of the doctor _*the doctor's sister*_

1. the locker of the employee ______
2. the supplies of the employees ______
3. the profits of the company ______
4. the directors of the companies ______

5. the house of Jan and Ted ______________________

6. the car of Omar and the car of Roy ______________________

CHAPTER 34

Using Apostrophes in Expressions of Time

When an expression of time (*day*, *week*, *month*, *year*) appears to possess something, use the possessive form of that word.

Singular: The customer won a **year's** supply of paper.

Plural: Mike Roy gave two **weeks'** notice before he left the company.

When writing the numerals of a decade or century, do not put an apostrophe before the final *-s*.

In the **1800s,** many immigrants arrived at Grosse Isle, Quebec.

Many Internet companies failed in the **1990s.**

Common Apostrophe Errors

Do not use apostrophes before the final s of a verb.

Simon ~~want's~~ *wants* to open a franchise.

Do not confuse contractions with possessive pronouns that have a similar sound. For example, the contraction *you're* sounds like the pronoun *your.* Remember that possessive pronouns never have apostrophes.

The company is growing. ~~It's~~ *Its* slogan is catchy.

That is my idea. It is not ~~their's.~~ *theirs.*

PRACTICE 5

Correct fifteen errors with apostrophes and possessive pronouns.

EXAMPLE:

If you ~~arent~~ *aren't* willing to work hard, ~~do'nt~~ *don't* start your own business.

1. If your thinking of starting a business, you should plan carefully. Spend a few year's learning about the business before your invest your life savings. In an interview with *The Record* in 2007, Lululemons chief executive, Christine Day, said that the company was planning to open fifteen stores the following year, even though they assumed they couldve opened thirty-five annually. She thought that their new pre-teen's clothing line would fill the markets needs, but she didnt see the venture as creating a mini-Lululemon.

2. Dennis "Chip" Wilson, founder of Lululemon, demonstrates that hes forward-thinking and a keen business person. The businesses success comes from foresight and close monitoring. In the companys past, though, they were criticized for claiming to promote seaweeds healthful benefits in their garments. The VitaSea line was tested to see if the products assets were indeed valid, but Canadas Competition Bureau returned negative results. The bureau stressed that Lululemon shouldnt have misrepresented its self, and the company complied. In an article by the Canadian Press, "the regulatory agency said the Vancouver-based yoga wear retailer has agreed to immediately remove all tags and other product notices that contain 'unsubstantiated' claims of therapeutic or performance benefits from its seaweed line of clothing in its nearly 40 retail stores across Canada."

Watch the Video
Quotation Marks
MyWritingLab

Quotation Marks (" ")

Use **quotation marks** to set off the exact words of a speaker or writer. If the quotation is a complete sentence, there are some standard ways that it should be punctuated.

- Capitalize the first word of the quotation.
- Place quotation marks around the complete quotation.
- Place the end punctuation inside the closing quotation marks.

... declared , "Complete sentence."

Here is an example of a sentence with a quotation.

> Poet William Butler Yeats declared, "Education is not the filling of a pail but the lighting of a fire."

Generally, when using quotations, attach the name of the speaker or writer to the quotation in some way. Review the following rules.

Introductory Phrase

Place a comma after a phrase introducing a quotation.

... says , "________________."

> David Suzuki states, "Our personal consumer choices have ecological, social, and spiritual consequences. It is time to re-examine some of our deeply held notions that underlie our lifestyles."

Interrupting Phrase

When a quotation is interrupted, do the following:

- Place a comma after the first part of the quotation.
- Place a comma after the interrupting phrase.

"_______________," ... says, "_______________."

"Just leap," Gordon Pinsent said, "because it's going to mean you are extending your possibilities from a standpoint of unlived experiences."

Ending Phrase

When you place a phrase at the end of a quotation, end the quotation with a comma instead of a period.

"_______________," says _______________.

"You're fired," said Donald Trump.

If your quotation ends with other punctuation, put it before the final quotation mark.

"_______________?" says _______________.

"You can't fire me!" she shouted.

"Why can't I fire you?" he asked.

Introductory Sentence

You can introduce a quotation with a complete sentence. Simply place a colon (:) after the introductory sentence.

She explains her views: "__________."

Susan Ward explains why small businesses fail: "People who start small businesses don't do the market research to find out if there's any genuine market for their product and/or services."

Inside a Quotation

If one quotation is inside another quotation, use single quotation marks (' ') around the inside quotation.

"Main quotation, 'Inside quotation.'"

According to Shannon Dowell, "Good parents always say, 'Clean up your own mess.'"

When the Quotation Is an Incomplete Sentence

If the quotation is not a complete sentence and you simply integrate it into your sentence, do not capitalize the first word of the quotation.

Olympic medalist Nancy Green once said that skiers "need intelligence to ski."

PRACTICE 6

In each sentence, the quotation is in bold. Add quotation marks and commas or colons. Also capitalize the first word of the quotation if necessary.

EXAMPLE:

Novelist Yann Martel explains his writing :"I ~~i~~ **trust my sense of the big picture, the overall design of what I'm working on, but the nuts and bolts of writing, the setting of sentences onto the page, is a struggle for me."**

1. According to Canadian astronaut Julie Payette **success is a mixture of skills, competence, luck and hard work: with a bit of effort, I believe the world can be at our feet.**
2. Canadian artist Emily Carr believed that you should create from your heart **that you do not write or paint anything that is not your own, that you don't know in your own soul.**
3. Fred Delaney proclaimed **a celebrity is a person who works hard all his life to become well known, and then wears dark glasses to avoid being recognized.**
4. **In the future, a wall could become a computer screen** according to journalist Kate McNamara.
5. Actor and comedian Jim Carrey believes that **you create your own universe.**
6. Diana Krall describes her profession as a musician **so much of what we do as artists is a combination of personal experience and imagination, and how that all creeps into your work is not so linear.**
7. **There's no life without humour. It can make the wonderful moments of life truly glorious, and it can make tragic moments bearable** observed singer and songwriter Rufus Wainwright.
8. **I'm never sure what's coming next** declared actress and director Sarah Polley **but I'm an open-minded person and I welcome any challenge.**

9. Canadian composer and jazz pianist Oscar Peterson once said **you not only have to know your own instrument, you must know the others and how to back them up at all times. That's jazz.**

10. Endocrinologist Hans Selye asserted **adopting the right attitude can convert a negative stress into a positive one.**

11. **We are looking to brands for poetry and for spirituality, because we're not getting those things from our communities or from each other** states author and social activist Naomi Klein.

12. **You have to dream dreams to live dreams** said former NHL player Eric Lindros.

Punctuation of Titles

Watch the **Video** Essay Introductions, Conclusions and Titles: Titles **MyWritingLab**

When using a title within a sentence, place quotation marks around the title of a short work, and underline or italicize the title of a longer work. Here are some guidelines for both.

Short Works	Long Works
Short story: "The Mask of the Bear"	**Novel:** *The Diviners*
Web article: "Arctic Sailor Sees Melting Sea Ice Firsthand"	**Website:** *CBCnews.ca*
Chapter: Chapter 1, "Mass Media"	**Book:** *Exploring Sociology: A Canadian Perspective*
Newspaper article: "Bad Habits Take a Decade Off Life: Study"	**Newspaper:** *The Vancouver Sun*
Essay: "Causes of the Rebellion in Lower Canada"	**Textbook:** *History of the Canadian Peoples*
TV episode: "Pizza and Promises"	**TV series:** *Due South*
Song: "New Ancients"	**CD:** *Mianca*
Poem: "The Permanent Tourists"	**Anthology:** *15 Canadian Poets X2*
	Movie: *The Five Senses*

Capitalizing Titles

Watch the **Video** Capitalization **MyWritingLab**

When you write a title, capitalize the first letter of the first and last words and all the major words.

The Catcher in the Rye *War and Peace* "Stairway to Heaven"

Do not capitalize .com in a Web address. Also do not capitalize the following words except as the first or last word in a title.

Articles: a, an, the

Coordinators: for, and, nor, but, or, yet, so

Prepositions: by, in, of, off, out, to, up …

Your Own Essay Titles

When writing the title of your own essay, do not put quotation marks around the title. However, you should capitalize key terms.

A Cultural Icon Is Born

PRACTICE 7

A. Add twenty missing capital letters to the titles in the next paragraph.

EXAMPLE:

C B

The magazine *canadian business* featured successful female entrepreneurs.

1. In recent years, some ambitious, multitalented women have become incredibly successful in different fields. Madonna, for example, has released about ten CDs, including one called *american life.* Her popular songs include "hollywood" and "like a prayer." She has written children's books, such as *the english roses.* She has also appeared in many movies, including *desperately seeking susan* and *swept away.* Critics have not always been kind to the Michigan native. In his article "no madonna is an island," *new york times* film critic A. O. Scott called Madonna a poor actress.

B. Underline or add quotation marks to the eight titles in the next paragraph.

EXAMPLE:

In 2005, the magazine <u>Ebony</u> featured an interesting article about Queen Latifah.

Allstar Picture Library / Alamy

Queen Latifah

2. Queen Latifah is a versatile performer. She is a rapper, model, and actress. In 1988, Queen Latifah got her big break with the song Princess of the Posse, which became a hit single on her album All Hail the Queen. She received a Grammy for another hit, U.N.I.T.Y. from the CD Black Reign. In the 1990s, Queen Latifah continued experimenting with her musical style, and she also ventured into acting. From 1993 to 1998, she had a role in a sitcom, Living Single. She also had a part in Spike Lee's hit film Jungle Fever. She became a household name when she received an Oscar for her role as Mama Morton in the film Chicago. Becoming an instant celebrity,

she was on the cover of many magazines, including Essence. She continues to achieve great success in her music and acting careers.

PRACTICE 8

Correct twelve errors with quotation marks, titles, apostrophes, or capital letters.

EXAMPLE:

S R

Paul Salopek, in an article titled "Children ~~s~~eeking ~~r~~oyalties," denounced the treatment of a South African composer.

1. Every time a song is placed on a CD or album, the writer receives a royalty. Lee Ann Arbringer, in an article called "How royalties work," says, "currently, the statutory rate is eight cents for each song." To combat illegal file sharing on the Internet, some legal music site's have opened up, but not all artists are happy about it. "I earn almost nothing from the legal file-sharing sites because the users just rent songs", says Jimmy Dee, a guitarist. Roz Hillman, an accountant, agrees, noting that the artist gets "Next to nothing."

2. Some artists have lost the rights to their own compositions. One of the greatest songs in the last century was written by a nearly unknown South African singer, Solomon Linda. Paul Salopek, of the Chicago tribune, wrote about him. In 1939, Linda wrote a song called "Mbube" and sold the rights to Gallo Records for a mere ten shillings, which is less than $2. Since then, Linda song has been rerecorded almost two hundred times, most famously in the 1961 version "The Lion sleeps tonight." The song is on the soundtrack of fifteen movies, including Disney's The Lion King. Solomon Linda died a pauper. "We are sad because he died without praise." said his daughter, Elizabeth.

REFLECT ON IT

Think about what you have learned in this chapter. If you do not know an answer, review that topic.

1. In contractions, which letter does the apostrophe replace in the word *not*? _______

CHAPTER 34

2. Write the possessive forms of the following phrases.

 EXAMPLE: the wife of my brother: *my brother's wife*

 a. the music of Joni Mitchell: ____________________

 b. the books of the professor: ____________________

 c. the house of Rob and Ann: ____________________

 d. the cases of the lawyers: ____________________

3. When a sentence ends with a quotation, the period should be

 a. Inside the final quotation marks.

 b. Outside the final quotation marks.

4. The titles of short works such as essays, articles, and poems should be

 a. Italicized.

 b. Set off with quotation marks.

5. The titles of longer works, such as magazines, newspapers, and movies, should be

 a. Italicized.

 b. Set off with quotation marks.

Final Review

Edit the following paragraphs for fifteen errors with apostrophes, quotations, or italics. Also, ensure that titles and quotations have the necessary capital letters.

EXAMPLE:

Musician Steve Miller complains, “My royalties have dropped 80 percent since 1999.”

1. In recent year’s, some recording artists and music companies have complained about the proliferation of music-sharing sites on the Internet. According to a reporter for *Fox News* “An estimated 60 million people participate in file-sharing networks”. Opinions about file sharing differ greatly.

2. File sharing among college students is common. Roz Mingue, a student at Grant MacEwan College, frequently downloads free music. Roz’ friend, Melissa Peng, says: “What is the big deal? They can’t stop us.” Some students think the record companies are simply too greedy. “Music companies say, “Don’t do that,’ but they still make a lot of money, so they should stop complaining,” argues Peng.

3. Recording companies have decided to fight back. Cary Sherman, president of the Recording Industry Association of America (RIAA),

compares file swappers to shoplifters. In a press conference, Sherman said, "there comes a time when you have to stand up and take appropriate action". In the 1990s, Napster was successfully sued and shut down. The recording industrys latest tactic is to take individual music file sharers to court.

4. The online magazine Wired News reports that hundreds of downloaders have been sued. Journalist Katie Dean writes "The defendants include a working mom, a college football player, and a 71-year-old grandpa." Joel Selvin and Neva Chonin are reporters for the *San Francisco chronicle.* Their article, "Artists Blast Record companies," contains quotations from artists who are unhappy with the lawsuits.

5. A prominent rocker points out that artists earn more from touring than from CD sales. "Bruce Springsteen probably earned more in ten nights at Meadowlands last month than in his entire recording career." said rocker Huey Lewis. Certainly music file sharing will not stop anytime soon. David Draiman of the rock band The Disturbed think's that artists should stop fighting because they can't win.

The Writer's Room

Write about one of the following topics. Ensure that your punctuation is correct.

1. What is success? Define success and, as a supporting example, describe a successful person whom you know.
2. What reasons do people give for downloading music and films? What are the effects of their actions? Write about the causes and effects of illegal downloading.

How Do I Get a Better Grade?

Visit MyWritingLab for audiovisual lectures and additional practice sets about the apostrophe, quotation marks, and titles.

Capitalization and Other Punctuation Marks

Section Theme **THE WORKPLACE**

michaeljung/Fotolia

In this chapter, you will read about topics related to **innovators.**

The Writer's Journal

Do you buy products online? Why or why not? Express your opinion about online shopping.

Capitalization

There are many instances in which you must use capital letters. Always capitalize the following words:

- **The pronoun *I* and the first word of every sentence**

  My co-workers and I share an office.

- **The days of the week, months, and holidays**

  Tuesday May 22 Labour Day

Do not capitalize the seasons: spring, summer, fall, winter.

- **The titles of specific institutions, departments, companies, and schools**

  Apple Computer   Department of Finance   Bodwell High School

  Do not capitalize general references.

  the company   the department   the school

- **The names of specific places such as buildings, streets, parks, cities, provinces, and bodies of water**

  Market Street   Dundas Square   Saint John, New Brunswick
  Robson Street   Newfoundland   Lake Ontario

  Exception: Do not capitalize general references.

  the street   the province   the lake

- **The names of specific languages, nationalities, tribes, races, and religions**

  Spanish   Mohawk   Buddhist   an Italian restaurant

- **The titles of specific individuals**

  Brigadier-General Jon Vance   Professor Molohon   Dr. Best
  Prime Minister Stephen Harper   President Barack Obama   Mrs. Ellen Ross

  Do not capitalize titles if you are referring to the profession in general or if the title follows the name.

  my doctor   the professors   Romeo Dallaire, a senator

- **The titles of specific courses and programs**

  Economics 201   Topics in Electrical Engineering   Nursing 402

  Do not capitalize a general reference to a course when you do not mention the course title.

  an economics course   an engineering program   a nursing class

- **The major words in titles of literary or artistic works**

  National Post   *This Land*   *Beautiful Losers*

- **The names of historical events, eras, and movements**

  World War II   Cubism   the Middle Ages

Capitalizing Computer Terms

Always capitalize software titles as well as the following computer terms.

Internet   World Wide Web   Microsoft Office

PRACTICE 1

Add fifteen missing capital letters.

EXAMPLE:

Oregon's
One of ~~Oregon's~~ best-known artists is Matt Groening.

1. Born on february 15, 1954, Matt Groening grew up with an interest in comic book art. In 1977, he moved to Los angeles with the intention of becoming a writer. He held many different types of jobs, including chauffeur and ghostwriter for an elderly movie producer. He started writing his own comic strip called *Life in hell*. The strip appeared in the *Los Angeles reader* in 1980 and went into syndication in 1983.

2. In 1987, Groening created a short animated series that served as extra material for the *Tracy Ullman show*. Picked up by Fox in 1990, *The Simpsons* has become the longest-running cartoon show in television history. The fate of the show was at first in doubt because many people, including former First lady Barbara Bush, criticized the show's portrayal of a dysfunctional family.

3. The show's characters are named after people in Groening's family. Groening's father is named Homer, his mother is Marge, and his two sisters are Lisa and Maggie. The show's central character is a scheming ten-year-old, and the name Bart was created by rearranging the letters in the word *brat*. In the television series, the Simpson family lives in Springfield next to Ned Flanders, a devout christian. Both families live on a street called evergreen terrace.

4. The show satirizes North american society. It contains stereotypical characters such as Wiggum, the corrupt, donut-eating police chief. In addition, at Ainsworth elementary school, principal Skinner takes orders from his mother and punishes students erratically.

5. Although the show is a cartoon, both adults and children enjoy it. To appeal to adults, some of the show's stories are based on famous literary works such as Edgar Allan Poe's "The raven." The show has been translated into spanish and other languages, and it has been watched by millions of people around the world.

CHAPTER 35

Watch the **Video**
Semicolons, Colons, Dashes and Parentheses
MyWritingLab

Other Punctuation Marks

Colon (:)

Use a colon for the following purposes:

- To introduce a quotation with a complete sentence

  The writer Lucy Maud Montgomery stated her opinion: "It wouldn't be half so interesting if we knew all about everything, would it?"

- To introduce a series or a list after a complete sentence

  Canada has produced some great writers: Margaret Atwood, Patrick Lane, Lynn Crosbie, Gary Geddes, Susan Musgrave, and Stephen Leacock.

- After the expression *the following*

  Please do the following: read, review, and respond.

- To introduce an explanation or example

  In 1929, investors witnessed a tragedy: the Stock Market Crash.

- To separate the hour and minutes in expressions of time

  The meeting will begin at 11:45 a.m.

Hyphen (-)

Use a hyphen in the following situations:

- When you write the complete words for numbers between twenty-one and ninety-nine.

  twenty-six ninety-nine seventy-two

- When you use a compound adjective before a noun. The compound adjective must express a single thought.

No hyphen: The new employee must work under high pressure.

Hyphen: The new employee has a high-pressure **job.**

(You cannot say a "high job" or a "pressure job." *High* and *pressure* must go together.)

No hyphen: Our boss is thirty years old.

Hyphen: We have a thirty-year-old **boss.**

(The words *thirty*, *year*, and *old* express a single thought. You cannot remove one of those words.)

If the adjectives before a noun function independently, do *not* add hyphens.

No hyphen: They renovated an old red barn.

(The two adjectives function separately.)

Nonhyphenated Compound Adjectives

Some compound adjectives never take a hyphen, even when they appear before a noun.

World Wide Web   high school senior   real estate agent

PRACTICE 2

Add ten missing colons and hyphens.

EXAMPLE:

The World Wide Web is a ~~top-notch~~ *top-notch* communications system.

1. Some revolutionary inventions in human communication are the following paper, the printing press, the personal computer, and the World Wide Web. Tim Berners-Lee, a respected fifty-three year old man, created the World Wide Web while working as a researcher for the European Laboratory for Particle Physics. His invention has had long term effects in the field of communications.

2. Born in 1955 in London, England, Berners-Lee showed an early interest in mathematics. He had many childhood hobbies designing cardboard computers, doing mental mathematical calculations, and experimenting with electronics. Because his parents were interested in computers, Berners-Lee became a computer savvy child.

3. In 1986, while he was working in Geneva, he had two great ideas designing a software system that linked information on his computer to information on his colleagues' computers, and sharing his program with scientists around the world. The system allowed scientists to communicate

with each other by accessing information on each other's computers. Berners-Lee envisioned a web like system of communications links. He named the new system the World Wide Web.

4. Since 1991, the Internet has become an extremely user friendly research tool. Berners-Lee did not profit monetarily from his creation. In fact, he fights hard to keep it free so that everyone can benefit from it.

Ellipsis Marks (...)

You may want to quote key ideas from an author, but you do not always want to quote an entire paragraph. Use ellipsis marks to show that you have omitted information from a quotation.

When you type an ellipsis mark, leave a space before and after each period. If the omitted section includes complete sentences, then add a period before the ellipses. In the next examples, notice how the quotation changes when ellipses are used.

Original Selection

Toronto is a dynamic, bustling city with several sports complexes, movie theatres, and music venues. Throughout the course of a day, you can experience several scenic attractions, from the CN Tower and the Rogers Centre by Lake Ontario to the Royal Ontario Museum and Yorkville shopping in the hub of the city; however, it will take you much longer to fully immerse yourself in Toronto life. With a small town like Mindemoya, on Manitoulin Island in Northern Ontario, you can experience all of the quaint town's offerings in one day. You can tour the town's central core first by chatting with locals at the Manitoulin Espresso Bar and then by relaxing near Lake Mindemoya, planning your next day's adventures to Providence Bay or South Baymouth to see or ride on the Chi-Cheemaun ferry. Both Toronto and Mindemoya provide engaging experiences; it just depends on whether you prefer city or small town life.

Quotation with Omissions

With a small town like Mindemoya . . . you can experience all of the quaint town's offerings in one day.

GRAMMAR LINK

For more information about quotations, see Chapter 34.

PRACTICE 3

Write quotations incorporating material from each of the next passages. Use ellipses to show where you omit words, and remember to keep important information.

Iyengar yoga focuses on concentrated movements to increase mobility, stability, strength and alignment ... [it] draws the attention inward, quieting and integrating mind and body, explains the Yoga Centre Toronto website.

—Aparita Bhandari, "Like It or Not, Yoga Is Here to Stay"

According to Bhandari, ___________________________________

____

____

2. Francine's study retreat is a recently converted sauna outside a cottage on the West Arm of Lake Nipissing. When Francine heard about her parents' decision to dismantle the malfunctioning sauna, she asked them if she could use it as a tiny studio. She built a bookshelf and desk out of cedar planks and assembled a corkboard with inspirational quotations and images—to motivate her and provide her with a quiet space to complete her Canadore College studies in the Building Construction Technician program.

____

____

REFLECT ON IT

Think about what you have learned in this chapter. If you do not know an answer, review that topic.

1. List five types of words that require capitalization. For instance, the days of the week begin with capital letters.

 ____

 ____

2. Add hyphens, where necessary, to the following sentences.

 He is a twenty five year old man who carries a small red book in his back pocket.

 He has a high pressure job, but he remains relaxed at work.

3. Correct the six errors in punctuation and capitalization.

 The famous canadian actress ellen page was born in halifax on february 21, 1987. She has made many films To Rome with Love, tilda, and Inception.

FINAL REVIEW

Correct fifteen capitalization and punctuation (colon and hyphen) errors in the next selection. Count each hyphen, colon, or capital letter as one error.

EXAMPLE:

highly motivated

Some ~~highly motivated~~ people risk their careers to become whistle-blowers.

1. The following people have all demonstrated the courage of their convictions by speaking up when they saw wrongdoing. Many helped

expose corruption that needed to be put right for the public good. A few have been recognized and publicly praised for their efforts—but most have suffered from harsh retribution from their employers as a result of their actions. Their stories demonstrate the value of whistleblowers, and the absolute need for strong legal protection for these people. The individuals listed here represent only a tiny fraction of the canadian whistleblowers that we know of. To avoid legal liability [the Federal Accountability Initiative for Reform] (FAIR) is only able to report what is already in the public domain, and most whistleblowers never manage to get their allegations entered into the public record.

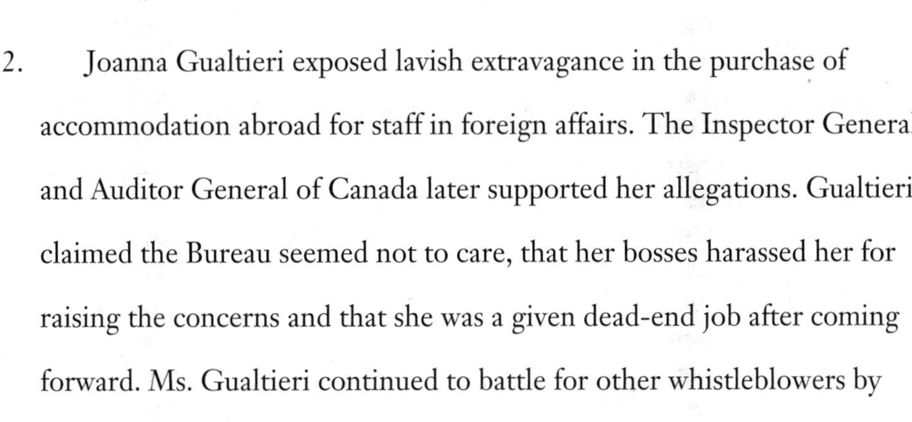

2. Joanna Gualtieri exposed lavish extravagance in the purchase of accommodation abroad for staff in foreign affairs. The Inspector General and Auditor General of Canada later supported her allegations. Gualtieri claimed the Bureau seemed not to care, that her bosses harassed her for raising the concerns and that she was a given dead-end job after coming forward. Ms. Gualtieri continued to battle for other whistleblowers by founding FAIR … and by serving as a director for almost 10 years.

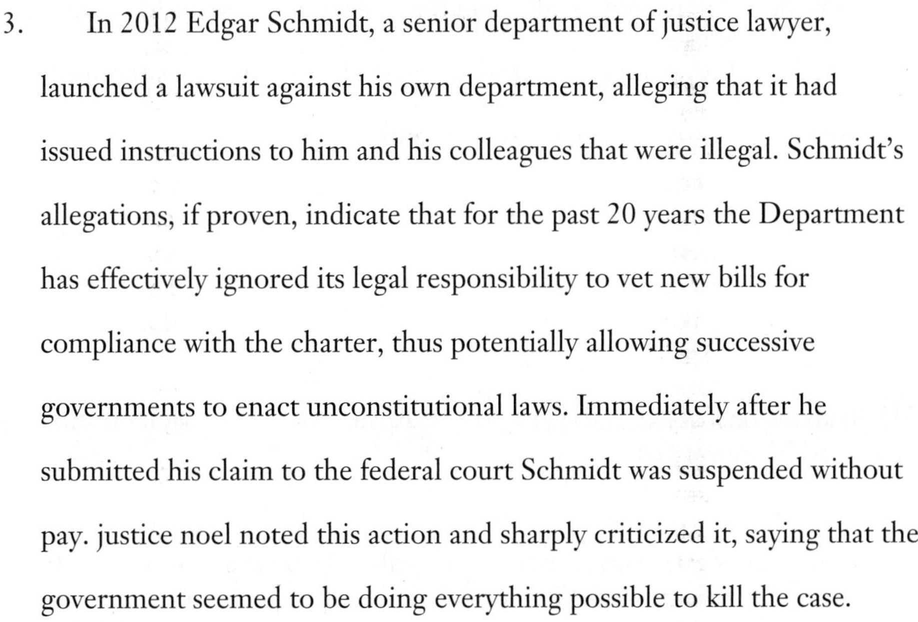

3. In 2012 Edgar Schmidt, a senior department of justice lawyer, launched a lawsuit against his own department, alleging that it had issued instructions to him and his colleagues that were illegal. Schmidt's allegations, if proven, indicate that for the past 20 years the Department has effectively ignored its legal responsibility to vet new bills for compliance with the charter, thus potentially allowing successive governments to enact unconstitutional laws. Immediately after he submitted his claim to the federal court Schmidt was suspended without pay. justice noel noted this action and sharply criticized it, saying that the government seemed to be doing everything possible to kill the case.

4. The RCMP Pension Fund scandal finally came to light through the efforts of five people, who all struggled on courageously in the face of apparent attempts by rcmp top brass to block investigations. **Denise Revine** was the human resource director who first uncovered the suspicious transactions and compiled a massive file of evidence. Her boss **Chief Superintendent Fraser Macaulay** tried to ensure that this evidence was properly investigated—and was removed from his position and given what he believed was a punitive secondment. Retired **Staff-Sgt. Ron Lewis** led persistent efforts to make someone in authority pay attention—first within the RCMP, then in outside agencies such as the Treasury Board and Auditor General, and finally to MPs and the media. **Staff-Sgt. Steve Walker** took part in the Ottawa Police Service's criminal investigation into the affair, and **Staff-Sgt. Mike Frizzell** was abruptly removed from the investigation as his inquiries got close to senior RCMP management.

5. In an unprecedented turn of events all five were given the RCMP's most coveted award, the commissioner's commendation, for outstanding service, and a Commons committee unanimously passed a motion that the five be publicly commended and that commendation be tabled in parliament. Prior to this, no canadian whistleblower had ever received formal thanks or recognition from the authorities.

ESSAY LINK

The Workplace

"The Beeps" by Josh Freed (page 570)
"This Boat Is My Boat" by Drew Hayden Taylor (page 573)
"Gone with the Windows" by Dorothy Nixon (page 576)
"Advertising Appeals" by Michael R. Solomon (page 578)

The Writer's Room

Write about one of the following topics. Ensure that your capitalization and punctuation are correct.

1. Describe your work environment.
2. What types of jobs does society value highly? Describe at least three different categories or types of workers who get a lot of respect.

Collaborative Activity

Work with a partner and think about a job that would interest you. Find a job advertisement from a newspaper, a magazine, or an Internet site. You could refer to one of the following sites:

www.monster.com www.jobs.net www.jobs.org

Compose a letter of application. In the first paragraph, explain what job you want and where you heard about the job. In the second paragraph, briefly detail your qualities and experience. Then, in a third paragraph, explain your availability and how you can be contacted. Ask your partner to help you compose each part of the letter.

Remember to be as direct as possible. After you finish writing, proofread your letter and ensure that you have used correct punctuation and capitalization. Exchange letters with your partner, and proofread your partner's letter.

How Do I Get a Better Grade?

Visit MyWritingLab for audiovisual lectures and additional practice sets about capitalization and other punctuation marks.

Editing Paragraphs and Essays

EDITING PRACTICE

In this chapter, you will have opportunities to edit different pieces of writing.

silver-john/Fotolia

After you finish writing the first draft of a paragraph or essay, it is important to edit your work. When you edit, you carefully review your writing to verify that your grammar, punctuation, sentence structure, and capitalization are correct. In this chapter, you can practise editing the types of written pieces that you see every day, including email messages, paragraphs, essays, and business correspondence.

Watch the **Video**
Revising and Editing Your Own Paragraph
MyWritingLab

PRACTICE 1 EDIT A PARAGRAPH

Correct fifteen underlined errors in the next selection. An editing symbol appears above each error. To understand the meaning of the symbol, refer to the chart on the inside back cover of this book.

Watch the **Video**
Editing a Paragraph
MyWritingLab

cap
1. Sergeant Leung Shiu-yuk's first experience with a chinese triad occurred
sp
when he was fourteen years old. The young Mr. Leung had an arguement
p
with an acquaintance. The classmates father aggressively claimed to be a
vt
triad member when he comed to see Mr. Leung's father about the
vt
schoolyard brawl. At that moment, Mr. Leung decided to became a police

officer to combat organized crime in Hong Kong. Over the years, he has
sp
become especialy knowledgeable about triad operations. Mr. Leung
agr wc
investigate powerful Chinese triads. He is a conscious expert witness for
the Hong Kong police.

vt
2. Chinese triads been involved in illegal activities in North America since
wc
the beginning of the twentieth century. There business includes the drug
trade, human trafficking, and extortion. Chinese triads also defraud public
pl
and private institution such as health care, insurance, and investment.

3. The triads can manipulate and transfer financial assets across
ad
international boundaries. Thus, they deceive investors real easily. Triads
sp
are responsable for much human misery. International police organizations
wc
are hopeful than they can erase these criminal organizations. Security
pro
forces must show perseverance to reach his goal.

PRACTICE 2 EDIT AN ESSAY

Watch the Video
Essays:Revising and Editing Your Own Essay
MyWritingLab

Correct twenty underlined errors in the next student essay. An editing symbol appears above each error.

Family Dynamics

Watch the Video
Essays:How to Edit
MyWritingLab

pro
1. One day, my brothers and me were discussing our childhood. We had
very distinct viewpoints about our experiences. We realized that our opinions
vt
were influence by our birth position in the family. Certainly, birth order
has an impact on a person's personality.

p agr
2. First time parents, unsure of what to do, tends to put a lot of pressure on
shift
the firstborn child. Although the oldest child benefited from the undivided
ad
attention of the parents, he or she also feels more stronger pressure than
the younger siblings. Oldest children are most likely to conform to their
p
parents expectations and are often compliant high achievers. For example,
m
my brother made my parents proud who became a lawyer.

3. Middle children have certains[ad] qualities that sets[agr] them apart. Immediately, they must fight for their place in the limelight, especially if they are the same sex than[wc] the eldest child. Middle children, therefore, tend to learn how to manipulate others to get what they want, they[ro] sometimes act out to get their parents' attention. I am a middle child, and I rebelled. Of course, the attention than[wc] I received from my parents were[agr] not always positive, but attention is attention, and I needed it.

4. By the time the youngest child is born, the parents are real[ad] relaxed and have less[wc] financial worries. Therefore, they tend to spoil the baby of the family, letting the youngest get away with mischief. In my family, my youngest brother did things that I would of[wc] been punished for. Including staying out late and taking the car without permission.[frag]

5. Being a parent is time-consuming, heartbreaking, and a reward[//]. Knowing about birth order can help people become better parents. Nancy Samalin, in her book *Love and Anger: The Parental Dilemma*, wrote, "Children will observe one another closely and take advantage of any edge they can achieve[P]".

PRACTICE 3 EDIT A PARAGRAPH

There are no editing symbols in the next paragraph. Proofread it as you would your own writing, and correct twelve errors.

Physicians overprescribe antibiotics and this practice is having a terrible effect on our health system. First, antibiotics are completely useless against viruses, yet alot of patients ask for and receive it when they have a simple cold. When drugs are overprescribed, some bacterial infections become drugs-resistant. Malaria and tuberculosis for example, are more difficult to treat than they were twenty years ago. The problem is especialy serious in hospitals. According to Dr. Ricki Lewis, antibiotic-resistant infections spread rapidly in a hospital environment. Furthermore, patients who are criticaly ill requires large doses of drugs who cause bacteria to mutate rapidly. We should remember that the body can fight many illnesses on its own. For instance, some common ear infections. Before accepting a prescription, consumers should ask whether antibiotics are necessary. There are problems enough in this world, the population does not need to create new illnesses by overusing antibiotics.

PRACTICE 4 EDIT A PARAGRAPH

There are no editing symbols in the next paragraph. Proofread it as you would your own writing, and correct fifteen errors.

Identity theft is the ilegal use of someones personal information. It is a serious crime, in fact, last year there was over one million cases of identity theft in Canada. To find identities, thieves go threw recycling bins, empty garbage cans, and stealing mail to obtain somebodys personal information. Computer hackers can even steal identities by tapping into personal information that persons keep on their computers. When a criminal has stolen a name, birthplace, address, and social security number, they can take out credit cards in the victim's name. For example, my co-worker, Nick Matsushita. He came home one day and found a large bill from a credit card company. Somebody had use his personal information to apply for credit. Nick and me are good friends, and I know that the identity theft has caused him alot of pain. He says that if he would have known about the way identity thieves work, he would have been more careful with his personal papers. Certainly, victims of identity theft loose time and money trying to fix the problem. To avoid being a victim, be prudent when sharing personal information.

PRACTICE 5 EDIT A WORKPLACE MEMO

Correct eight errors in the next excerpt from a memo.

Re: Summer vacations

As many of you know, each summers everybody wants to take their vacation at the same time. For this reason, employees are being ask to state your vacation preferences before next friday. Please sign the sheet posted on the bulletin board stating when you wanna take your time off. If you gotta good reason for needing a specific time period, please send Judy or I a memo explaining why.

Michael Rosen

Human Resources Department

PRACTICE 6 EDIT AN ESSAY

There are no editing symbols in the next essay. Proofread it as you would your own writing, and correct twenty errors.

1. Many courageous explorers has attempted expeditions to the Antarctic. Robert Falcon Scott did not want to become an explorer. In fact, he once said "I may as well confess that I had no predilection for polar exploration". However, he went on to lead two expeditions to the South Pole.

2. His first expedition, which took place from 1901 to 1904 was unsuccessful. Scott and his crew experienced many problems. Because of the harsh climate and terrain. For example many crew members develop scurvy due to a lack of vitamin C. They had travelled 960 miles and was only 480 miles short of the South Pole when they had to give up. In 1905, Scott wrote a book about his journey, *The Voyage of discovery*.

3. On June 10 1910, on a ship called the *Terra Nova*, Scott raced to the South Pole again. Unfortunately, when Scott reached his destination, he found that a norwegian expedition had arrived there first. Every member of Scotts team were disappointed.

4. On the return journey, Scott and his crew faced terrible blizzards. "Great God! This is an awful place." Scott wrote in his journal. One man, Captain Oates, had severe frostbite on his feet. Knowing that he would never make it to the supply camp Oates decided to leave the group and walk to certain death. So that he would not have to depend of his friends. When they were only eleven miles from the supply camp, Scott and the remaining crew members set up their tents. Their frozen bodies were discover a few months later. Forty-three-year-old Scott was the last to die.

5. Although Scott was not the first person to reach the South Pole his decision to undertake important and dangerous explorations inspired many others. In Cambridge, England, the Scott Polar research Institute was named after the explorer.

PRACTICE 7 EDIT A FORMAL LETTER

Correct ten punctuation and capitalization errors in the next formal letter.

Ari Praz
278 Rue St-Grard
Montreal, Qc H2Y 1M3

July 6, 2014

Montreal Department of Finance
Hearing-by-Mail Unit
P.O. Box 29201
Montreal, QC H2Y 3R3

Subject: Ticket #4089-01411

Attention: Finance Department

I am writing to explain why I am pleading "not guilty" to a parking ticket I received on the morning of friday, june 24, 2014. Please read the following explanation and refer to the enclosed documents.

On the evening of june 23, I parked a rented car on the south side of 18th street. I knew I could park there legally overnight until 8:30 a.m. At approximately 8:15 friday morning, I went to move the car from that parking space. When I arrived, I discovered that the front tire on the passenger side was flat. Unable to move the car, and unable to change the tire myself, I immediately returned to my apartment a few blocks away to phone the rental companys hotline. I estimated that I made the call at about 8:30 a.m. On the photocopies of Continentals service records, you will see they dispatched someone at 8:39 a.m. Unfortunately, while I was away from the car making that call, I received a ticket. The ticket was written at 8:40 a.m.

I'm sure you can see why I am pleading "not guilty" to this parking offence. I had every intention of moving the car by the specified time, I was not able to do so until roadside assistance arrived to replace the flat tire.

Yours Truly,

Ari Praz

Ari Praz

Enclosures: 2

PRACTICE 8 EDIT AN ESSAY

Correct twenty errors in the next essay.

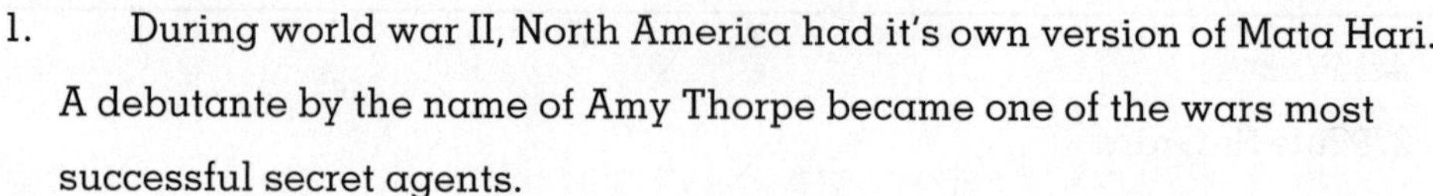

1. During world war II, North America had it's own version of Mata Hari. A debutante by the name of Amy Thorpe became one of the wars most successful secret agents.

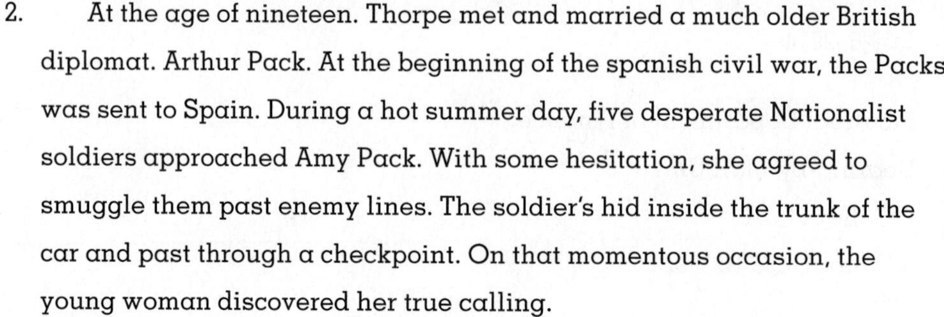

2. At the age of nineteen. Thorpe met and married a much older British diplomat. Arthur Pack. At the beginning of the spanish civil war, the Packs was sent to Spain. During a hot summer day, five desperate Nationalist soldiers approached Amy Pack. With some hesitation, she agreed to smuggle them past enemy lines. The soldier's hid inside the trunk of the car and past through a checkpoint. On that momentous occasion, the young woman discovered her true calling.

3. In a revolt against her sheltered upbringing, the diplomats wife desired a life of danger and excitement. In the summer of 1937, Amy Thorpe separated from her husband and becomes a spy for Britain. With the code name of Cynthia, she obtained secret information about Hitlers plans to invade Czechoslovakia.

4. One of her most dangerous mission occurred in Vichy, France. Posing as an American journalist, "Cynthia" seduced Charles Brousse, an official at the french Embassy, and convinced him to work with her. Thorpe's mission was to photograph secret Nazi codebooks. The couple met in the embassy for several nights and convinced the night watchmen that they were simply an amorous couple. On the third night, they enterred the code room, opened the window, and let a professional safecracker into the room. Suddenly, Thorpe had a hunch, and, to the surprise of the men, she decided to remove her clothing. Seconds later, the door opened, and the night watchmans flashlight beamed into the room. When he saw the naked woman, he apologized and retreated. Thorpe quickly dressed. The safecracking expert then opened the safe. Thorpe photographed the codebooks.

5. Although most Canadians have never heard of her, Amy Thorpe's wartime actions were extreme important. Amy Thorpe has been credited with saving more than 100 000 Allied lives.

PRACTICE 9 EDIT AN ESSAY

Correct twenty errors in the next essay.

1. Sports surround us every day in the papers, on television, and on the radio. Some people criticize our sports-driven culture. Sports critics say that university's put young athletes on pedestals and do not emphasize the achievements of students in academic programs. In fact, athletes do not receive enough praise.

2. First, colleges with good sports teams gets a lot of publicity. For example during the football season, two national television channel (CTV and CBC) and one specialty sports channel (TSN) covers the games. During the basketball playoffs, Canada's version of March Madness seen on television. The publicity that universities receive from sports bring more students to the academic programs. Sports help these programs, they do not harm them.

3. In addition, colleges and universities make money from their student athletes. For example, Canadian Interuniversity Sport (CIS) states, "An athletic scholarship can include, but is not limited to, scholarships, bursaries, prizes, leadership awards, merit awards, housing, and all other non-employment financial benefit received by an athlete from their institution." Millions of dollars in nonathletic monetary awards was also given to student athletes that same year. Clearly, colleges show long good-term planning when they promote star athletes.

4. Moreover, sports are a motivation for athletes to go to university. Significant financial contributions for Canadian athletes are from the University of Alberta, Queen's University, and Dalhousie University. Therefore, the student athletes were real motivated. To attend these postsecondary institutions.

5. Colleges and universities are right to pay special attention to athletes and sports programs. Because of the extra effort that student athletes must give to suceed, and because of the publicity and money that educational institutions receive from sports programs and their athletes colleges and universities have a serious obligation to encourage there athletes.

How Do I Get a Better Grade?

Visit MyWritingLab for audiovisual lectures and additional practice sets about editing paragraphs and essays.

Reading Strategies and Selections

In the first part of Chapter 37, you will learn strategies that can help you improve your reading skills. Later in the chapter, you will see a number of thought-provoking essays that present a wide range of viewpoints about topics related to popular culture, college life, psychology, health care, great discoveries, the workplace, political intrigue, and the legal world.

As you read each essay, think about how the writer achieves his or her purpose using one or more of these writing patterns:

- Illustration
- Narration
- Description
- Process
- Definition
- Classification
- Comparison and Contrast
- Cause and Effect
- Argument

From Reading to Writing

Pavel L Photo and Video /Shutterstock

Aspiring songwriters and musicians study different musical styles to determine which lyrics, notes, rhythms, and so on work well together. In the same way, by reading different pieces of writing, you can observe which elements other writers use and how they use them. Then you can try applying the same principles to your own writing.

Reading Strategies

When you read, you also develop your writing skills. You expand your vocabulary and learn how other writers develop topics. In addition, you learn to recognize and use different writing patterns. Finally, reading helps you find ideas for your own paragraphs and essays.

The next strategies can help you become a more successful reader and writer. They guide you through the reading process and provide useful tips for getting specific information from a piece of writing.

Previewing

Previewing is like window shopping; it gives you a chance to see what the writer is offering. When you preview, look quickly for visual clues so that you can determine the selection's key points. Review the following:

- The titles or subheadings (if any)
- The first and last sentences of the introduction
- The first sentence of each paragraph

- The concluding sentences of the selection
- The photos, graphs, or charts (if any)

Finding the Main Idea

After you finish previewing, read the selection carefully. Search for the **main idea,** which is the central point that the writer is trying to make. In an essay, the main idea usually appears somewhere in the first few paragraphs in the form of a thesis statement. However, some professional writers build up to the main idea and state it only in the middle or at the end of the essay. Additionally, some professional writers do not state the main idea directly.

Making a Statement of the Main Idea

If a reading does not contain a clear thesis statement, you can determine the main idea by asking yourself *who, what, when, where, why,* and *how* questions. Then, using the answers to those questions, write a statement that sums up the main point of the reading.

Making Inferences

If a professional writer does not state the main idea directly, you must look for clues that will help you **infer** or figure out what the writer means to say. For example, read the next paragraph and try to infer the writer's meaning.

> The band cost about $4500 for the night. The hall rented for $900, and we figured we got a good deal. We had to decorate it ourselves. There were flowers on every table ($25 for each bouquet), rented china and silverware ($1850), and tablecloths, tables, and chairs ($900). The catered food worked out to be $40 per person, multiplied by 300. This is not counting the dresses, the tuxedos, the photographer, or the rented limos. Sure, it was a special night. It is too bad the guests of honour split up three months later.

PRACTICE 1

Reread the preceding paragraph. Then answer the following questions.

1. What is the subject of the paragraph? ______________________
2. What is the writer's relationship to the guests of honour? ______________________
   ____
3. What is the writer's main point? ______________________

Finding the Supporting Ideas

Different writers use different types of supporting ideas. They may give steps for a process, use examples to illustrate a point, give reasons for an argument, and so on. Try to identify the author's supporting ideas.

Highlighting and Making Annotations

Watch the Video
Annotating Your Texts
MyWritingLab

After you read a long text, you may forget some of the author's ideas. To help you remember and quickly find the important points, you can highlight key ideas and make annotations. An **annotation** is a comment, question, or reaction that you write in the margin of a page.

Each time you read a passage, follow the next steps.

- Look in the introductory and concluding paragraphs. Underline sentences that sum up the main idea. Using your own words, rewrite the main idea in the margin.
- Underline or highlight supporting ideas. You might even number the arguments or ideas. This will allow you to understand the essay's development.
- Circle words that you do not understand.
- Write questions in the margin if you do not understand the author's meaning.
- Write notes beside passages that are interesting or that relate to your own experiences.
- Jot down any ideas that might make interesting writing topics.

Here is a highlighted and annotated passage from an essay titled "The New Addiction" by Josh Freed.

> 1 Is the cellphone the cigarette of our times? That's what I've been asking myself lately as the scourge of smokers slowly disappears from city life and a scourge of cellphone users takes their place. Everywhere you look, people hold cellphones up to their mouths, instead of cigarettes, and non-users react as intolerantly as non-smokers ever did. How does the cellphone resemble the cigarette? Let me count the ways.
>
> 2 It's an oral habit. For many users, the cellphone is an obvious substitute for smoking. It's a nervous habit that gives you something to do with your hands—whether you're dialing, checking your messages, or just fondling the buttons. Just like cigarettes, the phone sits in your breast pocket or on a restaurant table, ready to bring quickly to your mouth. Often, it's in a fliptop case that pops open as easily as a cigarette pack.

Why?
What is "scourge"?
General background
Main point suggests cellphones are like cigarettes.
Good example. I play with my phone.
"Fondling"?

Understanding Difficult Words

Watch the Video
Writing Vocabulary
MyWritingLab

When you read, you will sometimes come across unfamiliar words. You can try to guess the word's meaning, or you can circle it and look it up later.

Using Context Clues

Context clues are hints in the text that help define a word. To find a word's meaning, try the following strategies.

- **Look at the word.** Is it a noun, a verb, or an adjective? Sometimes it is easier to understand a word if you know how that word functions in the sentence.
- **Look at surrounding words.** Look at the sentence in which the word appears and try to find a relation between the difficult word and the words that surround it. Maybe there is a **synonym** (a word that means the same

thing) or an **antonym** (a word that means the opposite). Maybe other words in the sentence help define the word.

- **Look at surrounding sentences.** Sometimes you can guess the meaning of a difficult word by looking at the sentences, paragraphs, and punctuation surrounding the word. When you use your logic, the meaning becomes clear.

PRACTICE 2

1. Can you easily define the word *disseminates*? No Yes
2. Can you easily define the word *parity*? No Yes
3. If you do not understand the meanings of those two words, then read them in the context of the next paragraph. You will notice that it is much easier to guess their meanings.

> Christina Hoff Sommers, author of *The War against Boys*, argues that boys are being neglected in order to help girls succeed in school. For years, she argues, feminist groups have spread myths about the disadvantaged girls, yet boys are actually the disadvantaged sex. The Department of Education **disseminates** hundreds of documents about gender equity, Sommers says. While the documents suggest ways to help girls succeed, none of them explain how educators can help boys achieve academic **parity** with girls.

Now write your own definition of the words as they are used in the paragraph.

a. disseminates: ______________________________

b. parity: ______________________________

Cognates

Cognates, or word twins, are English words that may look and sound like words in another language. For example, the English word *responsible* is similar to the Spanish word *responsable*, although the words are spelled differently.

If English is not your first language and you read an English word that looks similar to a word in your language, check how it is being used in context. It may, or may not, mean the same thing in English as it means in your language. For example, in English, *assist* means "to help." In Spanish, *assistar* means "to attend." If you are not sure of a word's meaning, consult a dictionary.

Watch the Video Writing Vocabulary **MyWritingLab**

Using a Dictionary

If you do not understand the meaning of an unfamiliar word after using context clues, look up the word in a dictionary. A dictionary is useful if you use it correctly. Review the following tips for dictionary usage.

- **Look at the dictionary's front matter.** The preface contains explanations about the various symbols and abbreviations.

- **Read all of the definitions listed for the word.** Look for the meaning that best fits the context of your sentence.
- **Look up root words, if necessary.** If the difficult word has a prefix such as *un-* or *anti-*, you may have to look up the root word.

Here is an example of how dictionaries set up their definitions.

Word Division
Your dictionary may use black dots to indicate places for dividing words.

Stress Symbol (′) and Pronunciation
Some dictionaries provide the phonetic pronunciation of words. The stress symbol (′) lets you know which syllable has the highest or loudest sound.

Parts of Speech
The *n* means that *deception* is a noun. If you don't understand the parts of speech symbol, look in the front or the back of your dictionary for a list of symbols and their meanings.

de•cep′tion / [di-sep′shen] / *n* 1. the act of misleading. 2. a misrepresentation; artifice; fraud.

From *The New American Webster Handy College Dictionary* (New York: Signet, 2000), 606.

From Reading to Writing

Watch the Video
Summary Writing
MyWritingLab

After you finish reading a selection, try these strategies to make sure that you have understood it.

- **Summarize the reading.** When you summarize, you use your own words to write a condensed version of the reading. You leave out all information except the main points.
- **Outline the reading.** An outline is a visual plan of the reading. First, write down the main idea of the essay, and then note the most important idea from each paragraph. Under each idea, include a detail or an example.

Make a Written Response

Watch the Video
Critical Thinking: Responding to Texts and Visuals
MyWritingLab

Your instructor may ask you to write about your reaction to a reading. These are some questions you might ask yourself before you make a written response.

- What is the writer's main point?
- What is the writer's purpose? Is the writer trying to entertain me, persuade me, or inform me?
- Who is the audience? Is the writer directing his or her message at someone like me?
- Do I agree or disagree with the writer's main point?
- What aspects of the topic can I relate to?

After you answer the questions, you will have more ideas to use in your written response.

Reading Selections

Themes: Popular Culture and College Life

READING 1

The Market and the Mall

Stephen Henighan

Stephen Henighan is a journalist and professor of Hispanic Studies in the School of Languages and Literatures at the University of Guelph. He is also a novelist (*Streets of Winter*, *The Places Where Names Vanish*, and *Other Americas*); short story writer (*A Grave in the Air*, *North of Tourism*, and *Nights in the Yungas*); nonfiction writer (*A Report on the Afterlife of Culture*, among others); and writer of books in translation (*The Accident*—a novel by Romanian writer Mihail Sebastian, for example). In the following comparison and contrast essay, the author discusses aspects of Canadian culture that are present—and absent—in a Canadian market. As you read, also watch for elements of narration, description, and argument.

repertoire
whole list of techniques

provisions
food supply

1 In the downtown core of my southwestern Ontario city, the visit to the market is a Saturday morning ritual. There is no parking at the market, only bicycle racks outside the front door. The walk to the market building passes two-storey red-brick houses that recall the British engineers dispatched to Canada during the War of 1812, who remained in the colony after the war ended and fanned out across Upper Canada, constructing houses in this style wherever they worked. As I cycle to the market, the houses remind me of the red-brick house where I grew up, six hours' drive away in Ontario's easternmost reaches; farmers in those rural areas did not hold a market, yet the consistency of architecture over this geographical expanse confirms the coherence of a culture. Many of the family-owned businesses near the market operate out of buildings that date back more than a century. The **repertoire** of architectural styles, creative variations on a cluster of consistent themes, offers aesthetic pleasure and corroboration of cultural wholeness, reiterating the history that underlies even the most casual Saturday morning outing.

2 As I enter the market, I keep one eye on the cheese, honey, maple syrup and organic meat and vegetables, and the other on the yoga-trimmed middle-aged figures in the aisles. I'm here to buy **provisions** to take home in my cloth shopping bag, but also to be recognized as part of the community. I feel at home here. These people fit into the category that the French, with cynical aptness, characterize as bobo—bourgeois bohemians. Some of them are my friends; others I recognize from the audience at music festivals, literary readings, political speeches. As a student of my city and its neighbourhoods, I know these people's preferences. Consumers of culture, they volunteer for progressive causes and vote for one of the three political parties—Liberal, NDP or Green—that regularly claim between half and two-thirds of Canadians' votes, yet, over most of the last decade, have been incapable of forming a federal government. Echoes of this impotence rupture the Saturday morning amiability: next to a stall that offers gluten-free wheatgrass is a table where angry older men solicit signatures against the tar sands (which no one here calls "oil sands"); the guitarist outside the door strums venerable protest ballads. Yet the most disconcerting feature of the market is not these

expressions of frustration, but the fact that in this most **quintessentially** Canadian setting, much of Canada is not visible.

quintessentially pure

3 The market is where I find my friends and feel my history and values reinforced; yet how can I not be troubled that everyone here is white? Some weekends I hear French or German spoken, but never Cantonese or Punjabi. The "ethnic" food stalls are Italian or Polish. True, an Eritrean family has opened a stall, a neighbour arrives with her adopted African-American son, and last weekend one of my former students showed up in the company of a Chinese-Canadian man; but the market remains overwhelmingly, unrepresentatively white. There are women in starched Mennonite bonnets, but none in hijabs. I know from experience that among the people who surround me are agnostics, atheists, crystal-worshippers, lapsed Catholics and members of the United Church of Canada, but few practising Catholics, Jews, Muslims, Hindus or Evangelical Protestants. Those people are at the mall.

4 In the suburbs on the edge of the city, the visit to the mall is a Saturday afternoon ritual. A few people take the bus, but most drive to the vast parking lots. The drive passes ranks of identical new houses that are rammed up against each other. The sameness obliterates awareness of history, nullifying the possibility of a shared culture. Traits that undergird the present with a tangible past are dispersed by the cult of material consumption. Even the contours of many customers' bodies are influenced by this cult. Amid the dank-grease stench of the food court, franchises serve food that is global in provenance yet ersatz: national dishes are pumped up with additives, purged of unfamiliar elements and paired with huge soft drinks. The shops are transnational chains; a few insert a maple leaf—like a fig leaf of respectability turned red with embarrassment—into their familiar logos. People of all ages and ethnic backgrounds carry throwaway plastic shopping bags that announce the brands on which they spend their money. The shoppers illustrate every stage of immigrant adaptation, from Somali women in traditional robes to South Asian–descended teenagers in shorts and T-shirts and sixth-generation Scottish-Canadian men from the Legion Hall. The teenagers greet their friends; adults pass without speaking. I know from my reading on local issues that many of these adults volunteer with their religious or ethnic communities; they vote Conservative, sometimes Liberal, often not at all. Tables set out along the mall's main corridor urge passersby to sign up for loyalty cards or buy an apple to support the cadets. Here the scourge of life is taxes: advertising vaunts the allure of not paying sales tax; cubicles promise to process your income tax so that you pay the minimum.

5 At the mall, I may be spotted by my students, but I do not meet my friends. I sometimes forget where I am. The mall, though diverse, is severed from history. All of Canada is here, but Canadian culture and identity are absent. In Vancouver, Toronto or Montreal, the contrast between the market and the mall would be less stark: the market would be more ethnically mixed; the mall might serve better food. Yet the dilemma posed by the difference between them is present everywhere. Who still assumes that to become Canadian implies integration into a recognizable arc of history, as immigrant families like mine did in the 1960s? If some more recent immigrants are uncertain of where they are, of whether this place means anything beyond freedom to shop, this may be because those of us who got here earlier are no longer sure, either.

Vocabulary and Comprehension

1. In paragraph 2, what does *amiability* mean? Circle the best answer.
   a. Danger b. Awkwardness c. Pleasantness
2. What role does history play in the market?

   ______
3. List three ways in which the market is a place for connectedness. Give examples from the essay to support your answer.

   ______

Critical Thinking

4. In your opinion, what is Henighan's motivation for writing this essay?

   ______
5. What is Henighan's attitude toward his subject?

   ______
6. What is his purpose? Why is he describing a typical Canadian market?

   ______

Writing Topics

Write about one of the following topics. Remember to explore, develop, and revise and edit your work.

1. Compare the values and attitudes of contemporary society with the attitudes and values of your grandparents or people from that generation. How are they similar or different? Use examples to illustrate your point.
2. Describe in detail a market in your town or city.
3. Visit a local mall, sit in the food court, and convey the atmosphere with your words.

Reading 2

We Turned Some Sharp Corners: A Marriage Proposal in Durango

Nick Massey-Garrison

Nick Massey-Garrison lives and works in Toronto. He is a freelance writer and editor who has also worked at the publishing houses Random House and Doubleday. He is the senior contributing writer for *Green Power Magazine*. He has written many articles and short stories and co-edited *Carbon Shift: How the Twin Crises of Oil Depletion and Climate Change Will Define the Future*. The next selection is a cause and effect essay about travel. As you read, look for elements of narration, description, and comparison and contrast writing.

1 No sooner had I proposed marriage than I began to have misgivings.

2 We were standing in the *plaza major* in Durango, our knees already weak from hours spent reeling through the Sierra Madres on a stretch of treacherous highway known as the Espinazo del Diablo. We were wearing creaking motorcycle leathers and clutching a bottle of tequila. And the bells of the cathedral were booming away in the empty square to welcome in the

new year. The arcades were lit up with strings of lights, the **hulking** sixteenth-century basilica bottom-lit and lemon yellow against a black sky. Drunken singing came from a distant café. We were intoxicatingly alone, untold miles from friends back home who would be toasting and kissing.

hulking: large, bulky

3 We were truants from that familiar world, untethered under the whirl of unfamiliar stars and privy to the mystery hinted at by whatever we call **sacrament**—that the everyday world is not where the important things are happening. Travelling on a motorcycle through Mexico induces this feeling regularly. We had encountered other tourists only once in two weeks. We had crossed featureless purple deserts and shrieked recklessly down mile after scrubby mile of dusk-bordered nothingness scattered with lonely oil rigs, telephone poles with their sagging wires loping along beside us, silhouettes leaning irregularly into the flat sky. Of course, we couldn't talk on the bike, so we just held hands, squeezing every once in a while to draw attention to something interesting or to let each other know that we were happy.

sacrament: a sacred or mysterious symbol or act

4 We had stopped for gas in tumbleweed towns with rusty old pumps, and breakfasted on burritos and bitter coffee in roadside cantinas. We had dodged chickens in dusty villages with bloated fly-blown corpses of dogs strewn on the side of the road. Christmas night was spent drinking imprudently in Cuatrocienegas with a seedy mariachi band and a cowboy named Nacho. And each night we curled up in a lumpy bed in an unlikely hotel and reminded each other of how lucky we were to be there, far from everything familiar except each other.

5 We rode and rode. Crossing cold deserts on a motorcycle is a lot like drudgery, and eating burritos of indifferent quality day after day quickly loses its appeal. But we romanticized as we went along, quickened at every turn by the recurring realization: *This is us; we are here*. We were nothing like the swashbuckling adventurers we felt we were. But that didn't really matter.

6 I had heard, of course, of the fruity coolers and the SUVs that share the name, but I had never heard of the city of Durango before we saw the name on a map spread out on a table in a cantina somewhere in the Coahuila desert. It turned out to be a city of over a million people, a provincial capital, and when we emerged from the desert, we found it shimmering in the orange plains at the foot of the Sierra Madres. We had stumbled upon a city of ambiguous charm. Durango is a prosthesis of the Old World, built by people looking for gold, a place where the Inquisition was administered. From the plaza, all arcades and mosaic, you can see the spires of half a dozen **brooding** churches, each sheltering a mournful Madonna and a grotesquely lifelike Christ, some with human hair and painted rosy cheeks and **dolorous** blue eyes, his head mutilated by thorns the size of switchblades, dark blood dripping from his hands and feet. We marvelled at the dates on buildings—A.D. 1887, 1744, 1625—stupidly astonished that we could have gotten on a motorcycle and ridden to, well, this.

brooding: hanging over

dolorous: gloomy, mournful

7 Durango reminded me of some of the great cities of eastern Europe, like Belgrade; fashioned by carpenters and stonemasons and sculptors and architects of an unknowable past, then allowed to lapse into decay. The bottoms of intricately carved doors rotted away where centuries of rain had splashed, hinges rusting off. Sidewalks cracked and heaved. Friezes obscured by soot. Walls blackened by the centuries of bodies brushing by, hurrying somewhere.

8 But this is not squalor or decrepitude, or not quite. It has all the haunting love mess of ruins, which stand as testaments to their own lost mode of being, to uses to which they are no longer put, to the unforeseen nature of their desuetude. Ruins jut out of the irrevocable into the mundane, where tourists

like me stumble over them and consider them minor epiphanies. No one builds things to fall down.

9 Now battered, wretched cars lurch and jangle through the narrow cobbled streets where, presumably, the coaches of imperial functionaries once clattered. No doubt there had been torrid affairs, thrilling swordplay and knots of swooning women with heaving bosoms and scented handkerchiefs. Their coats of arms are still carved in the lintels of their decaying houses.

10 A few days before New Year's we had walked through a market. The vendors' booths were arranged according to the objects they sold: one aisle of garish clothes, knock-offs and sweatshirts with the logos of faraway sports franchises and nonsense slogans ("OKAY Boy Is Here To Jazz It Up"); a florists' aisle; an aisle of dry foodstuffs; a butchers' aisle, reeking of generations of offal; an aisle of ceramic madonnas looking heavenward.

11 In the leather goods aisle, among the saddle- and shoe-makers, we met an old man with the long hair and wild eyes of a locust-eating prophet. He stared as we approached. I warned Ange not to look. A glance would have made avoiding an awkward conversation impossible. But as we passed he called to us in Spanish. We turned to shrug innocently and mumble "No hablo Español" when he asked, smiling, earnest, "Are you married?" We conceded that we were not. "So young," he beamed. To Ange: "So beautiful! Why you're not married?!"

12 These were neither compliments we could return, nor questions we could answer. We stammered and looked at each other. "You have children?" We smiled uncomfortably. No. "So nice, so nice, so young." Shaking his head, but smiling. Then he pulled a yellowed photograph from the wall. He showed us a burly young man in a white shirt and a vest of indeterminate colour. The young man stares at the camera grimly, intently, as though trying to communicate something of grave import, like a euchre player trying to table-talk. His moustache is a push-broom and his hair is slicked back. One hand is on a hip.

13 "Is me," said the shoemaker proudly.

hale: healthy, strong

14 We've all seen pictures of our grandparents as **hale** youths, photos of our middle-aged parents as infants, irrefutable evidence that things have not always been what they are. Strange, then, our assurance that they will never change. We will always be young, we will always be happy.

15 We had left Mazatlan the morning of New Year's Eve, heading for Torreon. But we had dawdled a little. I stopped at a cathedral to buy a St. Christopher medal, only to be admonished by a baleful old woman in the mandatory black dress that the patron saint of travellers had been de-canonized. I settled for the protection of St. Michael. We spent hours stopped on the shoulder of the highway, tossing pebbles over the cliff. We stopped in Durango for dinner and decided halfway through that we would stay the night. We immediately ordered the beers we had been lusting after. The other patrons in the cantina were drinking heartily in anticipation of the night's festivities, and the man at the next table, who had earlier offered to share his salsa, invited us to a disco. We declined, asking him whether a crowd would gather in the plaza. He seemed to say yes.

16 We found a hotel room and set off through the narrow, exhaust-choked streets in search of a *liquoreria*. The city was abuzz, vendors selling peanuts and tamales. Street lamps cast cones of light through the haze of dust. We finally found a little shop, its iron grille almost shut, which sold only two brands of beer and two brands of tequila. We hurried back to our room through

the gathering bustle to nap and have a quiet post-prandial, and smoked in the elevator, just because it was permitted.

17 As midnight approached, we ran, hand in hand, toward the plaza. The narrow streets were quiet and dark. A car would pass and throw our shadows onto the sidewalk and the pocked walls with their peeling posters. We laughed and the tequila burned.

18 But the square was empty. All the shops were closed. Little white lights outlined the contours of windows and arches. The cathedral leaned into the sky. We sat on benches in the little park and waited. The sound of drunken singing came from a distant window. We felt, once again, that we had discovered this remarkable place, that our intrepidity and boldness had brought us here.

19 There is a mode of happiness that is the promise of happiness. Contentment in the moment is something that can be foreclosed upon by the thought of the future: the drinker contemplating his hangover. But to be happy because you expect to be happy, that horizons await—this happiness is not so easily extinguished.

20 When the bell rang out, Ange and I stood there embracing. For a long time. The world spun while I weighed like pebbles in my mouth the question that had at that moment occurred to me to ask.

21 The idea of proposing marriage had arrived uninvited and I had no words rehearsed. I stammered and shuffled my feet. Finally, exasperated, she told me to spit it out.

22 I could manage nothing better than a mumble.

23 "Are you joking?" was her reply.

24 Hence my misgivings. They lay not in my choice of bride but in my means of securing her. I had offered no ring. I had not dropped to my knee to ask. I feared that in the hierarchy of moments this blunder would wield tyrannical dominion over the years to follow.

25 But the best reason to propose from one's knees is that so little discourse is conducted from that position. Kneeling is a signal that something extraordinary is happening, that the succession of everyday moments is about to be interrupted. And in our case it already had been. Ange and I had stepped out of our everyday lives weeks before when we set off for Mexico, and we did not need rings or gravitas to know that we had entered a new order of experience.

26 This sense that the concerns that regulate the banal procedures of daily life have fallen away, that the inveterate world is hushed and dimmed and may have paused altogether, is just what you need when you are asking someone to marry you. When Ange said yes, this moment of perfect freedom and promise slipped coolly into memory, invulnerable to the encroachments of time.

27 My misgivings did not last long.

Vocabulary and Comprehension

1. Find a word in paragraph 3 that means "released." ____________________

2. Circle the best answer: The word *decrepitude* in paragraph 8 means

   a. disorder. b. worn out. c. poverty.

3. What examples does the author give to emphasize the passage of time?

4. How is the city of Durango compared to European cities?

5. Massey-Garrison states: "No one builds things to fall down." Why does the author stress this?

Critical Thinking

6. What is the significance of the title of this essay?

7. Why does the narrator mention the word *misgivings* at various points?

8. Why were the Nick and Ange "nothing like the swashbuckling adventurers" they felt like?

9. Basically, the author narrates what happened to him. What can you infer from the author's story? In other words, what is the deeper message?

Writing Topics

Write about one of the following topics. Remember to explore, develop, and revise and edit your work.

1. What can cause a person to have a transformative experience? List some examples.
2. When individuals travel, should they venture outside of tourist areas? Why or why not?
3. Reflect on Morissette's quotation. What do both Morissette and the essay writer seem to be saying about exploration? How are their opinions about the body (Morissette) and the ruins (Massey-Garrison) similar?

"I think of my body as an instrument rather than an ornament."

—ALANIS MORISSETTE, SINGER AND COMPOSER

READING 3

Stealing Glances

Sheila Heti

Sheila Heti is a Toronto-based author and playwright. Her most recent work includes *Ticknor*, *What It Feels Like for a Girl*, and *The Middle Stories*. She has also created a popular lecture series, "Trampoline Hall." As you read through this argument essay, also look for elements of cause and effect and comparison and contrast writing.

1 Sometimes I feel an urgent need to get out of Toronto, and this is one of those times. The strain does not come from difficult friendships or celebrity magazines or the noise, so much as my relationship to my fellow pedestrian. The crisis is almost always a crisis about strangers; it's a crisis of eye contact. Someone approaches and the problem of whether to look away or look at them—and if to look, how long to keep looking for—does not resolve itself easily, quietly, in the background. It becomes a loud problem, and as people pass by, the anxiety of how to act and this question about responsibility to my fellow humans, paid out in a momentary acknowledgement of our mutual humanity, prohibits me from thinking about anything else.

2 In such a state it is difficult to accept that we really are free on the streets of Toronto; free to look or not look as we choose, without consequence and without affecting anyone for the better or worse. In times like these, it feels as though what it means to look at someone and what it means to decide to not look is as central an ethical dilemma as any; that the question of our responsibility to each other really comes down to how we interact with people we do not know. What degree of regard are the hundreds of strangers we pass in a single day worth?

3 That walking among others should present itself as a dilemma is pathetic. Perhaps it is because we are primarily a culture of drivers, not pedestrians. Even if we do not drive, still we share the streets with many who do, who do not occupy the sidewalks with pleasure but rather are wishing there was less space to travel between the restaurant and their parked car. "Urbanity and automobiles are antithetical in many ways," writes Rebecca Solnit in *Wanderlust*, a history of walking. "A city of drivers is only a dysfunctional suburb of people shuttling from private interior to private interior." This is also true in a city of transit users—we rush to the streetcar stop, take a seat, look through whatever newspaper is lying closest. Walking is no longer, as Solnit points out, "a state in which the mind, the body, and the

world are aligned." As a result, we are jarred by our encounters. Eye contact is an irritation. It disrupts the work of getting somewhere.

4 Most of us accept as inevitable the sort of eye contact that is most pervasive, that rushed and fearful glance. You might argue that this way of looking is respectful; that since privacy is so scarce in a city, it is gracious to look away. But I have experienced such gentle looks away—giving them, getting them—and they're not what I am talking about and not the norm. There still remains that quick glance away, which often leaves me with a feeling of shame or a sense of the diminishment of my humanity. And as I sweep my eyes rapidly from someone's face onto the mailbox, I recognize that, in my wake, I may leave that person with this same anxiety.

5 For some people, it seems clear, if someone looks quickly and uncomfortably away as soon as eye contact is made, no matter. This crisis doesn't exist for them; the interaction barely registers. I wonder if such people are suffering from what George Simmel calls "the blasé attitude." He defines it as the result of the over-stimulation of nerves that accompanies life in a metropolis, which results in a "blunting of discrimination, [so] that the meaning and differing values of things, and thereby the things themselves, are experienced as insubstantial. They appear to the blasé person in an evenly flat and gray tone; no one object deserves preference over any other." The lamppost, that boy, same difference.

6 But for those of us who are not suffering from the blasé attitude, who are very conscious of the reality of the people we encounter, why do we look away embarrassed or scared, rather than gently, politely, in good conscience? Perhaps in every glance there is desire expressed. I don't mean sexual desire—though sometimes there's that—as much as the sort Constant Nieuwenheuys described when he wrote, in 1949, "When we say desire in the twentieth century, we mean the unknown, for all we know of the realm of our desires is that it continuously reverts to one immeasurable desire for freedom."

7 Perhaps the desire expressed in every glance, that we see in another person's face and they see in ours, is a desire for freedom—which on the street comes down to the freedom to look at each other. We are naturally curious about other people. From the start, as babies, we are drawn to the eyes of our parents. Imagine a cat, neurotically trying not to look directly at a passing cat. We need eye-to-eye contact. We want to see each others' faces. It is why we take and keep photographs, watch television, hang portraits in our homes. There is something terrible about looking at each other, only to have reflected back our own (and the other person's) **thwarted,** repressed desire to look. Somewhere we have failed magnificently.

thwarted: blocked, prevented

8 Our culture is such that a greater value even than freedom is productivity, utility. I was having a conversation with a friend about leisure, and she was saying how much she enjoys doing nothing, just wandering aimlessly around her house, thinking. "I find it so productive," she decided. Even an activity we enjoy precisely because it is not about production we must ultimately justify by way of its productivity. This being the situation we find ourselves in, how can we ever justify to ourselves or to each other the value of those most fleeting relationships, lasting at most two seconds long, with a stream of people we will never see again? What is the utility of the quarter-of-a-second-long relationship?

9 When we look and look away, we reveal what we want—**communion,** citizenry—and what we lack—communion, citizenry. It is not unreasonable to think the health of a culture can be judged by how many seemingly

communion: sharing, community

inconsequential encounters and experiences are shared among its citizens. Take the option of making real eye contact with strangers—frank, fully conscious, unafraid, respectful, not obtrusive. This level of engagement would be satisfying, but so exhausting to sustain; possibly too relentless and demanding for a city-dweller, since to look at someone in this way is to acknowledge and recognize how they're like you, how they are like everyone you know and love, and so to become responsible for them, just as you are responsible for those you love. But while your duty to your friend is directed only at your friend, as needed, your duty to a stranger can be paid only to the collective, constantly.

10 We need to learn how to look away well, but we cannot fake it. We cannot look from someone's face comfortably until we find what we are looking for in it.

Vocabulary and Comprehension

1. Find a word in paragraph 3 that means "jolted."

2. What does the word *blasé* in paragraph 5 mean? Circle the best answer.
   a. Unimpressed b. Plain c. Charged

3. According to the author, what prevents people from making eye contact in public? Give at least three reasons.

4. What is freedom, according to the author?

5. Look at the first two paragraphs, and underline the thesis statement.

Critical Thinking

6. Which words does Heti repeat throughout "Stealing Glances"? What effect does this have on the reader? Explain why.

7. The author begins the essay by expressing her need "to get out of Toronto." How is this desire to escape relevant for this essay?

8. In paragraph 8, Heti includes an anecdote about her friend. Explain why you think the author agrees or disagrees with her companion.

9. The author writes, "When we look and look away, we reveal what we want—communion, citizenry—and what we lack—communion, citizenry." What does she mean by this? (Look in paragraphs 9 and 10 for clues.)

___

___

___

___

___

Writing Topics

Write about one of the following topics. Remember to explore, develop, and revise and edit your work.

1. As a pedestrian or on public transportation, have you had any positive or negative experiences because of your choice to make eye contact with a stranger?
2. Do you agree or disagree with the author's argument? Support your point of view with specific examples.
3. Reflect on the Baldwin quotation. What is his deeper meaning? Do you agree with him? How does this quotation relate to Heti's observations about human isolation in cities? Give examples or anecdotes to support your views.

"Anyone who has ever struggled with poverty knows how extremely expensive it is to be poor."
—James Baldwin, Author

READING 4

The Great Offside: How Canadian Hockey Is Becoming a Game Strictly for the Rich

James Mirtle

James Mirtle, a native of Kamloops, British Columbia, is the Toronto-based hockey reporter for the *Globe and Mail*. He is also a co-host of *LeafReport*, a weekly radio podcast. In the following argumentative essay, the author stresses the high costs that young Canadian hockey players and their families encounter. As you read, also watch for elements of narration and cause and effect writing.

1 Karl Subban knows the cost of being a hockey parent in Canada.

2 The patriarch of one of Canada's most successful hockey families—his boys P.K., Malcolm and Jordan have all been drafted by NHL teams—he and his wife paid $5,000 each in one year just to register them in minor hockey in the Greater Toronto Hockey League (GTHL).

3 "And that's not including equipment and what not," Mr. Subban says. "It was very expensive. But you make sacrifices. That's what we did."

4 It's widely known that Canada's national winter sport is expensive to play. But various factors have conspired over the last 10 to 15 years to make minor hockey dramatically more expensive, pricing out many middle-class families. These days, more and more of the players that go on to play major junior, college and, ultimately, pro hockey are from wealthy backgrounds.

5 It's a development that threatens the sport's blue-collar roots, including the idea that the next Gordie Howe or Wayne Gretzky will come from backgrounds as modest as theirs were. Players of modest means in this generation must beat out peers who are often better trained and have spent many more hours on the ice, thanks to wealthy parents.

6 "The game has changed in this respect: It used to be that you had a right to play," long-time GTHL president John Gardner says. "Now it's can you afford to pay."

7 While there are still many examples of players of limited means who beat the odds and make the NHL, a sport that was once a true **meritocracy** is increasingly one where money talks, and a case study of how income inequality affects Canadians.

meritocracy
progress based on talent

8 According to a confidential survey commissioned by Hockey Canada last year and obtained by The Globe and Mail, the 1,300 parents surveyed had an average household income roughly 15 per cent higher than the national **median.** The majority listed their occupation as a "professional, owner, executive or manager," a reflection of hockey's new white-collar base.

median
midrange

9 "If you're doing eight, nine, 10 years of Triple A hockey from novice up, you're talking eight to 10 grand, minimum," says Jim Parcels, a long-time minor hockey coach and administrator who is the co-author of *Selling the Dream: How Hockey Parents and Their Kids Are Paying the Price for Our National Obsession.* "You do that for 10 years, that's almost $100,000. That's because it's six, sometimes seven days a week commitments."

10 Mr. Parcels recalls coaching teams of 14- and 15-year-olds through NHL-calibre seasons, where they would travel around the province and play 80-plus games between September and March. Every additional game added to the already considerable cost, but parents often wanted more chances for their kids to compete, not fewer.

11 "I was absolutely embarrassed I was part of a staff that did that," Mr. Parcels says. "And we weren't the only ones. Everybody did it."

12 The highest levels of minor hockey aren't the only ones that have become prohibitively expensive, however. According to the survey by Hockey Canada, the average hockey parent spent just shy of $3,000 on minor hockey in the 2011–12 season alone.

13 Those costs included $1,200 for registration and ice time, $900 for travel and accommodations and more than $600 for skates and other equipment. The expenses were also considerably higher as players got older, with parents paying roughly double—or about $3,700 a season—for children between the age of 11 and 17.

14 Among the parents surveyed by Hockey Canada whose children had recently stopped playing hockey, 46 per cent said lower costs would make them "much more likely" or "somewhat more likely" to resume playing. (Add the increased costs to changing demographics and concerns about **concussions**, and enrolment in hockey across the country has been down or flat, with only one in 10 Canadians between the age of 5 and 19 now playing, according to Hockey Canada.)

concussions
brain injuries

15 One of the biggest reasons for hockey's spiralling costs is the rise in the price of ice time. Municipal facilities have become overburdened in many parts of the country. Private arenas have begun offering more and more of the available ice time, often at a much higher cost. What used to cost a minor hockey team $50 an hour can now be upwards of seven times that.

16 Another factor is the enormous rise in the importance of rep or "travel" hockey teams: elite teams that draw on the best minor hockey players at each level to compete against teams from other towns or neighbourhoods. The travel costs and additional fees can add up quickly, but it's often kids on these elite teams that get noticed by scouts and drafted into the Canadian Hockey League, the NHL's primary feeder system in this country.

17 Then there is the emergence of so-called hockey academies—private boarding schools where parents pay $40,000 a season for their teens to incorporate hockey into their high-school education, all in a bid to improve their skills so they can compete in elite leagues and catch the eye of scouts. Add to that what some parents are now paying for skills-development programs and off-season training, and the cost can become mind-boggling.

18 "It's getting totally out of control," says Derek Popke, who deals with overzealous parents dreaming of their children making the NHL as the president of Vancouver Hockey School. "It's a crazy world. It's professionalized. And I think this really has to come to people's attention that it has to be dialled back. Everything."

19 Beyond the financial picture, playing minor hockey at the elite level has other bizarre implications, many of which only involve the super-rich. There are stories of parents moving into different neighbourhoods—or even legally separating from their partner in order to have two addresses—in order to allow their children to play on higher-profile teams.

20 "It's an ego thing for parents," says Mr. Parcels. "Their kids couldn't care less, but it becomes a status symbol."

21 Some of the solutions to the problems plaguing high-level minor hockey are novel. Mr. Parcels points to Thunder Bay, Ont., where the city's remote location makes travel hockey difficult. Hockey officials there devised a system where top players compete against older teams in the area in order to get an appropriate challenge.

22 With no need to travel for games and tournaments, the costs are more manageable. Thunder Bay has produced an impressive number of pro players despite its modest population.

23 Other ideas are more obvious, such as Mr. Gardner's call for governments at all levels to better subsidize arenas and ice time as a way to promote kids being active.

24 "If you don't invest in youth, if you don't plant the seeds, the tree isn't going to grow," says the GTHL president. "I mean, this is insane. How in the heck can you get kids involved in hockey with those kinds of costs? Especially people that are new to the country. When they find out how much it's going to cost, they get very nervous."

25 The Subban family has taken its own approach to the issue. Partnering with a corporate sponsor, they helped create the Hyundai Hockey Helpers program, which provides grants of up to $1,000 to children who can't afford to play hockey.

26 P.K. Subban, the charismatic, 24-year-old star with the Montreal Canadiens, has become the face of the campaign, appearing in television commercials that have played during *Hockey Night in Canada*.

27 "It's a great game," he says in one of the ads, "but it's an expensive game, too."

28 The program's first year helped 1,880 children get onto the ice last season, something that was important to Karl Subban, who immigrated to Sudbury from Jamaica when he was 11 and couldn't afford to play organized hockey.

29 He and his wife, Maria, were ultimately able to give their children that opportunity thanks to two successful careers, but he knows from experience that many will not get that chance without some help.

30 "Many of us afforded it with difficulty," says Mr. Subban, who recently retired after 30 years as a principal and teacher, at times in some of Toronto's poorest neighbourhoods. "Many people are making sacrifices, and I don't remember many parents not complaining about the cost.

31 "We have so many children who want to play but just can't afford it. The rising cost is just putting too many children on the sidelines."

Vocabulary and Comprehension

1. In paragraph 2, what does *patriarch* mean? Circle the best answer.
   a. Tribe (b.) Male head of a family c. Planetary
2. What is Mirtle's attitude toward his subject?
   ____
3. Underline the thesis statement in the essay.
   ____

Critical Thinking

4. Mirtle clearly outlines some of the reasons why hockey is affordable only for the wealthy. What are they?
   ____
5. What are the sacrifices that families have to make for their children and teens to play hockey?
   ____
6. What is Mirtle's solution to the problem of the high costs of playing in hockey?
   ____

Writing Topics

Write about one of the following topics. Remember to explore, develop, and revise and edit your work.

1. What types of sports have you participated in? Were they expensive or relatively inexpensive to play?
2. Select a sport that you enjoy, and describe how social media have enhanced the game.
3. Do you agree or disagree with the author's argument? Provide examples from the essay to support your point of view.

READING 5

Ten Beauty Tips You Never Asked For

Elizabeth Hay

Elizabeth Hay is an Ottawa-based writer whose third novel, *Late Nights on Air*, garnered the Scotiabank Giller Prize. Her other works include *A Student of Weather*, *Garbo Laughs*, *Crossing the Snow Line*, and *Small Change*. As you read this definition essay, also look for elements of classification, illustration, narration, and description writing.

1 When I was small and in love with Perry Como, I would sit on my mother's bed and watch her put on her clothes exactly as she took them off: in one fell **swoop.** Overnight those multiple layers of undershirt inside blouse inside sweater upon sweater cooled off and in the morning, when she slid them over her head, they were icy. What kind of mother was this? Where was the makeup? The high heels? The romance? It pretty much broke my heart that I didn't have a beautiful mother.

swoop: descend rapidly

2 Sometimes I would suggest that she wear one of her suits, and she would, but not until late in the day—she had the habit of wearing the same old clothes all day long and then changing into something better before my father came home. There was the butterscotch-coloured suit with a matching frilly blouse, and the soft greeny-blue suit with the cream-coloured blouse. Both jackets came in at the waist, both suits were a joy to behold. But two suits was not a lot of suits.

3 In those days, I had a friend with a glamorous, vividly high-strung mother who lived for playing the piano and going to Toronto, which she called the city, where she shopped on Bloor Street at the Colonnade. I will never forget the way she looked down at her new suede shoes, and, spotting a scuff on the side, said, "Look at that scuff! I'm going to have to get a new pair!" Nor will I forget the sight of her playing piano with such concentration that her beautiful face screwed up into a monkey's.

4 Beauty Tip #1: Don't **grimace** when you play piano.

grimace: distortion of the face, frown

5 At eighty, my mother—your grandmother—had become so beautiful that I couldn't stop looking at her. Her thick hair—her crowning glory, as she called it with amused derision—was the colour of fine silver. Her old satiny skin was walnut brown. Her hands with the Henry Moore thumbs—curving into backward C's as befits a sculptor, or, in her case, a painter—were gnarled but arthritis-free. She became beautiful after her four kids left home and she no longer had to pretend she was so damned happy about being a mother. She would dispute this, she always has disputed it, but I am the one writing this piece. Her cross face relaxed, her 1950s glasses came off in favour of gold-rimmed **specs** and she stopped putting her naturally curly hair into tight curlers.

specs: eyeglasses

6 Beauty Tip #2: It is never too late, as Churchill kept telling Garbo.

7 In the meantime, you came along. At the age of six you sat on my bed and said to me, "You always wear pants and you always wear the same pants."

8 Beauty Tip #3: Listen to your daughter.

9 If anything, my interest in beauty has only increased with the years. I notice skin more avidly than ever. The way many women work their skin with their fingertips, especially during the cold winter months, rubbing and tugging at it as if it were cheap dry goods. The overripe watermelon gleam that swollen old female knees acquire. The fine cross-hatching that afflicts blondes who swim in chlorinated pools, the furrowed upper lip that plagues auburns above all. In the name of research, I ask perfect strangers what they use on their skin, and they tell me. The ruddy newspaperwoman who pulled a wagon of *Ottawa Citizens* behind her bicycle, no matter the weather, said, "That vitamin E cream you get in the pharmacy."

10 "Vitamin E?"

11 "Yeah. Or C."

12 The cleaning ladies who were tromping up somebody else's steps, laden with buckets and mops, said, "Neutrogena when we can afford it, but usually Lubriderm." The Cambodian wagon vendor who was selling French fries during the ice storm said, "Vaseline. In Cambodia too." There's Vaseline in Cambodia? "Everywhere. All over the world." And you needed it over there?

"There it's worse, so cold and dry that even our cheeks would split." The thin, elderly woman working in a health food store on a hot summer's day said, "For years, I couldn't have a bath. I'm going to get that fly"—she was holding a swatter up in the air. "I'd have a bath and in the middle of the night I'd be scratching here"—across her belly—"so hard I'd bleed. Then we moved into the country and I realized I was allergic to the chlorine in city water. But I still couldn't be in the sun. I'd be in the sun, and it was like boiling water thrown over me. I burned so bad. Then I started reading in these books we have"—she pointed around the store—"and began to take flaxseed oil capsules, three of them three times a day, and in two and a half months I could feel oil on my skin. And this summer I could be in the sun without burning. This may not look like much of a tan to you"—stretching out her arm—"but if I held it up against my breasts you'd see how white the rest of me is. Now I'm down to one capsule twice a day. My hair looks 100 percent better. And my bowels! I just go into the bathroom and I'm out again before you know it."

13 I have tried her method in scaled-down fashion, a variation of my old childhood practice of dipping my finger in the butter dish every time I passed the dining room table. As someone who butters her baguette on both sides, you will be sympathetic. I have even framed Beauty Tip #4: Don't bother with skin cream, just eat oil. And added Beauty Tip #5, my favourite, as a corollary: Don't bathe so often. All a daily shower accomplishes is to remove a body's natural oils that then have to be replenished with expensive lotions, and what this furthers beyond lining the pockets of the beauty industry I don't know. But, in honesty, I have to add something else. As someone with a cupboard full of skin creams from as far away as Cuba and Germany, as someone who took a workshop on how to make my own herbal lotions and has a drawer full of ingredients and a willingness to try anything—motivated as I am by the highest scientific interest—take it from me, this is a shortcut: Beauty Tip #6: Nothing works.

14 Now on to hair. I have it on good authority that before the war, women used to wash their hair no more than twice a month, and it was "a job" conducted not in the bathroom but in the kitchen. With shampoo? I asked your grandmother. "Oh, my dear, no. Hand soap." But didn't your heads get itchy? "We scratched."

15 She remembers clearly the furor when Mary Martin, starring in *South Pacific*, washed that man right out of her hair every night on stage. "People were concerned that her hair would turn to straw." She remembers, too, the Canadian-Scottish sneering that occurred when the first beauty parlour came to town. This was in the Ottawa Valley in the 1930s. "Such nonsense," everyone said, to go to a beauty parlour to get your hair washed.

16 When I was a teenager like you, I had tragically oily hair and my own technique for dealing with it, something I was reminded of a year ago when I ran into an old school friend I hadn't seen in thirty years. She wanted to know if I still washed my hair with dish detergent. "No," I answered, "not any more. But I have observed that washing my hair every day is a mistake. It looks better on day two or three." Beauty Tip #7: Hair, like homemade bread, is always better on the second day.

17 Body hair is something else, and finally I have reached the unspeakable heart of the matter. I could have built a pyramid in the time I've spent regretting my own body hair and forecasting your hairy fate. Oh, the sorrows that await. But this is where the torch I'm ready to pass on gets so wisely refused. You dumbfound me by taking a different approach. At fifteen, when you have to give a speech in French class, you take the point of view of the despised and embattled leg hair: the hair on a woman's leg speaks to the hair

on a man's leg, asking why its existence is so much more threatened. You practise your speech in front of our French-speaking neighbour, who actually comes from Greece, and what follows on a beautiful June evening is an outpouring of body-hair confessions as informative as they are heartwarming, a United Nations of body hair enlightenment.

18 "I am hairy too," announces our Greek neighbour, a pretty thirty-year-old who dresses in revealing tops, petite and slender, though with a hearty appetite (she comes for a drink and stays for supper). "I am a very hairy woman," she says. "It is a curse. The Mediterranean curse of hairiness." She describes her trauma at sixteen when a man made a pointed remark about the hair under her arms. And she gives you the following advice about leg hair. Beauty Tip #8: Don't shave. Never shave. First: wax. Then, when the hair starts to come in again, use a depilatory instrument; they cost $100 at a department store.

19 She tells you, "Don't be jealous of other women. Well, I am jealous. But don't be."

20 Then, having accepted another glass of wine, she offers to wax your legs. Stepping back with a smile, she says, "This is not a conspiracy. But if you want …" She explains that she has a Greek product, no longer available under the new EU restrictions. "Now you can only buy expensive waxes. But this product used to be cheap. It is sugar, lemon and water. You paint it on and pull it off in strips."

21 "Will it hurt?" you ask.

22 "If it does, we stop."

23 You graciously decline. But when Irene moves to Europe to teach advanced linguistics at a famous university, I inherit her instrument, the famous hair plucker, since it operates on a North American current and will be useless to her over there. As a result, I can testify to the stoical thread that unites hairy women, whether they be of Mediterranean or of grim northern stock. Never do I use it without thinking of her and of her gentle, forthright urgings that you not make your life harder for yourself than necessary.

24 In the end, the delivery of your speech was anticlimactic. Your classmates laughed, but much more moderately than you had hoped, and you came home depressed. Beauty Tip #9: Square your shoulders and remember Irene.

25 A few other things I'll pass on: Noses grow. They keep growing long after everything else has stopped. This is not an illusion. Moles proliferate. They increase in number as you age and there will be no end to them. Brown ones, beige ones, red ones like flicks from a red paintbrush. They prefer your chest to any other place. Eyebrows flourish. Pubic hair thins. Wens removed from your scalp grow back.

26 Lately, you have taken to wearing your father's old pants, and I find myself thinking as I look at you, You always wear pants, and you always wear the same pants. I am filled with admiration and an almost atavistic—look it up—sadness, and say nothing.

27 But last week your father said to me, "If you are going to write about the beauty tips your mother never passed on to you, why don't you pass them on to our daughter?" And this seemed like a **revolutionary** idea, because, although I've been thinking about beauty for fifty years, it never occurred to me that I had anything to pass on. How wrong I was.

revolutionary: a dramatic change

28 Beauty Tip #10: Check out Audrey Hepburn in pants.

Vocabulary and Comprehension

1. Circle the best answer: In paragraph 9, *plagues* means
   a. fatal diseases. b. nuisances. c. afflicts.

2. Write a synonym for the word *avidly* in paragraph 9. ________________

3. How does Hay define beauty tips? Give examples from the essay.

____

____

4. Why does the author mention Mary Martin and Audrey Hepburn?

____

____

CRITICAL THINKING

5. Who is the main audience for this reading?

____

____

6. Why does the narrator offer helpful beauty tips in a humorous way? Provide examples.

____

____

____

____

7. In part two, how does the author advance the story?

____

____

____

8. Hay classifies beauty tips universally, crossing age and continent. How does she do this?

____

____

____

Popular Culture and College Life

Write about one of the following topics. Remember to explore, develop, and revise and edit your work.

1. What fads have you followed? Have you bought something silly, joined in an activity that was suddenly popular, or worn your hair in a trendy style? Describe one or more fads that you have followed.
2. Compare and contrast two holidays, ceremonies, or festivals.
3. Reflect on this proverb. What are some reasons that people have for believing in a god or a higher power?

"The believer is happy; the doubter is wise."

—Hungarian Proverb

***Themes:* Psychology and Health Care**

READING 6

New Evidence in "Diefenbaby" Case

Charlie Gillis

Charlie Gillis is an award-winning, Toronto-based national correspondent for *Maclean's* magazine, covering sports and politics. He has also written for the *National Post* and was a reporter at the *Edmonton Journal.* He was educated at Ryerson University as well as the University of British Columbia. In the following example of an argumentative essay, the author recounts the genetic link between George Dryden and John Diefenbaker, Canada's late prime minister. As you read this argumentative essay, also look for elements of illustration and cause and effect writing.

1 A Toronto man who believes he is the son of John Diefenbaker now has a persuasive piece of evidence to back his claim, Macleans.ca has learned: DNA analysis indicating that he is related to the late prime minister's family.

2 Last Tuesday, George Dryden received results from a DNA lab that compared his genetic profile to that of an unidentified male member of Diefenbaker's extended family who lives in southern Ontario. The relative's sample came from a discarded Q-tip, which was obtained without consent by a private investigator experienced in paternity cases. It was then sent directly to a Toronto firm where DNA analysts identified "genetic overlap" pointing to common ancestry.

3 "There is a familial linkage," Harvey Tenenbaum, president of Accu-Metrics, told *Maclean's* for a story appearing in this week's issue of the magazine. "I can't say what it is, but it's more than just strangers passing in the street."

4 Tenenbaum cautioned that the results don't definitively prove that 43-year-old Dryden was fathered by Diefenbaker, who was married twice and had no children by either of his wives. Dryden "could be fifth cousins" with the man from whom the sample was obtained, Tenenbaum said, adding: "You'd really need a sample from John Diefenbaker, or a member of his immediate family, to do an accurate comparison."

5 Still, the finding marks a huge stride forward for Dryden, who has tried **in vain** to obtain a **definitive** test against DNA that belonged to Canada's 13th prime minister, who died in 1979. Previous tests of cells gathered from personal articles that once belonged to the former PM, now stored at the Diefenbaker Canada Centre in Saskatoon, Sask., came back inconclusive.

in vain unsuccessfully

definitive complete

6 Dryden did test negative last winter against a sample of male DNA gleaned from the handle of a clothes brush that belonged to Diefenbaker. But the handle appeared to have been used by more than one person, so no one could be sure whether the DNA analyzed was, in fact, the late PM's.

7 Dryden refused to give up. Last spring, with the help of a professional genealogist, he tracked down more than a dozen members of an eastern branch of Diefenbaker's family residing mostly in the Kitchener–Waterloo area (they spell the name "Diefenbacher"). The other branch of the family which arrived in Canada from Baden, Germany in the early 1800s, died out with the Tory icon.

8 When none of those contacted were willing to provide DNA samples, Dryden enlisted Al Duncan, a retired detective who served with the Toronto police internal affairs unit, and who now runs a private investigation firm.

9 Duncan wouldn't say which member of the Diefenbachers used the Q-tip, or how his investigators obtained it. But he did tell *Maclean's* that his firm, Toronto P.I., is well-practised in identifying and gathering court-worthy evidence. "We bag it, we initial it, we photograph it, we seal it up with tamper-proof tape," he said. "We maintain control of it at all times, and we take it directly to the lab ourselves."

10 The team will take samples from garbage bins, Duncan acknowledged, but only if they believe they can link the items with reasonable probability to a specific individual. He would not say whether the swab came from a trash container.

11 Whatever the source, Dryden was elated by the results. "As far as I'm concerned, this proves it," he said in an interview. "I'm John Diefenbaker's son. I don't know that there's a whole lot more that I can do."

12 Dryden acknowledged the remote chance that the genetic co-mingling revealed by the test had nothing to do with Diefenbaker. His family and that of the unwitting donor have lived in the same region of the country, after all, for more than a century. But Dryden believes the more likely explanation arises from his mother Mary Lou's well-known friendship with the Saskatchewan politician, dating back to her time as a Progressive Conservative youth leader in the late 1950s and early '60s.

13 The two were seen together at public events and Dryden believes their relationship continued even after Mary Lou married Gordon Dryden, a senior figure in the federal Liberal Party, in 1967. Dryden was conceived three and a-half months after their wedding, but a DNA test performed last year proved that Gordon Dryden is not George's biological father. Mary Lou told friends she named her boy John George after the former PM. "The chance of the two families **intermingling** in any other way is very remote," Dryden said.

intermingling
one with another

14 The findings are certainly the closest he's come to proving his theory, which has suffered from a lack of useable evidence. Last week, the Diefenbaker Centre announced that staff had discovered cuttings from hair thought to have been clipped from the former prime minister when he was a child. But the hairs, Dryden has been told, do not have the root cells necessary for analysts to obtain a DNA sample.

Vocabulary and Comprehension

1. What does *genetic overlap* mean in paragraph 2?

   ____

2. What lead-in does the author use? Circle the best answer.

   a. Quotation b. Surprising or provocative statement c. Question

3. Who is the audience for this essay?

   ____

4. What is the author's main point?

   ____

   ____

Critical Thinking

5. Why does Gillis use the word *Diefenbaby* in his title?

6. What two arguments does the author give to acknowledge the opposing point of view?

7. What two examples does the author give to defend Dryden's own position?

8. The author mentions Harvey Tenenbaum's statement in paragraph 3. Why is this piece of information significant to Dryden's claim?

Writing Topics

Write about one of the following topics. Remember to explore, develop, and revise and edit your work.

1. Why has John George Dryden's paternity interest garnered so much attention?
2. Describe another celebrity paternity case.
3. Adopted children should have the right to contact their birth parents. Do you agree or disagree with this statement?

READING 7

The Catcher of Ghosts

Amy Tan

Amy Tan is an American writer. One of her most well-known novels is *The Joy Luck Club*. She has explored themes such as mother–daughter relationships and cultural issues. As you read this descriptive story, which appeared in her book *The Bonesetter's Daughter*, also look for elements of narration and cause and effect.

1 When we returned home, Mother and Father, as well as our aunts and uncles, were bunched in the courtyard, talking in excited voices. Father was relating how he had met an old Taoist priest at the market, a remarkable and strange man. As he passed by, the priest had called out to him: "Sir, you look as if a ghost is plaguing your house."

2 "Why do you say that?" Father asked.

3 "It's true, isn't it?" the old man insisted. "I feel you've had a lot of bad luck and there's no other reason for it. Am I right?"

4 "We had a suicide," Father admitted, "a nursemaid whose daughter was about to be married."

5 "And bad luck followed."

6 "A few calamities," Father answered.

7 The young man standing next to the priest then asked Father if he had heard of the famous Catcher of Ghosts. "No? Well, this is he, the wandering priest right before you. He's newly arrived in your town, so he's not yet as well known as he is in places far to the north and south. Do you have relatives in **Harbin**? No? Well, then! If you had, you'd know who he is." The young man, who claimed to be the priest's acolyte, added, "In that city alone, he is celebrated for having already caught one hundred ghosts in disturbed households. When he was done, the gods told him to start wandering again."

Harbin:
a large town in northeastern China

8 When Father finished telling us how he had met these two men, he added, "This afternoon, the famous Catcher of Ghosts is coming to our house."

9 A few hours later, the Catcher of Ghosts and his assistant stood in our courtyard. The priest had a white beard, and his long hair was piled like a messy bird's nest. In one hand he carried a walking stick with a carved end that looked like a flayed dog stretched over a gateway. In the other, he held a short beating stick. Slung over his shoulders was a rope shawl from which hung a large wooden bell. His robe was not the sand-colored cotton of most wandering monks I had seen. His was a rich-looking blue silk, but the sleeves were grease-stained, as if he had often reached across the table for more to eat.

10 I watched hungrily as Mother offered him special cold dishes. It was late afternoon, and we were sitting on low stools in the courtyard. The monk helped himself to everything—glass noodles with spinach, bamboo shoots with pickled mustard, tofu seasoned with sesame seed oil and coriander. Mother kept apologizing about the quality of the food, saying she was both ashamed and honored to have him in our shabby home. Father was drinking tea. "Tell us how it's done," he said to the priest, "this catching of ghosts. Do you seize them in your fists? Is the struggle fierce or dangerous?"

11 The priest said he would soon show us. "But first I need proof of your sincerity." Father gave his word that we were indeed sincere. "Words are not proof," the priest said.

12 "How do you prove sincerity?" Father asked.

13 "In some cases, a family might walk from here to the top of Mount Tai and back, barefoot and carrying a load of rocks." Everyone, especially my aunts, looked doubtful that any of us could do that.

14 "In other cases," the monk continued, "a small offering of pure silver can be enough and will cover the sincerity of all members of the immediate family."

15 "How much might be enough?" Father asked.

16 The priest frowned. "Only you know if your sincerity is little or great, fake or genuine."

17 The monk continued eating. Father and Mother went to another room to discuss the amount of their sincerity. When they returned, Father opened a pouch and pulled out a silver **ingot** and placed this in front of the famous Catcher of Ghosts.

ingot:
pieces of metal historically used as currency

18 "This is good," the priest said. "A little sincerity is better than none at all."

19 Mother then drew an ingot from the sleeve of her jacket. She slid this next to the first so that the two made a clinking sound. The monk nodded and put down his bowl. He clapped his hands, and the assistant took from his bundle an empty vinegar jar and wad of string.

20 "Where's the girl that the ghost loved best?" asked the priest.

21 "There," Mother said, and pointed to me. "The ghost was her nursemaid."

22 The priest said to me, "Fetch me the comb she used for your hair."

23 My feet were locked to the ground until Mother gave me a little knock on the head to hurry. So I went to the room Precious Auntie and I had shared not so long before. I picked up the comb she used to run through my hair. It was the ivory comb she never wore, its ends carved with roosters, its teeth long and straight. I remembered how Precious Auntie used to scold me for my tangles, worrying over every hair on my head.

24 When I returned, I saw the assistant had placed the vinegar jar in the middle of the courtyard. "Run the comb through your hair nine times," he said. So I did.

25 "Place it in the jar." I dropped the comb inside, smelling the escape of cheap vinegar fumes. "Now stand there perfectly still." The Catcher of Ghosts beat his stick on the wooden bell. It made a deep kwak, kwak sound. He and the acolyte walked in rhythm, circling me, chanting, and drawing closer. Without warning, the Catcher of Ghosts gave a shout and leapt toward me. I thought he was going to squeeze me into the jar, so I closed my eyes and screamed, as did **GaoLing**.

GaoLing: the girl's younger sister

26 When I opened my eyes, I saw the acolyte was pounding a tight-fitting wooden lid onto the jar. He wove rope from top to bottom, bottom to top, then all around the jar, until it resembled a hornet's nest. When this was done, the Catcher of Ghosts tapped the jar with his beating stick and said, "It's over. She's caught. Go ahead. Try to open it, you try. Can't be done."

27 Everyone looked, but no one would touch. Father asked, "Can she escape?"

28 "Not possible," said the Catcher of Ghosts. "This jar is guaranteed to last more than several lifetimes."

Vocabulary and Comprehension

1. Find a word in paragraph 7 that means "helper."

   ____

2. Why do Mother and Father need the services of the Catcher of Ghosts?

   ____

   ____

3. Who is the ghost and what relationship did it have with the family?

   ____

4. A simile is a comparison using *like* or *as*. Underline an example of a simile that the author uses to describe the priest.

5. The author uses imagery in this essay. Give an example of the following:

   Sight: ______________________________

   ____

Sound: ______________________________

____

Smell: ______________________________

____

Touch: ______________________________

____

Critical Thinking

6. Who is Precious Auntie?

____

____

7. What can you infer, or guess, about the Catcher of Ghosts when he asks for "proof of sincerity"?

____

____

8. What can you infer about the characters of Mother and Father from their actions?

____

____

____

Writing Topics

Write about one of the following topics. Remember to explore, develop, and revise and edit your work.

1. Describe an incident from your childhood or the childhood of your parents or grandparents. Try to use descriptive imagery.
2. Describe a family tradition. Give as many details as possible using the five senses.
3. What are some examples of superstitions that people have?

READING 8

A Shift in Perception

Cynthia Macdonald

Cynthia Macdonald is a Toronto-based journalist, author, and literary critic. She has written a novel (*Alms*) along with several short stories. Her nonfiction articles cover a wide range of topics in the arts and education. In the following example of a cause and effect essay, the author discusses perception and the five senses. As you read, also look for elements of narration, description, illustration, and argument.

1 When Constantine Caravassilis listens to stringed instruments, strange things happen. If he hears a chord played in the low range, his eyes might

suddenly flood with colour: "a G," he tells me, "is usually orange." At other times, this type of sound can cause him to experience sweet or bitter tastes.

2 Caravassilis, an accomplished composer and doctoral student at the University of Toronto's Faculty of Music, has an unusually strong case of synesthesia—a condition in which the stimulation of one sensory pathway leads automatically to the arousal of another.

3 Synesthesia isn't unique to musicians, although they may be disproportionately affected by it. It wasn't until his second year at university that Caravassilis learned that several other composers (such as Claude Debussy and Alexander Scriabin) shared what he thinks of as "an ability, not a malfunction. But you wouldn't describe it as a negative or positive experience," he says. "It just is."

4 Up until recently, it would have been easy to dismiss Caravassilis as delusional: after all, creative people are known for having active imaginations. Now, however, what **synesthetes** say they experience is backed up by science. Using functional magnetic resonance imaging (fMRI), neuroscientists have discovered that there is much more crosstalk among the senses than we ever imagined before. It just so happens that Caravassilis's is much louder than most.

synesthetes
individuals who perceive overlapping senses (sound is perceived as a colour)

neuroscience
various types of nervous system and brain studies

5 But if **neuroscience** is telling us that the most profound synesthetes truly "see" a colour invisible to most of us, then what exactly do we mean when we talk about vision? Or for that matter, about taste, hearing, smell and touch?

6 Professor Mohan Matthen is trying his best to answer this question. He is currently the principal investigator at the Network for Sensory Research, an international team of philosophers headquartered at U of T who believe it is high time we developed a new conceptual framework for the senses.

7 It seems natural that philosophers should be leading this investigation; after all, it was Aristotle who originally conceived of the five-sense model to which we rigorously cling. And until the scientific method was developed in the 17th century, investigation of the senses belonged to the philosophers alone. Today, they share the stage with neuroscientists, psychologists, medical doctors and biologists. And findings within these fields are reframing philosophical thinking in fascinating ways.

8 Matthen himself came to philosophy via the sciences: his first degree was in physics, and he has also taught the philosophy of biology. His first exposure to the domain that would shape his life came when a teacher in his native India recommended that he read *Appearance and Reality* by the British metaphysician F.H. Bradley. On his chatty blog, Matthen jokes that the book (and his teacher) actually caused him "much misery"; nonetheless, it spurred him to study human perception.

9 Other philosophers around the world have been probing the mystery of the senses for some time. Barry Smith, codirector of the University of London's Centre for the Study of the Senses, is best known as a specialist in flavour and smell. Fiona Macpherson, who is the director of the University of Glasgow's Centre for the Study of Perceptual Experience, is an expert in the nature of visual experience, including optical illusions. Matthen has brought these researchers together—in person, when possible—with like-minded thinkers from Harvard, M.I.T. and elsewhere. "We want people to communicate, share each others' work and get access to faculty members in other disciplines," he says. "We're particularly interested in multi-sensory integration and how the senses contribute to knowledge."

10 A key question the network wants to address is whether Aristotle's model is still relevant. "The traditional five senses are external, but we're also interested in the internal senses—those that have to do with a sense of what your own body is doing," Matthen says. These include proprioception (knowing where your body is in space); nociception (the feeling of pain); and thermoception (temperature sense), among others.

11 Matthen's colleague Fiona Macpherson points out that animals have certain senses that we lack. "There are fish who are sensitive to electric fields. And there's quite good evidence that some animals are sensitive to magnetic north, which we aren't." We humans might possess a vomeronasal organ—which animals famously use to sniff each others' pheromones—but the jury is still out on whether a human sense functions this way. So if we no longer have five senses, then how many do we have?

12 Like a practiced synesthete, I can see Matthen's head shaking over the phone. "There's not much point in counting them," he says. "What we're more interested in is how they come together." Barry Smith expands on this. "You could have more than one sense of smell, because you've got the smelling from the outside in when you take a breath. But you're also smelling aromas that enter the sinus cavity from inside the mouth."

13 An explanation: when I attend one of Smith's talks, he offers everyone in attendance a jelly bean, and tells us to hold our nose while chewing. My jelly bean is coconut flavoured; with my nose held, I can only perceive that it's "sweet" (in that respect, no different in any way from raspberry or chocolate). The coconut flavour only becomes apparent when I unplug my nose. Smith's point is clear: what we call "flavour" is a blend of tongue-taste and smell. "None of the parts operate separately anyway," he says. "So how can we think of them as parts?"

14 *None of the parts operate separately*. It's an idea that completely upends what we all learned as schoolchildren: there are five individuated senses, some more cherished than others. And yet we know from experience how integrated they all must be. When we have a cold, for example, taste and smell are equally diminished. And instinctively, we know that beautifully presented food somehow tastes better.

15 Sensory fusion is also illustrated by the McGurk effect, where you watch a mouth forming the sound "ga" while the sound "ba" is being played. What you will then hear is wrong: it's the sound "da," the midpoint between the two. (There are several video demonstrations of this effect on YouTube.) "So the question is, do we partly hear with our eyes?" asks Smith. "And the thought seems to be, yes. You're fusing hearing and vision to make some new product. The way we're talking about hearing and vision no longer depends on input from just one sense, and as a result we've had to tear up our old ideas."

16 And yet, it's not as if Aristotle was completely wrong: there are dividing lines, but where are they? On a sunny day in May, Matthen gathers members of the network at a winetasting in the Niagara region of Ontario. Smith is, among other things, an oenophile—wine-tasting being a discipline that naturally combines all the senses at once. "Smell this!" he demands, proffering a glass of Riesling. "It has notes of diesel and lime." This doesn't sound inviting, and Smith is right: what I inhale seems nothing less than mildly citric gasoline.

17 But tasting is a different matter altogether. On drinking the wine, I perceive it as sweet and floral, its flavour only a distant cousin to its scent. Smith says this disconnection is common in the flavour business. He points

out the example of Époisses cheese, which tastes delightful but smells like a "teenager's training shoe." It's clear that there are separate perceptual systems operating here. But the war may not be between smell and taste—instead, it could be one of my smell-senses rejecting the information from another.

18 It appears that we may have multiple sight senses, too. Take the remarkable example of Daniel Kish, a Californian who had his eyes removed as a toddler due to cancer. To navigate the world, Kish echolocates: he uses vocal clicks to activate a kind of sonar system more commonly associated with animals such as bats. A recent study showed that Kish's method can help him tell a car from a lamppost, or a flat object from one that is convex. He can also stand near your car and tell you how far it is from the curb.

19 Amazingly, brain scans show that Kish's visual cortex lights up when he is "looking" at something, even though he is echolocating the object instead of seeing it in a traditional manner. So in one very key sense, Kish has not lost the ability to see things—just the usual way of doing so.

20 And yet, as Fiona Macpherson points out, the very words "visual cortex" might be erroneous; after all, it's a given that a person with no eyes cannot see. "This area of the brain is clearly doing a lot of visual processing—but is it exclusively visual?" she asks. "It might be better to call it a spatial-processing cortex."

21 In any case, "when somebody loses a sense," says Matthen, "they often manage to get the same information in a different way. That's of vital interest to us."

22 Matthen points out that whether disabled or not, all human beings use their senses in concert all the time, though they may not be conscious of it. When one sense fails or feels untrustworthy, we automatically let another take over. "If you don't trust the colour of something, you might turn it over, use motion to manipulate the object and learn more about it," he says. "Vision can make mistakes, but generally by interacting with an object in a multi-sensory way we can check those mistakes."

23 So are we all synesthetic? Fiona Macpherson believes that a case such as that of Caravassilis—true synesthesia—is relatively rare. But she thinks we all experience cross-modal phenomena. Take the "Bouba-Kiki" experiment of 2001, in which people were shown two pictorial figures—one rounded, the other angular. Ninety-five per cent of participants assigned the name "kiki" to the angular figure and "bouba" to the rounded one, proving a link between visual and auditory faculties in the brain. Macpherson says we frequently make other synesthesia-like associations, too. "Suppose I gave you a blank piece of paper and a pen, and I asked you to draw how the days of the week were related to each other," she says. "How would you do it?"

24 I tell her that it's nonsense to think the days of the week are spatially related. But in her mind, they are. "I would draw a circle that goes anticlockwise, with Saturday and Sunday at the top," she says. I tell her that strikes me as frankly weird—but she returns the favour when I tell her the appearance of sloppily printed letters can sometimes make the skin on my thumbs feel itchy.

25 "One of the nice things about these studies," she says, "is that we're realizing the way human beings think about things is really idiosyncratic. What goes on in our heads is so unique, because of the rich, complex people that we are."

***

26 What is a "sense," anyway? As a verb, it means to grasp, or feel, or understand. As a noun, it has traditionally referred to a bodily faculty that enables us to do these things.

27 And yet, even those simple definitions are currently up for review. It might even be possible to sense something without being aware of it. "There is emotional communication through chemical signalling," says Smith, noting that researchers at the Weizmann Institute in Israel last year found evidence that chemical signals from a woman's tears lower men's sexual interest, even though tears give off no **discernible** odour.

discernible recognizable as different

28 Advances in science are not only doing away with how we view the senses, but how we view philosophy itself. Since the invention of the scientific method, a chasm has opened between the two disciplines. And unless philosophy works to keep up, a good deal of what we've traditionally thought risks invalidation.

29 "When philosophers start telling you how it is, I start to get worried," says Smith. "Especially if they're talking about the mind, or language or emotions, and they don't look at the relevant recent science on these topics." He points out that many outmoded philosophical views are vital links in a chain that is still snaking through history towards the truth. But if these views are no longer tenable, we should no longer teach them as gospel.

30 "We've given up the idea that the world is composed of four elements. Why do we hold on to Artistotle's view that there are just five senses?" Smith asks. "Somehow this is a bit of folk ideology that still remains."

31 Neuroscience has revolutionized philosophy. Technology such as fMRI offers a picture of the self that seems to contradict the fragile and unreliable accounts of it we like to give each other.

32 It may seem a broad statement, but Macpherson reminds me how fundamental these questions are to philosophers. "One of the big philosophical questions that everybody knows is, how do I know that the world around me really exists, and is as I take it to be? That question arose because people thought: well, maybe I'm just hallucinating it all. Maybe I'm in the Matrix, and sentient machines are tampering with my brain."

33 So if science is discrediting much of what philosophers used to think about the nature of perception, why should philosophers participate in this debate at all? Matthen says that the examination of subjective experience—how it feels to be human, regardless of what any lab test might tell us—is still very much the province of philosophers, and has always been a significant area of study. Our preference for viewing the world unscientifically may be annoying and frustrating. But it's also key to understanding who we are.

34 Smith agrees. "We all know the sun isn't really moving, but we still talk about it 'setting.' How do we connect the lived experience, the way things seem to us, with what's really going on? It's the job of the philosopher to do that."

35 *"If the doors of perception were cleansed, everything would appear to man as it is, infinite."* Since William Blake wrote that over 200 years ago, many (most famously, the writer Aldous Huxley) have tried to alter their perceptual experience with drugs. But instead of stumbling through a drugged haze, some modern-day Huxleys are now tweaking their senses with different kinds of substances.

36 One of these is miraculin, a derivative of a west African berry that strips lemons of their acidity and makes them taste as sweet as peaches. Miraculin has more serious uses too. People undergoing chemotherapy—who often find that food tastes unpleasantly metallic—can use it to positively alter the flavour of what they eat.

37 Flavourless jelly beans, sweet lemons and wine that smells like gasoline: it's not hard to believe Smith when he says that sensory research is "a lot of fun." Those attracted to it are quirky sorts, preoccupied with questions that wouldn't trouble most of us. "One of the things that's really nice about this work," says Matthen, "is that everything you do, even if it's terribly mundane, suddenly takes on more meaning. You might notice that when you're driving, you don't have to see the corners of your car to know where they are. The car responds to your own movements and when it does that, it becomes integrated into your own bodily sense."

38 Being most concerned with questions of taste, scent and flavour, Smith admits to having acquired an overdeveloped sense of smell. "I can't turn it off!" he laughs. "I walk into rooms and I smell people, or the rooms themselves; when people walk by I'm noticing their different sensory fingerprints."

39 Isn't that unpleasant? Not at all, he says. "You think: all of this was going on, and I've been missing it. To put yourself back in touch with your animal nature, your senses, your contact with the environment is wonderful. You feel healthier, more complete."

40 Back in Toronto, Constantine Caravassilis is working on something very special to him: a huge, colour-coded musical project, which he plans to finish in two or three years. "Instead of preludes and fugues in D major or C minor, we'll have preludes and fugues in green or orange," he says.

41 He uses software that converts his piano's sounds to string sounds, and shifts them into a lower range. When that happens, his synesthesia kicks in and his mind erupts in colour, tastes and emotions. "With the part I'm working on now, I'm trying to stick with beige," he says. "But it's very difficult. I'll spend days on just three bars, and then all of a sudden my fugue subject wants to turn red! So that's the challenge. I have to find a way to keep it going…in the same colour."

Vocabulary and Comprehension

1. What does the word *synesthetes* mean in paragraph 3?

   ____

2. What is the meaning of *neuroscience* in paragraph 3?

   ____

3. Macdonald uses descriptive imagery. Descriptive imagery includes active verbs, adjectives, and other words that appeal to the senses (sight, smell, touch, sound, taste). Underline at least six examples of descriptive imagery.

4. Which researchers are mentioned in Macdonald's article?

   ____

   ____

Critical Thinking

5. What does Barry Smith's experiment demonstrate?

   ____

   ____

6. Why can we no longer "dismiss [Constantine] Caravassilis as delusional" (paragraph 3)?

____

____

7. Why does Professor Matthen want to create "a new conceptual framework for the senses" (paragraph 4)? What might that include?

____

____

____

____

Writing Topics

Write about one of the following topics. Remember to explore, develop, and revise and edit your work.

1. Write about a time when you saw an event that changed your perception of someone.
2. Macdonald tells a story to make a point about living life to the fullest. Write about a moment in time when you felt that you were living life to its fullest. Use descriptive imagery in your writing.
3. Do you live in a clean, organized environment or a messy one? Describe a clean or messy room in your home—using all of your senses.

READING 9

The Sage: Gordon Smith Knows Painting

Eric Andrew-Gee

Eric Andrew-Gee is a Montreal-based journalist who has written for *Toronto Life* and *Canadian Art*. He is also the associate editor of *Maissoneuve* magazine. In the following descriptive essay, the author eloquently profiles a renowned West Coast painter, Gordon Smith. As you read, also look for elements of narration and cause and effect writing.

1 Gordon Smith is 93. Every morning, he wakes up early, then heads to his studio. It is a victory of sorts, if not a miracle. At seven o'clock, he uses his walker to cover the 20 or so metres from his house. There is something prehistoric about the grounds he walks, overlooking Howe Sound in West Vancouver: the primal screech of Steller's jays **ricochets** off sprawling ferns and glides along ponds stocked with huge, ancient-looking orange fish; the Douglas firs loom like titans. Entering the studio, Smith passes through a door frame whose upper corners are clotted with spiderwebs. Then, he lowers himself into his wheelchair; it is a Breezy 600 model, all black.

ricochets rebounds

2 His grin is mischievous, Pan-like, his hair soft and white as a virgin snowfall, and his big painter's hands grasp your forearm with the tender firmness of a baseball player holding his favourite Louisville Slugger. But his body bears the brunt of years and experience. Thanks to his service in the Second World War, he has to cup a magnifying hand around his left ear for it to be any good, and there is a steel brace on his right ankle.

bespoke
custom-made

3 He dresses in **bespoke** brown corduroy jackets and stylish blue pinstripe shirts, and his reedy, English-accented voice would not sound out of place coming from a pith-helmed *sahib* in the British colonial service. He and his Filipina assistant, Minnie, have this variation on the Jeeves-and-Wooster routine, with Smith forever calling out for Minnie to do this or that—water the plants, order a cab—and Minnie forever replying, "I already did it, Mr. Smith." He seems, at first blush, every bit the tweedy Edwardian gentleman.

4 But inside the small cedar outbuilding where he does his painting, time seems to stop. The walls are covered in burlap, painted white: a blank canvas. When he starts to work, he rarely pauses until three or four hours have passed. At nine o'clock, Minnie brings coffee. Otherwise, he is mostly alone.

5 Smith uses all manner of implements to shape the paint: brushes, scrapers, sponges—sometimes, even a yellow plastic pasta ladle. "He really does just love to push paint around," says the painter Attila Richard Lukacs. "Letting chance come through."

6 As the phrase implies, painting is never a sure thing. But Smith has a deep reservoir of faith in his work. I was startled when, over dinner at a quiet Japanese restaurant, he told me his current canvas-in-progress was the best thing he'd ever done. Later, his art dealer, Andy Sylvester, told me that Smith says the same thing about every new painting. "If you ask him what is the most important painting in this show," Sylvester said, as we walked through an exhibition of Smith's work at Equinox Gallery, which Sylvester curated, "he'll say, 'There's one at my studio. And I think I've made a discovery.'"

7 This makes Smith "a quintessential modernist," according to Sylvester. A modernist in that he believes in progress, and the future.

diminution
reduction

8 The photographer Christos Dikeakos, another friend, recognizes the improbability of this belief. Not only is Smith at an age that most people think is measured in terms of **diminution** and decay, but he also lives in an age short on faith in the progress of art. Dikeakos has a name for Smith that reflects this, like something out of a spaghetti western: "the surviving and ongoing modernist."

***

9 When Gordon Appelbe Smith was born, on June 18, 1919, in East Brighton, England, women younger than 30 couldn't vote, the Treaty of Versailles was 10 days shy of being signed, and Matisse and Picasso were still controversial. Modernism was dawning, but for most people it was no more than a pink blur on the horizon.

10 By 1951, you couldn't escape it. Smith was living in Vancouver with his wife, Marion, and had begun teaching at the Vancouver School of Art. He did some painting of his own, but most of it was shy and stilted, and shared the subject matter of Lawren Harris and Emily Carr. That year, Smith knew his art needed to be pushed off a cliff, so he went to San Francisco and enrolled in the California School of Fine Arts, then famous for housing members of the Bay Area school of Abstract Expressionism.

11 Elmer Bischoff was one of Smith's teachers. On the first day of class, a Friday, he told the students, "okay, start painting and I'll be back next Tuesday." Some were shocked by his flippancy. Smith went out and made some very earnest paintings of rocks.

12 Come Tuesday, Bischoff hardly looked at Smith's efforts. Instead, he told the students to gather around a student who had laid a stretcher on the floor and covered it in black paint with his hands. As Ian Thom recounts in "The Act of Painting," a biographical essay about Smith written in 1997, Bischoff spent the morning singing hosannas to the paint-drenched stretcher. He then told

the rest of the students to go to the school shop and buy big canvases—at least 60 inches across—and cans of Fuller's house paint, and "just start painting." As Smith tells it today, the sky opened up and the good light of modernism flooded in. Painting was about the paint itself, not pretty pictures, Smith realized. Bischoff had won a convert.

13 Smith's lifestyle did not take long to catch up to his art. He returned to Vancouver and was part of a cadre of modernists centred around the University of British Columbia and the Vancouver School of Art, most of them teachers as well as artists, who outshone everyone in the dreary world of mid-century Vancouver, people like Jack Shadbolt, B.C. Binning, Alistair Bell, Bruno and Molly Bobak, and Arthur Erickson.

14 Smith's group revolutionized living in Vancouver as much as they did the city's art. They started eating green salads, commissioning modernist homes, drinking martinis and sitting in Jacobsen chairs. "To buy a Jacobsen chair in 1955, it was kind of like buying hash in 2012," Douglas Coupland says.

15 In 1965, Erickson designed Smith a house in West Vancouver. You arrive in Smith's driveway, and, at first, you don't even think, "here is a house." It has a timeless, even a placeless, quality. Wood beams hover unobtrusively in midair, stained a camouflaging forest green. Whole walls are made of glass. The house is as much lens as it is habitation. As curator Scott Watson puts it to me, "The city went from Edwardian values and lifestyles to contemporary ones because of people like Gordon and his wife. They were proselytizers for the modern."

16 Not all of Smith's friends had tastes as brave as his. Bell and Bruno Bobak, especially, rejected Abstract Expressionism from the beginning, and never wavered. "They just didn't have any trust in it," Smith tells me at his dining room table. "They were wrong, they were wrong! They were wrong."

17 Smith launched himself headlong into Abstract Expressionism from the mid-1950s onward. *Blue & Black Painting*, from 1958, may be his most impressive work from this period. Featured prominently in the first room of the Equinox show, it moves with the buzzing turbulence of a swarm of wasps. The almost angry daubs of blue, black and white resolve into a menacing mass. It is a work of controlled fury.

18 But *controlled* was too often what his Abstract Expressionist paintings from the '50s and '60s were. They feel mannered, cautious. The paint does exactly what Smith demands of it—he fails to let chance come through.

19 Part of the reason for this can be traced to his teaching. In 1956, Smith took a position in UBC's faculty of education, teaching future teachers how to teach art. He was in a pedagogical state of mind. His painting often became a laboratory for theories he was expounding in the classroom.

20 This came to a head with Smith's hard-edge paintings. While teaching at UBC, he discovered the colour theory of Joseph Albers and Johannes Itten, and began applying it to his art. The results often didn't work. The neon pink and snot green of *Black Diamond* (1966) are as queasy as they sound. *Portfolio A: VI* (1968) radiates red and purple like an elaborate sunburn. Usually, seeking the new rejuvenated Smith's work. But with the hard-edge paintings, he was trend chasing. None of them made it into the Equinox exhibition, partly because Smith has come close to disowning them. One year in the 1970s, Smith threw a whole edition of hard-edge prints into a massive bonfire in his yard. Revenue Canada was nonplussed. "They came to do my income taxes one time," he remembers, "and they said, 'Where are all these paintings you've got?' And I said, 'I burned them.'"

***

21 It is 720 kilometres northwest from Vancouver to Haida Gwaii, the islands that inspired Smith's best work and his self-reinvention. People who have

made the voyage say that, whereas Vancouver is psychically penned in by Vancouver Island, Haida Gwaii feels like the end of the earth.

22 When Smith made the first in a series of visits to the islands in the 1980s, part of his world was ending. He had retired from UBC in 1982, bringing to a close a teaching career that he says was his true vocation. It was also, it now seems clear, a straitjacket.

23 Beginning with *TANU* (1985), Smith broke out of it. Named after a village in Haida Gwaii, the painting is a dark riot, a forest interior during a nighttime storm, the colours—ochres and mauves and mosses—clawed across the black backdrop like animals fleeing danger. All of this is merely suggested, or evoked: no literal figures emerge from the chaos. The work is primarily about what paint does if freely applied to a canvas, about paint's autonomous will. (Smith later admitted that he had tried painting with his left hand around this time, "so I wouldn't do anything too tasteful.") Smith let the paint take over.

24 The work only gets less inhibited from there. *Tanu* (1987) is all loose, fluid strokes, hanging raggedly together like a torn velvet curtain. It's an object lesson in not overpainting. (Its five vertical forms, in pink, white and grey, also seem to refer cheekily to Picasso's 1907 *Les Demoiselles d'Avignon*.) In *Shannon Falls* (1991), Smith masterfully recreates the experience of seeing agitated water turn to froth, a feat of realism, but also lets the paint bleed out of the falls' appointed path, blending with the colours of the rock as only paint could.

25 Smith kept emancipating paint with *Winterscape* (1991) and *Pond* (1996), done almost entirely in bravura black and white. Sadly, they did not make it into the Equinox show, nor did *Shannon Falls*.

26 What did make it in, overwhelmingly, were the paintings that have consumed Smith for the last decade: dense, tangled forest scenes (strangely, this bard of the BC landscape seems to have never painted a mountain) in a squintingly bright palette of orange and lime and white—what Smith calls his "boring" phase. Sylvester is right to point out that, despite these paintings' realism and seemingly picturesque subject matter, the madly flailing sinews of twig and grass that occupy most of their foregrounds create a visual barrier that prevents easy, passive immersion in the scene. These paintings are not *just* boring. But they lack the forceful, coherent vision of the 1985-to-1996 work.

27 Nonetheless—or maybe therefore—they have developed a following. Scott Watson, an art historian at UBC, and not a cynic by disposition, has this to say about Smith's collectors: "He's in fashion now, among people who want to spend substantial amounts on a painting."

28 The panjandrums were out in full force on the night of the Equinox collectors' opening last fall. In the parking lot of the converted warehouse where the show was being held, I parked next to a Maserati, a car that would set a Canadian member of Parliament back a year's salary before taxes. Inside, there were hors d'oeuvres—"Truffle and Asparagus Mousse in Edible Cone," "Cinnamon Rubbed Albacore Tuna on Lotus Chips with Sesame Brittle"—and an open bar.

29 If you wanted to get away from the crowd, you could go to the first room in the show, which contained Smith's "black paintings." In the early 1990s and then again around the turn of the last decade, Smith composed a series of dark, abstract canvases that treat his experience in the Second World War. On July 20, 1943, Smith had his right leg shattered in a Sicilian town called Leonforte, a week after disembarking at Pachino Beach. There is, somehow, a picture of him lying on the battlefield right after it happened—a ball of khaki—which hangs in his office.

30 Smith spent the 50 years after the war doing paintings as close to devoid of psychological content as you can get. Then, in 1990, with *Juno II*, he let out a howl of sublimated pain about his war experience. Referencing the beach where Canadians landed during D-Day (as well as a favourite dog), the painting has a scrawled red "2 +" that drips, or weeps, or bleeds, down the middle of the canvas. The canvas (and a small section in the top-left corner) is actually tarpaulin, from the kitbag Smith had when he landed in Italy. At the bottom of the painting is a white, spectral shape floating from the frame. It registers as the head of a drowned figure (which would make it the first and only human figure Smith has painted, as far as I can tell). The painting's presence in the show was like a having a man with his leg blown to pieces crawling through your cocktail party, bleeding on the carpet, crying for help.

31 Taken as a whole, the black paintings—which he continues to produce—are the most ambitious and fully realized of Smith's works. And they are a stark departure: the use of symbolism, collage and text is essentially absent elsewhere in Smith's catalogue. The psychological content is so dense as to almost be surrealist, something it's hard to imagine saying about a mere landscape painter.

***

32 After being wounded, Smith spent five months recuperating in a Tripoli hospital, lost to the world. Most painfully, he was unreachable by the blue airmail letters he had been receiving daily from Marion. It tells you a lot about a love like theirs that Smith mentions this detail—a month without Marion's letters—as prominently as he does in his war stories.

33 In 2009, Marion died. Her death devastated Smith.

34 When my mother heard the news, she sent Smith a condolence note. She was not just a fan: her parents, Geoffrey and Margaret Andrew, had been part of Smith's circle. Geoff was a professor at UBC, and Margaret had a fine eye for art, and they liked dinner parties. Smith remembered my mother as the little girl he used to put on his shoulders at Geoff and Margaret's house, and he invited her and her family to visit him, which we did, three summers ago. This is how I came to know him.

35 It bears mentioning. I never met my grandparents, but Smith was very fond of them, and spoke about them as real, formidable people. He says he was afraid of my grandfather, a commanding guy who could recite reams of Milton from memory. My grandmother, he says, over and over, was "tough"—a high compliment. In the spirit of full disclosure, you should know that I see Smith first as the man who brought my grandparents flickering temporarily to life for me, and that my gratitude for this remains incandescent. As I visited him in his mourning, he produced a reincarnation.

36 This is characteristic of his art: it is vital, life-giving. Now, perhaps, literally so. It is hard not to see his productivity as a form of sustenance at this late stage of his life. It casts Dikeakos's nickname for Smith—"the surviving and ongoing modernist"—in a new light: it could be that Smith is surviving *because* of his modernism.

37 Douglas Coupland, incongruously, is among Smith's closest friends, and understands his universe as well as anyone. Unlike Smith's serene modernist compound, Coupland's house in West Vancouver is like a toy chest. It's a small space, and to get anywhere in it you have to tiptoe through a jumble of exuberant Pop sculpture. Among the dozens of artistic obstacles that lie in one's path are text works that resemble vintage board games, translucent

globes, a model CN Tower and a four-foot column of multicoloured pencil crayons framed in glass, which has a twin in the threshold of Smith's kitchen.

38 "I think that when Marion died, people expected him to fall into a deep pit and promptly die six months later," Coupland tells me. "And, of course, he didn't. Everybody asked, 'How is Gordon?,' expecting some dark response. And I'd say, 'I think he went to London for three days the other week.'"

39 When I visited Smith last September, he had just returned from such a trip. He goes to Toronto, New York and London every year to keep up with the art world. And the morning I arrived, he had just started work on a new canvas. He took me to his studio to see it. A pink scar stares out at you from the middle of the picture; mists are suggested in grey, as in the hill scene of a Chinese ink-wash landscape; two tectonic plates of black have collided and crested like a mountain range. But it is pure abstraction: the raw physicality of paint is the real subject.

40 Gordon Smith is keen to show the new work to visitors. He's made a split with the past, he feels—broken new ground. He thinks it's the best thing he's ever done.

Vocabulary and Comprehension

1. In paragraph 15, *unobtrusively* means
   a. unaware. b. awkwardly. c. inconspicuously.
2. Write a synonym for the word *tectonic* in the last paragraph.
   ____
3. Why does Andrew-Gee mention the word *sage* in the title?
   ____

Critical Thinking

4. Who is the main audience for this reading?
   ____
5. What is the author's attitude toward his subject?
   ____
6. In the last paragraph, the author mentions that painter Gordon Smith "thinks it's the best thing he's ever done." Why does the author include this statement?
   ____

Writing Topics

Write about one of the following topics. Remember to explore, develop, and revise and edit your work.

1. Research Abstract Expressionism, and write an informative essay on it, highlighting one painter of the period.
2. What are some of the advantages of using painting as a form of self-expression. Use examples from Andrew-Gee's article to substantiate your point of view.
3. People cannot learn everything by reading books. Compare and contrast knowledge acquired through books to knowledge acquired through life experiences.

READING 10

The Sanctuary of School

Lynda Barry

Lynda Barry is a cartoonist, writer, and playwright. Her work includes graphic novels and the syndicated comic strip *Ernie Pook's Comeek*. As you read this narrative essay, also look for elements of description.

1 I was seven years old the first time I snuck out of the house in the dark. It was winter, and my parents had been fighting all night. They were short on money and long on relatives who kept "temporarily" moving into our house because they had nowhere else to go.

2 My brother and I were used to giving up our bedroom. We slept on the couch, something we actually liked because it put us that much closer to the light of our lives, our television. At night when everyone was asleep, we lay on our pillows watching it with the sound off. We watched Steve Allen's mouth moving. We watched Johnny Carson's mouth moving. We watched movies filled with gangsters shooting machine guns into packed rooms, dying soldiers hurling a last grenade, and beautiful women crying at windows. Then the sign-off finally came, and we tried to sleep.

3 The morning I snuck out, I woke up filled with a panic about needing to get to school. The sun wasn't quite up yet, but my anxiety was so fierce that I just got dressed, walked quietly across the kitchen, and let myself out the back door.

4 It was quiet outside. Stars were still out. Nothing moved, and no one was in the street. It was as if someone had turned the sound off on the world.

5 I walked the alley, breaking thin ice over the puddles with my shoes. I didn't know why I was walking to school in the dark. I didn't think about it. All I knew was a feeling of panic, like the panic that strikes kids when they realize they are lost.

6 That feeling eased the moment I turned the corner and saw the dark outline of my school at the top of the hill. My school was made up of about fifteen nondescript portable classrooms set down on a fenced concrete lot in a rundown Seattle neighborhood, but it had the most beautiful view of the Cascade Mountains. You could see them from anywhere on the playfield, and you could see them from the windows of my classroom—Room 2.

7 I walked over to the monkey bars and hooked my arms around the cold metal. I stood for a long time just looking across Rainier Valley. The sky was beginning to whiten, and I could hear a few birds.

8 In a perfect world, my absence at home would not have gone unnoticed. I would have had two parents in a panic to locate me, instead of two parents in a panic to locate an answer to the hard question of survival during a deep financial and emotional crisis.

9 But in an overcrowded and unhappy home, it's incredibly easy for any child to slip away. The high levels of frustration, depression, and anger in my house made my brother and me invisible. We were children with the sound turned off. And for us, as for the steadily increasing number of neglected children in this country, the only place where we could count on being noticed was at school.

10 "Hey there, young lady. Did you forget to go home last night?" It was Mr. Gunderson, our janitor, whom we all loved. He was nice and he was funny and he was old with white hair, thick glasses, and an unbelievable number

of keys. I could hear them jingling as he walked across the playfield. I felt incredibly happy to see him.

11 He let me push his wheeled garbage can between the different portables as he unlocked each room. He let me turn on the lights and raise the window shades, and I saw my school slowly come to life. I saw Mrs. Holman, our school secretary, walk into the office without her orange lipstick on yet. She waved. I saw the fifth-grade teacher, Mr. Cunningham, walking under the breezeway eating a hard roll. He waved.

12 And I saw my teacher, Mrs. Claire LeSane, walking toward us in a red coat and calling my name in a very happy and surprised way, and suddenly my throat got tight and my eyes stung and I ran toward her crying. It was something that surprised us both.

13 It's only thinking about it now, twenty-eight years later, that I realize I was crying from relief. I was with my teacher, and in a while I was going to sit at my desk, with my crayons and pencils and books and classmates all around me, and for the next six hours I was going to enjoy a thoroughly secure, warm, and stable world. It was a world I absolutely relied on. Without it, I don't know where I would have gone that morning.

14 Mrs. LeSane asked me what was wrong, and when I said "Nothing," she seemingly left it at that. But she asked me if I would carry her purse for her, an honor above all honors, and she asked if I wanted to come into Room 2 early and paint.

15 She believed in the natural healing power of painting and drawing for troubled children. In the back of her room, there was always a drawing table and an easel with plenty of supplies, and sometimes during the day she would come up to you for what seemed like no good reason and quietly ask if you wanted to go to the back table and "make some pictures for Mrs. LeSane." We all had a chance at it—to sit apart from the class for a while to paint, draw, and silently work out impossible problems on 11×17 sheets of newsprint.

16 Drawing came to mean everything to me. At the back table in Room 2, I learned to build myself a life preserver that I could carry into my home.

17 We all know that a good education system saves lives, but the people of this country are still told that cutting the budget for public schools is necessary, that poor salaries for teachers are all we can manage, and that art, music, and all creative activities must be the first to go when times are lean.

18 Before- and after-school programs are cut, and we are told that public schools are not made for baby-sitting children. If parents are neglectful temporarily or permanently, for whatever reason, it's certainly sad, but their unlucky children must fend for themselves. Or slip through the cracks. Or wander in a dark night alone.

19 We are told in a thousand ways that not only are public schools not important, but that the children who attend them, the children who need them most, are not important either. We leave them to learn from the blind eye of a television or to the mercy of "**a thousand points of light**" that can be as far away as stars.

a thousand points of light:
a spirit of volunteerism encouraged by former President Bush

20 I was lucky. I had Mrs. LeSane. I had Mr. Gunderson. I had an abundance of art supplies. And I had a particular brand of neglect in my home that allowed me to slip away and get to them. But what about the rest of the kids who weren't as lucky? What happened to them?

21 By the time the bell rang that morning, I had finished my drawing, and Mrs. LeSane pinned it up on the special bulletin board she reserved for

drawings from the back table. It was the same picture I always drew—a sun in the corner of a blue sky over a nice house with flowers all around it.

22 Mrs. LeSane asked us to please stand, face the flag, place our right hands over our hearts, and say the Pledge of Allegiance. Children across the country do it faithfully. I wonder now when the country will face its children and say a pledge right back.

Vocabulary and Comprehension

1. Find a word in paragraph 6 that means "uninteresting."

____

2. What type of narrator is telling this story? Circle the better answer.

   a. First person   b. Third person

3. When and where does the story take place?

____

____

4. Why did the author sneak out of her house and go to the school?

____

____

Critical Thinking

5. Describe the author's family life. You will have to infer or guess.

____

____

____

6. In paragraph 6, the author writes that she stopped feeling anxious when she saw the school. What are some reasons that she felt secure at the school?

____

____

____

7. In paragraph 9, the author writes, "We were children with the sound turned off." What does she mean?

____

____

8. What role did Mrs. LeSane play in the author's childhood?

____

____

____

9. According to the author, how does the public school system of her childhood compare to the public school system of today?

____

____

____

10. The author uses imagery—description using the senses—to depict her environment. Give an example of each of the following types of imagery.

    Sight: ______________________________

    ____

    ____

    Sound: ______________________________

    ____

    ____

    Touch: ______________________________

    ____

    ____

WRITING TOPICS

Write about one of the following topics. Remember to explore, develop, and revise and edit your work.

1. Narrate an event that happened in your childhood at school. How did you feel?
2. Who was your childhood role model? Was it a parent, a teacher, or another adult? Explain why you respected this person.
3. Describe what the ideal classroom would look like. Mention the space, the type of teachers, and the activities in an ideal classroom.

READING 11

Like It or Not, Yoga Is Here to Stay

Aparita Bhandari

Aparita Bhandari is a Toronto-based broadcast journalist from New Delhi. She is featured on CBC Radio's *Metro Morning*, covering arts and entertainment. As you read this process essay, look for illustration and cause and effect writing patterns.

acolytes: followers

1 It may have started out being popular only in select circles—new-age philosophy **acolytes**, neo-hippies or celebrities such as Madonna and Sting. But the yoga craze has since become part of the general consciousness.

2 At bookstores, yoga accessories such as bricks, mats and DVDs are just a stretch away from yoga magazines and books. Looking fierce in a warrior pose is a cinch in yoga wear offered by major clothing lines, as well as yoga-centric apparel companies such as Canada's own Lululemon, which went public with much fanfare in July.

3 Yoga centres have mushroomed in strip malls in Toronto's far-flung suburbs, nestled in between all-day breakfast restaurants, grocery chains and nail salons. It's not just a big city phenomenon either—you can find anything from mokhsa and hatha to shanti yoga in Elora, Ont., Iqaluit and Whitehorse.

The science of life

4 Despite its ubiquitousness, it's easy to be **sceptical** of the yoga phenomenon. Besides, yoga's many incarnations can confuse the novice. What's the difference between ashtanga and power yoga?

sceptical: critical, doubtful

5 But even if people initially try out one of the many types of yoga because it's trendy, the benefits will make them life-long practitioners, say yoga instructors of various backgrounds.

6 Yoga is the science of life, says Prahlada (he goes by one name), who runs the Sivananda Yoga Vedanta Centre in Toronto. The centre follows classical hatha yoga, popularized by Swami Vishnu-devananda. Hatha yoga uses asanas (poses), pranayama (breathing techniques) and dhyana (meditation) to bring about a healthy body and peaceful mind.

7 "Yoga is an exercise that does not stop at the body, it goes to the mind also," says Prahlada. "It synchronizes all the body movements with breathing. So as long as you can breathe, you can exercise."

8 "In a spiritual sense, yoga is the union of the individual soul with the supreme soul—but we don't tell that to the beginners," he adds. "We say yoga is a union between body and mind. If you have the awareness of body and mind together, you can function in a better way."

9 Born into a modest farmer's family in rural India, Prahlada started learning yoga as a teenager at the Sivananda Yoga Vedanta Dhanwanthari Ashram in Kerala. Initially drawn to the physical rigour of the asanas, he eventually found it a peaceful practice.

10 "People are constantly seeking yoga...We all want to know who we are and what we are doing," he says. "It keeps you more positive, and when you feel good about yourself, your physical ailments are taken care of."

11 Besides taking care of aches and pains, yoga gives you a feeling of calm, says Andy Orr, a teacher for 25 years at the Yoga Centre Toronto.

12 "A lot of people have sore lower backs, or they have sore necks from sitting at the computer all day long. There are various poses to deal with those problem areas," Orr says. "We've even worked in conjunction with doctors helping cancer patients and MS patients. Yoga helps them relax."

13 It boosts fitness levels, too. A former runner, Orr was taken aback by his inability to do some of the stretches at his first yoga lesson. Training in the Iyengar style of yoga, developed by B.K.S. Iyengar, Orr discovered there was more to yoga than a flexible body.

14 Iyengar yoga focuses on concentrated movements to increase mobility, stability, strength and alignment. The intense concentration draws the attention inward, quieting and integrating mind and body, explains the Yoga Centre Toronto website.

15 "Physically you feel good, but it's also helpful in dealing with other issues like anger, fear or arrogance," says Orr. "When a person does a headstand, it's very scary. But as you work one part before the next...the fear of the headstand goes away, and fear of other things also goes away. I'm more comfortable doing taxes. Or if I have one of those near misses on a bicycle, I'm more at ease."

Yoga's roots

Form of yoga

16 ▪ **Hatha yoga:** The most widely practiced form of yoga, hatha yoga uses bodily postures (asanas), breathing techniques (pranayama), and meditation

(dyana) with the goal of bringing about a sound, healthy body and a clear, peaceful mind.

17 ▪ **Ashtanga yoga:** Made popular by Pattabhi Jois, this method involves synchronizing the breath with a progressive series of postures. The process is supposed to produce intense internal heat and a profuse, purifying sweat that detoxifies muscles and organs.

18 ▪ **Iyengar yoga:** Created by B.K.S. Iyengar, this style is characterized by great attention to detail and precise focus on body alignment. Iyengar pioneered the use of "props" such as cushions, benches, blocks, straps and even sand bags, which function as aids.

19 ▪ **Anusara yoga:** Started by John Friend in 1997, this is a modern school of yoga with a Tantric philosophy. Attainable bliss and joy in practice and everyday life are an important aspect of the underlying philosophy of this school. Many western students with a modernist bent find this school attractive.

20 ▪ **Power yoga:** A general term used to describe a vigorous fitness-based approach to yoga. Most power yoga is modeled on ashtanga yoga, but does not follow a set series of poses. This form is said to have brought yoga into the gyms of America.

21 ▪ **Vinyasa yoga:** This term covers a broad range of yoga classes. The word Vinyasa means "breath-synchronized movement." In other words, the teacher will instruct you to move from one pose to the next on an inhale or an exhale. This technique is sometimes also called Vinyasa Flow or just Flow.

22 ▪ **Bikram Yoga:** Also known as hot yoga and developed by yoga guru to the stars Bikram Choudhury, this style is ideally practised in a room heated to 105°F (40.5°C) with a humidity of 50 per cent. The philosophy is that extreme temperature allows for deeper relaxation and stretching. Each class follows an unchanging pattern: A series of 26 poses done twice over 90 minutes.

23 ▪ **Mysore yoga:** Students are invited to practise whatever postures they please.

24 ▪ **Jivamukti yoga:** A physically challenging form that combines Sanskrit chanting and spiritual discussions—all performed to music.

25 ▪ **Kundalini yoga:** This style concentrates on psychic centres or chakras in the body in order to generate a spiritual power, which is known as kundalini energy.

26 A reason for the confusion around the various styles of yoga may be that they come from the same source, says Ron Reid, an ashtanga yoga practitioner.

27 Made popular by K. Pattabhi Jois, ashtanga yoga synchronizes breathing with a series of linked postures—a process that's supposed to purify the body through blood circulation and sweating. Initially developed to train teenage boys, the six series full of jumps and push-ups are physically challenging.

28 "Part of the wisdom of yoga is that it has different access points, just as people have different natures," says Reid, who started out learning from Swami Vishnu-devananda's *The Complete Illustrated Book of Yoga*. "Some people are very physical. Some are very devotional. Some are intellectual. Yoga seeks to have a pathway appropriate for everybody."

29 Along with Diane Bruni, who became interested in yoga after a chance meeting with a Sikh yogi, Reid now runs the downtown Toronto Downward Dog Yoga Centre. It's popular with ashtanga yoga enthusiasts—including many celebrities. Most recently, musician Sting dropped in on a special class

while he was in town. "At the time I started teaching, nobody knew it back then," says Bruni, who practised Kundalini and Iyengar yoga before teaching herself ashtanga yoga using books and videos. "Now, of course, there are thousands of people just in Toronto doing it."

The attraction

30 "People come to the classes for different reasons," Bruni says. "But what's fascinating is that when all those different people go into shavasana [relaxation pose], they all go to the same place...the same experience we are seeking. I'm not sure we can even articulate what we are seeking. It's an experience that's lacking in our culture."

31 "It's not something I can describe to you," says Reid. "You have to take a class. At the end of it, I ask how you feel, and you say—'Great'—that's yoga."

32 It doesn't matter what style you start out with, you will eventually come to yoga, says Prahlada. "It's only when I see it being used as a gym activity, that's a pain to watch," he says. "It's hard to find the roots of yoga in that... but people need to go and try out different types of yoga, and see what suits their temperament."

33 Orr of the Yoga Centre Toronto suggests asking questions.

34 "Ask the teacher if you can do yoga if you are menstruating or if you can do a headstand if you have a headache," he says. "If they say, 'I don't know,' or 'Follow along and take it easy,' go somewhere else."

35 Although yoga is currently a hot fitness trend, students will come to appreciate its philosophy, says Reid.

36 "Culturally, it's something we're all looking for," he says. "Ultimately, yoga connects each person with their own true self. It has everyone's best interest at heart. You can heal yourself. It can help you relax. It helps take harmful emotions away. Really, what yoga does at a very profound level is that it delivers."

Vocabulary and Comprehension

1. Find a word in paragraph 4 that means "presence everywhere."

   ____

2. Find an example of slang in paragraph 1.

   ____

3. What does this essay help readers do? Circle the better answer.

   a. Complete a process b. Understand a process

4. This essay does not contain an explicit thesis statement. In your own words, write a thesis statement for this text.

   ____

   ____

5. In your own words, explain why people take yoga classes.

   ____

   ____

   ____

Critical Thinking

6. What is the author's specific purpose?

7. How does the author add weight to her arguments?

8. In your opinion, how are the suggestions useful or impractical?

Writing Topics

Write about one of the following topics. Remember to explore, develop, and revise and edit your work.

1. Think about a time when you began a new activity such as yoga or another form of physical exercise. Describe the process that you went through during and after the event.
2. Bhandari describes the physical and emotional benefits of yoga. Write about yoga's spiritual element—and why, as Prahlada states (in paragraph 8), this is not mentioned to beginners.
3. Reflect on Queen Elizabeth's quotation. How is it applicable in your life? You might give examples of things that make you feel angry, or ways of dealing with anger constructively, considering the emotional benefits of yoga mentioned in Bhandari's article.

"Anger makes dull men witty, but it keeps them poor."
—Queen Elizabeth I, English Monarch

Themes: Great Discoveries and the Workplace

READING 12

The Beeps

Josh Freed

Josh Freed is an award-winning journalist and documentary film writer. In the following example of an illustration essay, also look for elements of comparison and contrast and cause and effect.

1 Uh-oh. Something in the house is beeping—but what? Is it the stove announcing that dinner is cooked? Or is the dryer proclaiming my clothes are ready? Is the fridge defrosting, the thermostat adjusting, the smoke alarm dying, or is my cell phone dead? I'm living in an electronic jungle, trained to leap at every beep—if I could just figure out which beep it is.

2 I grew up in a time of easier-to-identify sounds, when telephones ding-a-linged, cash registers ka-chinged, and typewriters clacked; when school bells clanged, fire alarms rang, and ambulance sirens wailed—instead of today's digital whooping. Now they are all being replaced by the beep-beeps and bing-bings that are the frantic soundtrack of the twenty-first century.

3 Many of these high-pitched beeps are strangely hard to locate, even when they are right beside me. I usually fumble around for my cell phone

when it rings because I can't figure out which pants pocket it's in—or which pants. Maybe it's lost under the armchair again? Several times a week, a mystery beeping goes off somewhere in our house, and I run around like a lunatic trying to find whatever it is. I listen to our bookshelves, to our laundry piles, and even to the inside of the fridge. But the beeping always stops long before I crack the mystery.

4 Meanwhile, I am bombarded on every side by other urgent electronic sounds. My car beeps constantly, nagging me to put on my seat belt, or turn off the lights, or lock the trunk, or whatever else it's trying to tell me—probably: "Wipe your shoes before you mess up my floor, mister!" My printer beeps identically when it's out of paper, or out of toner, or when something is jammed—but which is it? My microwave beeps all the time, just for fun.

5 Out in the world, elevators and ATM machines beep constantly. TV shows beep when they bleep out swear words. Store machines beep when they swipe your groceries, or you try to swipe theirs without paying. Then there are security beeps: the loud BEEEEP … BEEEEP … BEEEEP that says you're about to be run down by a city street cleaner that's backing up; the shrill beep-beep-beep-beep that says you have 15 seconds to punch in the house alarm code or an old-fashioned siren will go off alerting a security firm that you are an intruder in your own home. The simple but dreaded beep of an airline security wand means it's time to start your striptease act.

6 Even life itself is measured in beeps. Hospitals are full of machines whose soft beeps indicate you are still alive. "I beep, therefore I am." We are born into the world in a noisy jungle of beeping medical monitors and wires. We will probably leave it the same way—for most of us, the world will end with a beep, not a bang.

7 Who would have guessed the sound of the twenty-first century would be the cry of the cartoon Road Runner, the fast-stepping bird that was always pursued by Wile E. Coyote, crying beep-beep as it ran? Today we are all Road Runners, frantically beeping as we run for our lives, chased by our own high-speed machines and hectic lifestyles.

8 Beep-beep! Fasten your seat belt. Beep-beep! You have another new e-mail … NOW. "BEEP! BEEP! Hello, we value your call, but we can't be bothered to take it now, so please don't speak until the beep." Electronic sounds have become so widespread, ornithologists report many birds are now mimicking our beeps, buzzes, and chirps as part of their mating songs. There are parrots that sound like cell phones, mockingbirds that mimic microwaves, and white-bellied caiques that do perfect car alarms.

9 Will the entire animal kingdom eventually chirp, roar, and growl electronically? Or will a new generation of humans choose more soothing sounds, like a phone ring that sounds exactly like birdsong, instead of vice-versa? Or an alarm clock that sounds like a rooster? Or a cash register that once again makes a genuine ka-ching? Perhaps we will all have truly personalized ring tones made by gentle New Age mechanical voices that show some respect for our space: "Jossshhh … This is your sto-o-ove speaking. Dinner is ready whenever you are, but don't rush—I'll keep it warm. Sorry if I disturbed you." "Suu-ssan … This is your phone ringing. Suu-ssan. I'm in your brown purse, under your make-up and your dirty gym socks. Will you take the call … or should I?" To beep or not to beep? That is the question future generations must face. But for now, I've got to run. That beeping just started again, and I've just figured out what it is: my computer.

VOCABULARY AND COMPREHENSION

1. Find a word in paragraph 8 that means "imitating." ____________
2. Freed states that he is "living in an electronic jungle." What does he mean?
3. The author discusses three main locations where he is bombarded with electronic beeps. List at least three locations, and give examples of some noise-making machines in each category.
4. How has new office technology affected nature?

CRITICAL THINKING

5. Why is the author frustrated with the new technology? Give at least two reasons.
6. What is the tone of the essay? Circle the best answer.

   a. Serious   c. Humorous
   b. Angry   d. Neutral

7. The author is indirectly comparing two worlds. What are they?

WRITING TOPICS

Write about one of the following topics. Remember to explore, develop, and revise and edit your work.

1. In your daily life, what actions or objects frustrate you? List some examples to support your point.
2. What is your most valuable possession? Give examples of why it is valuable.
3. Does modern technology make life easier, or was life better when technology was simpler? Use examples to support your point of view.

READING 13

This Boat Is My Boat

Drew Hayden Taylor

Drew Hayden Taylor is from Curve Lake First Nations in Central Ontario. He is an award-winning playwright and novelist. His works include *The Berlin Blues*, *Toronto at Dreamer's Rock/Education Is Our Right*, and *The Night Wanderer: A Native Gothic Novel*. As you read this argument essay, also look for elements of the narrative and comparison and contrast writing patterns.

1 F. Scott Fitzgerald once wrote "The rich are different from you and I," to which everybody usually responds, "Yeah, they've got more money." On a similar theme, it's been my Ojibway-tainted observation over the years that "middle-class white people are different from you and I." Yeah. They're insane.

2 Much has been written over the years about the differences between native people and non-native people, and the way they view life. I think there's no better example of this admittedly broad opinion than in the peculiar world of outdoor recreational water sports and the death wish that inspires them.

3 As a member of Canada's indigenous population, I've cast a suspicious glance at all these waterlogged enthusiasts for several reasons. The principal one is the now familiar concept of cultural appropriation—this time of our methods of water transportation. On any given weekend, Canadian rivers are jam-packed with plastic and fibreglass kayaks and canoes, hardly any of them filled with authentic Inuit or First Nations people, all looking to taunt death using an aboriginal calling card.

4 Historically, kayaks and canoes were the life's blood of Inuit and native communities. They were vital means of transportation and survival, not toys to amuse bored weekend warriors. To add insult to injury and further illustrate my point, there is a brand of gloves used by kayakers to protect their hands from developing calluses. They are called Nootkas. To the best of my knowledge, the real Nootka, a West Coast First Nation, neither kayaked nor wore gloves.

5 Perhaps my argument can best be articulated with an example of the different ways these two cultural groups react to a single visual stimulus. A group of native people and white people sit in two separate canoes before a long stretch of roaring rapids—with large pointy rocks and lots and lots of turbulent white water. Watch the different reactions.

6 Granted, I'm generalizing, but I think I can safely say the vast majority of native people, based on thousands of years of travelling the rivers of this great country of ours, would probably go home and order a pizza. Or possibly put the canoe in their Ford pickup and drive downstream to a more suitable and safe location. And pick up pizza on the way. Usually, the only white water native people enjoy is in their showers. Hurtling toward potential death and certain injury tends to go against many traditional native beliefs. Contrary to popular assumption, **"portage"** is not a French word—it is Ojibway for "Are you crazy? I'm not going through that! Do you know how much I paid for this canoe?"

portage: carrying a boat between two bodies of water

7 Now you put some sunburned Caucasian canoeists in the same position, their natural inclination is to aim directly for the rapids paddling as fast as they can toward the white water. I heard a rumour once that Columbus was aiming his three ships directly at a raging hurricane when he discovered the Bahamas. I believe I have made my point.

anthropological: relating to the study of human beings

8 I make these observations based on personal experience. Recently, for purely **anthropological** reasons, I risked my life to explore the unique subcultures of white water canoeing and sea kayaking. There is also a sport known as white water kayaking, but I have yet to put that particular bullet in my gun. So for three days, I found myself in the middle of Georgian Bay, during a storm, testing my abilities at sea kayaking. I, along with a former Olympic rower, a Quebecois lawyer who consulted on the Russian constitution, one of Canada's leading diabetes specialists, and a six-foot-seven ex-Mormon who could perform exorcisms, bonded over four-foot swells and lightning. All in all, I think a pretty normal crosscut of average Canadians. The higher the waves, the more exciting they found the experience.

9 Still, I often find these outings to be oddly patriotic in their own way. I cannot tell you the number of times I've seen people wringing out their drenched shirts, showing an array of tan lines, usually a combination of sunburned red skin and fishbelly-white stomachs. It reminds me of the red-and-white motif on the Canadian flag. Maybe that's where the federal government got its inspiration back in the 1960s for our national emblem.

10 But this is only one of several sports originated by various indigenous populations that have been corrupted and marketed as something fun to do when not sitting behind a desk in a high-rise office building. The Scandinavian Sami, otherwise known as Laplanders, were instrumental in the development of skiing. Though I doubt climbing to the top of a mountain and hurling themselves down as fast as gravity and snow would allow was a culturally ingrained activity. The same could be said of bungee jumping. Originally a coming-of-age ritual in the South Pacific, young boys would build platforms, tie vines to their legs and leap off to show their bravery and passage into adulthood. I doubt the same motivation still pervades the sport, if it can be called a sport.

11 I have brought up the issue of recreational cultural appropriation many times with a friend who organizes these outdoor adventures. The irony is she works at a hospital. And she chews me out for not wearing a helmet while biking. She says there is no appropriation. If anything, her enthusiasm for the sports is a sign of respect and gratefulness.

12 That is why I think people should pay a royalty of sorts every time they try to kill themselves using one of our cultural legacies. I'm not sure if any aboriginal group has ever sought a patent or copyright protection for kayaks or canoes—that probably was not part of the treaty negotiations. But somebody should definitely investigate the possibility. Or better yet, every time a non-native person white water canoes down the Madawaska River, or goes kayaking off Tobermory, they should first take an aboriginal person to lunch. That is a better way of showing respect and gratefulness. And it involves much less paperwork.

Vocabulary and Comprehension

1. Find a word in paragraph 1 that means "feeling" or "point of view."

2. What lead-in does the author use? Circle the best answer.
   a. Quotation b. Surprising or provocative statement c. Question
3. Who is the audience for this essay?

4. What is the author's main point?

Critical Thinking

5. Why does Drew Hayden Taylor object to white-water sports?

6. What two arguments does the author give to acknowledge the opposing point of view?

7. What two examples does the author give to defend his own position?

8. The author writes about "respect and gratefulness" (paragraph 11). Why are respect and gratefulness so important to the author's argument?

Writing Topics

Write about one of the following topics. Remember to explore, develop, and revise and edit your work.

1. Why do some people engage in dangerous white-water sports?
2. What are some advantages of participating in canoeing and kayaking?
3. Reflect on the Desbiens quotation. Write a counterargument to the essay "This Boat Is My Boat."

"Living is like navigating. You take the waves, the weight and the wind into consideration. And also the North Star."

—Jean Paul Desbiens, For Pity's Sake

READING 14

Gone with the Windows

Dorothy Nixon

Dorothy Nixon, a freelance writer, has written for *Salon.com*, *Chatelaine*, and *Today's Parent* magazine. She is also the author of *Threshold Girl*, which can be read on Amazon's Kindle. In the next essay, she compares how information today is stored or lost compared to the past. As you read this comparison and contrast essay, also look for elements of cause and effect and narration.

1 The other day, I had trouble accessing Photoshop through our home network. The program was on my other computer, so I had to whip downstairs to see what the problem was. I discovered that my back-up computer was in pieces. My eighteen-year-old had pulled its hard drive apart, no doubt for some mischievous reason, and left the cannibalized carcass to air in the middle of the room.

2 When I asked, "What's up?" he said he needed a component to be able to play a computer game in his room with his friends—and some other people in Japan. Of course, my son has the most advanced computer in the house, by far. My son also visits all the usual Web sites so popular with teens and gets a lot of viruses on his computer. So he is always "wiping his hard drive," as he puts it.

3 I know this because he and his dad like to discuss such things. (That's definitely a good thing.) I seldom butt in on these conversations, but the other day I overheard a remark that distressed me. My son was oh-so-casually explaining to my husband how he had inadvertently erased all of his photographs from his grade 11 trip to Europe. The images had evaporated into the ether. All gone. Not to worry, he said, "Lots of other kids still have theirs."

4 Now, he had taken hundreds of pictures of Baroque fountains, messy hotel rooms, and bleary-eyed teens—and shown me the snapshots just once upon his return. I had intended to print out the best ones and mail them to his grandmother. Now she will never see that picture of her grandson Mark with that "gladiator" in front of the Roman Coliseum.

5 Digital technology makes it all just so easy. We can instantly capture our most intimate and spontaneous moments and effortlessly pass these images on to friends and family by e-mail or snail mail or post them on Web sites for the entire wired world to see. And, still, my son's record of his once-in-a-lifetime experience is lost forever.

6 I have a different perspective on things: About two years ago, I found some old documents saved by my husband's ancestors from Richmond, Quebec, in a trunk in my father-in-law's basement. There was a direct-mail ad for Crisco Shortening from 1915, when butter was getting costly. I found a National Drug Company promotional brochure with ads for bizarre remedies such as white liniment for ailments like "brain worry" and "fag" (what we might refer to as chronic fatigue) and impotency.

7 There were family documents, too. Hundreds of letters were tied up in ribbons. Great Uncle Herb's letters reveal he was always in debt. A newspaper clipping described British militant suffragette Barbara Wylie's arrival in Montreal in 1912. Reporters couldn't believe how attractive a feminist could be!

8 I also discovered booklets containing detailed household accounts. For the 1883 marriage, it cost 5 dollars for a lady's ring and 50 cents for a frying

pan. In 1884, after the baby's arrival, a toy cost 5 cents, but the doctor's bill was 51 dollars! In 1896, a house built in pseudo-Scottish Baronial style went for 2,712 dollars. Family expenses for the era averaged between 300 and 500 dollars a year. Wood for heating and dentist and medical bills (outside of childbirth) were the big expenses.

9 We're talking a lot of history here, of interest to family as well as to historians. I posted my findings on the Web, and the information has been very well received by the academic community. Some scholars have actually thanked me for making the effort. It was just luck, I tell them, just luck that one day while I was waiting for the washing machine to end its spin cycle, my gaze rested on an old Victorian trunk in a basement where I'd been hundreds of times before. I got curious.

10 Will future amateur historians be as lucky as I was? With all the runaway digital documentation going on in homes today, will today's family history be available or accessible to future inquiring minds like mine? We just recently transferred our baby videos to CD, but it's possible that in a few years the CD format will be as impenetrable as a **cuneiform tablet**. My son's experience with his high school pictures suggests that a lot of twenty-first century family history could be, well, gone with the windows. And that will indeed be ironic—and a great big shame.

cuneiform tablet: a stone tablet with the earliest known writing system in the world

Vocabulary and Comprehension

Complete additional reading comprehension questions for this selection at mywritinglab.com

1. In paragraph 1, what does *cannibalized carcass* refer to?

   ____

2. In paragraph 10, find a word that means "puzzling."

   ____

3. What event happened that made the author think about technology?

   ____

   ____

4. Nixon compares the present with the past. What comparison pattern does she use? Circle the better answer.

   a. Point by point   b. Topic by topic

Critical Thinking

5. Nixon actually compares more than the present to the past. List other topics she compares.

   ____

   ____

   ____

   ____

   ____

6. Why did the author put the information she found in a trunk on her website?

____

____

7. How does the author see the relationship between history and technology?

____

____

____

WRITING TOPICS

Write about one of the following topics. Remember to explore, develop, and revise and edit your work.

1. Compare one of the following: two decades, two discoveries, or your past to your present.
2. Imagine that you could time-travel to a period in your past. Where would you go and why? Would you change what happened?
3. Write about an event in history. Narrate what happened.

READING 15

Advertising Appeals

Michael R. Solomon, Greg W. Marshall, and Elnora W. Stuart

The next essay, which appeared in *Marketing: Real People, Real Choices*, focuses on advertising. As you read this classification essay, also look for the illustration and argument writing patterns.

1 An advertising appeal is the central idea of the ad. Some advertisers use an emotional appeal, complete with dramatic color or powerful images, while others bombard the audience with facts. Some feature sexy people or stern-looking experts—even professors from time to time. Different appeals can work for the same product, from a bland "talking head" to a montage of animated special effects. Although an attention-getting way to say something profound about cat food or laundry detergent is more art than science, there are some common appeals that are highly effective.

2 Testimonials are a useful type of endorsement. A celebrity, an expert, or a "man in the street" states the product's effectiveness. The use of celebrity endorsers is a common but expensive strategy. It is particularly effective for mature products that need to differentiate themselves from competitors, such as Coke and Pepsi, which enlist celebrities to tout one cola over another. For example, Michael Jackson and Shakira have been in Pepsi ads, and Bill Cosby and Bill Gates have endorsed Coke. Makeup and perfume companies also hire well-known faces to promote their brands. For instance, Penelope Cruz advertises L'Oreal mascara, and Nicole Kidman promotes Chanel.

3 A slice-of-life format presents a dramatized scene from everyday life. Slice-of-life advertising can be effective for everyday products such as peanut butter and headache remedies that consumers may feel good about if they

see "real" people buying and using them. Tide, for instance, regularly depicts ordinary kids playing a rough and tumble game and arriving home covered in dirt and grass stains. Old El Paso shows a family of four sitting around the kitchen table enjoying their tacos.

4 Fear appeal ads highlight the negative consequences of not using a product. Some fear appeal ads focus on physical harm, while others try to create concern for social harm or disapproval. Mouthwash, deodorant, and dandruff shampoo products play on viewers' concerns about social rejection. Also, life insurance companies successfully use fear appeals, as do ads aimed at changing behaviors, such as messages discouraging drug use or encouraging safe sex. Axe, for instance, has a humorous ad depicting a young man with very dirty, messy hair. The young fellow gets ambushed by a group of girls who wash his hair with Axe shampoo. Election campaigns make particular use of fear advertising. For example, during the country's health care debate, many political ads warned about seniors dying and about socialized medicine. Senators regularly warn voters about their opponents' tax plans.

5 Advertising creative types, including art directors, copywriters, photographers, and others, work hard on a "big idea"—a concept that expresses the aspects of the product, service, or organization in a tangible way. The best ads are attention-getting, memorable, and appealing to consumers.

Vocabulary and Comprehension

1. Find two words in paragraph 2 that mean the same thing as "promote."

   ____

2. Highlight the thesis statement in the essay.
3. What introduction style does the author use? Circle the best answer.

   a. General background b. Anecdote c. Definition

4. Underline the topic sentence in paragraphs 2 to 4.
5. What is the author's purpose? Circle the best answer.

   a. To persuade b. To inform c. To entertain

Critical Thinking

6. Add an appropriate transitional word or phrase to the beginnings of paragraphs 2 to 4. Write your ideas here.

   Para. 2 ____________________

   Para. 3 ____________________

   Para. 4 ____________________

7. Include an additional example of each type of ad. Think about some ads that you have seen.

   testimonial ____________________

   ____

   ____

slice-of-life ______________________________

____

____

fear appeal ______________________________

____

____

8. What are ethical problems with fear appeal ads? Think of examples to support your point.

____

____

____

____

9. Which type of advertising is most effective, in your opinion? Which type of ad is least effective? Explain your answers.

Most effective: ______________________________

____

____

Least effective: ______________________________

____

____

WRITING TOPICS

Write about one of the following topics. Remember to explore, develop, and revise and edit your work.

1. Develop another way to classify advertising into at least three categories. List characteristics and examples of each category.
2. Describe a very effective advertising campaign. Include details to support your point.
3. What products have been elevated into necessities when they are actually quite useless? Have you ever been influenced to buy a useless item because of a really good advertisement? Write about the power of advertising to influence people.

Themes: Political Intrigue and the Legal World

READING 16

What Adolescents Miss When We Let Them Grow Up in Cyberspace

Brent Staples

Brent Staples, a reporter for *The New York Times*, writes about culture and politics and has written an award-winning memoir called *Parallel Time*. In the next essay, Staples reflects on the effects of new technologies. The selection is mainly an example of cause and effect writing, but it contains elements of the comparison and contrast pattern as well.

1 My tenth-grade heartthrob was the daughter of a fearsome steelworker who struck terror into the hearts of fifteen-year-old boys. He made it his business to answer the telephone—and so always knew who was calling—and grumbled in the background when the conversation went on too long. Unable to make time by phone, the boy either gave up or appeared at the front door. This meant submitting to the intense scrutiny that the girl's father soon became known for.

2 He greeted me with a crushing handshake and then leaned in close in a transparent attempt to find out whether I was one of those bad boys who smoked. He retired to the den during the visit but cruised by the living room now and then to let me know he was watching. He let up after some weeks, but only after getting across what he expected of a boy who spent time with his daughter and how upset he'd be if I disappointed him.

3 This was my first sustained encounter with an adult outside my family who needed to be convinced of my worth as a person. This, of course, is a crucial part of growing up. Faced with the same challenge today, however, I would probably pass on meeting the girl's father—and **outflank** him on the Internet.

outflank: go beyond the reach of somebody

4 Thanks to e-mail, online chat rooms, and instant messages—which permit private, real-time conversations—adolescents have at last succeeded in shielding their social lives from adult scrutiny. But this comes at a cost: teenagers nowadays are both more connected to the world at large than ever and more cut off from the social encounters that have historically prepared young people for the move into adulthood.

5 The Internet was billed as a revolutionary way to enrich our social lives and expand our civic connections. This seems to have worked well for elderly people and others who were isolated before they got access to the World Wide Web. But a growing body of research is showing that heavy use of the Net can actually isolate younger socially connected people who unwittingly allow time online to replace face-to-face interactions with their families and friends.

6 Online shopping, checking e-mail, and Web surfing—mainly solitary activities—have turned out to be more isolating than watching television, which friends and family often do in groups. Researchers have found that the time spent in direct contact with family members drops by as much as half for every hour we use the Net at home.

7 This should come as no surprise to the two-career couples who have seen their domestic lives taken over by e-mail and wireless **tethers** that keep people working around the clock. But a startling body of research from the Human-Computer Interaction Institute at Carnegie Mellon has shown that heavy Internet use can have a stunting effect outside the home as well.

tethers: restraining ropes

gregarious: friendly

8 Studies show that **gregarious,** well-connected people actually lost friends, and experienced symptoms of loneliness and depression, after joining discussion groups and other online activities. People who communicated with disembodied strangers online found the experience empty and emotionally frustrating but were nonetheless seduced by the novelty of the new medium. As Professor Robert Kraut, a Carnegie Mellon researcher, told me recently, such people allowed low-quality relationships developed in virtual reality to replace higher-quality relationships in the real world.

9 No group has embraced this socially impoverishing trade-off more enthusiastically than adolescents, many of whom spend most of their free hours cruising the Net in sunless rooms. This hermetic existence has left many of these teenagers with nonexistent social skills—a point widely noted in stories about the computer geeks who rose to prominence in the early days of Silicon Valley.

quotidian: everyday

pseudonym: false name

deterred: discouraged; stopped

10 Adolescents are drawn to cyberspace for different reasons than adults. As the writer Michael Lewis observed in his book *Next: The Future Just Happened,* children see the Net as a transformational device that lets them discard **quotidian** identities for more glamorous ones. Mr. Lewis illustrated the point with Marcus Arnold, who, as a fifteen-year-old, adopted a **pseudonym** a few years ago and posed as a twenty-five-year-old legal expert for an Internet information service. Marcus did not feel the least bit guilty and was not **deterred** when real-world lawyers discovered his secret and accused him of being a fraud. When asked whether he had actually read the law, Marcus responded that he found books "boring," leaving us to conclude that he had learned all he needed to know from his family's big-screen TV.

11 Marcus is a child of the Net, where everyone has a pseudonym, telling a story makes it true, and adolescents create older, cooler, more socially powerful selves any time they wish. The ability to slip easily into a new, false self is tailor-made for emotionally fragile adolescents who can consider a bout of acne or a few excess pounds an unbearable tragedy.

12 But teenagers who spend much of their lives hunched over computer screens miss the socializing, which is the real-world experience that would allow them to leave adolescence behind and grow into adulthood. These vital experiences, like much else, are simply not available in a virtual form.

Vocabulary and Comprehension

1. Without using a dictionary, define *hermetic* as it is used in paragraph 9. Use clues in the text to help you.

____

2. Underline a sentence in this essay that sums up the author's main point.
3. What are the causes, or reasons, for young people's attraction to Internet technology, according to Staples?

____

____

4. Staples gives many examples of the negative effects of Internet technology. List at least three negative effects.

Critical Thinking

5. What does the story about Marcus (paragraphs 10 and 11) tell us about the world of the Internet?

6. Compare Brent Staples's childhood with the childhoods of young people today. How are they different?

7. What positive effect of Internet technology does Staples mention?

8. In your opinion, what are some other ways people benefit from the Internet?

Writing Topics

Write a paragraph or an essay about one of the following topics. Remember to explore, develop, and revise and edit your work.

1. Write about a new technology, and explain how it has affected your life.
2. Compare the effects of television and the Internet on you or on society in general. How are the effects similar or different?
3. Reflect on Brecht's quotation. Choose some inventions and write about their effects on our society.

"Today every invention is received with a cry of triumph, which soon turns into a cry of fear."
—Bertold Brecht, writer

READING 17

Is Anything Private Anymore?

Sean Flynn

Sean Flynn has written for *Parade magazine*, *Esquire*, and *GQ*. Notice that some newspaper and magazine articles contain short, one-sentence paragraphs. As you read this cause and effect essay, also look for elements of illustration.

1 Kevin Bankston was a closet smoker who hid his habit by sneaking cigarettes outside his San Francisco office. He expected anonymity on a big city street. But in 2005, an online mapping service that provided ground-level photographs captured him smoking—and made the image available to anyone on the Internet. This year, Google's Street View project caught him again.

2 Coincidence? Absolutely. Yet Bankston's twice-documented smoking highlights a wider phenomenon: Privacy is a withering commodity for all of us.

3 What you buy, where you go, whom you call, the Web sites you visit, the e-mails you send—all of that information can be monitored and logged. "When you're out in public, it's becoming a near certainty that your image will be captured," says the newly nonsmoking Bankston.

4 Should you care? I've interviewed numerous people on all sides of the privacy debate to find out just how wary we should be.

5 One thing is clear: In today's world, maintaining a cocoon of privacy simply isn't practical. Need a mortgage or a car loan? A legitimate lender is going to verify a wealth of private information, including your name and address, date of birth, Social Security number, and credit history. We all make daily trade-offs for convenience and thrift: Electronic tollbooths mean you don't have to wait in the cash-only lane, but your travel habits will be tracked. The Piggly Wiggly discount card saves you $206 on your annual grocery bill, but it counts how many doughnuts and six-packs you buy. MySpace posts make it easy to keep in touch with friends, but your comments live on.

6 So how do you live in a digital world and still maintain a semblance of privacy? Experts say it's crucial to recognize that those bits of data are permanent—a trail of electronic crumbs that is never swept away, available to anyone with the skills and inclination to sniff it out.

7 Privacy may not feel like much of an issue for those in their teens and twenties. They've grown up chronicling their lives on popular social networking sites like Facebook for easy retrieval by friends and strangers alike. But some young people don't realize that what was funny to college buddies might not amuse a law-firm recruiter. Employers regularly research job applicants on the Internet. Some colleges are helping students prepare: Duke University hosts seminars on how to clean up a Facebook account. "You learn why posting pictures of you riding the mechanical bull at Shooters is a bad idea," says Sarah Ball, a senior whose own page is secure and clean.

8 Amy Polumbo, twenty-two, restricted her page on Facebook to a hundred or so people who knew her password. "It was a way for me to keep in touch with friends all over the country," she says. But after she was crowned Miss New Jersey in June, someone downloaded pictures of her and threatened blackmail. She thwarted the attempt by releasing the photos herself (they're quite innocent) but suffered weeks of embarrassment.

9 "I know how easy it is for someone to take advantage of you on the Internet," says Polumbo. "The Web is a place where people can destroy your reputation if you're not careful."

10 In fact, all kinds of transgressions now are easily retrievable. An employee at a New York City bank watched his reputation shrink when his colleagues pulled up an article from a small-town newspaper about his drunk-driving arrest two years earlier. Divorce lawyers have been issuing subpoenas for electronic tollbooth records to use in custody cases. (You say you're home at 6 p.m. to have dinner with the kids, but Fast Lane says you're getting off the Massachusetts Turnpike at 7 p.m.) Abbe L. Ross, a divorce lawyer in Boston, finds a gold mine in computers: financial data, e-mails, what Web sites a soon-to-be-ex spouse looks at and for how long. "I love to look through hard drives," she says.

11 Details about you already are stashed in enormous databases. Unless you pay cash for everything, data brokers almost certainly have compiled a profile of you that will be bought and sold dozens of times to marketers and direct-mail firms. "There's almost nothing they can't find out about you," says Jack Dunning, who worked in the junk-mail business for thirty-five years. Right now, there are roughly 50,000 such lists for sale in a $4 billion a year industry. Now junk mail is going digital: Companies can use personal profiles and records from Internet search engines to tailor advertising—both what you see and precisely when you see it—to individual consumers.

12 And new databases are being created all the time. Most of the major proposals for health-care reform, for example, include compiling medical records into easily and widely accessible digital files. In July, the FBI requested $5 million to pay the major phone companies to maintain logs of your calls—information the Feds can't legally stockpile themselves but might find useful later.

13 Surveillance cameras are increasingly **ubiquitous** in our post-9/11 world. Indeed, New York City plans to ring the financial district with them, as central London did several years ago.

ubiquitous: everywhere

14 Of course, there are upsides. London's network of cameras helped capture failed car bombers in June. And streamlined electronic medical records would make health care safer and more efficient.

15 Still, most experts say we need to be vigilant about the increasing encroachments on our privacy.

16 The ability to collect information and images has outpaced the security available to protect them. Since January 2005, nearly 160 million personal records have been stolen or inadvertently posted online.

17 And even if information stays secure, the big question remains: Who should be allowed to access these databases? The FBI might find evidence against a few bad guys in millions of phone records, but the government could track all of your calls too. (President Bush has acknowledged that the National Security Agency tapped phone calls, though whose and how many is unknown.)

18 Even more disturbing: All of those data files can be linked and cross-referenced. At the 2001 Super Bowl in Tampa, fans were scanned with cameras linked to facial-recognition software in a hunt for suspected terrorists. Some privacy advocates worry that police could videotape anti-war marches and create a library of digital faces or start mining Web pages for personal information.

19 Kevin Bankston was only caught smoking, but he's worried about larger implications: "The issue isn't whether you have anything to hide," he says. "The issue is whether the lack of privacy would give the government an inordinate amount of power over the populace. This is about maintaining the privacy necessary for us to flourish as a free society."

Vocabulary and Comprehension

1. In paragraph 8, what does the word *thwarted* mean? Circle the best answer.
   a. Helped b. Answered c. Prevented
2. Highlight the thesis statement.
3. This essay was written in a journalistic style with very short paragraphs. Revise this essay by drawing lines to indicate where paragraphs could be joined.
4. Why do we accept invasions of privacy? Sum up the main idea of paragraph 5.
   ____
   ____
5. Which sentence best sums up the main idea of paragraph 7? Circle the best answer.
   a. Privacy may not feel like much of an issue for those in their teens and twenties.
   b. But some young people don't realize that what was funny to college buddies might not amuse a law-firm recruiter.
   c. Duke University hosts seminars on how to clean up a Facebook account.
6. According to paragraph 11, why do companies pay for information about you?
   ____
   ____

Critical Thinking

7. Why do people put potentially embarrassing photos and information on sites such as Facebook? Use your own ideas.
   ____
   ____
8. According to the essay, what are three possible consequences of posting personal photos online of partying, etc.? Provide examples from the text.
   ____
   ____
   ____
   ____

9. Why does this essay begin and end with a reference to Kevin Bankston? What does his example show?

____

____

____

Writing Topics

Write about one of the following topics. Remember to explore, develop, and revise and edit your work.

1. At the end of the essay, Bankston says, "The issue is whether the lack of privacy would give the government an inordinate amount of power over the populace." Write a cause and effect essay about the possible consequences if the government compiles private information about citizens.
2. Reflect on how social networking sites serve to make everybody feel famous in their own social circles. Illustrate how this is true with examples from your life.
3. How has technology changed during your lifetime? Trace some of the technological advances that you have witnessed, and explain whether they are positive or negative.

The Basic Parts of a Sentence

Parts of Speech	Definition	Some Examples
Adjective	Adds information about the noun	tall, beautiful, blue, cold
Adverb	Adds information about the verb, adjective, or other adverb; expresses time, place, and frequency	friendly, quickly, sweetly, sometimes, usually, never
Conjunctive adverb	Shows a relationship between two ideas	also, consequently, finally, however, furthermore, moreover, therefore, thus
Coordinating conjunction	Connects two ideas of equal importance	for, and, nor, but, or, yet, so
Determiner	Identifies or determines if a noun is specific or general	a, an, the, this, that, these, those, any, all, each, every, many, some
Interjection	A word expressing an emotion	ouch, yikes, oh
Noun	A person, place, or thing	singular: man, dog, person plural: men, dogs, people
Preposition	Shows a relationship between words (source, direction, location, etc.)	at, to, for, from, behind, above
Pronoun	Replaces one or more nouns	he, she, it, us, ours, themselves
Subordinating conjunction	Connects two ideas when one idea is subordinate (or inferior) to the other idea	after, although, because, unless, until
Verb	Expresses an action or state of being	action: run, eat, walk, think linking: is, become, seem

PRACTICE 1

Label each word with one of the following terms.

adjective	noun	verb	adverb
conjunction	preposition	pronoun	interjection

EXAMPLE:

Easy ___*adjective*___

1. Human ______________
2. With ______________
3. Below ______________
4. Herself ______________
5. Wow ______________
6. Whispered ______________
7. Quickly ______________
8. Because ______________
9. Children ______________
10. They ______________

Types of Clauses and Sentences

Other Key Terms	Definition	Example
clause	An **independent clause** has a subject and verb and expresses a complete idea.	The movie is funny.
	A **dependent clause** has a subject and verb but cannot stand alone. It "depends" on another clause in order to be complete.	Although it is violent
complex sentence	At least one dependent clause joined with one independent clause	Although the movie is violent, it conveys an important message.
compound sentence	Two or more independent clauses that are joined together	Some movies are funny, and others are deeply moving.
compound-complex sentence	At least two independent clauses joined with at least one dependent clause	Although the movie is violent, it is very entertaining, and it conveys an important message.
phrase	A group of words that is missing a subject, a verb, or both and is not a complete sentence	in the morning after the storm
simple sentence	One independent clause that expresses a complete idea	The movie is funny.

Irregular Verbs

Base Form	Simple Past	Past Participle	Base Form	Simple Past	Past Participle
arise	arose	arisen	feel	felt	felt
be	was, were	been	fight	fought	fought
beat	beat	beat, beaten	find	found	found
become	became	become	flee	fled	fled
begin	began	begun	fly	flew	flown
bend	bent	bent	forbid	forbade	forbidden
bet	bet	bet	forget	forgot	forgotten
bind	bound	bound	forgive	forgave	forgiven
bite	bit	bitten	forsake	forsook	forsaken
bleed	bled	bled	freeze	froze	frozen
blow	blew	blown	get	got	got, gotten
break	broke	broken	give	gave	given
breed	bred	bred	go	went	gone
bring	brought	brought	grind	ground	ground
build	built	built	grow	grew	grown
burst	burst	burst	hang*	hung	hung
buy	bought	bought	have	had	had
catch	caught	caught	hear	heard	heard
choose	chose	chosen	hide	hid	hidden
cling	clung	clung	hit	hit	hit
come	came	come	hold	held	held
cost	cost	cost	hurt	hurt	hurt
creep	crept	crept	keep	kept	kept
cut	cut	cut	kneel	knelt	knelt
deal	dealt	dealt	know	knew	known
dig	dug	dug	lay	laid	laid
do	did	done	lead	led	led
draw	drew	drawn	leave	left	left
drink	drank	drunk	lend	lent	lent
drive	drove	driven	let	let	let
eat	ate	eaten	lie**	lay	lain
fall	fell	fallen	light	lit	lit
feed	fed	fed	lose	lost	lost

*When *hang* means specifically "to suspend from a noose until dead," it is a regular verb: *hang, hanged, hanged.*

***Lie* can mean "to rest in a flat position." When *lie* means "make a false statement," then it is a regular verb: *lie, lied, lied.*

(continued)

Irregular Verbs *(continued)*

Base Form	Simple Past	Past Participle	Base Form	Simple Past	Past Participle
make	made	made	speed	sped	sped
mean	meant	meant	spend	spent	spent
meet	met	met	spin	spun	spun
mistake	mistook	mistaken	split	split	split
pay	paid	paid	spread	spread	spread
prove	proved	proved, proven	spring	sprang	sprung
put	put	put	stand	stood	stood
quit	quit	quit	steal	stole	stolen
read	read	read	stick	stuck	stuck
rid	rid	rid	sting	stung	stung
ride	rode	ridden	stink	stank	stunk
ring	rang	rung	strike	struck	struck
rise	rose	risen	swear	swore	sworn
run	ran	run	sweep	swept	swept
say	said	said	swell	swelled	swollen
see	saw	seen	swim	swam	swum
sell	sold	sold	swing	swung	swung
send	sent	sent	take	took	taken
set	set	set	teach	taught	taught
shake	shook	shaken	tear	tore	torn
shine	shone	shone	tell	told	told
shoot	shot	shot	think	thought	thought
show	showed	shown	throw	threw	thrown
shrink	shrank	shrunk	thrust	thrust	thrust
shut	shut	shut	understand	understood	understood
sing	sang	sung	wake	woke	woken
sink	sank	sunk	wear	wore	worn
sit	sat	sat	weep	wept	wept
sleep	slept	slept	win	won	won
slide	slid	slid	wind	wound	wound
slit	slit	slit	withdraw	withdrew	withdrawn
speak	spoke	spoken	write	wrote	written

Appendix 3
A Quick Guide to Verb Tenses

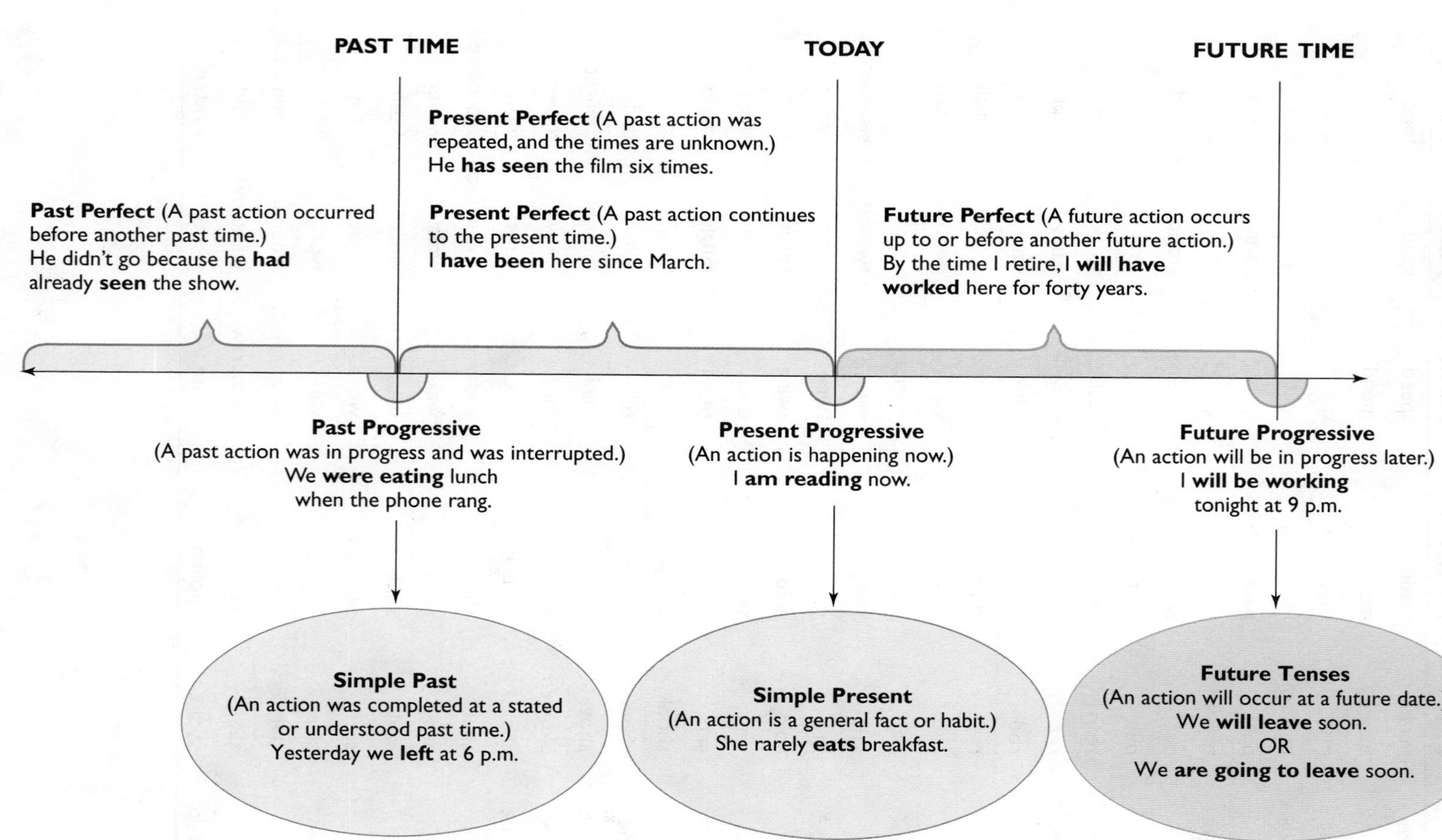
PAST TIME
TODAY
FUTURE TIME
Past Perfect (A past action occurred before another past time.)
He didn't go because he **had** already **seen** the show.
Present Perfect (A past action was repeated, and the times are unknown.)
He **has seen** the film six times.
Present Perfect (A past action continues to the present time.)
I **have been** here since March.
Future Perfect (A future action occurs up to or before another future action.)
By the time I retire, I **will have worked** here for forty years.
Past Progressive
(A past action was in progress and was interrupted.)
We **were eating** lunch when the phone rang.
Present Progressive
(An action is happening now.)
I **am reading** now.
Future Progressive
(An action will be in progress later.)
I **will be working** tonight at 9 p.m.
Simple Past
(An action was completed at a stated or understood past time.)
Yesterday we **left** at 6 p.m.
Simple Present
(An action is a general fact or habit.)
She rarely **eats** breakfast.
Future Tenses
(An action will occur at a future date.)
We **will leave** soon.
OR
We **are going to leave** soon.

Making Compound Sentences

A.

Complete idea

, coordinator
, for
, and
, nor
, but
, or
, yet
, so

complete idea.

B.

Complete idea **;** complete idea.

C.

Complete idea

; transitional expression,
; however,
; in fact,
; moreover,
; therefore,
; furthermore,

complete idea.

Making Complex Sentences

D.

Complete idea

subordinator
although
because
before
even though
unless
when

incomplete idea.

E.

Subordinator
Although
Because
Before
Even though
Unless
When

incomplete idea **,** complete idea.

Apostrophe (')

Use an apostrophe

- to join a subject and verb together.

  We'**re** late.

- to join an auxiliary with *not.*

  I **can't** come.

- to indicate possession.

  Ross's computer is new.

Comma (,)

Use a comma

- to separate words in a series (more than two things). Place a comma before the final *and.*

  The doctor is kind, considerate, and gentle.

- after an introductory word or phrase.

  In the evenings, Carson volunteered at a hospital.

- around interrupting phrases that give additional information about the subject.

  Alan, an electrician, earns a good salary.

- in compound sentences before the coordinator.

  We worked for hours, and then we rested.

- around relative clauses containing *which.*

  The documents, which are very valuable, are up for auction.

- in quotations after an introductory phrase or before an ending phrase.

  Picasso said, "Find your passion."

  "Find your passion," Picasso said.

Note: Do not join two complete sentences with a comma!

Colon (:)

Use a colon

- after a complete sentence that introduces a list or after *the following.*

  The course has the following sections: pregnancy, labour, and lactation.

- after a complete sentence that introduces a quotation.

  Picasso's advice was clear: "Find your passion."
- before an explanation or example.

  Carlos explained what he really needed: a raise.
- to separate the hours and minutes in expressions of time.

  The mall opens at 9:30 a.m.

Semicolon (;)

Use a semicolon to join two independent but related clauses.

Mahatma Gandhi was a pacifist; he believed in nonviolence.

Quotation Marks (" ")

Use quotation marks around direct speech. When a quotation is a complete sentence, capitalize the first word in the quotation. Place the end punctuation inside the closing quotation marks.

In his essay, Levi said, "**W**e were interchangeable."

If the end of the quotation is not the end of your sentence, end the quotation with a comma. If your quotation ends with other punctuation, put it inside the closing quotation marks.

"We were interchangeable," according to Levi.

"You can't be serious!" she shouted.

"What did you call me?" he replied.

Integrated Quotations

If you integrate a quotation in a sentence, add quotation marks around the words the speaker quoted.

Dorothy Nixon calls herself a "**t**errible mother."

"Inside" Quotations

If one quotation is inside another quotation, add single quotation marks (' ') around the inside quotation.

Bernice was forced to act: "She turned to Charlie Paulson and plunged. 'Do you think I ought to bob my hair?'"

Citing Page Numbers

If you are using MLA style, write the page number in parentheses, and place it after the quotation. Place the final period *after* the parentheses if the quotation ends the sentence.

In his essay, Levi says, "We were interchangeable" (4).

Capitalization

Always capitalize

- the pronoun *I* and the first word of every sentence.
- the days of the week, months, and holidays.

  Tuesday May 22 Labour Day

- the names of specific places, such as buildings, streets, parks, public squares, lakes, rivers, cities, provinces, and countries.

  Kelvin Street Lake Erie Halifax, Nova Scotia

- the names of languages, nationalities, tribes, races, and religions.

  Spanish Mohawk Buddhist

- the titles of specific individuals.

  General Dewitt Dr. Franklin Mr. Blain

- the major words in titles of literary or artistic works.

  Fifth Business *The Diviners* *The Tin Flute*

- the names of historical eras and movements.

  World War I Cubism the Middle Ages

Punctuating Titles

Place the title of short works in quotation marks. Capitalize the major words. Short works include songs, short stories, newspaper and magazine articles, essays, and poems.

The Beatles' worst song was "Help."

Italicize the title of a longer document. Long works include television series, films, works of art, magazines, books, plays, and newspapers.

We watched the classic movie *West Side Story.*

In many of your courses, you will have to answer exam questions with a paragraph or an essay. These types of questions often allow you to reveal your understanding of the topic. Although taking any exam can be stressful, you can reduce exam anxiety and increase your chances of doing well by following some preparation and exam-writing strategies.

Preparing for Exams

Here are some steps you can take to help prepare for exams.

- Before you take an exam, make sure that you know exactly what material you should study. Do not be afraid to ask the instructor for clarification. Also ask what materials you should bring to the exam.
- Review the assigned information, class notes, and the textbook, if any.
- Read and repeat information out loud.
- Take notes about important points.
- Study with a friend.

Predict Exam Questions

An effective study strategy is to predict possible exam questions. Here are some tips:

- Look for important themes in your course outline.
- Study your notes and try to analyze what information is of particular importance.
- Look at your previous exams for the course. Determine whether any questions or subjects are repeated in more than one exam.

After you have looked through the course outline, your notes, and previous exams, write out possible exam questions based on the information that you have collected. Then practise writing the answers to your questions.

Writing Exams

Knowing your material inside and out is a large part of exam writing; however, budgeting your time and knowing how to read exam questions are important, too. When you receive the exam paper, look it over carefully and try these test-taking strategies.

Schedule Your Time

One of the most stressful things about taking an exam is running out of time. Before you write, find out exactly how much time you have. Then plan how much time you will need to answer the questions. For example, if you have a one-hour exam and you have three questions worth the same point value, try to make sure that you spend no more than twenty minutes on any one question.

Determine Point Values

As soon as you get an exam, scan the questions and determine which questions have a larger point value. For example, you might respond to the questions with the largest point value first, or you might begin with those that you understand well. Then go to the more difficult questions. If you find yourself blocked on a certain answer, do not waste a lot of time on it. Go to another question, and then go back to the first question later.

Carefully Read the Exam Questions

It is important to read exam instructions thoroughly. Follow the next steps.

Identify Key Words and Phrases

When you read an exam question, underline or circle key words and phrases in order to understand exactly what you are supposed to do. In the next example, the underlined words highlight three different tasks.

1. Discuss how each time period differs from the others.

2. Organize the essay according to each period's date.

Distinguish among Paleolithic, Mesolithic, and Neolithic. Place these periods in chronological order, and describe how the people lived during those times.

3. Discuss what people did for shelter, food, and leisure activities.

Examine Common Question Words

Exam questions direct you using verbs (action words). This chart gives the most common words that are used in both paragraph- and essay-style questions.

Verb	Meaning
describe discuss review	Examine a subject as thoroughly as possible. Focus on the main points.
narrate trace	Describe the development or progress of something using time order.
evaluate explain your point of view interpret justify take a stand	State your opinion and give reasons to support your opinion. In other words, write an argument paragraph or essay.
analyze criticize classify	Explain something carefully by breaking it down into smaller parts.
enumerate list outline	Go through important facts one by one.
compare contrast distinguish	Discuss important similarities and/or differences.
define explain what is meant by . . .	Give a complete and accurate definition that demonstrates your understanding of the concept.

(continued)

Verb	Meaning
explain causes	Analyze the reasons for an event.
explain effects	Analyze the consequences or results of an event.
explain a process	Explain the steps needed to perform a task.
summarize	Write down the main points from a larger work.
illustrate	Demonstrate your understanding by giving examples.

PRACTICE 1

Determine the main type of response that you would use to answer each essay question.

narrate	explain a process	explain causes/effects	define
argue	classify	compare and contrast	

EXAMPLE:

Discuss the term *affirmative action*.

define

1. Distinguish between the interest rate and the rate of return.
2. Describe what happened during the Tet Offensive.
3. List and describe five types of housing.
4. What steps are required to improve your city's transportation system?
5. List the reasons for global warming.
6. Give a short but thorough description of narcissism.
7. Discuss whether religious symbols should be banned from schools.

Follow the Writing Process

When you answer paragraph or essay exam questions, remember to follow the writing process.

Explore
- Jot down any ideas that you think can help you answer the question.

Develop
- Use the exam question to guide your topic sentence or thesis statement.
- List supporting ideas. Then organize your ideas and create a paragraph or essay plan.
- Write the paragraph or essay. Use transitions to link your ideas.

Revise and edit
- Read over your writing to make sure it makes sense and that your spelling, punctuation, and mechanics are correct.

PRACTICE 2

Choose three topics from Practice 1 and write topic sentences or thesis statements.

EXAMPLE:

Discuss the term *affirmative action.*

Topic sentence or thesis statement: ***Affirmative action policies give certain groups in society preferential treatment to correct a history of injustice.***

1. ______________________________

2. ______________________________

3. ______________________________

PRACTICE 3

Read the following test material, and answer the questions that follow.

Essay Exam

You will have ninety minutes to complete the following test. Write your answers in the answer booklet.

A. Define the following terms (2 points each).

1. Region
2. Economic geography
3. Territoriality
4. Spatial distribution
5. Gross national product

B. Write an essay response to one of the following questions. Your essay should contain relevant supporting details. (20 points)

6. Define and contrast an open city with a closed city.
7. Discuss industrial location theories in geography, and divide the theories into groups.
8. Explain the steps needed to complete a geographical survey. List the steps in order of importance.

Schedule Your Time and Determine Point Values

1. What is the total point value of the exam? ______________________

2. How many questions do you have to answer? ______________________

3. Which part of the exam would you do first? Explain why. ______________________

____

4. Schedule your time. How much time would you spend on each part of the exam?

   Part A: ____________________ Part B: ____________________

   Explain your reasoning. ______________________________

   ____

Carefully Read the Exam Questions

5. Identify key words in Part B. What important information is in the instructions?

   ____

6. What two things must you do in question 6?

   a. ____________________ b. ____________________

7. What type of essay is required to answer question 7?

   a. Comparison and contrast b. Classification c. Process

8. What type of essay is required to answer question 8?

   a. Comparison and contrast b. Classification c. Process

In the first few pages of your writing portfolio or on the next pages, keep spelling, grammar, and vocabulary logs. The goal of keeping spelling and grammar logs is to help you stop repeating the same errors. When you write new assignments, you can consult the lists and hopefully break some ingrained bad habits. The vocabulary log can provide you with interesting new terms that you can incorporate into your writing.

Spelling Log

Every time you misspell a word, record both the mistake and the correction in your spelling log. Then, before you hand in a writing assignment, consult your spelling log. The goal is to stop repeating the same spelling errors.

EXAMPLE: *Incorrect* *Correct*

realy *really*

exagerated *exaggerated*

Grammar Log

Each time a writing assignment is returned to you, identify one or two repeated errors, and add them to your grammar log. Then, before you hand in writing assignments, consult the grammar log in order to avoid making the same errors. For each type of grammar error, you could do the following:

- Identify the assignment and write down the type of error.
- In your own words, write a rule about the error.
- Include an example from your writing assignment.

EXAMPLE: *Illustration Paragraph* *(Feb. 12)* *Run-On*

Do not connect two complete sentences with a comma.

accidents. Other

Bad drivers cause accidents, other drivers do not expect sudden lane changes.

Vocabulary Log

As you use this book, you will learn new vocabulary words. Keep a record of the most interesting and useful vocabulary words and expressions. Write a synonym or definition next to each new word.

EXAMPLE: *Exasperating means "annoying."*

Spelling Log

Grammar Log

Vocabulary Log

Credits

TEXT

Chapter 1

Page 5: Montreal is a vibrant city of extremes. Peaceful suburbs integrate ... (116 words) and revised paragraph: Wade Vong, college student; **Page 10**: Lomax also found a relationship between polyphony... (57 words): Carol R. Ember and Melvin Ember, Cultural Anthropology, 10th Ed., (c) 2002. Reprinted and electronically reproduced by permission of Pearson Education, Inc. Upper Saddle River, New Jersey.; **Page 11:** When dealing with club managers, it is imperative that ... (61 words): Reprinted by permission of Jake Sibley. Jake Sibley is an independent writer and musician. He can be reached at jakesibley.com; But there was no reason why everyone should not ... (76 words): Kate Chopin, The Awakening and Other Stories, 1899; **Page 12:** Work. I've only worked in a restaurant. A lotta reasons to ... (122 words) I think people should always tip in restaurants. Why. Well, the waitresses ... (112 words): Sandra **Ahumada**; **Page 13:** College student Chul Yee brainstormed about cities. He made a list of general ideas. (Bulleted List): Chul Yee; **Page 14:** College student Clayton Rukavina used a question-and-answer format to generate ideas about binge drinking: Clayton Rukavina; **Page 15:** College student Mahan Zahir used clustering to explore ideas about crime. He identified some main topics: Mahan Zahir; **Page 16:** "Keeping a diary is a way of making..." (15 words): Anaïs Nin; **Page 20:** The commercialization of traditional holidays helps our economy. First... (176 words): Catherine Niatum.

Chapter 2

Page 21: College student Sandra Ahumada practiced narrowing a topic by thinking of ideas about work. (Bulleted List): Sandra Ahumada; **Page 23:** Runners are a different breed. With much of our modern athletic... (99 words): "Dashing Through the Snow" by Jeff Beer and Jordan Timm. Canadian Business, February 14, 2011, p. 74. Printed with permission; Taking a proactive approach is especially important... (79 words): "Filling in the Gaps: How Emotional Intelligence Training can Combat Workplace Bullying" by Naomi Brown. HR Professional, November/December, 2012, p. 39. Reprinted with permission from HR Professional magazine and the Human Resources Professionals Association (HRPA). www.hrpa.ca; **Page 24:** Imagine a society without laws. People would not know ... (88 words): Frank Schmalleger, Criminal Justice Today: An Introductory Text for the Twenty-first Century, 6th Ed., (c) 2001. Reprinted and electronically reproduced by permission of Pearson Education, Inc., Upper Saddle River, New Jersey; Cosmetic surgery is not like fooling around with... (109 words): "Temp" Reprinted by permission from Maclean's Magazine. Patricia Chisholm, "The Body Builders."; **Page 28:** University student Mahan Zahir narrowed his topic and wrote his topic sentence. Then he listed ideas that could support his topic sentence. (Lists): Mahan Zahir; **Page 29:** College student Sandra Ahumada brainstormed ideas about tipping (List): Sandra Ahumada; **Page 31:** One day, some gentlemen called on my mother... (118 words): From The Story of My Life by Helen Keller, edited by Roger Shattuck. Copyright 2003 by Roger Shattuck. Used by permission of W.W. Norton & Company, Inc.; Although our thirst mechanism can trigger us to ... (147 words): Nutrition: A Functional Approach, 2nd Ce edited by Janice Thompson, Melinda Manore and Judy Sheeshk, 2010 (Page 237). Reprinted with permission by Pearson Canada Inc.; **Page 32:** Their house was even more elaborate than I expected. It was ... (78 words): F. Scott Fitzgerald, The Great Gatsby (c) 1925; **Page 33:** The tiny interior of the shop was in fact uncomfortably full... (131 words): George Orwell, 1984 (c) 1949; Many factors contribute to racist attitudes. First, there are often ... (101 words): Eliot Mandel, student; **Page 34:** Mahan completed his paragraph plan: Mahan Zahir; **Page 37:** People steal for many reasons. Poverty is a primary motivation ... (120 words): Mahan Zahir;

Chapter 3

Page 42: The discovery of insulin was certainly the most important event ... (158 words): Henry B.M. Best, Margaret and Charley: The Personal Story of Dr. Charles Best, the Co-discoverer of Insulin. Printed with permission from Dundurn Press Limited; **Page 45:** Celia Raines, a student, wrote the following paragraph ...: Celia Raines; **Page 49:** First, Poverty (Revision) On pages 37–38 in Chapter 2, you read the first draft of student Mahan Zahir's paragraph about crime. Look at his revisions for unity, support, coherence, and style: Mahan Zahir; **Page 50:** Now look at the first draft of Sandra's paragraph, and revise it for unity, support, and coherence….: Sandra Ahumada; **Page 51:** MAHAN'S EDITED PARAGRAPH. Mahan Zahir edited his paragraph about crime. He corrected errors in spelling, capitalization, punctuation, and grammar: Mahan Zahir.

Chapter 4

Page 59: Having integrity puts your ethics into day-to-day action. When you ... (208 words): Keys to Success: Building Successful Intelligence and Achieving Your Goals 5th Ce by Carol Carter, Joyce Bishoop, Sarah Lyman Kravits and Peter J Maurin, Toronto Pearson Canada 2010 (Page 379). Reprinted with permission by Pearson Canada Inc.; **Page 58:** Illustrations at Work (Text Box): Patti Guzman.

Chapter 5

Page 70: Narration Work: Joseph Roth, a boiler and pressure vessel inspector, used narrative writing in a memo he wrote to his supervisor: Joseph Roth; **Page 72:** There are a few memories of my childhood in Frobisher Bay... (140 words): —Alootook Ipellie, "Frobisher Bay Childhood", The Beaver, 310.4, Spring 1980 in Northern Voices: Inuit Writing in English, edited by Penny Petrone. Reproduced with permission of Canada's National History Society, Publisher of Canada's History (formerly The Beaver); **Page 73:** The economic ups and downs caused by expansion and contraction... (189 words): Karen Collins and Jackie Shemko, Exploring Business. Reprinted with permission by Pearson Canada Inc.

Chapter 6

Page 84: Description at Work (Text Box) One of the major selling features and fundamental advantages of an escorted coach tour is the complete and total absence of "hassle.": Printed with permission from TravelBrands Inc.; **Page 85:** For several days the wind blew, full of dust... (37 words/2365 word article): Josephine Johnson, "September Harvest" The Atlantic; They hooked wrist-thick hanks of laghmien noodles and shoveled ... (22 words/638 word article): Jeffrey Tayler, "A Cacophony of Noodles" The Atlantic online; We had crossed featureless purple deserts and shrieked ... (39 words): Nick Massey-Garrison, "We Turned Some Sharp Corners: A Marriage Proposal in Durango"; **Page 88: My** fifth grade teacher, at the time she taught me... (89 words): Robyn Sarah, excerpt taken from "Notes that Resonate a Lifetime". Printed with permission.; **Page 92:** Eight years ago, my first attempt at arc welding... (paragraph): Kelly Bruce;

Chapter 7

Page 97: A framed painting hanging on a wall creates its own imaginary world... (207 words): Philip E. Bishop, A Beginner's Guide to the Humanities, 2nd Ed., (c) 2007. Reprinted and electronically reproduced by permission of Pearson Education, Inc., Upper Saddle River, New Jersey.; Insert 7.1 Tsunamis, like the one that occurred in Indonesia in 2004, are....: Natalia MacDonald.

Chapter 8

Page 111: A standard baseball pitch—slider, curveball, fastball—seems to slavishly ... (146 words): Jay Ingram, "Pitch Perfect," The Walrus, From the June 2103 Magazine; **Page 119:** Slang is informal language that changes rapidly and exists ... (204 words): student.

Chapter 9

Page 125: There may be no way to rid the world of dishonesty, but ... (246 words): John J. Macionis, "Spotting Lies: What Are the Clues" in Sociology, 11th Ed., (c) 2006. Reprinted and electronically reproduced by permission of Pearson Education, Inc., Upper Saddle River, New Jersey.; **Page 133:** College students often confront many different types of difficulties... (113 words); Daniel Mirto, college student.

Chapter 10

Page 139: As with the work itself, there's always a chasm between my ideal... (95 words): Catherine Bush, First Chapter: The Canadian Writers Photography Project (ed. Don Denton). Printed with permission; **Page 140:** My frontyard in downtown Toronto is covered with dirty white stones... (246 words): Kristen den Hartog, "Sugar Beets & Roses," in Notes from Home: 20 Canadian Writers Share Their Thoughts of Home. Printed with permission.

Chapter 11

Page 153: Cause and Effect at Work: Luisa Suarez.

Chapter 12

Page 165: Argument at Work (Text Box): Kamal Natu; **Page 166:** Throughout Canadian history, immigrants have been the shock... (130 words): Harald Bauder, "Economic Crisis Bears Down on Vulnerable Immigrants". Printed with permission.; **Page 175:** With the increased traffic flow in Ottawa, speed bumps should be... (259 words): Craig Susanowitz;

Chapter 13

Page 180: Alternative Culture essay**:** Veena Thomas; **Page 194:** "I never saw the blow to my head come from Huck..." 140 words: Linda L. Lindsey and Stephen Beach, Sociology, 3rd Ed., (c) 2004. Reprinted and electronically reproduced by permission of Pearson Education, Inc., Upper Saddle River, New Jersey.; **Page 195:** Many practices in conventional medicine are safe and effective... (176 words): Mark Sherman, MD CM, CCFP, "Integrative Medicine: Model for Health Care Reform," Can Fam Physician. 2006 July 10; 52(7): 832–833. Reprinted with permission; High school is a waste of time. In fact, it is a baby-sitting ... (89 words): Adelie Zhang; **Page 196:** D. The story of how Christianity ultimately conquered the Roman Empire ... (81 words): Albert M. Craig et al., The Heritage of World Civilizations, 6th Ed., (c) 2003. Reprinted and electronically reproduced by permission of Pearson Education, Inc. Upper Saddle River, New Jersey.; **Page 197:** As soon as smoking is banned in all public places, we will ... (74 words): Jordan Lamott, "Butt Out!"; **Page 201:** Positive Messages in Hip-Hop Music essay (examples include introduction, drafts and final essay): David Raby-Pepin, "Positive Messages in Hip-Hop Music". Printed with permission.

Chapter 14

Page 208: After climbing a great hill, one only finds that there are many more hills to climb: Nelson Mandela, former South African president; Everything has its beauty, but not everyone sees it: Confucius, ancient Chinese philosopher and educator; We are, for all our diversity, a collective, more than we are Individuals: Aritha Van Herk, Canadian novelist; **Page 210:** "A Lesson in Humility" Essay: Printed with permission of Jeff Kemp. Jeff Kemp, ex NFL quarterback and V.P. of Family Life; **Page 212:** The suburbs are full of heroes: Camilla Gibb, Canadian novelist; When your mouth stumbles, it's worse than feet: Oji proverb; Those who cannot remember the past are condemned to repeat it: George Santayana, Spanish poet and philosopher; **Page 213:** Character, like a photograph, develops in darkness: Yousuf Karsh; The wind kicked the leaves: Kurt Vonnegut, Jr., "Next Door"; **Page 214:** "There is a legend that when the good people ... (39 words): Eric Nicol, 1970; **Page 215:** There is no need to go to India or anywhere else to ... (32 words): Elisabeth Kubler-Ross, Swiss author; The real voyage of discovery consists not in seeking new landscapes but in having new eyes: Marcel Proust, French author; Compassion is an act of imagination; a leap of faith into another's closed circle: Ann Marie MacDonald, Canadian writer and actor; Iron rusts from disuse, and stagnant water loses its purity and in cold weather becomes frozen; even so does inaction sap the vigor of the mind: Leonardo Da Vinci, Italian artist and inventor; **Page 218:** Steps to Music Success (Essay)**: Reprinted with permission from** Jake Sibley; **Page 220:** Treat the earth well. It was not given to you by your parents; it was loaned to you by your children: Native American proverb; Know how to listen, and you will profit even from those who talk badly: Plutarch, ancient Greek philosopher; Every child is an artist. The problem is how to remain an artist once he [or she] grows up: Pablo Picasso, Spanish artist; If you can spend a perfectly useless afternoon in a perfectly useless manner, you have learned how to live: Lin Yutang, Chinese author; **Page 223:** "Sports Fanatics" essay**:** Diego Pelaez; **Page 224:** A house is more than the sum of its beams and planks and two-by-fours and wires snaking through the walls: Diana Hartog, Canadian poet and novelist; Nothing in life makes you feel more in control than having choices: Gail Vaz-Oxlade Money Rules: Rule Your Money or Your Money Will Rule You.

Toronto: HarperCollins, 2012, p. 48; Rebelling against social control is what youth does: Judy Rebick, Canadian journalist and political activist; A leader who does not hesitate before he sends his nation into battle is not fit to be a leader: Golda Meir, former Israeli prime minister; **Page 227:** "Psychology" essay: CICCARELLI, SAUNDRA K.; WHITE, J. NOLAND, PSYCHOLOGY, 2nd Ed., ©2009, pp. 565–566. Reprinted and Electronically reproduced by permission of Pearson Education, Inc., Upper Saddle River, New Jersey; **Page 229:** Work saves us from three great evils: boredom, vice, and need: Voltaire, French author and philosopher; There are three kinds of lies: lies, damned lies, and statistics: Benjamin Disraeli, British politician; There appears to be three types of politicians: leaders, lobbyists, and professionals: R. Ravimohan, Indian journalist; We peer so suspiciously at each other that we cannot see that we Canadians are standing on the mountaintop of human wealth, freedom and privilege: Pierre Elliott Trudeau; **Page 231:** "Montrealers, Cherish your Clotheslines" Essay: Christopher DeWolf, "Montrealers, Cherish your Clotheslines". Printed with permission of Christopher DeWolf; **Page 233:** My grandfather once told me that there are two kinds of people: those who work and those who take the credit. He told me to try to be in the first group; there was less competition there: Indira Gandhi, Indian politician; People are more violently opposed to fur than leather because it is safer to harass rich women than motorcycle gangs: Unknown; Happy families are all alike. Every unhappy family is unhappy in its own way: Leo Tolstoy, Russian author; Soups fall into two camps: quick and simple water, veg, cook and hit the table, or classically made with time and love: Trish Magwood, Canadian chef and entrepreneur; **Page 235:** "Why Canadian Businesses Fail" Essay: "Why Canadian Businesses Fail", Kevin Bousquet, Corpa Group, Inc. Printed with permission.; **Page 237:** A word after a word after a word is power: Margaret Atwood, Canadian author, poet, critic, essayist; What I would say to my younger self is this: forget about fear: Erica de Vasconcelos, Canadian novelis; All human actions have one or more of these seven causes: chance, nature, compulsion, habit, reason, passion, and desire: Aristotle, ancient Greek philosopher; One of the symptoms of an approaching nervous breakdown is the belief that one's work is terribly important: Bertrand Russell, British author and philosopher; **Page 240:** "The Importance of Music" Essay: Christine Bigras; **Page 242:** An eye for an eye leads to a world of the blind: Mahatma Gandhi, Indian activist; Our history is partly what makes Canada unique in the world, distinct from other nations with different populations, traditions, political systems, myths and landscapes: Charlotte Gray, Canadian professor and writer;

Chapter 15

Page 244: David's Paragraph without Research, David's Paragraph with Research: David Raby-Pepin; **Page 250:** Summer barbecues and late-night drinks are a seasonal must for some people . . . (128 words): Material reprinted with the express permission of National Post, a division of Postmedia Network; **Page 251:** Unfortunately it turns out that hit men, genocidal maniacs, gang leaders, and violent kids … (64 words): written by Martin Seligman, appeared in the APA Monitor on Page 97; **Page 252:** Religious beliefs and practices are found in all known contemporary … (60 words): Carol R. Ember and Melvin Ember, Cultural Anthropology, 10th Ed., (c) 2002. Reprinted and electronically reproduced by permission of Pearson Education, Inc. Upper Saddle River, New Jersey.; **Page 253:** Human history abounds with legends of lost or deserted … (39 words): The selection, written by John E. Farley, appeared on Page 97 of his book, Sociology; The collapse of German communism began with the regime's desperate decision… (59 words): Daniel R. Brower, The World in the Twentieth Century, 6th Ed., (c) 2006, p.371. Reprinted and electronically reproduced by permission of Pearson Education, Inc. Upper Saddle River, New Jersey.; **Page 258:** Orcs, Mages, and Zerglings. Oh My! (essay): Printed with permission from Marie Lemieux.

Chapter 19

Page 302: Canadian corporations are not nearly as advanced as we like to think they … (272 words): "Temp" Reprint by permission from Maclean's Magazine. Rachel Mendleson, "Diversity or Death".

Chapter 34

Page 496: "the regulatory agency said the Vancouver-based yoga wear retailer has …" (44 words/309 words in article): Brenda Bouw "Lululemon to remove healthful claims" November 11, 2013. THE CANADIAN PRESS. Printed with permission.

Chapter 37

Page 496: "Gone with the Windows": Dorothy Nixon; **Page 527:** de•cep??tion/[di-sep??shen]/n 1, the act of misleading. 2. a misrepresentation; artifice; fraud: From The New American Webster's Handy College Dictionary by Philip D. Morehead and Andrew T. Morehead, copyright 1951 (renewed), (c) 1955, 1956, 1957, 1961 by Albert H. Morehead, 1972, 1981, 1985, 1995 by Philip D. Morehead and Andrew T. Morehead. Used by permission of Dutton Signet, a division of Penguin Group (USA) LLC; **Page 528:** "The Market and the Mall": Stephen Henighan, "The Market and the Mall" Geist Fall 2013. Printed by permission of Stephen Henighan; **Page 530:** "We Turned Some Sharp Corners: A Marriage Proposal in Durango": "We Turned Some Sharp Corners: A Marriage Proposal in Durango" (c) Nick Massey-Garrison; **Page 535:** "Stealing Glances": Sheila Heti, "Stealing Glances". Printed by permission; "I think of my body as an instrument rather than an ornament": Alanis Morissette, Singer and Composer; **Page 538:** "The Great Offside: How Canadian Hockey is Becoming a Game Strictly for the Rich," by James Mirtle (1,384 words): "The Great Offside: How Canadian Hockey is Becoming a Game Strictly for the Rich," by James Mirtle, The Globe and Mail (Canada), 8 November 2013, http://www.theglobeandmail.com/news/national/time-to-lead/the-great-offside-how-canadian-hockey-is-becoming-a-game-strictly-for-the-rich/article15349723/; "Anyone who has ever struggled with poverty knows how extremely expensive it is to be poor: James Baldwin, Author"; **Page 546:** "New evidence in 'Diefenbaby' case": Charlie Gillis September 5, 2012, Maclean's. http://www2.macleans.ca/2012/09/05/new—evidence—in—diefenbaby—case/.
Printed by permission; **Page 548:** "Ghosts": "Ghost" from The Bonesetter's Daughter by Amy Tan, copyright © 2001 by Amy Tan. Used by permission of G. P. Putnam and Sons, a division of Penguin Group (USA) LLC; **Page 551:** "A Shift in Perception": Cynthia Macdonald, "A Shift in Perception,"

University of Toronto Magazine, Autumn 2012. Printed with permission from Cynthia Macdonald; **Page 557:** "The Sage: Gordon Smith Knows Painting," by Eric Andrew-Gee (2974 words): "The Sage: Gordon Smith Knows Painting," by Eric Andrew-Gee, CANADIAN ART, Spring 2013, http://www.canadianart.ca/features/2013/05/06/gordon-smith-knows-painting/. Printed by permission of the author; **Page 563:** "The Sanctuary of School": Reprinted by permission from Lynda Barry "The Sanctuary of School" from the New York Times, January 5, 1992. Copyright © 1992 by Lynda Barry; **Page 566:** "Like it or Not Yoga is Here to Stay" by Aparita Bhandari: Reprinted by permission from CBC News (www.cbc.ca/news/background/exercise_fitness/yoga.html; **Page 570:** "Welcome to the electronic jungle and a life of beeping misery": Josh Freed, "Welcome to the electronic jungle and a life of beeping misery," The Gazette (Montreal), August 2, 2008. Printed with permission of Josh Freed; **Page 573:** "This Boat is My Boat": Written by Drew Hayden Taylor; **Page 578:** "Advertising Appeals" (455 words): SOLOMON, MICHAEL R.; MARSHALL, GREG W.; STUART, ELNORA, MARKETING: REAL PEOPLE, REAL CHOICES, 4th, ©2006. Printed and Electronically reproduced by permission of Pearson Education, Inc., Upper Saddle River, New Jersey; **Page 581:** What Adolescents Miss When We Let Them Grow Up in Cyberspace: From The New York Times, May 29 © 2004. The New York Times. All rights reserved. Used by permission and protected by the Copyright Laws of the United States. The printing, copying, redistribution, or retransmission of this Content without express written permission is prohibited; **Page 575:** "You take the waves, the and edit your work. weight and the wind into consideration. And also the North Star": Jean Paul Desbiens, For Pity's Sake; **Page 583:** "Today every invention is received with a cry of triumph, which soon turns into a cry of fear": Bertold Brecht.

Index

A

F

U

V

Y

Notes

Notes